PRODIGAL
SONS

PRODIGAL SONS

The New York Intellectuals & Their World

ALEXANDER BLOOM

OXFORD UNIVERSITY PRESS
New York   Oxford

Oxford University Press

Oxford   New York   Toronto
Delhi   Bombay   Calcutta   Madras   Karachi
Petaling Jaya   Singapore   Hong Kong   Tokyo
Nairobi   Dar es Salaam   Cape Town
Melbourne   Auckland

and associated companies in
Beirut   Berlin   Ibadan   Nicosia

First published in 1986 by Oxford University Press, Inc.,
200 Madison Avenue, New York, New York 10016

Oxford is a registered trademark of Oxford University Press

From *Making It,* by Norman Podhoretz. Copyright ©1967 by Norman Podhoretz. Reprinted
by permission of Harper & Row, Publishers, Inc.

Harold Rosenberg, "1776." Reprinted with permission of *Poetry* magazine.

Delmore Schwartz, "The Ballad of the Children of the Czar," Delmore Schwartz: *Selected
Poems: Summer Knowledge.* Copyright 1938 by New Directions Publishing Corp.; and
"Genesis," Delmore Schwartz: *Genesis.* Copyright 1943 by New Directions Publishing
Corp. Reprinted by the permission of New Directions Publishing Corporation.

Lionel Trilling, excerpted from *The Liberal Imagination.* Foreword copyright © 1978
Diana Trilling and James Trilling. Reprinted with permission of Charles Scribner's Sons.

Library of Congress Cataloging in Publication Data
Bloom, Alexander.
Prodigal Sons

Bibliography: p.
Includes index
1. Jews—New York (N.Y.)—Intellectual life.
2. Intellectuals—New York (N.Y.) 3. American
literature—Jewish authors—History and criticism.
4. Jews—New York (N.Y.)—Cultural assimilation.
5. New York (N.Y.)—Intellectual life. 6. United
States—Civilization—Jewish influences. I. Title.
F128. 9. J5B55 1986 974.7'1004924 85–5128
ISBN 0–19–503662–x
ISBN 0–19–505177–7 (pbk.)

2 4 6 8 10 9 7 5 3 1

Printed in the United States of America

For Stefan & Zachary,
who give me pleasure beyond words

Preface

That which is read first is written last. The author knows—or thinks he knows—what awaits the reader. The reader may have expectations but ventures into unknown territory. For an author, the book is done. For the reader, it is just beginning. The book is in the reader's hands.

I have been at this project for a number of years. Jokingly, I have said that I feel as though I had been assigned this topic when I started grade school. Seriously, I have told my older son that I have been working on it longer than he has been alive. He may be impressed; I am incredulous. This book is longer and took more time than I ever imagined necessary when I began. And yet, other individuals and events could have been included but were left out for reasons of space; other themes might have been developed; and further analysis of what is already here was possible. In this sense, this book—any book—is not done, only the writing has stopped.

Before the reading is to begin, a few comments. This book falls into a number of cracks between the divisions which usually mark the historical profession. It is intellectual history, but is more than a discussion of ideas. It is ethnic history, but the story of just one, unique group which emerged from an ethnic community. It is social history, but neither of the old nor the new variety. I do not claim however, that this is a new kind of history. In fact, it is probably the oldest kind. I have let my subject determine the approach. The New York Intellectuals have wandered through radicalism and literary criticism, cosmopolitanism and ethnicity, cultural discussions and political debates. And I have followed. A recounting of both their lives and their ideas is essential for a full understanding of their history.

I have not proceeded totally alone. I have received guidance and assistance in a number of forms over the years. The staffs and resources of several libraries have provided me access to the tremendous amount of material the New York Intellectuals have produced. I am grateful to the Boston College Library, the Wheaton College Library, the Boston Public Library, and the Harvard University Library—whether they were aware of my presence or not. The F. W. Dupee Papers at Columbia University were an important source, and I am grateful to Mrs. F. W. Dupee for giving me permission to use and to quote from the papers, including letters of her late husband. In addition, for permission to quote from letters written to F. W. Dupee, I would like to thank Clement Greenberg; Mary McCarthy; William Phillips; Norman Podhoretz; Farrar, Straus, and Giroux, for the estate of Edmund Wilson; Edward Mendelson, for the estate of W. H. Auden; and Mrs. Gloria Macdonald, for the estate of Dwight Macdonald.

I have made extensive use of *Partisan Review* and *Commentary* and am most grateful for the permission of these magazines to quote from them, as well as that of Irving Howe to quote from his 1946 *Commentary* article, "The Lost Young Intellectuals," his 1954 *Partisan Review* article, "This Age of Conformity," and his 1968 *Commentary* article, "The New York Intellectuals: A Chronicle and a Critique"; that of Irving Kristol to quote from his 1952 *Commentary* article "Civil Liberties: 1952—A Study in Confusion"; and that of William Phillips, to quote from his 1976 *Commentary* article, "How *Partisan Review* Began."

A number of the individuals about whom I wrote spoke openly with me and have allowed, in some cases with revision, their words to reappear here. This provided me with the opportunity to ask questions not answered in the literature, and their insights have added a texture and dimension unavailable from printed sources alone. I am certain that these individuals will not agree with all of my interpretations, but each encouraged me—during the interview—to pursue my own analysis and write my own book. This has been their style throughout their careers. The present book would be something much more limited without the benefit of these interviews. I am very grateful for the time taken—in the initial interviews and in the subsequent revisions and the approval of quotations—by Arnold Beichman, Daniel Bell, Midge Decter, Leslie Fiedler, Morris Fine, Clement Greenberg, Sidney Hook, Irving Howe, Alfred Kazin, Irving Kristol, the late Dwight Macdonald (reviewed by Mrs. Macdonald), William Phillips, Norman Podhoretz, Meyer Schapiro, and Diana Trilling.

Julian Bach agreed to serve as my literary agent and Sheldon Meyer agreed that Oxford University Press would publish this book long before I had any right to expect either representation or publication. Their faith saw me through the common condition of a graduate student—the feeling that no one really cares about a dissertation except the candidate and his or her advisers—and helped bridge the gap between a thesis and a book. Wendy Weil, Julian Bach's associate, helped finalize the initial publishing agreement. Their agency is a model of civility coupled with enthusiasm; their willingness to put an unknown graduate student on their list of best–selling authors bespeaks a commitment beyond financial reward. Everyone at Oxford University Press has been nothing short of splendid—supportive, patient, and excited, when appropriate. Sheldon Meyer remains the perfect editor—available, insightful, and encouraging. Otto Sonntag, the copy editor, dissected the manuscript with his red pencil, to my temporary exasperation and the book's substantial improvement. All of these people have my sincere appreciation.

In the years I have been working on this project, I have had the assistance of a number of extremely helpful individuals. My research assistants have done everything I have asked, from minute tasks to large–scale endeavors, and I am extremely grateful to them: Diane Beswick, Diedre Fogg, Laura Harding, Allison Perry, Susan Pulfer, Deborah Sedares, Christine Swenson, and, especially, Kim Kennedy and Kristin Robinson. The preparation of the manuscript for publication was facilitated by the work of the secretarial staff at Wheaton College, in particular Nancy Shepardson, Kathie Francis, and Emily Pearce, and by the Wheaton Academic Computer Center, including Gail Richardson and Linda Fitzpatrick.

A number of friends have floated in and out of this project over the years— reading sections, sending me clippings, alerting me to articles, listening to my ideas, or merely talking with me. They are a disparate group, spread over geography and time. As a whole they serve as a kind of personalized history of the years I have been working on this. They are true friends: Ann Banks, Paul Breines, Nancy Condee, Todd Endelmen, Paul Helmreich, Frances Maher, John Miller, Alan Rogers, Ellen Schrecker, Peter Warner, and Kersti Yllo.

Several friends read major portions of the manuscript and took the time to make careful and thoughtful comments. David Ennis and Marc Ferrara read the part which began as my dissertation—essentially the first nine chapters—and their comments helped in the revision of those sections. Peter Weiler read my dissertation as it was being written, and his intelligent criticisms improved the thesis and this book. David Vogler read the entire book and brought a critical and insightful eye to the whole work. All these friends have my heartfelt thanks.

My debts to Andrew Buni and Alan Lawson are great. Both read and commented on my dissertation, but their contributions only begin there. Andrew Buni provided consistent encouragement from the very beginning of my graduate school career, first as a teacher and later as a colleague and a friend. He made it clear that the profession of history was both exciting and accessible, even to graduate students. Alan Lawson encouraged this project from its start—in his seminar—and continued as a model thesis adviser. His detailed, challenging, and supportive comments improved every section of the book, as he provided the same careful reading of all that I wrote. I hope these two understand my indebtedness and my appreciation for all they have done for me.

Jill Betz Bloom took time from her own busy professional and academic career to discuss with me various crucial issues at important junctures in the thinking and writing of this book. Her psychological insights helped clarify particular discussions. In addition, she read the final work, helping to catch everything from errors in typesetting to muddled syntax and unclear concepts. Beyond all these, however, are contributions more intangible but even more important. Over the years, a great many of the things we have learned, beyond our specific disciplines, have been learned together. These are impossible to enumerate, but essential to recognize. The process of learning together has been as important and as satisfying for me as the knowledge gained. For all this—and for more—I am extremely grateful.

My sons, Stefan and Zachary, have grown with this book. The first was born when I was writing my thesis, the second when I was writing the book. They have provided a constant reminder of what is most important to me. Holding a book can be very satisfying, especially if one wrote it. Holding one's child is even better. What I owe my sons is inexplicable, but their contributions to my life continue to be wonderful.

Brookline   Alexander Bloom
May 1985

Contents

IV. MAKING IT

PRODIGAL
SONS

Introduction

"The Herd of Independent Minds"

The New York Intellectuals dislike being labeled, they can speak bitterly about each other's work and opinions, they may not see one another from year's start to year's end, but they are nervously alert to one another's judgment. Attention is paid— whether from warranted response or collective vanity or provincial narrowness, it hardly matters.

—Irving Howe

They were themselves, if not the only, the main people who knew what they were talking about. All of us, in fact, write to each other as an audience.

—Norman Podhoretz

A lot of people in the group hate one another like poison, and you have to be about eighty years old before you can look at your worst enemy and say he and I belong in the same place.

—Midge Decter[1]

Although they first came together in the 1930s the New York Intellectuals* began only recently to admit that they belonged "in the same place." They do not agree on much else these days, or at least large segments of the intellectual community have gone their separate ways so dramatically that it would be hard for anyone without a knowledge of their backgrounds to believe that they ever occupied the "same place." Perhaps the political distances which have grown, as well as advancing age and new intellectual groupings, have made it easier for

---

*Throughout this work, the New York Intellectuals have been designated with a capital I to distinguish them as a particular group, as opposed to the great number of other intellectuals who lived in New York during the period this study covers. The notion of the "intellectual world," for example, is very different from that of the "New York Intellectual community."

them to understand their common connections. But it is only lately—and with the community truly dispersed—that they started to talk about their common story.[2]

Outside observers have for years, however, seen them as a group and as identifiable players on the stage of American intellectual life. New York Intellectual became a label which could be affixed to a certain intellectual style by the 1950s.[3] But members of the group did not suddenly come together in the postwar years. They shared a common history which stretched back to the Depression and beyond. Public acknowledgement of their particular intellectual position marked the culmination of an effort which had been under way for two decades.

They had assembled on the edge of American society. Coming from the immigrant ghettos in which their parents had settled upon arrival in America, they moved toward the center of American intellectual life by a circuitous route through left politics and the avant-garde cultural life of the 1930s. They exchanged the peripheral world of the immigrants for the marginal world of radical intellectuals. But even here, among those who all considered themselves cosmopolitan and universalist, they felt different. They were young, Jewish, urban intellectuals whose radical politics became bound up with an assimilationist momentum begun when their parents left Europe. Whether as precocious youths in the city school system, as young radicals interacting with American leftists who came from generations of American native stock, or as intellectuals feeling that political constraints inhibited their cultural development—they did not integrate fully with the others. They frequently spoke of themselves as alienated. As Norman Podhoretz later put it, "They did not feel that they belonged to America or that America belonged to them." But neither did they feel that they belonged to the world of their parents, a world fated to fade before their eyes. Nor did they feel, Podhoretz noted, that they belonged "to the Jewish people" as a whole. What they did belong to was each other. They were, in Podhoretz's telling phrase, "the Family"—each other's intellectual relatives.[4]

"Almost all these individuals come out of themselves," Daniel Bell observed in the 1970s. "They had no *yichus*," which Bell translated from the Yiddish as "eminent pedigree."[5] They all made themselves who they were. They knew one another—in college cafeterias, on magazine editorial boards, from radical organizations—but they all achieved on their own. They became experts in different areas of American intellectual life. Some earned doctoral degrees, but in a variety of fields. Others functioned in a more traditional intellectual role, as free-lance critics or reviewers, often holding down regular jobs as well. Some found themselves drawn into the community because of literary issues, others because of political concerns. They published widely, often in the same magazines, but also in the more specific journals of their fields. They labored extremely hard to create their own individual places in the American intellectual world. But these efforts should not deflect us from understanding the common themes and threads which bind them together.

They remained, through it all, a feisty, battling community. "There's a lot of talk about back-scratching," Irving Howe remarked in the 1960s, "but I don't see much. Change the word 'back' to 'eye' and maybe you've got something." Only in those years did William Phillips, a founding editor of the essential New York Intellectual journal *Partisan Review*, come to see the impact of the tumultuous interactive style the New Yorkers adopted. "I realized," he said, "why New Critics such as [Allen] Tate and [R. P.] Blackmur and [John Crowe] Ransom enjoyed such fine reputations and nobody ever heard of us. They were always praising each other and we were always at each other's throats." But they also understood the benefits of their particular kind of personal interactions; moreover, they were not as unknown as Phillips suggested. When asked why he remained in New York, Irving Howe responded,

> It's because in New York I can talk with people like Meyer Schapiro, Daniel Bell, Harold Rosenberg, and Lionel Abel. They usually disagree with me, but they put me on my mettle. Outside of New York, I might be a big cheese in a small town. But the trouble with big cheeses is that they're probably full of holes and I want to be near people who can point them out.[6]

Since Howe made this assessment, Rosenberg has died, and Bell moved to Cambridge and Abel to Buffalo. Certainly, Howe has other friends who will evaluate his work. Meyer Schapiro is still one, but the rest may not be New York Intellectuals any longer. Death and geographical dispersion, as well as political and cultural schisms, have ended the cohesion of the New York Intellectual community. Its existence is now the province of history.

Lionel Trilling is in many respects my idea of the perfect New York intellectual . . . intelligent, curious, humane, well read, interested in ideas, fascinated by other times and places, immensely knowledgeable about European culture.   —David Daiches

[Harold] Rosenberg was . . . formidable and combative—in many respects, the quintessential New York intellectual, resourceful in polemic and sometimes dazzling in style. . . . His style, both in conversation and in writing, was nurtured on that special mixture of Marxism and modernism that came to constitute the distinct Weltanschauung *of the New York intellectuals.*   —Hilton Kramer

Yes, Virginia, there is a Santa Claus, Yes, there is such a figure as the New York Intellectual, and he is, or was, Philip Rahv.
                                                                —William Barrett[7]

Despite the community's dissolution and despite the fact that the three "quintessential" New York Intellectuals noted above have all died, New York

Intellectuals still exist. The living remain some of the most important figures in American intellectual and academic life. And they retain many of the attributes developed when they shared the margin with other members of their intellectual community. The entire group is most easily identified by the generational stages in which they emerged and by the institutional connections, especially to magazines, which developed. The first generation coalesced in the late 1930s around the "new" *Partisan Review*—"new" because it had broken its direct ties with the Communist left. Drawn by political and literary issues, as well as by a desire to define the place of intellectuals in society, the "new" magazine and the emerging community attracted a wide range of literary and political figures, including Philip Rahv, William Phillips, Lionel Trilling, Diana Trilling, Meyer Schapiro, Clement Greenberg, Harold Rosenberg, Dwight Macdonald, Elliot Cohen, and Sidney Hook. Among the readers of the "new" *PR* were young radicals still in college, a number of whom would become the second generation of the intellectual community. These included Irving Howe, Irving Kristol, Daniel Bell, Delmore Schwartz, Leslie Fiedler, Seymour Martin Lipset, Nathan Glazer, Alfred Kazin, Robert Warshow, Melvin Lasky, Isaac Rosenfeld, and Saul Bellow. As they came of age, these younger writers joined with the older ones, but just at the point when politics began to change for them all. They made the transition from thirties radicalism to postwar liberalism together. They also succeeded in establishing names for themselves after 1945, as well as several new journals, including *Commentary* and *Dissent*. A small, third generation attached itself after the war. Students rather than colleagues, they joined not when the community was on the periphery of American intellectual life but as it moved to the center. While a few of this third generation—Norman Podhoretz, Midge Decter, and Steven Marcus— grew to importance in the community, most of the others, including Norman Mailer, Philip Roth, and Susan Sontag, headed off in varying directions. The times and the changed status of the older members made the connections different and, often, much looser.*

The New York Intellectuals began as radicals, moved to liberalism, and sometimes ended up as conservatives. But they were always intellectuals. *Partisan Review* started as a magazine dedicated to radical literature and then rededicated itself to radical culture, only outside the world of proletarian literature and Communist party politics. The New Yorkers held out for the preeminence of art, not devoid of social context but reflective of it. They resisted both the perceived limited scope of the New Critics and their notion of the programmatic nature of proletarian literature. They brought the modernist

---

*As is evident from the listing of the individuals who comprise the community, this is essentially a male group. As such, when discussing the intellectual community itself, male pronouns are frequently used, as are the designations "bright boys" or "young men" to describe them in their early years. General societal descriptions are gender-free. The use of male identified terms is intentional and meant to be specific of the group.

heroes of the 1920s into the world of radical politics, without sacrificing cultural standards or radicalism, they believed. Furthermore, they held strongly to ideas about the special and crucial role for critics and for intellectuals in general. In the end their politics, rather than their cultural ideas or intellectual position, underwent the most dramatic changes. And with those changes they moved to the center.

Having been "stuck with one another" in the 1930s, as Podhoretz was to put it, they stayed with one another through the 1960s when political pressures and the passage of time finally began to undo the community. No sudden disruption occurred, just the moving away of various individuals at various points. Until this happened, however, the New York Intellectuals found themselves and kept themselves together. They held out for their personal independence but maintained their connections. All were strong, driven individuals, eager to create their own personal place, and they often saw their own achievements in personal terms. Yet they moved across the political landscape together, not in a single line advancing along a common front, but occupying the same large areas at the same time.

Harold Rosenberg once labeled his fellow intellectuals as a "herd of independent minds." He went on to describe his personal distinctions from the "herd." The others could have equally well set themselves apart from the rest. All of them, however, including Rosenberg, belonged for a long time. They resisted inclusion because they worked so hard to make themselves something and, in so doing, often lost sight of the common ties. And they were not always friendly in person or courteous in print with one another. Still, they all ran with the herd.

After reviewing the course of the first years of *Partisan Review*, Leslie Fiedler concluded that despite intellectual and, in his case, geographical distinctions, *PR* (at that time synonymous with the New York Intellectual community) was a part of him: "I have accepted my fate with all its contradictions: I stand somehow for *PR* and *PR* for me."[8] These individuals usually came to *PR* and, ultimately, to the New York Intellectual community from a common background, seeking certain intellectual and political goals, and eager to fulfill the ambitions of their youth. They shared much, differed on many particulars, and steadily advanced together. They were a varied and often extremely individualistic lot. There was no single, typical New York Intellectual, because no one of them fit all the characteristics the group possessed or shared all the community's wide–ranging intellectual interests. There is no question that some differed on certain points and that they have gone their separate ways in the last decade or so. Yet there is also no question that these individuals embodied many of the most important political and intellectual forces of recent years, that they helped shape what America thought—in its universities, its leading journals, and its political debates. And there is no question that despite personal animosities and differing attitudes on particular questions, they could for a long time be considered together. The discussion which follows does not aim to write the complete biography of any single member of the community, nor does it maintain that every member shared every position. Rather, it seeks to describe the intellectual herd as a mass and to follow it as it moved across the political and intellectual landscape. How the community came to be formed, what it thought important, how and why it moved and changed, and why it ultimately came undone are what we are after. Watching the community come together, develop, and adjust, we can learn about the motives which helped drive these children of immigrants to positions of intellectual eminence, about some of the ways in which intellectuals function and justify their own places, and something about the political and cultural terrain itself over which the New York Intellectuals passed.

Section I

PATHS TO PARTISAN

Chapter 1

Young Men
from the Provinces

New York had long been the center of American radicalism and artistic movements, the ideal place where young intellectuals could learn and develop, and come into contact with numerous styles and trends. The New York Intellectuals did not grow up, however, in that part of New York which mattered to radicals and artists. The New York where they did grow up proved just as essential to their maturation as the one to which they would eventually migrate. They lived on the periphery—in the Brownsville section of Brooklyn, in the Bronx, in Newark, or even in the neighborhoods on the edges of other large American cities. These places made up "for most American Jews the image of their group," Robert Warshow observed in 1946. "The New York pattern is the master pattern, repeated in its main outlines wherever there is a large Jewish population." In the immigrant ghettos in which their parents had settled, the young students were raised and schooled. Maturing in a half–English, half–Yiddish environment, they always carried with them some of that divided world. This world was more than their environment, however; it settled into the consciousness and the memories of young Jews. "It is what a Jew remembers, it is what he has in mind when he experiences his more private emotions about being a Jew—affection, pity, delight, shame," Warshow believed. It was their home, more than merely their address. The Jewish ghetto offered many of the New York Intellectuals what small towns had offered bright young Americans for decades, a place in which to grow and learn. And while "the life of the small town can be said in some sense to embody the common experience of the older Americans," Warshow concluded, "so the life of New York can be said at this particular stage in the process of acculturation to embody the common experience of American Jews."[1] The young New Yorkers came, in time, to reject and abandon this world, just as past generations

11

had fled the small towns. But this abandonment meant more than merely the departure from one's place of birth. The young intellectuals, like the future accountants, schoolteachers, salesmen, and social workers in their neighborhoods, carried with them the dreams of their parents, even as they rejected their world. The archetypal contest between the small-town life and the bright lights of the city describes the division which grows between parents and children, between basic beliefs and values. The immigrants in the ghettos wished strongly for the success and assimilation of their children. What developed was not a battle of systems but a joint venture in launching the younger group. This experience is by no means unique to the New York Intellectuals. Immigrant parents' ambition for the success of their children is a classic tale of American history. With this success, though, came a burden to be carried through adult life. The large number of New York Intellectuals who grew up in this environment carried these burdens. Their early, personal history was reflected in their later lives. Their ghetto youth influenced their adult concerns, reemerging as they sought to find their way in political and intellectual worlds. They shared childhood experiences with numerous young Jews. Their adult resolutions, however, were all their own.

ONE HUNDRED THOUSAND JEWISH PARENTS

We were the end of the line. We were the children of the immigrants who had camped at the city's back door, in New York's rawest, remotest, cheapest ghetto. How that was an extrordinary world to grow up in!
—*Alfred Kazin*[2]

To understand fully both how "extraordinary" and how "raw" this world really was required the perspective of both having been raised there and having left. "In New York the Jews still formed a genuine community," Irving Howe recalls, "reaching half-unseen into a dozen neighborhoods and a multitude of institutions, within the shadows of which we have found protection of a kind."[3] This community nurtured its sons, protected them, and dreamed for them.

The immigrants had come to make a place for themselves in America. Encountering poverty and prejudice, they spent their days trying to make a living. Life proved extremely hard. "When I was young, there were three words we dreaded," Sidney Hook recalled, "'diphtheria,' because that meant a child would die; 'pneumonia,' because that meant an adult would die; and 'slack,' because that meant six months without work."[4] Grand aspirations had to give way to the process of survival, the immigrants transferring their yearnings to their children. The young would take the final step, would enter and prosper in the larger American society. The security of the immigrant Jewish community provided the protective environment and the early preparation for this venture into the world. From an early age the expectation of a successful life beyond the bounds of the immigrant ghetto became one of the clear goals set for the young boys by their parents. The pressures of achievement for oneself and for one's parents became part of the psychological baggage they took with them.

Most American immigrant neighborhoods offered a communal sense to counter the feeling of isolation from the outside world. For the adults, community organizations, social interactions, cultural groups, and religious affiliations provided solace. The young found a tight-knit community, where some of the stigma of poverty and prejudice might be avoided. Although Irving Howe's father went bankrupt in 1930 and became a door-to-door peddler to support his family, Howe's recollections of those years offer an example of the insulating aspects of the ghetto environment.

> We were often very poor, living together with uncles, aunts, and grandmothers to save rent. Yet I had no very acute sense of being deprived, or any notions that I was the victim of social injustice . . . . The realization of what is meant to be poor I had first to discover through writings about poverty; the sense of my own handicap became vivid to me only after I had learned about the troubles of people I did not know. And surely this experience was typical.[5]

While the young intellectuals and their contemporaries matured, the ghetto cushioned their growth. As Alfred Kazin remembered, "In one sense I had a hundred thousand Jewish parents when I grew up in Brownsville." And Howe summarized the general nature of the ghetto as follows: "The Jewish community enclosed one . . . . We did not realize then how sheltering it was to grow up in this world. . . ."[6]

The cushioning, however, was mixed with expectations. Parents measured success by educational achievement, and as the young boys proved precocious, they were singled out in the public schools and shone in adults' eyes. While this marked a boy for educational heights at an early age it also brought with it personal pressure to succeed.

Other difficulties added to the contradictory sense of support and pressure. The young boys shone at school, yet the classrooms seemed overcrowded, constrictive. At home, where parents transferred their own aspirations to their children, families lived in a few rooms. Even beds were crowded. At school and at home the expectations pressed in. The only place of personal freedom was in the street. "The streets were ours . . . the streets belonged to us. We would roam through the city tasting the delights of freedom, discovering the possibilities far beyond the reach of our parents," Howe later recalled. Being streetwise grew to be a mark of these young students, sharp and mentally tough. It was mirrored in their intellectual styles. "Even those of us who later became intellectuals or professionals kept something of our bruising gutter-worldliness, our hard and abrasive skepticism."[7]

Within the Jewish community existed a wide variety of cultural and political offerings. The immigrants had transported a number of radical and socialist movements with them to America. Others had sprung to life in their new country. For the young students, the diversity of street-corner speakers, political meetings, and discussions of Yiddish literature or of the day's *Forward* filtered into emerging intellectual consciousness. They might wander through the numerous associations of impromptu discussions, picking up bits and pieces. Always quick to learn, praised in school for their verbal agility, considered bright young boys—many of the young intellectuals tested their political wings in their own environment long before they could have ventured out in the larger radical world. Having become an early convert to socialism, Daniel Bell recalls standing on street corners at the age of fourteen, championing the socialist position.[8]

The assimilation of this variety of cultural and political material had a second effect. The give-and-take of the street corner or the cultural association kept learning and education from compartmentalization. Ideas on political events flowed into those on philosophy or culture, issues of the street mixing with lessons of the classroom. "It was inconceivable to me that I could be simply an academic specialist," recalled Alfred Kazin. "I was swept up in all sorts of socialist and radical ideas, and I believed that modern art and modern history had come to be very much related."[9]

The passion of the intellectual interests of the Jewish neighborhoods added to their breadth. The electricity of the intellectual debates became a chief source of vitality among the immigrants. For others, set adrift in an alien world, the maintenance of a European tradition—religious, cultural, or political— helped compensate for the general isolation. Many Jewish immigrants came to America because of political beliefs, converts to socialism seeking a home where their ideas might take root. All these reasons contributed to immigrants' intellectual interests. Their passion, though, also increased through a con- vergence of theory and reality. "Always a voracious reader," Sidney Hook recalled of his youth, "I devoured the literature of the socialist movement at an age when righteous passion at the indignities of existence which surrounded me in the proletarian slums where my family lived, helped me to understand . . . the fundamental truths of the class-struggle."[10]

The European talmudic tradition and lives sharpened by poverty combined to create this intense, passionate environment in the Jewish ghettos. The streetwise young students learned much of their style from their elders. In a difficult life, intellectual pleasures offered a temporary escape. The street corner debates, the pointing of fingers, and the pounding on chests provided the stimulation as much as did the particular issues under discussion. Stifled at nearly every turn, the Jewish immigrants found some release in this combative atmosphere, aware that it was something of a game in which to spend pent-up energy. The young men as well as their elders, venturing into this world of verbal battles, found the give-and-take of the argument coupled with a sense of tolerance. "Attitudes of tolerance and permissiveness, feelings that one had to put up with and indulge one's cranks, eccentrics, idealists, and extremists, affected the Jewish community," Irving Howe later wrote. And for those like himself, "You might be shouting at the top of your lungs against reformism or Stalin's betrayals, but for the middle-aged garment worker strolling along Southern Boulevard you were just a bright and cocky Jewish boy, a talkative little *pisher*."[11]

They might be *pishers* and cocky, but being bright raised them above the level of potential "cranks" or "eccentrics." Youthful swagger would be tolerated. With the support and tolerance of the community, it could be turned into attributes which would lead them out of the ghetto. And nowhere were these expectations higher than at home.

WE WERE THEIR AMERICA

> O Nicolas! Alas! Alas!
> My grandfather coughed in your army,
>
> Hid in a wine-stinking barrel
> For three days in Bucharest,
>
> Then left for America
> To become a king himself.
>
> —Delmore Schwartz

> *My parents were Jewish immigrants and now, in retrospect, I can see how important this was to my life. It meant, on the one hand, a home atmosphere of warm and binding love, and it meant, on the other hand, an atmosphere of striving, of struggle to appropriate those goods of American life which to others come almost automatically.*
>
> *—Irving Howe[12]*

More than a cultural boundary surrounded Brownsville. Jewish immigrants stayed not only because of familiarity but also because a move would merely have been to someplace else, not to someplace better. Language, education, and poverty, as well as prejudice, kept the immigrants out of the mainstream of American life. "They were trapped in the limitations of their skills," wrote Irving Howe, "in the skimpiness of their education, in the awkwardness of their speech, in the alienness of their manners."[13] Singly and collectively, however, they saw their personal emancipation and full participation in American society through the success and assimilation of their children. Homes also provided support and a launching ground. To be schooled, to succeed, to go to the university, *and* to be a success—all this would complete the journey Jews had begun in the pale, as well as lead them out of Brownsville.

The immigrants transferred a second goal to their sons, their intellectual tradition. The high hopes placed on the bright boys came not only from successes in the first encounter with an American institution, the public school, but also from the potential fulfillment of the stifled intellectualism of their fathers. Many an immigrant father worked in a skilled or semiskilled job by day and became the household or neighborhood intellectual in the evening. Years later Irving Howe looked back on the attitude of fathers such as his own:

> The Jewish immigrant is the most intellectualized of the workers for a variety of reasons: the traditional forms of his religion are highly literary; the compensation of an urban, restless, and rootless people who can find sustenance only in the internalized, that is intellectualized, experiences, lead him to an overvaluation of the significance—as well as the cash value—of verbal and written activities.

The limits of language and an education inappropriate to the American intellectual marketplace kept the fathers in their working-class professions. Those few schooled in Europe had received a talmudic training, useful perhaps for mental agility but otherwise useless in America. The right kind of training was, however, being given their sons. In place of his own success, then, Howe saw how the frustrated intellectualism of the father worked itself out in his children. "Since he himself has not the opportunity to so develop but must, as he puts it, 'spend the rest of his days in the shop,' he centers his hopes on his favorite son."[14]

The young students felt the responsibility placed on them from the outset. While never articulated, their role in this process remained unconsciously perceived. It influenced the way they behaved in classes, determined the level of their academic motivation, and colored their relations with their parents. "My father and mother worked in a rage to put us above their level," Alfred Kazin has written; "they had married to make *us* possible. We were the only conceivable end to all their striving; we were their America."[15]

Living with these expectations did not always make for the easiest of childhoods. Along with the warmth and love of home and community came an increasing sense of the pressures as well. Alfred Kazin remembered,

> I worked on a hairline between triumph and catastrophe. Why the odds should always have felt so narrow I understood only when I realized how little my parents thought of their own lives. It was not for myself alone that I was expected to shine, but for them—to redeem the constant anxiety of their existence. I was the first American child, their offering to the strange new God; I was to be the monument of their liberation from the shame of being—what they were.[16]

Most of the contemporaries of these young students never perceived the choices so starkly, learning that more than a hairline existed between triumph and catastrophe. First-generation assimilation does not usually lead to immediate public prominence, but a smaller step into the larger middle classes—a move from Brownsville to Long Island, Westchester, or the New Jersey suburbs. The case of the New York Intellectuals is atypical. The intellectual heights they achieved met the dreams of their parents but proved exceptional for most other first-generation Americans.

There is a period in life when all children incorporate the values of their parents. By the time children begin to break away from their parents, they already carry many of these values with them. Many are able to adjust them, some deny them, and others consciously oppose them. Yet, they function in terms of them. For these young Jewish students, Alfred Kazin among them, the incorporation went even deeper than for others in their neighborhood. The high hopes placed on the brightest students matched the increased incorporation of the parents' outlook into their own.

> I was awed by this system, I believed in it, I respected its force. The alternative was "going bad." The school was notoriously the toughest in our tough neighborhood, and the dangers of "going bad" were constantly impressed upon me at home and in school in dark whispers of the "reform school." . . . Behind any failure in school yawned the great abyss of a criminal career. Every refractory attitude doomed you with the sound "Sing Sing." Anything less than absolute perfection in school always suggested to my mind that I might fall out of the daily race, be kept back in the working class forever, or—dared I think of it?—fall into the criminal class itself.[17]

The drive for absolute perfection, Irving Howe believed, led to "precocity, internality, moral quest and self judgment, a neurotic need for perfection." Against what seem overwhelming odds, the young students ultimately triumphed. The "neurotic need for perfection" and the high "hopes [placed] on the 'favorite son' " finally led to success and eminence.[18]

All the evaluations and assessments of these dynamics would come later. The immigrants, as Howe noted, "were seldom in a position to grasp the complex process by which ideas of collective fulfillment were transformed into goals of personal achievement." They reacted as individuals, responded personally—sometimes with expectations different from those of their children.[19] While academic achievement became the standard which established the beginnings of this process, the question of where to apply academic success proved a point of generational debate. Material worth became the tangible sign of American success, especially among impoverished immigrants. Intellectuality had its place, but the idealized model of European Jews was the man rich enough to have time to spend in the synagogue, not the impoverished, perpetual student. This model found its American counterpart. Mrs. Bauman, a character in a story by Delmore Schwartz, "dreamed that her sons would be millionaires and her grandsons rabbis and philosophers."[20] The future intellectuals, whether at the point of making career choices or, as we shall see, at the point of thinking no careers were really available to them, chose the path of Mrs. Bauman's grandchildren. They became philosophers, scholars, critics—intellectuals. Yet, they internalized the strivings of their parents and in the postwar years emerged neither as millionaires nor as impoverished intellectuals.

The compromise they achieved allowed for the best of both generations, the scholar and the success. They worked out a system of priorities which would guide them in career choices as well as in intellectual decisions. As Robert Warshow summarized for his contemporaries, "They evolved the three imperatives that govern them: be secure, be respected, be intelligent." He then elaborated the kind of career choices these imperatives would direct: "In their world a dentist is better than a machinist, a doctor better than a businessman, a college professor is best of all. But an unsuccessful intellectual is worse than an unsuccessful businessman: he should have known better than to try."[21] The option to be a machinist or a businessman might have existed for some of their generation. For the young intellectuals the high hopes held for them pointed to the highest places on this list of potential careers. In the resolution of career choices and directions, they carved a middle ground between personal goals and parental expectations. Before they settled in this position, however, the New York Intellectuals cast about in areas and activities far from the places their parents envisioned and far from the comfortable positions they ultimately achieved.

The overall relations between these young men and their parents provided an exaggerated example of the basic pattern of maternal closeness and paternal aloofness typical of the time. This form was not the sole province of the ghetto families. The atmosphere of the ghetto, however, added special elements to the role perceptions. While the father often was the symbolic figure of a household intellectual, this activity confined itself to his personal love of books or his interaction with the other men. His example more than his instruction accounted for the intellectual inheritance the young received. In addition, the father's self-perception of failure, his belief that his life lacked fulfillment, increased the disparity between the attention of the parents. Mothers are remembered for nurture and support as well as for overattentiveness and a smothering of their children with concern. Fathers are faulted for excesses in the other direction, for being too standoffish. They specifically desired that their sons *not* grow up like them. Sons might expand on the father's limited intellectualism, but otherwise the fathers hoped their children would turn out differently from themselves. The ultimate success of the fathers' ambition rested on the sons' achievemnt.

The relation of the mother to her child grew especially close in this atmosphere. "From infancy on," Irving Howe later observed, "the child is petted by his mother. She keeps him in the feminine pattern as long as possible." She doesn't want to cut his curls, Howe noted, or to have him enter atheletic activities, for fear he might be hurt. He is "burdened" with so many activities, such as music lessons, Hebrew school, family obligations, and schoolwork, that he has little time for the normal pursuits of childhood. "She constantly hovers over him, developing in him—as if with unconscious skill— the sense of dependence on her which he is later to find so difficult to overcome." Only in later life were individuals like Alfred Kazin able to sort out the roots of certain motivations. "I felt all my life," Kazin said in 1976, "that I was having to report back to my mother. I didn't feel I was a victim; I felt I was responsible for her."[22]

Relations between mothers and sons proved intense and deeply rooted, but relatively straightforward. The relations between fathers and sons never grew as close, and they evidence more complexity. During adolescent rebellion the sons found clearer targets in the overattentive and restrictive pattern established by their mothers. Never fully free of the ties to their mothers, the young could at least temporarily feel the bonds breaking. To resolve the internalized connections and hostilities they felt toward their fathers remained a more difficult task. Fathers provided multifaceted objects for the young men to confront—symbols of intelligence, aloofness, and failure. Mothers might dominate through cajoling, spoiling, and loving; fathers were figures of much less personal involvement. Fathers' sacrifices and hopes for their sons' success were not always translated into closeness. In reponse, the young men vacillated between reverence, resentment, disappointment, and conflict.

The immigrant father spent his life largely outside the home. At work, in the synagogue, or in a political meeting, he was a figure removed from a child's perception of the day-to-day events of the household. However, the father's public "pretensions," as Robert Warshow would call them, ultimately came to be seen as "nothing but nonsense," and the boy ultimately held him "responsible" for the family's hardships. Isaac Rosenfeld's novel *Passage from Home* is the fullest articulation of this generational conflict between Jewish fathers and sons. Bernard, the main character, speaks about this dilemma: "[I felt] forever disappointed in my father, just as I know he was disappointed in me. As far as I can remember, I was always denying him." Disappointment, Warshow later observed, "was often the only thing [fathers] could clearly communicate."[23]

As the young boys grew, resentments and disappointments moved toward the surface. Adolescent rebellion was fully manifest in the immigrant ghettos. The centrality of this conflict in the life of so many of his contemporaries led Daniel Bell to see it in vivid terms. For the "bulk of Jewish immigrants," he stated, "the anxiety was translated into the struggle between fathers and sons. Few generational conflicts have had such exposed nakedness, such depths of strain as this." The children of other immigrant groups, perhaps even those from long-established American families, might also believe their generational conflict highly intense. Bell's observation is less telling about the relative degree of "struggle" than about the impression it made upon his generation of Jewish youths. "In my time," Lionel Trilling wrote, "we all were trying to find a release from our fathers."[24] The same impression emerged in the responses to Isaac Rosenfeld's novel, published in 1946. Many New York Intellectuals were deeply touched by Rosenfeld's descriptions. Irving Howe's review in *Commentary* noted that "the helpless, tragic conflict [was] . . . a true and acute perception, the very stuff of which literature is made."[25] The perceptions of Bell, Howe, and others emerged in adult years. Time and space had offered the chance to gain perspective on the interactions. Yet, during the childhood years, signs of the differentiation, the first hints of the distance that grew between parents and children, began to appear. This divergence stemmed from the same source as the other difficulties—the problems brought on by immigration and the alien place of the parents in American society.

While the ghetto environment provided the parents a degree of familiarity in a strange land, it also allowed them to maintain old-world habits and customs. Language was one significant remnant. Many of these immigrants not only continued to read the foreign-language press but also spoke Yiddish at home. Many young children went to school either speaking only Yiddish or knowing Yiddish better than English. "Yiddish was my first language," Bell noted; "English was my second." Irving Howe recalled an awkward moment deriving from this home–school distinction.

> I attended my first day of kindergarten as if it were a visit to a new country. The teacher asked the children to identify various common objects. When my turn came she held up a fork and without hesitation I called it by its Yiddish name: "a *goopel*." The whole class burst out laughing at me with that special cruelty of children. That afternoon I told my parents that I had made up my mind never to speak Yiddish to them again, though I would not give any reasons. It was a shock for them, the first in a series of conflicts between immigrant and America.[26]

Immigrants believed school to be the arena where potential successes began, and thus the disparity of school–English and home–Yiddish grew more obvious. Delmore Schwartz saw this bilingualism as "produc[ing] in some a fear of mispronunciation; a hesitation in speech; and a sharpened focus upon the characters of the parents." Parents' stature clearly began to diminish. Norman Podhoretz contrasted his patrician high school teacher with his mother. "The idea of Mrs. K. meeting my mother was more than I could bear: my mother, who spoke with a Yiddish accent and of whom, until that sickening moment, I had never known I was ashamed and so ready to betray." Daniel Bell recalls similar feelings of "awkward shame."[27]

As the students increasingly interacted with the world outside the home and, especially, outside the ghetto community, their sense of separateness and shame grew. Howe's aversion to the Yiddish speech of his parents fed his sense of distance. He remembered playing in an abandoned lot and having his father call for him: "He would shout my name from afar, giving it a Yiddish twist: 'Oivee!' I would always feel a sense of shame at hearing my name so mutilated in the presence of amused onlookers. . . . I would always run ahead of my father as if to emphasize the existence of a certain distance between us."[28]

This physical separation, placing actual space between the generations, became a child's simple way of expressing something much more intricate. It was most pronounced when the interaction occurred outside the insular Jewish community. Bernard, in *Passage from Home*, feels no real shame interacting with his very traditional and Orthodox grandfather in Jewish neighborhoods.

> Once when he had come to our house—we lived farther North and West, among Gentiles—I had been ashamed to meet him at the elevated station and walk down the street with him, and had kept a few paces ahead, not letting him take my arm.[29]

As the young grew older, their sense of distance took on more mature and more cultural forms. The distinctions they saw between themselves and their parents continued to grow. They came to realize, Daniel Bell concluded "the fact that most of this generation, including myself, were ashamed of our parents."[30] They felt themselves pulled toward the center of American society, away from the edge where their parents lived. They grew ever more alienated from the world of the ghetto and from their own parents as well. No longer at home in this environment, they could not immediately find a home at the center either.

STANDING OUTSIDE AMERICA

The distance which developed between parents and children did not provide the younger generation with a sense of being at home in America. A sense of belonging, feeling part of the mainstream, remained as absent from their own consciousness as from their parents'. They felt somewhat removed from the old–worldliness of the ghetto and of their parents, but they neither felt totally accepted nor were totally accepted in the New World. They stood between, aware of what they were not—distancing themselves from one group, kept at a distance by the other.

They, too, were immigrants or branded by their immigrant connections. Philip Rahv emigrated from Russia as a small boy, first to Palestine and then to live with an older brother in Providence, Rhode Island. Mary McCarthy told how Rahv, older than the grade school students in whose class he was placed, "went to grade school still dressed in the old–fashioned European schoolboy style, in long black trousers and black stockings, looking like a somber little man among the American kids." Even for those born in America, the immigrant experience played heavily on the notions of who they were. "The basic element of Jewish life in America," Daniel Bell has commented, "has been the immigrant experience . . . . At times it led . . . to a sense of being a 'guest in the house.' "[31]

The feeling of being apart was reinforced by a second factor which proved crucial for defining the ghetto as different from mainstream America. In addition to being immigrants or immigrants' children, they were Jewish. These characteristics, given the motives for emigration and the places of residence in the New World, were interwoven but not identical. Immigration carried with it the hope or potential for assimilation. One desired to be an immigrant or an alien only a short time. Jewishness, however, was an ethnic tradition which it was wrong to abandon or to deny. These distinctions, to be sure, seemed less apparent to the young residents of the Jewish neighborhoods, where Jewish culture and immigrant life styles combined. Alfred Kazin found it necessary to write in a 1944 symposium on Jewish writers, "It is about time we stopped confusing the experience of being an immigrant, or an immigrant's son, with the experience of being Jewish."[32] The close coupling of Jewish and immigrant identities made it extremely difficult for the maturing young students to decide which portions of their inheritance to abandon and which to maintain. It became easiest to move away from it all.

This dilemma was further complicated by the fact that for their parents many of the immigrant institutions also served to maintain Jewish identity. Yiddish newspapers, cultural associations, neighborhood synagogues—all these provided social as well as ethnic identifications. For the young the move toward assimilation meant the rejection of many of these institutions; they consciously tried to shake off immigrant ways but in the process abandoned Jewish elements. It became difficult, though, to reject the institutions which provided Jewish as well as immigrant identity and then to maintain a clear sense of Jewishness. In their early careers, many New York Intellectuals found themselves grappling with this problem and with definitions. In the symposium on young Jewish writers in 1944, Lionel Trilling and Alfred Kazin provided two examples of attempts to redefine their Jewishness, definitions which lacked the specific attributes their parents might have included. "For me," Trilling noted,

> the point of honor consists in feeling that I would not, even if I could, deny or escape being Jewish. Surely it is at once clear how minimal such a position is . . . . [It] is perhaps the position of most American writers of Jewish birth.

Kazin put it this way:

> My parents are Jews—not particularly devout, not particularly conscious of being insincere in their occasional devotion; but Jews for whom the symbols have had a direct and tender meaning, and for whom the code had a plain integrity. I had no such luck. I learned that Jews were "different"—but different as I had to suppose, only because the ones I knew were always poor and usually scared. . . . I learned long ago to accept the fact that I was Jewish without being a part of any meaningful Jewish life or culture.[33]

Aware that they were Jews but unable to define clearly their Jewishness, the young intellectuals fell back on a "minimal" position, such as Trilling's. This stance kept pace with the cosmopolitan and radical style of the times. As they matured, they returned to these dilemmas and ultimately arrived at a personal identity which defined their Jewishness, as well as their general place in

American society. During their youth, however, the engima remained, unspoken and unresolved. Clearly perceived as Jews in the Gentile world, they felt less clear as to what that meant personally. In a series of short stories about a year spent teaching at a midwestern college (actually at Wisconsin), Trilling often returned to the theme of being a Jew in an essentially non-Jewish environment. This led his autobiographical character in one story to daydream of a rabbi whirling his arms excitedly. " 'What does it mean to be a Jew?' He repeated it over and over again." Being a Jew, Trilling's imaginary rabbi finally announces, has two aspects: "the Subjective and the Objective—What does it mean to be a Jew to Yourself and What Does it mean to be a Jew to Others?"[34] It was much easier for these young intellectuals to answer the second question, to give the objective definition, than the first. That others perceived them as Jews was undeniable. "A Jewish writer," Isaac Rosenfeld believed, "feels that he may at any time be called to account not for his art, nor even his life, but for his Jewishness."[35] If called to account, these Jews could not comfortably provide answers. Just as they were caught between the immigrant world and the center of American society, they found themselves similarly caught between a notion of Jewishness which their parents held and which they could not accept and a designation as Jews which the outside world imposed.

The sense that they were Jews and therefore different never became a matter of controversy. Personal experiences with anti-Semitism supplemented those of their parents, both in Europe and in America. Stories of Cossacks and pogroms formed a part of their heritage; encounters with anti-Semitism from non-Jewish teachers and interactions outside their neighborhoods were a part of their childhood experience. When they embarked upon careers, especially in the academic world, they faced open prejudice. It confronted them as they progressed into the non-Jewish worlds of academe, publishing, and criticism. After working as an instructor at Columbia for four years, Lionel Trilling was dropped, in 1936. "The departmental spokesman said he would not be reappointed for a next year because 'as a Freudian, a Marxist, and a Jew,' he was not happy in the department," Diana Trilling recalled. "Lionel said he *was* happy in the department. They said he would be 'more comfortable' elsewhere." Only in 1939, after his book on Matthew Arnold had been published, and only through the personal intervention of Nicholas Murray Butler, Columbia's president, was Trilling appointed the first Jewish assistant professor in the Columbia English department.[36]

This attitude was not, however, what Trilling had hoped would exist in academic life. In another of the stories of his year at Wisconsin, he described his desire to find a "cultivated" society in academe, "men living pleasantly, well-mannered, civilized, among whom he could be one . . . there would be no confinement . . . here there was no crying of 'Jew!' "[37] As Trilling's experience at Columbia proved, the academic world was no more tolerant than the rest of society. Trilling could only hope that it might be possible to live an existence free of the tensions of ghetto life, of the drive to raise oneself out of poverty, to be released from the daily struggle. This would be a life far different from the one being abandoned—and better as well. "Our families and teachers seemed tacitly agreed that we were somehow to be a little ashamed of what we were," Alfred Kazin recalled.[38] The achievement of a better life involved a denial or minimization of what they were—not a conscious rejection, but slow adjustments in perspective, until the parents' world seemed foreign, even inferior.

Schools, where the process of assimilation began, provided the initial comparisons. Delmore Schwartz recalled that, "contrast between the authority of the public school teachers and the weakness of the Hebrew school teacher [was] one which makes the child wonder what reason can justify the emphasis on Jewishness."[39] What they were to become was clearly defined. Where they came from remained unconsidered until, in later life, they discovered just how far they had moved away.

Anxious to abandon the world of which they felt a little ashamed, they began to include the characteristics of their parents and of Jewishness among the items to be rejected. Irving Howe found that statements beginning "I am a Jew and . . ." were very difficult for his fellow New York Intelletuals to utter. Lionel Trilling, one of the first successful Jewish professors of English, clearly discovered the division between his professional and personal background. While establishing his personal position as a "minimal" Jew, as he called it, he claimed,

> I cannot discover anything in my professional intellectual life which I can signifcantly trace back to my Jewish birth and rearing. I do not think of myself as a "Jewish writer." I do not have it in mind to serve by my writing any Jewish purpose.[40]

Apart from the world of their fathers as well as the society around them, the young intellectuals found themselves standing between the two. They maintained this position for a number of years, comfortable in neither place. Their sense of alienation, in fact, helped form their new grouping. "This is a generation," Daniel Bell noted, "which more than any other made itself."[41] Increasingly alienated individuals found that others shared the same position, that the dynamic which propelled them out of the ghetto propelled others. As young Jews, they might even focus on their alienation as a source of intellectual insight. Clement Greenberg believed that his appreciation of the abstract stemmed, in part, from

> a certain *Schwärmerei*, a state of perpetual and exalted surprise—sometimes disgust—at the sensuous and exalted data of existence which others take for granted. This is probably connected with the Jew's chronic conception of himself as a wanderer.[42]

The young Jews might look for sources of intellectual solace, might take joy, as did Alfred Kazin, in the other "aliens" from American culture, such as Emily

Dickinson or Walt Whitman. "Nevertheless," Kazin wrote, "I still thought of myself then as standing outside America."[43]

Even Lionel Trilling sensed that he did not belong in his arcadian dream of the cultivated midwestern college town, fearing it was "going to make him do things he must not do . . . . To prevent this he had use of a hitherto useless fact. He had said, 'I am a Jew,' and was immediately set free. He had felt himself the embodiment of an antique and separate race." Unable to define his own Jewishness in more than a "minimal" way, Trilling nonetheless had felt that connection strongly enough to realize that his place was not in the non-Jewish world of a midwestern college. He fell back not on the cultural or religious institutions of his parents' generation but on the place being carved out by young men like himself—a space created by their sense of apartness. "Lonely you were born and lonely you would die," Kazin remembered; "you were lonely as a Jew and lonely in a strange land, lonely, always lonely even in the midst of people . . . ."[44] Feeling apart from the community in which they had grown up, they pushed ahead toward the next stage of development. They emerged from the shadows of the protective Jewish neighborhoods and into the often frightening light of New York City. They did not find a home waiting; instead, they created one among those waiting to find a home.

YOUNG MEN FROM THE PROVINCES

> *Thus equipped with poverty, pride, and intelligence, the Young Man from the Provinces stands outside life and seeks to enter. This modern hero is connected with the tales of the folk. Usually his motive is the legendary one of setting out to seek his fortune, which is what the folktale says when it means that the hero is seeking himself. He is really the third and youngest son of the woodcutter, the one to whom all our sympathies go, the gentle and misunderstood one, the bravest of all. He is likely to be in some doubt about his parentage; his father the woodcutter is not really his father. Our hero has, whether he says so or not, the common belief of children that there is some mystery about his birth; his real parents, if the truth were known, are of great and even royal estate.*
>
> *—Lionel Trilling*[45]

Standing at the edge of manhood as well as the periphery of Manhattan, the young Jewish students probably sensed the possibilities for the future more clearly than their growing disconnections from the past. With the support and dreams of their communities behind them, they ventured into the new arena of their development. Looking ahead, they were not always aware of what was being left behind. "One of the longest journeys in the world," Norman Podhoretz wrote, "is the journey from Brooklyn to Manhattan." Although Podhoretz's journey came a few years after the others, in the motives for his progression and in the growing distance from his parents he was typical of those who had followed this path in the 1920s and 1930s. That all of them were moving beyond the confines and traditions of their parents and their childhood communities was obvious. That this movement embodied a growing sense of estrangement from their parents and neighborhoods was undoubtedly less clear. "It appalls me to think what an immense transformation I had to work on myself in order to become what I have become," Podhoretz continued: "if I had known what I was doing I would surely not have been able to do it, I would surely not have wanted to."[46]

These breaks were softened in part by their slow evolution and in part by the exhilaration of adolescent emancipation. The young men did not immediately conquer New York. Their continuing to live at home during college blurred the growing distinctions. Their successes came slowly; they eased their way in—through school, primarily, or small jobs and even smaller opportunities to write or review. Yet, they had been conditioned to move beyond their parents' world. The dynamic of immigrant assimilation propelled them as it has pushed scores of others. The spirit of the 1930s, the dreams engendered in the radical movements which sprang up in the aftermath of the crash, fueled their development. The American past, of which they were never a part, seemed as irrelevant as the Jewish past of their parents. Firstborn Americans always have a sense of themselves as new men and women. This sense of newness could now be shared by countless other Americans. The young New York Intellectuals found excitement in the cultural upheaval. They did not have to follow the standard path into traditional American society and culture. "They meant to declare themselves citizens of the world," Irving Howe remembered, "and that succeeding, perhaps consider becoming writers of this country."[47]

Part of this break was highly personal. In a number of cases, names were changed. William Phillips's father changed the family name from Litvinsky; Daniel Bolotsky's uncle chose "Bell"; and Ivan Greenbaum, using a variant of his mother's longer Russian name, took "Philip Rahv." Some rationalized changes because of their connections to radical movements and the search for a protective pseudonym. For others it was an attempt to escape Jewish identification in the "international" days of the 1930s. Irving Howe believed that it was quite likely a mixture of the two. Name changing had long been a part of the assimilative process and some of these young Jews followed a path taken by many others of their generation.[48]

In this entire estrangement, Norman Podhoretz came to feel that a "kind of treason" existed. That parents concurred in the decisions which led to it, he wrote in 1967, made it "sadder but no less cruel."[49] At the time, however, the movement into this new environment was filled with excitement, and the young Jewish writers saw in it great promise. This new life, free of old traditions and burdensome connections, not only provided an inspirational source for their writing but gave a new direction for Jewish literature as well.

Previous trends in Jewish writing had been confined to smaller Jewish circles. Lionel Trilling noted the differences between his own predilections and those expressed in a notable journal of Jewish culture to which he once had been attached, the *Menorah Journal*. Choosing the Jewish author Ludwig

Lewisohn as his case in point, Trilling believed that this "literature of self-realization" attacked the "sin of 'escaping' the Jewish heritage." The result of this was an easier acceptance of the "sin of 'adjustment' on a wholly neurotic basis. It fostered a willingness to accept exclusion and even intensify it, a willingness to be provincial and parochial." Even his own series of short stories about his year at Wisconsin, which appeared in the *Menorah Journal*, were, Trilling admitted, a part of this trend. The material of Jewish literature should come not from the acceptance of exclusion and heritage but from the flight and the discovery of the larger world. As Clement Greenberg put it, "Again and again they describe escapes or, better, flights from the restriction or squalor of the Brooklyns and Bronxes to the wide open world." This was in keeping with a great American theme, Greenberg maintained, but the concerns of the young Jewish writers added an extra dose of intensity and personal involvement. "His writing becomes essentially a career which provided him with the means of flight." This close interrelation between life and work propelled the young writer even more rapidly toward the outside world.[50]

A strong notion of class was also buried in this entire dynamic. Only subsequently did some of the young men come to see how clearly their own progress was tied to a desire to rise. Sociologists like Bell and Seymour Martin Lipset would view class and status anxiey as strong motivating factors in postwar American society. Norman Podhoretz recognized its application to his own life: "I was never aware [when young] . . . how inextricably my 'noblest' ambitions were tied to the vulgar desire to rise above the class into which I was born; nor did I understand to what an astonishing extent these ambitions were shaped and defined by the standards and values and tastes of the class into which I did not know I wanted to move."[51]

The process of maturation begun in the Jewish neighborhoods of the Bronx, Brooklyn, or Newark had taken these young students to the foot of the bridges to Manhattan. Entering Manhattan did not mean immediate prominence or a sense of full participation in the political or cultural life of the country. Rather, it introduced them to the next arena of their development. There—in the classrooms of the city's universities, in radical political meetings, or in the editorial offices of a few important journals—they would continue their education. But their life on the periphery had been their beginning, and they would carry with them, on the one hand, the benefits of those years and the burdens of their time spent there and, on the other, the burdens which accompanied their abandonment of that world. As Trilling wrote,

> The story of the Young Man from the Provinces is thus a strange one, for it has its roots both in legend and in the very heart of the modern actuality. From it we have learned most of what we know about modern society, about class and its strange rituals, about power and influence and about money, the hard fluent fact which modern society has as its being. Yet through the massed social fact there runs the thread of legendary romance, even of downright magic.[52]

Chapter 2

A New York Education

Crossing the bridges to Manhattan brought the young intellectuals to a world in which they felt more isolated. Manhattan was the real New York, Irving Howe recalled thinking, "the embodiment of that alien world which every boy raised in a Jewish immigrant home has been taught, whether he realized it or not, to look upon with suspicion."[1] The young Alfred Kazin saw it as the province of others.

> Why did they live *there* and we always in "Brunzvil"? Why were they *there*, and we always *here*. Why was it always *them* and *us*, Gentiles and *us*, *alrightniks* and us? Beyond Brownsville was all "the city," that other land I could see for a day. . . . Beyond was the strange world of Gentiles. . . .[2]

Like the emigrants of other generations or other parts of the country, they, too, made their trek—but often to return home each night. They came for school and for work. And they came to find a place for themselves. Their initial preparation in the ethnic ghettos of their youth gave way to the next phase of their education—be it the actual classroom learning of one of the city's universities or the lessons gained from their attempts to mark out a place for themselves in an alien environment. Their assimilation proved slow and erratic. But once they had begun the process, they found it impossible to turn back.

Those who ventured forth in the 1930s found the entire experience intensified by the disruption which affected all Americans during this period, the Great Depression. Making their way in the larger American society was never easy for immigrant youths, and it proved especially difficult after 1929. Whatever their political or social outlook—whether hopeful writers, struggling intellectuals, young radicals, or new undergraduates—they found that the depression unalterably adjusted their perspective. And it struck "them" as it struck "us"; it affected life in "the city" as well as "Brunzvil."

Thus, the next step in the progression of the New York Intellectuals proved to be an often uneasy intermixing of a college education and the beginning of a career with the tumult created by the Depression. The economic chaos and political instability complicated the already knotty dilemma of a personal sense of apartness coupled with a powerful ambition and drive. Questions about one's future were complicated by questions about the condition of society itself. Those who crossed the bridge to Manhattan after 1929 found a world shaken, as alien to its longtime residents as to its newest arrivals.

THE NEW RELIGION

> *It was a symbol of spiritual promotion. . . . University-bred people were the real nobility of the world. A college diploma was a certificate of moral as well as intellectual aristocracy.*
>
> *My old religion had gradually fallen to pieces, and if its place was taken by something else, if there was something that appealed to the better man in me, to what was purest in my thoughts and most sacred in my emotions, that something was the red, church–like structure on the southeast corner of Lexington and Twenty-third Street.*
>
> *It was the synagogue of my new life. Nor is this merely a figure of speech: the building really appealed to me as a temple, as a House of Sanctity, as we call the ancient Temple of Jerusalem. At least that was the term I would fondly apply to it, years later, in my retrospective broodings upon—upon my first few years of my life in America.*   —*Abraham Cahan*[3]

In *The Rise of David Levinsky*, Abraham Cahan's novel of Jewish immigrants, the main character laments that despite personal wealth he was never able to attend that citadel of learning he described so grandly—the City College of New York. Among the immigrants the notion of attaining a college education appeared the surest way to move into American society. If, like Levinsky, they could not attend themselves, they passed the hopes on to their children. The bright, precocious youths in the immigrant ghettos seemed fated to go on to college after high school, and, thereby, out of the ghetto. Teachers as well as parents spotted the potential and nurtured the development. In the early years of the twentieth century, immigrants' children followed this course with increasing frequency. By 1920 the number of Jewish students in New York's major universities had grown large. The proportion of Jewish students at Columbia reached 40 percent; the percentage at New York University was even higher. At tuition-free City College and Hunter, the figure grew to between 80 and 90 percent.[4] Some of the older New York Intellectuals were

among these Jewish students, including those at the private colleges. Meyer
Schapiro took his bachelor's degree from Columbia in 1924, Lionel Trilling in
1925. Diana Trilling, then Diana Rubin, graduated from Radcliffe in 1925.
Elliot Cohen, a child prodigy, graduated at eighteen from Yale. Sidney Hook
had been an undergraduate at City College and took his Ph.D. from Columbia;
William Phillips, another CCNY graduate, went to NYU for his master's.[5]

The pattern of Jews at major universities abruptly changed, however. In the
years following the First World War, many private schools began to perceive
what became known euphemistically as the Jewish problem. During the first
years of the 1920s Jews began to face, at many American universities, a system
of quotas, restrictions, and outright rejections. The techniques ran from the
sophisticated (Harvard's intricate geographical quota system) to the more
blatant (denial based solely and admittedly on Jewishness).[6] The oldest of the
New York Intellectuals had entered college before these restrictive barriers had
been fully established. By contrast, no members of the "second generation"
went to Columbia as undergraduates.[7] Between the college careers of these two
generations, during the middle 1920s, the lines of ethnic discrimination were
drawn firmly across American higher education, altering the direction which
the younger ghetto students would take. City College remained the one major
New York school that freely admitted Jews.

When Jewish students had gone to Ivy League schools or other private
colleges, they still confronted the problems of anti-Semitism, as prevalent on
college campuses as in American society. Clubs, fraternities, college dramatic
societies, and various other campus organizations remained closed or restricted
to Jews. Once graduated, young Jews found academe no more open than
Princeton's eating clubs or Yale's Skull and Bones. Lionel Trilling recalled the
difficulty Jews encountered when considering careers in the university.

> [Elliot] Cohen, after a brilliant undergraduate career at Yale, had given up the
> graduate study of English because he believed that as a Jew he had no hope of a
> university appointment. When I decided to go into academic life, my friends
> thought me naive to the point of absurdity, nor were they wholly wrong—my
> appointment to an instructorship at Columbia was pretty openly regarded as an
> experiment, and for some time my career in the College was complicated by my
> being Jewish.

Trilling was, in fact, fortunate—his experimental instructorship was an
exception. Clifton Fadiman, a member of Trilling's class, was told upon
graduation, "We have room for only one Jew and we have chosen Mr.
Trilling."[8] There were a few traditional scholars among the New York
Intellectuals. Several emerged from this first generation, those who entered
college before the Depression and before the spread of overt discrimination.
Hook, Schapiro, and Trilling pursued doctorates and academic appointments in
the well-established manner in which scholars are trained and employed. Their
publications reflect, in large measure, their schooling and employment.

Trilling, as was mentioned, had a more difficult time finding a tenured place, but that may have been because English departments were traditionally more anti-Semitic than others. Schapiro first applied to Princeton for graduate work but was rejected, he later learned, because he was Jewish. Even at Columbia, which accepted him, he remained aware of his ethnic distinction. There were then, he recalled, only four or five Jewish full professors on the entire university faculty.[9]

The flow of intelligent Jews into many American universities, either as students or as professors, declined markedly in the 1920s. Prejudice forced many young Jews to rethink and redirect their career goals. Daniel Bell recounts the story of his cousin Teddy Cohen, one of the most brilliant in his college class. Seeing the potential for an academic career severely limited, he chose instead to go into business, ultimately growing rich as an importer.[10] A few did become academics. Meyer Schapiro began as a lecturer at Columbia in 1928, Sidney Hook as an instructor at NYU in 1927. Both retired in the 1970s as professors emeriti from the same institutions. They remained the exceptions, however, during their early years. At the Washington Square campus of NYU, the *Menorah Journal* complained in the late 1920s, "over ninety percent of the students are Jews, but less than one percent of the instructors are Jewish." Although specific numbers may have been exaggerated, the journal's perception of the general pattern was accurate.[11]

In the 1920s it grew increasingly difficult for Jews to enter the more prestigious private colleges. Prejudice against hiring Jews to teach at these institutions remained strong. Thus, even in the period of economic prosperity, when most Americans believed in the limitless possibilities of social growth, restrictions and constraints lay across the paths of ambitious Jewish students. Some, such as Bell's cousin Teddy or Elliot Cohen, turned away from academic careers. Others, such as Hook, Trilling, and Schapiro, persisted—but not without confronting more difficulties than non-Jewish students encountered. For the younger students contemplating a college education and a career, the world made a sudden and dramatic shift after 1929. College degrees, along with almost everything else, came to be reevaluated amid the social chaos of the Great Depression. New barriers fell across the path toward success and prominence. And now other Americans, some not accustomed to such inhibitions, joined the young Jews in confronting the possibilities and the limits of future advancement.

AN EDUCATION BY SHOCK

The immigrant neighborhoods from which these young students came had little share in the general prosperity of the 1920s. Life was hard and money often scarce. Work came in the form of low-paying jobs as garment workers, housepainters, and unskilled laborers. These might not pay much, but at least they paid something. The young children of the immigrants replaced immediate gratification with the notion that a better world existed for those able to raise themselves out of the ghetto. The promise of a professional career based on a college education seemed one likely path to this end. For many families the minimal level of security and the hopes for the future ended with the stock market crash. Jobs, businesses, and small savings were lost. Compared with those of the large investors, the financial losses might have been minimal. For people living at the most marginal level, though, any loss had disastrous consequences. The resulting adjustment in personal lives often had a great impact on the young. "The great event of my childhood," Irving Howe recounted,

> came when, during the Depression, my father lost his little grocery business, and we were plunged into severe poverty. It was this which turned me to the world of books and ideas, which pulled me out of the unreflectable routine of ordinary childhood. From the cast of seriousness that was then thrown over me I have been unable to escape nor do I wish to.[12]

The Depression did not affect all the children of the immigrants equally. Delmore Schwartz's father lost a considerable fortune and soon died of a heart attack. Robert Warshow's family hotel business suffered some economic setbacks but avoided deep poverty.

More important, however, than the fact that a few immigrant families were unaffected by the Depression is the extent to which other American families began to experience many of the same hardships as the immigrants. In the 1920s many young intellectuals tended to turn toward traditional models, established styles. Alfred Kazin recalls that Lionel Trilling seemed to resemble the non-Jewish critics, such as Van Wyck Brooks, Carl Van Doren, and Lewis Mumford, all of whom had a "conscious air" of being "the voice of tradition." Kazin later distinguished between Trilling's "casual, gentlemanly style of the twenties" and that of his own contemporaries, a style which "had absorbed the social angers of the abrasive lower-class thirties."[13] Many non-Jews and nonimmigrants who might in earlier days have naturally fused with the "voices of tradition" now chose the style of the outsiders. This had always been the province of immigrants. Dwight Macdonald, after a career in prep school and at Yale, was forced to support his mother after the death of his father and the loss of family income in the crash. He first went to work at Macy's, later joined *Fortune*, and ultimately found himself more and more involved in radical politics, joining the Trotskyists. Mary McCarthy shuttled between relatives and foster homes as a child, after her parents' modest life-style crumbled.

Kazin's comparison of Trilling and himself demonstrates that more than economic changes differentiated the 1920s from the 1930s. Unavoidable hardship and suffering confronted many Americans. Caught up in the "lost generation" spirit of the twenties, Malcolm Cowley, for example, wrote poignantly of the slowly developing awareness which emerged by 1931. A small-town refugee, Cowley abandoned his detached literary stance of the pre-crash period and became deeply involved in radical politics and literary radicalism. Young men attaining maturity in the 1930s found these precrash days very distant indeed. At the end of the decade, Kazin remembered the twenties as "no more than a boisterous version of the Continental *fin de siecle*."[14] By contrast, the world of the 1930s seemed to be neither boisterous nor stable, but to be undergoing internal eruption. "Something happened in the thirties," Kazin concluded in 1941,

> that was more than the sum of the sufferings inflicted, the billions lost, the institutions and people uprooted: it was an education by shock. Panic, a panic often significantly disproportionate to the losses of those who were most afraid, became the tone of the period. . . . In the world after 1932, where everything seemed to be breaking up at once, the American had at first neither a sense of history nor the consolation of traditional values. He was oppressed by forces that were meaningless to him in operation and hence all the more humiliating in effect.[15]

Non-Jewish intellectuals, young men and women with long ties to American society, found the disruption shocking. It often threw them into radical political and cultural movements and thus into close proximity with the young Jewish intellectuals. The same is true of the young Jews, though with slight modification. They did not have deep roots in American society but had just made their first connections to it. Their parents, abandoning European values and traditions, fastened onto American ones, less out of a sense of patriotism than from the need for touchstones in an alien culture. Their children, on the verge of entering that society, saw it crumbling about them. The prize, seemingly within their grasp, had vanished. The Depression made political questions nearly unavoidable. The elder New York Intellectuals either found their pre-crash radicalism heightened or turned to politics instead of to more literary or scholarly interests. Lionel Trilling gave up his interest in Jewish cultural concerns, left the circle around the *Menorah Journal*, and began an uneasy period of involvement with radical movements. William Phillips graduated from City College in the late 1920s and in his first postgraduate years devoted himself to purely literary questions. During the first years of the Depression, however, Phillips grew increasingly interested in political matters. Philip Rahv, on the other hand, always possessed strong political interests, as did Sidney Hook. Many pre-crash radicals, such as Rahv and Hook, discovered that the intensity of their commitment and their radical activity increased during the 1930s. Parlor socialism gave way to more active pursuits. As Dwight Macdonald put it, whereas once "people would have voted for the [Socialist] Norman Thomas, by '32 Norman Thomas seemed much too mild."[16]

The younger students, just beginning to form their political and cultural attitudes and to map out career plans, found both areas clouded. "Most of us did not think seriously about careers," recalled Alfred Kazin. "Not only was there a depression, but we were all quite certain that a war was coming. I did not go on in graduate school and was too much an independent writer and free-lancer, living very hazardously indeed, until my first book came out in 1942, even to think of having a 'career.' "[17] During the latter part of the thirties, when he was writing *On Native Grounds*, Kazin supported himself by teaching night classes at the New School and at City College. Irving Kristol, who graduated from City College a few years after Kazin, found employment in a shipyard.

> To some extent there just weren't any other jobs. To another extent, it may have been colored by my radical inclination, the notion that proletarian work was good, healthy, redeeming work, which was easy to think since no one was offering me nonproletarian work.

Irving Howe later recounted that his first job after graduating from CCNY was in a factory, where he was fired within six weeks for attempting to organize the workers.[18]

Recent graduates were not the only individuals forced to take nonacademic positions. Many of the older intellectuals found it equally difficult to find "nonproletarian" employment. Clement Greenberg worked for the Civil Service Commission, the Veterans' Administration, and as a clerk in the New York customshouse. Remembering those days, Greenberg wrote,

> Worldly success seemed so remote as to be beside the point, and you did not even secretly envy those who had it . . . when I thought of taking up painting as seriously as I had once half-hoped to do before I went to college, the highest reward I imagined was a private reputation of the kind [Arshile] Gorky and [Willem] de Kooning then had, a reputation which did not seem to alleviate their poverty in the least.[19]

Others found the situation nearly as bleak as Greenberg did. A few like Kazin found occasional employment as part-time college instructors. William Phillips taught briefly at NYU; Lionel Trilling spent nearly a decade as a night school instructor at Columbia. Those who hoped to be writers and critics had to hustle. A few bits and pieces could be had at the popular journals, reviews for the *Nation* or the *New Republic*, occasional articles elsewhere, but little else.

The radical dislocations, economic disruptions, and personal disorientation visited upon many Americans by the Great Depression certainly took their toll on the young New York Intellectuals. Yet, for them the impact had its own, special twist. Rarely did the Depression end a prosperous existence, with breadlines replacing the country club. They had mostly been poor, their cultural orientation was of the outsider looking in, and they had been schooled to feel they were in the process of moving into the larger American society. The failure to feel fully a part of either their parents' society, which they had abandoned, or the Gentile society of mainstream America left them feeling disoriented. The Depression blocked their hopes for a resolution of this alienation. The sacrifices their parents had made and the ambitions which had been instilled were supposed to direct these young men toward a successful future. The achievement of that goal came into serious doubt. Their hopes for personal advancement did not decline, but their notions of how that advancement might be achieved changed. The sobering realities of the thirties forced the young New York Intellectuals to alter some of their attitudes, to redirect their ambitions and energies. William Phillips noted this change in 1934, in terms of all his radical contemporaries. Implicit in Phillip's assessment, however, is strong evidence of the changed attitude of his young Jewish contemporaries in particular.

> Most of us come from petty-bourgeois homes; some, of course, from proletarian ones. But the gravity of the economic crisis has leveled most of us (and our families) to meager, near-starvation existence. Opportunities for cashing-in are gone, and we have no illusions about their return. The kind of reputation which used to bring jobs as editors, lecturers, and readers in publishing houses holds no lure for us, because those jobs have been whittled down to a few sinecures for standpatters and tightrope walkers. The bourgeoisie does not want us, and we could not accept the double-dealing which these jobs require. All of us have worked, for some time at least, in factories, in stores, and at odd jobs. Some have had better paying jobs as teachers. But we are all in the same leaky boat now.
>
> Our economic experiences have stripped us of waverings, of side-glances toward prosperous avenues. Our aims have been linked to the proletariat.[20]

LUFTMENSCH

The Depression added a new barrier beyond that of discrimination to the educational difficulties and obstacles of Jewish students. Economic chaos put intellectual endeavors into new perspective. Lionel Trilling recalled the futility he felt while at work on his dissertation:

> I was trying to write a book about Matthew Arnold and having a bitter time of it because it seemed to me that I was working in a lost world, that nobody wanted, or could possibly want, a book about Matthew Arnold. . . . They wanted it even less because it was to be a doctoral dissertation . . . the university, it is true, was just then beginning to figure in people's minds more than ever before in America, but it did not enjoy the prestige, though ambiguous, which it now has, and I was much ashamed of what I had undertaken.[21]

The lack of a sense of usefulness which Trilling reported also affected the younger, second generation of New York Intellectuals. The economic difficulties caused by the Depression reinforced other factors which directed young Jewish students toward some colleges and away from others. Tuition-free and a subway commute from home, City College in the 1930s attracted Alfred Kazin, Daniel Bell, Nathan Glazer, Irving Howe, Irving Kristol, and Seymour Martin Lipset. In addition, young Jewish students found the atmosphere at City College appealing. In many ways it seemed a continuation of their past lives in the ghetto. It was, above all, overwhelmingly Jewish. More than this, Kazin recalls, the students shared the same motivation. "The urgency was very strong. The competition [of Jewish intellectuals] came as much from [fellow students] as from my parents. There were two Nobel Prize winners in my class, or three, not to mention personalities of some fame in later life, like Zero Mostel, Bernard Malamud, and Albert Wohlstetter."[22]

Despite these shared motivations, the onset of the Depression shifted the driving ambition of many of the Jewish students. No less intense or intellectually driven, they now lived in a world where "it was taken for granted that one would be unemployed," Howe remembered. What the students wanted from their education changed.

You went to college, and you didn't have to worry about career choices. You could study things that seemed impractical because one was as impractical as another. It made for a certain kind of airlessness, a kind of *luftmensch* outlook. You went to college; there was nothing else to do. It was considered by Jewish parents a good thing if you learned something, and perhaps it would have some use or value later on. But we had nothing to look forward to immediately.

At City College, whether in class or out, the competitive drives remained. They merely ceased to dominate one's entire life. "Very few of us took our academic careers seriously," Irving Kristol later noted. "The question of whether you got good grades, for instance, was one that never came up. No one gave a damn what grades they got so long as they didn't flunk out."[23]

The "airlessness" had its intellectual rewards. The ability or interest in floating about allowed for wide-ranging intellectual development. Courses and interesting professors could be sampled and uninteresting areas avoided. In many ways, this was the best training for the lives these individuals came to lead in the intellectual world. Switching disciplines, as Alfred Kazin did, or just sampling widely provided a measure of expertise in a variety of areas.[24] The facility with which many of the the New York Intellectuals handled diverse topics came, in part, from their undergraduate "airlessness." Irving Howe's importance in the worlds of literary criticism, socialist politics, and social history; Nathan Glazer's expertise in linguistics and sociology, plus occasional fiction reviews; the varied topics of Irving Kristol's essays—all these bespeak the widespread learning and interests of these men.

The City College education held an additional appeal for many young Jews. The intensity and competitiveness of the classroom often provided the natural arena for the streetsmart confidence they had developed in the immigrant neighborhoods. Nowhere was this more true or more put to the test than in the classroom of Morris Raphael Cohen. "In my time," Hook wrote, "Professor Cohen was the strongest intellectual force in the college. His full strength was felt primarily by the students and through them reflected upon the faculty." Of the New York Intellectuals only Hook and the "fellow traveler" William

Barrett could be considered students of Cohen's. Cohen is a figure extremely distant to students of the present, a figure of historical importance rather than one with philosophical impact. Unlike his contemporaries John Dewey and Bertrand Russell, he has become the subject of works of social and intellectual history rather than remained central to philosophical investigations.[25]

Morris Cohen's special appeal to the students at City College derived from the provocative combination of his own career, his classroom style, and his personal ideals. In many ways he provided a living example of the limits which constrained Jewish academics. A Russian-born Jew who emigrated to America at age twelve, in 1892, Cohen grew up on the Lower East Side and in Brownsville. He performed brilliantly in public schools and at City College, graduating in 1900. He took his Ph. D. from Harvard, rooming with Felix Frankfurter. To this point his life seems perfectly in keeping with American myths about immigrant assimilation and social ascent. Yet, after leaving Harvard, Cohen could not find a job teaching philosophy and had to return to the mathematics position he had held at City College before beginning his doctoral studies. There he stayed for five years, before transferring to philosophy, the first Jew to teach in that department. Cohen remained in the City College philosophy department until his retirement but never accepted the fact that he was unable to teach at a more prestigious school. He harbored ambivalent feelings toward Dewey, Hook reported, because he believed that Dewey could have found a place for him at Columbia. Hook later asked Dewey about this. Dewey claimed that by the time he knew Cohen he was out of power at Columbia. The real villain was F. J. E. Woodbridge, Dewey contended, Cohen's first graduate teacher in philosophy. This was the period of Nicholas Murray Butler's conservative presidency at Columbia, and Wood-bridge did not want to risk incurring Butler's antagonism by hiring a Jewish professor.[26] The young Jews saw in Cohen all the genius and all the potential which some Jews possessed, as well as the resistance they faced in Gentile society. Confronting exclusions of their own, from other colleges and many professions, these young men identified strongly with the exclusions someone as brilliant as Morris Cohen had endured.

Cohen's reputation for brilliance among the students rested not on his writings but on his classroom style. Admitting in later years that he was a poor lecturer, he adopted the Socratic method. Yet Cohen's classes were not like the patient dialogues Plato recorded. "The room was electrified," recalled one student; "we jumped to the defense of our fellow-student, but our teacher took us all on, in a razzle-dazzle of knowledge, of analytic power, of fighting intellect. But truth was the quarry and we were really fellow-participants in the hunt." Sidney Hook came to reevaluate Cohen's classroom style. He recalled Cohen's "insensitivity" and "cruelty," although he believed that Cohen was unaware of how he affected students. His religion, accent, and irascibility, Hook concluded, kept him out of the great universities. "He compensated for the bitterness and deprivation of his lot by playing God in the classroom." His manner was to dispense with student answers and positions with a "rapier or sledgehammer—and usually a wit that delighted those who were not impaled or crushed at the moment." Ultimately, Cohen's position prevailed. What astonished Hook, in retrospect, was the degree to which the students shared in his methods. In a tribute to Cohen written in 1928, Hook recalled that "it was sometimes painful to be . . . impaled on the horns of a dilemma; but it was a bleeding quite salutary for the soul." Recently, however, Hook modified his belief in the value of this bloodletting. Recalling an especially devastating remark Cohen made to one student ("The trouble with you is that you can't think!"), Hook noted that the student blanched and, more important, that "so great was Cohen's authority with us, we didn't hold this judgment against him but against his hapless victim." The wound left scars, some of which, such as this student's, did not go away.[27]

Students nevertheless flocked to Cohen. They became a recognizable group on campus, "distinguished by an intensity of ideas, but a catholicity of interests and by a keenness and persistency of logical analysis which often outran the limits of social discretion." The "mark of Cohen," Hook labeled it. They were challenging, argumentative, skeptical. To some the atmosphere of Cohen's classroom was "not unlike that of a yeshiva." To others it reflected the give-and-take world of immigrant neighborhoods. "Toughened as I was as a street brawler and political activist," Hook remembered, "I thoroughly enjoyed our give-and-take—although I almost always took more than I gave." A class by Morris Cohen could be "terrifying," Irving Howe has written. His was sometimes even a sadistic method of teaching and

> only the kinds of students that came to Cohen would have withstood it—Jewish boys with minds honed to dialectic, bearing half-conscious memories of *pilpul*, indifferent to the prescriptons of gentility, intent on a vision of lucidity. "He never let us down [Howe quotes a former student], we were always left a bit more confused, a bit wiser, always more hopeful, even giddy with hope, for he was a living example of the power of reason."[28]

For all of Howe's hyperbole—there have been other "cruel" taskmasters in American universities and other successful students from nonimmigrant backgrounds—his conclusion points to many of the special qualities of both Morris Cohen and the students he taught. They found in his life and in his classroom style personal connections. At a time when they were drawing away from their homes and their parents, even if they still lived at home, Cohen was a gravitational force of their new environment. His classes became rites of passage for many intelligent students, as well as forums where their special skills could be brought into play. Few stayed in the Cohen orbit long. He spawned no philosophical school or followers and begrudged the shifting allegiances of his former students as they moved to Dewey or G. E. Moore.[29] For most, however, a career in philosophy was never the goal. Rather, Cohen fit into a larger intellectual pattern which was growing among a number of his students. Howe believed that the City College education was marked by a sense of intellectual life as a form of combat, the sharp division, the polemic. Cohen certainly contributed to that. And this has its origins in the Jewish intellectual world, has its origins in the Jewish disputatiousness and the talmudic disputatiousness. Also [it] has origins in the Russian political-intellectual world, which was ferocious.

So all these styles came over. It was part of the style of the radical movement, which is certainly disputatious and polemical.[30]

As the young students progressed from youth to adulthood many passed through the classroom of Morris Cohen. There they were tested and abused, and they refined a number of the argumentative skills they had brought with them. His legacy is less in the ideas he imparted than in the intellectual style he chose. What many New York Intellectuals learned from Morris Cohen accounts, in part, more for their abrasive interactions than for any philosophical position they took.

It is unfair to dispense with Cohen's intellectual contributions entirely. If the style of Cohen had its immediate impact, some of his ideas and his intellectual approach seem to have been unconsciously absorbed. Cohen remained a steadfast liberal, while students, especially the future New York Intellectuals, grew significantly more radical. Although Cohen's classes were exercises in intellectual combat, his writings were decidedly less bombastic. Furthermore, he felt no hesitation about publishing in a wide variety of places—scholarly monographs in the *Journal of Philosophy*, reviews and articles in the *New Republic*. Like those of many of the New York Intellectuals, his books were often compilations of his essays.[31] Cohen also published on a broad range of topics. His *New Republic* articles between 1918 and 1920, alone, include discussions of Platonism, Zionism, Josiah Royce, John Dewey, Santayana, higher education, Einstein, and G. Stanley Hall and his "Slacker's Apology" about World War I. Thus, he represented an intellectual model which many of these intellectuals, wide-ranging in their interests and publications, later emulated.

To some degree, moreover, the political ideas of Morris Cohen resurfaced among the New York Intellectuals in later years. His arguments against Hook and other radicals in the 1930s found their way into the postwar liberalism many of these intellectuals adopted. Cohen was not credited as being the source of the thinking, but many of his students had come around his political outlook by the 1950s.[32]

The classroom of Morris Cohen provided one forum for a display of the specific talents of the smart young boys from the ghetto; a second arena was the highly charged atmosphere of the college cafeteria. The lunchroom occupied a large ground-floor space, where sandwiches and beverages were sold. Around the sides, under large windows, were the alcoves—a euphemism, Meyer Liben maintains. They were "kinds of booths, in the basement, adjoining the cafeteria." In these "booths" students congregated according to their own special interests, spent their lunch hours and the periods between classes, played Ping-Pong ("Sometimes with a net, sometimes without," Irving Kristol remembered), and, if it was the bent of the alcove residents, argued about politics. The budding New York Intellectuals occupied Alcove No. 1, that of the anti-Stalinists. Alcove No. 2 was the home of the Stalinists. In other alcoves were the Newman Club, the Zionists, Orthodox Jews, the few blacks and the "jocks." To the residents of No. 1 and No. 2, however, theirs were the only two which mattered. "It was between those two alcoves," Irving Kristol wrote in 1977, "that the war of the worlds was fought, over the faceless bodies of the mass of students, whom we tried desperately to manipulate into 'the right position.' "[33]

The actual number of radical students, even at a politically charged campus like City College, remained small. Kristol calculated that the Stalinists in Alcove No. 2 were more numerous, yet they could rarely mobilize more than five hundred students on a campus of twenty thousand. Alcove No. 1 had thirty regulars and could gather only fifty to a hundred for a rally. At City College, however, these small factions dominated student life, battling over student government and the college newspaper. "What happened at Berkeley, once in a lifetime," Meyer Liben concluded, "might happen . . . at City every Thursday between 12 and 2 in the afternoon." Outside speakers came to campus; meetings and demonstrations were held. In the alcoves the debates and discussions continued, the natural place for those with "the mark of Cohen" to practice their skills. "You isolated a monist position and hammered away," Liben remembered. "You caught your opponent in a fallacy, preferably a logical one, but a historical one would do. You smiled. Let him get out of *that* one. Then the bell rang, new period, changing of the guard in the alcoves."[34]

Many of the young New York Intellectuals congregated in Alcove No. 1. Irving Kristol, one of the inhabitants, later called Seymour Martin Lipset the most representative, "a kind of intellectual bumblebee." A member of the Trotskyist Young People's Socialist League, Lipset eventually became its national chairman and a delegate to the American Student Union convention. Another YPSL ("Yip-sel"), Irving Howe, was a Trotskyist leader and alcove "theoretician," Kristol recalled. Daniel Bell, among the mildest of the radicals, argued a social-democratic position. His "immense intellectual curiosity" and "amused fondness for sectarian dialectics" made him an integral part of the alcove, which Melvin Lasky and Nathan Glazer also frequented.[35]

Like the classrooms of Morris Cohen, the political environment of the anti-Stalinist alcove provided a particularly appropriate arena for the special skills of these young students. City College had a large number of equally intelligent students who avoided campus politics. Kristol remembered both the economist Kenneth Arrow and the historian David Landes as students who kept their distance from the political alcoves. They ultimately pursued more direct academic careers. To lead a vigorous intellectual life, however, Kristol felt it necessary to be political at City College. Only in the alcoves did this become possible.

After graduation Kristol spent a year in Chicago, where his wife, Gertrude Himmelfarb, had a graduate fellowship at the University of Chicago. In addition to working as a freight handler, he "hung around" the university. He discovered that Chicago had its own version of Alcove No. 1; it included Saul Bellow, Isaac Rosenfeld, Leslie Fiedler, H. T. Kaplan, and Oscar Tarcov.[36] Chicago, like City College and a few other schools, remained an exception among college campuses in the 1930s. The politically charged atmosphere of these institutions found few parallels elsewhere. However, it was to these schools that the young New York Intellectuals went. In part the same factors which prompted their choice of schools—urban, commuter, tolerant of Jews—created the political style.[37] A survey taken by *Fortune* during the 1930s found that only 5 to 10 percent of all college students were politically active. Daniel Bell concluded that just one-half of one percent took part in radical activity. Bell maintained though, that "like the drop of dye that suffuses the cloth, this number gave the decade its coloration."[38] Whether this was true for all the students of the 1930s is debatable. For the New York Intellectuals it seems likely. Of the first and second generations, only Elliot Cohen and Clement Greenberg, among the elders, and Robert Warshow, from the younger group, went to schools outside of New York or Chicago. Nearly half went to City College. For these individuals a unique atmosphere molded their college education. Isaac Rosenfeld drew a picture of the political life at Chicago which could portray City College as well.

> The political interest colored practically every student activity on campus, with the major division drawn between the Stalinists [who dominated the American Student Union] and the Trotskyists [who worked through the local chapter of the Young People's Socialist League]. The two Marxist groups, with their symps and associates, spoke bitterly about, but never to, each other and avoided all contact, except to heckle, and occasionally strong-arm, each other's meetings. Politics was everywhere, in a measure, one ate and drank it; and sleep gave no escape, for it furnished terror to our dreams; Hitler, Mussolini, the Moscow Trials, the Spanish Civil War, the plaguey bill of Stalinism, the stopgaps of NRA, WPA, and the New Deal, and the approach of inevitable war. We lived in the shadow of annihilation, drawing on the pattern of Guernica and Ethiopia to imagine what bombings would be like. Liaisons, marriages, and divorces, let alone friendships, were sometimes contracted on no other basis than these issues, and dominated, in a way that might seem incomprehensible to the present generation, by events of the world order. Even students who were *hors de combat* were involved, for everyone was called upon to justify their disinterest, and they had hard work convincing even themselves. Politics was form and substance, accident and modification, the metaphor of all things.[39]

The education which the New York Intellectuals received at City College, Columbia, NYU, and Chicago proved to be the second stage in their paths to *Partisan* and their personal and intellectual development. College classroooms and campus politics supplemented and refined the skills and ambitions they brought from their childhood environment. Those of the first generation took their degrees before 1929 and felt the impact of the Depression as they began to pursue intellectual and scholarly careers. Those of the second generation saw their attitude about their education itself become marked by the economic disarray of the 1930s. In both cases, the onset of the Depression turned the intellectuals toward political activities, on campus or off. They attended urban colleges which accepted Jews and offered scholarships. These same schools witnessed the growth of radical activity after 1929. Some New York Intellectuals served on their faculties, others sat in their classrooms. The elders began to write in the radical press, and the younger students read these works. A ghetto childhood and an urban education directed the young students in their earliest years. Radical politics brought the individuals together and formed a crucial element of the developing community.

Chapter 3

The Radical Vanguard

Isaac Rosenfeld's observation that politics formed the "substance" of college life in the 1930s, the "metaphor of all things," reflects the college he attended more than the national pattern. In Daniel Bell's view the number of campus radicals was small but their impact great. His "drop of dye" analogy is, like Rosenfeld's "metaphor of all things," applicable to more than just the student population of the 1930s, however. American radicalism flowered for one of the few times in American history during the Depression decade. Economic difficulties, personal distress, and the seeming exhaustion of solutions within the liberal capitalist framework prompted people to argue for radical alternatives. The actual memberships of the various radical parties may have been small, but their impact far exceeded their size. In the election of 1932, for example, the Socialist party candidate, Norman Thomas, polled nearly 900,000 votes, matching the previous high of Eugene Debs's Socialist candidacy in 1912. The actual membership in the Socialist party in 1932 was only 17,000. Thomas's vote evidenced a large sympathy or openness toward more-radical proposals. In the same election, the Communist party ran a highly prominent campaign. Its candidate, William Z. Foster, did not receive as many votes as Thomas, but 100,000 Americans did cast their ballot for him. In addition, Foster's campaign attracted a large number of prominent supporters, especially among artists and intellectuals.[1]

All through the decade radical meetings tried to organize the dispossessed, leftist journals were launched, polemics and critiques were published. Major shifts of policy and personalities occurred in the radical movements as did periods of hostility and of cooperation. The system appeared to have broken down, and many individuals saw the validity of new solutions to the major problems. Among leftists there erupted arguments over major points, such as collectivism and nationalization, or relatively minor disputes, over slightly different Marxist interpretations, for instance. A typical example of the variety of disputatious positions can be seen in the debate between Sidney Hook and John Dewey, waged mainly in their *Modern Monthly* articles, entitled, "Why I Am a Communist" and "Why I Am Not a Communist," respectively. While Hook defended his communism, Communists attacked Hook's brand of Marxism. Warfare among leftists probably undercut the potential success of any radical program, but it created a charged atmosphere in which most individuals could find a radical movement to fit his or her personal requirements.

Of the many radical groups which grew or expanded during the 1930s, several became increasingly prominent in radical and intellectual circles. Those uninterested in joining the Socialist or the Communist party could follow Leon Trotsky and belong to the Socialist Workers party, under Max Shachtman and James P. Cannon; join the Communist Party U. S. A. (opposition), known as the Lovestonites, under the former executive secretary of the American Communist party, Jay Lovestone; or support the American Workers party of A. J. Muste. Even within supposedly unified parties, discord frequently erupted. The Socialists broke down between the Old Guard, under Morris Hillquit and James Oneal, and the Militants, such as Jack Altman, Andrew Biemiller, and Alfred Baker Lewis. William Z. Foster lost his position as head of the American Communist party to Earl Browder, just as Lovestone had lost his job to Foster. Temporary coalitions developed, such as the short-lived alliance between the Musteites and the Trotskyists. All these movements and actions, often frenzied and often counterproductive, did provide a sense of dynamism within the radical world.

In addition to the particular radical movements, the general labor situation in America during the 1930s buoyed radicals. One after another, major American industries which had long resisted union organization capitulated to Congress of Industrial Organization unions. Radicals played large parts in this organizing effort—Communists, Socialists, Trotskyists, and Musteites. The aims of labor, coupled with the economic crisis, made a radical future appear possible.[2]

All this activity notwithstanding, the number of radicals remained low for the nation generally, as it did on college campuses. Norman Thomas's 900,000 votes in 1932 dropped to 187,000 in 1936. The Communists gathered their largest vote in 1932 and declined thereafter. Despite the success of various labor disputes, radical union aims soon gave way to traditional demands for wages, hours, and benefits. Still, as Bell observed about college students, the radicals also acted as a drop of dye in American society. If they did not color the decade itself, they certainly colored the perceptions of those who remembered or analyzed it. This coloration stems from a variety of factors. Most obviously, the flourishing of radicalism in America is so rare that when major developments do occur they are striking. Furthermore, the economic and political situation was extremely unstable, and the possibility of radical adjustments probably never seemed greater. In addition, for many of those involved in radical activity the levels did seem high and the interest great. In large urban centers, among like-minded individuals, it could appear that radicalism had a widespread following. Finally, the intensity of the experience lasted well beyond the period of active involvement. "Joining a radical movement when one is young is very much like falling in love when one is young," remarked the ex-radical Irving Kristol. "The girl may turn out to be rotten, but the experience of love is so valuable it can never be entirely undone by ultimate disenchantment." Irving Howe, less romantic but no less clear, believed that "for almost all New York intellectuals the radical years proved a decisive moment in their lives. And for a very few, the decisive moment."[3]

The sense that "everyone" was becoming involved in radical activity found reinforcement in the steady stream of writers, artists, and critics who joined various radical causes. Whereas in the 1920s intellectuals and artists had remained isolated, they now joined the left parties. In the first days of the Depression, the Communist party seemed to attract the largest share. In the election of 1932 many intellectuals lined up behind Foster's candidacy and issued a pamphlet, *Culture and the Crisis*, in support of the Communists. Written primarily by Malcolm Cowley, the pamphlet bore the subtitle "An Open Letter to Writers, Artists, Teachers, Physicians, Engineers, Scientists, and Other Professional Workers in America." The call went out for a union between intellectuals and the Communist party. Among the signers of *Culture and the Crisis* were a wide variety of American intellectuals and writers. The novelists Sherwood Anderson and Erskine Caldwell; the black writers Langston Hughes and Countee Cullen; the literary critics Malcolm Cowley, Granville Hicks, and Edmund Wilson; and the journalists Lincoln Steffens, Matthew Josephson, and Ella Winter—all were among the sponsors of the pamphlet. The diversity appeared impressive: blacks and whites, writers and critics, immigrants' sons and old-stock Americans.

The intellectual allegiance of so many leading lights gave communism in particular and radicalism in general a strong position among other, especially young, intellectuals. A socialist since his youth, Alfred Kazin remembered in 1965 the attraction of the Communist party, which rested on both its appearance of activity and its notable members, European as well as American.

> They had . . . Silone, Malraux, Hemingway, Gide, Rolland, Gorky, Aragon, Picasso, Eluard, Auden, Spender, Barbusse, Dreiser, Farrell, while the Socialists seemed to have only their own virtue. I was tired of virtue, and now I wanted to see some action.[4]

The critic Edmund Wilson proved a compelling example for young intellectuals. Wilson's journey from a nonpolitical stance in the 1920s to his political commitment in the 1930s provided something of a role model for many young critics. Not the man of culture who had to put down his studies and entered the political fray, Wilson exemplified the intellectual who would take his literary calling with him into the world of radical politics. He made it possible to imagine the union of politics and culture; he was, Irving Howe recalled, "the author of both *The Triple Thinkers* [a study of literary modernism] and *To The Finland Station* [on the development of socialist theory], he served as a model for emulation." Wilson's radical commitment coincided with the period of intense radical fervor in America. By the decade's end, like so many of his contemporaries, he had modified or moved away from his strong radical stance. Yet, Willliam Phillips remembered that Wilson "was close to being a spokesman for the critical conscience of the period . . . he did not want to immunize himself against the ideas and passions of what was taken as the presiding idealism."[5]

Dwight Macdonald's assessment of Wilson could apply to most of the radical intellectuals during the 1930s. To be "unpolitical [was] declassé," Macdonald observes. "An interest in *avant-garde* politics was expected of every proper intellectual." When the period of radicalism had passed, its heritage was not in the form of socialist programs or major new political parties. The impact was more often on the radicals themselves than on the society they sought to change. As he looked back on days of radical activity, Lionel Trilling recalled the importance of that activity for his intellectual contemporaries.

> In any view of the American cultural situation, the importance of the radical movement of the Thirties cannot be overestimated. It may be said to have created the American intellectual class as we now know it in its great size and influence . . . the political tendency of the Thirties defined the style of the class— from radicalism came the moral urgency, the sense of crisis, and the concern with personal salvation that mark the existence of American intellectuals.[6]

No matter what the relative impact of radicalism during the 1930s for American society, it marked the intellectuals who participated in it, coloring the decade in their eyes. Its benefits to society may have been marginal. These intellectuals, however, learned and gained a good deal—lessons and skills which later found use in nonradical settings.

Lionel Trilling's assessment of the relation between radicalism and the "American intellectual class" may be a bit sweeping. The impact of radicalism on the New York Intellectuals is surely more calculable. In a time of "intensity and fervor," Irving Howe remarked, radicalism "gave the New York Intellectuals their distinctive style."[7] Few attributes can be said to identify all the New York Intellectuals; participation in radical activity during the 1930s is one, although it involved different movements and different levels of commitment.

A number of the New York Intellectuals initially joined the Communist party or found themselves close to the Stalinists. Sidney Hook, in fact, signed the *Culture and the Crisis* pamphlet, and Meyer Schapiro would also have signed, had he not been out of the country when it was drafted. Schapiro did write a statement whose points were similar to the pamphlet's and which circulated among architects. A number of others, although not yet known well enough in radical circles to be asked to sponsor major writings, still worked closely with Communist groups, including Philip Rahv, William Phillips, and Harold Rosenberg. Lionel Trilling, according to his wife, "was committed to Communism for less than a year," in 1932 and 1933. Clement Greenberg recalls that though always a socialist, in the early 1930s he "had vague Bolshevik sympathies."[8]

The involvement and intensity of these radicals varied greatly. Sidney Hook, as was mentioned, became an important figure in American radical politics throughout the decade. His interest in political questions began before the stock market crash and crossed over into his studies in philosophy. In 1927, for example, his first two books were published, *The Metaphysics of Pragmatism*, his thesis, and an English edition of *The Collected Works of Vladimir Illich Lenin*. His work on pragmatism was augmented by studies of German philosophy in general and of Marx in particular. Philip Rahv, another individual whose radicalism predated the Depression, found his radical interest intensifying after 1929, but his focus remained different from Hook's grand philosophical investigations. As dogmatic as Hook, Rahv centered his attention more on literature, his considerations being more specific. Politics entered the world of the arts, snapped it into line, and gave it a coherent form.

The radicalism of some of the others grew after the crash. William Phillips, although the product of the "poor boy's land" of the Bronx, a graduate of City College, and a student of Hook's, later admitted that "despite the lack of money and worldliness, [he] had managed to avoid radicalism." His interests were more rooted in the twenties; the subjects of his intellectual pursuits were T. S. Eliot, Ezra Pound, James Joyce, and Cubist painters. In the early 1930s however, Phillips was teaching part-time at New York University.

> It was a lowly course in which we had to read some essays to learn something called expository writing. But the standard text was so bad, so pointless, so banal while pretending to be popular in the way academic collections can be, that I decided to use the *Nation* and the *New Republic* as our texts. And in the process of reading and discussing these magazines religiously as they came out each week, both teacher and students became radicalized.[9]

Lionel Trilling's radical activity offers another example of the various styles of commitment among the older New York Intellectuals. His childhood was less harsh than that of most of the others. He had grown up in a more prosperous home, his father being a skilled tailor. Trilling had once been drawn to the Jewish cultural community around the *Menorah Journal* but ultimately rejected its provincialism. During the 1930s he, too, found himself attracted to radicalism. With a number of other radical intellectuals, Trilling joined in a project entitled "Marxist Study of American Character," planning to write on cultural minorities. Several other New York Intellectuals also hoped to contribute: Hook would provide the "Preface to Marxism" and the section on philosophy, Meyer Schapiro the chapter on fine arts, and Elliot Cohen the contribution on sports.[10] All planned to use Marxist interpretations to evaluate contemporary problems, social as well as political. While the project fell through long before the essays had been submitted, the attitude and perspective of the participants demonstrate their radical concerns. Later in the decade Trilling served on the Trotsky Defense Committee, along with Hook. Despite these parallels between Trilling and Hook—an early association with communism, a later connection with Trotsky—they had very different experiences with radical politics. "For some intellectuals, politics was a very serious matter indeed, and their whole lives were shaped and formed by this," Irving Howe noted, citing Hook and Rahv as examples. "For others, say for a man like Fred Dupee," once literary editor of the *New Masses*, "the experience" may have been a great deal more marginal. "They were never as deeply involved." Trilling fits into this second camp.[11] Nonetheless, it is Trilling who later concluded that the radical politics of the 1930s could not be "overestimated"—that it "created the American intellectual class." At the very least, it created his class.

For the young college radicals, maturing in the 1930s, radicalism reflected both the tumultuous times and the style of youthful development. Daniel Bell, at City College in those years, spent his youth in various radical circles. His coming of age as a young Jew provided a symbolic moment for Bell's emerging radicalism, as well as an opportunity for one of his typical embroidered stories.

> When I was thirteen years old and being at that time an orthodox Jew, I had a *bar mitzvah*. One had to put on phylacteries. I had joined the Young People's Socialist League and I felt that I had found the truth. You see, I had lost my belief in God. So I went to the rabbi who had prepared me for the *bar mitzvah* and I said to him, "you know, I'm not going to put on *tvillim*. I've found the truth; I don't believe in God." He looked at me and said—"So *you* found the truth; *you* don't believe in God." He stopped, and he thought a moment, then said—"Tell me, do you think God cares?"

Despite his rabbi's chiding, Bell persisted with his teenage radical activities. In 1932 he gave street-corner speeches for Norman Thomas, serving as something of a warm-up for the older Socialist speakers. He memorized a speech of Eugene Debs, paraphrased in Upton Sinclair's *The Jungle* but not attributed to the Socialist. Bell delivered it from atop a stepladder around the Lower East Side. "At fifteen I was writing resolutions on the road to power," he recalled. "There were ironic discussions on battlefront tactics. One of the questions which used to amuse the YPSLs was 'How do you make revolutions since there are no longer any paving blocks in the streets?' "[12]

Bell's personal history, while altogether atypical of American youth, was a much more representative example of these immigrant boyhoods. Rather than expressing horror at a relative's commitment to radicalism, Bell's family became agitated only about the choice of which group he became allied with. A brief interest in a Communist youth group prompted an anarchist cousin to give Bell several pamphlets by Emma Goldman and Alexander Berkman. "They told how Trotsky had treacherously butchered the sailors of the Kronstadt fortress in 1921 . . . . The next time young Communist League kids came around, I said, 'What happened at Kronstadt?' "[13] Bell did manage to maintain more than a cordial relationship with the Trotskyists at City College. A number of his fellow students in Alcove No. 1 belonged to the Trotkyist YPSLs, including Howe, Kristol, and Seymour Martin Lipset.

The need for political action during the Depression clearly motivated these individuals—young and old, marginally or centrally involved—to join radical movements. Beyond the general causes lay individual motives. These often account for the choice of political groups and for the personal goals desired. In addition, these individual motives helped create differences among the radicals, attitudes and styles which "universalism" or "cosmopolitanism" could never overcome. One striking difference, clear to a young socialist like Alfred Kazin, grew between the children of immigrants and of old-stock America.

> Starting out in the Thirties under people who were "radical," like [John] Chamberlain and Cowley and [Otis] Ferguson, I could never identify myself with them, for they were so plainly with the haves, with the people who so mysteriously sat in positions of power. . . . It would never have occurred to me then to feel common cause with someone like Cowley, or to feel particularly close to Chamberlain, for writers from the business and professional class could only interpret in an abstract and literary way the daily struggle that was so real to me in Brownsville.[14]

What Kazin could not share with Cowley or Chamberlain, he could share with some of his fellow radicals who came from the Jewish ghettos. In part, many were only daytime émigrés, coming to Manhattan by day to study or work and returning to Brooklyn or the Bronx, often to their parents' homes, at night. They lived in two worlds, moving toward that of the "haves" but by no means there yet.

These young socialists did not rebel against the traditions of their families, as did many other radicals whose parents represented the business and professional class. Radicalism had always existed in the immigrant community and became part of the childhood experience of many of these Jewish youths. In Irving Howe's memory, the associations to his youth include "the Jewish slums of the East Bronx, endless talk about Hitler, money worries . . . the certainty bordering on comfort that [he] would never find a regular job, and above all, the Movement." At the age of fourteen, Howe recounted, he "wandered into the ranks of the socialist youth and from then on, all through [his] teens and twenties, the Movement was [his] home and passion." This youthful socialism was shared by others, Daniel Bell, Irving Kristol, and Alfred Kazin among them. In Brownsville, Kazin remembered, the immigrants' radicalism offered more than lessons in political theory. "The way anywhere those summer evenings led through the rival meetings on Pitkin Avenue. I could always find people there. Socialism would come to banish my loneliness."[15] As they grew older, the young Jews sought the same compensations elsewhere.

Having moved away from, if not totally out of, the world of their parents, they found in radicalism a bridge to overcoming their feelings of isolation. It became what "everyone" did, at least everyone they knew. Having been a youthful Socialist, Alfred Kazin considered the transition to adult radicalism perfectly natural. Being so natural, it often went unquestioned.

> Although I was a "Socialist," like everyone else I knew, I thought of socialism as orthodox Christians might think of the Second Coming—a wholly supernatural event which one might await with perfect faith, but which had no immediate relevance to my life. "Socialism" was a way of life, since everyone else I knew in New York was a Socialist, more or less; but I was remarkably detached from it intellectually. . . .

In contrast to Kazin's "detached" socialism is Irving Howe's "passion." Yet, Howe also recounted that, especially for young Jews, there was more than social reform to the appeal of radicalism.

> The "Jewish radical," who turned up in virtually all of the now happily forgotten "Marxist" novels, was a New York boy, of course; he came from poor parents and his father was usually a garment worker, he was a CCNY graduate, very brainy and rebellious though given to occasional lapses into petty bourgeois moodiness (Jews, it is well known, are very moody). In the end he always managed to overcome the handicaps of his background as well as the suspicions of the workers whose strikes he invariably led.

This stereotype of popular radical literature contained "just enough blurred truth," Howe admitted, "to make it easily recognizable." After his own graduation from City College, Howe's first job was in a factory, as mentioned above, from which he was fired six weeks later for attempting to organize the workers.[16]

Clearly personal elements drew both the passionate and the detached Jewish intellectuals toward radical causes. There certainly existed a belief in a better social order, in reform or revolution. Beyond this, there can also be found attempts to overcome their unique and often lonely position. The social aspect of American radicalism has often been demonstrated, from the communitarian societies of the mid-nineteenth century to the Communist-party summer camps of the 1930s. For these Jewish radicals, the movement provided a special community. Having drawn away from their former world, they sought grounding in a new one. The camaraderie of the City College lunchroom, where Ping-Pong went hand in hand with debate on the dialectic, is only the most obvious example. While they called for a utopian future of international brotherhood, they would settle, for the time being, for a utopian movement which embodied this goal. The cosmopolitan philosophy of the radical causes offered the hope of a world where being Jewish would not make any difference. Even within the cosmopolitan movements, however, the young Jews could still feel the distinctions. They sought to overcome their Jewishness not by trying to pass or convert but by putting it behind them, as they were putting the ghetto behind them. They thus came to radicalism with a personal agenda different from that of many other radicals. They shared a belief in the positions argued, surely; they joined because "everybody" they knew joined, because the times were marked by "intensity and fervor." Beyond this, however, they had their special reasons. Rather than forcing a total break with their parents, radicalism allowed for a degree of continuity with their own past and traditions and served as part of their transition from the ghetto margins to the larger society. They joined because the radical movements provided specific outlets for the particular talents developed in the youths and because they allowed them to apply their heritage in a new and appropriate manner, rather than requiring them to cast it off. In the end, they and their parents could still look to the same future. "Socialism," Alfred Kazin concluded, "would be one long Friday evening around the samovar and the cut-glass bowl laden with nuts and fruits. . . . " For Kazin and his contemporaries the coming future would be a day when "the heroes of the Russian novel—*our* kind of people— would walk the world."[17] They planned to be emissaries from their parents' world, not exiles.

Alfred Kazin's contrasts between the radicalism of the "haves" like Cowley, Chamberlain, and Ferguson with that of the "have-nots" like himself grew, in part, out of his understanding that these other radicals perceived a difference in his background and community. Recounting the time he brought Otis Ferguson home to dinner with the promise of an "exotic, mysterious, vaguely Levantine" meal, Kazin recalled Ferguson leaving him at the subway platform and asking, "What was so exotic about that?" Comparing their perspectives, Kazin ultimately saw the distinct differences between his perspectives and Ferguson's.

> Ferguson's boredom with us, with the crudity that had seemed to me positively sacramental in its significance for the future, with the worldly insignificance of poor Jews from whom had sprung the early passion of Christianity itself, shocked me; it seemed to send us all spinning into a world of actual dullness and tawdriness, where poverty was graceless and Jewishness merely a bore. I did not mind being poor, Jewish, excluded, for I knew that history was on the side of such things; what I could not understand was Ferguson's finding us dull.[18]

The young Jews came from a background quite distinct from that of the other radicals. Alfred Kazin could stroll among the socialist meetings on Pitkin Avenue, Irving Howe wandered into socialism at fourteen, and Daniel Bell stood on street corners giving radical speeches in his teens. By contrast, Malcolm Cowley writes that, at seventeen in Pittsburgh, "we were disillusioned and weary. In the midst of basketball, puppy love and discussions of life—washed down with chocolate sodas on warm afternoons—we had come to question almost everything we were taught at home and in school."[19]

The immigrant world was filled with a wide variety of radical causes and publications. At the turn of the century, radicals had found their greatest pockets of strength among the European immigrants. In 1928, of the 7,800 members of the Socialist party, over 3,400 were in foreign-language-affiliated organizations. For years the backbone of the Socialist party was provided by the immigrant radicals, especially the Jews in New York. The rank and file of the early New York socialists centered in the garment trade of the Lower East Side. In the 1920s the *Jewish Daily Forward*, the largest Yiddish newspaper in the world, subsidized the activities of the national office of the Socialist party by providing a monthly contribution of $500.[20] The Yiddish neighborhoods were not the exclusive domain of the Socialists either. From Emma Goldman's anarchism to the communism of the newpaper *Freiheit*, all types of radicalism flourished. For the young Jews, growing up in this world, radicalism was a constant element. Many parents were personally involved in one movement or another. Yet even those from nonpolitical families could hardly avoid the contact.

Despite the radical activity, the impact rarely spread beyond the immigrant world. The radicals spoke and wrote in Yiddish, restricting their message to other Jews. The cultural barriers which impeded the advancement of the immigrants on many fronts also applied to the dissemination of their radical ideas. Occasionally, there might be a bright spot, such as Meyer London's election to Congress as a Socialist in 1914. By and large, however, the fervor was restricted to the community itself.[21]

The young Jewish students and intellectuals never joined the radical movements of their parents. Once they had begun the pilgrimage to Manhattan, the provincialism and limitations of the ghetto became obvious. Yet, as part of the larger, English-speaking radical world, they sensed their differences from that milieu as well. Otis Ferguson's reaction to dinner in Brownsville not only angered Kazin but also demonstrated to Kazin his own sense of "doubleness, almost of duplicity, about the daily contrast of [his] personal life, [his] friends, [his] life in Brownsville, with those [radical] literary personages in Mid-Manhattan." The young Jews were not the escapees from *Main Street* and *Winesburg, Ohio*, but emissaries to the larger, nonimmigrant world. They left their Jewish communities with the approval of their parents and in joining radical movements found they could transfer a vestige of the immigrant environment to their new areas of activity. A Socialist or

Communist son would not cause parental horror—he might even be a source of pride. "The repetition of at least some of the ideological styles of immigrant Jewish socialism became," Howe concluded, "paradoxically, a way of breaking out of the confinements of immigrant Jewish life."[22] Less paradoxically than Howe believed, the radical movement provided the perfect means for the transition of the young Jews to American society. They could believe they were simultaneously conquering new worlds without abandoning old ones entirely.

Another vestige of their ghetto upbringing could be brought to their radical involvement. The streetwise style which had proved so appropriate in public schools and college classrooms also found a place in the radical movements. "We were clever and fast in responding to familiar cues," Irving Howe recalled. " . . . We were trained in agility rather than reflection. . . . " They used and refined these skills in the radical movements. "At a YPSL meeting you learned how to make a speech, even if sometimes a bombastic one . . . . At a meeting of a Socialist faction you learned how to 'theorize,' or at least mimic the posture of theory. . . . " These skills, Howe noted, did carry beyond the radical days, providing a "certain facility when you went on to college and became a sociologist or an English professor."[23] At all levels of their radicalism, from the City College lunchroom to the floor of the American Writers' Congress, they brought their ghetto training into practice.

Carrying vestiges of both their ethnic upbringing and the immigrants' radical tradition did not entirely smooth the transition of these young Jews. While avoiding the hostility which other radicals encountered from their elders, the Jews nonetheless still moved out of their community networks. Kazin's awareness of the clear distinctions between his Manhattan radical circle and life in Brownsville is one illustration of this divided sense—that despite some similarities the worlds remained different. Cultural connections helped span the move from the ghetto but could not fully cushion the feelings of disconnection many of the young radicals experienced. They had set themselves on a new course, and only a portion of their background could move with them. When young, they had found support within the ethnic neighborhoods, had a hundred thousand Brownsville parents, Kazin observed. As that world receded, new connections and associations needed to be developed. Skills and ideals learned in the ghetto helped them gain acceptance into radical movements. The closeness and sense of community in radicalism facilitated their move out of the ghetto. They became members of what Irving Howe describes as an underground city. This city consisted of

a series of stopping places where we could ease the strain of restlessness and feel indifferent to our lack of money. In the winter there were the numberless "socials" given by branches of the Movement to raise funds for their headquarters. . . . There were the movies on Forty-second Street where amid clouds of steam and stench our political virtue was compromised by sophisticated European art films. There were the free concerts at the Metropolitan Museum where—it was a matter of pride to know—the music was poor but one found a sort of comfort . . . allowing our romanticism to find a sanctioned outlet in Beethoven and Schubert.[24]

It was not only the socialist "youth" who found a strong social element in radical movements. The elders among the New York Intellectuals were themselves only barely into their thirties, and for them, as for the college-age students, the social aspects of radicalism were important. William Phillips remembered, "Our favorite hangout was not the Algonquin but Stewart's cafeteria on Sheridan Square, where for a dime you could get coffee and cake, and sit for hours arguing and solving the problems of the world."[25] One cynical observer of this period, Arnold Beichman, recalled a sense of "parlor revolutionarism." "You gave money, you went to a Madison Square Garden rally, where Norman Thomas or Earl Browder appeared, you sang the 'Internationale' (in different variations if you were a Socialist or a Communist), then you went to Bickford's Cafeteria." The more one became known in the movement, the better one's chances for social contact. "If you got into the movement," Leslie Fiedler remembered, "you could meet rich people, get invited to big parties—people you never saw otherwise, if you came from a working-class or petty-bourgeois background." Going to the parties and meeting these people often had other rewards. "In a funny way, it also opened publishers' doors to you and magazines as well," Fiedler recounted. Beyond the professional and even the political, there was the purely social. The radical world was like most other social networks; it had its salons, its hostesses, its internal customs. "You could meet a Soviet counsel at a party at Max Lerner's house," Arnold Beichman said. In the Popular Front period,

> you could see a living representative of the revolution before you. It was all very exciting. And it was also a good way to get laid. You met a lot of nice girls that way, and some not so nice. It was a very important outlet for sexual energies as well as intellectual energies.[26]

New York Intellectuals eventually formed their own social network, but in their first years in Manhattan they found one already in existence; it added an often exciting touch to the radical world they had just entered.

The prospect of nice girls, Soviet counsels, and opening doors—the entire social network—proved both a stimulus and a way to overcome the sense of disconnection felt by the immigrants' sons. Participation in radicalism offered another element of psychological support, this time more personal than social. Among these Jewish intellectuals, personal prospects appeared slim. They felt certain that few jobs were available. An "airlessness" molded their college careers. Their attitudes toward the future of the American system grew cynical. In addition, parental hopes about success in American society declined as the society itself teetered. Their goals seemed less attainable once the insular comforts of the ghetto were behind them. Seeking directions, touchstones, and even answers, they found some in radical ideologies. Radicalism gave the intellectuals more than "a 'purpose' in life," Howe recalled; "far more important," it gave "a coherent perspective upon everything that was happening to us." Compared with the belief and comfort in a Marxist future, radicalism was "a good deal more practical and immediate." "The Movement," Howe noted, "gave us a language of response and gesture . . . . It felt good 'to know.' . . . we enjoyed a privileged relationship to history." Amid all the disorientations, radicalism provided a "*dramatic* view of human experience," perfectly appropriate for the unconnected émigrés from the ghettos, Howe believed.

> With its stress upon inevitable conflicts, apocalyptic climaxes, ultimate movements, hours of doom, and shining tomorrows, it appealed deeply to our imaginations. We felt we were always on the rim of heroism, that the mockery we might suffer at the moment would turn to vindication in the future, that our loyalty to principle would be rewarded by the grateful masses of tomorrow.[27]

The immediate future looked dim—few jobs, economic despair, and a crumbling system. The plans which their parents had made for these young Jews suffered severe setbacks. No shining world awaited. Set adrift, they found solace in the world of radicalism, encouraged by the insights of their "privileged" understanding. For the moment this helped stay the disorientation. For the future, radicalism also offered hope. Unable to complete their anticipated journeys in traditional American society, they expected personal success in the coming world. "When the revolution came," when the shining tomorrow dawned, they would be rewarded by the "grateful masses," would become the heroes of the transformed society. The move from their marginality as immigrants' children to positions of central importance would be as complete as the reconstruction of the old society. Amid the disarray and disorientation of the Depression years, the security of this knowledge helped carry these young men. Radical dreams made the future look brighter. Perhaps more important, they made the present seem not so bad either.

The optimism of the new order for American society, the sense that "everyone" belonged to a radical movement, could not hide the fact that the numbers of radicals remained small. As radical votes decreased and Roosevelt's popularity rose, the smallness of the radicals' ranks became obvious. Undiscouraged, many radicals found a rationale for this development which allowed them at least to maintain their personal commitments and to continue to believe in their special sight. Growing out of their sense of "assuredness" was the belief of those within the movement that they held in their "pocket a skeleton key to History," as Dwight Macdonald put it in 1957. "Nothing is more frustrating for an intellectual than to work out a logical solution and find nobody is listening." The concept of a vanguard party perfectly suited both the intellectual and the practical reality of American radicalism. "We meta-politicians were the *illuminati*," Macdonald stated, whose esoteric knowledge enabled us to divine the real, hidden nature of events and, when the time came to Take Advantage of Revolutionary Situations. We were the "cadres of leadership" . . . and the masses would fall behind us as they followed the Bolsheviks in October. The smallness of Lenin's pre-1917 party was a great comfort—if he could take over Russia with a mere handful of disciplined comrades, why not . . . ?[28]

As intellectuals, they could see the need for radicalism and, thus, formed the core of the "vanguard party." This became a self-gratifying attitude. "*We* were not alienated," recalled Irving Kristol. "By virtue of being radical intellectuals, we had 'transcended' alienation . . . the 'elite' was us—the 'happy few' who had been chosen by History to guide our fellow creatures toward a secular redemption."[29]

More than intellectual arrogance, however, prompted this view and the radical participation. The intellectuals believed it necessary for them to join the radical parties. In the *Culture and the Crisis* pamphlet, addressed to all writers and artists, the place of the intellectual in the radical struggle was made explicit.

> We, too, the intellectual workers, are of the oppressed, and until we shake off the servile habit of that oppression we shall build blindly and badly, to the lunatic specifications of greed and ignorance. If we are capable of building a civilization, surely it is time for us to begin; time for us to assert our function, our responsibility; time for us to renew the pact of comradeship with the struggling masses, trapped by the failure of leadership in the blind miseries of a crumbling machine.[30]

As aspiring intellectuals as well as young radicals, the New York Intellectuals found the appeal of a radical intelligentsia compelling. When they later analyzed what had prompted Americans to become involved in various left causes, they often came back to the characteristics which were especially appropriate for them. The intellectuals attracted to Marxism were a "phenomenon," wrote Alfred Kazin in *On Native Grounds*, more than a group representing "a body of critical thought." Daniel Bell extended this analysis even further, concluding that the "main appeal of the Communist Party was to the dispossessed intelligentsia of the depression generation and to the 'engineers of the future' who were attracted by the elitist appeal . . . ."[31] They assigned to everyone the motives which moved them.

When Nathan Glazer assessed the "social basis" of American communism for one of the countless series on communism published in the postwar years, he too generalized about the radical appeal in terms which often seemed to fit the experiences of his fellow New York Intellectuals. "To be a Communist meant to shed the limitations of one's social reality, and to join a fraternity that transcends the division of the world," Glazer wrote. Particularly strong was the appeal to white-collar and professional classes, as they evidenced a "good deal of resentment of the difficulties for latecomers establishing a social base."[32]

Undoubtedly, Glazer's portrait describes the motives of some Communists and some non-Communist radicals. What is striking about his conclusion is that it suits his own group so well.

When the young radicals among the New York Intellectuals had aged a bit and the world had changed after the Second World War, they often looked back on their radical experiences. Like that of Bell and Glazer, the analysis dealt with *all* radicals or *all* Communists but frequently spoke most to the analysts' own experiences and motives. In his novel about the coming maturity of a young Jewish youth, *Passage from Home*, Isaac Rosenfeld wrote a bitter exchange between two relatives of the main character.

> "Any person who finds a cause he can devote his life to is a goner."
> "Oh, so now we're against causes."
> "Lay off, lay off sister. All I mean is a person either believes a certain thing because it's really in him—and then it's not a cause, it's his nature—or else he's faking. And trying to cover up a lot of dirt, most likely."[33]

The assessment is clearly more harsh and more critical than need be. The radicals among the New York Intellectuals were not "fakers." Yet, there is probably as much hidden truth in Rosenfeld's dialogue as in Bell's and Glazer's generalized descriptions. The problem was not a "lot of dirt" they were covering up but a wide array of personal motives which remained concealed. The young students and critics found in the radical movements new ties and connections which helped them overcome their personal isolation and reinforced their own sense of political and intellectual appropriateness.

To the young Jewish émigrés, thirties radicalism provided an appropriate outlet for their desires and personal needs. At least it seemed to for a time. Whether "passionate" or "disinterested," they all found themselves bound up with one of the various radical causes of the Depression years, seeking both social goals and personal fulfillment. When they later came to evaluate that experience, either for themselves or for others, they rarely painted portraits of altruism or sincere commitment. His young life had been wrapped up in "The Movement," Leslie Fiedler remembered, a phrase he considered "shockingly unanalyzed."

> *The* Movement, the epithet, all kinesis and no commitment, echoes in the enduring head like a reproach.
> The Movement . . . the symbolic flirtation at least with denying the whole universe that defined our intolerable exclusion, our outsideness—set against the counter-urge to belong, to infiltrate, become one at the world's center, the definition of its alienation.
> It was a pretty irony for boys, but in the end a mask for accommodation.[34]

The young Jewish intellectuals joined the radicalism of the decade, believing, or perhaps merely hoping, that it was possible to be a radical and an intellectual, that the children of immigrants and the children of the "haves" might come into radical alliance, and that a bright future awaited them. They also joined the radical causes because "everyone" did, from the ghettos to the Manhattan literary circles. In the end, most left the movements disappointed, finding that the goals could not *all* be achieved or that personal requirements remained unfulfilled. For a time, though, it formed the "substance" of all their lives and proved an essential element in forming the New York Intellectual community. It was not, however, "a deeply-grounded experience," Irving Howe concluded. "It lacked roots in a popular movement which might bring intellectuals into relationship with the complexities of power and stringencies of organization." They were captured by the spirit of the times, swept along by the prevailing current, fearful of being *"declassé,"* and attempting to simultaneously transfer and break free of the ghetto influences. It was, however, short-lived. "From a doctrine it became a style," Howe admitted, "and from a style a memory."[35]

AN ART "SUBVERSIVE AND DANGEROUS"

The young intellectuals who were drawn to the radical movements of the 1930s desired more than merely to bring their intellectual skills to the political battlefield. Writers and critics began to see new or newly revitalized literary styles as more appropriate than those which had held sway before the crash. They revived once-popular notions of social realism in literature, but in ways which took on new and intensified meanings. In 1930 Lionel Trilling called realism "the most relevant literature we are producing today. Looking about the world around him, he felt that "no person in the United States, save he be a member of the plutocratic class . . . is not tainted, little or much, with the madness of the bottom dog." Ultimately, Trilling believed, "the salvation of American art lies not in a greater rapprochement with the environment, but in its becoming subversive and dangerous to the social order."[36] Trilling was not alone is his view. As the literary atmosphere of the decade became increasingly politicized and the political atmosphere increasingly sectarian, the manner in which writers and critics attempted to fulfill this goal changed and adjusted. Nevertheless, the literary community's heightened awareness of the problems of its society *and* its belief that there was a significant role for it in the reformation of that society persisted.

Radical literature did not suddenly emerge in the wake of the Great Depression. Rather, the minority who argued for political art during the 1920s found their position coming into vogue. In February of 1921 Michael Gold had published an essay entitled "Towards Proletarian Art" in the *Liberator*. This was the first attempt to enunciate what became known as proletarian literature. In the flush of radical optimism after the Bolshevik Revolution, Gold saw the promise of a union of art and politics. "Now, at last, the masses of America have awakened, through the revolutionary movement, to their souls," he declared. "The method of erecting this proletarian culture," he concluded, "must be the revolutionary method—from the deepest depths upward."[37]

Gold's optimistic prophecy proved premature. By 1929, however, the nation was facing economic catastrophe. Now the time seemed ripe for the emergence of proletarian literature. Gold and Joseph Freeman, editors of the radical magazine the *New Masses*, helped to found an organization dedicated to perpetuating this revolutionary art. The John Reed Clubs, named after the former editor of the old *Masses* and the *Liberator*, who died in Russia in 1920, aimed to encourage both the creation of proletarian literature and the training of radical writers. The first John Reed Club was established in New York, and that branch remained the most important. By 1932, clubs had sprung up in twelve cities, sufficient to hold a national conference in Chicago. Out of that conference emerged the Draft Manifesto of the Clubs, which the *New Masses* reprinted. The integration of revolutionary politics and culture emerged as the central position.

> The general crisis of capitalism is reflected in its culture. The economic and political machinery of the bourgeoisie in decay, its philosophy, its literature, and its art are bankrupt. . . . Capitalism cannot give the mass of mankind bread. It is equally unable to evolve creative ideas.

This political crisis required that writer and artists join in the political activity.

> We call upon all honest intellectuals, all honest writers and artists, to abandon decisively the treacherous illusion that art can exist for art's sake, or that the artist can remain remote from the historic conflicts in which all men must take sides. We urge them to join with the literary and artistic movement of the working-class in forging a new art that shall be a weapon in the battle for a new and superior world.[38]

This explicit appeal to intellectuals to join the workers in the class struggle attracted a variety of young writers in the early years of the Depression. Richard Wright described his going to his first meeting of the Chicago club as an "amused spectator" but quickly finding himself both published in the left press and enmeshed in the club activities. Like many of the other radical organizations of the era, the clubs provided a social locus as well as an arena for the articulation of political beliefs. This seemed especially compelling for young writers whose already scant hopes of success had been dashed by the economic collapse. William Phillips recalled that many members came from "the army of magazine rejectees" or those "who tried to overcome their creative frustrations by attending endless meetings and making passionate speeches about such unreal subjects as the 'culture' of the working class."[39] In addition, like their counterparts in other radical movements, many club members felt they now possessed special knowledge, the key to history. Malcolm Cowley recently recalled an "imperious summons" to the national headquarters of the John Reed Club, in December 1932, to discuss an article Cowley had written for the *New Republic* about a national hunger march in Washington. Four young men waited for Cowley.

> They had before them a thick manuscript which, as they read it aloud, turned out to be a line-by-line criticism of the article. Not many comments were eulogistic. Roughly, they had concluded that the article failed to emphasize the correct leadership of the Communist Party in the struggle for bread, and it did not suggest the growing militance of the broad masses, that it did not mention the part in the struggle played by Negroes and other minority groups, that it did not explain how the Washington police were acting as agents of a capitalist conspiracy, and, in general, that it revealed my petty-bourgeois illusions and my insufficient grounding in the Marxian dialectic.

Cowley believed that part of the hostility of these four stemmed from the fact that they were "turning the tables on one of the editors [of the *New Republic*] who had rejected their work."[40]

Two of Cowley's inquisitors soon emerged as the dominant forces in the New York chapter. William Phillips had graduated from City College more interested in modernism than radicalism. His first publication had been a piece of non-Marxist criticism in *Symposium*. However, his radicalization in the early 1930s led him to reevaluate his literary position and directed him to the New York John Reed Club, of which he eventually became secretary. Philip Rahv, in Phillips's phrase, "had drifted into the John Reed Club from the West Coast." Rahv had always been interested in political questions, unlike Phillips. Joseph Freeman recalled receiving an unsolicited article on Plekhanov, by "an obscure boy in the Bronx." Liking it, Freeman invited the author, Rahv, to submit more, all of which he published in the *New Masses.*[41]

Rahv and Phillips approached Freeman in 1933, complaining that the *New Masses* was too political. They suggested founding a radical journal devoted to topics which were more directly literary. Freeman agreed, and under the sponsorship of the New York John Reed Club, *Partisan Review* made its initial appearance in the spring of 1934. Rahv, Phillips, using the name Wallace Phelps, and Freeman were listed as editors, along with nine others.[42] The opening editorial, apparently written by Freeman, restated the aims of the John Reed Club Draft Manifesto and the ultimate goals of proletarian literature.

> We propose to concentrate on creative and critical literature, but we shall maintain a definite viewpoint—that of the revolutionary working class. Through our specific literary medium we shall participate in the struggle of the workers and sincere intellectuals against imperialist war, fascism, national and radical oppression, and for the abolition of the system which breeds these evils. The defense of the Soviet Union is one of our principal tasks.

The first issue of the journal offered an array of articles which followed these guidelines. Several proletarian authors, including Grace Lumpkin, Alfred Hayes, and Joseph Freeman, contributed stories or poetry. James T. Farrell published an excerpt from *Studs Lonigan*, Phillips a critical essay, and Rahv and Granville Hicks book reviews.[43]

Partisan Review's initial concerns centered on radical literature and criticism, but from the outset the continual problem of financial support also occupied the young editors. To raise money, they instituted a series of social activities. The original funding for the magazine had, in fact, come from the sponsorship of a lecture on literature and dialectical materialism by the English Communist John Strachey. "The lecture turned out to be a smash hit," Phillips remembered, "and Rahv and I and our wives left the hall with our pockets stuffed with money, scared of losing it or of being robbed until we could get to the bank the next morning." The Strachey lecture netted *PR* $800, enough to keep the magazine going for a year. Expenses were low—no rent, no salaries, and low printing costs "made the Depression seem like a literary utopia."[44]

The financial health of the young journal continued to rely on revenues from lectures and dances. In his early years, Phillips recalled, they thought they had "finally made it" when he and Rahv were arrested for charging admission at a party and selling drinks without a license. As he remembers the event,

> It was a party one Saturday evening for the German composer, Hanns Eisler, who had been prominent in Communist activities and had just arrived in this country. The affair had been going full swing, when a man approached me as I was standing next to the table where the punch was being sold, and asked me the price of a drink. I told him it was twenty-five cents, and he asked whether I would pour one for him. I did and dropped the quarter he had ostentatiously given me in a box full of money on the table. He then asked me to step outside with him, informed me that he was a cop, and said that I had violated the ABC law. Apparently another cop had taken Rahv outside, too, and told him he was running an affair without a license. They took us to a nearby police station, where they said we could explain things to the captain and then go home. We then got our first lesson in police methods, for as soon as we got there they frisked us and put us in a cell for the night, while assuring us we could be released on bail in the morning. I was permitted to call my wife, but of course it was impossible to raise the bail money on Sunday. However, with remarkable resourcefulness she managed to find a friend who put up a Soviet government bond as bail.[45]

The dances and lectures which supported *Partisan Review* during its first years also helped create the world which was growing up around the journal. These events became part of the "underground city," as Howe called the radical social network. Although the world around *Partisan Review* remained small during these first years and fit into a larger radical milieu, the magazine did, from the outset, provide a social focus as well as an intellectual forum.

In the first years of publication, Rahv and Phillips continued to trumpet the radical literary cause, while seeking to establish some definitions and standards by which to evaluate the movement and to put it in its proper place in the literary tradition. They waxed optimistic about the prospects for proletarian literature. In the second number of *PR*, Rahv declared that the Marxist critics who had "busied themselves with the building of a theoretical scaffolding for a partisan literature expressing the revolutionary reconstruction of society" had succeeded. He saw "the new class novels coming off the press month after month, the new literary magazines spring up all over the country—all these signs of a promise fulfilled. They prove the fusion of theory and practice in American revolutionary literature and its leaving behind the incipient phase of creative helplessness."[46] To those critics who might scoff at this development, Rahv responded in the tough and streetsmart style which would characterize much of the early *Partisan Review* writing. "No hue and cry of propaganda, no lugubrious head-shaking of wiseacres, and no amount of sneering on the part of those who persist in their palsied hieroglyphics on the fly-paper of bourgeois class impotence, can arrest its progress."[47]

The young editors sought to define the place of this newly emerging literary form. Phillips, in a 1934 article entitled "Three Generations," expressed the belief that this new group of writers was the only unified literary movement of the period. Most of its members, he found, were related to the labor movement, the Communist party, and "the literature growing out of these forces." "Their activity," he announced, "marks a period in which revolutionary literature is the most significant and strongest literary current." Other movements of the past decade—those of "the exiles," including Hemingway, Cowley, and Allen Tate, and of the "pioneers," radicals like Freeman, Gold, and Joshua Kunitz—had been so entrenched in their particular pursuits that they were unable to incorporate the valuable qualities of the other. The younger, third generation could draw together the crucial elements of these previous literary movements. Thus, Phillips could incorporate the "heritage" of his old modernist interests with the revelations of his new political outlook. He was able to achieve what the "pioneers" could not, a fusion of the literary spirit of the 1920s with the political necessities of the 1930s.[48]

Feeling themselves at the forefront of a dynamic new movement in literature proved exhilarating for the young editors. "The proletarian writer, in sharing the moods and expectations of his audience," Rahv and Phillips announced in a joint essay, "gains the creative confidence and harmonious functioning within his class which gives him a sense of responsibility and discipline totally unknown in the preceding decade." The writer could fulfill the creative and the social impulse simultaneously, break free of the necessity of choosing between art and politics, and set his sights on a wider audience without lowering literary standards. "Indeed," they happily concluded, "it is largely this intimate relationship between reader and writer that gives revolutionary literature an activism and purposefulness long since unattainable by writers of other classes."[49]

Rahv and Phillips continued to exude optimism about proletarian literature, but in the middle years of the decade certain questions began to creep into their writings, and they began to express doubts about the movement they had founded a magazine to further. Despite brave declarations, they found themselves not entirely happy with the quality of the literature being produced. What was more essential and more personal, they began to express concern about the role of critics and criticism within the political context of proletarian literature; they found themselves caught on the dilemma of balancing radical aims and intellectual standards. Throughout 1935 and 1936 their writings were filled with questions and signs of discomfort.

They called attention to the immediate problem that journalism and pamphleteering were being mistaken for quality writing. In a 1935 article Rahv and Phillips tried to take stock of the movement and propose ways of limiting polemics disguised as literature. Proletarian literature lacked a crucial element, they believed, a cohesive and structured theoretical position against which works could be judged. "One factor in this chaos is the absence of an esthetic of our own which would find its practical application in the evaluation of writing and currents." The failure to develop such a theoretical structure proved one not of oversight, however, but of resistance. It was being "seriously hampered by the prevalent vociferous aversion to theoretical analysis," which was often "dismissed as 'bourgeois estheticism,' 'academicism,' and what not."

This led to a larger concern, their belief that the critical role had been minimized. "Another difficulty confronting Marxist critics is the servile role assigned to it by our writers. The critical faculty," they complained, "is narrowed down to the writing of what amounts to little more than publicity for new proletarian novels and plays." Having merged their own radical and literary commitments, they felt unable to put their commitment into practice. This led to more than feelings of neglect, they argued. True literary creation required something more than either literary talent or the understanding of ideology. "Ideology lights up the darkness, it does not grant the eyes to see," they asserted. Examples existed in areas beyond radical literature. T. S. Eliot, despite his great talent, had become a bête noire among leftists because of his conservative, Anglo-Catholic, anti-Semitic views. This Anglo-Catholic phase, Rahv and Phillips noted, "set up a wall between his poetic talent and its realization." The lesson for those on the left should be clear, they assumed. Only through the critical attention of those who could balance both these elements—the radical and the literary, the political and the cultural—could proletarian literature achieve its full potential. The Marxist critics, among whom Rahv and Phillips surely counted themselves, appeared the very individuals best able to carry out this task.[50]

These criticisms did not, however, cause Rahv and Phillips to abandon proletarian literature in 1935. They demonstrate, rather, the doubts and difficulties the two experienced. Rahv could still write of proletarian literature as "a new way of looking at life—the bone and flesh of a revolutionary sensibility taking on literary form." Although they called for an increased role for critics, they still felt that all individuals interested in literature should turn to politics. They warned other writers not to stand back from the problems of social actions and be content to strike the writer's classic pose of the interested observer. "The assimilation of this new material requires direct participation instead of external observation." It was the role of the critic "to point out the dangers inherent in the *spectator's* attitude."[51]

A final role for the critic, clearly the most important, emerged from the analysis of Rahv and Phillips. A critic must become "the ideologist of the literary movement." Citing Lenin as support, they maintained that

> any ideologist . . . is worthy of that name only when he marches ahead of the spontaneous movements, points out the real road, and when he is able, ahead of all others, to solve all the theoretical, political, and tactical questions which the "material elements" of the movement spontaneously encounter.[52]

Thus, they set themselves an enormous and important task, one which would surely raise them from the servile level they felt they had been assigned in the proletarian-literature movement.

One can only speculate as to how long Rahv and Phillips would have fought for their notions of a critical standard for radical literature, had the John Reed Clubs and the proletarian-literature movement continued on the same basis throughout the decade. As their attitudes about proletarian literature began to change in 1935, however, the movement itself, as well as the entire face of American radicalism, underwent significant adjustment. These changes in the movement did not drive Rahv and Phillips out. They merely made their departure easier and helped them resolve the ambivalence they had been feeling.

The most significant of these changes was the creation of the United Front Against Facism—or, as it was generally known, the Popular Front—and the concomitant dissolution of the John Reed Clubs. Even before the actual international call for the Front, in August of 1935, "the premonitory rumblings of the People's front were already spreading over the world," Malcolm Cowley later recalled. After battling with one another for the first half of the decade, and in fact for many decades, a number of radical groups attempted to form a coalition to resist the threatening rise of fascist parties. Beyond responding to the specter of fascism, the Front seemed to offer many radicals the hope of a political union of what the critic Newton Arvin called "the Left and the Center that bends left." As part of this attempt to broaden the radical base, the John Reed Clubs disbanded, replaced by the League of American Writers. The league aimed to be a less sectarian group which would incorporate already established writers rather than promote new talent, as had the clubs. "The kids had played the largest part up until that time," Cowley remembered. "Now the party had decided that the kids could be pushed to one side, and that the writers of 'some' standing would be invited."[53]

Partisan Review, which continued to publish despite the disbanding of the John Reed Clubs, did not resist this change initially. In fact, it printed the "call" for the league's first writers' congress, to be held in New York. "The editors of *Partisan*," they wrote, "not only endorse this Congress but also offer the pages of this organ for a thorough discussion of the problems which will be analyzed at the gathering of proletarian and sympathetic authors."[54] They added, two months later, that the congress would "set the frame for a more profound and more extensive revolutionary literature." Moreover, William Phillips attended several of the organizational sessions for the meeting.[55]

The League of American Writers held its first congress in the auditorium of the New School for Social Research in April 1935. Among delegates were an illustrious cross section of literary radicals, including a number of foreigners and a variety of representatives of the working class. Matthew Josephson, Langston Hughes, Malcolm Cowley, Earl Browder, and John Dos Passos presented papers. Other delegates included John Chamberlain, Richard Wright, James T. Farrell, Josephine Herbst, Clifford Odets, Lincoln Steffens, Van Wyck Brooks, and Lewis Mumford. Delegates came from across the country and from Mexico and Cuba.[56] The success of the writers' congress stemmed from the gathering of so many notable American writers, as well as from the general optimism about the potential success of revolutionary literature. Participants felt that the two trends which had existed in American literature over the preceding twenty-five years, the political and literary, were now merged. Harold Rosenberg, reporting on the congress in *Poetry*, wrote of the hopeful future of radical poetry on the basis of events at the congress.

> The ideas and arguments might have been exchanged anywhere. But when the representative of a group of Pennsylvania miners came forward to say: We are prepared to print and circulate 10,000 copies of any poem we can recite or sing together, and even if it is a difficult poem we will try to master it—that was a new thing. And when an appeal was made on behalf of 300 workers' theatres all over the U.S. for poetic monologues, group recitals, and plays of any length in verse or prose, it became possible to see how poetry might step forth from the little magazines and the tomb to which the publishers annually bring their half-dozen volumes of *Collected Works*, and walk once more upon the stage and the street; and the individual poet could begin to hope that perhaps soon he would no longer be compelled to lead a double life, through the need to maintain a social existence by some other means than poetry.*[57]

It seemed to Rosenberg, as to other delegates, that the proletarian-literature movement had finally approached fruition. Writers and workers, who in fact had always both been workers, would find liberation in the radical efforts.

---

*Perhaps Rosenberg tried to fill part of this request himself when he published "1776" in *Poetry*, May 1936, pp. 80–81 (see next page).

Even the Communist party secretary, Earl Browder, appeared to redress the image of left writers as either political hacks or Communist propagandists. "We do not want to take good writers and make bad strike leaders of them," he told the audience. And the league president, Waldo Frank, felt he was witnessing "the ferment, the warmth, the energy," and "the will to hard experiencing on our parts in the revolutionary struggle."[58]

A number of the papers presented to the congress reflect this optimism, most notably Granville Hicks's "The Dialectics of the Development of Marxist Criticism." Hicks allowed that a final, complete philosophy of proletarian literature had not yet been achieved but noted that the heartening development had been the union of two main trends in American writing—the fusion of what he called the spirit of the *Massses* and the *Liberator*, of the political and the artistic. It was, he contended, a dialectic process, and though the fusion had occurred, the ultimate refinements had not been achieved. In this context, he noted and praised some of the recent criticism being expressed about revolutionary literature, making particular mention of *Partisan Review*. Calling two weaknesses "especially serious," Hicks cited the argument of Rahv and Phillips on the technical problems of the writer and the relation between experience and creation.[59]

While Hicks noted the areas of concern which Rahv and Phillips suggested, he argued against the particular solutions they proposed. The resolution of these weaknesses would emerge more from the inherent nature of the dialectic, Hicks claimed, than from some forced attempt to mold a theory of literature. "Nothing . . . can be gained, and much may be lost, by sacrificing the strength of Marxism in an attempt to remedy its weakness," Hicks maintained. The diversity of recent proletarian writing pointed to signs of "a far more adequate unification [of politics and art]. But let us not suppose that the synthesis will be final." For Hicks, Rahv's and Phillips's article suggested the need for a Marxist aesthetic "that would be good for all time." Instead, Hicks argued, "new errors will arise. New errors have to be corrected. The dialectic process will go on."[60]

stands in	Revolution	they can't swallow	red
their throats,	holding their	it, it's	with the
like iron it'll	mouths open	sticking	sparks of
choke them	It was	in their	the Commune,
Nothing to	with this great	throats—	with the fire
sneak back to—	mace of	1776	of October.
no king	Revolution	hiss-	
like Greece,	stolen from	ssing	
no tyrant	the people	between their	
like Germany,	they built	jaws, turning	
nothing	everything	hot again.	
but a People's	Now	It's all	

Hicks's optimism about both the current state and the future of proletarian literature remained strong despite his awareness of the problems Rahv and Phillips suggested. The difficulties would be remedied without the creation of a formal literary aesthetic. To Rahv and Phillips, this meant that Hicks did not believe it necessary to rethink the role of critics, to change their assignment from servile publicists to ideologists, as they had argued. The problem of literary standards would work itself out in time and did not require the critical role the *PR* editors envisioned.

Rahv and Phillips remained caught between their belief in proletarian literature and Marxist criticism, on one hand, and the desire to reform or restructure radical art, on the other. Through 1936 they showed a continually ambivalent attitude, unwilling either to abandon or to embrace the movement fully. They defended radical art against critics who held that "the philosophy of social revolution straight-jackets the poet's experience," while at the same time they reiterated their belief in the need for a revolutionary aesthetic, the very theme which Hicks had called too narrow and constricted.[61]

As Rahv and Phillips began to express doubts about the turns the revolutionary-literature movement was taking, so too did others begin to question *Partisan Review*. One suggestion discussed by the executive committee of the League of American Writers was the creation of a new literary quarterly to replace the little proletarian magazines of the John Reed Clubs, including *PR*. "We'll tell them to stop publishing *Partisan Review*," Alexander Trachtenberg, head of cultural affairs for the Communist party, announced at one meeting. Malcolm Cowley objected. "Listen, Trachty, the kids have done a good job. They've gotten out a lively magazine and they've done it all themselves. Let them go ahead with it." Trachtenberg dropped his objection and did not carry out what Cowley assumed "to have been Party orders to kill the *Partisan Review*."[62] The party need not have bothered. For in the spring of 1936, armed with an emerging theory of radical literature different from that of the proletarian writers, Phillips and Rahv suspended publication of *PR* and broke with the Communists and the League of American Writers.

Adrift in the radical and literary world, they looked for new connections and new associations upon which to reestablish their magazine. They had joined the world of radical literature full of the optimism of true believers, only to feel increasing doubts about the movement to which they were committed. They now set out to revive *PR* on a basis which would more fully represent their new ideas about literature and politics. They sought out other disenchanted writers and intellectuals also feeling disconnected from "orthodox" radicalism. They found a good many, and among these "apostates" an intellectual community was formed.

Section II

THE PARTISAN MIND

Chapter 4

The *Partisan* Family

The break of *Partisan Review* from the Communist left, the *New Masses*, and proletarian literature allowed Philip Rahv and William Phillips to recast their magazine in an image and style more congenial to their own point of view. Although free of the dictates of a cultural approach they found constricting, they still faced one crucial problem with their declared independence: How could they revive the magazine without the financial backing of their old allies? In the year between the suspension of the "old" *Partisan Review*, in 1936, and its rebirth, in 1937, Rahv and Phillips cast about for sources of monetary support. In the process, they discovered a number of other intellectuals who shared their unhappiness with Stalinist politics and its cultural expressions—individuals who were seeking an appropriate forum to express their ideas. From this group of unaffiliated radicals, Phillips and Rahv were able to fashion a new editorial board, secure financial support, and collect a stable of writers to contribute to the "new" *Partisan Review*.

Frederick W. Dupee, the *New Masses'* literary editor, was one of those unhappy with the Communists. A midwesterner, Dupee had attended the University of Illinois and the University of Chicago before finishing his degree at Yale in 1927. Like many of his contemporaries, he was caught up in the radical and literary politics of the Depression years, joining the Communist party and rising to an editorship at the *New Masses*. By 1936, however, he was experiencing the same kind of uneasiness as Rahv and Phillips. Phillips told Dupee of the plans for reviving *PR* on a non-Stalinist basis and persuaded him to leave the *New Masses* and become an editor of the "new" journal. In a letter to the radical critic Newton Arvin, Dupee tried to explain his move. "Feeling that political strife is poisoning the intellectual atmosphere just now, we plan to effect a partial divorce settlement between literature and politics to pursue an independent Marxist investigation into American culture and culture in general," Dupee explained. "Complete independence is perhaps impossible," he realized. "But at least we shall work free of the immediate, day-to-day political pressures which have made my job [at the *New Masses*] so very difficult." Bitterness did not accompany Dupee's change, as he and Arvin visited one another during the summer of 1937 and had "many amiable arguments about Stalinism."[1]

Dupee, in turn, suggested two old friends from his Yale days as possible additions, Dwight Macdonald and George L. K. Morris. They had edited a small, literary journal at Yale called the *Miscellany* and had remained in touch since then. Macdonald came from a relatively prosperous middle-class family, his father being a lawyer and his mother the daughter of a well-to-do Brooklyn merchant. He went to private schools and then to Yale, graduating in 1928. The Depression dealt his family a severe blow, however, causing harsh financial losses, which in turn contributed to his father's death in 1929. Forced to enter business to support his mother, Macdonald briefly joined Macy's management program. Unhappy there, he moved to the staff of *Fortune*, where he remained throughout the early 1930s. The change in his own economic condition, coupled with the larger changes in American society, led him to study the radical writers he had previously avoided and ultimately to join with the radical left.[2]

The third Yale graduate, George L. K. Morris, was less interested in political questions than either Macdonald or Dupee. His primary concern was modern art. *PR*'s commitment to high culture and modern art drew Morris to it. He possessed another attribute which made his inclusion indispensable: "Morris was the guy that had the money."[3] He thus joined the early meetings among the prospective editors. "We arranged to get together at my house one Sunday," Phillips remembered, "which we referred to for a long time as 'Bloody Sunday.'" Given the hard-nosed style which characterized both radical politics and the Jewish intellectuals, this early meeting was hardly a congenial discussion about organizational problems. "As I recall," Phillips wrote in 1976, "we were at it all day long; and I still have in my mind a picture of Rahv and myself backing Macdonald up against a wall, knocking down his arguments, firing questions without giving him time to answer, and constantly outshouting him."[4]

The *PR* style was set in these first meetings. Out of the sessions with these five individuals, a new editorial board took shape. Seemingly woven into the makeup of the board were the conflicts and tensions of that early gathering at Phillips's house. Neither disinterestedness or impartiality ever became a guiding principle. Rather, politics and personality continually intermixed. The personal drives of these vital and voluble individuals sparked the creative energy which powered the "new" journal. This merger of the personal and the political and cultural helped make *Partisan Review* and the people around it seem exciting. William Phillips remembered the editors as willing to take on

Stalinists, "double-talking liberals," conservatives, and "unhistorical" New Critics. "False reputations were cut down. . . . On the whole, the magazine was raucous, impious, and intransigent."[5]

The work at the beginning also proved long, hard, and distinctly nonremunerative. Rahv took a weekly salary of $12.00 for doing the mundane office work. The other editors were unpaid, as were the contributors in the early years. "We lived on nothing; we scrounged," Phillips recalled. "Lunch could be a bag of peanuts."[6]

Despite the poor pay and the internal disputatiousness, from the birth of the "new" *PR* it was apparent that more than the publication of a journal was involved. *Partisan Review*, for all its intrinsic importance, served as the locus for a developing intellectual coterie—a shifting, tempestuous family of intellectuals. The inclusion of a sixth editor illustrates the blurring of personal and editorial lines. In 1937, at a party at James T. Farrell's, Rahv met Mary McCarthy, not yet the well-known literary figure of later years. Their affair occasioned gossip among the radical-literary community in New York. In the first summer they borrowed an apartment on Beekman Place and in the fall moved into their own apartment on East End Avenue. Although she was unknown, Rahv brought McCarthy to *Partisan Review* as an editor; her duties were to handle theater criticism. McCarthy claims she received the assignment because she had once been married to an actor and was "supposed to know something about theater." Although she was clearly a woman of intellectual skills, it is also clear that her position on the *PR* editorial board derived essentially from her relationship with Rahv. When she left him, she left the magazine. The personalities at *PR* fueled outside interest as well. "Why is everyone always talking about her?" one "disgruntled listener" is reported to have asked. "Do you know that I once knew more about Mary McCarthy and Phillip Rahv than I knew about myself."[7] The journal as well as the articles it printed became topics of interest, and the editors attracted as much notice in the intellectual world as the ideas they were expressing.

By December of 1937 the new nucleus of *Partisan Review* had been assembled and the first issue of the reborn magazine published. The effort to launch, or relaunch, a journal kept some of the volatility of the editors in check, but the harmony did not last long. The editorial board of *PR* soon broke down into two main factions. Initially, the difficulties involved personal more than political issues, again demonstrating the frequent overlap of the two at *PR*. Anti-Stalinism was "really the main extent of our politics," Macdonald recalled. "[In politics] we had no general disagreements. We tried to turn it into a cultural thing." The points of debate, in the first years, were relatively minor, concerning editorial style or particular cultural questions. More instructive than the issues themselves were the camps into which the board split: "Rahv and Phillips on the one hand, and myself [Macdonald], on the other hand, with Morris as a kind of sleeping partner. And Dupee held the middle, swing vote."[8] When the issues grew more substantive in the next few years, it was precisely along these lines that the board divided. Rahv and Phillips had founded *PR*, suspended its publication, and reestablished it. Their alliance remained strong throughout these early years.

In the 1930s, and for some years thereafter, the precise relationship between Phillips and Rahv and their relative influence were difficult to assess. For years they seemed extremely close. One long-employed secretary remarked to William Barrett "that it was too bad William [Phillips] and Philip [Rahv] were not of opposite sex, for then they could have gotten married and had babies instead of *Partisan Review*." In terms of personal style, Rahv was clearly the dominant force. Phillips once half joked that Rahv, a man of intense dynamism, was a "manic-impressive." There was no point in Rahv's entering psychoanalysis, Phillips told Barrett. "Most of us, under analysis, break down and admit our shortcomings. Philip would break down and confess he was a great man." "He couldn't help thrusting himself forward," Barrett himself observed. "Philip could orate to you over a point on which you were already in agreement with him."[9]

In a group of alienated intellectuals, Rahv was in some ways the most alienated. Born in the Ukraine, he emigrated to America when he was fourteen, settling in Providence. After high school he went to the West Coast, where he worked in advertising until his return to New York in 1932. Whereas many contemporary intellectuals held unusable bachelors' degrees, Rahv had not even been to college; whereas the others had come from the immigrant ghettos, he was an immigrant. "Though he knew America intimately," Mary McCarthy remembered at his death in 1973,

he remained an outsider. He never assimilated. When he lived in the country . . . he was an obstinate city man . . . . He never learned to swim. This metaphysically summed up his situation: he would immerse his body in the alien element . . . but he declined or perhaps feared to move with it.

It was Rahv's very physical and intellectual presence which, as much as any other factor, shaped and propelled the magazine. At times he did so by "the sheer rudeness of his personality," Barrett concluded. The magazine "was an extension of his personality—one might say, of his body; and his personality was not a shrinking one." Rahv thus provided a personal center, as well as much of the physical drive behind the magazine. "He was naturally a talker rather than a writer," Alfred Kazin remembered, " . . . an intellectual master of ceremonies and dominator . . . the Doctor Johnson of his small group of radical intellectuals."[10]

The position of William Phillips in this relationship therefore did not always appear clearly. "There is no question that when I was around, and for some years after, Rahv dominated Phillips," Dwight Macdonald observed. "He would have anyway; he was a much stronger personality and a much more original and vigorous mind." Phillips was no mere hanger-on, however. He and

Rahv held the same political positions, and Phillips was to demonstrate his own intellectual abilities on numerous occasions. Regarding their characters, Macdonald observed, "Phillips is a weak and mild guy, whereas Rahv was an almost eccentrically powerful personality." Yet, when one could get beyond the Rahvian bravado, other personal attributes of the two editors became apparent. "Phillips was the man of action," Clement Greenberg remembered. "If someone had to dicker with a publisher, Phillips did it. Philip [Rahv] would lose track of things in a business deal." William Barrett also came to understand and appreciate Phillips's special role, that of providing "the oil and grease to keep the human parts of the machine going."[11] Amid the strong personalities who edited and wrote for the magazine, keeping the parts functioning smoothly was no small task. A measure of Phillips's intangible skills is the manner in which he continued to run the magazine in recent years, long after all the more bombastic personalities departed.

Phillips was not a silent partner or merely an efficient office manager. He fashioned his own, independent career in radical politics and literary criticism. He came from the same background as his peers, with slight modifications. Although an East European immigrant, his father seemed more interested in a variety of political and personal pursuits than most immigrants. He was, for a time, a Christian Scientist and turned to different self-help alternatives. "He went through various things—yoga, Coué, and a Fletcherizer," Phillips remembered. When he arrived in America, at age thirteen, he had gone to an Owenite community in Oregon and, although he remained a socialist, he was not "an intense radical." Coming from a slightly different home style, Phillips also followed a slightly different path to radicalism, as has been discussed.[12] In addition to his bachelor's at City College, Phillips took a master's from NYU and did additional graduate work at Columbia. He turned from an academic career to writing and then to radical politics—a route which led through the John Reed Clubs to *Partisan Review*.

While less the pontificator than Rahv, Phillips nonetheless engaged heartily in the give-and-take of personal argument, as did many of these intellectuals. Bothered by a writer's block which kept his written output small, Phillips poured his energy into the magazine and the personal connections of his radical and literary circle. He was "brilliant in argument," William Barrett remembered, but both Barrett and Phillips ultimately came to see the energy he wasted. "The long nights during the 1930s," Barrett recently wrote, "and indeed much of the days, had been consumed in argument; and while there had been zest and excitement in it at the time, there came the later moments when it all would seem suddenly hollow." One night Phillips confessed to Barrett and Delmore Schwartz, "I pissed my life away in talk."[13]

From modernism as well as radicalism, the *New Masses* as well as the "old" *Partisan Review*, Yale as well as City College—the editors found themselves joining to bring out a journal devoted to their shared interest in a newly defined cultural radicalism. The intention of creating a literary journal with a strong radical commitment was clearly stated in their first editorial:

Any magazine, we believe, that aspires to a place in the vanguard of literature today, will be revolutionary in tendency; but we are also convinced that any such magazine will be unequivocably independent. PARTISAN REVIEW is aware of its responsibility to the revolutionary movement in general, but we disclaim obligations to any of its organized political expressions.

An unwillingness to become "obligated" to any organized movement offered a clear declaration that this *Partisan Review* would avoid the pitfalls which, for them, marked Communist intellectual efforts—and philistinism. In addition they argued that despite their maintenance of a "revolutionary tendency," they were unwilling to continue in the style of the previous radical literary attempts of the decade.

The tradition of aestheticism has given way to a literature which, for its origins and final justification, looks beyond itself and deep into the historic process. But the forms of literary editorship, at once exacting and adventurous, which characterized the magazines of aesthetic revolt, were of definite cultural value; and these forms PARTISAN REVIEW will wish to adapt to the literature of the new period.[14]

They hoped to link the best of both worlds—the political awareness of the proletarian movement with the literary contributions and excitement of the modernists.

The editors discovered a number of writers willing to pursue this dual goal of a revolutionary stance coupled with a commitment to high cultural standards. They tapped the personal networks which had been established in previous years to solicit material, contacting friends and colleagues from radical organizations, college campuses, and other journals to ask them to write for *PR*. In the initial years of the revived journal, nearly all of the first-generation New York Intellectuals contributed, as did some from the second generation. The very first issue included pieces by Macdonald and McCarthy and reviews by Rahv, Morris, and Dupee, as well as articles, stories, and reviews by Lionel Trilling, Delmore Schwartz, Lionel Abel, and Sidney Hook. In addition, the editors were able to draw on other anti-Stalinist and noncommitted intellectuals like Edmund Wilson, Wallace Stevens, James T. Farrell, James Agee, William Troy, and Arthur Mizener. A contribution by Pablo Picasso, "Dreams and Lies of Franco," rounded out the first issue.

For a fledgling journal, edited by intelligent but not enormously well known individuals, the array of talent in this first issue proved impressive. In the readjusting world of radical politics in the late 1930s, *Partisan Review* filled a newly created intellectual vacuum. The attempt to combine anti-Stalinism and high culture was appealing for two groups seeking to find new homes and new forums. One group found itself frustrated with proletarian literature; the other was unhappy with Stalinist politics. Some, like Rahv and Phillips, clearly belonged in both camps. The combination of the two, however, attracted a large number of writers. Prior to their break from Stalinism, *PR* had been perhaps the most literate, but certainly not the only, journal interested in cultural radicalism. Now it largely owned the field and found, atypically for new small magazines, a number of prominent writers and critics taking a serious interest in its efforts.

Given all the well-known persons who contributed to the first "new" issue, it is anomalous that the article which met the highest praise was by an unknown young writer. "In Dreams Begin Responsibilities," published as the lead piece in the first issue, remains Delmore Schwartz's best-known and most highly praised story. Schwartz was younger than the other New York Intellectuals who joined *PR* in the late 1930s. He burst upon the American cultural scene like few before him. Schwartz's first volume of poetry, also titled *In Dreams Begin Responsibilities*, received glowing praise. Allen Tate compared it to the breakthroughs of Eliot and Pound; Eliot sent a laudatory note, and it put Schwartz into the literary limelight. Schwartz's career declined steadily after the highpoint in his youth. He never regained the unanimous critical acclaim he achieved in these first years, although he continued to work and eventually became an editor of the *PR* in the 1940s.

Schwartz's career took the opposite track from that of most of his intellectual contemporaries, and his personal life followed its own, distinctive course as well, especially before he wrote for *Partisan Review*. The child of immigrants, like most of the New York Intellectuals, he did have a more prosperous childhood than other such children. He suffered less from material hardships than from family instability. His parents frequently separated and reunited during his earliest years and parted permanently when he was nine. Schwartz's father left New York for Chicago, and for the next six years Schwartz moved back and forth between the relatively modest home of his mother and the quite prosperous world of his father. The stock market crash had a permanent effect on the fortunes and health of Harry Schwartz, as it did on those of Dwight Macdonald's father. He died of a heart attack in June 1930. A millionaire on paper, Harry Schwartz left his family practically nothing. For several years Delmore Schwartz awaited the inheritance which never came. Later he wrote,

> You too,
> O New York boy,
> Fell with the market that October day,
> In New America in 1929![15]

The Depression did not have the same intellectual effect on Schwartz as on the other New York Intellectuals. He was not immediately thrust into political awareness, but he continued for most of the decade to be more interested in literary matters than in radicalism. Furthermore, unlike that of his contemporaries, his high school record was relatively uneven. He gained admittance, however, to the University of Wisconsin in 1931. Distinctly unlike

City College or Columbia, the Madison campus was characterized by an "aroma of Bohemianism" rather than by a spirit of revolution. It was, for Schwartz, an appropriate environment. He continued his own study of poetry and European writers, his formal classes being of lesser concern. Always erratic and impulsive, he left Wisconsin the night before his last examination in June, intending to return in the fall. At home, ostensibly for the summer, he undertook the project of translating a book by the conservative French intellectual Julien Benda, author of *La Trahison des clercs*. In September, with family finances tight, Schwartz chose not to go back to Wisconsin. Instead, the following spring he entered NYU. A philosophy major, Schwartz took courses from James Burnham and Sidney Hook. He flirted with radical politics —this was the period of Hook's Marxism and Burnham's Trotskyism. Still, his focus remained essentially literary.

After graduating from NYU with a degree in philosophy, Schwartz spent a year at Harvard. He left in 1937 without taking a degree, but fame was about to come to him. He submitted his story to *Partisan Review* and was invited to lunch with Rahv. Macdonald remembers that the editors "had the sense to recognize it as a masterpiece." Schwartz was intrigued by the personalities and impressed by the *Partisan* community as well as by the journal. "You should have seen Philip Rahv—He looked like the Paris Commune," he reported to his friend William Barrett. With Mary McCarthy, Schwartz was "fascinated . . . to the point of obsession," his biographer concluded. Schwartz was, in many respects, the first intellectual drawn to the *PR* world which the others had been working to create.[16]

The other contributors to the first issue of the reborn *PR* often had established reputations earned in other settings. Columbia was always a source for the editors. Through Dupee, Lionel Trilling had been encouraged to review and soon contributed a full article.[17] Trilling, as discussed, had entered Columbia before the rigid barriers against Jews were erected, and he had chosen an academic career before the Depression created a sense of "airlessness" among undergraduates, but he would experience anti-Semitism before gaining a full appointment at Columbia.[18] Trilling had also fallen in with the radicalism of the times, although he was "committed" to communism for "less than a year," Diana Trilling later recalled.[19] After a decade of cultural and political activity, his fame in no measure matched its postwar level. His book on Matthew Arnold had not been published, and he was still only an instructor at Columbia. Trilling rose to prominence along with *PR*. By contrast, Sidney Hook, only two and one-half years older than Trilling, had achieved wide fame by the late 1930s. Born in Brooklyn and graduated from Brooklyn Boys High, Hook had gone from the City College classroom of Morris Cohen to the Columbia seminars of John Dewey, James Montague, and Frederick Woodbridge. He finished his Ph.D. in 1927, taught briefly at NYU, and then spent 1928 and 1929 studying in Berlin, Munich, and Moscow. He returned in 1931 to an assistant professorship at NYU, where he remained until his retirement. Hook's renown grew from his studies in German philosophy and, especially, his works on Marx. His intellectual reputation complemented his importance as a radical writer and debater. He had signed the endorsement of Foster and Ford in 1932, before breaking with the Communists. His verbal agility as a debater became legend. Wallace Markfield called upon Hook's reputation in one novel; one of his characters "knew five or six languages," "made special trips for the State Department," and "could hold his own against Sidney Hook."[20] A prolific author, Hook published in a wide variety of periodicals: the *New Republic,* the *Saturday Review,* and the *American Mercury,* as well as the *International Journal of Ethics,* the *Journal of Philosophy,* and the *American Journal of Sociology.* He had served as an editor for V. F. Calverton's *Modern Quarterly* and helped found the short-lived *Marxist Quarterly* in the late 1930s. By the time he came to *Partisan Review,* he was an important American intellectual and well known in the world of radical politics. His inclusion proved crucial to the journal's quest for legitimacy as both a political and a cultural undertaking. Hook began with a book review but soon wrote articles for *PR* as well.[21]

The problem of gaining political and cultural legitimacy, central to the claims *PR*'s editors made for their version of radical literature, was overcome by both the arguments offered and the individuals who offered them. The degree to which *PR* could attract well-known radical intellectuals would aid the acceptance of their positions and the development of their audience. Hook's contributions served this function, as did the articles of several "fellow travelers," especially Edmund Wilson and James T. Farrell. What Wilson and Farrell wrote about in *PR* is less important than the fact that they wrote for it at all. Farrell's renown had grown during the 1930s with the publication of his *Studs Lonigan* trilogy. He had also been closely associated with the League of American Writers and with the proletarian-literature movement. His joining *PR* offered a clear example of an important, radical writer who moved away from the Communists and toward the new position that *PR* argued. *PR* hoped to become a focus for unhappy literary radicals, and Farrell's participation fostered that image.

Edmund Wilson's place among the *Partisan* contributors provided a dual service for the journal. Like those of Farrell, Wallace Stevens, and Picasso, Wilson's name helped light up the table of contents and establish the journal's intellectual and cultural importance.[22] For the editors and young contributors, Wilson's participation surely had a second benefit. Wilson had long been the model many of these intellectuals aspired to follow. In the mid-1930s Wilson had, like the *PR* editors, broken with the Communists, maintaining an interest in radical politics, but of a non-Stalinist variety. Thus, he retained his position as both a man of culture and a man of politics. Even more than before, Wilson now served as a demonstration of what correct-thinking intellectuals might become and might accomplish. Irving Howe remembered that, although Wilson was not much older than the *Partisan* editors, "for many young

Americans who reached the crucial years of mid-adolescence in the Thirties,"
he was someone to be admired and emulated:

> Edmund Wilson's *Axel's Castle* introduced us to modern literature. Remembering
> our admiration for Wilson's blend of avant-garde culture and social radicalism, we
> can easily understand why we thought of him as the kind of intellectual we too
> should like to become.

Chance alone did not cast Wilson into this role as intellectual model. "To be, to
become an intellectual," Howe also noted, "that was the implicit purpose of
Wilson's career." At least in the eyes of the *Partisan* writers, he succeeded.
Wilson appealed to them because of their parallel paths through radicalism,
because of his early interest in modernist literature, and because of what Howe
characterized as his concern with "the human imagination and the human
predicament."[23] Wilson's early contributions to the "new" *Partisan Review*
provided the editors with an occasion for self-congratulation. Their own
approach appeared vindicated by the inclusion of the intellectual they felt best
exemplified their own ambitions. There is, undoubtedly, some circular logic
here—we think we are correct because Wilson is doing what is right; Wilson
agrees to write for us, therefore we must be correct—but the conclusion was
reassuring nonetheless.

The "elders," as well as the thirties adolescents, saw Wilson as a model.
Years later Lionel Trilling recalled moving into a Greenwich Village apartment
in 1929, across the street from Wilson. "Someone had pointed out his
apartment to me and I used to take note of his evening hours at his desk."
Wilson's presence in the Village was sufficient "to validate its present dignity,
to suggest that what the Village stood for in American life was not wholly a
matter of history." During the early 1930s, Trilling recounted, encouragement
from Wilson broke Trilling's depression over the seeming narrowness of a
dissertation on Matthew Arnold. Trilling found himself buoyed by Wilson,
who "with his involvement in the life of the present . . . was so clearly not at
odds with his natural and highly developed feeling for scholarship."[24] For many
young intellectuals like Trilling, Wilson's decision to combine radicalism with
literary criticism in the early 1930s helped affirm the rightness of their radical
path. His move to *PR* buttressed the editors' beliefs in their undertaking and in
themselves.

The second issue of the revived journal brought other contributors from the
literary and the left movements and added them to the *PR* constellation. Meyer
Schapiro's background in both academe and radical politics—as a Columbia
professor with close ties to the anti-Stalinist left—made him an ideal *PR*
contributor. Furthermore, as one of the radicals detaching themselves from the
Communist party, Schapiro naturally gravitated to the emerging intellectual
community. "They approached me," Schapiro recalled, intending "to submit
Communist ideas to criticism and to be open in areas of literature, art, and
philosophy." For two years he neglected his own scholarly work to contribute

to this effort. He believed that an important undertaking, beyond the mere sustaining of a magazine, was at hand. Although Schapiro may have turned from his own writing in art history, he continued his dual role as radical-intellectual and professor of fine arts. He has been described by numerous friends, including Irving Howe and William Barrett, as a great teacher. Schapiro was just as naturally a talker as any of his contemporaries, but his interpersonal style differed from theirs. Barrett recently repeated Mary McCarthy's characterization of him as a "mouth in search of an ear." For Barrett, "the flow of his eloquence was not confined to the classroom. Encountered almost anywhere, on a street corner or a subway train, his discourse would pour effortlessly forth as if all the while he had simply been waiting for your receptive ear."[25] His inclusion among the *Partisan* writers further cemented the ties between the journal and the academy, as well as those between the journal and the anti-Stalinist left.

Thus, by the second issue of the "new" *PR*, Rahv, Phillips, Macdonald, Dupee, Trilling, Hook, Schapiro, and Schwartz—all later identified as New York Intellectuals—were contributors. Only as the ebb and flow of political and cultural issues began to shift and adjust perspectives on the left did this group become especially distinctive. In the first year or two of publication, it belonged to a larger group of unhappy radicals and intellectuals. Political doubts about Stalinism had surfaced in the mid-1930s, especially with the revelations of the Moscow trials and the Spanish civil war. To large numbers of literary radicals, uneasiness with the cultural positions and artistic creations of the radical art movement aggravated political problems. Anxious to continue in a radical mode, but seeking a new focus for their efforts, many of these radicals found *Partisan Review* the place to initiate the discussion. This group of disaffected intellectuals provided the *PR* editors with a roster of writers which helped establish the journal's reputation and create its audience. The readership of *PR* remained small, its circulation never exceeding 5,000 in the 1930s. Yet, it served the radical intellectuals drawn to it in the vacuum created by the moves of many radicals away from Communist politics and art.

One particular group of young readers sat around Alcove No. 1 at City College, where *PR* held an "intimidating presence," Irving Kristol recounted. For Kristol, reading the magazine was not always easy, but he found it worth the effort: "It was a great educational experience . . . it introduced us to culture. As a result, we all began to read Thomas Mann and Proust, Gide and Kafka. I worked harder reading *Partisan Review* than I worked reading any required reading in my courses." Kristol remembered needing to read each article twice, "in a state of awe and exasperation—excited to see such elegance of style and profundity of mind." Unknowingly, the elder New Yorkers, now forming into an intellectual community, sowed the seeds for their second generation. "In our younger years," Daniel Bell recollected, "*Partisan Review* was the place we wanted to publish. Appearing in *Partisan Review* was a sign of acceptance."[26]

Meanwhile, the *PR* editors themselves continued to discover well-known Americans and Europeans willing to contribute to the fledgling journal. Critics like Kenneth Burke, R. P. Blackmur, and F. O. Matthiessen; Hook's philosophy department colleague and Macdonald's Trotskyist comrade James Burnham; and young poets like Elizabeth Bishop and John Berryman—all began to appear in *PR*.[27] John Dos Passos wrote Rahv, "I'm very glad you are starting up the *Partisan Review* again. Something is certainly needed to keep a little life in the left. . . . Here's a story I dug up out of my desk drawer."[28] Posthumous works by famous Europeans—Kafka, Rimbaud, Rosa Luxemburg—were printed along with pieces by renowned living authors—Gertrude Stein, André Gide. Auden sent an unsolicited article to Fred Dupee, with an accompanying note which said, "In case it would interest you for *Partisan Review*." He added, "I assume you pay your contributors."[29] Thus, within its first years of independent publication, *Partisan Review* amassed a roster of important contributors, which helped it achieve a place in the radical intellectual world of the late 1930s. "We saw ourselves," Phillips later said, "as a rallying ground or center, where the best intellectuals would come."[30]

The developing stature of *PR* was not, however, unanimously hailed in radical circles. As might be expected, the defenders of the "orthodoxy," the *New Masses* and the *New Republic*, greeted the "new" *Partisan Review* with harsh denunciations and critiques. A *New Masses* editorial blasted both the abandonment of revolutionary goals by the *PR* editors and their acceptance of a Trotskyite position.[31] As evidence the editorial cited the expulsions of Rahv and Dupee from the Communist party as Trotskyites. The *PR* editors responded by reiterating their distinctiveness from the *New Masses*, claiming the two journals were "always at loggerheads on the problems of revolutionary literature." The *PR* editors steadfastly denied any connection with the Trotskyists. *Partisan Review* was not like the *New International*; it never directly attached itself to the Trotskyist movement. Yet in the public mind, *PR* was associated with Trotsky because of its anti-Stalinist positions, the Trotskyist affiliations of Dwight Macdonald and Mary McCarthy, and Trotsky's own contribution to the August–September 1938 issue.[32]

This issue included Trotsky's "Art and Politics," as well as several other pieces which struck some readers as placing *PR* squarely in the Trotskyist camp. Writing in the *New Republic*, Malcolm Cowley found this development especially objectionable. Cowley attacked *PR* for failing to live up to its stated goal, that of creating a literary journal with radical underpinnings. The August–September 1938 issue, he held, demonstrated a different trend. Five of the eight articles were anti–Soviet political statements written by Trotsky, Dupee, the anti-Bolshevik Russian émigré Victor Serge, and two American Trotskyists, Macdonald and Burnham.[33] The drift of *PR* toward strident political issues was not, Cowley held, an intentional subversion aimed at wooing the literati to Trotskyism. Rather, "in the midst of their battles against the Communist Party press, [the editors'] opinions solidified into hatreds, fixing their minds into one frozen mold, so they scarcely realized they were committing all the literary crimes they charged against their opponents."[34]

Cowley attempted to chastise *PR* for the very shortcomings it often pointed out in Stalinist publications, and with some justification. Facing a barrage of criticism from their former allies, the *PR* editors felt they were under siege and exaggerated their own place in the political and literary battles of the decade. "As our readers know," the editors wrote in the second issue, "the Communist Party seems to consider the destruction of *Partisan Review* as important an effort as the destruction of Franco—perhaps a bit more important."[35] As an example of this hostile campaign, they raised the case of William Carlos Williams. Williams had, they claimed, agreed to publish some poems in their magazine. They listed his name along with those of other "future contributors" in the first issue. Williams did not publish in *PR* and, in fact, wrote a short note to the *New Masses* claiming he had no intention of doing so. The *PR* editors saw this as evidence of an attempt to make them look foolish and of the coercive tactics the *New Masses* employed among writers on the left.

It is obvious that the interest the Communist party took in the destruction of *Partisan Review* in no way matched its interest in Franco. Even if one makes allowances for poetic exaggeration, the position of *PR* nevertheless strains believability. What this hyperbole demonstrates is not the attitude of the Communists but the pressure those at *PR* felt. The charges and countercharges which raged between the Communist literary camp and *Partisan Review* point to the ever-hardening lines which divided the literary left. *PR* stepped into the intellectual vacuum which developed when some radicals abandoned communism and proletarian literature. The variety of important writers who contributed to the fledgling journal testifies to the size of the need which *PR* filled. Potential contributors on either side of the debate needed to choose one position—to choose, as in the case of Williams, the *New Masses* or *Partisan Review*. While *PR* claimed it never kept any writer from publishing anywhere else, the young magazine could not have exerted that kind of influence in any event. More important, no explicit ban on writing for Communist publications became necessary. By virtue of joining the *Partisan* circle, writers automatically excluded themselves.

These hardening lines helped create the notion of a separate group of *Partisan* writers, identifiable by their political and social leanings as well as by their anti-Stalinism. Beginning with the positions sketched in their first editorial of the "new" journal, *Partisan Review* became a central focus for a new version of radical culture, one which sought to avoid the problems of the Stalinist attempt at political art. Out of the discussions which surrounded this undertaking, an identifiable position—the "*Partisan* mind"—emerged. The philosophy of a magazine led to a philosophy of an intellectual community.

Chapter 5

The *Partisan* Mind: Cultural Turns

The "new" *Partisan Review* took shape as more than a vehicle for the presentation of lively writers and erudite authors. It consciously sought to place itself in the intellectual void which the editors believed Stalinism had created. Major segments of the American literary community had sacrificed their art for a faulty radicalism, the editors concluded. They hoped that those opposed to Stalinism and disabused of the virtues of proletarian literature might look to *PR* as a new point of radical focus. The perceived problem with the previous attempts at radical art during the 1930s had been a subjugation of literary quality and cultural standards to political expediency. The "new" *PR* sought to readjust the priorities and to restore the proper place of literature in the radical movement. Now outside the proletarian movement, Rahv and Phillips were free to launch the critical reevaluation which had been stifled in the League of American Writers, to set standards and establish a radical aesthetic. In the course of this effort, the *Partisan* critics redefined their own roles as critics and intellectuals as well, emerging with a literary school and a critical position much more in keeping with their own predilections.

REVOLUTIONARY MODERNISM

A decade after their revival of *Partisan Review*, Rahv and Phillips recalled their initial aim for the "new" journal. They hoped "to bring about a rapprochement between the radical tradition on the one hand and the tradition of modern literature on the other." They sought something new. Virtually all left-wing magazines had in the past done their utmost to prevent the rapprochement. The proletarian-literature movement tried to convert one tradition to the other, leading "to a false show of unity," the editors maintained. Instead,

> it seemed to us that a reconciliation could be effected only by so modulating the expression of both traditions as to convey a sense at once of the tension between them and of their relevance to each other within the common framework of civilization.[1]

In place of the old "falsity," the *PR* critics aimed to establish a new harmony. The "modulation" they sought would maintain a radical base, without adversely affecting the literature or banishing important writers because of conservative political tendencies. The definition of radical activity came into question, as did the requirements for revolutionary literature. Rahv and Phillips found themselves "frankly skeptical of the old imperatives." To them, novels and poems, were "rarely weapons in the class struggle." Instead, a new, intermediary position seemed necessary, one between the apolitical independence of the twenties writers and the programmatic hard line which Rahv and Phillips saw in proletarian literature. Radicalism remained vitally important, as did good literature. Marxism might be a guide for action and for literature, but whether literature itself could be a guide for action was a different matter. This emerged as "one of the problems that *Partisan Review* [was] dedicated to explore."[2]

The *PR* critics found that though literature did not create labor strikes, it still might change consciousness. "Our program is the program of Marxism," they declared in their first editorial.[3] Along with this, however, they found it perfectly legitimate to reawaken their interest in modernist heroes of their younger days. In the next few years they explored both of these areas and tried to "modulate" between the analysis of the Marxists and the insights of the modernist writers. The attempt to bring modernism into the revolutionary fold raised the question of the relation between the avant-garde and society. Modernism had begun as an artistic revolt, as the efforts by various artists to break free from the constraints they felt had been imposed by traditional literary forms. In a recent review of the history and nature of modernism, the English critics Malcom Bradbury and James McFarlane described modernism as a "movement towards sophistication, technical display, internal self-scepticism," with parallel technical features appearing in various artistic movements, "anti-representationalism in painting, atonalism in music, *vers libre* in poetry, stream-of-consciousness narrative in the novel." In the late 1930s the *PR* critics attempted to bring that spirit of liberation into the world of revolutionary politics. This appeared particularly appropriate, given the second set of modernist attributes which Bradbury and McFarlane noted: "Experimentation does not simply suggest the presence of sophistication . . . it also suggests bleakness, darkness, alienation, disintegration. . . . The crisis is a crisis of culture; it often involves an unhappy view of history—so that the Modernist writer is not simply the artist set free, but the artist under specific, apparently historical strain."[4] Amid radical politics, economic dislocation, and highbrow literary tastes, a more politicized modernism might provide the best frame through which to analyze society and its art.

The concept of identifying and understanding the interrelated roles of radical politics and literary modernism proved attractive to other members of the emerging *PR* community. Lionel Trilling, uncomfortable with proletarian literature, agreed with this less overtly political style. "We learn not to expect a political, certainly not an immediately political, effect from a work of art," Trilling wrote in *PR*, "and in removing from art the burden of messianic responsibility which it never discharged and cannot discharge, we may leave it free to do whatever it actually can do." Writers as well as literature would be freed. No longer conscience-bound to write for the masses, Trilling felt he could now write for the intellectual class.[5]

The achievement of literature's fullest potential—the discovery of what literature "actually can do"—required something new, the critics believed. "A decade of fellow-travelling and revolutionary manipulation has drained American writing of so much of its energy," Rahv maintained. And the chief culprit of this deprivation was, obviously, the proletarian-literature movement. "Ostensibly a literature of the working class, it was really nothing more than a cultural publicity-agency for the Stalin mob in this country."[6] Because so many influential critics remained with the "mob," the first task was its discrediting.

The *PR* critics castigated proletarian literature along two main lines. They held the proletarian writers and critics who unswervingly praised the movement responsible for the sorry state of American letters. Rahv mocked the presentations of Joseph Freeman and Malcom Cowley at the American Writers' Congress of 1937. Freeman had hailed the literary revival as equal to that of 1912 to 1916, while Cowley spoke of the richness of the radical literary movement. Whereas only a few years earlier Rahv had hailed the outpouring of radical literature, now he said this "renaissance" was "manufactured . . . an imaginary crop of masterpieces." "Actually, of course," he wrote, "literature in America has seldom been so stagnant as it is at present."[7]

In addition to their fabrication of masterpieces, Phillips found the literary styles of American radicals contributing to the sad condition of American writing. Socialist realism, he claimed, was "really a throwback to the 'slice-of-life' formula of popular fiction—a method that could not possibly carry the weight of new sensibility and a new consciousness." This defect lowered both the quality of literary works and literary tastes. The constant praise for "conventional, mediocre, and culturally backward authors" reduced general literary standards, Rahv argued. "Even intelligent readers appear unable to discriminate between genuine literary art and that which is patently commercial and popular in character."[8]

The other major difficulty with proletarian literature derived from the treatment of the writers themselves and the role assigned to literature in the

Stalinist movement. Writers were being asked to ally themselves not with the working class but with the Communist party disguised as the working class. Rahv saw this as a contract with "all the specific stipulations . . . left to be written in." The humbling of writers within the party structure revealed more than an unfortunate instance of the subjugation of art to politics. It also provided a microcosmic example of the tactics which marked Stalinist behavior everywhere, "a miniature version of the powers which in Russia had resulted in the replacement of the dictatorship of the proletariat by the dictatorship of the Communist Party."[9]

Rahv and Phillips felt it insufficient to admit that they had merely been wrong about radical literature, that their high hopes had been dashed on the tensions between political goals and cultural standards. Instead, they chose to portray themselves as the defenders of the duped and abused artists, as men interested in quality literature *and* radical politics fending off both the philistine and the dictatorial notions of the Stalinists. Once this position was articulated, however, their own claims to the carrying of the radical literary mantle became much more secure. By dispensing with proletarian literature as it existed, they hoped to clear the decks for their own formulations about the proper approach for radical literature.

They had not, as we have seen, abandoned their beliefs in radicalism or their interest in Marx. They did seek, however, a redefinition of the role of Marxist criticism and the entire Marxist perspective in literature. "The truth of the matter," wrote Phillips, "is that Marx was not a literary critic, and no amount of textural research can convert him into one. Nor was Engels . . . so far as I know, they were silent on those questions of literature which occupy western criticism." What Phillips did find in Marx and Engels regarding literature, he believed directly contradicted the notions of the proletarian-literature camp: "At no time did Marx and Engels either state or imply that art is but a class weapon, nor did they sponsor a proletarian art to educate the workers in the theory and tactics of communism." Phillips discovered instead that both Marx and Engels saw literature as qualitatively different from other elements in the political process—in fact, wrote Phillips, quoting Marx, "certain periods of highest development of art stand in no direct connection with the general development of society, nor with the material basis and the skeleton structure of its organization." He cited examples from Engels which reaffirmed this position and freed the poet of any obligation to furnish the reader with ready-made historical solutions for the future. Phillips concluded that "many of the statements . . . read like direct polemics against the kind of 'Marxist criticism' advocated by Michael Gold and Granville Hicks."[10]

Phillips's interpretation of a proper Marxist position of the relation between literature and politics allowed the *PR* critics to pursue their own critical arguments while believing their Marxism still valid. In view of this new Marxism, the restrictions which were implicit in the brand of criticism offered by Granville Hicks at the American Writers' Congress could be loosened. Marxism, Phillips found, was "not a closed system, nor a formula for declaring that all ideas inspired by other ways of thinking are false." That had been the problem with the proletarian critics. Marxism was a *"method,"* and it proved more fruitful "to speak of Marxist *criticisms* in the plural, or of *ventures in Marxist criticism.*" For Marxism to maintain any validity in literary pursuits, it would surely have to operate in a less structured and more open atmosphere, one in which critics would assume a new role and escape the reins which had been placed on their potential in the movement for proletarian literature.

The function of critics showed another central failure of proletarian literature. Radical critics had been the "pawns" of the Stalinists, Rahv held. The potential for the revitalization of literature had been stifled, and this resulted in a general decline of American art and writing. Phillips offered a contrast: "The major impulses of European art can be traced in practically every instance to the existence of an active intelligentsia." Since the Renaissance, Phillips believed, the immediate sources of art had been this intelligentsia, which made up "a distinct occupational grouping in society."

The outstanding failure of American national culture was precisely "the inability of our native intelligentsia to achieve a detached and self-sufficient group existence." At no time was this more evident than during the Stalinist-dominated days of proletarian literature. Rather than denigrating critics and other intellectuals and placing them in servile roles, Phillips, Rahv, and other *PR* critics called the critical role essential. The American environment, however, militated against this development, Phillips found. American intellectuals evidenced an "ambivalent psyche, torn between the urge toward some degree of autonomy and an equallly strong tendency to self-effacement." The Stalinists exploited this second tendency. In an effort to become part of a popular movement, critics had willingly sacrificed their rightful role. They wrote "publicity" for Stalinist hacks, rather than the criticism which would improve literary standards. Phillips called for a reversal of form, a reaction against the "natural inclination to merge with the popular mind." Only through the active leadership of intellectuals could the complexities of modern life be explained. Thus, intellectuals ought not to submerge themselves in political and cultural movements but to lead them from above. "Modern art with its highly complicated techniques, its plaintive egotism, its messianic desperation, could not," Phillips concluded, "have come into being except through the formation of the intelligentsia of a distinct group culture, thriving on its very anxiety of being an elite."[11]

The editors perceived this elite as standing not outside of radicalism but in the vanguard of radical literature. The critics at *Partisan Review* continued to hold out the hope of a revolutionary impact for creativity, only now in a much less politicized sense. In the summer of 1939 *Partisan Review* published a call from the League for Cultural Freedom and Socialism, an anti-Popular Front coalition. Many of the signers were members of the intellectual community around *PR*, including all the editors. The position of the league was not only that Russian, German, and Italian culture was dominated by totalitarians but also that in America the cultural gains of recent decades were being sacrificed.

"In the name of 'spurious' anti-fascist unity, numerous intellectuals are deserting their hard-won critical independence. . . . In the name of a 'democratic front' against tyranny abroad they put up with increasing tyranny at home." To counter these forces and this worrisome trend, the signers claimed "to unite to defend their independence."

> The defense of intellectual freedom requires, moverover, that we reject all theories and practices which tend to make culture the creature of politics, even revolutionary politics. We demand COMPLETE FREEDOM FOR ART AND SCIENCE. NO DICTUM BY PARTY OR GOVERNMENT. Culture not only does not seek orders but by its very nature cannot tolerate them. Truly intellectual creation is incompatible with the spirit of conformity; and if art and science are to be true to the revolution, they must first be true to themselves.[12]

The best that could be done—the radical thing to do—was thus "to infuse literary life with a revolutionary spirit," as Rahv and Phillips would later claim to have accomplished. In the process, they found that all the modernist and avant-garde writers, neglected or attacked during the days of proletarian literature, could be brought back into the fold. Thus, the requirements for revolutionary denotation could now be significantly broadened, and writers without a direct political philosophy or even with a conservative one could be viewed as revolutionary, in the new sense. Philip Rahv discovered the revolutionary spirit in Henry Miller, whom he identified as "the artist as desperado" and the "biographer of the hobo-intellectual and the poet of those people at the bottom of society."[13]

Even so conservative a figure as Dostoevsky took on revolutionary characteristics. *The Possessed* provided contemporary society with a "pre-Marxist" picture of revolution, Rahv argued, Stalinism a "post-Marxist" view. In the character Verkhovensky and his philosophy of Nechayevism could be seen an early equivalent of Stalinism. "Verkhovensky's attempt to overthrow the Czar without the active intervention of the masses is equivalent to Stalin's attempt to build socialism in Russia in isolation from the fate of the international working-class." Despite the enormous questions raised by this interpretation, Rahv continued to proclaim Dostoevsky's revolutionary importance and insight. Admitting that he "labored to give his genius a religious sanctification" and "that his philosophical and political views . . . ran counter to progressive thought," Rahv nonetheless found that Dotoevsky

> discovered inversions and dissociations in human feeling and consciousness which to this day literature but imperfectly assimilated. Reactionary in its abstract content, in its aspect as a system of ideas, his art is radical in sensibility and subversive in performance.[14]

Artistic sensibility could be radical and subversive, Rahv claimed without further definition, and all the heroes of the modernist movement—Joyce, Eliot, Pound, Kafka—could be put into this revolutionary corps. Thus, the favorites of the critics' youths, the writers whom the twenties exiles had favored and the thirties radicals dismissed, could be called men of literature and of radical insight. In fact, it was discovered that they possessed previously unnoticed radical sensibilities.

Having witnessed the failures of radical literature within the social-realist movement, the *PR* critics now focused on the avant-garde as the truly revolutionary force. Dwight Macdonald, in his review of Soviet cinema, held that its decline was a result of the replacement of avant-garde artists with Stalinist bureaucrats. This paralleled the replacement of the Old Bolsheviks; "whole advance political theories clashed with a backward society." Similarly, Soviets with progressive notions in art found themselves "opposed by conventional, even reactionary artists."[15]

Macdonald's articles on Soviet cinema prompted the response of an artistically minded clerk in the New York customshouse. Clement Greenberg had held a variety of jobs since his graduation from Syracuse in 1930, none using his artistic training or interests. Born in the Bronx, of an immigrant family, he "spoke Yiddish as soon as [he] did English." His father, a small shopkeeper and then a manufacturer of metal goods, provided the family with a comfortable, if not prosperous, existence. Graduating from college as the Depression struck, Greenberg spent the next two and a half years at home, where he independently studied German, Italian, French, and Latin. Married and divorced in the mid-thirties, he finally secured regular employment with the Civil Service Commission in 1936. In 1937 he moved to a position in the Appraiser's Division of the Customs Service. Like Melville and Hawthorne before him, he used his spare time to write, including a letter to *Partisan Review*.[16] Macdonald thought the letter worthy of a fuller presentation and arranged to meet Greenberg for lunch. The letter became Greenberg's first contribution to *PR*, "Avant-Garde and Kitsch," published in 1939. The luncheon meeting and the expansion of the letter into an article prompted Macdonald to joke that he had "invented Clement Greenberg."[17]

"Avant-Garde and Kitsch" was significant not just because it launched the career of one of America's important art critics. Greenberg's argument added to Rahv's notion about the radical impact of modern culture. Going beyond Rahv's identification of writers with radical "sensibilities," Greenberg offered a schematic guide for an understanding of which art forms actually aided radicalism and which impeded it. "The true and most important function of the avant-garde was not to 'experiment,' " as might traditionally be thought, "but to find a path along which it would be possible to keep culture *moving* in the midst of ideological confusion and violence." While the avant-garde propelled society, "kitsch"—middlebrow culture, movies, comic books, Tin Pan Alley, Coca-Cola, Luce publications, and rayon stockings—helped perpetuate the capitalist system of class interests. Furthermore, kitsch could be dominated by dictators, whereas the avant-garde could not. Proletarian literature—middlebrow and dominated by a variety of dictators—fell into the category of kitsch, in Greenberg's view. True avant-garde art and literature, by contrast, was "too innocent" and "too difficult to inject [with] effective propaganda." Kitsch was "more pliable to this end."

Avant-garde culture did possess one essential attribute which kitsch did not, one which became very important for radicals. Kitsch proved incompatible with true socialism. Only when socialism had been instituted could a true, meaningful global culture be achieved, Greenberg argued, and only the avant-garde could bring about this development. Offering a bit of circuitous logic, Greenberg made two assumptions—only the avant-garde moved society along and only when society had moved to socialism would culture fully flourish—and then used each to justify the other. Like Rahv's equation of Verkhovensky and Stalin, it required the acceptance of the authors' propositions as truths.[18]

These various propositions and assumptions combined to form a literary and artistic position, one which defined the roles of literature and of critics. Discovering the radical sensibilities of the modernist writers, it restored them to places of importance. Their belief that the avant-garde was the force which propelled culture and society toward socialism justified the radical writers' abandonment of proletarian literature and their renewed focus on modern literature. An interpretation of Marxist criticism, counter to the *PR* critics' notions of what Stalinists believed, similarly pointed to the radical truth of revolutionary modernism. Finally, artistic and critical independence emerged as a cardinal principle. Only when a writer was able to wander off in his own direction—to follow his own muse—could his contribution achieve full meaning for society at large. Thus, the process by which a writer came to speak for and to society was reversed. Misguided proletarian novelists had consciously set out to speak to a preconceived mass audience. The modern writer had to feel his way toward his rightful audience. Lionel Trilling summarized this position in the introduction to a collection from the first decade of *Partisan Review*:

> The writer who defines his audience by its limitations is indulging in the unforgivable arrogance. The writer must define his audience by its abilities, by its perfections as far as he is gifted to conceive them. He does well, if he cannot see his right audience, within immediate reach of his voice, to direct his words to his spiritual ancestors or posterity, or even, if need be, to his coterie. The writer serves his daemon and his subject. And the democracy that does not know that the daemon and the subject must be served is not, in any ideal sense of the word, a democracy at all.[19]

In Trilling's analysis we can see the changed literary position which the *Partisan* critics advanced. At the same time that Trilling saw the potential of a large audience for writers, he also justified the necessity of restricting an audience. Rather than seeking a mass audience by striving for the lowest denominator, the writer should aspire to the audience's highest qualities, its "perfections." If this was not immediately apparent, then a limitation of audience rather than literary quality should follow. "Spiritual ancestors," such as the modernist writers, or a "coterie," such as the *Partisan* crowd, should become the focus. Ultimately, the larger audience and democracy, itself, would be best served. At the same time, all proscriptions which had been placed on the artist during the days of proletarian literature were removed; yet, the potential benefits remained.

In revolutionary modernism the New York Intellectuals argued a theory of literature and of culture which satisified their intellectual demands while allowing them to believe they had not sacrificed their radicalism. They justified the notion of a coterie, even if only as a temporary grouping awaiting a true mass audience. Finally, revolutionary modernism would produce better literary achievements as well as a better balance between intellectual endeavors and radical politics. "In view of what has happened," Philip Rahv concluded, "is it not clear that the older tradition [of artistic independence] was a thousand times more 'progressive'—if that is to be our criterion—was infinitely more disinterested, infinitely more sensitive to the actual conditions of human existence, than the shallow political writing of our latter days?" Proletarian literature was inferior *and* significantly less radical. Turning the tables on his old allies, Rahv accused them of the very shortcomings they had once attributed to the modernists. "Whether we choose Soviet novels by orthodox authors," he observed,

> or recent "militant" works by the Frenchmen Aragon and Malraux; or the revolutionary prose and verse of American writers like . . . Michael Gold, Clifford Odets, John Howard Lawson, [and] Albert Maltz . . . in none of them shall we find an imagination or sensibility which is not of a piece with some variety . . . of the bourgeois creative mode.[20]

Thus, in revolutionary modernism, in the belief that through avant-garde culture and literary insight subversive activities could accompany literature of high standards, the *PR* writers found a position which was more congenial to their own notions of literary radicalism than was proletarian literature. The hesitations and ambivalence which had prompted their abandonment of proletarian literature were gone and the basic priorities of art and politics set straight. Furthermore, they could apply the old radical criticism of progressive and social-realist writers—that they were acting within a bourgeois frame—to their former radical associates.[21]

Revolutionary modernism offered the *Partisan* writers and others a version of literary criticism which criticized proletarian writing without abandoning the radical ground. In addition, the critics rescued and promoted the names of leading modernist writers and established a base from which to proclaim their position. Most important, this newly articulated philosophy promoted the role of the intellectual as well as that of the artist. Perhaps as much as anything else, this was the key element which drew the young New York Intellectuals to the

Partisan position. The literary critics of the community's second generation would begin from the position carved out by the elders in the late 1930s. The creation of new radical criticism had been the ostensible reason for a "new" *PR*. Revolutionary modernism and the promotion of the avant-garde became the first perceptible position with which the reborn magazine became identified. From the outset, it characterized the philosophy of the critics who wrote for the journal and became a pillar of New York Intellectual thinking.

THE MODERN TRAGIC HERO

The revitalized role of the critic in revolutionary modernism helped overcome the frustration the *PR* critics felt in the proletarian-literature movement. Granville Hicks had argued not for conscious intervention but for unconscious dialectic forces to change and refine cultural movements. The skill and insight needed to recognize and explain the subversive component of Dostoevsky's work, for example, required the special talents of the critic. The formation of a radical literary aesthetic, one which could sift through both conservative writing with "radical sensibilities" and political novels of dubious literary merit, could not be accomplished by impersonal means. This undertaking demanded an active and central role for critics, who in the context of identifying good radical writing also helped direct the avant-garde toward true socialism. This view turned Hicks on his head and reversed the priorities held by the critics of the writers' congress.

The contentions of the *PR* critics rested on a larger belief in the importance of intellectuals in general and of critics in particular. The intelligentsia, William Phillips argued, were responsible for the existence of modern art. The true function of America's intellectuals had eroded over the decade, he maintained. "How shall we characterize the modern intellectual?" he asked rhetorically in 1938. His answer did not paint a glowing portrait of some of his contemporaries:

> [The intellectual's] condition, today, seems to be that of a liberal anti-fascist; indeed this is the dominant type. Yet it is he who in the name of progress suppressed insurgency, in the name of peace clamors for war. He has forgotten his vital function in society; to safeguard the dreams and discoveries of science and art and to champion some political movement insofar as it fulfills the requirements of an intellectual ideal.[22]

The reassertion of this "vital function" emerged as the second major task the *Partisan* writers took upon themselves. How should an intellectual function? What impact did his activities have on literature? On culture? On society? All these became questions of central importance for *PR*, because the answers went far beyond abstract beliefs. Like that of their critical role, the notion of the intellectual's proper function clearly helped define their own place in society.

Beginning, again, with the literary questions which had caused the creation of a "new" *Partisan Review*, Philip Rahv carried his analysis of the "slump in American writing" beyond the immediate problems with proletarian literature. As intellectuals grew increasingly politicized and allied themselves with various political movements, they lost their position as "a special group maintaining a separate existence on the basis of superior cultural values." The attachments to political movements caused them to disperse, and this "signaled the beginning of the end of modern literature."[23] Once eager to join the main current of the times—radicalism—the *PR* writers now called for intellectual retrenchment. An intellectual should still be radical, but in the context of an intellectual milieu, a "special group."

Abandoning this special group for one radical movement, communism, brought intellectual humiliation as well as a loss of perspective. They had been used, Rahv believed, and found themselves in a position similar to that of some of the founders of the Soviet Union now being purged by Stalin. "It is not only the Old Bolsheviks who are on trial," Rahv declared; "we too, all of us are in the prisoners dock . . . these are trials of the mind and of the human spirit." Seizing the most inflammatory issue in the debate between Stalinists and anti-Stalinists—the Moscow trials—Rahv attempted to apply it to the situation of American intellectuals. "Much is being said about the 'moral collapse of Bolshevism,' but how little about the moral collapse of the intellectuals." Among intellectuals, the "moral collapse" manifested itself in "smugness," an "abandonment of the values of culture," and the fact that "everywhere they place themselves under the surveillance of authority, they rationalize, they explain away." These crimes, Rahv believed, placed the American intellectuals on a level with the Old Bolsheviks confessing in Moscow. "The monstrosity of my crime is immeasurable," Bukharin had admitted during the trials. Rahv applied the words to many of his intellectual contemporaries.[24] However monstrous Rahv believed the "treason of the intellectuals" to be, their plight was hardly comparable to that of the individuals standing in the Soviet courtrooms. Rahv painted the picture more starkly than necessary to reinforce the importance of his position or, perhaps, to convince the skeptical. The lack of a literary aesthetic in proletarian literature or the need to save the world from second-rate Stalinist poets hardly merited the type of societal role Rahv and Phillips declared for intellectuals. This new role provided the critics with the means of securing the central position denied to them in Communist literary circles. Unwilling to function in "servile roles," they fashioned a newly assertive and self-conscious place for all intellectuals and justified it with references to broad social questions.

The reassertion of the role of literary critics thus became only the starting point in this reevaluation of the importance of intellectuals. "Only insofar as this minority [the intellectuals] recovers its independence," Rahv predicted, "will literature regain its vitality." The realization of this goal would be no simple task, however. Rahv and Phillips argued that intellectuals had to win back the independence the *PR* editors claimed had been lost amid the radical ties of the decade. Furthermore, the American environment, Trilling argued, was extremely inhospitable to intellectuals; it was "haunted by a kind of social fear of intellect." Thus, in addition to the effort to revive literature and criticism, the New York Intellectuals set themselves a dual project, to rescue the good name of intellectuals in America and to establish their proper place in American society—one which left them unconstrained, fully appreciated, and markedly nonservile.[25]

This reassessment of the intellectual's role never considered a return to any sort of isolation. Given the instability of the capitalist system and the threat of fascism to whatever order still existed, the political nature of intellectual commitment remained an essential underpinning for this new mentality. The intelligentsia had to "think seriously of its future," Rahv maintained in 1939; it could "afford no longer to belittle and neglect political creeds and action." The crucial question became a balancing of intellectual and political roles. The scales had tipped too far toward the political side, Rahv believed. The intellectual had allowed "his political faith to affect him as a craftsman." Too much isolation and insularity would lead to problems as well. This danger, however, paled in comparison with "the international Tammany Hall that Stalinism had turned into." When he was independent, the artist's "stupidities" were at least his own. After all, Rahv concluded, the ivory tower was "an infinitely more commendable home for literature than Tammany Hall."[26]

Reacting to their sense of the coercion existing in the Communist camp, the *PR* intellectuals proclaimed independence as the essential ingredient in their redefined intellectualism. More than any other element, critical independence and critical detachment would foster a true intellectual identity. Rahv quoted Wilfred Owen: "All a poet can do today is warn. That is why the true poets must be truthful." He added, "All we have left to go on is individual integrity—the probing conscience, the will to repulse and to assail the forces released by a corrupt society."[27] The *PR* critics concluded that the dream of proletarian writers to engage directly in revolutionary activity had failed. Rather than abandoning politics, however, they lowered their sights, calling for a role as political analysts or commentators, separate but involved. Breaking with the classic stereotype of an intelligentsia, they believed they should not remain aloof from political action. Conversely, unlike the proletarian writers and critics, they argued they should not abandon their separate identity as intellectuals. Perhaps it was not possible for poems to move workers or for novels to bring revolutions. But as diagnosticians of the modern ailment, intellectuals could at least help awaken interest in pressing problems. Simultaneously, they would earn the respect and position which their training and personal inclination led them to believe they deserved. The artist, Phillips argued, had to stand against barbarism and, in so doing, carry on the highest tradition and achievements of civilization.[28]

The notion of an intelligentsia serving as a group to diagnose the modern condition and the belief in critical detachment and independent thought might appear to be contradictory. However, when all intellectuals functioned freely and properly, an atmosphere emerged in which artistic and cultural endeavors flourished and the society grew more cohesive rather than more diversified. Intellectuals "throughout their history and despite growing tendencies toward atomization," Phillips declared, "have maintained the kind of institutional stability vital to the production of art." Stressing the important of this cohesive vitality, Phillips concluded that "obviously . . . through such a unified and self-perpetuating group . . . our national cultural community has been preserved and the individual artist has been provided with a sustaining tradition of convention and experiment."[29]

The existence of independent, yet unified, intellectuals provided a stable atmosphere for social progress. This traditional aspect of intellectualism, Phillips maintained, needed constant reassertion. Modern life presented a new role, however, for intellectuals to fill. Seeking touchstones in a tumultuous world, society turned to intellectuals as never before.

> As society has lost its earlier unity of belief, which the artist shared and took as his starting point, the very plight of the intelligentsia and the more or less homogeneous outlook it had acquired served as a philosophical mooring for the modern artist . . . the intelligentsia, in their role of intellectual conservatism and in their tightly knit traditions, perform for modern times a function that an institution like the Church, for instance, had in the medieval period. And, in an historical sense, the Church was actually the organized body of intellectuals in the Middle Ages.[30]

Like critics in revolutionary modernism, intellectuals in general were now assigned positions of enormous importance. Beyond the escape from the previously felt bonds of Stalinism, Phillips argued for the placement of intellectuals at the very center of modern society, in the roles of stabilizers and spiritual guides.

Whereas they had once shunned a sense of specialness—the creation of intellectual elites—the Partisan writers now championed the concept of intellectual uniqueness and the view that the intelligentsia was just such a self-conscious elite. The difference between previous elites and the one being organized stemmed from the current political climate. "The most advanced sections of the elite," Phillips observed, "tend to be radical, dissident, and uncompromising, and to relate themselves, however indirectly or uncon-sciously, to those social forces that challenge the economic and cultural exploitation of man." Societies needed and created intellectual elites. To deny their existence stifled normal creative development and, more important, ran the risk of promoting philistinism and cultural destabilization. Praise, rather than scorn, should greet the emergence of a coterie—an emergence which was natural and crucial. As one young second-generation intellectual, Issac Rosenfeld, wrote, quoting another, "In every society, in every group, there are what Saul Bellow has called 'colonies of the spirit.' " And in a highly prophetic conclusion—to a large degree self-fulfilling—Rosenfeld declared, "Artists create their colonies. Some day these may become empires."[31]

The fame of the New York Intellectuals did not fully emerge until after World War II, when a number of them would achieve a level of prominence equal to their ambitions. For the moment, however, they contented themselves with notions of society which placed the intellectual at its core. "The modern tragic hero, from Hamlet to Joseph K.," Phillips argued, "has been an intellectual, or, more precisely, a man of sensibility, who has taken upon himself the burdens of civilization as a whole, and in his various guises and mutations has reflected the changing stresses of Western thought." Such a view placed a grave responsibility on intellectuals. The *Partisan* writers willingly accepted their own call. Battle-hardened by the experiences of the 1930s, they felt well suited to the task.

> The political person is in this sense a central figure today. . . . The really significant political figure is therefore a man of consciousness who has been crucially implicated in the major turns, who had been made and unmade by them. The conversion to the cause, the days of faith and the days of conscience, and, more recently, the great exodus, the atonements, and the overhauling of beliefs—all have left their mark on him.[32]

Armed with a self-justifying notion of true intellectual calling and social relevance, the New York Intellectuals saw themselves as both tragic and heroic. After the political storms of the Depression years and their bouts with party and conscience, they were ready to assume their rightful place and to follow their calling to the center of American society.

Chapter 6

The *Partisan* Mind: Political Turns

In the opening editorial of the revived *Partisan Review*, the editors reiterated several basic premises of the original magazine, now set in a new context. Cultural concerns, modified by the shift from proletarian literature to revolutionary modernism, remained central. These cultural discussions continued to assume a political framework, just as the new role for intellectuals required not academic isolation but an awareness of and concern with political events. The radicalism of the "old" *PR* carried over to the "new," although it was now independent of party connections. Wary of the direct hand of any organized political group, the editors still argued that writers must be "frankly revolutionary." Achieving this required a radical position more congenial with their cultural pursuits. For the remainder of the prewar years, the writers who gathered around *Partisan Review* continued to feel themselves a part of the American radical community—at least of its anti-Stalinist wing. The ex-Communists, such as Rahv, Phillips, and Schapiro, joined with those like Macdonald who had never been close to the Communist party, in an effort to create an independent cultural radicalism to promote intellectual ends.

One significant difference between the cultural positions and the political discussions emerged in the writing of the *Partisan* crowd. The emphasis on the revival of interest in modern literature and, especially, on the reassertion of the proper role for critics and intellectuals lasted into the postwar years. These cultural positions, moving away from the politicized world of proletarian literature, formed the core of the *Partisan* stance both in the 1930s and afterward. The political issues which helped define the community in the late 1930s were, by contrast, transitory. They demonstrate not a convergence on a single position but the beginnings of a process of political reevaluation. By the 1950s, though the cultural elements remained largely intact, the political perspective had changed again. The political positions which identified *Partisan Review* and the New York Intellectuals in the late 1930s served as way stations on their travels away from the radicalism of their youth.

Obviously, some of the change was tied to world events. The threat of fascism loomed large before 1940 but was of little relevance after 1945. In addition, changes during the 1930s, buffeted all the radical movements. The organization of the Popular Front, which resulted in the disbanding of the John Reed Clubs, also created realignments among various groups. While hostility still raged between Stalinists and Trotskyists, other radical groups found themselves in closer alliance with Communists than even before. Despite avowed denials, the claim in the *New Masses* and elsewhere of *PR's* "Trotskyite" connections caused the editors to evaluate their relationship to Trotsky.

Fundamental to the political reevaluation taking place in the minds of the *Partisan* writers was their commitment to and interpretation of Marxist theory. Although nearly all the *Partisan* writers continued to identify themselves as Marxists, they were much less sure of its precise meaning. Phillips's arguments about "ventures" in Marxist criticism or "criticisms" in the plural found parallel interpretations in areas other than Marxist literary criticism. Continuing to be quite "respectful to Marx," Irving Kristol recalled, the young students reading *Partisan Review* at City College demonstrated a willingness "to question Marx as the ultimate revealer of radical truth." The pages of *Partisan Review* evidenced this same willingness. There emerged no single position in this discussion of Marxism, analogous to revolutionary modernism or the role of intellectuals. Rather, the discussions and revisions point toward developments after the war, when most New York Intellectuals dropped Marxism entirely. Clear definitions of a cultural position emerged, but the *Partisan* writers began to revise and reinterpret Marxism, in a way which ultimately led to its abandonment. It continued to provide a "bite and edge," in Irving Howe's words, long after it ceased to be a specific doctrine.[1]

Thus, the *Partisan* community's most publicly identifiable political stands did not yield any new position which carried over into the 1950s. Rather, while cultural arguments firmed, political beliefs loosened. In part, the transition from pre- to postwar political views reflects the changing issues which confronted these intellectuals. It also evidences the political reevaluation going on in the minds of the intellectuals and demonstrates that, despite claims to the contrary, it was not merely the Stalinist version of radicalism which was being reconsidered.

THE MARXIST CURE

Unlike those on literary criticism, the political discussions which the New York Intellectuals entered were under way by the time the "new" *Partisan Review* appeared. In contrast to the abrupt shifts which marked the cultural debates—

over modernism and artistic isolation in the 1920s, proletarian literature in the 1930s, and *PR*'s emerging revolutionary modernism—the questioning and discussions in Marxist circles had gone on for years. Following in the footsteps of their European brethren, American Marxists engaged in a series of interpretative and revisionist endeavors, seeking to adjust Marx to the American setting or modify beliefs in keeping with political affiliations. The writers in the *New Masses*, arguing the Communist position, battled the Trotskyists, who published in the *New International*; the debates reflected the allegiances to the two sides of the great Soviet schism. In other journals, such as the *Nation*, the *New Republic*, and the *Modern Monthly* (later the *Modern Quarterly*), various American Marxists offered different Marxist positions, based on personal philosophical positions rather than on 'party affiliations.

One debate which raged in the pages of V. F. Calverton's *Modern Quarterly* demonstrates the intensity as well as the special circumstances which affected American Marxist thinking. In 1926 Max Eastman published his *Marx and Lenin: The Science of Revolution*. Eastman, once the darling of the prewar Greenwich Village set and editor of the "old" *Masses*, had been a young instructor at Columbia in the same department as John Dewey. His book on Marxism sought to humanize Marx and, in the process, to argue against the incorporation of German idealism into Marxist thought. Specifically, Eastman contended that Marxism must be divested of its Hegelianism. The dialectic, he argued, allowed individuals to assume a passive role. Instead of some abstract force of "inner logic" promoting history, Eastman asserted, an active human component must enter. The task as he saw it, was "to take the revolutionary motive out of 'history,' where Marx and Engels surreptitiously projected it, and locate it in the human breast where it belongs."[2] To accomplish this humanizing, Eastman turned to Freud's insights into the human personality. Eastman felt that the one great figure of Marxism to understand this, implicitly, was Lenin. His activism, his call for a vanguard party, and his unwillingness to wait out the historical process all demonstrated his grasp of the personal, psychological component which Marxism needed.

Eastman's work raised a storm of debate in Marxist circles, both in America and in Europe. Attacks came from William Z. Foster, the head of the American Communist party, and Michael Gold, as well as from Leon Trotsky. But the severest opposition, and the longest lasting, came from another student of Dewey's, Sidney Hook. Believing that Eastman had "bungled a great theme," Hook began his response with a defense of Hegel and the dialectic. The significance of Hook's arguments has several dimensions. First, the longevity of his debate with Eastman is remarkable. For five years they battled one another, in the pages of the *Modern Quarterly*, at times employing combinations of philosophical argument and personal assault. "Poking fun at a terminology he has not taken any trouble to understand," Hook jabbed his opponent, "Eastman plays at being a wit and succeeds as the Irishman said, in only being 'half a one.' "[3] Second, Hook did not seek to defend orthodox or party-line

Marxism; rather, he wanted to develop a Marxism truly in keeping with the insights of his mentor John Dewey. Finally, Hook's prolonged engagement with Eastman helped propel him to the front line of American Marxist thinkers. A young academic when the debates began, Hook had by 1933 firmly established his importance in American philosophical and radical circles.

In contrast to Eastman, who thought himself a left critic of Deweyan pragmatism, Hook always maintained a strong element of Dewey in his thinking, transposed to a Marxist frame. "Dewey's idea is a socialized America," Hook wrote in 1931. His only quarrel with his mentor was with his "failure to appreciate the instrumental value of *class struggle* rather than class collaboration in effecting the transition from Corporate America to Collective America." Whereas Dewey's independent liberalism carried him to support Norman Thomas and the Socialists in 1932, Hook's Marxism led him to Foster and Ford. Although Hook could write in 1934 that the "fundamental issue of modern times is not democracy versus dictatorship but capitalism versus Communism," he nonetheless claimed to be an "unorthodox Marxist." For Hook, though, Marx himself was not an "orthodox" Marxist. "One cannot be orthodox at any price and a lover of truth at the same time."[4]

Hook's "unorthodox" approach included a parallel argument to Eastman's call for a human element in Marx, but it rested on distinctly different grounds. Hook never had any use for Freudianism, "a scientific mythology," as he has called it.[5] More important, Hook saw the incorporation of pragmatic insights as a means both of overcoming the antihumanistic elements which Eastman criticized and of accurately understanding the Hegelian component. "The 'dialectic' for Marx," Hook wrote in 1928, "is not something working *exclusively* in things and inevitably destined to bring about socialism, but it is *primarily* in things as a condition precedent to human action." Marxism, contrary to programmatic and absolutist notions of historical inevitability, was a "method," Hook maintained, concerning itself only with what was directly dealt with—a "realistic method of class action." It was "not the whole universe," nor did "it profess to have a final truth about what it [did] not concern itself with." In fact, Hook admitted, "its specific conclusions may turn out to be wrong," but many Marxists by "refusing to distinguish between the essential method and tentative results of Marxism have revealed a common ignorance as to what scientific method means."[6]

The dialectic, which Eastman had wanted to drop, remained integral to Hook's philosophy, though defined in such a way as to mesh with his pragmatism. The dialectic, he wrote in 1933, was a "method"—in fact, "the philosophical rhythm of a conscious life." Thus, Hook chose to direct his Marxism toward the instrumental elements which called for human action and to defend the dialectic as a part of that "method." Ultimately, Hook concluded in an analysis ringing with Deweyan phraseology, "Marxism must be interpreted as a voluntaristic humanism rather than as the theological fatalism embraced by Social-Democrats everywhere else." The theory of what Hook called "economic predestination" was a "mischievous myth." He characterized Marxism instead as "a realistic evolutionary naturalism, strongly voluntaristic in its social implications." Hook saw this as the true meaning of dialectical materialism and claimed that its acceptance and the belief in socialism were the two essential requirements for true Marxism.[7]

By the end of his debates with Eastman, halted when Calverton concluded they had become an "obscene enjoyment of the bourgeois world,"[8] Hook possessed a well-established reputation in American radical circles. He signed the 1932 pamphlet for Foster and Ford but soon found himself at odds with the Stalinists. Not yet the apostate Eastman had become, Hook appeared more an American interpreter.

To radical intellectuals, interested in human souls as well as economic needs, Hook's interpretation offered the prospect of a Marxism mindful of an individual's limitations and perfectibility. The dialectic did "not sanction the naïve belief that a perfect society, a perfect man, will ever be realized." Rather, the dialectic propelled humanity onward and upward, not alleviating all problems, but "transforming problems to higher and more inclusive levels." "Under communism," Hook wrote, "man ceases to suffer as an animal and suffers as a human. He therewith moves from the plane of the pitiful to the plane of the tragic."[9] The fullest statement of this early position appeared in 1933, in the first major book Hook published on Marx, *Towards the Understanding of Karl Marx*. "The dialectic method," he maintained there, "was genuinely experimental." Marx had succeeded in doing what Hegel had not, applying the dialectic to human history and society. "Without denying the enormous complexity of the factors involved, he offered a guiding thread into the mazes of the social process." Using a Hegelian concept which Marx had never explicitly employed, Hook brought the dialectic into conjunction with his own notions of voluntaristic Marxism.

> Marx tries to show how social change arises from the interacting processes of nature, society, and human intelligence. From objective *conditions*, social and natural (thesis), there arises human *needs* and *purposes* which, in recognizing the objective possibilities in the given situation (antithesis) set up a course of action (synthesis) designed to actualize these possibilities.[10]

As a demonstration of his integration of conditions and needs, Hook used the example Eastman had selected to defend his position. "How would the [Russian] revolution have developed if Lenin had not reached Russia in April, 1917?" Hook asked. Lenin's willingness to alter the party line and, even more, the fact of Lenin's existence seemed to Hook verifications of the relation between personalities and events. All was not chance, however. Rather, Hook argued, "one might very well say that the Russian Revolution of November 1917 was due in part to Lenin's belief that Marxism must be interpreted as a voluntaristic humanism."[11] Although this interpretation stressed personal roles, Hook was neither so naïve nor so shortsighted as to fail to see a potential difficulty in his position which might undermine his Marxism entirely. Given his belief in human involvement and the examples which pointed to Lenin's crucial participation, might not that human involvement be seen as central and the Marxist perspective and dynamic as secondary or even superfluous? Admitting a certain necessity of choice in social action, Hook nonetheless viewed this choice as emerging only at a point well along the path to revolutionary activity and ultimately bound up with the dialectical process. "The choice is intelligent only if it takes note of Marx's analysis; but once the choice is made, it *itself becomes an historical factor in making the revolutionary ideal come true* [italics Hook's]. The objective truth of Marxism," he concluded, "realizes itself in the informed revolutionary act. Marxism is neither science nor myth, but a realistic method of social action." Thus, Hook dispensed with those theorists who saw personality as the single, crucial element. "In terms of Marx's philosophy of history it is easy to make short shrift of any conception such as Carlyle's which sees in the development of civilization nothing but the deeds of heroes and the thoughts of genius."[12]

Many radical intellectuals in the 1930s found Hook's interpretation of Marxism especially meaningful and his demeanor and erudition very impressive. By dint of his prolific writing, the force of his argumentative abilities, and the appropriateness of his brand of Marxism for personal activities, Hook emerged as a dominant figure in the political discussions among the individuals who eventually formed the New York Intellectuals. He was, in William Barrett's analysis, "the acknowledged master of Marxist theory . . . everybody leaned on Hook politically." Barrett recalled a party at which Dwight Macdonald stated, "Look, there are a hundred and twenty million people in the United States and Sidney Hook is America's Number One Marxist!"[13]

While Macdonald's accolade would have met with opposition in a number of radical circles, Hook nonetheless emerged as a leading figure on the American radical scene. His writings, Irving Howe later recounted, "influenced many of us as providing the possibility of an intelligent American Marxism." For Daniel Bell, "Hook was the first person among American Marxists, to trace the historical evolution of Marx's thought. For many people, Hook was a political mentor. He certainly was for William Phillips." In addition, never a distant oracle emerging only in print to slay the Eastmans or to duel the Stalinists, Hook actively participated in New York political and intellectual life. He spoke at rallies and argued at parties. "Don't lecture them so much," his wife once chided him.[14] The intensity of his beliefs, coupled with his learning, added to his overall stature. Alfred Kazin, who much later still expressed a personal dislike for Hook, felt his influence.

> It was not Hook's logic that impressed me . . . ; it was his passion for . . . ideas. He was humorless, but never petty; obstinate, but not malicious; domineering, but not self-centered. . . . It was his commitment that impressed me. He was a believer. He wanted to change society totally, to overturn disproven ways of thought, to discard all the encrusted superstitions, to give mankind the new chance that it hungered

for. . . . He made the choice stark and the issue dramatic. . . . Here was logic, here
was science, here was experimentalism. Here were instruments of social analysis that
exposed all the contradictions in capitalist society and could give me all they needed
for creating a society practical, sensible, harmonious and just. His method, wholly
and entirely rational, would become the lever of revolution. How could one not
grasp it?[15]

Beyond his passion and his scholarship, there was a final reason for Hook's
appeal for the young Jewish radicals. He symbolically staked the claim of his
generation of radicals. Max Eastman represented the prewar socialists and
bohemian radicals. Hook represented the newer men of the 1930s, coming of
age in the Depression years. The son of immigrants, Hook had been Morris
Cohen's student at City College, but he moved beyond Cohen's liberalism to
thirties radicalism. He moved beyond the intellectual framework of his true
mentor, John Dewey, as well. Never abandoning the pragmatic lessons he had
learned, he applied them to a position Dewey never adopted, Marxism. In the
April 1934 issue of the *Modern Monthly*, Hook's generational separation was
clearly in evidence. The central issue, "Why I Am [or Am Not] a Communist,"
took on a symbolic meaning and a political one, as Hook responded in the
affirmative both to his teachers Cohen and Dewey and to Bertrand Russell.[16]
Some Marxist intellectuals, unhappy with the limits they felt Stalinism
imposed, found Hook's addition of a voluntaristic element attractive. To
literary critics like Rahv and Phillips, eager to posit a critical function for
literature and to enhance the role of critics, Hook's call for positive interactions
was very congenial. Hook offered political arguments which paralleled the
literary considerations being advanced in *Partisan Review*. He found that
individuals engaged in political action had erred in the same way in which *PR*
critics accused radical literary figures of erring. "I have come to the conclusion
that the cause of freedom would have been better served if scholars and artists
had remained faithful to the integrity of their crafts," Hook concluded, "if they
had carried over into the holiday fields of their political enthusiasm some of the
professional discipline, caution, sense of evidence, and elementary feeling of
justice which they took for granted in their workaday world."[17] It is not
surprising that, as the circle which developed around *Partisan Review* began to
form, even before the appearance of the "new" journal, Sidney Hook found a
central place in it. His interests were never literary, and he always perceived
marked differences between himself and the "literary boys" at *PR*. He became
a member of the *Partisan* community, however, because of his anti-Stalinism,
because of his intellectual skills, and, most important, because his Marxist
interpretations permitted the very theoretical loosening which Rahv, Phillips,
and other literary critics desired.

Hook's Marxism, though, proved no firmer than that of the other radicals who joined *Partisan Review*. In the years between the founding of the "new" journal and America's entry into World War II, Hook continued to argue his own brand of Marxism, built on its Deweyan foundation. As the anti-Stalinism of the New York Intellectuals grew more intense, Hook reiterated the distinctions between his Marxist vision and the Stalinist party line. The publication of Marx's early *Economic and Philosophical Manuscripts* prompted a "systematic re-study" of all of Marx, Hook reported. This investigation renewed his sense that the "dialectic method by which Marx strove to combine realism and activism . . . involved a nascent experimental naturalism. This was essentially the same position which John Dewey had independently arrived at in a different idiom and developed so impressively in psychology, logic, science, and esthetics." Hook cautioned against the misinterpretation that Dewey was a Marxist or "Marx the John the Baptist of pragmatism," though they did share "fundamental metaphysical and logical positions."[18]

In addition, Hook began to shed what appeared to him superfluous or misguided. He even turned against the dialectic which he had defended against Max Eastman a few years before. By 1937 Hook was viewing the dialectic as just "an abbreviated synonym for scientific method." Because the notion of the dialectic often became the tool of muddled thinking and mistaken conclusions, Hook argued, "it would be more conducive to clear thinking if the phrase were dropped."[19] A perfect example of an improper application of the dialectic was the programmatic approach to literature advanced by the proletarian critics. The active role of the investigator in the scientific method corresponded nicely to the active role of the critic in the *Partisan* concept of literature.

Beyond the intrinsic modification that Hook put forward, his dropping of the dialectic carried significant symbolic value. Most obviously, among those who followed the Hook-Eastman battles, Hook's new position demonstrated the degree of revision occurring in his thinking. Furthermore, other Marxists in the New York Intellectual community, such as Meyer Schapiro, had never felt comfortable with the idea of the dialectic.[20] Although the intellectuals' Marxism contained numerous distinctive qualities, a large element of difference was now eliminated. Finally, Hook's recalculations pointed to a larger development. Marxism was in need of a cure. In the face of Stalinism and its improper Marxist notions, salvation remained possible, Hook maintained,only through a "reinfusion with a democratic spirit (and not the phony kind the Communist Party is talking about)." Moreover, this reinfusion had specific requirements. It had to be "explicitly scientific" and contain a "conception of socialism not only as a program of economic activity but as a way of life." As always, for Hook, a solution lay at hand—"the experimental philosophy as expressed in the major works of John Dewey."[21]

Although they never embraced all the specific features of Hook's Marxism, other intellectuals in the *Partisan* community did contribute to the changes in Marxist thought. In this atmosphere of revision, a number of these individuals came together to establish the *Marxist Quarterly*. Published by the American Marxist Association, it had a board of editors which included important figures on the non-Communist left. Hook, Schapiro, James Burnham, Lewis Corey, Louis Hacker, Will Herberg, Corliss Lamont, and Bertram D. Wolfe were among the initial sponsors. Lasting only three issues, the journal did publish a number of articles demonstrating the developments in Marxist circles. Hook's "Dialetic and Nature," in which he formally abandoned the dialectic, appeared in the second number.

For the intellectuals gathering around *Partisan Review*, the different approaches to and conceptions of Marxist thought served not as a divisive factor but as one which reinforced the notion that Marxism was a "method" rather than an absolute truth. William Phillips, who argued for Marxist criticisms "in the plural," expanded his notion of Marxism in general, reflecting a more wide-ranging approach:

> While its method remains constant—radical, empirical, materialistic—it is necessary, as it absorbs new discoveries and opposes new dangers, for it to discard some of its original philosophical emphasis. . . . The text of Marxism is not absolutely fixed, but must be constantly recreated to keep step with the ever-changing world of politics and culture. And at any given time, the question of what is living and what is dead in Marxism is not an abstract one, for it can be determined only by applying the old theories to new ideas and situations.[22]

Lionel Abel's assessment of Harold Rosenberg's Marxism serves as a kind of symbolic summary of the new approach these radicals followed. "Rosenberg took the view that Marxism was two things: it was Talmud, to be sure. But it was also Cabala. And he thought that the role of the literary men should be to develop the arcane, cabalistic side of Marxist doctrine."[23]

The publication in *PR* of an excerpt from Edmund Wilson's study of the development of socialist thought, *To The Finland Station*, illustrates how much had happened in the world of Marxist thinking over the decade. Wilson had read a copy of Eastman's *Marx and Lenin*, the initial occasion of the Hook-Eastman melee, and written to Eastman that it was "the best critical thing [he had] read of this philosophical aspect of Marxism." In his own article Wilson followed the Hook of 1937 and the Eastman of 1926 by dropping the dialectic, which he called a "religious myth . . . disencumbered of divine personality and tied up with the history of mankind." The editors evidently tried to build a *PR* symposium around Wilson's contentions, with Hook, Schapiro, James Burnham, and Bertram Wolfe responding. The idea was shelved, however, when William Phillips discovered the difficulty of finding a "100% dialectical materialist."[24]

The Marxist positions of the *Partisan* writers demonstrate the ever-growing looseness of the interpretations. *Partisan Review*'s rebirth came at a time when many of its contributors were reassessing their Marxism, not yet abandoning their beliefs but surely relaxing their commitment. Ever aware of the active role of the individual—especially of that of the critic and intellectual—within the political process, they discovered in the Marxism of Sidney Hook an interpretation which required *voluntary* human action and allowed for variations of viewpoint within a larger Marxist framework. Hook's position, however, proved no more hard than that of others. All these intellectuals continued the process of revision into the war and postwar years. Ultimately, most of these intellectuals abandoned their Marxism for other political positions. In the late 1930s, however, they remained committed to Marxism, in some form. As a result, the political philosophy of *Partisan Review* was much less precise and firm than its cultural stance. This proved a benefit rather than a problem. Political requirements needed to be relaxed if literary pursuits and intellectual endeavors were to be broadened. The focus on individualistic roles in radical politics offered just such a loosening. The ills of contemporary Marxist thought could be cured by an injection of human involvement, argued Sidney Hook. This remedy would also relieve the suffering state of American literature, a condition which the *Partisan* writers felt Stalinist charlatans had induced.

THE MAN IN MEXICO

It became common coin in the world of radical politics and literature to chart the progression of *Partisan Review* from a Stalinist journal in the middle 1930s to a Trotskyist one by the end of the decade. Steadfastly denied by the editors, then and since, charges of Trotskyism emanated from Communist circles. Michael Gold blasted the "new" *PR* in the *Daily Worker*, under the heading "A Literary Snake Sheds His Skin for Trotsky."[25] In truth, the ties between Trotsky and the journal never proved as close as the Communists argued. Save for the personal membership of one editor and the sharing of several political positions, *Partisan Review* and the Trotskyists steered relatively independent courses during the late years of the decade. Each expressed some reservation about formal connections with the other, and each thought the other more desirous of establishing actual ties. "Trotsky tried very hard to get us to become 'serious,' as he put it, about politics—in essence to make ourselves into an organ of the Trotskyists," recalled Dwight Macdonald. " 'After all,' he said, 'you are left-wing and radical and anti-Stalinist, so what's the difference.' " Although Macdonald himself was an active Trotskyst, he later said "We definitely turned him down, because one thing we all agreed on was that we should have absolutely no political connections at all."[26] By contrast, Isaac Deutscher, Trotsky's biographer, believed that the resistance came from the other camp. "The editors invited Trotsky to contribute. He refused at first, and treated the venture with reserve. 'It is my general impression,' [Trotsky] wrote to Macdonald, 'that the editors of *Partisan Review* are capable, educated, intelligent, but have nothing to say.' " Trotsky himself, Deutscher contended "wondered just how serious was the *Partisan Review*'s commitment to revolutionary socialism."[27]

These hesitations and these differences between PR and Trotsky would seem to undermine the Communists' contention and to vindicate Rahv and Phillips. At PR's tenth anniversary, the editors summarized the relationship:

> Though in some quarters—where people took their cue from the Stalinists—we were quickly stamped as Trotskyite, the truth is that only Dwight Macdonald was a member of that party, and he but for a short time. Our editorial position could then be said to have been Trotskyite only the sense that we mainly agreed with Trotsky's criticism of the Soviet regime and that we admired him as a great exponent of Marxist doctrine. Beyond that we were not willing to accept many of the specific theories and practices of the Trotskyites.[28]

Despite this formal independence, the connections between the Trotskyists and the *Partisan* crowd proved much more intricate than the PR editors claimed. As the magazine became increasingly identified with a particular group of intellectuals, as well as with cultural and political positions, the relationship between many of the individuals and Trotsky brought the two sides closer together. In addition to Macdonald, Mary McCarthy was close to the Trotskyists during the late 1930s. While McCarthy recalled that "the 'boys' were 'too wary of political ties,' " she added, "[I] was myself a great partisan of Trotsky, who possessed those intellectual traits of wit, lucidity, and indignation, which I regarded, and still regard, as a touchstone."[29]

Others in the *Partisan* community, though not active members of the party, took public stands identified with the Trotskyist camp. Supporting Trotsky against the claims of the Moscow trials, the American Committee for the Defense of Leon Trotsky numbered among its members James T. Farrell, Edmund Wilson, V. F. Calverton, and Lionel Trilling, in addition to Macdonald and McCarthy. When Sidney Hook attempted to form an alliance between the American Socialist party and the Trotskyists, he argued that it would be a distinct advantage for the Socialists to include their ranks a number of prominent American intellectuals currently associated with Trotsky. Among those Hook listed were Louis Hacker, Max Eastman, John Dos Passos, Lionel Trilling, Lionel Abel, and John Chamberlain.[30] In Alcove No. 1 at City College, the Trotskyist organ, the *New International*, often served as a companion to PR in the late 1930s. Irving Kristol recalled that whereas the *New Masses* rarely found a place, the *New International* seemed a "distant cousin" to *Partisan Review*.[31] If PR itself remained independent of Trotskyist connections, many of the intellectuals gathering around it did not.

The course of world events also thrust the Trotskyists and the PR circle into close proximity. In 1937, the year of PR's rebirth, the Moscow trials moved into high gear. Trotsky's trial in absentia and the conviction of his "conspirators" fueled the debate between Stalinists and anti-Stalinist in America. The *New Masses* stood behind the conclusions of the trials and called for a boycott of the Joint Commission of Inquiry, headed by John Dewey, which investigated the charges against Trotsky. The American Committee for the Defense of Trotsky, cited above, assembled in support of the Dewey commission. In the *New Masses*, many of the same individuals who had been attacking *PR* signed the boycott, including Granville Hicks, Theodore Dreiser, Corliss Lamont, and Nathanael West. As the lines were being drawn in the late 1930s, *PR* and Trotsky found themselves, despite personal reservations, on the same side of the demarcation. Rahv noted this similarity of position when he equated the role of anti-Stalinist intellectuals in American and Old Bolsheviks in Moscow. "We too, all of us are in the prisoners' dock."[32]

All of these personal and psychological connections placed the *PR* writers and the Trotskyists in the same general region of the American radical landscape, but that does not mean the two groups were one. Rather, personal attachments varied, as did attitudes toward the fallen Russian leader. *PR* maintained its steadfast independence from the Trotskyist movement, even as some *PR* writers moved into Trotsky's orbit. Formal ties never became real. Informal connections, however, remained. In part, these interactions were prompted by the relatively small plot of radical ground which both the Trotskyist and the *Partisan* crowd felt comfortable occupying. Eager to maintain their radical commitment outside of Stalinism, the *PR* writers sought a political position from which to argue their case. Their opposition to the Popular Front further restricted the number of groups and individuals whose perspective they shared. For some, such as Macdonald, Trotskyism provided a left position from which to oppose Stalin and the Popular Front. For a young student like Irving Kristol, the choices grew increasingly slim.

> It would be hard for Jews, most of us coming from poor, working-class families, not to be radical. So we wanted to be radical. On the other hand, many of us realized that the Stalin regime in the Soviet Union was not our conception of what a radical politics was supposed to create. Well, if you wanted to be radical, what was left— Trotskyism or a variant. American socialism just wasn't radical enough. It was an older, non-Jewish tradition.[33]

The prevailing anti-Stalinist ethos had not yet turned anti-Communist. Stalinism, not communism, emerged as the enemy. "We had been brought up to believe," William Barrett wrote, "that Lenin and Trotsky were heroes, *sans peur et sans reproche*, and that Stalin was the arch-villian solely responsible for all the evils wrought in the name of Marxism." This attitude allowed the radicals to hold "a kind of devil theory of history which, by pushing all the evil on to one individual, allowed one to keep one's Marxist faith intact."[34] Among the young readers of *PR*, newly testing their radicalism on an anti-Stalinist basis, Trotskyism emerged as the movement most often chosen. In addition to Kristol, Irving Howe, Seymour Martin Lipset, Leslie Fiedler, and Nathan Glazer belonged to the Trotskyist Young People's Socialist League. Having been through one movement already, the "elders" usually chose not to become directly affiliated. Nonetheless, their sympathies and inclinations led them into close association with Trotsky, whose anti-Stalinist Marxism fit their radical requirements. Moreover, the hostility and abuse *PR* editors suffered at the hands of the Stalinists drove them, perhaps unwittingly, closer to the Trotskyist camp. Resisting formal connections, they discovered that maintaining their anti-Stalinist radicalism required some political alignment with the Trotskyists.

This political cohabitation with Trotskyism did not prove entirely un-comfortable for *Partisan Review*. On cultural questions, many of Trotsky's views matched those of the editors. In the same year as the "new" *PR*'s rebirth, Trotsky published his assessment of Stalinism and the course of recent Soviet history, *The Revolution Betrayed*. Trotsky's analysis of the Stalinist impact on Soviet art echoed the cultural position of the *Partisan* critics. Trotsky's appraisal of Soviet writers paralleled the *PR* view of proletarian literature. Trotsky concluded that the Stalin era would "go down in the history of artistic creation preeminently as a epoch of mediocrities, laureates, and toadies." His overall description of the state of the arts reads like the *PR* criticisms of the American Writers' Congress writ large.

> The literary schools were strangled to death one after the other. . . . The process of extermination took place in all ideological spheres, and it took place more decisively since it was more than half unconscious. Their present ruling stratum considers itself called not only to control spiritual creation politically, but also to prescribe its road of development. The method of command-without-appeal extends in like measure to the concentration camps, to scientific agriculture, and to music. The central organ of the party prints anonymous directive editorials having the character of military orders, architecture, literature, dramatic arts, the ballet, to say nothing of philosophy, natural science, and history. The bureaucracy superstitiously fears whatever does not serve it directly, as well as whatever it does not understand.[35]

Thus, the circle of *Partisan* writers found in Trotsky a radical who shared their views on the independence of art. On this topic, Trotsky ultimately made his one contribution to *PR*, "Art and Politics." "Art, like science," Trotksy argued, "not only does not seek orders, but by its very essence, cannot tolerate them. . . . Truly intellectual creation is incompatible with lies, hypocrisy and the spirit of conformity." Trotsky's argument reappeared in only slightly altered language a year later, in the statement of the League for Cultural Freedom and Socialism, which *PR* printed and which all the editors and a number of other New York Intellectuals signed. That statement included these sentences: "Culture not only does not seek orders but by its very nature cannot tolerate them. True intellectual creation is incompatible with the spirit of conformity." Trotsky concluded his 1938 article with the declaration "Art can become a stong ally of revolution only in so far as it remains faithful to itself." The LCFS statement claimed, "If art and science are to be true to the revolution, they must first be true to themselves."[36]

The alliance with Trotsky thus extended beyond the political arena to the realm of culture. In the traditional political battles between Stalinists and

Trotskyists, the central arguments usually focused on such questions as "permanent revolution" versus "socialism in one state" and "the Old Bolsheviks" versus the Stalin bureaucracy. The *Partisan* writers, though, could also see the battle between the two Russian revolutionaries as a battle over culture. "Art has its own laws," Dwight Macdonald wrote, quoting Trotsky, praisingly. "Such trifles mean nothing to Stalin, 'the practical realist.' . . . Stalin is a philistine, so unconscious of his own limitations that he does not hesitate to interfere in the most intimate way in all fields of culture."[37] To the already long list of crimes of Stalin, Macdonald now added the destruction of the Soviet cinema, which he also tied directly to the demise of Trotsky.

> In 1928, Eisenstein and Pudovkin issued a manifesto denouncing the realistic use of sound in the cinema and outlining a new "contrapuntal" approach, based on montage, which promised to revolutionize the sound film as their theories had already recreated the silent cinema. In 1928, Trotsky was exhiled, the other makers of the 1917 revolution were humbled, the Stalinist clique assumed full power, and the first Five Year Plan was launched. In 1930 the Plan was extended to the cinema. . . . Everyone except a few Trotskyist grumblers expected that great things would be done with sound. . . . But even the severest critics of Stalinism could hardly have been prepared for the debacle that followed.[38]

In Philip Rahv's analysis, the political and the cultural questions augmented one another, anti-Stalinism reinforcing revolutionary modernism. His analysis of *The Possessed* stressed Dostoevsky's "revolutionary insight," even in the absence of radical ideas. In Dostoevsky's nineteenth-century work, Rahv found lessons about Stalinism. "Stalinism is, in one sense, Nechayevism [the political movement in the novel] plus state power. Stalinism, too, acts 'for the masses' instead of with and through them." The attempt to overthrow the czar without mass support "is equivalent to Stalin's attempt to build socialism in Russia in isolation from the fate of the international working class." The central split between Trotsky and Stalin, the question of extending socialism or strengthening it in the Soviet Union, became a guide for Rahv's evaluation of Dostoevsky. And Dostoevsky's pre-1917 insights became a guide for the understanding of postrevolutionary ideas. In a conclusion he italicized, Rahv declared, "If Nechayevism represents the pre-Marxist stage of revolution Stalinism represents its post-Marxist one."[39]

A series of personal considerations supplemented the political and cultural issues tying the *Partisan* writers and Trotsky. Again, these did not prompt any mass enlistment in the Socialist Workers party, but they sustained the intellectuals' inclination toward the fallen Soviet leader. Trotsky himself, quite apart from his political or culture notions, was an appealing figure for the young radicals—a man of words *and* a man of action. He not only wrote, as many radicals do, but wrote brilliantly—a serious political thinker as well as a polemicist. "Even his critics recognized Trotsky's brilliance as a writer," James T. Farrell wrote in *PR*, "but his work is more brilliant—it is furtive, suggestive, illuminating. Compared to its method, acuteness and high seriousness, the productions of our American political scientists and journalists seem morally flabby, spineless, full of facile improvisations." Farrell's sentiments were echoed by many other *PR* writers. "Trotsky is indisputably the most brilliant Marxist in the world today," Sidney Hook acknowledged, "a Marxist in blood, temperament, and concrete logic."[40] As an intellectual and a writer, Trotsky belonged in the first rank.

His personal appeal, however, went beyond his intellectual capacities. He applied his brilliance to the real world of practical politics, bringing his insights and intellect to bear on the problems which faced him in czarist Russia. "Trotsky made history, and kept an eye on history," Irving Howe would later conclude. "He was a man of heroic mold, entirely committed to the life of action, but he was also an intellectual who believed in the power and purity of the word."[41] No brief characterization could more clearly define the personal ambitions of these young radicals as they moved through the political and cultural movements of the 1930s and found their eventual home around *Partisan Review*. Trotsky's example demonstrated the possibility of pursuing both intellectual and political goals.

Many *Partisan* writers fastened onto Trotsky in an uncritical way, idolizing his skills, overvaluing his contributions, and finding reflections of their own calling in his actions. It was Trotsky, Rahv declared, "under whose direct leadership the October insurrection was carried through." Dwight Macdonald proclaimed the Russian's virtues in terms fitting the *Partisan* model of the radical intellectuals.

> This passionate doer, this incarnation of revolutionary will and energy who planned and directed the October revolution and created the Red Army, was also a literary man, with all the professional delight of a man of letters opening books and in turning over the pages of a freshly printed volume. For relaxation on the military train that bore him from one front to another, he read French novels.

Trotsky's career, Macdonald later concluded, "showed that intellectuals, too, could make history."[42]

A final attribute of Trotsky's helped cement the *emotional* relationship between him and many of the young radical critics and writers. He was a Jew. Trotsky, like the young men from immigrant ghettos, was not devout—this was an age of radical cosmopolitanism. Still, childhoods in the Jewish communities created invisible ties which would continually direct the young radicals' lives. So, too, did the unstated awareness of Trotsky's Jewishness provide a final psychological link. He was all they were or wished to be—a young Jew who coupled his radical commitment with his intellectual abilities to lead what *PR* writers deemed the most important event in radical history, the Bolshevik Revolution.

As a role model, Trotsky had the perfect combination of radicalism and intellectuality, and thus he would very likely have been held in high regard by the *Partisan* writers no matter what the circumstances. The limited plain of radical anti-Stalinism, his willingness to contribute to *PR*, and his correspondence with a number of the individuals around the journal only served further to tighten the connection. In a period when *Partisan Review* attempted to establish its own credentials in the turbulent world of radical political journalism, any link with a figure as important as Trotsky proved heartening. After receiving Trotsky's 1938 article "Art and Politics," William Phillips wrote to F. W. Dupee, "The Trotsky piece certainly justifies our having wanted something of this kind from him." The entire issue, which caused such consternation in the radical literary world, seemed "pretty well balanced and exciting" to Phillips.[43] The New York Intellectuals were still young and relatively unknown. Trotsky was old, famous, and a giant of twentieth-century radicalism. To correspond with the great man, to have him as a contributor, helped put *PR* on the radical map, as surely as their stands on literature and art did. "May your magazine take its place in the victorious army of socialism," Trotsky wrote to *Partisan Review*.[44] Although they denied the Stalinist contention that *PR* was a Trotskyite organ, nonetheless, for personal as well as political reasons, the editors and many contributors were closer to Trotsky than their denials of formal attachments indicate. In a period when *Partisan Review* sought to define its place among radical intellectuals and when political positions often centered on attitudes about Stalinism and the Popular Front, Trotsky and Trotskyism formed a crucial element of the intellectual complexion of the journal. While never a "Trotskyite organ," *Partisan Review* spent several years within the orbit created by Trotsky, thrown into that circle by the flight from the Stalinist world and drawn by the gravitational force of the great man.

THE AMERICAN BOURGEOIS FRONT

The histories of the United Front Against Fascism and *Partisan Review* intertwined even before *PR*'s break with the Stalinist camp. The formation in 1935 of the Popular Front, as it was called, led to the dissolution of the John Reed Clubs and their replacement with the League of American Writers. While not initially opposed to this change, *Partisan Review*'s editors discovered that their position was relatively smaller in the impressive world of the American Writers' Congress than it had been in the John Reed Clubs. When Rahv and Phillips began to articulate their criticisms of proletarian literature, Granville Hicks presented this countercritique at a congress session. In the very period when radical literature, like radicalism in general, attempted to widen its base of support, *Partisan Review* began its move away from radical literature. The "new" *PR*'s identity derived, in part, from differences with the Popular Front and its cultural arm, the League of American Writers. From the inception of the Popular Front, the *PR* writers reacted with a good measure of ambivalence, which ultimately turned into hostility. Once the *Partisan* editors broke with the Communists, their joining the Popular Front never was a serious possibility. A variety of personal, political, and cultural differences kept the *PR* writers out of the alliance. This steadfast resistance to any connection with the united antifascist effort proved their most publicly recognizable attribute. Other political positions were less precise. The revisions of Marx varied, and the connection of Trotsky remained vague and undefined. Even the positions concerning literature and intellectual activities emerged only over the course of several years' writings. Their attitude toward the Popular Front, however, remained clear and consistent. They opposed the Front directly on political and cultural grounds. Among many pro-Fronters, the opposition of *PR* provided an additional verification of *PR*'s Trotskyist ties, because the followers of Trotsky also opposed the Popular Front. Although both groups were against the Front, their rationales often differed.

The *PR* writers were opposed not to the idea of a united front but to this front at this time. In the *Modern Monthly* of July 1934, for example, Sidney Hook described the failure of the German left to unite in the face of fascism: "The tactic of the united front in its classic form of organization . . . should have been followed all along the line." It should have been official, public, and clear, Hook maintained. Communist resistance to joining other non-Communist leftists, whom they branded as social fascists, proved self-destructive. In the June 1934 issue of the *Modern Monthly*, Elliot Cohen, former managing editor of the *Menorah Journal* and later founder of *Commentary*, called for an American united front. Commenting on the May Day parade in New York, Cohen noted that "every capitalist newspaper" would be "gleeful" over the divisions among the marchers. "The 'Communist parade' . . . was a parade of the offical Communist Party," While "the 'Socialist parade' was no better, no worse, than the Stalinists . . . . As a genuine broad proletarian united front, it achieved little more than the Communist parody."[45] In the early 1930s the idea of a left front was less alien to some of these intellectuals.

By the late 1930s Socialists and Communists had come together, along with the New Dealers and other moderate and leftist groups. *PR* now opposed the common front. Uppermost in the minds of the *PR* intellectuals was the role of the Communists. This anti-Stalinism paralleled the Trotskyist opposition. Yet the differences between the *PR* and Trotskyist critiques of the Popular Front provide another example of the distinctiveness of the camps. Trotsky was mistaken, Philip Rahv argued, in his assumption that Stalin had capitulated to the bourgeois democratic states by joining the Front. Rather, Rahv maintained,

it is plain that only in appearance did the People's Front strategy indicate the relinquishment of independent positions in favor of democratic capitalism. In reality it was a strategy of deception calculated to extract from capitalism what it could give by way of political and material aid while withholding all return-payments except verbal promises and such purely formal concessions as the dissolution of the Comintern.

The other members of the Front compromised principles, Rahv believed. Having long since abandoned theirs, the Stalinists remained free to manipulate others. "Instead of Stalin it was his allies who grovelled," Rahv contended.[46]

Prior to 1935 the Communists resisted all attempts at forging a left unity. The new call for unity, Sidney Hook later contended, was actually "the tactics of the Trojan Horse," organizing "mass infiltrations" and "speak[ing] the language of the New Deal." They hid their communism under a more appealing umbrella, Diana Trilling believed, offering "anti-fascism or peace or some other decent abstract ideal virtually indistinguishable from the traditional ideals of liberalism." Full of deception, "the Communist Party learned to keep a safe distance from the gullible souls it was manipulating to its own purposes." It became the self-assigned task of the *Partisan* intellectuals to expose this manipulation. "The handful of liberals . . . who had sufficient experience" tried, according to Trilling, "to warn the innocents in this country that they were being used."[47] The warnings fell on deaf ears. Isolated because of their radicalism and ethnic background, the *Partisan* crowd, as a result of its opposition to the Popular Front, was moved closer to the periphery. Whatever they thought of the Communists, large segments of the American political and intellectual community in the late 1930s did not agree with *PR*'s stand.

Opposition to the Popular Front did give these intellectuals the opportunity to reclaim the mantle of radical purity and to restate their position about the actual nonradicalism of the Communists. The sight of Communists and New Dealers joining forces provided easy targets. On the one hand Rahv disagreed with Trotsky's claim that Stalin had capitulated to the bourgeois democracies; on the other hand Rahv saw the Stalinists as selling out their radicalism by supporting the Popular Front. "To lead writers to abandon their revolutionary direction for the sake of defending the bourgeois democratic order," Rahv accused the Second Writers' Congress, "is nothing short of betrayal. The Stalinists have converted anti-fascism into the latest rationale for defending the status-quo."[48] Depending on the issue, the *PR* criticism of the Popular Front tried to have it both ways. Anxious to proclaim their own radicalism, the *PR* writers charged that radical groups who joined the Popular Front were capitulating. Sidney Hook held that a "socialist who calls for the formation of a Popular Front cannot do so without in effect surrendering socialism." In fact, the Popular Front's "defense of capitalism . . . may open the gates to the fascists who are even more resolute defenders of capitalism." Of the Popular Front mind, Rahv would later write, "I see that mind not only as unrevolutionary but as profoundly bourgeois in its political amorphousness, evasion of historical choice, and search for formulas of empty reassurance." A mind willing to accommodate, it proved totally unprepared to deal with the Communists, "particularly so when the [Communists] oblige by playing the game of not being 'real Communists' at all but democrats of the extreme left."[49]

An additional dispute developed between the *Partisan* intellectuals and those connected with the Popular Front, one which spoke directly to the basic issues prompting *PR*'s break with Stalinism. This argument continued after the breakup of the Popular Front in the wake of the Nazi-Soviet pact of 1939. Under the influence of the Popular Front, the notions about radical literature within the proletarian-culture movement expanded, as the League of American Writers sought to broaden both the base and the membership of the movement. Several of the emerging literary trends and cultural notions disturbed the *PR* critics.

At the First Writers' Congress, Kenneth Burke had provoked a storm of criticism by suggesting that a literary focus on "the worker" was too narrow and that he favored broadening the symbol to "the people." This had met with a hailstorm of abuse, including allusions to Hitler's use of the concept *Volk*. By the time of the Second Writers' Congress, in 1937, the cultural notions of the Popular Front had moved in the direction Burke had suggested. Newton Arvin's paper, printed first in the published collection from the proceedings, typified the new approach. Entitled "The Democratic Tradition in American Letters," it sought to capture the "spirit [of the] inheritance . . . we have in common with a long series of men and women in all generations of American literature." While leftists study Pushkin, Dostoevsky, and Proust, Arvin complained, "we have not yet heard quite enough—or have heard from the wrong quarters—of Thomas Hooker and John Woolman . . . of Parker, of Howells, of Hamlin Garland." He concluded by quoting Whitman: "I speak the password primeval, I give the sign democracy."[50]

The *Partisan* critics, still committed to a cosmopolitanism devoid of national identities and still champions of the modernist cause, singled out this trend as an example of the wrongheadedness of the Popular Front's cultural program. This controversy drove straight to the basic conceptions of art which distinguished the two groups. A cosmopolitan culture, rooted in the dynamics of the interplay between society and the avant-garde, emerged as a cornerstone of the *Partisan* conception of "revolutionary" art. The call for a uniquely American literature undermined this position.

Personalities, as well as positions, shifted in the battles between *PR* and the Popular Front. As the League of American Writers attracted well-known literary figures, the individuals subjected to critical assessment changed. In addition, many of the more famous members were the very intellectuals arguing the new "American" line. Thus, *PR* abuse of Communists like Gold and Freeman declined, replaced by criticisms of more prominent critics like Archibald MacLeish and Van Wyck Brooks. Furthermore, the patriotism and drumbeating for war, which swelled in the late 1930s and which the Popular Front joined, fit easily into the revived interest in "American" themes. Even after the Popular Front had fallen apart, the renewed interest in American culture continued. Brooks, in the midst of writing his massive account of nineteenth-century New Engand culture, and MacLeish, the poet and the Librarian of Congress, became frequent *PR* targets.

F. W. Dupee sounded the first major *PR* attack on this position in 1939, shortly before the breakup of the Popular Front, in an article entitled "The

Americanism of Van Wyck Brooks." After praising, with some reservations, Brooks's early work, Dupee took exception to the turns Brooks's criticism had taken. Dupee noted that Brooks had once characterized the nineteenth century as "an age of rude, vague, boisterous, dyspeptic causes." Now Brooks described it as a period of "a noble chivalry to which provinciality was almost a condition." Brooks's prose, Dupee wrote, "evokes images of mountain streams, his passage through the New England world is accompanied by the springing up of greenery and flowers." To Dupee this was more than the rediscovering of a glorious past; he called Brooks's attitude "anti-modernist" and accused Brooks of employing Spengler's "celebrated antinomy between 'culture' and 'civilization.'" Beyond this crucial question lay an even more disturbing trend, Dupee argued.

> Brooks' latest utterances suggest that a further shift has occurred and that in his mind the antithesis between New England and the megalopolis may have been replaced in importance by the antithesis between America, conceived as a politico-cultural totality, and fascist Europe.

This conclusion once again demonstrated the misapplication of culture, Dupee believed. As the proletarian critics bent their literary notions to a Stalinist political end, so the critics calling for a uniquely American culture fit their cultural notions to their political goals. As evidence, Dupee pointed to a speech Brooks had delivered before a chapter of the League of American Writers. "We are Americans," Dupee quoted Brooks as having said, "and Americans are born free. We are prepared to show that this country can do something better than fascism or communism."

Brooks began as a critic who called into question the prevailing American standards, Dupee concluded. "Today [he] ends by affirming them. The powerful critic of the United States has turned into a zealous curator of its antiquities." Not only is the Brooks thesis inappropriate; it is a fiction. "In order to finally accomplish his great purpose of reconciling the artist with American society he has had recourse to an already distant past, and a past, moreover, which is largely the projection of his own fancy." A past which provides keys to the present does exist, and that past has an American component, Dupee believed. To counterpose Brooks's view, Dupee called on one of the heroes of modernism. "In the end the United States has become to Van Wyck Brooks the fairy-tale it never was to Henry James; for whatever may have been the attitude of James to Europe, it is certain that he had no illusions about middle-class America." Just as Brooks is no Spenglerian, the world which Brooks believes "flowered" is not the same late-nineteenth-century America which Henry James rejected. Nonetheless, Dupee underpins his criticism of Brooks with references to *Partisan* villains and heroes alike. If Brooks can be shown to be both pro-Spengler and anti-James, his position is further diminished.[51]

Another supporter of the renewed interest in American culture, Archibald MacLeish, came under severe criticism in *PR* for his views both on literature and on intellectuals. Early in the decade MacLeish had argued stongly against intellectuals aligning themselves with political movements, especially with the Communists. During that period the future *Partisan* writers had done exactly this. By the decade's end the positions had been somewhat reversed. *PR* did not abjure politics in the way MacLeish had previously suggested, nor did he commit himself to a particular political movement as radical writers had done earlier. Nonetheless, *PR* now favored independence as a central prerequisite for intellectual activity, and MacLeish attacked "irresponsible" intellectuals who failed to respond to the fascist challenge. "The men of intellectual duty, those who should have been responsible for action, have divided themselves into two castes, two cults—the scholars and the writers," MacLeish wrote. "Neither accepts responsibility for the common culture or for its defense."[52] The scholars, he argued, dwelt only in the past, writers only in the present. They failed to grasp the truths and insights offered by the other and thus failed to fulfill their intellectual calling.

Brooks presented an assessment parallel to that of MacLeish, dividing writers into primary and secondary camps. The primary writer became the "responsible" intellectual in MacLeish's assessment. "A great man writing," Brooks claimed,

> is one who bespeaks the collective life of the people, of his group, of his nation, of mankind; and every great man writing knows what men and women are and what they have it in them to become—through him humanity breathes and thinks and sings.[53]

These arguments about Americanism and intellectual calling met with derision in *Partisan Review*, lumped into what became known as the Brooks-MacLeish thesis. Dwight Macdonald rose to respond to this position, calling it *Kulturbolshewismus*. Hidden in the Brooks-MacLeish thesis, Macdonald argued, were problems which extended beyond good and bad writng. Their arguments in fact pointed to "an official approach to art" and had as their aim "the protection of a historically reactionary form of society against the free inquiry and criticism of the intelligentsia." The Brooks-MacLeish thesis, if successful, would undermine basic tenets of the *Partisan* position—the primacy of high culture and the special role of intellectuals in society—and would lead to the legitimizing of Stalinists in the American intellectual and cultural community. In addition, using the attributes Brooks cited for his support of primary writers, Macdonald drew a composite of the secondary writer. Not only was the picture which emerged negative but this view of a secondary or "coterie" writer appeared very much like a hostile portrait of modernist and, especially, *Partisan* writers. The coterie writer, Macdonald said,

> is a thin-blooded, niggling sort of fellow, whose work reaches a "mere handful of readers." His stuff has brilliant "form" but lacks "content." He is a "mere artificer or master of words," who perversely celebrates the "death-drive" instead of the

"life-drive." He is a doubter, a scorner, a sceptic, expatriate, highbrow and city slicker.

Finally, as though the preceding problems were insufficient, Macdonald leveled the ultimate charge at Brooks and MacLeish. If this official approach to art took root, Macdonald prophesied, America would witness the first stirrings of totalitarianism. "Where have we seen this all before?" he asked. "Where have we known this confusion of social and literary values, this terrible *hatred* of all that is most living in modern culture? . . . I say these are the specific methods of the Moscow Trials."[54] Thus, Macdonald reunited the two strains in the League of American Writers which *PR* opposed—Stalinism and the promotion of a uniquely American culture. The ideas were wrong, and the political potential embodied in the ideas was wrong.

The war in Europe only intensified the problem. Even before Brooks's and MacLeish's articles appeared, *PR* published the response of the League for Cultural Freedom and Socialism to the coming war. The league's position pointed in the direction of Macdonald's *Kulturbolshewismus* conclusions:

> If in the totalitarian state intellectual life is an affair for the police, in America it is preparing, under the pressure of anti-fascist hysteria, for voluntary abdication. Cultural circles, formerly progressive, are now capitulating to the spirit of fascism while ostensibly combating its letter. They fight one falsehood with another. To the deification of Hitler and Mussolini they counterpose the deification of Stalin, the unqualified support of Roosevelt. The mysticism of "Aryan" supremacy they match with a national-democratic myth conjured out of America's historic infancy. To the war drive of the fascist powers they reply with a drive of their own.[55]

The league statement can be seen as the clearest articulation of the anti-Front position taken by *PR*. The Popular Front, as the New York Intellectuals saw it, proved crass, bourgeois, and hostile to modern culture. Its sponsors were themselves Stalinists hiding their own political ambitions behind benign phrases.

Until America's actual entry into the war, *Partisan Review* maintained this independent position. War and the pressure it brought changed the situation. In the years between the revival of the journal and Pearl Harbor, however, the *Partisan* intellectuals marked out a largely definable territory for themselves and occupied the space with relative consistency. Some issues, such as Marxist revisionism, underwent change and readjustments, but the large perimeter remained. General agreement among themselves, however, did not mean immediate acceptance of their positions in the larger intellectual or cultural world. That recognition came in future years. They were a herd of independent minds, as Harold Rosenberg later called them, but at least by 1940 they ran as a herd.

Within a few years, the questions raised by the war and the postwar world once again caused them to readjust and rethink their positions. They also discovered that a number of crucial concerns which had gone unspoken during the 1930s, questions carried from childhood and from the immigrant neighborhoods, emerged to cause additional reevaluations. The seeming resolution of the "*Partisan* mind" proved temporary. Personality clashes would reshuffle the "*Partisan* family" as intellectual debates redefined the "mind." By 1940 the intellectual migration of the New York Intellectuals had come not to a halt but rather to a rest. They had established a position which gave their beliefs the solidity of a philosophical stance and had founded a magazine in which to argue that position. After the tumult of the 1930s—personal, political, and cultural—they achieved something of a stasis, even if one which proved remarkably short-lived.

Section III

PRODIGAL SONS

Chapter 7

Partisan Warfare

The solid base which the "new" *Partisan Review* offered the New York Intellectuals helped them resolve a number of basic difficulties and questions which had plagued them for years. The magazine carved a place for itself on the intellectual left, as its contributors mapped out their own political and cultural positions and priorities. As a capstone to their anti–Stalinist and anti–Popular Front efforts, the stunning announcement of the Nazi-Soviet nonaggression pact in 1939 allowed the *PR* intellectuals to gloat a bit over this seeming vindication of their position and allowed them to return a measure of the scorn which had been leveled at them by the Popular Fronters. An editorial of the fall of 1939 reminded the readers which group best served radical interests:

> The exposure of Stalinism as the implacable enemy of the international working class had to come sooner or later, and it will be in the long run a healthy and progressive development. But the immediate effects are shattering and demoralizing. The labor and socialist movement the world over has hardly been in a century in such a state of collapse as today. For this tragic situation the Kremlin and its dupes and agents—the [Earl] Browders [American secretary of the Communist party] and . . . the [Corliss] Lamonts and [John] Stracheys and [Malcolm] Cowleys and [Max] Lerners and [Granville] Hicks . . . must bear full responsibility.[1]

Years later Lionel Abel noted a second effect of the pact: "It was the shock of this event, I think, which started New York City, bitter and demoralized, back from the U.S.S.R., to America."[2]

The period of the Second World War did not, however, bring as much harmony or unity for the New York Intellectuals as the ideas and events of 1939 had promised. Just as the world was thrown into tumult, so was this intellectual community. Personalities clashed, and ideas changed. As ever, outside events influenced internal actions. Also as ever, the volatile individuals clustered around *PR* continued their personal frictions and their constant shuffling of friends and sleeping partners. At the center of both the personal and the political interactions sat Philip Rahv, his personal life and politics inextricably bound to the magazine. Mary McCarthy's leaving Philip Rahv might normally have prompted some gossip. For her to leave Rahv for Edmund Wilson added the kind of intellectual and political dimension which often energized the community but blurred the lines between gossip and intellectualism. Wilson had been the consummate intellectual model, a figure inspiring awe and envy. Now he had taken Rahv's "girl." In a world in which the personal and the professional are more clearly separated, Rahv as well as Wilson and McCarthy might have gone their own ways. But in the incestuous intellectual world in which they all lived, relations with one another had to be revised so that they could all go on. Wilson and McCarthy still published in *PR*, and *PR* still needed and liked Wilson's inclusion. Yet relations grew strained. In 1940 Wilson wrote to F. W. Dupee complaining about the treatment he and McCarthy were receiving at the hands of the *PR* editors. "I've thought there was something wrong in your shop ever since you passed up that short story of Mary's," Wilson wrote. "You people owed her a chance to develop, since she was one of your original group." Concerning his own issues, Wilson felt miffed that after Dwight Macdonald had kept after him for months to do a piece on Lenin, he was being sent back this piece with the suggestion that he do "a little something on the younger novelists." "You are developing all the symptoms of the occupational disease of editors," he concluded his letter, "among them, thinking up idiotic ideas for articles that you want the writers to write instead of printing what they want to write."[3]

If Wilson still needed to publish in *PR*, Rahv could still make use of Wilson. During the same period, McCarthy mentioned in a note to Dupee, "We got Philip's Guggenheim project. Edmund gave him a very strong recommendation. I thought the project sounded wonderful." And then, with a typical personal-political transition, in her next sentence she asked Dupee, "What do you think of Trotsky's new line?"[4]

The early 1940s also almost separated Rahv from the magazine he founded. After breaking up with Mary McCarthy, Rahv married an architect, Nathalie Swan. In the spring of 1941 they went to Chicago, where she had a job. "It was not clear whether they would stay there and thus he would have to leave the magazine," Phillips recalled. The ties proved too strong. Rahv wrote back to his fellow editors, "You've probably heard that we plan to return East in October . . . keep my name on the masthead." Even after leaving Chicago, Nathalie continued to find work, and Rahv could stay doing what he loved best. "In Nathalie," William Barrett observed, "he had a perpetual Guggenheim."[5]

Personality shifts, changing partners, and new friendships are often easier to chart than intellectual developments. The generally difficult problem of following political and cultural lines becomes even harder for the World War II years. A nation at war proved a very different influence from a society in economic disarray. Questions of patriotism supplemented considerations of social reform. And the passage of time, often unnoticed amid the concerns of war, took its effect. From the beginning of the European war until the final victory over Japan, six years elapsed—as much time as *PR* had been publishing before the war. The editors grew older, new individuals joined the magazine and the community, and ideas which had been shifting before the war continued their evolutionary process. Yet, one gets a sense that real time was frozen during war, as though the society at home had been on hold, waiting for the international situation to resolve itself. Despite continuing political debates and serious internal changes, something of this sense of frozenness pervaded the intellectual world around *Partisan Review*. We can chronicle the intellectual debates and the shifting roster of personalities, but the full impact of these changes did not become apparent until after 1945.

At war's end *Partisan Review* and the New York Intellectuals entered a new phase, a new era. They left behind the world of Depression America and sectarian radicalism. Before them stretched not a newly unified and harmonious nation but a society tensed by new concerns. For the intellectuals themselves, the postwar years presented the opportunity to argue and act their intellectual position in an atmosphere largely uncluttered by the debates of the thirties. New questions arose, and, out of the war, an essential component of their character—their Jewishness—reemerged to demand attention. More than they knew, much of their intellectual and personal agenda quietly underwent significant rewriting during the war, the implications of which would become fully understood only in years to come.

PROPOSITIONS ABOUT THE WAR

Throughout the late 1930s the *Partisan* writers steadfastly opposed involvement in the travails of European politics. Their stand against the Popular Front combined with their radical beliefs to form a position of neutrality. "Fascism in bourgeois countries is not inevitable," Sidney Hook had written as early as 1936, "but it cannot be staved off by a united front for *bourgeois* democracy." The Munich crisis did not stir *Partisan Review*. In fact, the journal attacked those intellectuals who called for war. "If the Czech crisis did not come to war," the editors wrote in 1938, "it was certainly not the fault of the intellectual left. . . . It would almost seem that the peculiar function of the intellectuals is to idealize imperialist wars when they come and debunk them after they are over." Radical intellectuals had no business, Philip Rahv argued, taking sides in "this contest of national imperialisms. Who will annihilate the potential German revolution, if not the French and British imperialists—once they have removed Hitler?"[6]

Reasserting the same claim to radical purity which marked their opposition to proletarian literature and the Popular Front, the *PR* editors maintained that once intellectuals became involved with the bourgeois order, they could not escape it. "Tying themselves to the bourgeois war machines, the intellectuals have given up their privilege—and duty—of criticizing class values," Dwight Macdonald warned. Even though intellectuals assumed they could return to their dutiful paths and progressive goals after the war, Macdonald cautioned, "In politics, however, the mask molds the face. You become what you do and say; you don't become what your reservations are."[7]

With the outbreak of the European war, the position of the New York Intellectuals proved consistent with their prewar position. The League for Cultural Freedom and Socialism, which had initially been formed to defend artistic independence among radicals, now added nonparticipation in the war to its political program. In a statement signed by all the previous signers, save one, and by a number of new individuals, the LCFS outlined its position in the pages of *Partisan Review*:[8]

We loathe and abominate fascism as the chief enemy of all culture, all real democracy, all social progress. But the last war showed only too clearly that we can have no faith in imperialist crusades to bring freedom to any people. Our entry into the war, under the slogan of "Stop Hitler!" would actually result in the immediate introduction of totalitarianism over here. Only the German people can free themselves of the fascist yoke. The American masses can best help them by fighting *at home* to keep their own liberties.

The war issue most intimately concerns American intellectuals. . . . What can American artists and writers do at this time?

In a practical, immediate sense, they can help make articulate the strong opposition which the great majority of the American people still feel to our entry into the war. . . . In a more general sense, American writers and artists must put themselves on record against the war as a symbol of their acceptance of the responsibilities of their profession. In the last war, a whole generation of writers committed spiritual suicide by taking part in the orgy. If only for the sake of their own integrity, American intellectuals must now signalize their opposition not only to war in the abstract but specifically to American entry into this war. It would be a betrayal of the human spirit for them to keep silent at this time.[9]

Partisan Review echoed the general themes of the LCFS statement in various editorials and articles during 1940. "The more the allies are exhausted by the war," *PR* argued, "the better for the interests of American capitalism."[10]

The period of the "phony war," between the German invasion of Poland in September 1939 and of France in June 1940, allowed Dwight Macdonald to reiterate the basic antiwar theme. "The most hopeful thing about this war is that the masses on both sides of the battle-lines seem to have already reached the same state of apathy and sullen war-weariness as came only after two or three years of the last war," he observed. Macdonald attributed this development to the inability of the masses to accept either alternative. "Tomorrow," he hoped, "they may find a common revolutionary destiny in that 'Third Camp,' whose interests lie with neither of the two warring imperialist camps."[11]

The future held, however, not a swing of the masses away from the camps of the belligerents but a swing of a good number of the *Partisan* neutrals to the side of the "imperialist powers." While Macdonald continued to argue his antiwar stand, others at the magazine began to hedge on the position of the LCFS statement of 1939. In 1941 Macdonald and Clement Greenberg, now an editor of *PR*, published their "Ten Propositions on the War," a major restatement of the radical antiwar position which had been argued since the late 1930s. Once again they dissociated themselves from the war effort, saying it would lead to a strengthening of American capitalism and, ultimately, to the arrival of fascism. Only revolutionary mass action could achieve the socialist alternative. Macdonald and Greenberg attacked the "line which most of the left today favors" and named the liberal weeklies, the labor bureaucracy, and ex-Marxists like Max Eastman, Lewis Corey, and Sidney Hook as examples. These liberals argued the "lesser of two evils" position, which opted for Roosevelt and Churchill over Hitler. "The lesser evil policy meant toleration of the existing system," Macdonald and Greenberg held, and "capitalism is *intolerable*."[12]

Rather than one of these liberals answering Macdonald and Greenberg in the pages of *PR*, opposition came from an unexpected figure, Philip Rahv. In the first clear, public break by a *PR* editor from the antiwar line, Rahv responded with "Ten Propositions and Eight Errors." He began by arguing against the "morally absolutist" position of Macdonald and Greenberg. In an un-characteristically modest tone, Rahv chastised his coeditors for feeling "still sure they knew all the answers." Which side prevailed should not become a matter of indifference, Rahv argued. Although a "bourgeois-democratic victory . . . will not bring socialism," he wrote, "it will, on the other hand, bring us quite a few steps nearer 'the real solution' by giving the labor movement an opportunity to take stock of itself, to regroup its forces, and, if so minded, to resume the struggle for a fundamental reconstruction of society." Having argued only three years before that taking sides in this "contest of national imperialisms" was not the business of radical intellectuals, Rahv now concluded that "whereas a Nazi victory would bury the revolution for good, the chances are that a Nazi defeat would recreate the conditions for progressive action."[13]

Even before America's actual entry into the war, it became evident that the previously solid position of the League for Cultural Freedom and Socialism (which both Rahv and Phillips endorsed) was eroding in the editorial meetings of *Partisan Review* and among the members of its intellectual community. There is little doubt that the once abstract questions of war, fascism, and survival now became very realistic. By late 1941 the European war was fully raging; France had fallen, and the German invasion of the Soviet Union had begun. The coalition of the Stalinists and the Nazis, which seemed so appropriate for the worldview of the left anti-Stalinists, had given way to a strong united front among the antifascist allies, including Stalin's Russia. The issues in the debate grew increasingly intense, and the personalities as well as the perspectives of the debates influenced the arguments. "When it comes to anything practical," Macdonald recalled, "I must say I never expected either Rahv or Phillips to be heroic or, even, reasonably courageous. They were quite timid in anything having to do with possible dangers of any kind."[14] In Macdonald's opinion, the danger of being highly unpopular proved too great for Rahv and Phillips. To argue against imperialist wars being fought by other nations is vastly different from opposing one's own nation once war is declared. The issue went beyond questions of principle, as the editors discussed the possibility that the magazine might be shut down by the government for an antiwar position.[15] Having worked so hard to define their own position in American society and to establish the place of *Partisan Review* among American intellectuals, Phillips, Rahv, and many of the others considered the risks of opposition to the war too great.

When the war came, the divergency of views which had developed among the editors was evident in the ambivalent position taken in the *PR* editorial. "It is clear," they wrote, "that PARTISAN REVIEW can have no editorial line on the war. Its editors will continue to express themselves on the issue as individuals . . . . Our main task now is to preserve cultural values against all types of pressure and coercion."[16] This general statement, with reference to the disagreements among the editors, masked the intense debates at *PR*. To many outside the magazine, *PR* began to "stumble and equivocate," as Irving Howe criticized in 1942. In-house, civil war raged—the most serious split to occur at the magazine since the break with proletarian literature. The war pulled the editors apart. Macdonald later remembered, "I didn't feel I had any support. I offered that either you [Phillips and Rahv] take it over or I will. I said, 'If you can get financing by fall or something like that, you do it, and if you can't then I'll try to do it.' "[17] By fall Phillips and Rahv had found it, and Macdonald resigned from the magazine.

In his resignation letter, published in the July–August 1943 issue, Macdonald argued that he favored a less exclusively "literary" approach. The political attributes of *PR*, he argued, had always distinguished it from literary journals like the *Southern Review* and *Kenyon Review*. The war changed all this. "Not only has the Marxist position been reduced to a minority of one—myself—but since Pearl Harbor there has been a tendency on the part of some editors to eliminate political discussion entirely." In their response Rahv and Phillips fell back on the position used during the last significant upheaval in the *PR* editorial board, that over the criticism of the Stalinists in 1936 and 1937:

> We regret . . . that Macdonald allowed himself to be carried away by his political passions. What he wanted was to abandon the cultural policy of *PR* and to transform it into a political magazine with literary trimmings. The use of literature as bait is a familiar strategy of left-wing politicians.[18]

Macdonald went on to found his own magazine, *Politics*, maintained his opposition to the war, and moved out of the core of the New York Intellectual community, although remaining a part of the New York scene. While other members went on to found *Commentary* and *Dissent* in the postwar years, Macdonald joined the *New Yorker*. His writings, especially those on mass culture, remained influential. Dwight Macdonald's closeness to the *Partisan* circle, his split from the magazine, and his subsequent endeavors illustrate the further development of the community. Just as new members moved to the center, older ones moved to the periphery.

NEW NERVE AND A NEW CAPITAL

Dwight Macdonald's claim that by abandoning politics *Partisan Review* lost its distinctiveness from other literary magazines was not entirely accurate. Political articles still appeared in *Partisan*, though Macdonald was quite accurate in his castigation of his fellow editors for dropping Marxism. As the various editors and writers continued to shift and revise their Marxist notions, the trend pointed away from Marx rather than toward a renewed faith. Once again, Sidney Hook emerged as the central figure in this ongoing debate. His political voice soon replaced Macdonald's at the magazine, and his contributions in the middle 1940s offered a clear sign of how thinking had changed.

In 1943 Hook published *The Hero in History*, the book which marked the end of his Marxist period and set forth a worldview he would have shunned only a decade earlier. "Either the main line of historical action and social development is literally inescapable or it is not," Hook wrote at the beginning of his work. "If it is, any existing leadership is a completely subsidiary element in determining the main historical pattern of today and tomorrow. If it is not inescapable, the question asks itself: to what extent is the character of a given leadership causally and, since men are involved, morally responsible for our historical position and future?" Hook chose the second alternative and denied the inescapability of the future. The case for determinism, he believed, had demonstrated only that "a great man cannot influence history until the times are 'ripe' for him."[19] Hook had argued this theme for years. In the contest between personal and social forces—in a rough sense between Hook's Deweyism and Marxism—he had always kept the balance between them, tempering the influence of one with the influence of the other.[20] In *The Hero in History* Hook tilted to the side of the hero. Even if the times were "ripe," a number of alternative developments would be possible. This situation, Hook believed, was "the presupposition of significant heroic action." He elaborated:

> What we are asserting is that in such situations the great man is a relatively independent historical influence—*independent of the conditions that determine the alternatives*—and that on these occasions the influence of all other relevant factors is of subordinate weight in enabling us to understand or predict which one of the possible alternatives will be actualized.

Lenin, Hook's frequent example, now emerged as a typical "hero." Hook
argued that "had it not been for the work of one man we should be living in a
different world today."[22]

In a democracy, Hook concluded, the problem of the hero proved more
knotty. The "potential hero" does not want to make himself independent of
the majority, but by his vision, his will, and his knowledge he is more likely
than not to be in the minority. "His sense of his vocation impels him to fight
for his insight. His loyalty to the democratic ideal compels him to make this
insight the common faith of the majority." Thus, the individual must not
renounce politics as a sphere of action but must continually work to influence
others.[22]

In addition to vintage Deweyism, Hook's argument about the role of
"potential heroes" in democratic society reflects a second concern, one which
he argued in *Partisan Review*, also in 1943. "The New Failure of Nerve," Hook
called it, and he identified as the nerveless such contemporary thinkers as
Reinhold Niebuhr and Jaques Maritain. This attitude cropped up in a number
of modes and in a variety of idioms, but Hook drew a composite of it. These
thinkers, he wrote, are marked by a belief in

> the original depravity of human nature; prophecies of doom for western culture, no
> matter who wins the war or peace, dressed up as laws of social dynamics; the
> frenzied search for a center of value that transcends human interests; the mystical
> apotheosis of "the leader" and elites; contempt for all political organizations and
> social programs because of the obvious failure of some of them, together with a
> belief that good will is sufficient to settle thorny problems of economic and social
> reconstruction; posturing about the cultivation of spiritual purity; the refurbishing
> of theological and metaphysical dogmas about the infinite as necessary pre-
> suppositions of knowledge of the finite; a concern with mystery rather than with
> problems, and the belief that myth and mysteries are modes of knowledge; a
> veritable campaign to "prove" that without belief in God and immortality,
> democracy—or even plain moral decency—cannot be reasonably justified.[23]

Against this "obscurantism" grown "precious and willful," this "fun-
damentalism [which] has donned a top hat and gone high church," Hook
offered a reaffirmation of the scientific method and rational investigation. The
causes of this turn from rationalism were obvious: "economic crises, world
war . . . the tidal wave of totalitarianism." The solutions being offered seemed
inappropriate to Hook. "The new failure of nerve in contemporary culture is
compounded of unwarranted hopes and unfounded beliefs. It is a desperate
quest for quick and all-inclusive faith that will save us from the trouble of
thinking about difficult problems." This failure extends beyond faulty
philosophy or theology; it points to a "disillusion in the possibility of intelligent
human effort so profound that even if Hitler is defeated, the blight of Hitlerism
may rot the culture of his enemies."[24]

The immediate political application of Hook's critique became apparent in
the next issue of *Partisan Review*. An original section of the first article had been

edited for reasons of space. Presented as a separate piece, "The Failure of the Left" clearly indicated the path which Hook thought best to follow—resolute, if qualified, support for the war. Leftists who opposed the war, including those Hook called "Romantic Revolutionists," sealed the defeat of democratic socialism. Among these "Romantics" Hook cited Dwight Macdonald by name. The erroneous belief that fascism was only a form of capitalism must be replaced by an "immediate program [where] *in the very interest of a complete military victory over Hitler* all the submerged interests of the nation [are] given a great stake in that victory."[25]

Hook's articles appeared in the first and second numbers of PR in 1943. Macdonald's letter of resignation appeared in the fourth. The split had been growing long before Hook's contributions and had become acute with Rahv's response to Macdonald and Greenberg's "Ten Propositions." Both Phillips and Rahv *and* Macdonald were already searching for independent financial support. In 1943 Greenberg left the magazine to join the Air Force. Although this further isolated Macdonald, Greenberg's departure proved more symbolic than material to the editorial shake-up. Most found themselves moving to support the war. In an answer to pacifist critics, George Orwell wrote to PR from London:

> Pacifism is objectively pro-Fascist. This is elementary common sense. If you hamper the war effort of one side you automatically help that of the other. How is there any real way of remaining outside such a war as the present one. . . . The idea that you can somehow remain aloof from and superior to the struggle . . . is a bourgeois illusion bred of money and security.[26]

Macdonald's resignation, Hook's contributions on rationalism and in support of the war, and the shift of PR to a position resembling Orwell's marked an important turning point for the journal and for the intellectuals associated with it. Having long argued for political purity and against any compromise on principles, they now took a prowar line based on a lesser-evil notion. Once vehemently anti–Popular Front, they threw their support behind an Allied coalition which included the Soviet Union. Finally, having always felt themselves to be marginal men in American society and always been more interested in European affairs and culture, they made their support of the American war effort their first commitment to American government policy and to the maintenance of American society as it existed. Just as Europeans underwent changes during the war which irreversibly altered their society, so did Americans, including the New York Intellectuals. The New Yorkers' notions of the world shifted, politically and culturally. Their cultural stance of the late 1930s proved relatively more stable than their political ideas. In politics the readjustments continued, the war prompting reevaluations of the balance between absolute principles and realistic alternatives. Having begun as cosmopolitan radicals, interested more in Continental culture than in American society, they found that the Second World War helped turn that perspective away from universal radicalism and toward America.

An early sign of the war's impact on this shifting geographical focus came in Harold Rosenberg's *PR* article "On the Fall of Paris," in late 1940. As Rosenberg starkly began his essay, "the laboratory of the twentieth century has been shut shown." Paris, he argued, was the capital not of France but of world culture: "Paris represented the International of culture." The process which undermined Parisian dominance actually began before the Nazi invasion. The political and cultural battles of the late 1930s initiated the decline, especially as antifascism subsumed all other concerns—"Anti-fascist unity became everything; programs, insights, spirit, truth, nothing." The Germans merely completed the destruction.[27] What Rosenberg hinted at, subsequent *PR* articles reaffirmed. In place of Paris, New York became the logical cultural capital, and America was now central, rather than peripheral, to modern culture. The realities of war made this an obvious conclusion. War tore Europe, while American soil remained safe. Many European intellectuals had fled the Nazis and come to the United States. And now New York, like Paris before it, could serve as a center for international intellectual activity. As an element in this process, *Partisan Review* published a list of European intellectuals under the title "What Has Become of Them?" By groups—painters, writers, and musicians—they identified the whereabouts of 113 Europeans, ranging from antifascist partisans like Andre Malraux and Louis Aragon to Salvador Dali, "reportedly on good terms with the Spanish government," and Richard Strauss, who lived "in peace with the authorities in Munich."[28] *PR* set itself up as the clearinghouse for such information: "We invite our readers to supplement and correct the information given." The relationship between America and international culture underwent realignment in the minds of the *PR* intellectuals, just as their relationship to America changed during the war.

The intellectual and cultural interests of a number of the *Partisan* writers in the 1940s reflect this geographical relocation. There was no abandonment of European letters, only a new awareness of America. Philip Rahv continued his interest in Dostoevsky, but now Henry James also became a frequent subject of his considerations. Rahv edited an anthology of James's short fiction in 1944. This volume and a second one by Rahv "touched off" the "James boom," as Rahv described it a few years later.[29] Lionel Trilling, whose career began with books on Arnold and Forster, wrote his famous essay on William Dean Howells. It was typical of the caustic interactions among these intellectuals that even this turn toward new themes was not without its personal frictions. When Harold Rosenberg first saw Rahv's anthology of James's stories, he called it "the Henry James delicatessen," a remark which worked its way back to Rahv, who made a characteristically abusive response.[30]

The decision to rally actively behind the American government coincided with the shedding of radical beliefs and the relocation of the world's cultural center. This new view was the most significant philosophical change among the "elder" New York Intellectuals during the war years. Whereas the war effort itself probably benefited little from the support of *Partisan Review*, that effort had an important effect on the intellectuals. For all their ambivalence and hesitation, the intellectuals decided they cared which side won the war, and they saw in an American victory a maintenance of their cultural goals as well as the defeat of fascism.

OUR FORESTS

> Orwell said there are a range of questions over which ordinary people never have any doubt; only intellectuals are crazy enough to ask these questions. The question of whether the United States should enter World War II is a perfect illustration of George Orwell's remark. Nat Glazer, Irving Kristol, and Dan Bell did not take part in that debate.
>
> —Midge Decter[31]

The battles among the elders of the *Partisan* community over support of American entry into the war were not repeated among the maturing "second" generation of New York Intellectuals. Irving Howe did chastise *PR* for its "equivocation" on the war issue and noted that "their failure . . . to move leftward resulted in an abrupt turn right."[32] For this younger group, however, the war was the event which marked the passage from youth to adulthood, just as the Depression had been for the elders. The Depression had evoked radical responses, including critical reassessments of the American system and calls for a revolutionary reconstruction of society. The war effort, by contrast, gathered intellectuals behind Roosevelt and the American government. It mustered the younger intellectuals into the service of a government which had once been the target of radical abuse. The reaching of maturity for the second generation coincided with a lessening of radical enthusiasm.

The war also had a significantly different effect on the personal lives of this next generation. Older intellectuals like Trilling or Hook had just begun their careers when the Depression came. The stock market crash was a disrupting event in their early lives. The second generation spent the latter part of their childhood amid economic chaos. The politics of their youth, their attitudes toward education, and their career objectives had all been molded by their growing up during the 1930s. For them it was the war which disrupted this pattern.

When the war broke out, the "second" generation had graduated from college and had generally found employment conditions little improved over those of the early 1930s. Alfred Kazin, graduating a few years earlier, had obtained some free-lance writing, as the result of an audacious encounter with the *New York Times* book reviewer John Chamberlain. Kazin discovered that among his friends the same pressures which had once moved the parents now moved their children. Many, Kazin included, married. "In the day-to-day uncertainty," he recalled, "the young radicals were becoming family-minded, security-minded . . . . My friends were going exactly the way of their parents—now that there was nothing to rebel against except their own poverty." Unlike many of his contemporaries, Kazin himself resisted the temptation to head for the public school system, the civil service system, or the welfare department. He spent five years after graduation in the New York Public Library, researching a book on the roots of modern American literature. It was not until 1942 that he found a full-time job, as a book editor of the *New Republic*. For most of the other young intellectuals, graduation from college meant looking for "proletarian work," as Irving Kristol later observed, because that was all that was available. Kristol worked in the Brooklyn Navy Yard and then as a freight handler in Chicago, where his wife was a graduate student. Irving Howe took a job in a factory, while Melvin Lasky was a "junior historical archivist," a position which qualified him to be a guide at the Statue of Liberty.[33]

Leaving school did not mean abandoning politics. In fact, Kristol did not actually join the YPSLs until after graduating from City College, although he had been "a very close fellow traveler." He was a member for about a year, then he "quit and/or got expelled, since any time you quit on ideological grounds they promptly expel you."[34] "In radical movements," Daniel Bell later noted, "you rarely come in as an individual or leave as an individual; you are usually involved in a small circle." The small circle that left the Trotskyists with Irving Kristol were called the Shermanities. As Bell recalled,

> Sherman was a party name for Philip Selznick, the older person in the group and the intellectual leader. The others in the group were a man who used the name William Ferry, another who used the name of Perry. One used the name Martin Lewis, and another used the name Martin Eden. They were all YPSLs at City College. Ferry was Irving Kristol, Perry was Earl Rabb. They used the name Ferry and Perry as a joke. They had been members of the [Max] Shachtman group, which was being attacked by James P. Cannon, whose English wasn't very effective. He would say, "There are all these young students who are on the *peri-feri* of the movement," by which he meant the periphery. Because of this, the two decided to take the names Perry and Ferry. Martin Lewis was Marty Lipset, and Martin Eden was Martin Diamond.[35]

First in New York and then in Chicago, the Shermanites began to publish a magazine in 1943 called *Enquiry*, with Selznick listed as editor, under his own name, and "William Ferry" as a contributing editor.

Enquiry appeared in fits and starts for several years, its editorial staff "disorganized" by, as one issue explained, the "inroads of the selective service system."[36] For a time Kristol took over as acting editor, finally appearing under his own name. While many of the articles in *Enquiry* offered assessments on traditional topics for radical journals, such as those entitled "Union Structure and Democracy" or "Workers Ideology under Fascism," several of Kristol's articles are notable for their connection to the New York Intellectual world. He frequently wrote on literary themes, on Auden and Silone. His awareness of and response to issues surrounding *Partisan Review* is also striking. Kristol wrote a review of Lionel Trilling's *E. M. Forster*, in the course of which he quoted from *PR* as well as from Trilling's book. In addition, Kristol contributed a long analysis of the "Failure of Nerve" discussion which appeared in *PR*. As a young radical, Kristol was not yet ready to follow Hook's latest turn. In fact, he pointed out the inconsistency between Hook's 1943 united-front argument and his 1939 anti–Popular Front position. Nonetheless, the degree to which Kristol was paying such close attention to what was going on in *PR* speaks to his awareness and intellectual connections.[37]

Although the war upset the editorial operation of *Enquiry*, for the young men who came of age in the early war years, the coming induction notice proved the only real certainty in their futures. The arrival of the draft call ended the uncertainty and the aimlessness they often felt. The feeling of the hero of Saul Bellow's first novel that he is "dangling" as he awaits induction reflects this attitude. *Partisan Review* published the first segment of that novel in 1943. Having resigned a job to await an impending induction call, the main character of the book finds that "bureaucratic red tape" has stalled his notice.

> I have thought of going to work but I am unwilling to admit that I do not know how to use my freedom and have to embrace the flunkydom of a job because I have no resources, in a word, no character. . . . There is nothing to do but wait and dangle and grow more and more dispirited.[38]

Bellow and the other younger New York Intellectuals were not alone in their attitude toward the war and the draft. Their entire generation found itself swept up in the events of war. Unlike their intellectual elders, they saw personal adjustment, not ideological debate, as the central issue. Verbal support of the war joined with the necessity of actively participating in the war effort. Irving Howe spent three and a half years in the Army, a year and a half stationed in Alaska, where he read voluminously. Clement Greenberg also found time to read and even to review while stationed in Oklahoma. "I have taken to reading Henry James from one end to the other," he wrote Fred Dupee. "I discovered in my last months at the Customs House that he's the best antidote to institutional boredom." Greenberg also told Dupee that he was reviewing a book by Stefan George for the *Nation*. Melvin Lasky followed an Army assignment from Fort Dix to Europe and then varied activities in postwar Germany. Irving Krisol served in the Army, Leslie Fiedler in the Navy, and Robert Warshow as a civilian in the Army Signal Corps. Alfred Kazin, classified 4-F because of a stammer, later recounted his joy at securing a civilian assignment which would take him to Europe: "War, blessed war, had come to the rescue of my generation, and nothing would ever be the same."[39]

The changed perspective brought by the war similarly influenced the second generation. The shift of focus from a Europe-centered notion of culture to one which at least considered America's importance found wide support among the younger group. Most of the creative work of this second group came after the war, but examples of the shift can already be seen before 1945. Most notable is Kazin's massive literary study *On Native Grounds*, published in 1942, the result of his five years of research. The work analyzes American literature from the late nineteenth century through the Depression years. The famous writers of the twentieth century, Kazin recalled, seemed to him "part of a continuing, hopeful, forward movement in American life," rooted in "American prophets like Emerson and Lincoln and Whitman."[40] Even the political literature of the 1930s appeared much more *American* for Kazin than for the cosmopolitan, universalist intellectuals he followed. In the thirties writing he found "evidence of how deeply felt was the urge both of the crisis to recover America *as an idea*—and perhaps only thus build a better society in the shell of the old."[41] Kazin's work reflects the further steps his generation would take with regard to their American outlook. Whereas the older critics began to accept gradually the role of American culture, Kazin took it as his main focus. When the former wrote about it, as Norman Podhoretz later put it, "it was with the eye of the learned outsider." For Kazin, "it was with the aggressive conviction that this literature was *his*." This difference is best captured in an anecdote Podhoretz recounted, telling of Kazin's being teased over a phrase he used in a piece on Francis Parkman's *Oregon Trail*: "*Our* forests, Alfred?"[42]

Other distinctions setting apart the two generations now emerged among the New York Intellectuals. The very emergence of two generations points to the changes taking place. The younger writers read *Partisan Review* at City College or Chicago and found themselves drawn to the journal and the coterie of intellectuals gathered around it. Their paths to *PR* differed from that of the elders. The young did not help form the community; rather, they moved from campus politics to an intellectual group already in existence. Their battles with Stalinists took place on street corners, in college cafeterias, or in the National Students' Union. They did not personally confront the *New Masses'* editors and were only peripherally involved in proletarian literature. For most of them the war debate remained a matter for the elders.

That things changed during wartime while nothing seemed to change is evidenced by the arrival of this new generation of writers on the *Partisan* scene. During the early 1940s many younger writers added their names to the list of contributors to *PR* and to the roster of New York Intellectuals. Only at the war's end, when everyone came home and editorial boards and lists of contributors resettled, was the change manifest. A new generation firmly planted itself in the New York Intellectual world, completing the solidification of the community as the individuals secured their own places in it. They were different from the elders and from one another. Irving Howe was "very dogmatic and sharp-tongued," Bell recalled, and Irving Kristol, "very rarely aggressive," with a "ready wit" but taking things "less personally," he would "make a crack and let it go." He himself, Bell noted, "was much more aggressive, rough-and-tumble," in his early years.[43] Leslie Fiedler studied in

Chicago and taught in Montana but remained a New Yorker all the same. Melvin Lasky never really returned home to America from World War II but became one of the community. Robert Warshow had begun at the *New Leader* in the late 1930s and ended up with *Commentary* after the war. Then there was Isaac Rosenfeld. Of all the young literati, the precocious critics, and the budding novelists, Rosenfeld seemed to hold the most promise. Even with Kazin and with Bellow, Rosenfeld was, as David Bazelon put it, the *"shoyne boychick"* of the newer generation, "the most prized Jewish son in a world replete with prized Jewish sons." Rosenfeld's story is ultimately pathetic, for his career never vaguely approached his promise. But for a time he held center stage among the bright, new arrivals.[44]

As the community grew, it changed and adjusted its perspective. This had been the pattern in the 1930s and would remain so after 1945. But during the war a number of changes occurred, many of which could not be fully realized until the peace. No longer the loyal opposition, the New Yorkers gradually abandoned their abrasive criticism of America and its culture and replaced it with a qualified acceptance of both the system and its cultural creations. This shift developed over the course of the war years, at a time when attention focused on compelling political events in Europe and Asia. When the New York Intellectuals could finally turn their full attention back to the issues at home, they discovered that their own perspective had undergone significant change over the preceding six years. As intellectuals, they found their ideas and works gaining increasing prominence. As individuals, they found their sense of separateness—the degree of alienation they had once felt from American society—essentially overcome.

A SILENT COMPLICITY

The New York Intellectuals' feeling more at home at war's end was marred by one haunting legacy. At the same time when many of them came into their own and secured positions closer to the heart of American society, they confronted a new reality which raised significant personal issues and called into question many of their cultural beliefs. "At one moment we emerged," recalled Alfred Kazin, "but who could have foreseen that this emergence would have coincided with the most terrible event in Jewish history." The impact of the Holocaust struck these Jewish intellectuals as it struck many others—Jews and non-Jews alike. An event incomparable in modern experience, it begged for a rational explanation, and none seemed available. While inexplicable, the Holocaust did produce a shattering reawakening of Jewish consciousness, not tied to any particular religious or ethnic notions, but as Irving Howe later observed, "We knew but for an accident of geography we might also now be bars of soap."[45] This reawakening remained relatively unarticulated among the New York Intellectuals. No outpouring of confessional, declaratory, or ethnocentric pieces ensued. Rather, the impact of the terrible events began to make itself evident only over a period of years, in part because of the magnitude of the tragedy and in part because it meant coming to terms with their own Jewishness.

Their sense of universalism, so appropriate for their intellectual notions, left little room for the expression of Jewish themes or even for much comment on Nazi anti-Semitism before the war. Given Hitler's anti-Semitism and the dislocation of Jews, it is remarkable how rarely the pages of *Partisan Review* and the various other writings of the New York Intellectuals contained references in the late 1930s to the persecution of the Jews. Although the extent of the horror remained unknown until after the war, evidence about Nazi actions abounded. Jewish intellectuals—persons of the stature of Freud and the Frankfurt philosophers—left their homelands. Various individuals and agencies in Europe and America sought to help Jews suffering under the Nazis.

Among the few prewar articles to deal with the theme of German anti-Semitism was Sidney Hook's "Tragedy of German Jewry," published in a November 1938 issue of *New Leader*. Immediately, Hook set out a "cosmopolitan" disclaimer. "Let us bear in mind that in protesting against Hitler's anti-Jewish brutalities we are also protesting against the hounding of other religious and political minorities." The thrust of Hook's article, however, proved to be not about Hitler at all. Rather, returning to anti-Stalinism, Hook wrote mostly on the relation of German events to activities in Russia and in the American Communist party. "In all totalitarian countries the Jews and other minorities are treated as the exigencies of power politics demands," he wrote, adding,

> Let us also remember that it was from Stalin that Hitler learned the art of uprooting and wiping out whole groups and classes of innocent citizens. We cannot with good conscience protest against Hitler's treatment of the Jews and remain silent about the six million . . . who fill the concentration camps in Russia . . . . Stalin has killed more Jews in the last two years than Hitler has since coming to power.[46]

Whatever the truth or distortion of Hook's information, his overall position is remarkable in its perspective. So entrenched was he in the anti-Stalinist campaigns that he could not discuss the questions of Hitler's anti-Semitism and Jewish persecution without entanglement in his anti-Stalinism.[47] It is equally remarkable that Hook's article was almost the only discussion of the topic during the prewar years—a period in which the *Partisan* writers kept busy attacking the Stalinists, proletarian literature, and the Popular Front.

Factors other than politics were at work. "Let's face it," Alfred Kazin later admitted. "If these intellectuals had gone on a great deal for stuff about the Jews and the war, the way, for example, the Yiddish press did, they would have seemed a good deal less 'American,' less assimilated." In addition, "they were very proud of their radicalism, people like Rahv and the others, they thought of themselves as super Lenins and Marxes. They had the most fantastic conceit about their ability to master the world situation." Daniel Bell recalled, "There was a great awareness of anti-Semitism, but a great fear of open discussion. Mel Lasky and I argued with Sol Levitas about the unwillingness of the *New Leader* to criticize British Home Secretary Herbert Morrison and FDR for not admitting Jews."[48]

The outbreak of war did not witness a significant increase in the discussions or the analysis of Jewish themes. The one notable exception was a short piece by Kazin in the *New Republic*. "In Every Voice, In Every Ban," like the few previous forays into this area, avoided the direct question of the Nazi persecution of the Jews, but a different rationale accounts for Kazin's hesitations. The haunting sense of inplausibility and incredulity with which many observers and analysts came to view the treatment of the Jews first appeared in his piece. The enormity of the horror pointed beyond revulsion or criticism. "Something has been done—and not by the Nazis—which can never be undone," Kazin wrote. "The tragedy is in our minds, in the basic equality of our personal culture; and that is why it will be the tragedy of the peace." Kazin became the first New York Intellectual to argue for an extended sense of guilt for the Nazi crimes. He catalogued the variety of ways and types of individuals who had averted their eyes. There are those, he said, who "believed utterly that society is always the prime cause of what we are," those who "pass the buck so persistently to everyone but [them]selves." He scored radicals, reactionaries, and liberals.

> But it is above all . . . all those—not liberals, not radicals, certainly not reactionaries—who want only to live and let live, to have the good life back, and who think that you can dump three million helpless Jews into your furnace, and sigh in the genuine impotence of your undeniable regret, and then build your Europe back again.

Kazin concluded his article with a prophetic view of the impact all of this would have on his fellow humans: "Something has been set forth in Europe that is subtle, and suspended, and destructive . . . . That something is all our silent complicity in the massacre of the Jews."[49]

The feelings expressed by Kazin's short analysis were often recapitulated by other Jewish writers in the postwar years. During the war, however, the response to his article remained more in keeping with prewar attitudes. "I was horrified by the response," Kazin later remembered "the *New Republic* was faintly embarrassed because it didn't seem to them to be particularly urgent."[50] Other intellectuals still argued from the universalist position, still expressed more interest in world trends or general themes. Whatever the specific validity of these analyses, the lack of discussion on the topic of Jews and their persecution stands out starkly. When the full story of the horror of the Nazi crimes began to unfold, the shock of their magnitude affected all individuals. Even Kazin had underestimated the slaughter by half. The others had not dealt with it directly at all. Only slowly did the realization of what this meant begin to sink in—of what this meant not for Europe's Jews but for Americans and especially for these young Jewish intellectuals. "There were men and women in other lands who raised their voices in protest, who lent helping hands," lamented Elliot Cohen in 1945. "But we also record the fact: the voices were not many, the hands not many. There was a strange passivity the world over."[51]

Some of the New York Intellectuals tried to maintain their cosmopolitan position. While aware of the "uneasiness" which the murder of six million created in most American Jews about their own position, Hook thought the feeling unjustified.[52] At one time others might have been hesitant to speak out; now they were unable to do so. "To recognize that we were living after one of the greatest and least explicable catastrophes of human history," Irving Howe wrote years later, "one for which we could not claim to have adequately prepared ourselves either as intellectuals or as human beings, brought a new rush of feelings, mostly unarticulated and hidden behind the scrim of consciousness." Having neglected their own roots in the pursuit of intellectual prominence and political goals, they found themselves face to face with their origins and a reality larger than any they could have envisioned. "We still don't understand what happened to the Jews of Europe, and perhaps we never will," Isaac Rosenfeld wrote in 1948.

> We know all there is to know. But it hasn't helped; we still don't understand. . . . There is nothing but numbness, and in the respect of numbness we, the innocent and the indignant, the relatives and coreligionists or friends of the victims, liberals all of us, who want anything from a reasonable settlement and a forgetting to outright revenge—when it comes to numbness we are no different from the murderers who went ahead and did their business and paid no attention to the screams.

The intellectual arguments and political reassessments of the late 1930s and the early 1940s set the New York Intellectuals in a position to respond to the political and cultural exigencies they perceived. As universalist intellectuals, they had not put their own relation to Jewishness among these central issues. They found that their newly carved position stood them in poor stead against the revelations of the Holocaust and left them with a "low charged guilt," Howe remembered, "a quiet remorse." They cried for the European Jews and for themselves. "We could no longer escape the conviction that, blessing or curse, Jewishness was an integral part of our life, even if—and perhaps just because—there was nothing we could say or do about it."[53] Unable to talk about the Holocaust itself, they began in the postwar years to talk about themselves as Jews, something they had rarely done before. Initially with some trepidation, they turned back to look at their own past and their connection to it. This investigation took them directly to the questions of who they were and where they were headed.

Chapter 8

Heart In—Head Out

By 1946 the New York Intellectuals had returned to America. The soldiers had come home, as had the universalist intellectuals. Their commitment to the war effort and their reawakened interest in things American brought them into a new relationship with their native land. Having spent the 1930s on the periphery, they now began to move into positions nearer the center of American society. *Partisan Review* had gained a position of intellectual prominence which small magazines strive for but seldom achieve. Academic positions and intellectual renown awaited many of its contributors. Still, for all the outward signs of achievement, the immediate postwar years did not prove a period of confidence or stability among the New York Intellectuals. Many of the issues of the 1930s had been resolved, while others ceased to command center stage. New concerns, however, arose to challenge the intellectuals and the community.

As the New York Intellectuals became important individuals and the community took on a public shape, questions about personal self-definition emerged. The magnitude of the Holocaust, coupled with the questions which naturally accompany maturity, carried these individuals back to their roots and brought the issue of their own Jewishness to the fore. Among writers and critics usually quick to analyze and philosophize, there developed a curious tongue-tiedness on the question of the Nazis and the destruction of the European Jews. Unable to consider the question in its largest frame—one which began with the figure six million—they chose instead to reduce it to its smallest terms and begin with themselves. In the postwar years a series of articles, symposia, and discussions appeared, focusing on the question of Jewish identity.

This series of investigations into Jewish identity became the first attempt of the New York Intellectuals to come to terms with their own early lives, and with their ambivalent attitudes toward their parents and backgrounds. All the labels and self-definitions of the 1930s appeared inappropriate in the aftermath of the war and the stunning reawakening of their Jewish identification. For many of these intellectuals, the one attribute they had never fully considered now came to the fore. The New York academic at the midwestern college, in Lionel Trilling's short story of twenty years before, "had said, 'I am a Jew,' and was immediately set free."[1] For many New York Intellectuals in the 1940s, the personal admission of Jewishness and the recognition that this mattered, that it helped define who they were, did not bring about instant salvation. It initiated, however, the reinvestigation of their own place and heritage. By the 1950s, as Norman Podhoretz observed, many had become "enthusiasts of Martin Buber, while the whole of the New York literary world was ringing with praise of the Yiddish storytellers, the Hassidim, Maimonides, medieval Hebrew poetry, and even Rabbis of the Talmud."[2] They admitted fully what they had never actually denied but had not totally confronted. Having admitted the fact of their Jewishness, they set out to discover what it meant.

NOT ALTOGETHER NOBODY, NOT ALTOGETHER SOMEBODY

The universalism or cosmopolitanism of the 1930s had been, for most, more style than substance. Alfred Kazin recalled feeling estranged from the other kind of radicals he knew, the small-town Protestants represented by Granville Hicks or Malcolm Cowley. Trilling felt out of place at the University of Wisconsin; the CCNY students knew the limits anti-Semitism placed on their educational careers. Still, they had tried to overcome the differences in a variety of ways, without ever facing the real question before them. Radicals, scholars, or critics, they all felt the stigma of difference. In the postwar years, they began to evaluate the unevaluated factor. "Since the Jew possessed a unique identity which springs from his origin and his story, it is possible for him to be any kind of man—rationalist, irrationalist, heroic, cowardly, Zionist or good European—and still be a Jew," Harold Rosenberg asserted in 1949. "The Jew exists but there are not Jewish traits." One might try to deny this, Rosenberg observed, but, on the other hand, "the Jewish identity has a remarkable richness for those who rediscover it within themselves."[3]

The question of what constituted this Jewish identity and to what extent it was different from that of preceding Jewish generations was not a simple one. These American-born Jews, the children of immigrants, were a unique generation. They had not fallen into a traditional pattern, largely because none existed. Over two generations, a family might have moved from an East European ghetto to an immigrant neighborhood in Brooklyn and then to Manhattan. "Few of us are duplicates of our grandfathers, in either thought, feeling, speech, or appearance," Rosenberg wrote, in an essay on Jewish identity. "Very often we even differ from our fathers, too, in most of these respects. We are, to a large extent, new people." To be a new person meant to "lack a given identity, to be in the deepest sense, anonymous. We can 'make a name for ourselves.' " This describes the path of many of these intellectuals in the 1930s, as they sought to create a place for themselves. "Until we have made a name for ourselves, we are 'nobody.' " Yet, having come through this first period, having ventured away from the neighborhoods of their youths, they found themselves less "anonymous" than they had once believed. Instead, "some particular form has been rather heavily, if not ineradicably, engraved upon them. Be it preferred or not, we are not altogether Nobody. Nevertheless, we are not altogether Somebody either." Somewhere between the rigid proscriptions of a specific Jewish identity and the infinite random choices of purely anonymous beings, Rosenberg saw the development of contemporary American Jews. "Jewish birth may confer an identity upon us that is quite empty of content. . . . Perhaps American Jews, to the discomfiture of assimilationists, are born with less group anonymity than most other Americans. Still it must be granted that they tend to be born with a least as much anonymity as Jewishness."[4]

American Jews reading Rosenberg's somewhat complex description of their identity—and his only one of a number of similar attempts—found little solace or security in his analysis. It did not offer the easy path of blind allegiance or ethnic ritual, nor did it praise total individuality. Rather, it called for self-analysis and self-definition, a process already under way among the New York Intellectuals. The slow process of defining their own place in terms of American society and their own Jewishness loomed as the next task.

The discussion of their own Jewishness began with the attempt to understand what had raised the issue in their own minds. Obvious causes existed—"the Holocaust and the founding of the state of Israel," for Irving Kristol; the Holocaust, Freudianism, and self-acceptance, for Norman Podhoretz. Personal factors supplemented these social pressures. Leslie Fiedler found that "the conscious beginnings of [his] reaching 'back' toward Judaism did not depend upon the successes of Hitler, but on the failures of Stalin."[5] Others, such as Clement Greenberg and Irving Howe, discovered an increasing awareness of an informal heritage, "transmitted mostly through mother's milk and the habits and talk of the family," Greenberg observed. More recently, Howe went back to generalize about this awareness, noting "a recognition in the fifties and sixties that no matter how hard you might try to shake off your past, it would still cling to your speech, gestures, skin, and nose; still shape, with a thousand subtle movements, the way you did your work and raised your children."[6]

One after another, under the influences of political pressure, social analysis, and personal awareness, the intellectuals began to reassess and reconsider their Jewish past. Some resisted this trend. In the early 1940s Lionel Trilling argued that the Jewish community could "give no sustenance to the American artist or intellectual who is born a Jew." He also claimed, "I know of no writer in English who has added a micromillimetre to his stature by 'realizing his

Jewishness.' "[7] When one of the next generation tried to do just this, Trilling objected. Alfred Kazin later recalled the reaction to the publication of the first volume of his autobiographical writings, *A Walker in the City*: "Trilling sniffed, without reading the book, and amused me by airly dismissing (presumably not my book but the topic itself) as something he called 'shmo.' "[8] Trilling's slightly different background—lower middle class and Columbia-educated rather than working class and City College–educated—may account for his different perspective. In a larger sense, the tendency to "shy away from Jewish subjects" or to feel that few benefits derive from mining one's Jewish background points to a larger trait prevalent among many Jews. Clement Greenberg attacked this attribute head on, in "Self-Hatred and Jewish Chauvinism."

Only in the postwar years, in the time of reappraisal and new self-definition, could many of the first generation begin to understand fully the subtle but intense impact their background had on them. Age, as well as events, propelled them toward these reconsiderations and to understandings with which they might not always feel comfortable. In a large admission about his personal attitudes, Greenberg wrote of "the realization of the Jewish self-hatred in myself . . . [of] the devious ways in which it conceals itself," and how this realization "explains many things that used to puzzle me in the behavior of my fellow Jews."[9] Self-hatred, he concluded, "is almost universal among Jews." Greenberg then cited an article by Kurt Lewin which appeared in 1941 in the *Contemporary Jewish Record*. Lewin reported,

> In the case of the underprivileged group . . . their opinions about themselves are greatly influenced by the low esteem the majority has for them. This . . . heightens the tendency of the Jew with a negative balance (i.e., the Jew who finds his identity as a Jew too much of a psychological handicap) to cut himself loose from things Jewish.[10]

This attitude described the position of the Jewish intellectuals in the late 1930s. However, Lewin added a further conclusion which spoke directly to the concerns of the late forties. "Being unable to cut himself entirely loose from his Jewish connections and his Jewish past, the hatred turns upon himself." This situation, Greenberg felt, required the attention of the Jews. Some alternatives were unsatisfactory. "What we might ask of our new Jewish self-consciousness is that it liberate rather than organize us," Greenberg hoped. "What I want to do is accept my Jewishness more implicitly. . . . I want to overcome my self-hatred in order to be more myself, not in order to be a 'good Jew.' "[11]

Greenberg's self-appraisal, Rosenberg's analysis of the somebody-nobody duality of Jewish existence, the explorations in personal history of Alfred Kazin—all were attempts to come to terms with elements in their background which had long remained unexplored. The failure to confront it had not made it disappear. Kazin felt the difference from "them"—the WASP radicals—in the 1930s. "The sense of Jewish inferiority is there," Greenberg concluded, "but less of it will be there the moment we acknowledge it and begin to realize just how and where we act upon it." The new emphasis of cultural programs or public displays of Jewishness would not, in Greenberg's analysis, solve the problem. "These tend to become means rather of evading and hiding the problem. For though they are designed to combat Jewish self-hatred, their sponsors are too afraid of naming it to know where to seek it out. We fool ourselves with fine-sounding phrases."[12]

Thus, problems existed beyond that of personal definition, deciding who you were and what it meant. Questions of social definition also arose, deciding where you stood. The modern pressure to be "one-hundred-per-cent-something" makes Jews "uncomfortable when they debate whether one can be an American and a Jew," Harold Rosenberg noted. "Being twice identified seems embarassingly ambiguous." Furthermore, this social ambiguity corresponded to a religious-cultural problem. "The area covered by the Jewish-history-mass [Rosenberg saw modern history as a moving mass] cannot be delineated by any static concept of Judaism nor represented monopolistically by any 'organized group.' "[13] It would be too easy and, more important, insufficient to cast one's lot with the blind acceptance of either Jewish religion or the particular notion of a "Jewish community" offered by the "orthodox" Jewish leaders. Few of these intellectuals immediately grasped at a religious faith. Their investigations and new allegiances focused on rediscovering Jewishness, not Judaism. They were "groping to establish rapport with the Jewish tradition," as Irving Kristol wrote in 1948, "standing at the synagogue door, 'heart in, head out.' "[14] To help establish some rapport, Kristol, Daniel Bell, and Nathan Glazer joined in 1949 with Milton Himmelfarb, director of information and research for the American Jewish Committee and Kristol's brother-in-law, for a study group reading Maimonides's *Misneh Torah*. Bell later recalled, "We'd meet every Sunday for dinner and then sit around the table reading Maimonides. The question of belief . . . was not merely a matter of obeying but a question of skepticism, of intellectual inquiry, of philosophical discourse."[15]

Bell discovered in Maimonides questions about the community and its cohesive elements. This same issue spurred other intellectuals, especially when groups claimed to speak for or represent the community. Harold Rosenberg found that the "organized group" in the cultural and social worlds of the Jewish community in America did not comprise the entire "community." Perhaps thinking of his fellow intellectuals in the 1930s, Rosenberg argued for the inclusion of "the Jew whom the Jewish past has ceased to stir, whom every collective anguish or battle for salvation passes by." It is this Jew who "may tomorrow find himself at the center of the movement toward the future." And in a conclusion which proved not only prophetic, but extremely optimistic, Rosenberg recalled that "like the reputation of the *zaddik*, a community is often built by surprise. Perhaps it is just those Jews who arrive from nowhere who will come to resemble most closely their remotest and most venerable grandfathers."[16]

Thus, the ultimate path to "realizing" one's Jewishness lay not only in outward commitment but also in inner admission. A willingness to tie one's own life to a common Jewish tradition proved necessary. This admission might seem a minor point in the postwar world of Israel, memories of the Holocaust, and ethnic awareness, but for the "universalist" intellectuals and radicals of the Depression years it marked a significant shift from past perspective. The reaction and barriers of American society had defined their Jewishness in the twenties and thirties. In the postwar years "the *common story* of the Jews and not 'the hostility and disdain' of others is the principle of their togetherness," Harold Rosenberg concluded. "Every Jew, regardless of class or even blood origin, is included equally in the entire common account." More than a historical epic, the story remained "alive in the individual," a "collective identity . . . of the miraculous founding of a cult or of the exploitation and struggles of trade union members." The story of the one was the story of all, "the history of a people, not of a cult, since the participation is not metaphysical but in an actual past." "Lacking faith," Daniel Bell wrote, "I myself can only 'choose' fate. For me, therefore, to be a Jew is to be part of a community woven by memory." Bell found verification of his memory in the *yizkor*, a community "summed up by the holy words: *Yizkor Elohim nishmas ahoh moi*: 'May God remember the name of . . . ' " The memory of the *yizkor*, Bell said, tied him to the larger community. It connected him to the whole and reaffirmed his specific links to that community. "In the *minyan* of my fellows, I am linked to my own parent. In the *Yizkor*, through memory, I am identified as a Jew."[17] In the late 1940s the New York Intellectuals sought the full meaning of Jewish history and their own Jewishness, hoping to come to terms with their specific links to the Jewish tradition. Once they understood themselves, they hoped to understand and appreciate their parents and the world from which they came.

WHAT ABOUT FAGIN?

Central to the appeal of thirties cosmopolitanism had been a sense of connection between the young radical writers and the great literary figures and cultural trends of the times. The *Partisan* critics championed revolutionary modernism and helped rescue Eliot and Pound. However, the postwar interest in questions surrounding Jewishness brought into clear focus an essential problem with the tie between the New York Intellectuals and several of these writers. In 1946 the Bollingen Prize for poetry went to Ezra Pound. The award caused a great debate, including a war of words between William Barrett and Allen Tate in which Tate seemed to be challenging Barrett to a duel. In general, Pound's wartime profascist activities and his anti-Semitism caused consternation among many intellectuals, especially among Jews.[18]

Beyond the worth or appropriateness of Pound's award, two more-essential questions grew out of the discussion over the Bollingen Prize. The first, most obvious consideration was a coming to terms with the persistent and often virulent strain of anti-Semitism in much of modern literature. Not only the most obnoxious reactionaries—few writers carried their sympathies as far as Pound—were anti-Semitic. Anti-Semitism went back to Dickens and even Shakespeare, was strong in Henry James, and surfaced in one of the guiding lights of modern culture, T. S. Eliot.[19] The second, deeper question concerned the relationship of these young intellectuals to a culture whose high priests included so many anti-Semites. The allegiance to this very culture helped create the New York Intellectual community. They could not simply boycott Eliot's works, as they might boycott the presentation of the Bollingen Prize to Pound. "The Jewish intellectual of my generation," Leslie Fiedler observed, "cannot disown him [Eliot] without disowning an integral part of himself. He has been a profounder influence on a good many of us than the Baal Shem Tov or the author of Job. We are not willing to resign from Western culture."[20]

Each of these questions—what to do about important anti-Semitic writers and how the anti-Semitic strain in literature affected Jews in Western culture—found full discussion during the postwar years. The first problem led to a *Commentary* symposium in 1949, in which a variety of writers responded to a general question.

> As a Jew and a writer working within the Anglo-American literary tradition, how do you confront the presence in that tradition of the mythical or semi-mythical figure of the Jew, as found, for example, in the works of such writers as Chaucer, Marlowe, Shakespeare, Walter Scott, Trollope, T. S. Eliot, Evelyn Waugh, Thomas Wolfe, Henry Adams, etc.? Do you find this an important block or barrier to your full participation and integration, as a writer or a person, in the literary or cultural tradition involved? In what ways, if any, does this constitute a real problem for you and how do you deal with it, or think it should be dealt with? If you do not find it a problem or think it a problem, why not?[21]

The responses to the symposium questions varied widely. Some people, such as William Phillips, dealt with the matter directly. As a Jew, he said, he was made "uneasy by any kind of anti-Semitism, whether [he found] it in a bar, a summer resort, his friend's grandmother, or in the avant-garde cadences of Ezra Pound." To ignore anti-Semitism for purposes of justification of literary merit, Phillips argued, was "a form of weaseling." Isaac Rosenfeld echoed some of Phillips's sentiments but emphasized that other kinds of anti-Semitism were "of much greater moment to him" and listed the anti-Semitism of his neighbors, shopkeepers, subway crowds, and, especially, governments as examples. "I expect to be able to get along as a writer, even in an anti-Semitic tradition in English and American literature," Rosenfeld claimed. "So they don't name streets after me." Anti-Semitism, he concluded, "is not a literary problem. It is a disease."[22]

Diana Trilling, not Lionel, participated in the symposium. She was no "stand-in" for her husband, because her literary credentials matched those of the other participants. Yet, Lionel Trilling was the New York Intellectual who had most prominently denied the role of Jewishness in his own literary background, and he became a leading apostle of non-Semitic high culture in the 1950s. Diana Trilling's contribution to the *Commentary* symposium proved consistent with ideas expressed elsewhere by her husband. She attempted to draw extremely fine distinctions among the writers cited as anti-Semitic. The difference between Pound and Eliot, for example, she felt to be significant. The Jew, in Eliot's work must, she believed, "be understood as a figure of speech; the Jew as metaphor for alienation, for the spirit which stands outside Eliot's particular design for a good society." Pound, on the other hand, "has a whole context of social irresponsibility. Even the Jew himself" can learn a great deal from Eliot, "whereas from Pound both Jew and gentile can only learn hatred." While it is true that Eliot did not broadcast over the radio for the fascists, as did Pound, and that Eliot's anti-Semitism is certainly less virulent than Pound's, Trilling's distinctions nonetheless appear derived more from her literary tastes than from her political or ethnic awareness. This seems an example of what William Phillips saw as the attempt of certain critics to "turn somersaults" to defend anti-Semitic writers they like.[23]

Diana Trilling carried her distinctions a step further, aiming to separate bad ideas from good literature. Authors often hold unpopular or inaccurate notions. "I see no reason to give more weight to, say, Dickens' anti-Semitism than to his anti-parliamentarianism: the latter is just as much a threat to my security as the former." Yet, she argued, there is no call to boycott Dickens for his antidemocratic utterances. Certainly, Jews have died because of the anti-Jewish myth, Trilling contended, but so have parliamentarians died in the face of antidemocratic forces, even Jewish parliamentarians. "The process of cause and effect is not so direct as we sometimes like to make out. There is unquestionably a clear path from Shylock or Fagin to Dachau," Trilling held, "but is there not also a discernible path between Marx's formulation of a socialist absolutism and the concentration camp of National Socialism?"[24] In this second argument, Trilling introduced so many varied and incompatible elements that the reader might rather accept the position than unravel all her threads. To begin with, a similar symposium on antidemocratic attitudes among literary figures might elicit equal condemnation of Dickens for this failing. More central to the question under discussion, and avoided by Trilling's equation, is the place of anti-Semitism in literature—the racist portrait of Jews in novels and poems and how that creates stereotypes. Furthermore, equating the line between European prejudice toward the Jews leading to Nazi concentration camps, on the one hand, and the somewhat dubious path between Marx and Nazism, on the other, strains credulity. Faced with the odious choice of either chastising writers once held in great esteem or accepting anti-Semitic elements in their works, Trilling attempted to draw distinctions which do not exist.

This attitude, and the contradictions which lie beneath it, affected individuals other than Diana Trilling. Confronting rather than avoiding this general paradox, Alfred Kazin found that it haunted and plagued Jewish intellectuals: "We cannot let them go [the anti-Semitic writers] nor can they let us go, for they imitate us, they are obviously fascinated by us . . . . And think how, in turn, *we* are fascinated by their resemblance to us." Jewish intellectuals do not turn to the "humanists," Kazin observed, not to the "truly Christian, like Bernanos and Mauriac. But precisely to the nasty ones, the clever modern ones—a Dostoevsky, a Henry James, a Henry Adams, and André Gide, a Santayana, a Cummings, a Celine, an Eliot, a Pound. How we love them, though they love us not!" The figures of modern culture were so much like the Jewish intellectuals that the differences between them seemed especially striking. "How we squirm and strain to get into Eliot's City of God . . . though he has barred us from it in advance! . . . In fact, if it were not for their *unfortunate* attitude about the Jews, some of us would be indistinguishable from them, if we are not that already."[25]

Kazin had struck the central chord in this discussion, but his conclusion pointed to a further dilemma. In their striving to be intellectuals, to align themselves with the ideas and apostles of modern culture, the Jewish intellectuals had found themselves in proximity to a number of important figures who were strongly anti-Semitic. In the universalist days of the 1930s, this could be overlooked or made to appear less important. Amid the personal questioning and attempts at self-definition aimed at developing a Jewish identity, anti-Semitism among one's heroes proved clearly unsettling. Moreover, many of the Jewish intellectuals had built their reputation defending a mode of culture which now appeared to have either strongly anti-Semitic strains or, at least, anti-Semitic practitioners. And finally, as Kazin hinted, the entire question of the relationship of Jews to modern culture itself surfaced in this discussion. Had the thirties intellectuals so completely identified with a Western culture, as opposed to their own, Jewish heritage, that they found themselves inextricably bound up with a culture which helped define their place as intellectuals, while attacking them as individuals? For many Jewish intellectuals, the larger problem of the attitude of non-Jews toward Jews, especially in the wake of Hitler, was now compounded by the undercurrent of anti-Semitism which flowed through modern culture. With Nazism and non-Jewish prejudice, the Jewish intellectuals could more easily deal. They had never had any illusions about popular anti-Semitism, whether in Brownsville or in Manhattan. By contrast, the culture to which they had firmly committed themselves posed much more difficult enigmas.

A SPECIALIST IN ALIENATION

The anti-Semitic strain in modern culture presented a further problem for the emerging Jewish intellectuals. Their desire to become an integral part of that culture conflicted with the exclusionist sentiment buried in anti-Semitism. After defining their own position vis á vis anti-Semitism itself, they faced a second task. To demonstrate the fallacies of the anti-Semites' claims, they argued for reversal of conceptions. These intellectuals posited that Jews had a central place because of their Jewishness. They now felt that Jewishness, once a source of scorn among some writers, offered a special sight, useful in the analysis of the modern condition. "What makes this especially different is that a Jewish writer has a kind of dual being," William Phillips observed. "He is both a Jew and a Western man. As a Jew, he bears the wounds of the stranger, as a Western man, he is part of the mind of Western civilization, sharing its values and contributing to its advances." "The theme of Jewish life," Alfred Kazin later noted, is "the pariah versus the central position—a constant mystery to other people."[26] This very sense of mystery, the dual perspective, could provide a special vision with which to discuss and analyze the problems of an anxious world.

Leslie Fiedler argued this position in several essays in the late 1940s, including his contribution to a *Partisan Review* symposium, "The State of American Writing, 1948," and a provocative piece in *Commentary*, "What Can We Do about Fagin?" in 1949.[27] Geographically, Fiedler posited, the Jew stood between American and European culture and offered a perspective on the "traditional dilemma of the artist in America, the conflicting claims of an allegiance to Europe and to the American scene." In the 1930s the American was played down as against the European, modernist perspective. During the war, as we have seen, an increasing sense of "Americanness" began to emerge. The children of immigrants found themselves in an excellent position to mediate between these two strains. "The second-generation Jewish writer has learned to be aware of a tradition immediately his, that is European and American at once; he is *himself* the guarantee of the singleness of Europe and America."[28]

The emerging Jewish writers bridged a second chasm, Fiedler suggested. Whereas the "typical American author in most periods had been almost aggressively anti-intellectual," the young Jewish writer, emerging from both an intellectual background and ideological politics, was well equipped to deal with intellectual matters. "He was convinced of the unity of his vocation from conversation to creation." The urban Jewish writer became a leader in the "attempt to close the gap between criticism and creation."[29]

Ultimately, Fiedler believed, the real value and importance for the young Jewish intellectuals lay in their ability to articulate their experience. The New York Intellectuals had stressed throughout the late 1930s their importance as intellectuals and the special role and insight intellectuals brought to the modern world. In the postwar context of reawakened Jewishness, they transposed that position to their new area of concern. "In this apocalyptic period of atomization and uprooting, of a catholic terror and a universal alienation, the image of the Jew tends to become the image of everyone; and we are perhaps approaching the day," Fiedler concluded, "when the Jew will come to seem the central symbol, the essential myth of the whole Western world."[30] This position, postulated by Fiedler and others in the late 1940s, enjoyed increasing repute during the 1950s. The emergence and general popularity of Jewish-American literature in these years points to the acceptance of Fiedler's theme. This achievement reflects the growing critical importance of these intellectuals perhaps more than the intrinsic value of the argument does. There had always been isolated artists, from the New Yorkers' modernist hero Franz Kafka to Sylvia Plath, Kazin's student at Smith. These Jewish intellectuals attempted to enlarge the scale from individual isolation to group isolation and to argue that a shared, lonely experience endowed them with special sight. They did not claim to have solutions, but merely previous experience with the dilemmas of modern existence.

Whereas they had earlier argued for a role as the modern "cleric" and arbiter of modern culture because of their intellectual calling, they now claimed to offer a uniquely appropriate view of modern society, thanks to their ethnic background. In both cases the goal remained the same—recognition by society at large of their particular talents—but the new focus no longer required them to minimize their Jewishness and to strike a cosmopolitan pose. In this manner, they adjusted their ambitions of the 1930s to their personal reorientation of the postwar period. Intellectuals should still unravel the twists and knots of modern society. In a world of alienated individuals, Jewish intellectuals had the best training and the most to offer. There is an inherent irony in this argument, however. In the process of presenting themselves as pathfinders in the modern world, these Jewish intellectuals overcame many of the exclusions and the feeling of marginality which they believed qualified them to be guides. The moment their arguments won acceptance, their peripheral status ended. Undaunted by this internal contradiction, they staked their claims.

The New York Intellectuals did not think themselves America's first alienated intellectuals. As intellectuals, in fact, they felt part of a long tradition, including many of the modernist heroes they had resurrected in the late 1930s. In addition to their notions of group marginality, which differed from individual feelings of aloneness, they also attempted to carry their alienation with them to the central position they felt they should occupy. Here they broke new ground. Alienation and marginality became the common stock of a society rather than the province of an intellectual or cultural minority. To have this argument take hold, the society had to be convinced that alienation and tenuousness defined its lot. The challengers to this thesis came not from the intellectual world but from among those who continued to believe in the promise of American life. In fact, in the 1950s these defenders began to point to a wide variety of social developments which they argued testified to the achievement of that promise. American prosperity—suburbs, schools, family security, television, automobiles—was hailed as tangible evidence of the arrival of the good life. Numerous glorifications of American life and money appeared on the best-seller lists during the postwar decades. In one sense, nothing was new. Popular literature which hailed the virtues of American prosperity went back to Horatio Alger's dime novels in the late nineteenth century, if not further. This tradition, however, underwent two significant adjustments which confronted the claims of the New York Intellectuals. First, Jewish authors became part of the cadre of popular writers praising American prosperity while writing about Jewish characters. Hardly intellectuals, they nonetheless shunned their "special sight" as members of an alienated group and chose, instead, to champion the notion that life was good. More important, their novels often pretended to a high-mindedness rarely claimed by popular literature, and they contained themes directly contrary to those under discussion among the New York Intellectuals.

In the face of these problems, especially the countervailing themes which underlay the novels, Leslie Fiedler could not, for example, merely dismiss Herman Wouk's *Marjorie Morningstar* as a second-rate, popular novel pandering to mass tastes. A subtle theme Fiedler found in Wouk's plot line made *Marjorie Morningstar* more subversive than it might appear. Wouk offered a countermyth to the one being argued by the New Yorkers. One of his characters, initially attractive to Marjorie and the reader, is set up as an example of the Jew as wanderer, the "artist," the representative of the avant-garde. Fiedler contended that there was also a contrasting character, the Jew as settled suburbanite. According to Fiedler the second character's triumph illustrated Wouk's "contention that the Jew was never (or has, at any rate, ceased to be) the rootless challenger, the stranger, which legend has made him, but instead is the very paragon of the happy citizen at home, loyal, chaste, thrifty—and successful."[31]

The writings of the Jewish intellectuals, in social science as well as literature, opposed these rosy portrayals of contemporary America. It was not that once-aliented Jews now joined the ranks of the "happy citizen" but that all individuals now lived alienated lives, Nathan Glazer maintained—a "*systematic* alienation involved in modern social organization as we know it: complex, large-scale industrial society."[32] No one felt truly at home in the modern world. The Jew had never felt at home, not before the war and not after. To fool oneself into thinking otherwise was to avoid reality. Furthermore, society at large now shared what the Jew had always experienced. To pretend the opposite only minimized the chance for Jews to use their insight to aid the larger community.

During previous periods when Jews felt excluded from society, they had sustained themselves by finding meaning and identity in their community on the periphery. This had been true for the residents of the immigrant ghettos as well as for the young radical intellectuals gathering about *Partisan Review*. Now society as a whole suffered from a sense of alienation, and this brought changes for everyone. It is the "unique fact of our [postwar] times," Glazer observed, that societal perceptions have changed; "there has been a revolutionary change in the psychological condition of man, reflected in the individual's feeling of isolation, homelessness, insecurity, restlessness, anxiety." It was no longer a matter of not being a part of the main cohesive center of society; now individuals felt that no such community existed. "Man's presumed oneness with his fellows and with the world is no more," Glazer contended. The history of the Jew's "life and his wanderings are, in a sense, the image of the world's destiny," Daniel Bell concluded. "His heightened sense of his own alienation is a prescient tremor of the quake to come."[33]

From their beginnings in ethnic ghettos, these intellectuals were always aware of their separateness, of their position between two cultures. As the shape of the modern world began to come into focus—when the utopianism of the thirties gave way to the pessimistic harshness of the postwar era—their perspective now seemed to offer a guide for the contemporary world. Already during the war, Isaac Rosenfeld began to argue for the special vision of the alienated Jew. In his section of the "Under Forty" symposium in 1944, Rosenfeld noted that the young Jewish writers "are bound to observe much that is hidden to the more accustomed native eye." The Jew is "a member of an internationally insecure group," and as such "he has grown personally acquainted with some of the fundamental themes of insecurity that run through modern literature. He is a specialist in alienation [the one international banking system the Jews actually control]." This specialty has become increasingly prevalent. Alienation puts him in touch "with the present predicament of almost all intellectuals and, for all one knows, with future conditions of civilized humanity." If alienation has become the common condition, Jews have emerged as its best analysts. "Since modern life is so complex that no man can possess it in its entirety," Rosenfeld concluded, "the outsider often finds himself the perfect insider."[34]

In the late thirties and early forties, these intellectuals had argued that their position as intellectual critics of society put them in a special place in that society—a place similar to that of medieval clerics, William Phillips argued. They believed themselves to be well situated for cultural arbitration and comment. In the postwar years, they added a new ingredient. They continued to maintain their intellectual standards, but now a social element furthered their claim. As Jews—and especially as alienated young Jews, standing apart from both their roots and the general society—they were in a unique position as commentators for the larger society. They were the outsiders who became the "perfect insiders," the perfect outsiders.

An intellectual model existed for this "perfect outsider." In the late 1930s *Partisan Review* had done much to introduce Franz Kafka to America. Leslie Fiedler argued in 1948 that, among major literary figures, Kafka "belongs particularly to us." Viewing Kafka as the archetypal alienated artist, Daniel Bell, in his discussion of alienation, quoted Auden on the Czech writer. "It was fit and proper that [Kafka] should have been a Jew," the English poet wrote, "for the Jews have for a long time been placed in the position in which we are now all to be, of having no home."[35] Kafka, tormented and isolated, offered all people a vision of the modern world, albeit an unhappy one. The one element

which distinguished him from most other modern writers provided his extra
insight—his Jewishness. To have full insight into Kafka himself and, by
extension, into modern life it was thus necessary to possess a Jewish
perspective. In an essay on Kafka written in *Commentary* in the mid-1950s,
Clement Greenberg argued the essential Jewish foundation of Kafka's thinking.
"Though Gentile history has finally brought Kafka emancipation, it still
remains Gentile, therefore essentially dangerous to the Jew, emancipated or
not." Instead, Greenberg asserted, Kafka held a steady belief in halakic order,
the belief that Jewish history stopped with the extinction of Palestine and will
begin again when the Messiah comes. Until then, Jewish life is to be kept
"humdrum, thoroughly prosaic, and historically immobile within the fence of
the law. Such history as persists is Gentile history." The problem for Kafka, and
for other modern Jewish intellectuals, stemmed from a lack of religious faith.
Kafka replaced religiousity with a reliance on "the most general and self-
evident features of the traditionally Jewish way of life: middle-class orderliness,
routine, sedentary stability, application to daily tasks—and chronic anxiety
about the future." Thus, this most "modern" of modernist writers, the one
who "belongs particularly to us," coped with the problems of contemporary
alienation through a reaffirmed interest in Jewish traditions and the details of
Jewish middle-class existence. "Marx and other emancipated Jews," Greenberg
continued, "tried to hurry the Messiah by looking for him in Gentile history
and foreseeing the imminent conversion of the Gentiles—not exactly to
Judaism, but to a kind of humanity to which Jews could assimilate themselves.
Kafka, the Jew of Prague, could not be so disloyal to what his immediate
experience told him."[36]

Greenberg's analysis rings true not only for Kafka's Prague but also for
Depression New York—for the young "emancipated" Jewish émigrés from
Brooklyn seeking a cosmopolitan "humanity" in Manhattan radical circles.
Kafka provided insight into the modern world, whether Europe in the 1920s or
America after 1945. His writings yielded an explanation of, if not a solution to,
the disorientation of alienation. "His sense of the world around him was the
sense of a trap," Greenberg concluded, "and as a Jew he was right, as the Jews
of Europe had reason to know twenty years after his death, and as those in
Prague ten years later still had reason to know."[37] Understanding Kafka and the
modern condition came most easily to the Jewish intellectual, Greenberg
implied. Having followed analogous intellectual paths, having rejected the
messianic hopes of "emancipated Jews" and others, and bringing with them the
unique perspective of the perfect outsider, the Jewish intellectuals found in the
relevance of Kafka's writings for the postwar world another verification of
their own critical superiority.

Once again, the New York Intellectuals showed a particular flair for arguing
that historical reality placed them in a unique situation for making insightful
criticism and comment. As radical intellectuals in the 1930s, alienated Jews in
the 1940s, and, as we shall see, ex-radicals in the 1950s, they frequently

discovered their own position remarkably appropriate for the contemporary situation. In the postwar years many Jewish writers discovered the value of their once-marginal existence as a guide to modern life, and large segments of non-Jewish society agreed with them. Beginning their reevaluations on personal grounds—shocked by the Holocaust into redefining their own identities—they later found a public application for the results of these investigations.

As was true of Kafka, their Jewishness, political past, and ethnic background intertwined. Kafka's "Jewishness is by no means incidental," Leslie Fiedler maintained.

> In America, in particular, where the impulse of the Frontier has become the doubtful strength of cities, a generation of writers and critics whose thirtieth year falls somewhere in the forties has appeared; Delmore Schwartz, Alfred Kazin, Karl Shapiro, Issac Rosenfeld, Paul Goodman, Saul Bellow, H. J. Kaplan, typically urban, second-generation Jews, chiefly ex-Stalinists, ambivalently intellectual but for all their anguish insolently at home with ideas and words.[38]

In the final analysis, the two central elements which connected these individuals, which defined their past lives, came together as one. They had been Jews first, the young boys from the ghetto, the sons of Jewish immigrants. Kazin had felt himself a "Jewish radical" among the WASP's, Trilling a "Jewish professor" alienated from a midwestern environment. By the late 1930s they had become intellectuals, arguing against the proletarian writers and for high culture and intellectual independence. In the postwar years, as part of their attempt to understand themselves and their place, these two essential characteristics united to provide the basis of their incipient public identities. They had never denied these attributes, although some like Trilling had minimized the impact of Jewishness. Now it became elemental. They defined, modified, and adjusted their perceptions to suit individual needs.[39] But they had all come to accept and, largely, to proclaim their Jewishness. Their ethnic identity overcame their former universalism just as their intellectualism had taken precedence over their radicalism a decade before. Now self-defined Jewish intellectuals, they laid claim to a special appropriateness for their personal viewpoint and to a high value for their insight.

It would have been impossible for the New York Intellectuals to embrace immediately the whole of Jewish culture or of Judaism. They chose to take from the Jewish tradition and add its positive elements to the intellectual position they had been developing. They had once been, as Harold Rosenberg argued, both nobody and somebody. The "somebody side" of their personalities—their Jewishness—had been neglected, while they overcame their "nobody side" and made a "name for themselves." Having established themselves, they looked back to discover that they had not been blank slates. They had come out of a cultural tradition, and they now sought to reattach themselves to it, in a manner befitting their intellectual calling. Having once linked themselves to radical movements, they were wary of becoming either dependent or subservient—of losing intellectual autonomy for the sake of political or institutional attachment. Elliot Cohen, the founding editor of *Commentary*, offered an appropriate solution in an article entitled "Intellectuals and the Jewish Community," published in 1949. Applauding the revived interest in Jewish culture and "things Jewish," Cohen felt that nothing better attested "the genuineness of this new impulse than the community's excited interests in the younger Jewish intellectuals, and their rumored revived concern with 'things Jewish.' " Part of the excitement, Cohen felt, stemmed from the community's awareness of the reevaluation going on in the mind of such an intellectual. "He is addressing himself to one or another phase of a larger task—the retesting and reevaluation of the intellectual and spiritual values of his own life and of the culture and society."[40]

What is remarkable about Cohen's article is that it called less on the intellectual to function for the community than on the community to recognize and appreciate the work of these intellectuals. "This is something new, this focus on the culture-maker and the culture-bearer himself, rather than on institutions or ideologies, or even 'cultural products,' " Cohen admitted. Yet, "if we are interested in the future of the Jewish heritage in America, that future depends primarily on them . . . . No bees, no honey." The intellectual whom Cohen described was clearly a product of the political and cultural battles of the preceding decades. His young intellectual was interested "in social betterment, but, for the most part, he approached society on the cultural and social, rather than political, level." Furthermore, he was "no utopian," for he weighed societal goals against potential sacrifices in human values and liberties.[41] The intellectuals themselves, Cohen was pleased to report, are already becoming aware of the potential convergence of the intellectual and the Jewish community.

> One of *Commentary's* writers, a member of the avant-garde in very good standing, reported the other day, with the sense of an important personal discovery, that whenever an article of his appeared it seemed to be read and argued about "by the most amazing variety of people in all kinds of circles," and for the first time as a practicing intellectual he had the sense of being a part of some kind of community in which his ideas counted for something. Similar testimony has been voiced by others, non-Jewish as well as Jewish, on more than one occasion; and warily some have begun to live with the idea that maybe one could find some closer relation with that community.[42]

Although Cohen's political viewpoint was no longer utopian, his picture of the future influence of these intellectuals was exceedingly rosy. He added a prophetic appraisal of the "Jewish-intellectual-religious tradition" in the later twentieth century. It may, Cohen observed, "flower in ways that will stand comparison with Spain, Germany, Eastern Europe, and elsewhere." "The intellectuals are there," he concluded. "If the marriage is to be made it is only for Jewish communal-minded people to show by *their actions* that their intentions are honorable—and serious."[43]

Cohen was very likely referring to a much larger grouping than the New York Intellectuals affiliated with *Commentary*. However, he was describing the situation of these very intellectuals, and their past and future. They sought a place where their intellectual abilities would be recognized and appreciated and their positions affirmed. During an era when the search for personal definition led them to reassess the Jewish community from which they had emerged years before, that very community seemed to offer the institutional base upon which to develop their public careers. In the late forties, as one "member of the avant-garde in good standing" discovered, the arguments of these Jewish intellectuals could find an audience outside the narrow confines of their intellectual community. Their first task in the postwar years had been to reevaluate and redefine their own identity as Jews, to try to work out the precise relation between their intellectual side, which had been growing, and their Jewish side, which had remained dormant. They enlarged their personal view to a general vision they felt society required. They claimed a special sight based on their unique position as Jewish intellectuals and argued that others should grant them the privileges attached to this status. Having created an intellectual identity among themselves in the late 1930s and having reassessed their personal identities in the immediate postwar years, they found their public influence expanding, first to the "Jewish community" and increasingly to society at large. Having rediscovered their personal connections to Jewishness, they discovered a Jewish community increasingly interested in them. This wider audience proved the beginning of a fuller recognition in the next years. This is hardly surprising, however. Having once been the pride of a Jewish community—the "bright *pishers* from Brownsville"—they found themselves the objects of increasing adulation among the new, postwar Jewish community, among the kind of people who had known all along they would turn out all right.

Chapter 9

Into the
Promised Land

The commitment of the New York Intellectuals, however tenuous, to a renewed interest in their own Jewishness had two strikingly different results. Atop the issues which had marked their intellectual investigations for a decade—questions of cultural priorities and political analysis—a new set of topics arose, centered on the relating of Jewish questions and identities to other intellectual themes. Jewishness became an intellectual problem as well as a matter of identity. In addition, many of the questions which stirred these intellectuals also stirred Jews in general. Following Elliot Cohen's hopes for the emmerging relationship between young Jewish intellectuals and the Jewish community, many Jews turned to the intellectuals for guidance or insight into contemporary Jewish questions. Cohen fulfilled his own prophecy, for a main focus of this intellectual discussion developed in the journal he edited, *Commentary*. While *Partisan Review* continued along the political and cultural road it had taken during World War II, *Commentary* met the political-cultural-ethnic questions head-on. Drawing on the same pool of talent as *PR*, *Commentary* grew in the postwar years to rival its "cousin" in intellectual prominence. The larger world perhaps perceived *Commentary* as a Jewish-intellectual magazine, while thinking of *Partisan Review* as a literary journal. To the New York Intellectuals the distinctions became minor. The journals both functioned as "family publications," as Norman Podhoretz would call them—in-house organs of an intellectual community on the verge of wide-scale success.

The second result of the renewed interest in Jewish themes concerned personal rather than intellectual investigations. The returning to their Jewishness brought these intellectuals back to their own beginnings. They aimed to understand not the attachment to the Jewish community at large but the attachment to their past. The true discoveries of the attempts to define Jewishness and their own identities had to end with a mature understanding of their parents and their own place in the generational tide of which they were surely a part. It was in keeping with their intellectual style, however, that these endeavors in self-discovery took place not only in the minds of the searchers or on analysts' couches. *Partisan Review* and, especially, *Commentary* published numerous quasi-autobiographical articles, which tried to extend the experiences of one or a few Jews to young American Jews in general.

These two developments—the rise of *Commentary* and the coming to terms with their own background—marked the final steps in the maturation of the New York Intellectuals. They emerged as clearly identified Jewish intellectuals, facing the political and cultural problems of the present, on the basis of a personal resolution of their past.

THE WORD, THE SAGES, AND THE GRAND DESIGN

> *We (Jews) believe in the Word. We believe in study. . . . We have faith in the intellect, in the visions of visionary men, in the still, small voice of poets, and thinkers, and sages.*
> —Elliot Cohen

> *The main difference between* Partisan Review *and* Commentary *is that we admit to being a Jewish magazine and they don't.*
> —Elliot Cohen[1]

The desire to create a Jewish-intellectual magazine did not begin with *Commentary* in 1945. There had been earlier attempts in America, some of which involved New York Intellectuals. The *Menorah Journal*, of which Elliot Cohen had once been managing editor, began publishing in 1915. Although he published his first fiction and criticism in the *Menorah Journal*, Lionel Trilling later called its Jewishness "parochial." In the radical, cosmopolitan period of the Great Depression, the insular Jewishness of the *Menorah Journal* hardly suited the intellectuals who ultimately joined *Partisan Review*. The American Jewish Committee sponsored the publication of the *Contemporary Jewish Record*, from 1938 until 1945. Both Philip Rahv and Clement Greenberg served as managing editor of this journal in the early 1940s. It pointed to the type of journal *Commentary* would become. The "Under Forty" symposium of young Jewish writers appeared in the *Contemporary Jewish Record*, for example. Yet, the magazine remained a small-scale operation, not consciously meant to serve the larger Jewish community.[2]

Commentary, also published by the American Jewish Committee, superseded the *Contemporary Jewish Record* both in scope and, more important, in reputation. Making its initial appearance in November 1945, *Commentary* set itself the task of becoming a successful intellectual magazine which extended beyond the

traditional themes or audience of small Jewish magazines. A crucial element in
the success of this venture was *Commentary*'s ability to draw on a large roster of
American intellectuals, especially those seeking to bridge the divisions in their
own minds between intellectual roles and Jewish heritage. Among the New
York Intellectuals these issues had become exceedingly poignant, and they
filled the pages of *Commentary*. Like *Partisan Review* before it, *Commentary*
happily published articles from many prominent intellectuals. Also like *PR*, it
became clearly identified, in its main intellectual endeavors and its chief
writers, with the New York Intellectuals.

The initial choices about personnel reflect this basic position. Given a large
measure of freedom from the Committee, as the American Jewish Committee
is always called, *Commentary* could go its own intellectual way. Although subtler
pressures continued to exist, the magazine never functioned as either a public-
relations journal for Committee activities or a forum for Committee
philosophy and position papers. The Committee generally respected the
editorial independence of the journal's editor. Elliot Cohen combined a
number of skills which made him an appropriate choice to direct the new
magazine. After leaving the *Menorah Journal*, in 1931, Cohen had spent a
number of years as a fund-raiser for Jewish organizations. A Stalinist in the
early 1930s, Cohen had maintained close ties with many student radicals during
the first years of the decade. His downtown office became a frequent gathering
spot for uptown college radicals of the National Student League, Meyer
Schapiro later recalled. "Elliot Cohen was their guru." Abandoning his
Stalinism in the same period when other New York Intellectuals did, Cohen
continued to interact and maintain close ties with the growing circle around
Partisan Review.[3]

When he selected his staff for *Commentary*, his choices often mirrored these
connections. Clement Greenberg became managing editor and Nathan Glazer
one of the two editorial assistants. Sidney Hook sat on the board of
contributing editors. In the first months and years, titles changed and jobs
shifted, but a heavy representation of New York Intellectuals remained a
Commentary constant. Within a short time both Robert Warshow and Irving
Kristol joined the magazine's staff.[4]

Cohen's magazine drew many of its contributors from the same community
of writers as the "new" *Partisan Review* ten years earlier. *Commentary*'s initial
number not only featured Cohen's "Act of Affirmation" and Glazer's "The
Study of Man" but also contained reviews by Harold Rosenberg and Mary
McCarthy as well as pieces by Paul Goodman and George Orwell, both of
whom had frequently written for *PR*. The second number featured an article by
Alfred Kazin and reviews by Hannah Arendt and Saul Bellow. Robert Warshow
made his first *Commentary* appearance in the third issue, Sidney Hook and Isaac
Rosenfeld in the fourth, and Daniel Bell in the fifth. By the end of
Commentary's first year, Diana Trilling, Irving Howe, William Barrett, Irving
Kristol, Philip Rahv, and Clement Greenberg had also published articles or
reviews.[5]

The first issue of *Commentary* sold only 4,341 copies. Funding by the Committee freed the magazine from the concerns about profit and financial stability, and as late as 1950, when its circulation reached 20,000, *Commentary* still lost $104,000 a year.[6] Cohen set out to create an important intellectual journal and focused his enormous editorial energy on the task of giving the journal a fairly clear direction and philosophy. *Commentary* often struck sympathetic nerves among many of the potential contributors and readers, as articles drove right to the center of the crucial questions Jewish intellectuals and Jews in general, asked themselves. *Commentary*'s tone, Norman Podhoretz later observed, "was, of course, the family [New York Intellectual] tone, and . . . it repelled public-relations minded Jewish readers." Those like Harold Rosenberg bothered by the chauvinism of certain Jewish zealots, found *Commentary* speaking to more subtle and personal questions. The journal, according to Podhoretz,

> attracted intellectuals to whom the idea had never before occurred that things Jewish could be talked about with the same disinterestedness, the same candor, the same range of reference, and the same resonance as any serious subject. Cohen thus helped to make an interest in things Jewish intellectually and culturally respectable within the family. . . .[7]

Not every member of the "family" responded positively to Cohen's venture. In its initial phase, Lionel Trilling expressed hesitations about becoming involved in the magazine. Although his wife reviewed for *Commentary*, Trilling turned down Cohen's request that he serve on its advisory board. He based his refusal on his experience as a contributor and editorial staff member of the *Menorah Journal*, of which Cohen had been, as Trilling put it, "managing editor and presiding genius." "I had had my experience of the intellectual life lived in reference to what Cohen called the Jewish community," Trilling wrote, "and I had no wish to renew it by associating myself with a Jewish magazine."[8] Trilling's ambivalence about "things Jewish" emerged in other contexts, as we have seen. Once *Commentary*'s intellectual position had been established, however, Trilling joined the impressive list of writers whose work came under the editorial scrutiny of Elliot Cohen.

A poor writer himself, Cohen saw his reputation as an editor grow to enormous proportions. Writing for *Commentary* became a labor, not always of love. "He was a demanding, doctrinaire intellectual," recalled his old friend Arnold Beichman. He was a great editor, Beichman added, "because he was so demanding." Cohen did not write much on his own. Instead, "he bullied everybody," Midge Decter later remembered. As Cohen's secretary, she witnessed much of the friction which could develop between the editor and the writers. "He pushed people around; he had many enemies. Editors always have enemies, but he had more than anyone ever needed to have. Everybody hated him at least once a year for something." To the outside world, *Commentary* probably appeared as Cohen characterized it for *Time* in 1951, when he said that the "idea of *Commentary* was not to tell people what to think but to give them the material to think with."[9] Clearly, Elliot Cohen had a fairly precise notion of what that material should be.

Cohen's background differed slightly from that of his Jewish intellectual contemporaries, which surely added to the intensity of his personality and the personal difficulties he ultimately faced. Born in Iowa, he moved to Mobile, Alabama, as a young boy. A child prodigy, he went to Yale at fourteen. As Midge Decter summarized this remarkable beginning, "To be a fourteen-year-old who goes to college is traumatic. To be a fourteen-year-old Jew from Mobile who goes to Yale [in 1914] is triply traumatic." His early experiences largely confirmed the high promise of his youth. In 1917, while still at Yale, he won the Intercollegiate Menorah Medal of the year, for his essay "The Promise of the American Synagogue," which the *Menorah Journal* reprinted. On graduation from Yale in 1918, Cohen received the John Addison Porter Fellowship in English ("one of the highest distinctions at Yale," the *Menorah Journal* reported) for graduate study. As Lionel Trilling later noted, Cohen declined to pursue his graduate studies, feeling the intense barriers placed against Jews in university English departments. Instead, he entered the field of journalism.[10]

Becoming attached to the *Menorah Journal*, Cohen rapidly rose from assistant editor in April 1924 to associate editor in November 1924 and managing editor in June 1925. In addition to his editorial skills, he contributed reviews and, from 1924 until 1927, wrote a column entitled "Notes for a Modern History of the Jews." A collection of assorted tidbits on the Jewish community, "Notes" contained current events, gossip, political and athletic events involving Jews, obituaries, and weddings. Only twenty-five when he began as managing editor, Cohen oversaw many tasks more important than his "Notes" column. During his tenure he introduced the first publications of Trilling, Tess Slesinger, Clifton Fadiman, Meyer Levin, and Herbert Solow. He fell out, however, with the editor in chief, Harry Hurwitz, and left the magazine. From 1931 until the appearance of *Commentary*, Cohen supported himself through his fund raising activities. Although he appears to have been moderately successful in this line of work, he never adjusted. "The misery he must have endured during those dark days is gruesome to contemplate," Podhoretz observed. Dwight Macdonald recalled lunching with Cohen in the early 1940s, when Macdonald had begun editing *Politics*. "I can see one reason he was impressed [with *Politics*]—it was so extremely free and independent. I was wondering how this guy—obviously a very brilliant guy with a lot of charisma, charm, and personal force—how he could possibly be satisfied milking all these fat cats."[11]

Cohen obviously was not satisfied, for when offered the chance to edit *Commentary*, he jumped at it, willingly taking a large cut in pay. He attacked his work with an intensity aimed at "mak[ing] up those fifteen lost years . . . with the compulsiveness and drive of a much younger man," Podhoretz noted.[12]

Within the magazine's staff, Cohen ruled autocratically. "It was Elliot's magazine," Irving Kristol recalled; "he was the boss." While writing very little, Cohen fashioned *Commentary* into the kind of publication he had envisioned and the committee very likely had not. They wanted a "Jewish *Harper's*," Podhoretz believed. Instead *Commentary* became a "Jewish" *Partisan Review*, with one exception. Podhoretz distinguished between *PR* as a journal for "producers" of ideas and *Commentary* as one of "consumers."[13] It is clear that Cohen and the Committee anticipated a wider audience, especially in the Jewish community, than *PR* had ever gained. The different eras of the journal's births offer an explanation for this distinction, especially since both employed the same cadre of writers. In the late 1930s *Partisan Review* developed on the periphery of American radical and literary circles, a bastion of high-culture radicals defending standards against Stalinists and philistines. By the postwar years the position of these intellectuals had undergone a significant change. More willing to participate in American society in general, they also grew much more conscious of their Jewishness and their relation to the Jewish community. They believed that their role should combine their Jewishness and their intellectualism, and Cohen, specifically, called on the Jewish community to seek the guidance of these young intellectuals. *Commentary* became a deliberate means to that end.

Although Cohen thus readjusted the direction of *Commentary* away from the initial plans of the Committee, Macdonald recalled that Cohen was "always kind of unhappy because he could never really break away from [the Committee]." "He survived," Macdonald believed, because "his nature involved a tremendous respect for authority and power." Despite his editorial independence and dominance of the staff, Cohen suffered from a lifelong sense of inferiority. His alma mater, Midge Decter recalled, was his most sensitive point. "You'd think that he wasn't the editor of the most distinguished intellectual magazine in America," Decter said. "He kept going up there all the time and then he sent his son there. Every time he spent a weekend there, he came back with the marks of suffering on him."[14]

As an editor, Cohen accepted the implicit authority of the Committee, while maintaining theoretical and, for the most part, actual autonomy. Political issues never arose to cause conflict. But occasionally the relation between the organization and the magazine became clear, for example, in the case of a short article by Isaac Rosenfeld, "Adam and Eve on Delancey Street." A whimsical essay on Jewish dietary habits, Rosenfeld's piece combined some popular anthropology with a measure of tongue-in-cheek satire to relate the food customs of Jews to the sins of sexuality. His initial premise, the fascination of crowds on the East Side with Kosher Fry Beef ("Jewish bacon") led him to speculate on the rationale behind the kosher proscriptions. "Here at the delicatessen store the crowd stands in a sexual trance . . . the businessman stops in his rounds to look at kosher bacon, and the housewife stops at his side, and in their minds thoughts of the golden *shiksa*, wild and unrestrained, and the husky *shaigetz . . . shaigetz* and *shiksa* are our yin and yang, the poles of sex." Rosenfeld also "analyzed" the secret roots of the milk and meat division: "*Milchigs*, having to do with milk, is feminine; *felishigs*, meat, is masculine. Their unction in one meal, or within one vessel, is forbidden, for their union is a sexual act."[15]

Although the editorial note accompanying the article said that the section of the magazine where the article was printed welcomed "informal explorations—i.e., *kibbitzes*—on matters high and low," nonetheless an uproar over the piece broke out at the Committee. Cohen found himself in a difficult position. "There was even a move to oust him," Macdonald remembered. Instead, Cohen printed several letters, including two from rabbis who characterized Rosenfeld's article as "disgusting" and "hav[ing] no place in any Jewish periodical." Cohen then ran a two-paragraph apology. Despite his reputation for absolute editorial control, he claimed there were "limits beyond which editors cannot go in editing writers." He admitted, "There is one anecdote that was in very bad taste."* This represents, he publicly acknowledged, "a lapse in editorial watchfulness, which the Editor deeply regrets."[16]

The ultimate authority of the Committee thus caused Cohen to make a public apology for an article which, among the New York Intellectuals, had probably seemed relatively harmless, partially insightful, and certainly witty. Macdonald, in his "usual superfluous way," as he put it, "got up a little round-robin in support of Elliot." When he showed it to Cohen, Macdonald assumed the editor would be pleased. "On the contrary, he was livid. It rather embarrassed him."[17]

The pressures of being a child prodigy, early intellectual successes followed by fifteen years of "milking fat cats," the intensity with which he molded *Commentary*, and his ambivalences about authority—from Yale to the American Jewish Committee—all combined to place an enormous burden on Cohen. Despite personal problems and with a driving ambition, however, Cohen pushed the magazine into prominence. His abrasive and intense nature may have been a foreboding of later troubles—in his early fifties he was "old and crabbed," Decter recalled—but in the first years of his editorship his achievement was considerable. At Cohen's death a friend wrote a letter to *Commentary* which nicely captured what Cohen had done. The friend told a story of a visit by Cohen's father. The old southern gentleman "recounted how during his childhood in Lithuania, he was the only Jew who could write

---

*Cohen did not specify which anecdote he found in bad taste, but it was quite likely the retelling of an old Yiddish joke as a demonstration of the milk-meat relation to sexuality which caused the stir: "The Jewish joke about the man with cancer of the penis bears this [sexual theory] out. He is advised by the doctor to soak his penis in hot water. His wife, finding him so engaged, cries out, 'Cancer-shmancer. *Doz iz a milchig teppel!*—Who cares about cancer? You're using a *milchig* pot.'" (Rosenfeld, "Adam and Eve on Delancey Street," *Commentary*, Oct. 1949, p. 387).

Lithuanian," so he quite automatically became important—the letter writer for his community. "And now," he said to Elliot, "it's all come full circle for us Cohens. You are the letter writer for your community."[18]

Cohen's respect for authority and established traditions and the newly emerging focus of the New York Intellectuals easily merged in one area. In the philosophy and tone which he brought to the magazine, Cohen sought to bridge the gap between intellectual pursuits and "things Jewish," as well as to discuss American and world politics. Among those arguing the liberal anti-Communist line, *Commentary* moved to the fore. The items Cohen offered his readers as "material to think with" included increasingly hard-line articles on communism and the Soviet Union. While not atypical of other magazines of this period, from *Partisan Review* to the *New York Times Magazine* and *Time*, Cohen's possessed multiple intentions. He not only shared the anti-Stalinist commitment of the New York Intellectuals but also saw in it further benefits. This theme, Podhoretz later observed, was "also part of a secret program to demonstrate that not all Jews were Communists." This argument found counterparts in other anti-Communist writings of this period, as liberals and socialists also tried to break down stereotypical notions which lumped various groups with Communists. Cohen, however, had an even larger conception; his anticommunism became a part of what Podhoretz called

> a Grand Design whose precise details were known only to Cohen, though guessed at accurately enough by others, to lead the family out of the desert of alienation in which it had been wandering for so long and into the promised land of democratic, pluralistic, prosperous America where it would live as blessedly in its Jewishness as in its Americanness.[19]

It took the perspective of several years for Podhoretz to be able to summarize the exact aim of Cohen's "design." Yet, for many of the New York Intellectuals, the underlying motives for many of their recent investigations and arguments fit precisely with Cohen's aim. They were moving toward the center of American society, politically and socially. Their long-standing position on the periphery gave way to institutional and cultural attachments at the heart of the society. In this effort *Commentary* clearly played a key role, discussing the place and importance of Jews and intellectuals in modern America. Beyond these immediate questions lay more complex goals. For as Podhoretz summarized at Cohen's death, the *Commentary* editor's aims went beyond either the stated goals of the magazine or even those discussed in his early *Commentary* article entitled "The Jewish Community and the Intellectuals." Cohen attempted to help resurrect a broader tradition, to prove wrong the notion prevalent in the 1920s and 1930s "that the Protestant-liberal-bourgeois synthesis which had formed the basis of Western civilization since the early 17th century was disintegrating." In the 1950s, Podhoretz added, a "revulsion set in against the idea that the West was 'finished.' . . . This revulsion expressed itself very strongly among young philosophers, historians, and sociologists of the postwar period, many of whom found *Commentary* hospitable to the kinder conceptions they were developing." "The 50s," Podhoretz concluded,

> undertook to demonstrate that the Protestant-liberal-bourgeois synthesis had *not* broken down—that, in fact our civilization was proving itself capable of adapting to new circumstances without losing form or identity. In this undertaking, *Commentary* was an important participant.[20]

For many members of the "family," this approach proved very meaningful. Lionel Trilling, a leading figure in the reassertion of the Western tradition and Western values, remembered Cohen as having "a sense of the subtle interrelations that exist between the seemingly disparate parts of a culture." While bearing what Trilling called "the heavy pain of genius," Cohen thus helped articulate the cultural goals Trilling and others strove to achieve. Not all of the New York Intellectuals rushed to embrace Cohen's or Trilling's vision. Some overtly resisted, Irving Howe branding the era an "age of conformity."[21] Others felt themselves pulled along by the current without fully accepting or evaluating the major propositions. Yet an overall impression emerged. The center could hold—or at least in *Commentary* one could believe that it could.

Without shedding the previous claims to insight from their experiences with alienation, the intellectuals writing for *Commentary*, under the close scrutiny of the journal's editor, offered what solace could be found in contemporary society. Understanding the modern condition as well as the historical truths, the Jewish intellectuals came out of the desert. They had moved from their marginal position in the 1930s, in school or in the radical parties, and had begun to find a new home at the center. One final step remained to complete the journey, a full resolution of the questions about the home they had left behind.

THE PRODIGAL SONS

> *[The] typical Jewish intellectual of the late 1940s . . . is a cultural child of the Great Depression, of the defeat of social reconstruction that followed it, of the great human cataclysm of World War II, and of the present period of peace which is not peace. Culturally he feels himself the survivor of a long series of routs and massacres. Insecurity is his portion, and doom and death are to him familiar neighbors. . . . He thinks of himself as wary, unhopeful, isolated and alienated. . . . Rather than ranging the whole country or the many continents, he is thrown back on himself. Skeptical of large claims of political ideologies, he is neither a joiner nor a devotee. He has almost no humor, little wit, and a kind of self-absorbed solemnity. . . . In contrast to his prototype of the 20s, he is not likely to be a*

novelist, short-story writer, or, least of all, a dramatist. His turn of mind seems to be reflective and analytical, and, as you would expect, his talents are directed toward philosophy, psychology, literary criticism, the social sciences, and religion.
—Elliot Cohen[22]

The immediate postwar years initiated a series of personal investigations and reconsiderations. The New York Intellectuals began the process of self-definition by looking back at their Jewishness and trying to understand their heritage. They furthered the creation of a cultural synthesis which allowed them to enter fully into American society while maintaining the special position of intellectuals and critics. Finally, they helped launch a journal dedicated to discussing both of these issues. *Commentary* tackled political, cultural, and Jewish themes, as well as the interrelation among them. The natural convergence between young Jewish intellectuals and the Jewish community which Elliot Cohen called for seemed to be at hand. Not yet possessing absolute answers, they should at least have had a good measure of consolation in the knowledge that the process of reevaluation was well under way. Instead, the questioning and the searching continued.

Mostly in the pages of *Commentary*, there appeared a succession of articles and self-analyses which sought to describe and explain the current condition of young Jewish intellectuals. While the New York Intellectuals gained increasing success in the postwar years—offers to write, teach, review, edit—contentment did not prevail among them. A measure of personal distancing from society had always marked their existence, especially in the 1930s when *Partisan Review* found itself on the periphery both of the radical movement and of society. The postwar years brought a sense of growing isolation along with the development of their new reputations and positions of importance. In an attempt to "make it" in the larger world, the bright young Jews had cut themselves off from their ghetto environment, beginning their journey to the larger society. After 1945 the end of that journey came into sight, and tangible evidence of success accrued. The intellectuals discovered, however, that their arrival was accompanied not by a sense of fulfillment but rather by some uneasiness. Having begun the journey by separating themselves from their parents and background, they found that it did not end in new, equally strong attachments. Theirs was not the sense of alienation felt by the larger society; the sense of estrangement of the New York Intellectuals was atypical of Americans in the postwar world and of a traditional Jewish life.

The estrangement began before the war, Daniel Bell would observe. "As he grew up, the young Jew confronted with the pressures of secularization gradually detached himself from [the immigrant environment]. But the secular world, stripping him of kinship, could offer no other unity or purpose in its place."[23] The full impact of this alienation had been cushioned during the Depression decade, with its radical optimism, universalism, and the growing cohesion of the *Partisan* crowd. Much of this optimism had yielded to a more limited and wary perspective after 1945. The young intellectuals—now not so young any more—began to try to find an appropriate place for themselves. They had fully accepted their intellectual calling, had claimed for it a central function in American society at large, and had initiated the attempt to come to terms with their own Jewishness. However, trying to orient themselves on the dual coordinates of Americanness and Jewishness, they found it difficult to place themselves exactly. Neither attribute seemed totally appropriate, and they saw themselves caught, as Irving Howe wrote at the time, "between an origin [the young intellectual] can no longer accept and a desired status he cannot attain."[24]

The distances which had grown in the Depression years between these intellectuals and their roots were somewhat conscious creations. They had pulled away from their communities to move across the bridges to Manhattan. In the postwar years a more personal sense of distance developed. In the 1930s the refugee from Brownsville had joined isolated groups—radical movements or the *Partisan* crowd. The Jewish intellectual now considered himself an isolated individual. He felt estranged from his cultural heritage and found few answers in the modern world. His "lack of external buttresses," Howe wrote in 1946 in *Commentary*, "forces [the intellectual] to turn to his own inner resources for intellectual and emotional sustenance—the more he does so, the more he does withdraw, and the more he feels unhappy about his withdrawal and desires a sense of community." The young intellectual, Howe continued, is never fully at home in either place. He is aware of the dilemma which confronts him but unable to resolve it. The word which best describes the situation, Howe thought, is *"Angst."*

> What makes *his* situation more unbearable is that he often cannot take even his own misery with complete seriousness.
>
> The biting sense of irony he has acquired from his family associations and from Jewish cultural tradition forces him to observe his own ridiculousness, his own posturing, his objective insignificance in relation to his self perception. *He is a victim of his own complexity.*[25]

While the writings in *Commentary* by Bell, Howe, and Cohen raised questions about Jews, intellectuals, and alienation in modern society, they spoke most specifically to young Jewish intellectuals like themselves. And the three were hardly alone in these investigations. In a variety of styles and approaches, many of the intellectuals wrestled with these questions. Sociological discussions, literary analysis, and literature itself were used to probe this matter.

A good measure of this activity emerged in larger discussions of alienation and human isolation in the modern world, as well as in the attempt to discover true Jewish identity. Yet, amid the general topics, there developed more-specific investigations of the relation between these intellectuals and their own past. Jews, they claimed, possessed an expertise in marginality, based on hundreds of years of experience. These American Jews, however, encountered a different phenomenon. Only the first, immigrant generation had been forced to live in the ghetto. The second or third might choose, but no longer felt constrained, to do so. Thus, a new sense of alienation rose, that of individuals alienated not from the society but from their own past. As these American-born sons grew increasingly distant from the immigrant environment, they found that more than customs and language faded. Arriving in a strained, disoriented society, these children of immigrants discovered they could not find relief by returning to the world of their fathers, a world receding into history.

In the ethnic world of their parents, Daniel Bell recounted, "the personal environment of the immigrant generation was defined by a pervasive love that emerged out of the concreteness of family experience, since ritual and social life were one." The move out of the ghetto undid this sense of connectedness. The larger world offered no substitute. "Today," Bell wrote in 1946, "the Jew feels the loss of concreteness of love so necessary for all moral life. As a result he turns into himself . . . . It is this loss of communal love which is the source of the self-love and the self-hate, the arrogant chauvinism and the cringing sycophancy so characteristic of Jewish life in our time."[26] Thus, for all Jews of his generation, Bell felt, the lack of support and the increased sense of personal alienation from the immediate past formed a common story.

The young Jewish intellectuals confronted a compounded problem. They had consciously and aggressively moved out of the world of their childhood. Furthermore, their belief in the proper functioning of intellectuals required a certain distancing from society at large—namely, the critical perspective. While this may have provided necessary elements for their work, it did not make their personal lives any more comfortable. Caught between two worlds, as Irving Howe noted, the Jewish intellectual "has largely lost his sense of Jewishness, of belonging to a people with a meaningful tradition, and he has not succeeded in finding a place for himself." Having moved away from his roots before the war, the young intellectual found it impossible to reestablish connection with them after it. His attitude toward "the Jewish culture on which he was reared," Howe continued, was "an ambiguous compound of rejection and nostalgia." "Of late," Elliot Cohen wrote in 1949, "one detects a new note in [the young Jewish intellectual's] sense of personal isolation and alienation which formerly he wore as a badge of distinction. There is a hunger for some group attachment . . . . He has a growing hankering for a smaller community of his own—for shelter and security, appreciation and support."[27] Fully aware of his own growth and maturity, the young Jewish intellectual also became aware of just how far he had come. He waxed more than a little wistful about the journey he had undertaken. Each one "suffers as a man, intellectual, and Jew," Howe reported. One factor which had traditionally lessened this difficulty had vanished. "The compensations he might acquire from a vital tie with his folk-past are also unavailable to him," Howe noted. "*He has lost the sense of continuity which was such sustenance to his forefathers* [italics Howe's]." Nine years later, amid what Howe called "this age of conformity," he would chastise those intellectuals who talked about "the need for roots"; he claimed that it veiled "a desire to compromise the tradition of intellectual independence, to seek in a nation or religion or party a substitute for the tenacity one should find in oneself."[28] In the years immediately following the war, however, it proved extremely difficult to find that personal tenacity. Rather, a sense of personal loss, as well as societal alienation, marked this period. Although not all the intellectuals actively saw the need for new roots, many of them bemoaned the loss of the old ones.

In a second sense many of the intellectuals attempted to "return home" in the postwar years. Their cosmopolitanism had been replaced by a renewed interest in Jewishness; their radicalism had given way to a general acceptance of American society. They called more for adjustments to the system than for its total reconstruction. Generalizing for his contemporaries, Daniel Bell wrote in the mid-1950s, "A radical is a prodigal son. . . . He may eventually return to the house of his elders, but the return is by choice. . . . A resilient society, like a wise parent, understands this ritual, and, in meeting the challenge to tradition, grows." Yet, several years earlier, Bell had offered a different portrait of prodigal sons, this time Jewish ones. In the original parable (and in Bell's general description as well), "the prodigal son returns home, his question revealing to him that home, the concreteness of family love, is the greatest truth." However, Bell noted, "The Jew cannot go home. He can only live in alienation." No home awaited the return of the young Jewish intellectuals—physically or intellectually. As assimilated Jews and as disenchanted radicals, they discovered they could not go back or even rely on the stability or support of their abandoned past. Having lost the shelter of his immigrant home, the young Jewish intellectual "may momentarily yearn for it," Howe admitted, but "he knows he can never find it again. Literally homeless, he has become the ultimate wanderer."[29]

The feeling of loss of their connection to the immigrant communities led these intellectuals to the next logical consideration, the reassessment of their ties to their parents and the process by which they had broken away. A large measure of this reevaluation clearly emerged because of their age. By the late 1940s and early 1950s, no longer the young radicals of earlier days, they undertook the natural reevaluation of parents which is a part of maturation. They discovered, in addition to the traditional pattern of children moving away from their parents and rejecting their life style, that these parents had actively participated in this process. This element of self-denial and sacrifice made its evaluation more difficult and the ultimate pangs more severe. "The greatest risk of memory," Daniel Bell wrote in 1961 in a remarkably revealing passage,

is its repression—the past allowed to come back in the form of self-hate, shame of one's parents, the caricaturing of Jewish traits (most notably verbal agility), the exaggerated thrust of ambition, the claims of superiority by the mere fact of being a Jew, and all the other modes of aggression that arise from the refusal to accept the tension of being in a minority, and the need to balance the insistent demands of the past with the needs of the present.[30]

In a single listing of traits, Bell had captured many of the characteristics of the coterie of intellectuals of which he was a part. It was precisely their verbal agility which had been praised in their youth; they also had felt shame about their parents' immigrant qualities, been enormously ambitious, and often claimed superiority on a number of fronts. They had dealt with these conflicts in the 1930s by repressing them and by abandoning their Jewishness. They now found this old stance to be more a defense mechanism than an intellectual commitment.

These Jewish intellectuals began to see themselves as both connected to and disconnected from their beginnings. The alienated Jew, Bell noted, "is the Jewish orphan. He comes out of himself, rather than out of a past. He is homeless. The present is his only reality." Although the personal links with the past might be broken and reliance on the support of that environment an impossibility, it still became possible to establish some sense of relationship and provide a semblance of order. "In the awareness of his rejection," Bell concluded, "his life is Jewish, too: he is one of a community of exiles whose common experiences are molded by the common fate—and this becomes his parochial tie."[31] Unable to reconstruct the world of their parents, they at least could understand it and appreciate it.

The old antagonisms of ghetto life fell under new light, and the most basic of their personal struggles—those between parents and children—underwent reassessment. The normal tensions between generations took on added strength in the ghetto environment, where parental desires for the assimilation of their children reinforced more-traditional frictions. The Jewish intellectuals finally began to understand what their development had entailed and how much their parents—overbearing mothers or aloof fathers—had participated in that process. They turned back to their own early lives in fresh ways, bringing this new understanding to their professional as well as their personal investigations.

In these years a remarkable outpouring of work by these intellectuals reflects this new awareness, which clearly lay at the root of all the articles on young Jewish intellectuals and alienation and which also motivated a wide variety of other endeavors. Alfred Kazin recounted the difficulty he experienced in finishing his second book, nearly eight years after the success of *On Native Grounds*. His plan had been to write about New York, on the basis of walks about the city. After struggling with the manuscript for several years, he found he could finish the book only when he decided to focus on his own growing up in New York. *A Walker in the City*, Kazin's highly praised autobiographical sketches of his childhood, was the book he "had wanted to write without knowing that [he] did." Recalling his early years in Brownsville in the 1920s,

Kazin drew portraits of his parents and neighborhood and made brief sketches of his early life. "I began to write *A Walker in the City* because my parents led totally anonymous, insignificant lives. It was up to me to speak for them." On a more traditional plane, Irving Howe began the series of publications of anthologies from Yiddish writings. Along with his coeditor Eliezer Greenberg, Howe first published *A Treasury of Yiddish Stories* in 1954, followed in later years by *A Treasurey of Yiddish Poetry* and *Voices from the Yiddish*.[32]

The connections between one's personal past and professional activities did not restrict itself to memoirs and anthologies. The interest which social scientists like Bell and Seymour Martin Lipset showed in questions of social mobility and status anxiety derived at least in part from the same source which animated the works of Kazin and Howe. What is partly true for social science, though, is central to literature. The American-born generation, Bell noted, "found meaning in Isaac Bashevis Singer . . . counter-pointed to such revelations as Isaac Rosenfeld and Saul Bellow made, in their unsentimental, even sardonic narratives of Chicago Jewish life."[33]

Rosenfeld's one novel, *Passage from Home*, affected these intellectuals deeply. While largely ignored by the general public, it received great praise from the New Yorkers when it appeared and continued to do so.[34] Important works often fail to get a wide response on publication, such as James Agee's *Let Us Now Praise Famous Men*, Nathanael West's *Miss Lonelyhearts*, or Henry Roth's *Call It Sleep*. Rosenfeld's work may fall in this category of works wrongly neglected. These books do, however, frequently gain a wider reputation in later years. Nearly forty years after publication, Rosenfeld's novel still has not attained the place the New York Intellectual reviewers initially claimed for it. Perhaps that is because it speaks to them in a much more personal way than it does to a wider audience. Rosenfeld's novel revolved around the ambivalent feelings between immigrant fathers and precocious sons. While a plot does exist to provide dramatic interest and while several other interesting characters emerge, the father-son relationship sits at the fulcrum of the work. In this first-person novel of his youth, Rosenfeld offers a very detailed description of the tensions which existed and the most succinct example of the changed attitude of these intellectuals toward their parents. They now understood how much of their own development had been fueled by personal desires and how much by parental. They began to perceive the intricate relation between their lives and those of their parents. For Bernard, the main character in *Passage from Home*, the recognition comes in a dream.

> One night I dreamed of my father. It was a simple dream, but stronger than I had ever known dreams to be. I dreamed I had become my father. I had reached his age, my hair was gray, my eyes were his shape and color, and when I looked through his eyes I saw the world, not differently, but yet altered as if it were by his own perception. I felt a melancholy that was utterly unlike my own, and yet it was mine—this was no longer the sadness that divided fathers and sons but the one that bound them. I went about with a sense of loss, of great bereavement; the world was

strange, never before entered. But it was not I who was lost, but rather someone else looking for me. When I awoke, still feeling the identity that had been established in my dream, I thought that now at last I had bridged the gulf between this life and the other, and that everything I had hitherto believed about my father was illusion. For without knowing what else the dream signified, I knew that I was indeed his son, and that his life had been meant, at the peril of my own, to live itself out in me.

Alfred Kazin's observation "I didn't feel I was [my mother's] victim, I felt responsible for her," provides the maternal counterpart to Rosenfeld's account. Together, they embody the new understanding to which the New York Intellectuals had come.[35]

Acknowledging rather than resisting one's parents—an incorporation which included an acceptance of parents and of self—is a sign of the maturity the New York Intellectuals achieved in the postwar period. Having mapped out an intellectual territory for themselves in the late 1930s, and refining and adjusting the positions in the 1940s and 1950s, they also arrived at a change in personal identity. Their coming to terms with their Jewishness in general, with their sense of personal alienation, and with their relationship to their parents symbolizes this resolution. The fruits of their postwar investigations did not harden into final answers. Personal inquiries continued. They had, however, come to grips with some basic questions they needed to ask themselves. Some of these investigations became more public than others. Kazin continued his autobiographical works, bringing out *Starting Out in the Thirties* in 1962 and *New York Jew* in 1978. Sidney Hook, by contrast, "confess[ed] to some perplexity in understanding laments about 'alienation' of the creative artist in American culture."[36]

By and large, the others did offer some glimpse of the changes taking place in their own minds. The novels of Rosenfeld and Bellow, the sketches of Kazin, and the articles of Howe, Bell, Cohen, Rosenberg, Greenberg, Warshow, and, later, Podhoretz all illustrate the personal reevaluations under way. While the Jewish intellectual found it impossible to "return home," Howe concluded, this did not make his lot hopeless. He cannot change things; "he must continue as he is; the rootless son of a rootless people. He can find consolation and dignity, however, in the consciousness of his vision, in the awareness of his complexity, and in the rejection of self-pity. To each age its own burdens."[37] The degree of self-pity Howe offered here shows that the process was not over. The more these intellectuals understood their relationship to their parents, the less "rootless" they would become. Although the world of their fathers was disappearing, personal foundations remained. Howe, for one, would continue the search over the next thirty years.

As the search went on, the understanding of the late 1940s proved an enormous beginning. The New York Intellectuals had come to accept what they were, where they had come from, and what had driven them. They had come to recognize that this was not a reality they could escape—or should even want to. Their nature did not easily accept the notion of "accepting." It had been their style to "take," to pursue actively their goals. The coming to terms with their own motives and their own place marked a crucial turning point in their development. They began to understand their place in the process, their role in the trek which began in the pale but did not end in the Village or on the Upper West Side. "I write as one of the middle generation," Daniel Bell concluded, "one who has not faith but memory, and who has run some of its risks. I have found no 'final' place, for I have found no answers." Rather, Bell added, "I was born in *galut* and I accept—now gladly, though once in pain— the double burden and the double pleasure of my self-consciousness, the outward life of an American and the inward secret of the Jew." Bell did not carry the burden alone. "I walk with this sign as a frontlet between my eyes, and it is as visible to some secret others as their sign is to me."[38] A shared awareness and acceptance did at least provide some measure of commonality with those feeling the pangs of isolation. Adrift in the postwar world, they found they shared essential attitudes beyond intellectual concerns. In fact, they had always shared them. They now accepted their parents and, in so doing, accepted themselves. The momentum of their early years had been spent, and they looked back to see from where they had come and by what path. When they moved on again, it would be under their own power.

Section IV

MAKING IT

Chapter 10

The Postwar Mentality: Imagination & Affirmation

A clear sign of the concerns which swirled in the New York Intellectual world at any given time could always be found in the various symposia which *Partisan Review* and *Commentary* published. The editors would invite a number of intellectuals to reply to a series of questions on a particular topic. In the late 1930s, amid the debates on proletarian literature versus high culture, *PR* sponsored a symposium entitled "The Situation in American Writing." In the late 1940s *Commentary*'s "The Jewish Writer and the English Literary Tradition" appeared, part of the coming to terms with Jewishness and the anti-Semitic strain in modernist literature. Yet no symposium so clearly demonstrated a changed perspective as strikingly as "Our Country and Our Culture," which ran in *PR* in 1952. The editors admitted that American intellectuals, once-fervent outsiders who reveled in their marginality, "regard America and its institutions in a new way." Just how far they had come was evident in the paragraph which introduced the symposium.

> Until little more than a decade ago, America was commonly thought to be hostile to art and culture. Since then, however, the tide has begun to turn, and many writers and intellectuals now feel closer to their country and its culture . . . . The American artist and intellectual no longer feels "disinherited" as Henry James did, or "astray" as Ezra Pound did in 1913 . . . . We have obviously come a long way from the earlier rejection of America as spiritually barren, from the attacks of Mencken on the "booboisie" and the Marxist picture of America in the thirties as a land of capitalist reaction.

Their past notions of radical utopianism had given way to a general acceptance of the broad outlines of American life, just as the individuals had come to accept themselves. "More and more writers have ceased to think of themselves as rebels and exiles," the *PR* editors concluded. "They now believe that their values, if they are to be realized at all, must be realized in America and in relation to the actuality of American life."[1]

The New York Intellectuals had labored long and hard in the 1930s to gain a place on the intellectual left and stake out a series of cultural and political positions which defined that place. In their move from the periphery toward the center, it became clear that these intellectual beliefs would have to undergo reevaluation and restatement. Some of the older positions, particularly those on political topics, had always been evolving, as may be seen in the attitude toward Marx. But the cultural positions, especially those concerning cultural standards and the role of intellectuals, remained more solidly rooted. The primary intellectual task of the first years following the war became the transposition of the *essential* elements of the thirties radical thinking to a newly defined political and cultural position appropriate for their place and perspective in the postwar world. This task proved doubly hard yet doubly important, as contrary trends also developed in American society. In the 1930s the *Partisan* crowd had advanced an alternative radical position against the Popular Front–style radicalism which dominated the American left. In the first decade after the war, they proposed a redefined liberalism to counter growing right-wing attitudes. This newly emerging liberal position preserved the crucial pieces of their previous radical mentality, applied to their new place. They had struggled with opponents on the left, and they continued that struggle. They now had to counter powerful forces on the right, both political and cultural. In the process they created a "vital center," which would ultimately carry the day and them along with it.

In the preface to *The Liberal Imagination*, Lionel Trilling sketched out the political world he found in postwar America. Liberalism, he argued, was "not only the dominant but even the sole intellectual tradition." Trilling noted the conspicuous absence of conservative ideas in general circulation, his notion of proper conservatism being vastly different from the philistine and reactionary ideas commonly associated with these years. We can note the absence of radicalism as a third potential source for an intellectual tradition. Only liberalism and conservatism seem available for Trilling, which bespeaks a telling change. Having committed themselves to a radical position in the 1930s, the New Yorkers found their politics moving toward the center in the 1940s. Yet, as these intellectuals showed in innumerable circumstances, intellectual changes were always made to seem mere adjustments or retoolings—seamless, logical transitions. They had always held liberal beliefs, they now argued, even during their radical days. In the 1930s Sidney Hook told his mentor Morris Cohen that liberal goals could be achieved only through radical programs.[2] Now the *real* goals of their radicalism could be achieved only through redefined liberalism. The major problems had been with the older, traditional form of liberalism.

The postwar world, with the changed status of American power and the shocking horrors of the past decade, required a new kind of liberalism, one able to cope with the new realities. A number of New York Intellectuals set about the task of defining this new position, of offering a guide for this new world.

The old liberalism possessed a kind of innocent enthusiasm, an "attitude toward life which was characterized by the free play of the intellect," Diana Trilling maintained. The postwar years were no time for innocence, for free play. All became seriousness, requiring newfound truths. The implicit assumption of liberalism's unfailing righteousness—a belief which Leslie Fiedler characterized as "the liberal is *per se* the hero"—had been modified during the decade of failed hopes.[3] The old liberalism had seemed too tame in the 1930s. In the postwar years it seemed vague and directionless. It should not be an attitude but a program, not a response but an initiative. It should learn from the radical efforts of the 1930s, while dispensing with the radical philosophies themselves. And it would be a liberalism which suited the intellectual history and needs of the New Yorkers who argued for it.

In 1949 Daniel Bell noted that, for the first time in two decades, new names were finally coming "to the fore among left-wing and liberal thinkers." It is striking that Bell dismissed the entire generation of the thirties, including elder New York Intellectuals like Harold Rosenberg, Clement Greenberg, Philip Rahv, and Lionel Trilling, all of whom began to publish in the 1930s. Among the few hopeful prospects, Bell included Arthur Schlesinger, Jr., one of "the harbingers of a new political generation."[4] Schlesinger had just published *The Vital Center*, one of the crucial works in the new, emerging liberalism. Schlesinger moved into the New York Intellectual orbit, although he was never fully assimilated into the heart of the community. He came to this place in the late 1940s by roads very different from those taken by the other New Yorkers.

Schlesinger's grandparents were German immigrants, but his father, Arthur Schlesinger, Sr., was one of America's leading historians. Rather than growing up the son of working-class parents in Brownsville or Newark, Schlesinger moved to Cambridge at the age of seven, following his father's appointment at Harvard. The senior Schlesinger had earlier taught at Ohio State University and the University of Iowa. The younger Schlesinger attended Phillips Exeter and entered Harvard as an undergraduate in 1935, while the young YPSL's were inhabiting Alcove No. 1 at City College. Tutored by Perry Miller and F. O. Matthiessen, Schlesinger graduated in 1938, expanded his honors thesis on Orestes Brownson into a book, and then spent a year at Cambridge. He returned to Harvard in 1939 as a junior fellow; this gave him time to begin the research which would result in his acclaimed work *The Age of Jackson*, published in 1945. Unlike a number of others at Harvard in the 1930s, such as the historian Daniel Boorstin or his tutor Matthiessen, Schlesinger never flirted with radicalism. In fact, he later argued that "while the New Dealers were saving the system," the radical intellectuals "were paralyzed by the hysterical vision that democracy and capitalism were through and the proletarian revolution was about to take over."[5] Only in the postwar years, when the New York Intellectuals came to argue for a liberalism which would succeed in achieving the basic goals of their prewar radicalism, could they move into an alliance with Schlesinger.

If liberalism *had* provided the base for political thought in the past decade, for radicals and New Dealers alike, how had it strayed so far off course? A significant part of the problem stemmed from a number of the political groups whose claims of liberalism these current analysts found either inappropriate or vague. "Communism has been the greatest threat," Schlesinger wrote, "because Communism draped itself so carefully in the cast-off clothes of a liberalism grown fat and complacent . . . ." But in addition to Communists others had also let liberalism down. Sidney Hook felt that "totalitarian liberals," had poisoned the climate "for most progressive-minded people to distinguish between the friends and the foes of the democratic tradition."[6] Schlesinger saw those liberals who tolerated communism less totalitarian than self-indulgent. The "Doughface progressives," he called them, liberals who shirked power in favor of personal satisfaction, who found "ample gratification in words" rather than in "getting things done." These were the "sentimentalists, the utopians, the wailers," for whom "liberalism is the mass expiatory ritual by which the individual relieves himself of responsibility for his government's behavior."[7]

In place of inappropriate liberalism, a new kind of liberalism had to be erected, steeled for the onslaughts of authoritarian radicals and hysterical reactionaries, as well as toughened to resist the weak strain which traditional liberalism often evidenced. No longer could liberalism exist in its innocent state, defending diversity and free inquiry. Liberalism needed positive characteristics set in a particular context, "a definite set of mind," Diana Trilling believed, "an attitude toward life which operates upon a whole series of preconceptions and imperatives." The old luxuries no longer appeared possible. Liberals had to come out of idealistic gardens and into the ominous, real world. To "keep alive the liberal tradition," Sidney Hook explained, it was necessary to "fill it with the social context."[8]

In order to toughen liberalism and make it battle ready, one had first to strip away its impractical, overly idealistic tendencies. Without this purging, other alterations would prove impossible. "The age of innocence is dead," Leslie Fiedler proclaimed.

> We who would like to think of ourselves as liberals must be willing to declare that mere liberal principle is not in itself a guarantee against evil, that the wrongdoer is not always the other—"they" and not "us"; that there is no magic in the words

"left" or "progressive" or "socialist" that can prevent deceit and the abuse of power.[9]

This kind of innocence only led to political impotence and to the victories of "totalitarian liberals" or philistine reactionaries. The liberal intellectual "lamenting his favorite myths," Schlesinger complained, "has failed wretchedly to live up to his obligation to provide intellectual leadership." It became necessary to move, as Fiedler put it, "from a liberalism of innocence to a liberalism of responsibility."[10]

Two components of the political position argued by New York Intellectuals during the late 1930s and the war years became essential to this new liberal stance. One myth which had to be directly confronted again concerned the Soviet Union and Stalinism. In the 1930s, as part of their radical critique, the New Yorkers had spoken out long and hard against the horrors of the Russian system. Moving away from radicalism, they focused on liberal susceptibility to the Soviet myth and the Stalinist appeal. "Europe—and the 'advanced' thinking throughout the world—had been Stalinized," William Phillips observed, "infiltrated by the Marxist ideology," which affects "many people who do not follow the Marxist line in every respect and in many cases even regard themselves as anti-Marxists." The problem with this distorted view, for Phillips, was that "the identification with this myth has come to be synonymous with enlightenment, with the triumph of humanism—with simple decency."[11] This "Stalinization" had to be rooted out, in part because the crimes of Stalin had been a consistent New York Intellectual theme and in part because liberalism and radicalism had to be separated. Enlightenment, humanism, and decency—standard liberal attributes—were not to be associated with radical beliefs.

The second perception which grew during the war was the measured acceptance of American society by the once-radical intellectuals. This attitude also challenged an older "liberal myth," Dwight Macdonald maintained, one "which glosses over Soviet Communism's shortcomings and correspondingly exaggerates those of American capitalism." This delays the "political reorientation that our liberal ideology has so long needed."[12] The New Yorkers drew those two emerging features together, reinforcing the anti-Soviet, pro-American position. More important, though, they moved their pro-American considerations from the cultural to the political and economic arena. The description of criticisms of American capitalism as exaggerated marks a significant shift from the rediscovery of virtues in Walt Whitman, William Dean Howells, or Henry James. Although the rhetoric and tone of the intellectual discussions carried vestiges of their thirties style, the substance of their political arguments about the American system became more defensive than critical.

A clear dose of practicalness entered the political argument. Liberals who took a nonpartisan view of the struggle between America and the Soviet Union engaged "in a form of mere self-indulgence," William Phillips claimed, "gambling on an American victory in a war with Russia, which will preserve for them all the existing freedoms, including the freedom to remain politically uncontaminated." The desire to remain uncontaminated had been the essence of the *Partisan* position on the Popular Front. Now this kind of thinking was the idle pastime of "bohemian radicals . . . more concerned with making a show of their purity and intransigence."[13] This notion of practical versus self-indulgent liberals pervades much of this developing political thought, as in Schlesinger's distinction between "true liberals" and "Doughface progressives," "doers" and "wailers."

Schlesinger had never had any real trouble with supporting the American system, not in the 1930s or the 1950s. For the others, however, the move to an affirmation of the country was a significant shift from prewar positions and had to be developed more gingerly. Rather than wholesale approval, a more moderate position began to develop among the ex-radicals. "Most of us have made a 'lesser evil' choice," Dwight Macdonald admitted. "And since the imperfect democracy of the West is clearly a lesser evil than the perfected tyranny of the Communists, we have chosen the West." Macdonald did note that the compelling passion which characterized thirties radicalism had diminished, but ambivalent acceptance provoked less enthusiasm and re-volutionary commitment. The intellectuals now accepted, even if less passionately and not always with a whole heart, what they had once shunned. "One inclines to endure familiar evils rather than risk unknown and possibly greater ones," Macdonald concluded. "Even private property, detested by every right-thinking, that is left-thinking, intellectual in the thirties . . . even this bete-noire of Marxism now presents a democratic aspect."[14]

Coming to terms with liberalism meant coming to terms with America's economic reality—the "democratic aspect" of private property—and accepting it, even if cautiously. "Business is less pecuniary and acquisitive," Daniel Bell argued, "although more manipulative and security-conscious: it has achieved a certain social-mindedness and become decent. . . ."[15] The New York In-tellectuals did not immediately become apologists for big business or cheerleaders for capitalism, as some would do in later years. Rather, they believed that a new working relationship between capitalists and liberals provided the basic strength of American society. All alone, Schlesinger claimed, capitalists fail politically. "Capitalism at once strengthened economic cen-tralization and loosened the mere bonds of society." This development led to instability, "which invites collectivism as a means of restoring discipline." At times of disorder, capitalism has been "bailed out by radical democracy, often under aristocratic leadership—Jeffersons, Jacksons, Lincolns, Wilsons, Roose-velts."[16] Looking back at the political experience of the 1930s, Schlesinger argued that liberal beliefs provided the framework for contemporary society and that liberals ought to understand their crucial role in the modern world.

Since that March day in 1933, one has been able to feel that the liberal ideas had access to power in the United States, that liberal purposes, in general were dominating our national policy. For one's own generation, then, American liberalism has had a positive and confident ring. It has stood for responsibility and for achievement, not for frustration and sentimentalism; it has been the instrument of social change, not of private neurosis.[17]

For Schlesinger the New Deal saved the system. Its continuance in the postwar years provided the best hope for continued improvement. While significant segments of the American populace, right and left, lambasted Harry Truman, most New York Intellectuals gave him their qualified support. On the basis of the radical democracy of the New Deal, Daniel Bell championed Truman's cause. "Here is no Thermadorian reaction against FDR, as many liberals feared, but the continuation of a revolutionary impulse, however vague and confused." Truman's limitations turned into attributes. His "limited imagination" seemed to Norman Podhoretz "astonishing and yet wonderful."[18]

Support of the New Deal, which they had previously mocked, did not create much internal debate among these ex-radicals, for once again they offered justifications which smoothed the abrupt shifts in their arguments. "There is no inherent obstacle to the gradual advance of socialism in the United States through a series of New Deals," Schlesinger contended in the 1947 symposium "The Future of Socialism," in *Partisan Review*. He envisioned various forms of governmental ownership and control, from TVA-like federal agencies to municipal ownership, cooperatives, and expanded governmental regulation. In the same symposium Sidney Hook looked toward a similar development. Unhappy with the notion, held by some socialists, that "a socialist economy [is] planned in its entirety" Hook opted for "some form of mixed economy," which could "secure the goals of democracy without the inefficiency, bureaucracy, and evasion of responsibility that seems attendant upon a completely planned system of production."[19] Hook's preferred prototype was the "evolving pattern of British socialism, now shedding its rather mangy coat of imperialism." In fact, he envisioned an "Anglo-American economic policy" incorporating "democratic countries outside the Russian orbit." This would enhance economic reform while defending democratic freedoms. "The future of socialism," Hook concluded, "depends upon the preservation to the last ditch of political democracy."[20]

The New York Intellectuals had taken their past and present and wound them into a overly neat view of the New Deal as a blend of social democracy and evolutionary socialism, a view which allowed them to approve the current American situation without rejecting wholesale the general aims of their youth. Someone like Hook might continue to maintain, down to the present, that his socialist commitment never disappeared, despite a growing conservative outlook. For the others, however, support for the New Deal as evolutionary socialism proved short-lived.[21] Rather, this assessment helped ease the transition from radical to liberal. At the time, however, the prospect of socialist development from within the established system held enormous appeal. They could now engage fully in the East-West struggle, support elected officials, and offer their own version of contemporary liberalism as a logical advancement from both the mainstream politics of the 1930s and their own radical beliefs of the past decade.

The calls went out not for uncritical chauvinism but for tempered, yet clear, support of the system. Elliot Cohen, writing one of his few articles in *Commentary*, claimed he would not be happy if all intellectuals immediately became 100 percent pro-American. But they should at least "admit the possibility" that the American system offered the best chance for the future. "Maybe *here*, right on our doorstep, is the long yearned-for political alternative, after all." Despite his initial disclaimer, Cohen concluded by arguing that the American system did offer the best alternative and that intellectuals should recognize the fact and support the nation.[22]

In the 1960s Irving Kristol recalled the twenty-year period immediately after the war as being the " 'bourgeois-ificaton' of society": "Where once we had the bourgeois confronting the masses, we now have the bourgeois masses."[23] What Kristol claimed for American society certainly happened to the New York Intellectuals. They began to support a society they had once criticized mercilessly and an economic and political system about which they had all harbored serious doubts. This support brought them into a new relationship with their native land, making them liberal intellectuals for the nation rather than radical intellectuals critical of it.

Moving closer to the center of American society forced them to readjust their views to correspond to their new proximity. Their standing at a distance in the 1930s had offered a wide-angle perspective and led to large-scale theorizing and solutions. They now maintained more-intimate connections with society, and, as a result, a narrower focus replaced sweeping generalities. The new issues concerned specific situations, trouble spots within a larger context. Revision rather than revolution became the guiding spirit. The New Yorkers attempted to tie this attitude, like many others, to positions of the past, making the new arguments seem less novel. Twentieth-century America's liberal heroes Oliver Wendell Holmes and John Dewey "bequeathed to American liberals . . . not merely a passion for freedom and a distrust of absolutes, but a *sense of problems*," Sidney Hook, always a Deweyite, observed.[24] Liberal responsibility required an addressing of these problems. Piece-by-piece analysis and step-by-step solutions might be less appealing than the flamboyant grandeur of radicalism, but the importance of the undertaking could not be denied.

One significant intellectual development which coincided with this changed social perspective was the emergence of the social sciences after World War II. No member of the "older" generation of New York Intellectuals could truly be classified as a social scientist. The "second" generation included Daniel Bell, Nathan Glazer, and Seymour Martin Lipset, who represented a new academic group in the intellectual community. While other second-generation members like Alfred Kazin or Leslie Fiedler might find the results of social science consistently boring, the approach and appropriateness of the social sciences neatly fit the new, internal political analysis. It also proved easier for Jews to enter the emerging fields in the social sciences than it had been to storm the bastions of civilization embodied by college English departments in the 1920s and 1930s. Finally, social science had changed. In *Commentary*'s first issue Nathan Glazer noted that "social scientists can no longer be reproached for burying themselves with theoretical issues while ignoring major problems confronting mankind." Like the gardens of innocence now emptied of liberals, "the ivory tower now stands abandoned." Sociologists, psychologists, and anthropologists, Glazer concluded, concern themselves "with how the studies devoted to the extension of man's knowledge of man may advance solutions to the problems of a free society."[25]

Glazer understood that the attraction of social science would be less powerful than that of other intellectual disciplines, lacking "obvious dramatics . . . staggering figures . . . or pictures . . . or immediate personal relevance." But historical precedent, as well as current political perspective, pointed to the importance of the social sciences. The possibilities seemed immense.

> Their most important discoveries are as simple, non-technical, and "commonsensical" as their detractors say they are. So were the discoveries of the 16th and 17th century physicists and doctors that helped destroy a feudal order and create a bourgeois one. . . . The social sciences, with their war-developed techniques, may well influence history as importantly as have the physical and biological sciences.[26]

Past thinking, especially past radical thinking, lacked concreteness. It did not possess the modern, hardheaded approach necessary for the understanding and incorporating of contemporary complexities. Marxists, for example, "did not spell out what they wanted," Daniel Bell argued, "they did not think through the consequences of what 'the Revolution' would mean." Instead, they possessed a "myopic rationalism," assuming "that 'History' or 'the Future' would settle all problems."[27] A commonsensical, clear-sighted approach was therefore necessary. This corresponded to the liberal and intellectual arguments being worked out by New York Intellectuals as well as to the more general attitude evident in postwar America. Lionel Trilling noted a change among his students parallel to that among his intellectual colleagues. "Present-day students accept the image of society as a rather good thing," Trilling wrote.

"Certainly they like to rebel, but the rebellion must be selective. In my time we protested everything there was."[28]

In Trilling's time, however, he and his contemporaries had felt themselves estranged from American society and had, in fact, turned their sense of exclusion into a positive attribute. In both periods the drive for recognition proved consistent. They always saw their intellectual calling as a ticket to some form of prominence. The rise of the social-science or problem-solving approach offered a new application of intellectuality. It is significant that Trilling noted this change in perspective because he was definitely not a social scientist. Another non–social scientist, Sidney Hook, also advanced a view of how adjustments in intellectual functioning changed social perceptions. Commenting on the general social distrust of intellectuals, Hook observed that often status and not function generated the hostility. "I would count lawyers as a class of intellectual sometimes distrusted by people." Once society perceived the direct utility of an intellectual, the distrust vanished. "Physicians . . . were never distrusted because their function came before their social status."[29] If society understood that intellectuals were the physicians of the social order, ambivalence about them would similarly disappear.

Hook's insight about the attitude toward physicians points to a much larger result of the new notions of intellectual problem solving and social utility. Without undermining the critical role of intellectuals, championed in the 1930s by the *Partisan* critics, the social-science, commonsense approach offered a second way for proclaiming the intellectuals' vital role in contemporary society. It reinforced and broadened claims of expertise and provided another argument in the persistent campaign to convince American society of the special importance and unique capabilities of the New York Intellectuals.

As a result of both the abandonment of a radical orientation and the new hardheaded view of contemporary problems, the larger question of a philosophical outlook required rethinking. The redefined liberal perspective argued by Schlesinger, the Trillings, and others provided a part of the answer. In scope, however, it differed fundamentally from past notions. No matter how strong the commitment to liberalism grew, it could never approach the fervor of radical commitment. That lack of fervor, though, could be changed from a detriment into an asset, neatly joining the turn to liberalism with a more practical approach to modern life. The two decades between 1930 and 1950 possessed "an intensity peculiar in written history," Daniel Bell observed, listing all the tumultuous and horrible events of these years. "For the radical intellectual who had articulated the revolutionary impulses of the past century and a half," Bell concluded, "all this has meant an end to chiliastic hopes, to millenarianism, to apocalyptic thinking—and to ideology." And in a concept associated with him ever since, Bell proclaimed that "ideology, which once was the road to action, has come to a dead end."[30]

Bell's most famous work, *The End of Ideology*, appeared in 1960, but it collected essays first published between 1951 and 1959. Its subtitle, "On the

Exhaustion of Political Ideas in the Fifties," spoke to the decade of its orientation. As Bell subsequently pointed out, the notion that ideology had ended was not his alone. Raymond Aron, Edward Shils, and Seymour Martin Lipset also advanced one form or other of the basic conception throughout the 1950s. Bell remained its most famous advocate, however, and he chose or was forced to defend and define its meaning in subsequent years. In keeping with their changed attitude toward America, Bell argued, intellectuals in the Western world now joined in a "rough consensus," accepting the Welfare State, decentralized power, a mixed economy, and political pluralism.[31] In a mid-1960s clarification of the basic concept, Bell reiterated the essential position in terms perfectly suited to the new political and intellectual perspective of the 1950s. Those who advocated the notion of an end to ideology, he believed, "decried the use of ideas as . . . secular religions. . . . In a democracy, moreover, ideological politics . . . can only be disruptive of society and lead to violence." This might once have been the radical goal, but it no longer served the liberals committed to America. "A democracy can exist only where there is 'civil politics.' " Furthermore, the end of ideology corresponded to the changed conceptions of the problem solvers. It was not, as some held, "a defense of the status quo" but rather "an emphasis on rational social change"—exactly the kind of activity liberal social scientists argued would best serve America.[32]

A frequent criticism of the concept of an end of ideology concerned its seeming absence or rejection of utopianism. Bell responded by saying that he favored a new kind of utopian thinking, not its total abandonment. Reflecting the new hardheaded, practical approach, Bell posited a kind of empirical utopianism. "There is now, more than ever, some need for utopia," he claimed, "in the sense that men need—as they have always needed—some vision of their potential, some way of fusing passion and intelligence." Only now the components of utopian thinking proved vastly different from those of past utopianism. "The ladder to the City of Heaven can no longer be a 'faith ladder,' but an empirical one," Bell asserted. In a prescription ideally suited for the new mentality emerging in the postwar world, he suggested that "a utopia has to specify *where* one wants to go, *how* to get there, the costs of the enterprise, and some realizaion of, and justification for, *who* is to pay."[33]

The notion of an "empirical ladder" to the "City of Heaven" reinforced the status of the empiricists while it attacked the goals of radical ideologies. Humanity would be saved not by general social upheaval but by attention to a variety of particular problems. The prominence enjoyed by this notion served as one sign of the acceptance which New York Intellectual thinking had gained. As Harold Rosenberg commented, outsiders were finding this viewpoint compelling and its conclusions significant. In an analysis of a book and a *Partisan Review* article by the French social critic Raymond Aron, Rosenberg noted that "by the end of ideologies M. Aron means an end to an interest in political theories and of 'nostalgia for a universal idea.' " Instead, "the model for how nations shall think in the future is America—and the model intellectual for M.

Aron is none other than the contemporary American." One kind of intellectual stood out, "the intellectual as 'expert' engaged in doing his job and suspicious of abstractions and systems."[34] In his one novel, *The Middle of the Journey*, published in 1947, Lionel Trilling made his central character just such an intellectual. In his youth, John Laskell "had planned a literary career. . . . He had wanted what young men of spirit usually want, freedom and experience." But as he matured, "Laskell discovered in himself gifts for practicality and detail which, in his dream of literature, he had never suspected." While Trilling himself never abandoned literary criticism, he had Laskell discovering his own ability to deal "not only with social theories, but also, as was necessary, with rents and rules and washing machines." As Norman Podhoretz later described it symbolically, they doffed "the intellectual's equivalent of the gaberdine" and donned "a well-cut business suit."[35]

Although they now accepted rather than criticized the American system, these postwar intellectuals found their enthusiasm and optimism somewhat tempered by the realities of the contemporary world. The economic and political chaos of the 1930s had given rise to radical utopianism and enthusiasm. Political and economic stability after World War II brought a quieter, more tentative attitude toward humanity's fate. In part this resulted from the disenchantment with radicalism and from the calamitous and inexplicable events of recent history. "The degeneration of the Soviet Union taught us a useful lesson," Schlesinger observed. "It broke the bubble of the false optimism of the nineteenth century." The emergence of revisionist liberalism coincided, Irving Kristol felt, with a rebirth of liberalism's more sober qualities. This meant, in addition to a return to a "celebration of plain evidence and rational judgment," a "premium on sobriety, orderly sensation, and conservative thought."[36]

Thus, two new elements in the emerging liberal position marked an abrupt shift in the style, as well as the substance, of the New York Intellectuals. While they maintained a sense of personal certainty, they were less convinced of the general social stability. "The grounds of our civilization, of our certitude, are breaking up under out feet," Arthur Schlesinger wrote. "Even those people who hastily traded their insecurities for a mirage of security are finding themselves no better off than the rest." The New York Intellectuals became more sober, in keeping with the limited goals they now aimed to achieve but also with a changed sense of human character and motivation. "The Soviet Experience," Schlesinger wrote, "on top of the rise of fascism, reminded my generation rather forcibly that man was, indeed, imperfect. . . ."[37]

The admitting of human imperfection marked another intellectual shift, one which not all the New Yorkers would make. A belief in human progress diverted by inappropriate conditions or historical aberration might still provide a useful frame for someone like Sidney Hook. But many of the others began to find alternative explanations more compelling. "What to Sidney would be an historical aberration," Daniel Bell later noted, "would be for Reinhold Niebur a theological example. And Niebuhr's explanation became much more congenial to us." In Niebuhr's arguments, Bell recalled, there existed the appropriate contemporary mix of "a kind of tough-minded attitude about human nature, a complex view of society, a complex view of human motivation, and a willingness to talk about politics."[38] Hook had seen this general trend emerging in the early 1940s and had spoken out against it. In the 1950s many of these intellectuals moved away from Hook's arguments of the certainty of scientific method and toward Niebuhr's darker prophecies. "The excessively optimistic estimates of human nature and of human history with which the democratic credo has been historically associated are a source of peril to democratic society," the theologian had written in 1944, "for contemporary experience is refuting this optimism and there is a danger that it will seem to refute the democratic ideal as well."[39]

A world view must not fall into the traps of a myopic view of human nature; rather, it must stand ready to combat the assaults by those Niebuhr called the "children of darkness" and to avoid the hazards of "hard" and "soft" utopianism. Civilization had been built by "foolish children of light" and was now "under attack by children of darkness, by the moral cynics." Disaster threatened because the children of light have underestimated "the power of self-interest, both individual and collective, in modern society. . . . The children of darkness are evil because they know no law beyond the self. They are wise, though evil, because they understand the power of self-interest." Continued belief in human perfectibility only perpetuated the naïveté of eighteenth- and nineteenth-century utilitarians, an expression of "the stupidity of the children of light in its most vivid form." Rather, "the children of light must be armed with the wisdom of the children of darkness but remain free from their malice. They must know the power of self-interest in human society without giving it moral justification. They must have this wisdom in order that they may beguile, deflect, harness and restrain self-interest, individuality and collectively, for the sake of the community."[40]

In the modern world two strains of political thought "underestimate the complexities of history and both . . . fail to understand the tragic character of human history." Niebuhr saw communism as "hard utopianism," which could easily be labeled as threatening. But pitfalls also existed with "liberal soft utopians," who "expect perfection to emerge out of the ongoing process of history." While not as "dangerous and fanatic as the communist hard utopians," soft liberals "do not understand that history makes the problems of man's togetherness more, rather than less, complex."[41]

This view neatly meshed with the emerging liberalism of the New Yorkers. Some revisionist liberals, such as Arthur Schlesinger, took Niebuhr as an essential cornerstone of their thinking. In the *PR* symposium on the future of socialism, Schlesinger scorned "official" (traditional) liberalism for rejecting "the dark and subterranean forces in human nature." "There are moody and destructive impulses in man of which official liberalism has taken no serious account," he noted.[42] Niebuhr's critique of hard and soft utopianism also paralleled Schlesinger's attack on communism and "Doughface" progressivism.

The call for an understanding of the evil forces in human society fit in with the notion that liberalism must be a doctrine applied to the contemporary reality, not a utopian vision. Finally, Niebuhr's assessment helped explain where past philosophies had erred. Thirties radicals and myopic liberals shared the responsibility for the current state. "Whether or not we avoid another war," Niebuhr proclaimed in 1952,

> we are covered with prospective guilt. We have dreamed of a purely rational adjustment of interests in human society; and are involved in "total" wars. We have dreamed of a "scientific" approach to all human problems; and we find that the tensions of a world-wide conflict release individual and collective emotions not easily brought under rational control. We have hoped to make neat and sharp distinctions between justice and injustice; and we discover that even the best human actions involve some guilt.[43]

Sidney Hook's unbending rationalism left no room for Niebuhr's belief in the dark forces of human nature. Despite political shifts, Hook's philosophical outlook remained rooted in the determinism of his youthful Marxism. People "like Kristol or myself," Bell recounted, "who had suddenly become interested in Kierkegaard or in Judaism became too broad for Hook."[44] Niebuhr's focus on the nonrational and the demonic did, however, complement an interest in religion or existentialism. For those seeking new explanations, Niebuhr's arguments about the darker side of human nature proved appealing. The positive absolutes and sweeping views of the past decade had been replaced by the more limited and more pessimistic views of the present. Immediatism supplanted utopianism; practicality seemed more important than grand schemes. Liberalism needed a particular context in which to prove effective, and that context had to account for the ghastly events of recent years. This darker view of nature served as a substructure for the more limited hopes of contemporary liberalism. Given human imperfectibility, the possibilities for success seemed restricted. The best that could be achieved might be no more than limited reform in the current society.

A LIBERALISM OF IMAGINATION

No book more clearly marks the emergence of the New York Intellectuals into the postwar than Lionel Trilling's *The Liberal Imagination*. Appearing in 1949, it was actually a collection of a number of essays written during the 1940s, all revised, and given coherence only by the brief preface Trilling included. As a result, his arguments were provocative rather than comprehensive. He aimed at stimulating and redirecting his readers, pointing down new paths and toward various reconsiderations. He left the filling in and following out of the arguments for later work—his own and that of others. His topics ranged widely, from Wordsworth to Sherwood Anderson, from Huck Finn to Kinsey. Nonetheless, Trilling succeeded in his central task, to stimulate his contemporaries. *The Liberal Imagination* sits at the center of the emerging postwar positions of the New York Intellectuals because of both its instrinsic and its symbolic importance. Trilling's two previous works of nonfiction, studies of Matthew Arnold and E. M. Forster, though well received, had failed to earn him the sweeping reputation he would gain in the 1950s and 1960s. This all changed with *The Liberal Imagination*. He became, in Norman Podhoretz's characterization, the "single most influential" New York Intellectual, a man "exactly in tune with the temper of his period."[45]

Central to the concerns of the radical critics around *Partisan Review* in the late 1930s had been the attempt to bring literature into the world of radical politics in a manner which reinforced its importance and maintained high standards. Trilling's appropriateness for the 1950s stemmed directly from his ability to stake out the area in the postwar world in which the same questions could once again be addressed. In addition to bringing past considerations to bear on the present discussion, he was able to expand on the issues at hand. The *Partisan* critics had turned against the subservient and derivative role of literature they perceived in radicalism. Trilling offered an argument which found a significant role for literature, and for critics, in the new liberalism.

He agreed with the perception that liberal politics offered the best prescription for the modern world. As was noted above, he found liberalism the sole intellectual tradition available for Americans. Liberalism's isolation on the political landscape elicited not a longing for the radicalism of years past but a desire for a counterbalancing conservative tradition. America did not lack for conservative impulses: "Such impulses are certainly very strong, perhaps even stronger than most of us know." These conservative impulses did not, "with some isolated and some ecclesiastical exceptions, express themselves in ideas but only in action or in irritable mental gestures which seek to resemble ideas." Trilling recalled that John Stuart Mill, whose liberalism was at odds with Coleridge's ideas, "nevertheless urged all liberals to become acquainted with this powerful conservative mind." Trilling explained that Mill believed that "the intellectual pressure which an opponent like Coleridge could exert would force liberals to examine their position for its weaknesses and complacencies."[46] The postwar need for liberalism to harden itself and abandon its innocence paralleled Mill's advice to nineteenth-century liberalism.

What Mill found particularly illuminating in Coleridge, Trilling went on to argue, was his "nature and power as a poet." Liberalism "stood in a paradoxical relation to the emotions." For Mill, liberalism's central concern may be with "happiness"—an emotional state—but "in its effort to establish the emotions . . . liberalism somehow tends to deny them in their full possibility." Here Trilling saw both Mill's attraction to Coleridge and the means by which literature might attach itself to liberalism in a manner meaningful to the critic. Trilling cited a passage which he did "not know whether or not Mill had particularly in mind," to illustrate his contention. For the epigraph of *The Ancient Mariner*, Coleridge chose

> the sentence in which [Thomas] Burnet says that a judicious belief in the existence of demons has the effect of keeping the mind from becoming "narrow, and lapsed entirely into mean thoughts." . . . Coleridge wanted to enforce by that quaint sentence from Burnet what is the general import of *The Ancient Mariner* . . . that the world is a complex and unexpected and terrible place which is not always to be understood by the mind as we use it in our everyday tasks.[47]

Mill was too much a nineteenth-century person and Trilling too much a twentieth-century one to believe in medieval demonology. Yet modern demons abounded. For Reinhold Niebuhr they existed in the evil of the children of darkness and even in the unconscious of the children of light. While Niebuhr argued his contemporary Calvinism, Trilling turned to a different source to explain the existence of the demons, the insights and critical devices of Freud. For Trilling, Freudian psychology offered not only a guide to the contemporary human predicament but also illumination about its possible resolution. Trilling's Freudianism shared with Niebuhr's theology an awareness of dark, hidden forces in human nature. With Freud, however, Trilling could see glimmers of light in the darkness of the human condition.

Freud's insights helped Trilling explain why "the simple humanitarian optimism" of the last two decades proved "politically and philosophically inadequate," an essential starting point for the ex-radicals. "Despite popular belief to the contrary," Trilling held,

> man, as Freud conceives him, is not to be understood by any simple formula (such as sex) but is rather an inextricable tangle of culture and biology. And not being simple, he is not simply good; he has, as Freud says somewhere, a kind of hell within him from which rise everlastingly the impulses which threaten his civilization.

Psychological thinking, as well as political, had suffered from optimistic failings. Parallel with traditional liberalism are the "reformulations of the analytic psychology which Dr. [Karen] Horney and Dr. [Harry Stack] Sullivan make in the name of reason and society and progress, which are marked by the most astonishing weakness of mind, and which appeal to the liberal intellectual."[48] A healthy and needed dose of pessimism, an admission of human imperfectibility, and an acceptance of evil's constant presence in the world and in human consciousness would all help to overcome the hopeful, but inadequate, thinking in both the political and the psychological camps over the past several decades.

Trilling had expressed his disapproval of the relation between faulty liberalism and neo-Freudianism throughout the 1940s. A 1942 discussion of

Karen Horney called her "symptomatic . . . of one of the great inadequacies of liberal thought, the need for optimism." Her revisions of Freudian theory were "the response of the wishes of an intellectual class which has always found Freud's ideas cogent but too stringent and too dark." This class wants, instead, "a less tragic and strenuous psychology, a more reasonable, decent and cooperative psyche, and Dr. Horney . . . has given them what they want." In the 1950s, when more and more intellectuals accepted human unreasonableness, a lack of decency, and a sense of tragedy, the Freud who probed the inner darkness seemed more appropriate. And for Lionel Trilling an additional attribute of Freudianism became crucial. Out of that hidden wellspring of human emotions—dark and light—came the insights and ultimate achievements of literature. "Not I but the poets . . . discovered the unconscious," Trilling quoted Freud as having said. The overly optimistic, rational approaches to the human condition had been found wanting, and new approaches or insights were called for. Trilling thought that two different routes were available, leading to the same essential answers. "The Freudian psychology is the only systematic account of the human mind which, in point of subtlety and complexity, of interest and tragic power, deserves to stand beside the chaotic mass of psychological insights which literature has accumulated through the centuries."[49]

The unlocking of the secrets of human existence, including the dark impulses which had burst forth in the twentieth century, required the active involvement of those willing to journey into the unknown recesses. Freud had done this scientifically, the poets instinctively. Literature provided the rays of light to illuminate the darkness, and Freud had catalogued and organized the random visions of the poets. "Freud has not merely naturalized poetry; he has discovered its status as a pioneer settler, and sees it as a method of thought."[50]

While admitting the applicability of Freudian thought to art and literature, Trilling found himself ultimately unhappy with the manner in which Freud and other psychologists approached art. Eventually, Trilling said, "Freud speaks of art with what we must indeed call contempt." Freud, Trilling noted, called art "substitute gratification" and "an illusion in contrast to reality." As for the artist, according to Freud "he is virtually in the same category with the neurotic" and "belongs to that race of beings whose realm is not of this world."[51]

Trilling's view of the relation between literature and reality countered this Freudian attitude. Instead of retreating from the real world, the artist can bring clarity to it, by enlarging the frame of understanding and providing visions of human activity unapproachable by any more-systematic means. The addition of this crucial element to the developing politics of the postwar era allowed liberals to understand fully the human condition and avoid the pitfalls of the overly optimistic approaches of previous years. In this manner, as well, an essential internal paradox of traditional liberalism can be overcome. One of liberalism's tendencies is to simplify, Trilling argued, "natural in view of the effort which liberalism makes to organize the elements of life in a rational way." However, this "organizational impulse" leads to "delegation, and agencies, and bureaus, and technicians." In this process it is difficult for ideas to survive delegation, but they are passed on to bureaus and agencies which "incline to . . . ideas of a certain kind and of a certain simplicity." As a result, "they give up something of their largeness and modulation and complexity in order to survive. The lively sense of contingency and possibility . . . does not suit well with the impulse to organization." Thus, liberalism itself experiences an internal "discrepency between . . . the primal imagination of liberalism and its present particular manifestations." Contemporary life requires both liberal elements, the programmatic and the critical. Those who preach and practice the emerging liberal politics are carrying out the requirements of the first.

> The job of criticism would seem to be, then, to recall liberalism to its first essential imagination of variousness and possibility, which implies the awareness of complexity and difficulty. To the carrying out of the job of criticizing the liberal imagination, literature has a unique relevance, not merely because so much of modern literature has explicitly directed itself upon politics, but more importantly because literature is the human activity that takes the fullest and most precise account of variousness, possibility, complexity, and difficulty.[52]

With the abandonment of radical politics, the concept of radical criticism which had developed in the 1930s needed to be revamped to become suitable for the new liberal mentality. A liberal cultural position, however, already existed—one which grew out of the traditional liberalism and one which needed correction. For Trilling, this older view found its most influential exponent in Vernon Parrington, especially in his *Main Currents in American Thought*. This book had educated a generation, and its influence persisted, despite the travails of the past decade. Parrington's sensibility corresponded to the historical notions of progressivism, focusing on democracy as a "fighting faith." Trilling argued that Parrington took a single-minded approach to literature and exhibited an always too predictable, rough-hewn social and economic determinism.

Parrington's focus on the progress of history seemed too often to lead him to favor particular styles of writing. "Society is after all something that exists at the moment as well as in the future," Trilling noted, "and if one man wants to probe curiously into the hidden furtive recesses of the contemporary soul, a broad democracy and especially one devoted to reality should allow him to do so without despising him."[53] Such a probing of the contemporary soul or the human unconscious was precisely the undertaking Trilling thought essential.

Parrington died in 1929, the last volume of his *Main Currents* only partially completed. Trilling was not concerned with why Parrington, a product of the Progressive Era, thought the way he did. But he did say, "Parrington lies twenty years behind us," years in which "a body of opinion aware of his inadequacies" has developed. "Yet Parrington still stands at the center of American thought." Trilling's explanation for Parrington's persistent importance highlights a basic division Trilling aimed to overcome. Parrington "expressed the chronic American belief that there exists an opposition between reality and mind and that one must enlist oneself in the party of reality."[54] This division mirrors Trilling's perception about the unnatural split between the rational and the emotional. He believed that revitalized liberalism required a literary and critical component. He also believed that the critic could best serve by delving into the mind, the emotions, the unconscious. If a new liberal criticism was to emerge alongside the new liberalism, this perceived separation had to be overcome.

Trilling sought to demonstrate that the separation of "mind" and "reality" was inappropriate. He noted the differing attitudes which prevailed toward Theodore Dreiser and Henry James. Dreiser had been "indulged" by liberal intellectuals, despite his literary inferiority, while James had been accorded nothing but "liberal severity." A more appropriate sensibility would have understood Dreiser's weaknesses, but "our liberal, progressive culture tolerated Dreiser's vulgar materialism . . . feeling that perhaps it was not quite intellectually adequate but certainly very *strong*, certainly very *real*." James, on the other hand, suffered because Americans instinctively believe that "an art which is marked by perception and knowledge . . . can never get us through gross dangers and difficulties." The sad truth, Trilling concluded, is that "in the American metaphysic, reality is always material reality, hard, resistant, unformed, impenetrable, and unpleasant." This attitude has led Americans to place the most trust in that mind "which most resembles this reality by most nearly reproducing the sensations it affords."[55]

Parrington found fault with James for withdrawing from "the external world of action . . . to the inner world of questioning and probing," dealing "more and more with less and less"—in the end, becoming "concerned only with *nuances*."[56] That is just where Trilling wants us to go, just what he wants us to be concerned with. This is the realm in which literature can now serve and which critics can describe.

Trilling's choice of Dreiser and James as his examples also resonates of past issues in the New York Intellectual world. Dreiser, in addition to representing the "vulgar materialism" of a reality-oriented mind, had himself been deeply involved with the Stalinist left, linked to the *New Masses*, critical of the Dewey commission on Trotsky, and a member of the League of American Writers. In the *Partisan* revival of modernism, the championing of Henry James had been an important element. James was one of the writers resurrected in revolutionary modernism, a perfect example of the kind of intelligent writing the *Partisan* critics felt had been neglected in the programmatic approach of proletarian literature. Trilling knew that contrasting these two writers did more than just point to the critical questions in a liberal mentality. This was the "dark and bloody crossroads where literature and politics meet," Trilling claimed. His adjectives were telling, for the once-radical critics surely remembered that some of their own blood had been spilled in this debate in the 1930s.[57] Their arguments in the thirties carried over to the fifties. Henry James was no more a liberal—redefined or otherwise—than Dostoevsky a radical. Yet Philip Rahv had argued for the "subversive sensibility" of Dostoevsky. Similarly, Henry James's dissection of the subtleties of individual actions could prove more enlightening than Theodore Dreiser's critical assaults on economic exploitation. Modernism and the critical function could be saved, along with liberalism.

The preconceived notions of critics and readers about American literature brought other problems to the surface—problems more significant than that of undue adulation for an author like Theodore Dreiser. Recent European literature, Trilling argued, has an "active" quality. "It does not, at its best, consent to be merely comprehended. It refuses to be understood as a 'symptom' of its society. . . . " American literature, on the other hand, "seems to me essentially passive: our minds tend always to be made up about this or that American author." American literature as an academic subject emerged as an *object* of study rather than as a *subject*. We are all too comfortable and secure with our appraisals. Like the problem-solving social scientists, literature itself needs to be more active, to engage society more directly. The achievement of this end requires an infusion of ideas into literature, not in lockstep applications of particular notions, but in making literature compete "with philosophy, theology, and science, [seeking] to match them in comprehensiveness and power and seriousness."[58] As in the 1930s, Trilling sounded the call for a primary, rather than derivative, role for literature. Once more, the problem of sifting through literary works emerged as a central difficulty. And once again, the critic stood in the best position to accomplish the task.

The progressive mentality, infecting radicals as well as cultural analysts like Parrington, foundered on its basic conceptual description of culture. Parrington's notion of a current symbolized this weakness. "A culture is not a flow," Trilling claimed, but a dialectic. Another old radical theme was introduced, but Trilling immediately moved the discussion to new ground. In a given culture, certain artists may possess a large part of the dialectic within themselves—"they contain . . . the very essence of the culture, and the sign of this is that they do not submit to serve the ends of any one ideological group or tendency." The best American writers, those of the late nineteenth century, "were such repositories of the dialectic of their times—they contained both the yes and no of their cultures, and by that token they were prophetic of the future." If the cultural dialectic existed within the artist, the creations which emerged are symptomatic of the state of the culture in general as well as of the quality of work within a particular artistic area. "The novel," Trilling wrote, "is a kind of summary and paradigm of our cultural life, which is perhaps why we speak sooner of its death than of the death of any other form of thought." In addition to artistic expression, novels devote themselves to "the celebration and investigation of the human will; and the will of our society is dying of its own excess. The religious will, the political will, the sexual will, the artistic will—each is dying of its own excess."[59]

The great task facing novelists, given this cultural decline, was "the restoration and reconstitution of the will." Against the traditional American notion of reality versus mind, Trilling offered an opposing view, drawn from Henry James. James, echoing his pragmatist brother and John Dewey, defined reality as "the things we cannot possibly know." The road to understanding and insight is thus left to the romantics, the very same group which Parrington derided. Trilling quoted James: "The romantic stands . . . for things that, with all the facilities in the world, all the wealth and all the courage and all the wit and all the adventure, we never *can* directly know; the things that can reach us only through the beautiful circuit of thought and desire." Previously, social class and its conflicts fueled novelists' motives. The loss of this compelling subject did not mean the end of the novel. "The organization of society into . . . groups presents a subject scarcely less absorbing," Trilling believed. It has "nearly as full a range of passion and nearly as complex a system of manners . . . ." Thus, this "opportunity of the novel clearly leads to its duty." The novel brings together most ably the two strains of reality and romance, Trilling noted from James, "a genre with a very close and really very simple relation to actuality, to the things we cannot possibly know . . . side by side with thought and desire." The novel "is the form which provides the perfect criticism of ideas attaching themselves to their appropriate actuality . . . . The novel passionately concerns itself with reality, with appearances and reality."[60]

After stressing the crucial function of the novel for contemporary American society, Trilling returned to his description of the passive state of contemporary American literature and to methods for overcoming this state. The problem centered on the seemingly contradictory attitudes of literature and liberal-democratic beliefs, difficulties he noted at the outset of his book. The European "active" writers provided no models, for they seemed hostile to the tradition of democratic liberalism. Trilling offered no easy solution to this problem, believing that all he could accomplish was to pose the basic question, but he did offer a tentative answer in the last paragraph of *The Liberal Imagination*. The difficulty, he suggested, stems from the writers' relation "toward the ideas we claim as ours." Too often, American writers use ideas as "pellets of intellection or crystallizations of thought, precise and completed, and defined by their coherence and their procedural recommendations."[61] This attitude leads to the sorry state of America's prose literature. It is necessary "to revise our habit of conceiving ideas in this way and learn instead to think of ideas as living things, inescapably connected with our wills and desires, as susceptible of growth and development by their very nature." If we effect this revision, "then we shall stand in a relation to ideas which makes an active literature possible."[62]

Several years later, in a lecture on Freud, Trilling briefly returned to the question of the relation between the artist and his culture. "For literature, as for

Freud, the test of the culture is always the individual self," Trilling suggested. "The function of literature, through all its mutations, has been to make us aware of the particularity of selves, and the high authority of the self in its quarrel with its society and its culture." And, echoing Philip Rahv of fifteen years past, Trilling concluded, "Literature is in that sense subversive."[63] For the old radicals, Trilling revived the idea of a dynamic relationship with one's culture, transferred to a liberal framework. Like the revolutionary modernists of the thirties, Trilling believed that literature held the potential for societal development, only now spurred by a liberal imagination.

Trilling's book was more speculative than comprehensive, his generalizations were frequently undocumented, and his conclusions were tentative rather than proven. Nonetheless, his themes proved crucial to the emerging liberal mentality among the New York Intellectuals. Liberalism had certainly lacked the excitement of a radical stance and apparently serious literary or cultural components as well. *The Liberal Imagination* changed all that. Trilling's eminence among literary critics in the postwar years derived from his ability to provide an appropriate intellectual and cultural dimension to the political position which had sprung up. Just as liberalism required positive actions in a particular context, rather than a passive set of beliefs, so a liberal imagination required an active relation with liberal culture. In the 1930s intellectuals had attempted an active relation in the radical movements and found themselves unhappy with the subservient position to which intellectual ends were relegated. In the postwar years they set out to establish firmly a more equivalent relation between politics and culture and to ensure the central place of intellectuals in it. The redefinition of liberalism, in political terms, and then the suggestion of an appropriate cultural dimension created a situation more congenial than that of the 1930s and perfectly suited to the political, intellectual, and personal requirements of these individuals. On this political and cultural foundation, they could once again argue their belief that intellectuals should play an important role in contemporary society. This time people listened.

MEN OF AFFIRMATION

The intellectuals invited to participate in the 1952 *Partisan Review* symposium "Our Country and Our Culture" responded to a series of questions, based on the initial premise of the discussion, which was cited at the beginning of this chapter. A new atmosphere existed, and intellectuals needed to assess their place in it. The questions put by the editors neatly laid out the various threads of a discussion about the role of intellectuals in American society. The proper function of intellectuals had clearly been a recurrent theme since the New Yorkers had first come together. But their ideas now took on a geographical and societal aspect. Personal aims became interlaced with larger social issues.

The editors' questions touched on the main areas of intellectual readjustment and the possible results of this newly emerging relation between the intellectual and the nation.

1. To what extent have American intellectuals changed their attitude toward America and its institutions?
2. Must the American intellectual and writer adapt himself to mass culture? If he must, what forms can his adaptation take? Or, do you believe that a democratic society necessarily leads to a leveling of culture to a mass culture which will overrun intellectual and aesthetic values traditional to Western Civilization?
3. Where in American life can artists find the basis of strength, renewal, and recognition, now that they can no longer depend fully on Europe as a cultural example and a source of vitality?
4. If a reaffirmation and rediscovery of America is under way, can this tradition of critical non-conformism (going back to Thoreau and Melville and embracing some of the major expressions of American intellectual history) be maintained as strongly as ever?[64]

These questions intrigued the New York Intellectuals for the first decade or so after the war. The answers provided in the *Partisan Review* symposium did not end the discussion. In various places—essays, lectures, books, as well as replies to symposia—these individuals evaluated their newfound intellectual position. On the whole, their attitudes toward their own function as intellectuals did not drastically change. Rather, they applied the personal requirements they had marked out in the 1930s to the new social realities of the 1950s, and found a more congenial place for their ideas to take root. In no clearly systematic manner, they sought to define their own place. Their attitudes and answers roughly fell along the lines indicated by the *PR* editors, but the discussion ranged far beyond the confines of a single intellectual symposium.

Regarding their new relation to America and its institutions, the intellectuals' response fanned out into several crucial areas of concern. Suffusing it all was a sense of a new awareness or even of maturity. Philip Rahv once told William Barrett that he often thought of writing a novel about the people around *Partisan Review* in its first decade, to be called *The Truants*. "The point of his title, [Rahv] explained, was that in those years we had all been playing truants, escaping for a brief while from the harshness of whatever practical reality would finally claim us again."[65] The practical reality proved not to be "harsh" as Rahv anticipated, at least not in terms of material or professional gains. They felt they could no longer escape current political affairs at a time when world events severely restricted intellectuals' choices. "I cannot understand why American intellectuals should be apologetic about the fact that they are limited in the effective historical choice," Sidney Hook complained in the *PR* symposium, "between endorsing a system of total error and *critically* supporting our own imperfect democratic culture with all its promises and dangers." Diana

Trilling found herself equally perplexed. by intellectuals' difficulties in throwing their support to America and against the Soviet Union. "We need not fully understand the genesis of an attitude in order to oppose it," she said. Moreover, Trilling argued, coming down on the wrong side carries serious intellectual ramifications. "The belief that a choice between America and the Soviet Union is a choice between anything except democracy and totalitarianism obviously does not disqualify the intellectual for political action. It merely disqualifies him as an intellectual."[66]

Rather than repelling intellectuals, America seemed to be attractive to them—at least to some of them. "The American intellectuals found new virtues in the United States," Daniel Bell wrote in 1959, "because of its pluralism, the acceptance of the Welfare State, the spread of education, and the expanding opportunities for intellectual employment. And in the growing Cold War, they accepted the fact that Soviet Russia was the principal threat to freedom."[67] The cold war, they believed, limited intellectuals' choices to two (one real choice, Diana Trilling argued), while new developments and compensations awaited those who moved into American society. The conception of American society thus underwent substantial change, now offering political and personal refuge.

The newly opened university life gave some escape from the perpetual financial worries they had experienced. For them, it also signaled a changed attitude on the part of Americans in general.[68] Certainly, some had been college professors before, but they were the ones with scholarly training. Now American universities welcomed those who were just intellectuals, including Phillips and Rahv, whose appointments Nathan Glazer remembered as "symbolic of the changing status of intellectuals." There emerged, Daniel Bell believed, a "cultural elite," and this was primarily a "university culture." "In contrast to fifty years ago," he wrote in 1959, "it is a 'liberal culture,' receptive to ideas, critical in outlook, and encouraging of (sometimes nostalgic for) dissent."[69]

The notion of elites extended beyond campus boundaries. "Many of the new cultural arbiters," Bell argued, "have affected not only serious painters and novelists but the standards of the larger public as well." As examples, Bell pointed to four New York Intellectuals: Clement Greenberg, Harold Rosenberg, Lionel Trilling, and Alfred Kazin. The impact of intellectuals extended upward as well as downward, toward those who ran the society as well as the popular masses. "The needs of society have brought to the top of the social hierarchy a large class of people of considerable force and complexity of mind," Lionel Trilling argued in the *PR* symposium. "Intellect has associated itself with power as perhaps never before in history, and is now conceded to be itself a kind of power."[70] Both Trilling's belief in the new connections between intellectuals and power and Bell's notions of essential elites point to a conception of the intellectual's place different from that of the 1930s. The apparent contradiction between the pre- and postwar attitudes actually turns on questions of appropriate forums rather than on a changed concept of role. As Harold Rosenberg suggested, intellectuals had previously thought of "getting into the game of authority," but in the 1930s intellectual activity had "associated itself with revolution; intellectuals dreamed of their emergence as commissars after another Ten Days That Shook the World." In 1951 Rosenberg discovered a changed mental climate, wherein " 'the permanent revolution' is used as the title of a special issue of *Fortune* . . . dedicated to the American tradition." Differences have become evident, and "ambitions have been at once solidified and reduced in scale." Intellectuals no longer "are thinking of running America. Strictly speaking, their urge is for place and role rather than for power."[71]

Born on the periphery, in immigrant ghettos, and living in the marginal world of radical intellectuals, the New Yorkers had once felt that their best hope of access to intellectual prominence and authority lay with a reconstructing of society. In the postwar years, they found the very society which they once scorned, and which had once scorned them, much more hospitable. They discovered a "place" and a "role" for themselves in it. "We are witnessing a process that might well be described as the *embourgeoisement* of the American intelligentsia," Philip Rahv observed. This change, coupled with the new liberal politics, "accounts for the fact that the idea of socialism . . . has virtually ceased to figure in current intellectual discussion."[72] These intellectuals now identified with American society intellectually as well as politically. A belief that American power was necessary for confrontation with the Soviet Union could be rationalized as a political expedient. What is more striking is the emerging sense of personal relatedness, especially among individuals previously bound up with their own exclusions. Intellectuals, Rahv observed, felt a part of the "national environment," having gained "a sense of what is concretely even if minimally our own." Philip Rahv—the Russian émigré, the fourteen-year-old boy who felt so out of place in the schools of Providence, the wanderer from the West who received his education on park benches and in public libraries—now concluded that "one can indeed speak of a 'reconciliation' of the intellectuals."[73] They really regarded this as a new world, one in which they felt at home.

In another sense, however, a great continuity existed between the attitudes of intellectuals in the 1930s and those in the postwar years. In 1941 William Phillips claimed that intellectuals performed a role in the modern world parallel to that of clerics in the Middle Ages; the church, in fact, was "the organized body of the intellectuals."[74] In 1966 Irving Kristol quoted approvingly from the Columbia philosopher Charles Frankel. "To a considerable extent, the secular intellectuals of modern nations have supplanted the clergy as the principal suppliers and endorsers of the symbols of legitimacy." In the same year, Daniel Bell agreed that "every society has usually had a class whose social function has been to transmit the cultural heritage and enduring values of civilization."

Over the years, Bell noted, these have been "the priests, the clerks, the mandarins, and the scholars . . . the *intelligentsia*." This basic sense of the social function of intellectuals had not changed since the 1930s, even as the New Yorkers changed their own relation to the society whose cultural heritage and values they felt they must now transmit. In fact, this new relation to society magnified the belief in an intellectual's importance for that society. "The name 'intellectual,' " Lionel Trilling suggested, implied a "certain intensity of commitment, the belief that the existence and the conduct of the intellectual class are momentous in and essential to the life of the society, the acceptance of intellectual activity as a mandate, a status, a personal fate."[75]

The problems for intellectuals acting with and in the society also represented a return to concerns voiced in the late 1930s. Overidentification with political movements had stripped intellectuals of some of their critical distancing, the *Partisan* intellectuals had once argued. While unhappy with the ivory tower, Philip Rahv found it more compatible than "the international Tammany Hall of Stalinism."[76] The issue of the masses diluting or weakening intellectual endeavor emerged in the criticism of proletarian literature and the arguments about the philistine nature of Stalinist-dominated arts in general. The New York Intellectuals argued for intellectual uniqueness and tipped the scales in the direction of academic exclusiveness, while still trying to maintain a social role for intellectuals. Their new relation to the whole of American society, after World War II, required a reassessment of the relative merits of these two positions. They had always argued for some modulation between the two, only now they had to push intellectuals back toward a closer relation with the masses, without undermining their unique position. Trilling believed that intellectuals possessed the qualities to preserve their own uniqueness and that the times had eliminated the worst fears of mass culture. The "large intellectual elite," Trilling held, "will not be—is not—content with mass culture as we now have it, because for its very existence it requires new ideas." Self-conscious of his role, the intellectual could uphold the values of high culture in the face of the threats of mass culture. The mass, however, proved less threatening than intellectuals believed. Writing a few years later, Trilling argued that the intellectual's "sense of an inert mass resistant to ideas, entirely unenlightened, and hating enlightenment, is part of the pathos of liberalism in the Twenties and Thirties." This attitude remains, "despite the fact that the liberal ideas of the Twenties and Thirties are . . . strong and established, truly powerful."[77]

In the 1930s the *Partisan* intellectuals feared the loss of intellectual uniqueness. In the postwar years William Phillips feared the opposite. He chided intellectuals who believed their task was presumably "to brood about absolute moral and political values." "But this is a luxury for American intellectuals," he said, "who have been able to depend on the strength and the prosperity of the United States to keep intact their present way of life while they occupy themselves with eternal questions." Although he did not "mean to disparage all forms of specialization," Phillips wrote that "the narrowing of interests" tended "to make the classic ideal of an educated man an anachronism and to reduce the writer to a craftsman."[78]

The best way to maintain the values of Western civilization and to avoid the pitfalls of mass culture—the second question of the *PR* symposium—was not through intellectual exclusiveness but through involvement with the guidance for the society at large. Intellectuals could not isolate themselves amid the political tensions and problems, nor should they do so in the face of feared associations with mass culture or lowbrowism. Rather, they should be ready to provide ideas and moral leadership, in order to guide society. With their close relation to the larger American society and their belief that American society had gained a new respect for intellectuals, the fulfillment of a dream of the 1930s—and of their lives—seemed at hand.

If American society appeared more hospitable to intellectuals, they in turn, had to act in a more appropriate and distinctive manner. Intellectuals needed to look at themselves in a new light, just as they viewed their society from a changed perspective. Old myths about themselves had to give way to truths. The feeling of bourgeois guilt became the foremost area for reevaluation. The myth of the proletariat appealed to intellectuals, Arthur Schlesinger argued, because an intellectual possessed a "sense of guilt over living pleasantly by his wits instead of unpleasantly by his hands." Furthermore, previous identification with workers helped an intellectual "to compensate for his sense of alienation." Diana Trilling echoed this second theme, concluding that despite the incorporation of intellectuals into government and policy-shaping roles in the New Deal years, "the liberal intellectual minority . . . still conceived itself an ineffectual little group . . . lonely even while its ranks swelled, and isolated even when it stood at the apex of public life." Trilling concluded that a salient feature of the intellectual mentality, one which existed despite current developments, was a feeling that "once unpopular, always unpopular; once weak, always weak."[79]

The new world called for a new awareness of an intellectual's society as well as self. Feeling out of place in one's home created attractions to other alternatives, which produced the wrong kind of political idealism. "The idealist finds virtue only where he is not—in the country which is not his country, in the class which is not his class," Diana Trilling remarked, "in the races and religions which are not his race and religion. Also in the occupations which are not his occupation." The masquerade of overidentifying with other groups or nations leads to an undermining of the proper intellectual function. "Why does the idealist middle-class think so little of itself and everything that pertains to it?" Trilling asked. Her answer pointed to the new self-worth being generated among intellectuals: "Could it be that we have lost our sense of our own worth because we have lost the sense of our creative power?" In fact, faulty idealism has led intellectuals down the wrong path, serving ends not their own. "By idealism, indeed, we precisely mean *not* creating, but serving—and serving a good which is not our own."[80]

To this inappropriate intellectual style, Trilling proposed an alternative, one which fit better the newly perceived position of intellectuals in America. "The most powerful and destructive myth operating among decent and supposedly thoughtful people to rob them of their freedom [is] the myth of selflessness." Communists were the chief propagators of this myth, exploiting it for their own ends.

> When we deny, as Stalinism insists that we do, a full sense of our own value, when we deny the worth of ourselves, then inevitably we must substitute for our own worth the worth of something which is not ourselves. This is the psychology of subservience; we become servants. And where there are servants there are masters. This is the path by which an ideal politics, a politics of supposed freedom, becomes a real politics of repression. It is the path by which Communism has become a totalitarianism as bad as fascism.

The alternative required a new intellectual direction, Trilling advised, a turning away from selflessness "to a life of self-interest . . . not to stop being an idealist—but just stop being the wrong kind of idealists." She added, "I believe it is dangerous to undervalue what is our own."[81]

Thus, the intellectuals needed to look to themselves before looking elsewhere. The difference between a scholar and an intellectual, Daniel Bell noted, revolves around the central focus of each one. A scholar "seeks to find his place in [a tradition], adding to the accumulated, tested knowledge of the past as to a mosaic." The intellectual, on the other hand, "begins with *his* experience, *his* individual perceptions of the world, *his* privileges and deprivations, and judges the world by these sensibilities."[82] And while looking to themselves, the intellectuals must also look out for themselves and their society. "We do not become chauvinists," Diana Trilling concluded; "we continue to criticize our country as we must." Yet, contemporary realities temper judgments—"we take into account the welfare of our own nation as well as the welfare of the community of nations." Finally, intellectuals must act as they have never acted before, must be self-aware without neglecting the needs of society, avoid selflessness without being egocentric. They must understand the needs of groups with which they once aligned themselves, without forfeiting their own special role.

> We do not give ourselves over to the false or mean values of class—our instincts to justice and generosity remain—but we cherish the privileges we would wish to extend to a class which does not have them. We do not become intellectual prigs, but we value our minds; we feel we have as much right to be heard on our highest level of development as others have on theirs; we insist that we, as intellectuals, have as much to contribute to civilization as farmers or mechanics—and, as a corollary, we accept our duty to think clearly.

Trilling's call for intellectual self-awareness seemed simple on the surface. Who could argue with the minimal characteristics she asked intellectuals to develop? "All I am asking for," she concluded, "is simply pride—a decent pride as the basis and guarantor of our political virtue. To value ourselves, and then because we value ourselves, also value others." Other alternatives seem bleak, she suggested, for unless intellectuals show a "new respect for the self . . . we conspire in our own extinction."[83] Yet, the results would hardly be simple. The call of Diana Trilling, Daniel Bell, Arthur Schlesinger, and others in the postwar years for a new position and self-perception among American intellectuals may have been continuous with attitudes of *Partisan* intellectuals of the late 1930s, but it marked a serious turn from other conceptions of the role of American intellectuals—from ivory-tower isolation to deep political commitment. The New Yorkers desired the best of both worlds—activism and distance, social importance and group uniqueness. They wanted to function as intellectuals and still contribute in a regular and intimate way to the workings of the society. They wanted to be not commissars but consultants, not the spearhead of a vanguard party leading the society toward a new utopia but a ready resource to which contemporary society turned for periodic guidance. No longer enrolling in the causes of others, they created their own movement. Although this movement aimed to improve the society in which they lived, it would also substantially improve the standing of the intellectuals who signed on.

With the benefit of this intellectual position, the New York Intellectuals looked about and discovered the degree to which their conception had already been incorporated and appreciated by American society and how much they were needed. "The social function of the American intellectual is to think, and to act in such a way that the results of his thinking are brought to bear on the great issues of our time," Sidney Hook believed. It became necessary to enlighten the "many American intellectuals unaware of the extent to which the social climate and objective possibilities for a democratic welfare state have improved in the last twenty years."[84] A second task was to change intellectual style, from the bombast of the thirties to a tone more appropriate for their newfound role. In part, maturity and the achievement of social position had already begun the process of softening styles. After a famous reading by the Beat poets at Columbia in 1958, Diana Trilling returned home to her "comfortable living room," emblematic of "a certain point in a successful literary career [which] confirms the writer in his sense of disciplined achievement and well-earned reward." Having moved far from the marginal existence and willing combativeness of the 1930s, Trilling now felt that "taste or style dictates that most intellectuals behave decorously, earn a regular living, disguise instead of flaunt any private digressions from the conduct society considers desirable."[85]

Taste and style, as well as comfortable living, frequently came to these intellectuals by the end of the 1950s. The attitudes which led to these changes had developed a decade before. In a long analysis of the case of J. Robert Oppenheimer, in the early fifties, Diana Trilling summed up Oppenheimer's attractiveness for American intellectuals. Had the description been written in the late 1930s, Oppenheimer might have been praised for his balance of politics and science, for the way his radicalism had influenced his commitment to help tame atomic power and use it to destroy fascism. Now his attractiveness derived not from his political views but from the manner in which his academic and public roles fit together.

> Dr. Oppenheimer had of course been something of a culture hero for American intellectuals, especially for literary intellectuals—our contemporary scene does not offer many figures so exciting and sympathetic to the humanistic imagination as this most theoretical of physicists so apt for decisiveness in practical affairs, this genius of science who knows how to read and write English, this lean handsome aristocrat bred in the indulgent Jewish middle class, this remote man of civilization called from the academy into the fiercest of worlds—a world of inventions to destroy civilization—only to return at will into that purest of academies, the Institute for Advanced Study at Princeton.

The phrases which leap from this description—"lean handsome aristocrat," the product of the "Jewish middle class," the "remote man of civilization"—all serve to reinforce the ideal intellectual style being promoted by the New York Intellectuals. They might not want to be scientists or to join the Institute for Advanced Study, but in Trilling's appraisal it is easy to see why she believed that "in identification with Oppenheimer, the American intellectual had been able to identify himself with an idealism whose most elaborate effort it had been to reconcile individual freedom with governmental responsibility, whose peculiar torment it had been to cherish the private gift while subduing it to the social need and will."[86] American intellectuals might not all share in this identification, but the personal requirements and new perceptions of the New York Intellectuals fit this characterization exactly.

The New Yorkers had always had intellectual heroes, individuals they wished to emulate. Unlike their ambitions of the prewar years, those of the present, they discovered, might be achieved more readily. The "growing complexity of the administering of our society," Lionel Trilling observed, had helped create a new intellectual class, which stood in a new relation with power. In addition, intellectual life itself took on a new character, "providing a new means of social mobility or social ascent." Intellectual endeavors brought one closer to the workings of society, to a responsible position in the culture, and offered the tangible benefits of influence and position. In the intellectual world, the possibility of outside rewards increased the appeal of intellectual pursuits. Commitment to an intellectual life still implied contemplation and humanism, but it now also meant status. Typical of this development was "the increased prestige of the universities," Trilling wrote, adding, "The university teacher now occupies a place in our hierarchy which is considerably higher than he could have claimed three decades ago."[87] Academic careers became a new road to power, even for those who did not use a professional post as a springboard to public employment. One could sit in an ivy-covered building— but not in an ivory tower—and still keep an important place in the society at large.

If the New York Intellectuals needed any public affirmation of the correctness of their ideas about intellectual activity and influence, it came in 1956, when *Time* ran as its June 11 cover story an article entitled "Parnassus— Coast to Coast." Although Jacques Barzun appeared on *Time*'s cover, the story and the accompanying pictures surely warmed the New Yorkers' hearts. "What does it mean to be an intellectual in the United States?" *Time* asked. It offered as a straw man the old stereotype of the intellectual which the New Yorkers had dispensed with long ago. "Is he really in such an unhappy plight as he sometimes thinks—the ridiculed double-dome, the egghead, the wild-eyed, absent-minded man who is made to feel alien in his own country?" No, *Time* proclaimed, times have changed.

> Ever since World War II, U. S. intellectuals have, as never before, been debating these questions. But in the course of the debate, one note has been struck time and again. . . . If there is a traditional distrust of ideas in the U.S., says Barzun, the nation's men of ideas have still "won recognition in tangible ways beyond any previous group of their peers." And more important, many have come at last to realize that they are true and proud participants in the American dream.

The New York Intellectuals did not have to content themselves with a philosophical restatement of their position in the *Time* article to feel their message gaining prominence. Pictured next to Barzun, were Trilling and Hook, along with three individuals closely related to them, W. H. Auden, Reinhold Niebuhr, and J. Robert Oppenheimer.[88] Hook and Trilling were quoted in the article, as were Irving Kristol and Leslie Fiedler. In characterizing Barzun, *Time* might have been drawing a portrait which could apply to any one of a number of the New Yorkers or which was a composite of them.

> If he is not the typical American intellectual—for no such person exists—he represents a growing host of such men of ideas who not only have the respect of the nation, but who return the compliment . . .
>
> Their time may be subdued, but their apparent lack of passion does not mean any lack of concern for America's destiny. The Man of Protest has to some extent given way to the Man of Affirmation—and that happens to be the very role that the intellectual played when the nation was new.[89]

"Affirmation," in *Time*'s conception, meant the intellectuals' positive attitudes toward America. But the *Time* article also confirmed the New York Intellectuals in their ideas about their proper function. They had been men of protest, and in that former world, they felt, their intellectual aims had failed or been neglected. In the postwar years they moved from opposition to participation, once again claiming their own special role. The roads to influence had changed since the 1930s, as had political realities. The constant remained the ambitions of the New Yorkers and their conception of the importance of intellectual life. The change was in the area where they could ply their trade most successfully. The deflation of hopes in the radical movements lessened not their intellectual resolve but their radical commitment. Armed with a new liberal political philosophy, a new attitude toward the positive virtues of American society, and a new sense of their own self-worth, they succeeded after World War II in creating the kind of intellectual environment they had always desired.

Chapter 11
Liberal Anticommunism

The uncertainty facing postwar America became the first problem the New York Intellectuals addressed with their redefined liberal mentality. The Allied victory in World War II had been absolute, the surrender of the enemy unconditional. America had invented the ultimate weapon; its security should have been complete and its power uncontested. And yet, Americans' sense of security proved extremely short-lived, as wartime allies became postwar antagonists and atomic weaponry proved to be the ultimate insecurity. With barely a break, America moved out of the hot war with Germany and Japan and into a cold one with the Soviet Union. Whereas after World War I there had been talk of a return to normalcy, after World War II there was no desire to pull back, no attempt to resort to a position of neutrality. America was committed to a global presence, to sustaining its vision of the world, and to maintaining its international interests. America took an active, aggressive role in the world, ready to confront its enemies with a hardheaded approach to world problems.

This desire to be direct and aggressive should have neatly dovetailed with the redefined liberal program being advanced by the New Yorkers. They had sought to replace the older style of liberal thinking, based on tolerance and principle, with a tougher approach directed at specific problems. The aims of American foreign-policy makers and those of the new liberals seemed perfectly matched. The intellectuals' hoped-for roles of influence now appeared to have found the perfect area for actualization.

One serious storm cloud, however, darkened this otherwise bright horizon. The Soviets had to be transformed, in the American popular imagination, from America's wartime ally to its postwar foe. Opposition to communism now burst upon the domestic scene as a major political issue. This, in and of itself, should also have given the New York Intellectuals little pause, as their own opposition to Stalinism went back many years and their criticism of the Soviet Union was exceptionally strong. But once anticommunism became a major pillar of postwar thought, it expanded as a domestic issue. The decision of the liberal Truman administration to intensify its anti-Communist rhetoric in the wake of the intensifying antagonisms of the cold war, stimulated a widespread and often hysterical outpouring of anti-Communist activities. Secretary of State Dean Acheson, for example, had been a chief architect of the cold-war planning, "present at the creation," as he later put it. In a few years he would be attacked by those on the right as being "soft" on communism and accused by McCarthy of having a "secondary allegiance to the Kremlin," after his primary one to the British Labour government.[1] The liberals in Washington and the liberal intellectuals in New York had argued for a more direct, more confrontational style, especially in discussions of communism and the Soviet Union. Having set the tone, however, they watched and worried as the focus of the anti-Communist sentiment spread; eventually they feared not only for their principles but also for their persons.

In the hysteria which developed during the cold war, anticommunism ran rampant, threatening ex-Communists as well as current ones, non-Communist radicals as well as Stalinists. From college campuses to Senate hearing rooms, from public libraries to Hollywood studios, Americans became obsessed with the dangers of communism. Despite their early and vehement anti-Stalinism, many liberals and intellectuals found themselves actual or potential targets of reactionary "witch-hunters." Liberals believed that no one left of center was entirely safe from the inquisitors. Subsequently lumped under the umbrella term "McCarthyism," this reactionary anticommunism posed a serious problem for many Americans, including the New York Intellectuals. They felt threatened as individuals and feared that the creation of an irrational right-wing mentality would supplant the new liberalism they had created.

The New Yorkers could not, however, oppose the right wing through a reliance on civil liberties or by discounting the Communist threat. Their own political philosophy, rooted in anti-Stalinism, precluded the possibility. Too many of their attitudes derived from their abandonment of radical politics, and the "I choose the West" pronouncements reflected their antagonism toward the Soviet Union. On the other hand, they could not sit by passively and watch as the right wing either eclipsed their place in the political arena or undercut their credibility with flagrant charges of un-Americanism. In response, the New York Intellectuals joined in the formation of an alternative anticommunism—a liberal version. In helping to articulate the essential planks of the liberal anti-Communist platform, they fended off the McCarthyite threat while finally closing the door on their own radical past. Most important, this anticommunism became the first real test of their newly emerging liberalism—its application to the contemporary political stage.

Before the details of their anticommunism could be developed, the New Yorkers had to establish firmly several basic positions. They had, first, to reiterate their own anticommunism and, second, to define precisely the "true" Communist threat. Finally, they had to make clear that unless an alternative anticommunism grew, liberals would be swept away with the Communists by the reactionary forces caring little about distinctions between moderate and leftist groups. Emblematic of the first point—the reiterating of their anticommunism—is Diana Trilling's declaration that "staunch anti-Communism was the great moral-political imperative of our epoch," as forthright a statement as could be made.[2] The New York Intellectuals issued countless warnings about the dangers of communism and the need for a strong resolve against the spread of its influence and power. One hard-line example came from William Phillips in 1948. He restated his basic opposition to Stalin, argued the importance of anticommunism in the contemporary world, and, finally, offered an appraisal which described the current situation, while resonating with his old radicalism.

> The desperate situation is simply that the Russian drive for world power is sweeping across the entire European continent, enslaving the populations of the occupied areas, and threatening to disintegrate the political and intellectual life of those countries as yet out of reach of the Red Army. Hence the main political and human problem is how to stop the advance of Stalinism, without losing sight of our radical goals.

Opposing Stalin while assisting radicalism had been the *PR* position for years. But Phillips added a further explanation, which demonstrated how the postwar position differed from the prewar one. The old radical panaceas no longer appeared attractive. "The alternatives of the third political camp and the third moral camp [the position held by *PR* in the late 1930s], which have been dangled before us all these years while Stalin kept adding to his collection of both the living and dead, can be regarded at this point as political and moral rituals of self deception."[3] Now that the third alternative was gone and the second alternative was Communism, the only thing left to do was to choose America.

When questioned why he had sponsored a stringent anti-Communist law, Illinois's liberal senator Paul Douglas responded that the Republicans did not really want to destroy the Communist party. "They keep it in existence and use it to smear Democrats like myself. We liberals must destroy the Communists if this dirty game is to stop."[4] The New York Intellectuals joined the ranks of such liberals out to destroy communism in order to stop the "dirty game." Providing many of the essential philosophical and political arguments used to strike at the Communists and to blunt the impact of the reactionaries, the New Yorkers emerged as an essential group in the liberal anti-Communist coalition—the kind of intellectual counsels they aspired to become. William Phillips may have felt in 1948 that anticommunism kept radical hopes alive, but in reality it drew him and his friends into the liberal establishment, for which their postwar political and intellectual position had been designed.

The final preliminary issue before the creation of liberal anticommunism was how to respond to the right-wing anticommunism which flourished. Here the liberals had to be careful to contest the methods and targets of the reactionaries without undermining the need for a more appropriate brand of anti-communism. Their fears were not only stylistic but also personal. Long before McCarthy made his appearance, William Phillips wrote to Arthur Koestler, "The Left must not permit the struggle against Stalinism to be appropriated by the Right." *PR* editorialized, also in 1946, that if liberals continued to defend Communists, "they would fall as the first victims of a terror of the Right . . . condemned to fall into reactionary hands by the 'liberals' themselves because they have failed to provide their own leadership." The editorial included an appeal to liberal comrades who "insist on digging their own graves": "We hope they are not past pleading with that they are dragging down in their own ruin everyone else who genuinely desires the values that have been an essential part of traditional liberalism."[5]

As the anti-Communist hysteria grew and with the arrival of Senator McCarthy, this theme was reiterated often. Liberals must be roused to join the cause for their own protection, but only by admitting past errors could they face both the Wisconsin senator and the Kremlin. "If American liberalism is not willing to discriminate between its achievements and its sins," Irving Kristol warned, "it only disarms itself before Senator McCarthy, who is eager to have it appear that its achievments *are* its sins."[6]

McCarthy represented the wrong *kind* of anticommunism. Some New Yorkers criticized McCarthy's methods rather than his destructiveness. For Kristol, anticommunism remained an "ineluctable liberty," so long as no one was libeled. The problem with the reactionaries was their violation not of the canons of liberty but of "the canons of charity, humanity, and—often—intelligence." Two important figures at *Commentary*—its editor, Elliot Cohen, and its assistant editor Nathan Glazer—concurred in this assessment. In 1952 Cohen called the Wisconsin demagogue merely a "second-string blowhard," adding that "his only support as a great national figure [was] from the fascinated fears of the intelligentsia." From *Commentary*'s point of view, Cohen found the threat from McCarthy actually less than expected, given the "steadily improved" status which "alien or 'minority' groups" like Jews experienced. These groups were "customarily subject to suspicion and scapegoating in times of tension." Since this had not happened, Cohen regarded the McCarthyite threat as milder than it might be. In a long article on the methods of McCarthy, published in 1953, Glazer agreed that McCarthy had made some people's lives unpleasant and that it was "a shame and an outrage that Senator McCarthy should remain in the Senate." Yet, Glazer continued, "I cannot see that [his staying in office] is an imminent danger to personal liberty in the United States."[7]

For other New Yorkers the best way to isolate McCarthy was to demonstrate his threat both to individual Americans and to America's postwar aims. Diana Trilling, one of the strongest anti-McCarthyites among the liberal anti-Communists, recalled listening to McCarthy over the radio. "All the time McCarthy spoke last night I found myself waiting for it to be my name he blared out over the air in that awful accent of righteous condemnation." Trilling feared the complacency of her "liberal friends who can persuade themselves that because they are unequivocally anti-Communist they have nothing to fear from the Communist-hunters." These liberals "exhibit naïveté which is scarcely credible."[8]

Beyond personal fears, another problem suggested by Trilling and others was the use which Communists themselves made of McCarthyism. Despite her anxieties about McCarthy's tactics, Trilling believed that "our intense fear of McCarthyism has been nurtured by the Communists and directly serves the Communist purpose." As in the 1930s with regard to Hitler, their opposition to reactionary forces could never escape their opposition to the Communists. McCarthy's methods did "incalcuable harm . . . to the reputation of the United States abroad," Sidney Hook declared. In fact, Hook argued, "The harm which McCarthy has done to the American position abroad [is] far graver than the harm he has done at home." Communists benefited from this side of McCarthyism, Hook argued, as McCarthyism provided an "obstacle to counteract Communist lies about the true nature of American society."[9]

Moreover, McCarthyism threatened intellectuals as well as liberals. *Commentary*'s managing editor, Robert Warshow, came away from the anti-Communist film *My Son John* fearing its anti-intellectual message. In the film the position of an anti-intellectual father is ultimately vindicated when his college student son renounces communism and suffers a gangland-style assassination in retribution. "What is being upheld is, precisely, stupidity," Warshow declared. "All through the film no effort is spared to emphasize the limitations of the father's thinking and his hatred and contempt for the mind." This irrational approach would lead to hostility toward various forms of intellectual endeavor, political and cultural. "The hidden logic seems to be: since we cannot understand Communism it is likely that anything we cannot understand is Communism." Thus, Warshow concluded, the film's strongest message is "that we must fear and hate the best potentialities of the human mind."[10]

Right-wing anticommunism thus threatened the two primary pillars of the New York Intellectuals' postwar position, liberalism and intellectualism. The New Yorkers could not defend the Communists on civil-libertarian grounds. Hard anticommunism was woven into their political philosophy. Yet, they could not join the reactionaries in bombarding all liberal and radical positions and individuals. Caught in the middle, they adopted an intermediate position, sufficiently anti-Communist to provide political legitimacy in the mainstream of American society, yet carefully defined to protect liberals and anti-Stalinist ex-radicals, while leaving the Communists exposed and discredited. Two arguments from the first years of the 1950s capture the liberals' dilemma and developing position. Writing in *Encounter*, Irving Kristol asked if liberals should "oppose Communism the less in order to allow General Franco, in splendid isolation, to oppose it the more." And Kristol agreed that liberals had a large agenda before them, concerned with a variety of reforms.

> But it is a fact that communism today rules one-third of the human race, and may soon rule more; and that as such it is the most powerful institution which opposes such changes and reforms as liberalism proposes. Why, then, should not liberals, and liberals especially, fear and hate it?[11]

Diana Trilling expressed an even more basic problem. Once liberals accepted the need for anticommunism—demonstrated by a belief in the guilt of Alger Hiss, for example—they had to "acknowledge the fact that had it not been for the un-American Activities Committee Hiss's guilt might never have been uncovered." This led to the "possibility that a McCarthy, too, may turn up someone who is as guilty as Hiss." Liberals thus had to "lament the tragic confusion in liberal government which leaves the investigation of such important matters to the enemies of liberal government."[12] Liberal anti-communism, as espoused by the New York Intellectuals, aimed to resolve this "tragic" confusion.

They approached the sorting out of the contemporary liberal confusion over McCarthyism and communism with a characteristic mixture of determination and verbal flair. While acknowledging the need to "retire" Senator McCarthy from public life, Sidney Hook believed that the undertaking would be much less strenuous than others imagined: "Our own vigilantes and reactionaries are much more like witches and straw scarecrows than are the paid and unpaid agents of the Kremlin." Liberals could "clear out" the reactionaries with "a little courage and a sense of humor."[13] Despite Hook's seemingly cavalier approach, he and his contemporaries knew well the seriousness of their undertaking. William Phillips identified the current problems: "In practice there are two equally dangerous forms of confusion: the failure to recognize a Communist unless he has a party card in his hand; and the irresponsible designation of any nonconformist as a Communist." Reactionaries frequently committed the latter offense; those "soft" on communism were often guilty of the former. The New Yorkers set out to demonstrate that one could be "hard" on communism without being reactionary; they sought an alternative to the destructive path of hysterical reactionaries and the myopic passivity of unthinking liberals. Naïve liberals, Phillips argued, "cannot disengage themselves from the progressive myths that have served to camouflage the nature of Communism"; reactionaries "cannot distinguish between genuine liberalism and Communism."[14] The New York Intellectuals felt they could do both.

The success of the liberal anti-Communist endeavor promised to do more than repel the McCarthyite threat or strike another blow against Stalinism. If a reasoned and reasonable alternative to McCarthyism could be developed, one which would be accepted as more befitting both America's values and the current world crisis, then the stock of these intellectuals would gain immeasurably. While never a clearly stated goal of liberal anticommunism, this became one of its by-products. By the second half of the 1950s, McCarthy himself had been disgraced and the more virulent reactionary anti-Communists were increasingly isolated on the right. Liberal anticommunism predominated. It would continue to permeate American thinking into the 1960s, even after its architects had begun to move to other positions or to forget that they had built it.

THE PRIME LIBERAL FALLACY

Liberal anti-Communists adopted an offensive stance in their battle against McCarthy and the Communists, offering their own version of anticommunism rather than defending the rights of others. Nonetheless, the liberal anti-Communists knew that their arguments about their own loyalty or morality would go unheeded if they could not convince the public that despite their radical past and their opposition to reactionaries, they did not themselves threaten society. The campaign contained elements of both an intellectual investigation and a propaganda effort. They needed to articulate a position at once intellectually valid and easily grasped. Issues had to be clear, comparisons understandable, and the distinctions between friends and enemies drawn to avoid all misunderstandings.

An early and essential part of this campaign was thus the public equation of communism with America's most recent and, until 1945, most hated enemy. The notion that Communists and fascists shared a number of primary qualities—were in fact two variants of the same basic tendency—became an essential touchstone of liberal anticommunism. America had mobilized to fight fascism in World War II. In the postwar years the Soviets supplanted the Nazis as the world's chief villains—Stalin was the new Hitler, the supreme symbol of evil. Similarities between the political systems were stressed, differences neglected.

The effort to repaint wartime allies as postwar enemies did not rest solely with the liberal anti-Communists. The rhetoric of the cold war, the public statements accompanying such government programs as the Truman Doctrine, the use of the "Munich analogy" to describe American resistance to "Communist aggression"—all became part of this effort. American foreign-policy makers perceived the international Communist movement as a single entity aimed at territorial aggression and internal subversion. The same attitude which had once been applied to the fascists was now applied to the Communists. America had resisted such a unified attempt to conquer and subvert before; it could do it again.

For liberal anti-Communists, the equation of Nazis and Soviets also solved a more personal problem. If Stalin could be likened to the Nazi leader, if the Communists could be portrayed as the "fascists" of the postwar years, then the thrust of anticommunism would immediately be turned away from the notions of left versus right. A new terminology would grow which would stress the distinctions between Communists and others on the left, and which would illustrate the similarities between the Soviets and the Nazis. Melvin Lasky put the case most directly when he wrote in 1952, "The historical uniqueness of Stalinism should not blind us to the fact that *morally* and *politically* it is identical with Nazism."[15]

Architects of American foreign policy and various anti-Communists might readily assent to Lasky's view, but for many others agreement required a significant change of perspective. While Sidney Hook blasted the notion that "Communists are an integral part of the indigenous progressive movement, instead of a cancerous growth upon it," other liberals and progressives took additional convincing to move from one world view to another. The acceptance of the fascist-Communist equation required an abandonment of a conception liberals had held since the Russian revolution and before. Many liberals and radicals had grown increasingly unhappy with the Soviet government. The 1930s optimism of a Lincoln Steffens—"I have seen the future and it works"—rarely found expression after 1945. Still, though critical of the Soviets, liberals and radicals continued to perceive communism on a continuum with liberalism, left of center. Fascism occupied the extreme in the opposite, rightward direction. To criticize Stalin or the Soviet Union did not necessarily require changing one's notion of the political spectrum. Thus, despite the bald assertions of Hook, Lasky, and others, the debate about the equation of fascism and communism was one over the defining or the charting of the political landscape.

Liberal anti-Communists did not contend that communism and fascism sprouted from the same philosophical roots or that Soviet socialism and National Socialism had the same economic goals. Rather, the anti-Communists argued that the similarities between fascism and communism became clear when the two systems were viewed in new ways. The *PR* editors chided the *Nation* and the *New Republic* for failing to see the similarities between Franco's Spain and Soviet Russia—both were "totalitarian" and "anti-democratic," "gave aid to Hitler," and "menace[d] world peace." Differences in economic goals, for example, fell out of this comparison, as did an awareness of the massive losses Russia sustained in fighting the Nazis. This same attitude prompted Diana Trilling's criticism of Simone de Beauvoir, voiced during a visit by the French critic to America. Trilling accused de Beauvoir of falling "victim to the prime liberal fallacy of our time," of seeing "no resemblance at all between Communism and Fascism."[16]

With this equation the tone of the political discussion, as well as the sources which could be brought into the argument, changed markedly. It now became possible to draw analogies between the fascists and the Communists and to discredit the latter by the actions of the former. Thus, as the government would use the Munich analogy to promote resistance to Communist aggression, the anti-Communists would recall examples from the prewar years for the postwar world. Responding to civil libertarians like Henry Steele Commager who defended the rights of Communists to present their political views, Irving Kristol asked, "If a Nazi had, in 1938, addressed a high school audience in this country, extolling the accomplishments of Hitler's regime," would the civil libertarians favoring free speech for Communists have found "in such a speech 'nothing that any normal person could find objectionable'"? (Kristol was quoting Commager's words about a pro-Communist speaker.)[17] Objectionable or not, the defense of the *right* of Communists to speak was the aim of the civil libertarians, and Commager would very likely have defended the Nazi in 1938 on the same civil-libertarian grounds. But Kristol neatly slid across the free-speech issue to the question of whether the remarks were objectionable, which rested entirely on the presumption that a Nazi's words in 1938 paralleled a Communist's in 1952.

With the Nazi-Soviet equivalency in place, it became possible to bring the actions of the antifascists into play, as well as those of the Nazis. To critics suggesting that communism posed little threat since it possesses such a weak international organization, Sidney Hook replied that anyone voicing a similar opinion about fascism in the 1930s "would have been branded an apologist for fascism by the Popular Front Liberals."[18] Hook's use of the analogy of the Popular Front is ironic because it was the *Partisan* crowd which had argued against the Front, while many of the postwar "apologists," as Hook called them, had been its active supporters. By the 1950s the New Yorkers had appropriated the Popular Front arguments, but substituting communism for fascism. In the 1930s they had held out against the Front, favoring a radical alternative and being critical of the Soviets and the Americans. In the 1950s Hook lambasted those critical of both: "To conclude from this [critique of American society] that Truman and what he represents is as bad as Stalin . . . is just as much the mark of political cretinism as to conclude that Roosevelt's America was as bad as Hitler's Germany."[19]

No anti-Popular Fronter ever made this point, but the *Partisan* editors' position in 1939 had been that Roosevelt's America was not praiseworthy enough for them to support the Allied side. This attitude did change with the outbreak of the war and the split between Macdonald and the other editors, but that was not until 1942. In the late 1930s the kind of "cretinism" Hook identified fit more closely the *PR* attitude than that of the Popular Front. Never bothered by adjustments in their own positions, however, these anti-Communists attacked liberals unwilling to join their united crusade in the 1950s. Their own independence during one period could not be duplicated by others during another.

An unwillingness to join a united effort against the Communists was more than an exercise in independence, however. There is no doubt that those at *PR* in the late 1930s believed fascism to be a serious, immediate threat. They opposed the Front's form, not its purpose. Many of those opposed to anticommunism thought that the threat from communism, especialy do-mestically, was exaggerated. But the anti-Communists treated the Communist threat as an absolute fact. From the anti-Communist viewpoint, only the naïve or the fellow traveler could fail to see it.

Armed with the Nazi-Soviet equation, the anti-Communists could now use prewar and wartime activities to explain and chart postwar events. The most important diplomatic event along the path to World War II quickly found its place in analyses after 1945. "It is clear," the editors of *Partisan Review* wrote in 1946,

> that the "liberals" [*Nation* and *New Republic* variety] are embarked upon nothing less than a policy of *appeasement of Russia*. . . . We are not surprised to find appeasement repeating itself, and the new instance already shows all the features familiar from the appeasement of Hitler. . . . Was war against Hitler avoided by appeasement? On the contrary. . . . If war between Russia and the United States is not inevitable, then perhaps the only way to avoid it is to stop licking Stalin's boots.[20]

For American foreign-policy makers and defenders, the Munich analogy provided a justification for actions taken against Communists and revo-lutionaries, on the basis of America's experience with fascists and counter-revolutionaries. For the liberal anti-Communists, it served this function, but it also contributed to their general attempt to isolate communism from other leftist groups. "The rise of fascism and Communism," Arthur Schlesinger wrote in *The Vital Center*, "illustrated vividly the fallacies of the linear conception of right and left." To many the world now looked different—in Schlesinger's analysis, circular. Right and left had come around to meet at the extremes. Anti-Communists focused on elements they thought common to Nazism and Stalinism, Schlesinger citing "the single party," "the leader," "the secret police," "the consuming fear of political and intellectual freedom."[21] Again, they rarely considered the differences in the philosophies of the systems, their economic goals, their intellectual foundations. Redefined liberalism had abandoned ideology and replaced it with a more practical, realistic approach to society. This view was extended to analyses of other systems as well. The tangible manifestations, the day-to-day political processes, the governmental structures—the sum of all these—established the nature of a political system. By focusing on these aspects, the anti-Communists could make Nazism and Stalinism meet.

This new political reality—the convergence of positions once considered polar opposites—brought a descriptive phrase into increasing usage. To-talitarianism became the convenient label by which the previous left-right disparity could be bridged. The "liberals" who tolerated the Soviet Union,

Diana Trilling noted, for example, "are the same people who were resolute against fascism, but they cannot admit that the socialist revolution has produced an equally virulent totalitarianism."[22] The term had been used before the war by individuals horrified by the excesses of Hitler's Germany or antagonistic to Stalin's Russia. But after 1945 it became common coin in the rhetoric of political debate and, in 1951, received its formal exposition in Hannah Arendt's massive *The Origins of Totalitarianism*.

Arendt occupied a special place among the New York Intellectuals. While offering an intellectual explanation or justification appropriate for current concerns and thinking, she never became an "insider" in the community. A number of the New Yorkers grew close to Arendt, but she maintained both her distance and her distinctiveness from the general group and from the general philosophical position which characterized the New York Intellectual world. Her background differed markedly from that of the others. She had left Nazi Germany for Paris in 1933 and fled Paris for America in 1940 as the Germans drove into France. She had a formal German education, including a Ph.D. in philosophy from Heidelberg, where she had studied with Karl Jaspers and written her thesis on Saint Augustine. In France and in her first years in America, Arendt did not teach, but worked for Jewish relief organizations and in publishing.[23] Only after the publication of *The Origins of Totalitarianism* did Arendt move to the university campus, to Princeton, Berkeley, Chicago, Columbia, Northwestern, and Cornell, before settling at the New School. "She was an extraordinarily trained scholar, a great classical scholar," Alfred Kazin, one of her good friends, remembered. She "had gone into political science from a point of view utterly unkown to the New Yorkers."[24]

In the 1960s Arendt's observations on the extensions of totalitarianism enraged a number of individuals who had praised her earlier work.[25] But in the postwar world of rapidly adjusting political reference points, her detailed explanation of the roots and attributes of totalitarianism found a ready and appreciative audience among anti-Communists seeking intellectual justification for their notions of the Communist-fascist duality. Arendt's work begins with two long sections, tracing the origins of contemporary totalitarianism in nineteenth-century anti-Semitism and imperialism. She offered intricate and intriguing analyses of Disraeli and Dreyfus, theories of race, and the rise of bureaucracies. In her last section, entitled "Totalitarianism," Arendt provided the material which anti-Communists awaited. Her first paragraph begins with the assumption of the Nazi-Bolshevik equation and offers three sentences which compare Hitler and Stalin. The remaining 130 pages lead from there. One finds, for example, references to "attitudes which confirm a Nazi or Bolshevik in his belief," "evidence . . . can be found repeatedly in Nazi or Bolshevik literature," or "Nazi Germany and Soviet Russia . . . two essentially identical systems." Even structural differences could be ironed out. "Nazi totalitarianism started with a mass organization which was only gradually dominated by elite formations, while the Bolsheviks started with elite formations and organized the masses accordingly. The result was the same in both cases."[26] *The Origins of Totalitarianism* served as the capstone of the effort to destroy the old notion of communism as just another leftist movement and to link it with the most horrific of recent political movements, Nazism. Arendt's arguments became the philosophical cement which firmly set this new view of political realities.

Anti-Communists most frequently employed the Nazi-Soviet equation as an analytical and metaphorical tool. Some, though, went beyond these approaches. Melvin Lasky, for example, believed that only the color of the soldiers' shirts had changed in East Germany. Originally stationed in Germany during World War II and then editor of the State Department–sponsored, German-based magazine *Der Monat*, Lasky often reported on German affairs in English-language publications. In *Twentieth Century* in 1951 he described an East German military parade:

> The official announcer of the Soviet-controlled *Berliner Rundfunk* was almost hysterical as the drum-beats echoed down the *Brandenburger Tor* (gateway between East and West Berlin). At one point his tongue slipped as he spoke of "this mighty brown force"; it was an accident; he corrected it immediately to "red force"; but the point was not lost on his listeners. This was a revival of Prussian militarism decked out in new colors. . . . The *Volkspolizie* [*sic*] is the new *Reichswehr*.

In German society, Lasky continued, "the SSD (*Staatssicherheitsdienst*) is in its structure and operations the successor to Hitler's *Geheime Staatspolizei* (Gestapo)." It had, Lasky believed, "the very same task of the 'destruction of the internal enemy.' It controls the very same concentration camps."[27]

The Nazis had become the Communists in this extreme view, not only as a comparable threat to world peace but as the same force under different banners. Lasky's conception carried the Nazi-Soviet equation to its ultimate conclusion, but not, given the basic argument, to an illogical one. If personal attributes, attractions, institutional elements, and appeals to human irra-tionalism spurred the development of totalitarianism, then the easy flip from fascist to Communist or back again seemed very likely. If political or ideological arguments were considered irrelevant, then the notion of a mass of individuals easily swayed from one totalitarian movement to another did not seem illogical at all. The Germans, recruits of the most despised totalitarian movement before the war, could easily fall victim to the most hated postwar movement.

American society moved from a fear of the Nazi menace to a fear of the "Red menace" during the first years of the cold war.[28] For liberal anti-Communists this endeavor took a variety of forms: the use of analogy, a recalling of the lessons of history such as Munich, and a redrawing of the political spectrum. This effort had the cumulative effect of distancing the liberals from the Communists. With the separation achieved, the rest of their task became that much easier. After communism was isolated, they sought to discredit it and those who believed communism was a legitimate political position and who wished to defend the civil liberties of their fellow Americans.

CAPTIVES OF THE IDEA

Once Communists could be severed from their traditional left-wing connections, the second task was to isolate them intellectually and personally. Again, anti-Communists aimed to demonstrate Communists' "difference" from other leftists. Communists were not political individuals who assessed situations and applied analyses in a reasoned and philosophical manner. Instead, overzealous and fanatical, they went *beyond* reason. In addition, if Communists were distinguished from "true" intellectuals, the distinction between Communists in general and the ex-radical anti-Communists would be further clarified in the public mind. One could thus refute anti-intellectual notions of right-wing anticommunism without defending Communists and while protecting socialists and other Marxists.

A number of individuals of differing political persuasions combined to paint a picture of communism as "blind faith." An essential distinction, argued Irving Howe, prompted his decision not to join an organization called the American Forum for Socialist Education. Howe stated that had this been an anti-Stalinist left-wing group, he would have participated. But since it included Communists, he felt he had to decline. "We do not believe that the Communist Party forms a part of the Left," he explained. "[It] represents a totalitarian political system and outlook. . . . Communists are not free agents."[29]

Lacking freedom, the anti-Communists believed, all Communists lost the independent judgment which comes from a proper intellectual perspective. For Sidney Hook, a Communist was "a dedicated person working with fanatical zeal and prepared to make great personal sacrifices in the grip of this belief."[30] This went beyond commitment or devotion to a cause. The words "fanatical" and "in the grip" give Hook's description an added intensity, for they suggest total lack of critical reasoning and sound judgment. Nathan Glazer, illustrating the same point, chose an analogy which even those unfamiliar with communism would find understandable. "To be a Communist means, ideally, and in large measure in reality, to be enlisted as a soldier in an organization. One hesitates to call it a 'cause.' " In this context, Glazer believed, Communists acted and were treated like soldiers, unthinking in their response to orders, highly organized and rigidly structured. "They accept the discipline and orders of their superiors, [and] are called by the military term of 'cadres.' "[31] The notions of Communists' lack of freedom, overzealous commitment, and submission to a highly disciplined and rigid organization came together most clearly in Irving Kristol's analysis of Communists and their activities, in his famous *Commentary* article "Civil Liberties, 1952: A Study in Confusion."

> Communism is an idea, beyond question. Indeed it is an Idea that is also a conspiracy to subvert every social and political order it does not dominate. . . . A

person who is captive to this Idea can at any time, in any place, be called upon to do whatever the Idea, i.e., The Party, thinks necessary.[32]

Kristol looped back to the basic anti-Communist argument of the Nazi-Stalinist duality to cement his point about Communists' lack of freedom and the potential danger they posed. Admitting that his picture of the mental captivity of Communists "sounds exaggerated, as it must, being so foreign to the nature of American political experience," Kristol even allowed that Communists "conveyed no impression of being conspirators." Still, Roosevelt "didn't see in Stalin any symptoms of blood lust," and "Herman Goering in jail struck one as a clever clown." Kristol did agree that "in a showdown" some Communists would "break free of the Idea and rally to the democratic cause." But Americans could not wait.

Unfortunately it is quite impossible to tell the citizens of Oshkosh, some of whom have suffered personal loss as a result of the war in Korea, that there is no harm in having their children taught the three R's by a Communist, as it would have been to persuade the citizens of Flatbush in 1939 that there was no cause for excitement in their children being taught by a Nazi.[33]

Committed to "the Idea," Communists lacked any critical intelligence, this line of argument ran. Their one shred of hope for convincing others of their intellectual credentials, anti-Communists believed, remained their idealism. These anti-Communists had abandoned vague utopian notions in their own postwar political reevaluations, but they continued to understand the potential appeal of an idealistic vision. This accounted, Daniel Bell surmised, for the "tremendous emotional hold that communism has on tens of thousands of persons," resting on "a mythopoeic and psychological level," involving "an acquiescence in the mysterious and imperative law of history" and a "resignation to a future deemed even more inevitable than glorious."[34] Idealism, rather than political experience, usually brought people to communism, Sidney Hook maintained, and this element—"the apparent offspring of moral idealism and scientific law"—was the last attractive feature of a movement stripped of its political and intellectual legitimacy.[35]

Robert Warshow, among others, set out to demonstrate that even the idealism of Communists was faulty.

Whether he cheers the Yankees or the Dodgers, whether he damns Franklin Roosevelt as a warmonger or adores him as the champion of human rights [examples from Julius Rosenberg], the Communist is always celebrating the same thing: the great empty Idea which has taken on the outlines of his personality. Communists are still "idealists"—perhaps the more so because the "idealism" is by now almost entirely without content—and the surprising degree of sympathy and even respect that they can command among liberals is partly to be explained by the liberal belief that idealism in itself is a virtue.[36]

This was not true idealism, not an idealism based in intellectual considerations and reasoned analysis. Utopian idealism had fallen out of favor among many of these intellectuals, having given way to more-practical goals based on realistic approaches. The idealism which remained must rest on feasible goals, as well as on intellectual analysis. Communist idealism failed to meet these new requirements. A Stalinist remained unthinking and uncritical, accepting the "party line" and thus abrogating any claims to intellectualism. One might think oneself intellectual, but, as Harold Rosenberg would point out, a Communist "belonged to an elite of knowing," and "since all truth has been automatically bestowed upon him by his adherence to the party, he is an intellectual who need not think." Rosenberg concluded sarcastically, "What good is mental activity if one can know more by giving it up?"[37]

When they attempted to assess why individuals might sacrifice intellectual and political independence to sign on with the Communists, the New Yorkers engaged in a bit of armchair psychologizing. A Communist's participation derived from unconscious needs and personal inadequacies. To Irving Howe, Communists "replaced the denied fraternal sentiments of their youth with a hard-headed valuation of industrial power." Thus the party represented a "managerial *camaraderie* resting upon a joint esteem for the gestures of power, the wonders of technology, and bureaucratic planning."[38] Arthur Schlesinger carried Howe's argument a step further. More optimistic about the state of American society than Howe, Schlesinger wondered why individuals would join the American Communist party. "Where cruel oppression affords little choice," such as in Chiang Kai-shek's China or in South Africa, Schlesinger could understand why individuals became members. In America, however, there had occurred "the longest period of liberal government in its history." Some other explanation must account for a person's denying the fruits of American society and embracing the Communists' "intolerable discipline of party membership." The answer could be found in the personalities of the members, not in current political issues. "Even America has its quota of lonely and frustrated people, craving social, intellectual and even sexual fulfillment they cannot obtain in existing society." For Schlesinger, neurosis lay at the root of the commitment to communism in Western countries. "For these people, party discipline is no obstacle; it is an attraction. The great majority of members in America, as in Europe, *want* to be disciplined."[39]

The Communists could thus be dismissed as failing to offer a viable political argument. Personal inadequacies had led them to a movement which remained intellectually faulty and strictly regimented. Ideas about the party and its members reinforced one another with a kind of circular logic. Weak, nonthinking individuals joined a movement which offered personal "fulfillment," despite its philosophical pitfalls. The Communist party lacked credibility because of its flawed members, subjectively bound by an emotional bond rather than objectively committed to political positions. An analysis of members and of ideas pointed to one conclusion—that the entire fabric of the Communist movement was overwhelmingly flawed.

Having been driven from the left in the anti-Communist analysis which equated them with fascists, the Communists were now expelled from the intellectual community as well—isolated from those with whom they had been clearly connected in the public mind, and identified as inadequate human beings. In the process, anti-Communists felt they could rescue the "good name" of intellectuals from the assaults of the reactionary right. The removal of Communists from the liberal-intellectual orbit provided protection for the remaining liberals without denying anticommunism its major target.

CLEAR AND PRESENT DANGER

Having separated the Communists politically and intellectually, the anti-Communists argued over how to isolate them legally. Communists might be political extremists akin to fascists and they might lack critical and intellectual attributes, but by themselves these points were insufficient to warrant legal action. Communists had to be placed far enough outside the pale that their existence constituted a perpetual threat rather than just a frequent annoyance. Sidney Hook most succinctly enunciated a method of viewing political movements in general and communism in particular which would fulfill this need. In 1953 Hook published *Heresy, Yes—Conspiracy, No*, in which he contended that a qualitative difference existed between what he defined as a heresy and a conspiracy. This distinction offered a key to an understanding of which groups should be afforded protection and which existed outside the bounds of the law and of tolerability.

> A heresy is a set of unpopular ideas or opinions on matters of grave concern to the community. The right to profess a heresy publicly on any theme is an essential element of a liberal society. . . . A conspiracy, as distinct from a heresy, is a secret or underground movement which seeks to attain its ends not by normal political or educational processes, but by playing outside the rules of the game . . . a conspiracy cannot be tolerated.

Hook believed that a society not only should but must make this distinction. The failure to do so, he argued, "is fatal to a liberal civilization, for the inescapable consequence . . . is either self-destruction, when heresies are punished as conspiracies, or destruction at the hands of enemies, when conspiracies are tolerated as heresies."[40] Society needed to protect the liberals and punish the Communists, advocates of the heresy-conspiracy position declared, countering both the McCarthyites and the civil libertarians.

Hook's position proved ideally suited for liberal anticommunism. Irving Kristol, for one, in 1952 found "it obvious to almost everyone, by now, that Communism is not, properly speaking, an 'opinion,' not even an erroneous opinion. . . . It is a fanatical conspiracy."[41] To give this argument the weight of an overarching theory, however, one had to apply it to a variety of associations possessing "conspiratorial" characteristics, not just to communism. Furthermore there were attempts to tie this view to the traditional American principles of free speech and thought as well as to notions about society's right to self-protection. Presented as a means for easily walking the fine line between dissident thought and threatening activities, the heresy-conspiracy distinction actually proved more derivative of postwar American society than Hook would admit. Attempts to expand the discussion beyond the pressing concern at hand—communism—led to difficulties. Hook had originally included several other examples of conspiracies to balance the picture—groups other than Communists who fit the conspiratorial requirements. Fascists, of course, easily met the criteria, and their similarities to Communists had already been well established in the anti-Communist argument. The Ku Klux Klan became another identifiable conspiratorial body. Yet, given his own definitions, Hook ran into trouble because groups not threatening to American society could also be labeled as conspiracies. Roman Catholics offered an unsettling example. Here Hook backpedaled a bit, admitting that some similarities did exist between Communists and Catholics, such as privileged access to truth, internal organization, methods of deification, education, and propaganda. However, crucial differences existed, as Hook explained:

> Whereas, from the standpoint of democracy, Stalinism is both a heresy and a conspiracy which justifies seizure of power by a minority to impose the will of the Party on the population by force and violence, Catholicism is only a heresy, since the full programme . . . is to be introduced only when a majority of the population has been won to the Catholic position.[42]

Hook's defense of Catholicism as *only* a "heresy" reveals the thin ice on which his theory was sitting. His elaboration raised more questions than it answered. Can the stipulation that Catholicism will present its "full programme" only when it wins a majority of the population to its position apply to other non-Communist "conspiracies"? Does the Klan become "only a heresy" since its "full programme"—absolute white supremacy eliminating Blacks, Jews, and Catholics from American society—can be achieved only when a majority of the white population has been won to its position? Hook was clearly not arguing this, nor did he really consider Catholicism a "heresy." He was trying to establish the rights of diversity and difference, to foster some sort of pragmatist democratic pluralism, but one which would exclude communism. What Hook's explanation reveals is the basis on which his view was predicated. The heresy-conspiracy concept attempted to drop legalistic dividers between groups already in existence, to supply a disinterested legalistic theory to match a highly charged current political perspective.

Whatever trouble critics might have with Hook's arguments, many anti-Communists readily accepted his basic distinction. Kristol, for example, argued that a conspiracy "had no right to be circulated outside of jail," while Robert Warshow pointed to communism as a "conspiracy ready to employ almost any means to its ends." In reviewing the course of Marxism in America, Daniel Bell noted in 1952 that in the postwar years "the Communist movement stood revealed before the American people not as a political party but as a conspiracy."[43]

The establishment of the heresy-conspiracy distinction was only half the battle against communism, however. It remained necessary to make sure communism was assigned the proper label. Individuals might use Hook's distinction to oppose the Klan or the Nazis and yet continue to defend Communists, on the grounds that they were merely exercising their personal, though unpopular, belief. Hook met this criticism head-on, challenging those who mistakenly believed Stalinism "an unpleasant heresy just a little worse than a crotchety theory of disease or finance."[44] He rejected the idea of communism as an extreme heresy by linking American Communists to an international conspiracy. "Without its organic ties to the Soviet state apparatus with all its machinery for war, espionage, and terror," Hook contended, "the American Communist Party would have only mundane value, its members would be ineffectual." Ideas alone, no matter how "crotchety," do not make Communists dangerous. "Their organizational ties; these make them the paramilitary fifth column of a powerful state, obligated to strike whenever their foreign masters give the word."[45] Communists thus clearly qualified as conspirators in a network which extended beyond America to another nation, whose leaders controlled the Americans' actions. Captives of "the Idea," American Communists remained a part of a perpetual conspiracy, dominated by "foreign masters."

To further strengthen the legalistic aspect regarding the danger of this conspiracy, the liberal anti-Communists turned to well-established principles on the limitations of free speech in America, as well as to the modifications now being handed down by the American judiciary. Hook favored toleration of heresies because a part of America's strength derived from what Justice Holmes called "free trade of ideas"—a notion Hook thought in keeping with liberalism "from Socrates to John Dewey." The only permissible checks on this "free trade" occurred when it became necessary to keep "the competition . . . honest and openly conducted" and "when a clear and present danger to the public peace and security" exists.[46] The nature of a conspiracy itself abrogated the "free trade of ideas," the anti-Communists believed, as did the nature and organization of the Communist party. The question of what constituted a clear and present danger or whether some other standard should apply elicited arguments from many legal quarters, including that of the liberal anti-Communists.

For Hook the old test established by Holmes was sufficient. "That a danger to our national security exists which is clear, present, flourishing, and extremely powerful seems to me to be undeniable." He pinpointed its source: "This danger flows from the unremitting campaign of the Kremlin . . . and the American Communist Party, no matter what its size or influence (which is not inconsiderable), forms an integral part of that movement."[47]

The courts, as well as some anti-Communists, had already begun to move beyond Holmes, however. In his appellate decision upholding the conviction of the leaders of the American Communist party in 1949, Judge Learned Hand had introduced the notion of a "clear and probable" test. The Supreme Court upheld both the conviction and Hand's view. Chief Justice Fred Vinson wrote that though the danger of revolution need not be present, it was "probable" and thus present in "the inflammable nature of world conditions."[48] Arthur Schlesinger, drawing on this "clear and probable" theory and on the notion of a conspiracy and the fascist-Communist equation, reaffirmed the need for new civil-liberties guidelines. "We are not just confronted with unpopular opinions, with eccentrics, zealots or bigots, with the fantasies of A. Mitchell Palmer's deranged imagination," Schlesinger asserted. "We are confronted with the spread of ruthless totalitarianism abroad. . . . A fanatical minority is engaged in a cruel conspiracy to end forever the whole conception of a society based on free discussion." Therefore, he concluded, the danger was "real," and the opposition's chances for success were significant. These were not merely quacks or idealists. "Is there not," Schlesinger asked, "some point in advance of 'clear and present danger' where free society must draw the line if it is to preserve its own inner moral strength?"[49]

In this line of thinking, then, the notion of conspiracy superseded the notion of an immediate danger; it was a matter of identifying a potential danger, clear if not present. Irving Kristol in 1952 summarized this position:

An opinion that urges its listeners to evade the draft, or not to send their children to school, or to blow up buildings, or to organize a conspiracy for the violent overthrow of government, has no right to be circulated outside of jail, and the state has every right to see that it is circulated nowhere else. And all this, regardless of any "clear and present danger"; for as our antitrust laws maintain concerning conspiracy, the very planning of it is a crime; and as Learned Hand said of the Communist conspiracy: "The conspirators will strike as soon as success seems possible and obviously no one in his senses will strike sooner."[50]

The designation of communism as a conspiracy liable to prosecution completed the political isolation of the Communists from other left-wing groups. It drew the clearest distinction between tolerable and intolerable ideas, Communists and ex-Communists, Communists and socialists, Communists and liberals. Liberal anti-Communists could continue to attack the Communists without having to join the McCarthyites. These liberals could defend the right of free speech for themselves and others without having to join the civil-libertarian defenders of Communists. Their anti-Communist position, from the fascist-Communist equation to the heresy-conspiracy distinction, gave them a platform from which to argue the case as liberals and anti-Communists. It also provided them a basis for judging the actions of other critics and commentators on the American scene. In 1954 Sidney Hook praised a study called *American Security and Freedom*, by Maurice J. Goldbloom, because it made "all the relevant distinctions—between heresy and conspiracy." Goldbloom's work contained "more common and uncommon sense" than all the writings of "ritualistic liberals."[51] "Realistic liberals," as Hook called himself and his compatriots, considered themselves the best judges of the current conditions in American society and the best anti-Communists.

SECURING THE LIBERAL CENTER

The effort to help create a liberal anticommunism—the best form of anticommunism—provided a new, cohesive force for many of the New York Intellectuals. It gave them a distinctive vocabulary and position in the preeminent political discussion of postwar America. And it offered them a philosophy of their own, free of the disquieting notion that they might be quasi-McCarthyites and, they hoped, free of lingering suspicions about their own past activities. Previously, people might have preferred "to risk being wrong with Stalin for fear of being right with Hearst," as William Barrett put it in 1949, "though they never put the alternative to themselves so starkly."[52] Now the alternative did not have to be so stark, at least on the surface. The middle ground had been smoothed by the new, liberal anti-Communist position. The liberals regarded their position as both personally fulfilling and politically correct—as satisfying intellectual requirements as well as international realities.

William Phillips, for example, found that "the defense of Western democracy against the Soviet threat should not present any special problems, since the recognition of one's roots does not preclude the free play of the imagination or the dissident spirit either in literature or in politics." Rejecting the idea that all anti-Communists must be anti-intellectual and lowbrow, Phillips argued just the opposite: "I, for one, do not see why the American writer need yield to any of the academic or philistine pressures in order to define either his national identity or his anti-communism."[53] Liberalism, intellectualism, and anticommunism—as interpreted by the New York Intellectuals after World War II—combined nicely to form a complete intellectual and political package.

This anticommunism offered a haven for other anti-Communists uncomfortable with the right wing. Anticommunism has "thrown the liberal in the same camp with the forces he detests, or should detest," complained Diana Trilling. Continuing her opposition to McCarthy and to Stalinism, Trilling urged her friends "to make a clean break" with the reactionaries.

> Just as the pro-Hiss liberal claims his right not to be smeared as a Communist just because the Communist agrees with him in this case, so the anti-Hiss liberal must insist on his right not to be labeled a reactionary just because reactionaries agree with him in this case.[54]

With the liberal anti-Communist alternative, these distinctions appeared much easier to make. Now at the center of things, the liberal "sets the tone of moderation and respectability in the intellectual community," Daniel Bell noted. Those on the radical right, as Bell would call them, "find themselves outside the pale."[55]

A central aim of the New Yorkers in redefining liberalism was to place themselves at the center of American politics—moderate and respectable. Liberal anticommunism helped them achieve just such a position. Furthermore, they now felt protected from the potentially harmful hysteria of anti-communism. They claimed that they—rather than the paranoids who found Communists under every bed or the political opportunists who attempted to ride anticommunism to high office—were the "real" anti-Communists.

In keeping with their new notions about liberalism as a political movement and their new practical approach to the problems of society, the liberals found in anticommunism a perfect test case. It avoided hysteria, idealism, and naïveté. The reactionaries were hysterical, the civil libertarians idealistic, and the American Communists naïve. "Those who have succumbed to the Soviet myth," Sidney Hook claimed, "were devoid of political experience. They were led to their first political affair by emotional compulsion rather than by sober computation of the consequences of adopting a given proposal and its alternatives."[56] The liberal anti-Communists saw themselves as overcoming the inherent weaknesses of these opposing groups. "Most anti-Communists have been through the Communist mill or frighteningly close to it," Diana Trilling believed, "which has given them first-hand knowledge of the Communist technique." This doubly qualified them to enunciate the proper anti-Communist position. In keeping with the popular image of the most effective anti-Communists, such as Whittaker Chambers or Elizabeth Bentley, they could be seen as insiders who came outside to tell the world the truth. In Alfred Kazin's words, these "old revolutionists constitute not a party, but an information service. They are the ones who 'know'—or knew first: it was they who once saw the totalitarian beast face-to-face."[57] In addition, and often unlike these flamboyant, right-wing "old revolutionists," the New Yorkers brought their levelheaded and unemotional intellectual attributes to bear on their personal experiences. "To be a decent person and to have had proof, in one's own political past, of one's power for self-deception is to be forever charged to self-awareness," Diana Trilling observed. "It means that at least one tries to put evidence before prejudice."[58]

Intellectuals could now comfortably become anti-Communists. In fact, it became essential for them to do so. Like redefined liberalism, liberal anticommunism emerged as more than an intellectual position. "The task of the intellectual," Sidney Hook instructed his peers, "is still to lead an intellectual life," but always in the larger frame of the world situation. Criticism of America remained legitimate, Hook maintained,

> without forgetting for a moment the total threat which Communism poses to the life of the free mind. Our own vigilantes and reactionaries are much more like witches and scarecrows than are the paid and unpaid agents of the Kremlin. . . . The

democratic West will require the critical support, the dedicated energy and above all, the intelligence of its intellectuals if it is to survive as a free culture. . . . Let the neutralists of the world remember. In the West non-comformists, no matter how alienated, can always win a hearing. . . . In the land of Purges and Brainwashing, the only thing a non-conformist can earn is a bullet in the neck. This is the historical premise of our age whose recognition is binding on all.[59]

Having established this "premise of our age," though often in terms less dramatic than Hook's, the New York Intellectuals succeeded in countering the threat of McCarthyism with a political response of their own. They had redefined anticommunism just as they had redefined liberalism, staking their claims not just to a position in the discussion but to the final word.

They had dismissed the Communists as totalitarian, anti-intellectual, neurotic, and conspiratorial, and the McCarthyites as "blowhards," "witches," and "scarecrows." But two other identifiable groups stood between the liberal anti-Communists and their secure hold on the liberal position. For very different reasons, these two groups chose to defend the Communists against anti-Communist attacks and to see anticommunism as the greater threat. One group, fellow travelers, had long been a nemesis for the New Yorkers, as far back as the Popular Front days. The other, those defending basic notions of civil liberties, were new combatants. With their newly defined liberal and anti-Communist arguments, the New York Intellectuals set out to discredit both of these opponents and to make their own position appear as the only logical choice.

Whereas it seemed easy to dismiss Communist party members as weak individuals bound to an authoritarian movement for neurotic reasons, it proved more difficult to dispense with fellow travelers. To some liberals, they posed a more insidious threat than the Communists themselves, because they served as unconscious agents for Communist activities. They offered a knottier problem for analysis. No simplistic psychological or intellectual profile would suffice. The central problem arose from the many similarities between fellow travelers and anti-Communists. Members of the two groups often came from the same ranks of writers, scholars, critics, and intellectuals. As Sidney Hook pointed out, "Statistical studies show how to this day members of the professoriate constitute the strongest and most influential group of Communist fellow-travelers in the United States."[60] Often having academic credentials to add respectability to their cause, fellow travelers like the critic F. O. Matthiessen and the astronomer Harlow Shapley, of Harvard, the philosopher Corliss Lamont, of Columbia, the political scientist Fredrick Schuman, of Williams College, and the artist Rockwell Kent could not be portrayed so easily as woeful underground men or conscious agents of a foreign power.

The problem of the fellow travelers persisted, in fact multiplied, with their personal prominence. They constituted, for Hook, "the most loyal battalion of that little army of 'progressive' intellectuals who are invariably found lending their names and prestige to Communist party front organizations." They championed Soviet foreign policy and "defend[ed] Communists against even the mildest and most justified of administrative measures." The motives of the fellow travelers did not come in for questioning, only the results of their actions. Their ideas, "generous in intention even if vague in expression, centered around ideas of equality, freedom, and peace." Holding on to erroneous Popular Front conceptions, they wielded a "profound influence on the attitudes of students."[61] Their impact went beyond student populations, to American policy. Offering his own version of the American role in the Chinese revolution, Irving Kristol provided an alternative to the reactionary view, which included McCarthy's charge that the John Hopkins professor Owen Lattimore was the top Soviet espionage agent operating in America. "By 1945," Kristol wrote,

> "vulgar" anti-communists . . . were pushed out of the State Deparment and their places taken by sophisticated "progressives" led by Mr. Lattimore's old and valued friend, John Carter Vincent. These new men did not, as has been charged, "sell China down the river." They merely borrowed from Mr. Lattimore a policy—of denying aid to Chiang until he formed a coalition with the Communists—which had this as an inevitable consequence, and which they smugly and foolishly thought to be the only "constructive" programme suitable for their advanced political sensibilities.[62]

Fellow travelers caused the liberal anti-Communists an additional concern. By standing between liberals and Communists, fellow travelers made it appear that the line from the center to the left passed through them to the Communists. Furthermore, if those on the right shared this perception of the political spectrum, they might blur the distinctions between liberals and fellow travelers. Amid the intensity of the McCarthyite campaigns, the label fellow traveler was as much of a stigma as the label Communist. Thus, support for the notion of the relative political proximity of liberals, fellow travelers, and Communists undermined the anti-Communist campaign to isolate and discredit Communists. "Every time a genuine democrat or liberal is called a fellow-traveler," Hook declared, "there is great rejoicing in Communist quarters."[63] Fellow travelers therefore had to be identified, isolated, and discredited, just as Communists had been.

In a 1949 issue of the *New York Times Magazine*, Sidney Hook undertook this task. Hook contrasted what he considered the fellow travelers' position with that of the liberal anti-Communists. Hook argued that fellow travelers believed "that the Soviet Union is a progressive social order, whose imperfections are relatively minor," and "that the United States is a greater threat to world peace than the Soviet Union." The anti-Communists offered directly opposing viewpoints. Fellow travelers also believed, according to Hook, that "the Communist Party is a legitimate part of the great movement of liberal reform" and that "it is desirable to work together with Communists in any good cause or organization, no matter by whom controlled." This attitude represented the "prime liberal fallacy," and only by revising it, liberal anti-Communists argued, could liberals be protected and America improved.[64]

Intelligent men and women, often possessing impressive academic training and experience, looked at the world situation and arrived at conclusions far different from those of liberal anti-Communists. Explanations of naïveté or desires for discipline would in this case be unconvincing. Instead, the liberals fell back on the precepts of their redefined postwar liberalism to illustrate the wrongheadedness of fellow traveling. Rather than relying on rational inquiry, the fellow traveler, Hook believed, "knows in [his] heart that it is all in a good cause, and in the interests of human welfare it is not necessary to put too fine a point on the truth." Like the Communists, fellow-traveling intellectuals had abandoned true intellectualism. "Intellectual integrity," Hook noted, "becomes the first victim of political enthusiasm."[65]

Other liberal anti-Communists contributed to the discrediting of fellow travelers, similarly drawing on the precepts of revised liberalism and liberal anticommunism. Arthur Schlesinger contrasted "progressive" fellow travelers negatively to New Deal–oriented "radical democrats." "Sentimentality" emerges as the "defining characteristic" of these "progressives." It distinguishes them, "on the one hand, from the Communist; for the progressive is soft, not hard," and, "on the other, from the radical democrat; for the progressive, by refusing to make room in his philosophy for the discipline of responsibility or for the danger of power, has cut himself off from the usable traditions of American radical democracy." These "progressives" reject both the pragmatic tradition and the "pessimistic tradition," which stretches "from Hawthorne to Reinhold Niebuhr. . . . The type of the progressive today is the fellow traveler or the fellow traveler of the fellow traveler." To these sentimentalists, "the USSR keeps coming through as a kind of enlarged Brook Farm community, complete with folk dancing in native costumes, joyous work in the fields and progressive kindergartens." Their failing to understand the darker passions left the fellow travelers with "a soft and shallow conception of human nature." Their position became "politically inadequate" and "intellectually inadequate." "Ideologies which exploited the darker passions captured men by appeals unknown to the armory of progressivism."[66]

Irving Howe took a slightly different tack in opposing the fellow travelers. While Howe was never a Communist, his radical commitment lasted longer and went deeper than that of many of his peers. He could empathize, if not agree, with the fellow-traveling position before the war, seeing "the Stalinist sympathizers of the thirties [as] often naïve and idealistic." In the postwar years the fellow travelers had moved from naïveté to callousness. Soviet sympathizers in the 1930s "would have been horrified at the accusations against Russia which Matthiessen blandly accepts as true." That the Soviet Union is "dictatorial and corrupt," he "does not seem to care." Fellow travelers failed, according to Diana Trilling, to comprehend the one central fact which would undercut their position, "the single criterion of a proper knowledge of the nature of the Soviet

Union—the awareness of the Soviet Union as a totalitarianism." Trilling treated this assertion, as the liberal anti-Communists did all their points, as unarguable. The fellow travelers' inability to recognize this truth thus discredits their entire position.[67]

An additional problem posed by fellow travelers was their place in the heresy-conspiracy question: Did their dissent cross the line Hook established as demarking intolerable activities? Liberals possess the right to social and political criticism, Hook argued, but fellow travelers "have revived and strengthened the old suspicion against all dissenters." For Hook, this emerged as the fellow travelers'

> gravest evil . . . that of giving all dissent an appearance of treason. Thus they make difficult the work of public criticism which genuine liberals must always direct against the errors and shortcomings in their own countries' policies, domestic, and international.

As they did not actively participate in the "conspiracy," fellow travelers might claim that their position constituted only a radical heresy. However, an acceptance of the fellow travelers' political legitimacy carried with it the negation of several central arguments in the liberal anti-Communist arsenal. Communism could not be considered a tolerable position on the extreme left, its proponents could not be labeled rationalists, and its criticism could not be seen as a mere heresy. If these views gained acceptance, the middle ground between the McCarthyite right and the Communists would vanish. "In many ways [the fellow travelers'] activities constitute a more serious threat to democratic life than those of Communist party members," Hook argued.[68] Americans may have considered fellow travelers a less serious threat to democratic life than Communists. To the liberal anti-Communists, however, the potential harm of the fellow-traveling position seemed more closely to match Hook's portentous analysis.

One direct campaign against fellow travelers involved Clement Greenberg. In February 1951 Greenberg sent a letter to the *Nation*, protesting the line taken by its foreign editor, J. Alvarez del Vayo. The *Nation* refused to print Greenberg's letter. The *New Leader* ran it instead, adding a preface of its own and one by the art critic. In his initial letter, Greenberg protested that del Vayo's column in the *Nation* "invariably parallels that of Soviet propaganda . . . and presents the point of view of the Soviet Union with a regularity that is quite out of place in a liberal periodical." Greenberg's stated subject in the letter was journalistic ethics, not politics: "I am not concerned here to discuss where the right lies in the differences between East and West." He did go on to say, however, "I abhor the Stalin regime and cannot see why anyone is obligated to consider both sides of the question any more in its case than in Hitler's."[69]

Two weeks after publishing the Greenberg letter, the *New Leader* published a one-page precis of del Vayo's views over the preceding five years. In the spring they continued to publish numerous letters about the *Nation* and del Vayo— some written to the *New Leader*, others written to the *Nation* but unpublished— under the head "Letters *The Nation* Wouldn't Print." Finally, in June, the *Nation* sued the *New Leader* and Greenberg for libel, setting off another round of editorials in the *New Leader*. The *Nation*, claiming legal restrictions, had printed little about the fight. The *New Leader*, attributing other motives to their opponents' actions, printed a good deal. In July the *New Leader* ran an article by the journalist Richard Rovere, entitled "How Free Is *The Nation?*" Rovere accused the *Nation* of presenting a form of "doughface anti-McCarthyism." Rovere's critique rang with the phrases of liberal anticommunism. Although as unhappy with the government loyalty program as the writers in the *Nation* were, Rovere nonetheless believed it necessary in order "to distinguish between liberals and Communists." He admitted that "some shameful things" had occurred in the preceding five years, but he maintained that the threats to civil liberties in America described by the *Nation* constituted a "fraud . . . a half-truth . . . passed off as *the* truth," adding, "What we have here, in the *Nation*, is no more than a half-truth, perhaps no more than a tenth part of the truth." The *New Leader* accompanied Rovere's critique with a box listing "*The Nation* Experts on Civil Liberties . . . brief political biographies of some of the contributors to *The Nation's* special issue" on civil liberties in America. Among the biographies were the following:

> *Matthew Josephson*: backed Henry Wallace in 1948, contributor to *New Masses*, affiliated with various Communist fronts;
> *Lewis Adamic*: backed Henry Wallace . . . affiliated with . . . Communist fronts;
> *Kirtley F. Mather*: affiliated with such Communist fronts as American Committee for Protection of Foreign Born and Mid-Century Conference for Peace;
> *Ben Shahn*: (cover artist for the *Nation* issue): backed Henry Wallace . . . affiliated with various Communist fronts;
> *Carey McWilliams*: affiliated with several score Communist fronts;
> *Arthur Eggleston*: labor columnist for the fellow-travelling New York *Daily Compass*.[70]

The suit was finally settled out of court in 1955, the journals agreeing to call off the litigation and to publish the same statement. The "defendants assert that they published said matters not with the intention of committing an act of defamation but, according to their conception of free journalistic discussion."[71] More than free journalistic discussion was involved in the *Nation–New Leader* dispute. A clear battle between political camps erupted over basic issues of the liberal anti-Communist view. While the battle extended beyond the border of the New York Intellectual community, its members could be found close to the front lines. Clement Greenberg had, in fact, provided the spark which ignited the conflict. *Partisan Review* supported him and attacked the *Nation*; the magazine's failure to respond to Greenberg in print, it asserted, "looks very much like an attempt to shut off political discussion of its policy when it touches its most sensitive spot." Schlesinger supported Greenberg in a letter to the *Nation*, and Reinhold Niebuhr resigned as one of its contributing editors.[72] Battlers in their youths, the New Yorkers continued to be aggressive in the political and intellectual battles of middle age, as in the attack on fellow travelers.

The critiques of communism and fellow traveling had been part of the effort to distinguish between liberals and Communists, two groups under attack by McCarthy and the right. Liberal anti-Communists sought to carve out a middle ground, with the aim of discrediting Communists, containing reactionaries, and protecting liberals. Another group also sought to occupy a middle position, on the basis of an entirely different set of priorities. Believing that the primary threat came from the McCarthyites rather than from the Communists, anti-anti-Communists offered an alternative liberal position. The times did not call for a "better" anticommunism, they argued, but for the discrediting of McCarthyism and the preservation of traditional American liberties. Neither Communists nor fellow travelers, anti-anti-Communists believed that they best represented true liberalism. To the liberal anti-Communists, this remained old-fashioned, "unrevised" liberalism as the anti-anti-Communists retained the old principles of liberalism—civil liberties, due process, and individual rights.

In the rough-and-tumble world of politics, especially as Senator McCarthy and other reactionary anti-Communists played in it, the cool voice of liberal moderation might offer an appealing alternative. The liberal anti-Communists, not unaccustomed to strident political discourse themselves, saw that a quieter tone might sway Americans by harking back to idealized liberal virtues. A series of books and articles, critical of McCarthy and anticommunism, emerged from these anti-anti-Communist liberals.[73] The satisfactions which these works provided struck Irving Kristol as harmfully lulling. "The more scholarly sections of American opinion have been so delighted to see the Senator get his, and so soothed by the cadences of a familiar tone," Kristol wrote in 1952, "that they have not so much read these books as permitted themselves to be enchanted by them."[74] This position, Kristol and the other liberal anti-Communists believed, neither faced the contemporary realities nor responded to the anti-Communist sentiment rampant in America. "Many Americans find themselves baffled and exasperated by 'anti-anti-communism,' which sees in overvigorous efforts to expose the Communist menace a growing threat to American freedom no less dangerous than Communism," Robert Warshow observed. "Their bewilderment is understandable, for such an equation is clearly absurd." Liberal anti-Communists had moved beyond the point of debating whether anticommunism should exist to discussing which kind of anticommunism was most appropriate. As Warshow saw it, "There *is* a wrong way, a dangerous way, to be anti-communist."[75] Opposition to communism had to become an axiom of American politics, the liberal anti-communists believed, not a subject of debate. To allow the anti-anti-communists to raise the question only reexposed liberals to attacks from the right. "There is one thing the American people know about Senator McCarthy," Irving Kristol noted in an oft-cited remark; "he, like them, is unequivocally anti-communist. About the spokesmen for American liberalism [the anti-anti-Communists], they feel they know no such thing. And with some justification."[76]

Liberal anti-Communists, faced with the anti-anti-communist alternative, set themselves the task of undercutting that position without allowing McCarthyites to rampage unchecked across the political landscape. Sidney Hook sought to discredit the anti-anti-Communists by applying to them some of his favorite adjectives. The realistic anti-Communists were "pragmatic," while the myopic anti-anti-Communists were "ritualistic." Those in the second group

> are the same "professional" liberals who are more hostile to anti-communism than to Communism, some inhumanists who called themselves Humanists, some irrationalists who think of themselves as Rationalists, some who have actively cooperated with Communist front organizations and who still regard Communism as a kind of left-wing liberalism, some absolute pacifists and that extreme wing of the Quakers which believes in peace at any price—even the price of freedom. . . . Men and women full of the milk of human kindness. Unfortunately they carry it to their head instead of their heart.[77]

Hook's brief attack brought many of the principal elements of revised liberalism and liberal anticommunism into opposition against anti-anti-communists. "Irrationalists," unthinking "humanists," naïve "pacifists"—they all represented the ritualistic liberalism of previous generations, a kind of liberalism oblivious to the changing realities of the modern world. The *Partisan* writers had had to contend with this kind of naïveté before. "Did not the major segment of American liberalism, as a result of joining hands with the Communists in a Popular Front, go on record as denying the existence of Soviet concentration camps?" Irivng Kristol asked. "Did it not apologize for the mass purges of 1936–38, and did it not solemnly approve the grotesque trials of the Old Bolsheviks?"[78] Liberal naïveté once again pointed toward faulty conclusions. The anti-Communists set about to stop this drift.

One additional attribute of the anti-anti-Communists called the special claim of the anti-Communists into direct question. An essential prop for the anti-Communists' position had been their intellectual and critical approach—their insistence on the need for a liberal, rational position against the McCarthyite irrationalism. The anti-anti-Communists represented the same constituency as the liberal anti-Communists. Writers, academics, and intellectual themselves, they competed for intellectual as well as liberal ground. In striking ways, however, the differences between the liberal anti-Communists and their anti-anti-Communist opponents demonstrated divisions which extended beyond the immediate issues. Irving Kristol identified several anti-anti-Communists by name and as "men of intellect and sensibility": Alan Barth, Henry Steele Commager, Zechariah Chafee, Howard Mumford Jones, Ralph Barton Perry, William O. Douglas, and Francis Biddle. In one sense, they represented the "other" liberals of the postwar years, just as Malcolm Cowley, Granville Hicks, and John Chamberlain had represented the "other" radicals during the thirties. They came from the old intellectual establishment, being more Yankee, more Harvard (save Commager), more Washington-oriented. Once again, the line between "them" and "us" could be drawn between the New York, City College, immigrants' sons and the "allrightniks." To a degree, the style of these "other" liberals reflected attributes normally associated with their social stratum as well as their political beliefs. They took a defensive position, seeking to protect civil liberties rather than attacking Communists and fellow travelers. The liberal anti-Communists took the offensive, as they had in most stages of their personal development and in most of the positions they had argued over the years.

Henry Steele Commager came in for particular abuse in these debates. An academic, like a number of the New York Intellectuals, and a fixture at Columbia for many years,[79] Commager came to epitomize the anti-anti-Communist position. Liberal anti-Communists attacked his view of political realities as being blurred, deriving from a tendency to look at communism "out of the *left* corner of his eye," Kristol commented. He seemed "seduced by the insidious myth according to which Communism is a political trend continuous with liberalism and democratic socialism." This "myth" had been exposed in the development of the liberal anti-communist philosophy, but obviously not so as to change Commager's mind. "It is a myth that Senator McCarthy, for his own ends, is happy to accept," Kristol wrote, "since it allows him to tag a New Dealer as being by nature an embryonic communist." Commager's viewpoint sustained this dangerous situation. "The conclusion 'any normal person' will draw from such behavior," Irving Kristol asserted, "is that, for whatever reason, [Commager's] critical faculties are less alert when he looks out of the left corner of his eye."[80]

Sidney Hook took an even more blunt line concerning Commager. Responding to Commager's view that a Communist should not be fired because of political beliefs per se, Hook asked, "Would Commager argue that to deny a fervent apostle of euthanasia a post as director of a home for the aged and infirm is necessarily to deny him his rights?"[81] Hook's conclusion was built entirely on the axioms of liberal anticommunism, laced with implications about the murderous intent of Communists. Without the structural framework he and others constructed, Hook's logic falls apart. Years later, Lionel Trilling took a softer tone, but the intensity still showed. "Anti-anti-communism was not quite so neutral a position as first it might seem to have been," he recalled in 1975; "it said that although, for the moment at least, one need not be *for* Communism, one was morally compromised, turned toward evil and away from good, if one was against it."[82]

The problems with Commager reflected the difficulties with all the anti-anti-Communists. The wrong kind of anti-McCarthyites and the wrong kind of liberals, they were thought to be playing into McCarthy's hands with their "ritualistic" liberalism. When "Mssrs. Commager, Barth, and Chafee defend [Owen] Lattimore's pro-Communist record in order to defend . . . independence and nonconformity," Irving Kristol asserted, they "play the Senator's game on the losing side." Similarly, assuming that communism existed on a left continuum with liberalism and that it was necessary to defend communism in order to defend liberalism, both evidenced the fallacious thinking of these old-style liberals. On these mistakes "McCarthyism waxes fat."[83] The failure to understand the realities of the situation, Kristol argued, only made the liberal task more difficult.

Kristol cautioned the anti-anti-Communists that unless they adjusted their thinking, their arguments would prove counterproductive. They must accept the axioms of liberal anticommunism in order to restore their credibility.

> If a liberal wishes to defend the civil liberties of Communists or of Communist fellow-travelers, he must enter the court of American opinion with clean hands and a clean mind. He must show that he knows the existence of an organized subversive movement such as Communism is a threat to the consensus on which civil society and its liberties are based. He must bluntly acknowledge Communists and fellow-travelers to be what they are, and then, if he so desires, defend the expediency in particular circumstances allowing them the right to be what they are. He must speak as one of *us*, defending *their* liberties. To the extent he insists that they are on our side, that we can defend our liberties by only uncritically defending theirs, he will be taken as speaking as one of them.[84]

Beyond the treatment of liberal anti-Communist tenets as given truths, Kristol's assessment is notable for the veiled threat it hurled at all liberals. They must either accept the revised liberal position or risk being smeared by the right. With more sophistication than their right-wing counterparts showed, Kristol and Hook did daub a bit of mud around, though they did not quite smear Commager. In making the "euthanasia" analogy or in accusing Commager of "looking out of the left corner of his eye," they did more than just directly rebut ideas. Having only slightly soiled the anti-anti-Communists, the liberal anti-Communists offered the means by which their liberal counterparts could cleanse themselves—"enter the court of American opinion with clean hands and a clean mind." They could become "one of *us*" only by accepting the liberal anti-Communist position. A consensus was forming, and if these liberals wanted to maintan their liberalism, they had to join it. Individual diversity, like individual rights, had to give way to public opinion and a shared position. For liberals to be liberal—according to the standards of redefined liberalism—they had to become anti-Communists. In the minds of the New York Intellectuals, another of their propositions soon took on the character of undeniable truth.

THE LIMITS OF LIBERALISM

The liberal anti-Communists cautioned the anti-anti-Communist liberals about the growing consensus over communism and individual rights, warning that the absolute civil-libertarian position was not part of this shared viewpoint. Staunch support for traditional civil liberties like free speech, free thought, and First and Fifth Amendment protections was the cornerstone for the arguments of Commager, Barth, and other anti-anti-Communists. The liberal anti-Communists argued from a "revised" position, believing the new liberalism to be an emerging political movement rather than a set of philosophical beliefs. Part of this revision was a willingness to question the sanctity of several basic tenets of old-style liberalism and to modify them. Just as contemporary realities required the development of a point "in advance" of clear and present danger to draw the line for free speech, so other traditional notions might need rethinking. Liberalism had to undergo adjustments to fit the modern world. As a passive repository of humanistic intentions and individual rights, it might retain all its tenets of toleration but grow politically impotent. To become an active, aggressive movement within the political mainstream, ready to cope with the real world, it had to be honed to battle readiness. "Liberalism," Sidney Hook declared,

> cannot be identified with the traditional beliefs in specific, absolute or inalienable rights, since every such right is in fact evaluated in terms of its consequences for society and is therefore subject to modification. . . . To say that we cannot preserve our freedom by sacrificing [rights] is an empty piece of rhetoric, because a *particular* freedom must sometimes be sacrificed to preserve other freedoms.[85]

The list of "particulars" that Hook and the others drew up eventually included a number of the most cherished liberal beliefs. In the area of civil liberties, the liberal anti-Communists proved increasingly willing to sacrifice some rights, arguing that this preserved others. In the process, however, many of those held most sacred were abandoned or, at least, severely limited.

The basic anti-Communist belief in a Communist's captivity to "the Idea" allowed Irving Kristol to argue that interactions with Communists must be qualitatively different from those with other individuals. A Communist was, "all appearances to the contrary," Kristol claimed, "a person with different loyalties, and with different canons of scrupulousness, from ours." As a result, to grant Communists an "immunity of silence" would be "to concede the right of conspiracy." This could not be tolerated. Kristol willingly limited individual civil rights, with no more tangible evidence of dangerous behavior than party membership or a belief in communism. In one sweep he denied the rights of free thought and of innocence until guilt is proven, and was ready to assess guilt by association. Anticipating civil-libertarian objections, he reiterated basic liberal anti-Communist conceptions to support his position: "No doubt there are some present members of the Communist Party who would, in a showdown, break free of the Idea and rally to the democratic cause. Unfortunately, we have no way of knowing who they are." Another limitation of basic rights emerges from Kristol's example. No longer must a teacher be found guilty of introducing subversive elements into the classroom, or a worker of planning sabotage, two examples Kristol cited. A belief system is now sufficient to establish the potential for action, a potential which can be actualized whenever "the Idea, i.e., the Party, thinks necessary."[86] As a result, due process now joined the other civil liberties being proscribed by the anti-Communist campaign.

Sidney Hook tackled the question of guilt by association from the same preconceptions as Irving Kristol did. Arguing that attitudes toward individuals invariably derive from subjective criteria, Hook claimed that people recognize "that under certain circumstances membership in the Society of Friends, Ethical Culture, and similar groups may be relevant in favorably assessing individual worth"; he asserted that these same people "will passionately deny that membership in a conspiratorial party . . . is ever relevant in making an unfavorable assessment."[87] Just as one's good associations shed favorable light, so one's negative associations prompt an unfavorable impression. Hook's logic here not only takes his own heresy-conspiracy concept as valid but offers a justification for discrimination. "Bad associations" in other contexts might include the Socialist party, the Knights of Columbus, or orthodox Judaism. Associations are always in the minds of evaluators, and for decades they had been the source of discrimination in American society. Implicit in Hook's argument is the common acceptance of communism as something *everyone* abhors, not merely one prejudiced individual or group. This kind of sweeping antagonism is usually reserved for criminals or moral degenerates rather than for political groups. In the liberal anti-Communist view, Communists had stepped beyond the status of a political party and moved toward that of the criminal or at least the conspirator. The analogies proved telling, such as Hook's equation of Communists and mercy killers, in his rebuttal to Henry Steele Commager. Irving Kristol offered a comparison between public disfavor visited on Communists and that shown to pederasts or proponents of infanticide.[88]

Closely connected to the acceptance of the principle of guilt by association was another limitation of a civil liberty. The use of Fifth Amendment protection against self-incrimination prompted wide discussion during the McCarthy years. Called before congressional committees or other investigatory agencies, individuals often chose to plead the Fifth Amendment rather than admit membership in the Communist party or provide information concerning the political activities of others, or as means of registering general disapproval of the investigation. Witness after witness took the Fifth, often to the frustration of the interrogators and other anti-Communists. Although protection against self-incrimination involved knotty legal questions—especially when claimed before congressional hearings rather than in judicial proceedings—a second debate emerged concerning the implications of pleading the Fifth. If guilt might be presumed from an individual's associations, could it not also be presumed from unwillingness to testify? Amid the anti-Communist hysteria, many individuals found that though their legal rights remained protected, their personal lives and reputations suffered severly as a result of their exercising their constitutional rights. The civil libertarians argued that the exercise of this right should not endanger an individual's personal affairs. Sidney Hook disagreed, devoting an entire book to the subject. In the introduction to *Common Sense and the Fifth Amendment*, published in 1957, Hook did state his belief in "retaining the privilege against self-incrimination as a legal procedural principle." He proposed to show, however, "that its invocation establishes a presumption of guilt or unfitness *with respect to the issue in question* which is relevant to inferences made in a non-legal or moral context." He went on to develop his thesis over five chapters, relating "logic," "psychology," "ethics," "politics," and the "individual" to the Fifth Amendment. Hook concluded his long discussion with classic liberal anti-Communist hardheadedness. "Truth has a sharp and uncomfortable edge but in the long run is more useful than the comforts of illusion."[89] Chief among these illusions was the notion that Communists merely exercised their constitutional right when they pleaded Fifth Amendment protection. As Irving Kristol added, "Communism . . . has not the faintest interest in a genuine resistance to the despotism of public opinion. These martyrs whose testament [is] 'I refuse to answer on the grounds that it might incriminate me' . . . [what] are they in danger of—being excluded from well-paying jobs!" Rather than strengthening constitutional rights, Kristol argued, the duplicity he believed Communists exhibited actually threatened basic privileges. Americans needed to distinguish clearly between those truly facing potential harm and those undeserving of legal protection. "No greater spur to the despotism of public opinion can be imagined," Kristol believed, "than this identification of free thought with underground conspiracy."[90]

Kristol thought it necessary to make a second distinction, between the demands for liberty and for equality. There was a difference between job discrimination against Communists and that against blacks, Kristol argued, reiterating the point that personal associations created bad impressions. Government protection for the rights of blacks remained essential, but it should not be extended to those of Communists. Although "the color of a man's skin has no bearing upon his character and moral and social worth," Kristol held, the same could not be said of one's communism. "The climate of opinion more highly values the liberty of an employer—even if he only makes grade B movies—than the claim to job equality of a Communist, because it has a low estimate of the character and moral worth of the Communists."[91] Once again, Kristol constructed his assertions on liberal anti-Communist declarations treated as absolutes, such as the question of guilt by association. Furthermore, he returned to the themes of a "climate of opinion," opting for social conformism over individual diversity. Despite his declarations against the "depotism of public opinion," Kristol participated in the creation and continuance of that depotism.

By virtue of their beliefs, Communists had forfeited the protection of basic American rights, Kristol believed. "Rights are not a matter of principle, but rather applying principles to concrete problems," he argued, echoing the relativism of revised liberalism. "It depends on *which* right and *what* time and place." Kristol illustrated this point with a subject widely discussed during the 1950s, the issuance of passports. He admitted that it is a "traditional" right of every citizen to obtain a passport but asserted that "it is nothing less than common sense to withhold this right from a person suspected of being a Communist courier." Of course, those who are denied it will protest their innocence, as no one will publicly admit to espionage. Likewise, the FBI will not have sufficient evidence to indict the suspect, otherwise this would have been done. So the situation remains unresolved. "In such cases it seems reasonable to give our government the benefit of the doubt," Kristol decided.[92]

In each of these issues involving civil liberties—free thought, innocence until guilt is proven, guilt by association, the limiting of the Fifth Amendment privilege, the countenancing of job discrimination, the restricting of passports—the position taken by the anti-Communists stressed the relativity of the problem and reflected the "commonsense" solution. The modern world forced a tempering of ideals with contemporary realities. Beneath this relativism lay several other motives, however. A reaffirmation of the basic positions of liberal anticommunism was evident in these arguments. Furthermore, a conception of Communists as different from other left-of-center persons reinforced the idea that they required special handling. True leftists, heretics, those not captive to "the Idea"—all deserved the protection of civil liberties. The defending of civil liberties, in the manner of the anti-anti-Communists, left anticommunism for the McCarthyites alone. Instead of opposing the limitation of rights, liberal anti-Communists argued for a *reasoned, moderate* limitation. They hoped to create a moderate consensus and to draw public opinion to their cause. In so doing, they could again isolate Communists, undermine McCarthyites, and secure the place of liberal anticommunism.

The notion of relativism extended beyond principles to legislative actions. Sidney Hook, for one, argued that though the passage of the Smith Act evidenced "doubtful wisdom," the wisdom of repealing it was "even more doubtful." The act, originally passed in 1940, made it unlawful to advocate or teach the forceful overthrow of any government in the United States or to belong to any group advocating or teaching such action. For all his reservations, Hook felt its repeal would strengthen an improper illusion "whose widespread and pernicious character was partly responsible for the original enactment of the Act." This pernicious illusion was "that the Communist party is a political party like any other on the American scene and therefore entitled to the same rights and privileges as all other American political parties."[93] The maintenance of the act so as not to strengthen an illusion—a central issue for liberal anti-Communists—outweighed its negative aspects.

To help sustain this tone of moderation and reasonableness, Hook offered, in the *New Leader* in 1954, what he called the "ground rules" essential to a maintaining of the "ethics of controversy." He cited ten items with which no political discussant should disagree. The liberal anti-Communists, including Sidney Hook, violated these ground rules frequently, however. "Criticism should be directed to policies," read one ground rule. Another cautioned debaters, "Do not treat an opponent of a policy as if he were a personal enemy of the country or a concealed enemy of democracy."[94] The aggressive attacks on Communists, fellow travelers, and, especially, anti-anti-Communists deviated from these guidelines. The accusations against Commager by Hook and Kristol took the form of strongly personal assaults, attributing characteristics to Commager which he did not possess.

Hook's final "ground rule" held that "the cardinal sin, when we are looking for truth of fact or wisdom of policy, is refusal to discuss, or action which blocks discussion." This reiterated Hook's argument in *Heresy, Yes—Conspiracy, No* that a "free trade of ideas" was an essential requirement for true liberalism.[95] Liberal anti-Communists frequently failed to live by the guidelines of trying to promote the most open discussion. Anti-anti-Communists had specific prerequisites to fulfill before they could "enter the court of American opinion," Kristol had written. They had to admit that communism was "an organized subversive movement." Discussing the Rosenberg case, Nathan Glazer noted that he could listen to arguments for clemency only from individuals who had admitted the Rosenberg's guilt. Kristol, in fact, summarized the attitude of anti-Communists toward those who defended Communists:

> Anyone who wishes to defend the right of a Communist to teach or to direct motion pictures will be listened to respectfully so long as he makes clear that he knows he is defending Communists, *that he despises them*, but that he defends them nonetheless. (Italics mine)[96]

When Elliot Cohen began *Commentary*, he wrote that he saw its primary function as providing materials which would help people to think and decide. As this developed, however, it became clear that Cohen had a precise notion of what those materials should be and what kinds of information should be excluded, especially in the area of anticommunism. There existed at *Commentary*, Norman Podhoretz recalled, an

> explicit ban on . . . "anti-anti-Communist" writers. All articles were carefully inspected for traces of softness on Communism: a crime of the mind and character which might even give itself away in a single word, or in some remark having no

apparent connection with politics at all. I was also increasingly bothered by the disposition inherent in the hard anti-Communist position . . . to place everything American in a favorable light. *Commentary* . . . could always be trusted to tell its readers what was right with American society more frequently than what was wrong.[97]

This attitude violated Cohen's stated aims as well as Hook's ground rules for debate. It demonstrates, however, the degree to which liberal anticommunism was a direct political movement rather than a philosophical position. A liberal alternative to McCarthyism became the overarching goal, protecting liberals while continuing to attack Communists. The planks of the liberal anti-Communist platform had all been fashioned to achieve this end.

Beyond the creation of a liberal anti-Communist position, however, existed a second, larger aim. Frequently, the anti-Communists offered notions of a general public consensus to buttress their points of agreement. They desired a "climate of opinion" which held communism in moral and political disrepute. While personal deviations—heresies—needed protection, Communists had to be perceived as conspiratorial and, thus, excluded. "Organized society is," Irving Kristol concluded,

> by its very nature, and even without taking into account its laws, coercive of public opinion to some extent: by religion, by morality, by custom, by conscience. A man who in our country openly praises pederasty or publishes a pamphlet in favor of infanticide has little chance of being nominated for President, or of holding any position for which public favor, explicit or implicit, is essential; his opinions will bring upon him this penalty. This fact it is foolish to deplore as an instance of "conformity." Conformity, if we mean by that profound consensus on moral and political first principles, is the condition for a decent society; without it, blunt error must rule.[98]

The New York Intellectuals had persistently added moral questions to the political discussion about anticommunism. They frequently called on the force of public opinion to support their contentions about communism's un-American character. Given their intellectual training, their political expertise, and the hardheaded realism of their political approach, the New Yorkers saw themselves as perfectly suited to help create the "profound consensus" Kristol deemed essential. Their anticommunism became both a political defense of liberalism in the face of McCarthyism and communism and the most obvious public display of their qualifications to help maintain a "decent society."

ANTICOMMUNISM AND THE UNIVERSITY

Central to the refutations of the fellow traveling and anti-anti-Communist positions was the necessity for liberal anti-Communists to discredit groups whose members included others in the intellectual community. In the postwar years the function of intellectuals and academic institutions changed. Along with intellectuals, anticommunism arrived on college campuses after 1945. Questions about the political views of American professors cropped up in congressional investigations, hearings by state legislatures, loyalty oath requirements, and numerous court cases. Although many states had loyalty oath statutes for teachers dating from before World War II, the pressure on American colleges and universities intensified with the cold war. Recent estimates have put at six hundred the number of professors and teachers dismissed during the McCarthy years for suspected un-Americanism. The disarray caused on college campuses by investigations and battles over academic freedom is incalculable.

Like the anti-Communist campaign in general, the issue of anticommunism and the university took a variety of forms, was inspired by a number of individuals, and proceeded along several different paths. The University of Washington opened its campus to the state's Joint Legislative Fact-Finding Committee on Un-American Activities, agreeing to dismiss any subversives the committee uncovered. Both McCarthy's Permanent Subcommittee on Investigations and the Senate Internal Security Subcommittee carried on investigations at Harvard. Harvard also exercised its own internal controls, as in the case of Dean McGeorge Bundy's withdrawal of a job offer to Sigmund Diamond, because of Diamond's past political activities. Around the country various college employees similarly lost their jobs as a result of their pleading the Fifth Amendment when called to testify. The University of California, in an attempt to head off state intervention, created the most controversial academic episode of the period by imposing a loyalty oath on all its faculty in 1949. The issue sparked a tremendous debate with the University of California system, leading to the dismissal of twenty-six faculty members. Another thirty-seven resigned in protest, and the university lost an additional forty-seven scholars who turned down academic appointments as a result of the crisis. As the dean of the College of Chemistry concluded, "No conceivable damage to the university at the hands of the hypothetical Communists among us could have equaled the damage resulting from the unrest, ill-will and suspicion engendered by this series of events."[99]

The assessment by the California dean contrasted sharply with the views of most New York Intellectuals. As intellectuals, academics, and anti-Communists, they felt themselves particularly well suited to comment on and, in some cases, to participate in the discussions and activities surrounding the question of communism in the university. These debates took on particular importance for the New Yorkers. They had claimed that the professoriat contained the largest percentage of fellow travelers. They regarded these subversives as insidious as Communists, if not worse. Furthermore, in the discussions about the protection of civil liberties, the liberal anti-Communists had argued that individuals should expect to suffer the consequences of personal beliefs, such as losing their job, especially when the community found those beliefs intolerable. Finally, the university emerged as the primary institution to support the rising prominence of intellectuals in general, and that was a separate issue of extreme importance for the New Yorkers. Public perception and support of the university remained crucial, if "intellectualism" was to be understood to possess social importance.

Two essential questions developed in the course of the debate over communism and the university. On both issues the New York Intellectuals took strong positions. The first concerned the fitness of Communists to teach. The basic tenets of liberal anticommunism clearly spoke to this problem, at least to the satisfaction of its proponents. By joining the Communist party an individual called his professional competence into immediate question, Sidney Hook argued. "A man may have a constitutional right to be a member of the Communist Party, but he has no constitutional right to be a college professor." A Communist failed to meet the basic requirements for college teaching, Hook claimed; "he is not a free mind." Moreover, Americans could not wait for this Communist to abridge some specific canon of intellectual activity. Waiting, as civil libertarians might suggest, until the professor was "caught in the act" of propagandizing would be too difficult, Hook held. This would require an elaborate spy system. In addition, "it would be very difficult to determine when a teacher was defending a conclusion because he honestly believed it followed from the evidence and when he was carrying out his task as a good soilder of the party cause."[100] Hook's analysis is replete with liberal anti-Communist themes. Echoing Kristol's and Schlesinger's belief that free speech should be restricted at a point in advance of clear and present danger, Hook argued for the abridgment of the rights of all Communists to teach. While an independent scholar might arrive at the same conclusion as a Communist, the latter could never be independent. The danger of these captives of "the Idea" rested not with their specific beliefs, Hook held, but the context from which they developed:

> It is not because of his *ideas* that a Communist party member is unfit to teach but because of his *professional misconduct* in joining a conspiratorial organization, one of whose declared purposes is corruption of the teaching process for political purposes.[101]

Fellow travelers presented, as always, a more complex problem. Their undoubted naïveté, the anti-Communists believed, could hardly be grounds for dismissal. "On any view of academic freedom," Hook admitted, "these men and women have every right to be members of the academic community." Fellow travelers did pose a serious threat, however. Because of "their numbers and because of the passivity of their colleagues, they have had and still have far more influence upon students' political habits than any other group," wrote Hook, who labeled them "ideological 'typhus Marys.'" Legislation against these "carriers" had proven ineffectual. Hook believed that the problem fell to "educators who must solve the problem within the framework of democratic education."[102]

Hook's arguments point to the second and, for these intellectuals, more crucial question raised by the issue of Communists on campus. They had little doubt about Communists' lack of fitness to teach, holding a low view of their ability to do anything worthwhile. More important, in light of the general motivation for the creation of a liberal alternative to McCarthyism, the questions about how to identify and deal with the problem became central. Among the New York Intellectuals, only Philip Rahv—not yet an academic himself—argued against intellectuals' actively engaging in the process of rooting out campus Communists. Declaring that communism did indeed present "a grave danger *to* America," Rahv felt it "scarcely the function of political-minded intellectuals, however, to serve as an adjunct to the FBI."[103] The other New Yorkers who publicly commented on the question took a view opposite to Rahv's. As with McCarthyism in general, the liberals feared the intrusion of outside, right-wing forces into another of their bailiwicks, the college campus. Again as with McCarthyism, the solution which emerged called for an alternative anticommunism rather than for a defense of traditional rights. "In general, the intrusion of the state in affairs of the school involving professional misconduct is to be deplored," Hook declared, "but if the teaching profession (like labor) fails to clear up its own sore spots—and no one can reasonably deny that there are evils to be remedied—such intervention is to be expected."[104]

Irving Kristol shared Hook's position, basing his arguments on pragmatic as well as philosophical grounds. "I am opposed to all loyalty oaths," Kristol declared, but he did not like them, because "they serve no purpose whatsoever. The first to sign are always the Communists, and it is those non-Communists who oppose them as a matter of conscience who are 'rooted out.'" The California case created an "undue amount of hysteria," Kristol believed, for the issue did not concern acadmic freedom at all. "A university has, in my opinion, the right to establish a policy of not hiring Communists (or Nazis) or Communist (or Nazi) sympathizers," Kristol argued, with classic liberal anti-Communist logic. But it would be much better to allow department heads to carry out the policy than to rely on such "a foolish bureaucratic measure as a special loyalty oath."[105]

The liberal anti-Communist solution for the problems at the university was to keep the decision making out of the hands of the right-wing anti-Communists and on the campus in the hands of academics. Outside invesigations carried with them an anti-intellectualism, as McCarthy often demonstrated. Furthermore, "cultural vigilantes," as Hook called them, made few distinctions between liberals, "heretics," and Communists. While Harvard's president Nathan Pusey declared that a Communist had no right to belong to any university faculty, McCarthy described one Harvard professor as one of "Pusey's Fifth Amendment Communists."[106] Finally, the liberals argued that outside forces invading college campuses actually strengthened the Communist hand. The California loyalty oath controversy had only raised cries of "witch hunt" across the country, Kristol noted, and this was "to repeat a term that is of Communist invention and whose purpose is to persuade people that the Communist investigation is only a figment of a distorted imagination." Hook noted the same problem with a New York State law requiring the dismissal of all subversive teachers. He feared that one mistaken application would create an incident which the Communist party would exploit, "swelling its ranks with fellow travelers and imbuing them with crusading self-righteousness." Such an incident could be created by "some zealously reactionary superintendent." If it was not, the Communist party would certainly "do its best to create one."[107]

The problem of Communists on campus called for the creation of another liberal anti-Communist alternative to the right—a technique to weed out only the real "witches." Those within the university seemed best suited to the task. The scholar had to remain ever vigilant to defend against the "radical philistinism" of fellow travelers and to counter their influence among the students. This influence "in its most vicious forms softens students up for participation and membership in the Communist movement and all that implies," Hook warned. He suggested changes in the curriculum and in the attitude of anti-Communists. The "theory and practice of Communism" should become an integral part of college learning. Furthermore, professors had to "break with the genteel tradition of suffering intolerance, disingenuousness, and intellectual dishonesty in silence." Presumably, Hook referred here only to Communists and fellow travelers, for he had little to say about anti-Communist disingenuousness or intellectual duplicity. Ultimately, the scholar must come down from the ivory tower, "must be prepared to take up the struggle." Echoing the attitude about revised liberalism and redefined intellectual activity, Hook cautioned academics that they would have to "fight on many fronts—against misguided patriots, clerical fascists, and those who are maddened by Communist intrigue into foolishness that may be harmful to free institutions." Hook's call to action resounded with the phrases of calls to war.

> It is a pity that so much intellectual energy must go into the defense of values which in happier times were taken for granted as integral to the life of scholarship. But it is precisely these values which are today under attack. If they die, academic integrity does, and with it academic freedom.[108]

While Sidney Hook led in the creation of the liberal anti-Communist position on university life, one New York Intellectual enlisted directly in the process of evaluating teaching on his campus. Lionel Trilling chaired a committee at Columbia which sought to deal with the problem of Communist academics. Amid the McCarthyite hysteria of 1953, the report of Trilling's committee earned praise as a statement of reason. The *New York Times* story hailed the committee's position in support of hiring and firing only on the basis of academic standards. "The basic test for fitness of a teacher should be his professional competence and personal integrity," the committee declared. "Membership in an organization, unless it is specifically illegal, should not be thought to constitute ground for disqualifying a person from continued membership in an academic institution." The committee also felt that all decisions should be made by the faculty or faculty committees. The *Times* report suggested that Trilling's committee reaffirmed traditional interpretations of academic freedom, and it applauded this position.[109]

Eight days later, however, the *Times* carried a letter from Trilling clarifying and expanding the story about the committee's report. The part of the report quoted in the earlier story came from a section concerning faculty members who did not claim Fifth Amendment protection. For those who did plead the Fifth, the committee set different guidelines, not reported initially by the *Times*. "The [Fifth] Amendment, to be sure, can scarcely extend its powers beyond the courts and the legislative committee room," the report declared. Drawing on a basic liberal anti-Communist argument, the Columbia committee believed that a pleading of the Fifth "cannot prevent inferences being drawn from the actions of those witnesses who claim its privileges." Trilling felt it necessary to clarify the committee's statement even further. "In short, it was the intention of the statement not only to say that a refusal to testify must not be automatically condemned but also to say that a refusal to testify must not be automatically condoned."[110] In April 1953 a Columbia anthropologist's contract had in fact not been renewed, after she had taken the Fifth the preceding September. The university denied any direct connection between the two events.[111]

Trilling went on to explain another area which the committee discussed, the right of Communists to teach. "We are not concerned to affirm that right . . . [as] we should not be concerned to affirm the right of Fascists to teach." However, the committee did take a philosophical position regarding the competency of Communist teachers. It asserted that the civil rights of a member of a totalitarian group should be defended, but added that it did "not believe that these civil rights include the right of a person to hold a particular academic post when the implied conditions of holding that post have been broken." Despite his declaration that the committee did not concern itself with affirming or denying the rights of Communists to teach, Trilling argued that Communists had transgressed the conditions of their posts and had thereby forfeited the right to them: "It is clear to us that membership in Communist organizations almost certainly implies a submission to an intellectual control which is entirely at variance with the principles of academic competence as we understand them."[112]

Trilling's letter is revealing in several ways, beyond his reaffirming of several central notions of liberal anticommunism. It is striking that he felt a need to publish it at all. The initial story on his committee's statement emphasized in-house evaluation of leftist professors and pointed to professional competence as the crucial factor in assessing the quality of faculty members, reiterating the traditional position of the liberal intellectuals on academic freedom. Trilling's clarifications all concern issues of anticommunism itself rather than academic freedom. The misunderstandings he wanted cleared up had to do with the general attitude in the *Times* report, which might have left the impression that civil liberties took precedence over anticommunism, opening the committee to attacks of being "soft" on communism. His restating and clarifying of the committee's report in clear liberal anti-Communist terms sought to put this misunderstanding to rest.

The Columbia faculty statement and Trilling's leadership in its drafting and in its public clarification are only the most obvious examples of liberal anti-Communist efforts in the area of academic freedom. Academic freedom, however, never really emerged as the central concern, at least not in a traditional sense. The New Yorkers again drew the lines so as to identify which groups should be investigated and dismissed. The danger of outside investigations, like McCarthyite activities in general, threatened others than Communists and fellow travelers. By supporting internal evaluations and setting boundaries of professional competence in liberal anti-Communist terms, these intellectuals once again turned a potential threat into a reinforcement of their basic position. The best anti-Communists for the general society also turned out to be the best evaluators of their own small world.

"EXILING GUILT": THE ROSENBERGS, HISS, AND OPPENHEIMER

Amid the hysteria of postwar anticommunism, two explosive cases emerged as the most compelling of the period. The accusations against and the trials of Julius and Ethel Rosenberg and Alger Hiss riveted the attention of Americans. Direct questions of guilt or innocence were compounded with other issues, the cases growing from criminal trials to causes célèbres. Positions on Hiss or the Rosenbergs became symbolic statements about more general feelings concerning anticommunism. Convictions in both cases and the executions of the Rosenbergs did quiet the debate. Despite thirty years of investigations, trials, appeals, polemics, scholarly research, novels, and, now, the Freedom of Information Act, both cases still arouse heated discussion. To this day, Alger Hiss and the Rosenbergs have their staunch defenders as well as those who have consistently thought them guilty. As a recent sampling of opinion about Alger Hiss suggests, attitudes have changed little over the years, despite numerous recent publications. Those who considered Hiss guilty in the 1950s still do so; those who proclaimed his innocence have steadfastly maintained that opinion.[113]

By the time the cases had run their full course, Americans knew minute details of the defendants' lives—about Alger Hiss's typewriter or a piece of a Jell-O box belonging to the Rosenbergs. The cases did differ in legal questions, basic accusations, and the style and background of the accused. Alger Hiss was a young man moving up the social and political ladder in the 1930s. A student of

Felix Frankfurter at the Harvard Law School, Hiss clerked for Oliver Wendell
Holmes at the Supreme Court, worked in the State Department in the 1930s,
and went on to be president of the Carnegie Endowment for International
Peace. He helped organize the San Francisco conference which gave birth to
the United Nations and had been at the Yalta conference. Amid the accusations
and confessions before the House Un-American Activities Committee in the
late 1940s, Whittaker Chambers, a senior editor at *Time* and an ex-Communist,
claimed to have received stolen documents from someone in the State
Department during the 1930s. Under pressure, Chambers named Hiss as his
former contact. Hiss's denials led to charges of perjury, the statute of
limitations for espionage having run out. The first trial ended in a hung jury;
the second convicted Hiss, and he received a five-year prison sentence.

Julius and Ethel Rosenberg began life in circumstances far different from
those of Alger Hiss. A young radical in the 1930s, Julius was among the
Communist crowd which ate lunch in Alcove No. 2 at City College. In the
wake of the anxiety following the announcement of the successful Soviet
explosion of an atomic bomb in 1949, rumors circulated about espionage which
had contributed to the Soviet achievement. In 1950, warrants went out for
Julius and Ethel Rosenberg and Morton Sobell, charging them with treason.
The charge against the Rosenbergs stemmed from the arrest for espionage of
Klaus Fuchs, a British scientist who had worked on the atomic bomb, and the
subsequent arrests of Harry Gold and David Greenglass, Ethel Rosenberg's
brother. Greenglass implicated his sister and brother-in-law. On their
conviction in federal court, the presiding judge told the Rosenbergs, "I
consider your crime worse than murder," and sentenced them to death. After
the failure of numerous appeals, including the calling of a special Supreme
Court session to overturn a last-minute stay by Justice William O. Douglas, the
Rosenbergs were electrocuted on June 19, 1953.[114]

The New York Intellectuals exhibited few doubts about the guilt of either
Hiss or the Rosenbergs, then or later. "I cannot believe that reasonable men
should fall out so widely when presented with the same evidence," Nathan
Glazer wrote in 1953. "I cannot believe that a truly careful consideration of the
evidence can lead one to doubt the guilt of the Rosenbergs." "The court
evidence is quite conclusive," Daniel Bell concurred in the *New Statesman*, that
same year. The view that their guilt had never been proven, he called "sheer
nonsense."[115] The statements about Alger Hiss took the same absolute line.
Diana Trilling declared in *Partisan Review*, "I speak from the point of view of
someone who argues . . . that Chambers told the truth and Hiss lied." Sidney
Hook found the internal evidence of Whittaker Chambers's memoir, *Witness*,
"so overwhelmingly detailed and cumulative, it rings with such authenticity,
that it is extremely unlikely that any reasonable person will remain
unconvinced by it." Irving Kristol's acceptance of Hiss's guilt is implicit in his
comparison of Hiss with Owen Lattimore, who, Kristol believed, "was no spy
in the sense that Alger Hiss was one." William Phillips attempted to explain

why "so many respectable people seem to have sworn allegiance to the innocence of Hiss, in the face of all the evidence."[116]

In their declarations about the guilt of Hiss and the Rosenbergs, the New York Intellectuals shared the beliefs of many other anti-Communists of the era. Even some anti-anti-Communists believed them guilty, and some still do. A number of anti-Communists have argued for their innocence. What is most striking here is not the actual position the New Yorkers took. It is unsurprising that, as staunch anti-Communists, they argued as they did. Revealing in these discussions are the issues they chose to address as demonstrations of the guilt of the accused and the lessons and conclusions they drew from the cases. Among these intellecuals each case touched nerves or personal issues which did not stir other anti-Hiss and anti-Rosenberg writers. As with much of their other thinking, they read their own lives and positions into the Hiss and Rosenberg discussions.

The accused themselves aroused strong feelings because of their political views as well as because of their alleged crimes. They presented positions the New Yorkers had argued against, and the convictions seemed a vindication of the New Yorkers' stance. When Irving Kristol recalled the battles which raged between Alcove No. 1 and Alcove No. 2 at City College, the only individuals he could remember from the Stalinist alcove were an unnamed university professor and Julius Rosenberg. At City College, among the Stalinists, Julius Rosenberg began the journey which ultimately led him to the electric chair. "It is about seventeen years since Communists told the truth about themselves," Robert Warshow wrote in 1953; "the 'popular front' was inaugurated during Julius Rosenberg's student days at City College." As a result, Warshow observed, "one is forced to wonder whether the literal truth had not in some way ceased to exist for the people."[117]

The Hiss case also resounded with old political issues. Hiss possessed "the Popular Front mind at bay, incapable of honesty even when there is no hope of anything else," Leslie Fiedler noted. Philip Rahv elaborated: "The fierce resistance which Chambers encountered . . . was essentially a symptom of the anguish of the Popular Front mind and its unreasoning anger at being made to confront the facts of political life." With the Hiss case, Rahv believed, the old battle over the Popular Front had been settled, with the hardheaded realism of the anti-Communists (once the anti–Popular Fronters) prevailing over those who "fought to save Hiss in order to safeguard their own illusions and to escape the knowledge of [their] gullibility and chronic refusal of reality."[118]

Rahv further associated the prewar *Partisan* opposition of the Popular Front with the postwar anticommunism of the New York Intellectuals and tied both to Alger Hiss. He found the crucial revelation from Chambers's memoir to be the degree to which Soviets had infiltrated the "top headquarters of the U. S. government," as in the cases off Hiss and Harry Dexter White.[119] This infiltration—"more extensive, probably, then we shall ever know"—resulted from "the political attitudes that prevailed in this country for a whole decade . . . between 1938 and 1948." William Phillips reiterated a basic point of liberal anticommunism in his explanation of the Hiss case. "The inability to understand the Hiss case has been at bottom a failure to grasp the nature of the Communist movement," Phillips observed. Liberal anti-Communists truly understood why Hiss was guilty.[120]

The New Yorkers also saw in the confusion and heated debate swirling about the protagonists of Hiss a number of the key issues of their anticommunism and the need to restate some of their basic principles. Sidney Hook suggested that one had to understand communism in order to evaluate Whittaker Chambers. After claiming that a "freedom from partisanship is essential" to view the case properly, Hook described the main theme of *Witness* as "the communist movement . . . and the logic of the commitment which led [party members] into an eager faithlessness not only to their country but to the moral values in which they were nurtured." These conclusions, Hook believed, represented a lack of partisanship on his part. His only hesitation about Chambers's analysis was that Hiss's accuser "recklessly lumps Socialists, progressives, liberals, and men of goodwill together with the Communists." This was an obvious transgression of a basic liberal anti-communist precept, and Hook faulted Chambers for not considering "the opposition of genuine American liberals to the cultural and physical terror of the Kremlin."[121]

Political issues only served as a backdrop for the New Yorkers' evaluation of the Rosenbergs and Hiss. These cases acquired a compelling immediacy because of the personal relations and comparisons between the accused and these anti-Communist accusers. Julius and Ethel Rosenberg grew up in the same environment as the young men from the provinces, Julius attending City College in the same period as many of the second-generation New York Intellectuals. Starting where many young Jews began, the Rosenbergs followed the well-worn path into thirties radicalism. Because their continued allegiance to communism, the Rosenbergs' route diverged from that of those who ended up at *Partisan Review*. For the New York Intellectuals this meant that the Rosenbergs wound up both politically flawed and subjugated to "the Idea." In an attempt to keep Julius Rosenberg from confessing and exposing other espionage agents, Daniel Bell argued, the *Daily Worker* "so martyrises him that confession becomes psychologically difficult."[122] As a result he will go to his death as a silent martyr rather than "logically" confess. "The Idea," Bell implied, has been called upon. In the life and death of Julius Rosenberg, it became possible for these ex-radicals to see a course their own lives might have followed. In an imaginary dialogue about the Rosenberg case, Leslie Fiedler allowed one character to express these feelings:

> Thank God, I've faced up long ago to the part of me that's guilty in the same sense the Rosenbergs are. Fortunately I never had the chance to do what they did, though once I would have given a lot to have had it. So I don't have to pay publicly for a crime, only internally for an intention.[123]

If Julius Rosenberg's direction might have been taken by the young Jewish radicals, Alger Hiss's career offers an example of a path permanently shut off to them. The personal connections in this case are with Whittaker Chambers, who although a steadfast Communist during the years when the New Yorkers broke with Stalinism and established *Partisan Review* nonetheless came from the same milieu and knew personally a number of these individuals. Meyer Schapiro was Chambers's closest associate among these intellectuals. Friends at Columbia in the early 1920s, they went to Germany and Belgium together in 1923 and saw each other during the 1930s. An expert in fine arts, Schapiro purchased four rugs for Chambers, one of which Chambers claimed to have given Hiss. In the summer of 1935 Chambers and his family occupied Schapiro's Greenwich Village apartment. All this came out during the Hiss trial, at which Schapiro testified.[124]

Schapiro was not the only one to have personal connections with Hiss's accuser. Lionel Trilling, also a Columbia student in the early 1920s, knew Chambers, or at least they knew about one another. Trilling did know Chambers personally by the 1930s, for Sidney Hook later recalled that his first meeting with Chambers was in 1934, at Trilling's request. Trilling invited Hook to lunch with him and Chambers, so that Hook could present his "criticisms of the theory of 'social-fascism' to Chambers." Although Hook had not met Chambers, he "had already known of his existence for some years through mutual political friends." Elliot Cohen was another of Chambers's friends during these years. In Lionel Trilling's only novel, *The Middle of the Journey*, one character was "more consciously derived from actuality than any of the others." Into the character of Gifford Maxim, Trilling wrote, went "a considerable amount of recollected observation of a person with whom I had long been acquainted . . . Whittaker Chambers."[125] Trilling published his novel just a few months before Chambers emerged from relative obscurity with the explosion of the Hiss case.

Friendships or political associations do not alone account, however, for the personal attachments between the New York Intellectuals and Chambers. Strong sentiments emerged in the negative appraisals of Alger Hiss. Some intellectuals were haunted by the possibility that they, too, might have done what Hiss did—troubled by how close their beliefs and Hiss's supposed actions had been. Both the pro-Hiss and the anti-Hiss liberals thought that "there but for the grace of God [went] themselves," Diana Trilling believed, although she added that the anti-Hiss liberal also meant Chambers as well as Hiss."[126]

Apart from the feeling that they might have followed the same course, the attitudes and the status of the groups opposing and supporting Hiss diverged sharply. "The first thing we observe," Diana Trilling noted of the Hiss supporters, "is that they have certain shared social and cultural characteristics." People of "the middle and upper classes, of education, breeding, professional solidity and distinction; people of great probity, thoughtful and conscientious citizens. Judged by the conventional criteria of class, Hiss's defenders come off rather better than his accusers." Here the full underlying dynamic of the opposition to Hiss emerges. In contrast to the "respectibility of those who are on the Hiss side," Trilling argued, "those who think him guilty have a taint of the bohemian, of the unconnected." She thought it possible to make some social distinctions between "Hiss's Harvard and Chambers' Columbia."[127] Trilling's analysis is replete with overgeneralizations, not the least of them being her equation of "bohemian" with Columbia. Chambers's supporters included many others beyond the intellectual world of New York, from Richard Nixon, the FBI, and William Buckley to his fellow ex-Communist accusers, Elizabeth Bentley, William Remington, and Herbert Philbrick. Furthermore, the description of Columbia in the 1950s as "bohemian" stretches credibility. Allen Ginsberg may have been Lionel Trilling's student, but Ginsberg's notoriety at Columbia in these years grew from his nonconformism. Even the Columbia of the 1930s could hardly be described as bohemian, given Diana Trilling's own discussion of the institution's anti-Semitism and the regal atmosphere created by Nicholas Murray Butler.

Diana Trilling's class analysis, though, reveals more about the New York Intellectuals' attitudes toward Hiss than about the case itself. She is not alone in dividing the Hiss camp and the Chambers camp along social lines, which often served to hide religious or ethnic divisions. To Leslie Fiedler, Hiss was "just the type that does not normally get caught in the indiscriminate 'witch hunt.'" Rather, the "visible outsiders" were usually made the targets, such as Assistant Secretary of Defense Anna M. Rosenberg (no relation), "both foreign-born and a Jew." She was much more likely to be haled up without any evidence against her." Someone with Alger Hiss's credentials could usually "slip past the ordinary Congressman, to whom 'Red' really means loud-mouth or foreigner or Jew."[128] Here reappeared the old exclusions of their younger days—us versus them. Alger Hiss, undoubtedly an allrightnik, possessed a Harvard Degree and a Holmes clerkship. As William Phillips put it succinctly, "The roster of Hiss supporters reads like a page out of the social register." To these people with impeccable credentials, the rallying to Hiss demonstrated

> not the right of Hiss to be a spy, but their faith in American institutions and in a clean-cut young man, tall, lean, with sloping relaxed shoulders, a good mixer, a career man with principles—a symbol of the new type of liberal executive in a Brooks Brothers suit. (What would have happened if Hiss looked like Peter Lorre and Chambers like Gary Cooper?) *He was one of them*; and if he was guilty then any one of them could be guilty, and nothing could be believed in, for anything was possible[129]

The contrasting styles of the New Yorkers, who had aggressively sought all the goals they achieved, and of the "haves," to whom success seemed to fall naturally, colored the perceptions. More than a bit of resentment emerged in Leslie Fiedler's denunciation of Hiss as playing "the honest man confronted by the 'rat.'"

Really, Hiss kept insisting, they'd have to call the Harvard Club, say he'd be a few
minutes late to dinner—after taking care of this unpleasantness. For a while it came
off quite successfully, coming from one who visibly belonged, whose clothes
beautifully fitted, whose manners were adequate to all occasions.[130]

The Hiss case seemed to provide these immigrants' children with a dramatic
representation of the fallacies of lineage in American society. Those too closely
tied to the system, the insiders, often let their emotions overcome their reason,
let personal feelings outweigh logical conclusions. The Communists rallied
behind Hiss because he had been one of them, the New Yorkers maintained,
and his guilt implied theirs. But these defenders were usually dismissed
casually. "Apart from known fellow-travelers," Diana Trilling began one
description of Hiss supporters; "in addition to the usual quota of fellow-
travelers," William Phillips wrote in another.[131] The rallying of the old-line
families, the people of breeding, those in the social register—their support of
Hiss provoked the New York Intellectuals much more. These forces saw in
Hiss's fall the tarnishing of their own image, or so the New Yorkers claimed.
These defenders of Hiss might actually believe he did "transmit secret
documents to Chambers," Robert Warshow held. "But they believe also that
this was somehow transmitted into innocence by the inherent virtue of Alger
Hiss's being."[132]

Much of this attitude the New York Intellectuals projected onto Alger Hiss.
Despite his credentials and the eminence of his supporters, his life had not
moved as easily toward social and political success as it initially appeared. "We
learned later, of course, how much the genteel aspect of Hiss was itself a
mask," Leslie Fiedler wrote. Instead, Fiedler found that Hiss possessed an
additional, hidden motivating force, beyond the publicly perceived attributes of
radical politics and the social register. "It was as if Alger Hiss had dedicated
himself to fulfilling, along with his dream of a New Humanity, the other dream
his father had passed on to him with his first name—from rags to riches. How
strangely the Marxist ideal and the dream of Horatio Alger blended into the
motives of treason. . . ."[133] Personal ambition was not limited to either the
Communists or the social elite. In Hiss's drive for success, the New Yorkers
could see a reflection of their own character—his combination of ambition and
communism mirrored their thirties coupling of ambition, intellectualism, and
anti-Stalinism. By the 1950s they had shed their radicalism for postwar
liberalism. But the questions about their own past continued to haunt them.
They might publicly proclaim the logical transition between pre- and postwar
attitudes, offer examples of the seamless shifts from radicalism to liberalism,
but in the explanations and analyses of various postwar investigations, their
own sense of guilt appeared just below their surface complacency.

Regarding the Rosenberg and Hiss cases, the New York Intellectuals could
not remain content with public declarations that the evidence proved the guilt
of the accused. The issues went far beyond overt espionage. "Certainly a
generation was on trial," Fiedler argued, "for having substituted sentimentally

for intelligence." In his internal dialogue on the Rosenberg case, Fiedler has one character argue,

> You know why most of the protesters are protesting. It has nothing to do with the Rosenbergs. They only want to save *themselves* in their own eyes, to acquit their own youth: pretend to themselves that *they* really wouldn't have done—or that their Communist friends whom they sponsored and protected in the Popular Front days, wouldn't have done it, couldn't have done it, *didn't* do it.

The same character later confesses,

> It's no use. I just feel guilty. I want to cry when I think of their dying—really cry, because *I'm* not dying, because they're paying alone the bill for the rest of us. To hell with their foolish or hypocritical defenders, and with their hypocritical or foolish opponents. I know what they mean![134]

The same sentiments emerged from evaluations of the Hiss case, which Diana Trilling suggested faced "the liberal with the most cogent representation he has yet had of the kind of responsibility he must take for his thoughts." Fiedler found the Hiss case "painful" because in it he "live[d] again through events of ten years gone." It became painful "to admit one's identity with a person who bore one's name in a by now incredible past." Finally, the real difficulty according to Fiedler, was "confess[ing] that one is responsible for the acts of the past, especially when such acts are now placed in a new and unforseen context that changes their meaning entirely. 'Not guilty,' one wants to cry, 'that is not what I meant at all.' "[135]

The feelings of guilt which surfaced during the Hiss and Rosenberg cases could be assuaged by a reiteration of the basic differences between the political attitudes of the accused and of the New Yorkers or held down by a return to the narrower question of criminal culpability. Another case captured public attention in the 1950s and aroused the same personal feelings as the Hiss and Rosenberg cases, but it lacked some of the particulars which helped keep conscience at bay. The investigation surrounding the granting of a security clearance to J. Robert Oppenheimer—the distinguished scientist, wartime leader of the Los Alamos project, and at the time head of Princeton's Institute for Advance Study—raised fears unallayed by extenuating circumstances. Oppenheimer represented a model intellectual, as in Diana Trilling's belief that he united the man of the academy with the man of action. Furthermore, the accusations against Oppenheimer were precisely the kind which might be raised against any of the ex-radical liberals. Once a fellow traveler and a financial contributor to the Communist party, Oppenheimer had become a moderate cold warrior in the postwar years. During 1952 and 1953 the government increasingly restricted Oppenheimer, first removing classified documents from his custody at Princeton, then issuing a presidential order limiting the data he received, and finally denying him all government clearance. A consultant to the Atomic Energy Committee, Oppenheimer was offered the chance to resign. When he refused, his phone was tapped, his mail sorted, and his home and office bugged. A subsequent hearing before an AEC-appointed board delved into Oppenheimer's past. While most of the American scientific community came to his defense, the board voted two to one that Oppenheimer represented a security risk and should have no further access to classified documents.

Oppenheimer's interrogation and the assessment of guilt did not result in his execution or in a prison term. But in this investigation the New York Intellectuals could see most clearly their own vulnerability. The labels ex-radical, anti-Stalinist, and postwar liberal applied to them as well as to Oppenheimer. According to "the strict standards by which Dr. Oppenheimer is now judged," Diana Trilling perceived, "virtually anyone might fail." Unlike Hiss or the Rosenbergs, Oppenheimer repented his past errors. "To have granted him clearance [when he was a fellow traveler] only to take it away from him now . . . seems to me at best to be tragic ineptitude," Trilling argued. But in generalizing about the verdict, she hit upon the distinctive lesson of the case. This "tragic ineptitude" in the end "constitutes a projection upon Dr. Oppenheimer of the punishment we perhaps owe to ourselves for having once been so careless with our nation's security."[136]

Not all the New York Intellectuals joined in this mass expiation of guilt. Harold Rosenberg, for one, found the proclamations of past culpability and present punishment unconvincing, although he understood their source: "If Americans spoke in order to escape from a dungeon, it was from the dungeons of their own selves." Despite Oppenheimer's current anticommunism, Rosenberg complained, these declarations of mass guilt leave the impression that "we are unreliable types and deserve to be fired, regardless of actual service to our country."[137] Few intellectuals went as far with their public confessions as Leslie Fiedler or Diana Trilling, but few felt as secure in their rejection of that position as Harold Rosenberg.

The cases involving Hiss, the Rosenbergs, and Oppenheimer aroused more than the standard declarations one might expect from anti-Communists in the 1950s, even from liberal anti-Communists. Certainly, the New Yorkers believed that the accused spies were guilty, and defended Oppenheimer. But beyond the basic issues appeared personal questions and hints of their own past and ideas. Each application of liberal anti-Communist belief—the Rosenberg's captivity to "the Idea," the naïveté of the Popular Front mentality, the false idealism of the Communists—was supplemented with discussions of social class and ethnic origins, issues about "bohemianism" and New York's intellectual world, and questions concerning liberal guilt in general. The self-satisfaction of revised liberalism and the assuredness of liberal anticommunism belied the haunting fears emerging from these anti-Communist investigations, especially clear in Oppenheimer's fall. The degree to which the political past of the New

York Intellectuals was bound up in their current political thinking is demonstrated by these questions. They had lived in an era with a completely different political and intellectual ethos. They had successfully made the transition from being prewar radicals to being postwar liberals, keeping their intellectual reputation intact. The McCarthyite hysteria threatened that smooth adjustment, threatened to call their past into the present. Despite outward assuredness, it kept them internally restless. In one of William Phillips's few short stories, written in 1949, the narrator is questioned by a supposed Army intelligence officer about another tenant in his building. The narrator's suspicions grow about who is actually under investigation. He becomes concerned over how others' statements about him might sound to an investigator.

> I became very tired and went into my bedroom to take a nap. But I could not sleep. And as I lay awake, in the twilight of the afternoon, I kept asking myself over and over again, how a man who may or may not be guilty of being an imposter could stir up so much guilt in me over the question of whether Miss Caruso [the neighbor] was guilty or innocent of a charge that had never been made. If I could only sleep, I thought, then I could exile my guilt to my dreams, like everyone else.[138]

THE SHEPHERDS OF CULTURAL FREEDOM

New York Intellectuals spread the gospel of liberal anticommunism through the time-tested approaches of their intellectual activity. The pages of *Commentary, Partisan Review* and the *New Leader* brimmed with anti-Communist articles, including a number of the essential formulations of their arguments. In addition, new journals and magazines opened to these intellectuals. They spelled out their position in the *New York Times Magazine* and *Book Review*, in *Saturday Review*, in the *Twentieth Century*, and in the *American Mercury*. Sidney Hook, always the most prolific of the group, poured out books as well as articles on the subject.

They did not stop at the printed word, however. In the postwar years, these intellectuals also participated in another effort to argue and promote their liberal anti-Communist outlook—an effort which marked the completion both of their transition from thirties radicalism and of their campaign to bring intellectuals into the public arena. They helped create an organization for anti-Communist intellectuals. Aiming to defend intellectual freedom, they helped found the Congress for Cultural Freedom and the American Committee for Cultural Freedom.

The structural relation of these two groups appears, at first glance, relatively simple. The congress attempted to become an international, non-Communist association of intellectuals, with national affiliates, such as the American committee, under its organizational umbrella. In fact, the roots and development of the two are a bit more complex and murky. The earliest incarnation occured in the late 1930s, when Sidney Hook and several other intellectuals resisted the creation of the Trotskyist-oriented League for Cultural Freedom and Socialism. Hook thought the LCFS "too left wing," according to Dwight Macdonald, and sought to create a "right-liberal counterpart." This organization went into eclipse during the war, reviving, according to Hook, in the anti-Communist intellectual uproar accompanying the famous Cultural and Scientific Conference for World Peace, held at the Waldorf-Astoria in 1949.[139]

The Waldorf conference was in one sense the last gasp of the Popular Front, as intellectuals from around the world gathered in New York. Soviet delegates attended, including the composer Dimitri Shostakovich. Among the American sponsors were such diverse individuals as Albert Einstein, Rexford Guy Tugwell, Leonard Bernstein, Aaron Copland, Marlon Brando, Harold Rome, Clifford Odets, Lillian Hellman, Henry Wallace, Frank Lloyd Wright, F. O. Matthiessen, and, of central importance for the anti-Communists, the Harvard astronomer Harlow Shapley. Coexistence rather than cold warriorism marked the tone of the conference. In opposition to it, Hook and Norman Thomas revived their prewar organization, calling on the support of a variety of intellectuals now much more receptive to a "right-liberal" alternative. Many individuals viewed this new group, called Americans for Intellectual Freedom, as a spontaneous development rather than the rebirth of a dormant organization. The *Nation* reported that a "new organization called the Americans for Intellectual Freedom (A.I.F.) was quickly created by a number of well-known anti-Soviet intellectuals. . . . The press agent for Local 802 of the Musicians' Union, Arnold Beichman, took over as publicist and anonymous 'spokesman' for the A.I.F." Beichman himself remembered the group as being "purely ad hoc" and as getting "some money" from David Dubinsky, head of the International Ladies Garment Workers Union, "who financed it with a few thousand dollars." The money went for "some rooms at the Waldorf, some typewriters, and some telephones. . . . It became a sort of sociopolitical headquarters for anti-Communist activity."[140]

The struggle which emerged between the forces for and against the conference grew heated and acrimonious. On March 20, six days before the conference's opening, Hook blasted its bias and demanded that he be placed on the program. Harlow Shapley replied that Hook's request came too late for him to change the program, but he offered Hook a position on one of the panels. Hook refused. Two days later, amid the spate of information which began to flow from the typewriters and telephones in the rooms at the Waldorf, Hook accused members of the Russian delegation to the conference of being agents sent to watch over Shostakovich. Furthermore, Hook announced an alternative rally to coincide with the opening of the conference. The next day, the twenty-third, Hook and George Counts, education professor at Columbia's Teachers College, publicly announced the creation of the Americans for Intellectual Freedom. Calling the Waldorf conference "a perfect case study of how

Communist propaganda is carried to writers, artists, scientists, and other intellectuals," they questioned the financial backing of the conference, implying that funding had come from the Soviets. Finally, they displayed a telegram from T. S. Eliot, who believed that the conference was "an attempt to demoralize intellectual and moral integrity everywhere." The public reading of Eliot's telegram appears to have been a countermove against the publication of a telegram from Thomas Mann supporting the Waldorf conference.

The next day brought further details of the counterrally. Accusing the conference of being "a gathering of specially selected apologists for Russian communism—designed to provide a platform for attacks upon American and Western democracy," the AIF promised to hold its counterrally "in the spirit of free inquiry and honest difference of opinion." Although no New York Intellectual had signed as a sponsor of the Waldorf conference—for obvious reasons—a large number joined in sponsoring the AIF rally. Among the two hundred listed sponsors were Daniel Bell, Clement Greenberg, William Phillips, Philip Rahv, Harold Rosenberg, Arthur Schlesinger, Jr., Delmore Schwartz, Lionel Trilling, and Diana Trilling.[141]

The conference proceeded as planned, as did the counterrally. During the panel on writing and publishing, Mary McCarthy, Dwight Macdonald, and Robert Lowell raised caustic questions from the floor, while Norman Mailer, a panelist, attacked both the United States and the Soviet Union for failing the socialist cause. Outside the hotel, the Americans for Intellectual Freedom and other anti-Soviet groups staged demonstrations. In the end, all the events went ahead in relative quiet, considering all the preconference emotion. Within the ad hoc coalition organized in opposition to the Conference, Arnold Beichman later remembered, there emerged "a desire to sort of formalize themselves. That led to the Congress for Cultural Freedom and then the American Committee for Cultural Freedom."[142]

If the impetus for the Congress for Cultural Freedom grew out of the anti-Waldorf demonstrations, the actual organization of the group stemmed from the actions of two Americans living in Europe. Michael Josselson, formerly with the wartime Office of Strategic Services, had served as a cultural affairs officer for George Patton. At war's end he met Melvin Lasky, a habitué of Alcove No. 1 at City College in the late 1930s. Also part of the wartime OSS, Lasky stayed on in Germany after the war, as the American correspondent for the *New Leader* and *Partisan Review*, though these were hardly lucrative positions. Chosen to give the Western response at a Soviet-organized writers' conference, Lasky attacked Soviet censorship, drawing parallels with Nazi book burning and concentration camps. "The proper place for the new generation is on the right side of the Rhine, not the left side of the Seine," he proclaimed. Attracting the attention of American officials, Lasky began to edit a German magazine, *Der Monat* (The Month) under the State Department's aegis.[143] Among the revelations of the 1960s concerning the activities of the Central Intelligence Agency came the information that both Josselson and Lasky had been part of the CIA "cultural affairs" program. Thus, the final element in the creation of the congress came from the financial support of the United States government, channeled through protective foundations.

In 1950 the Congress for Cultural Freedom called its first meeting, to be held in West Berlin. In May the planning committee for the congress declared its aim "as the first major offensive against Soviet propaganda. The gathering will attract literary and scientific personages of international repute." Among those said to have accepted invitations were Julian Huxley, Arthur Koestler, Haakon Lie, James T. Farrell, Ignazio Silone, and Denis de Rougemont.[144] The Soviet army's official newspaper in East Berlin denounced the meeting, calling Lasky the "chief agent of atomic strategy in Berlin.[145] In June the American delegates were chosen: David Lilienthal, Arthur Schlesinger, Jr., the actor Robert Montgomery, Tennessee Williams, the author Giuseppe Borgese, James Burnham, and Sidney Hook, as well as Farrell. By the time the congress convened, three other Americans had joined—George Counts, the Nobel Prize–winning geneticist H. J. Muller, and Irving Brown, of the American Federation of Labor.[146] These Americans joined nearly one hundred other delegates.

The actual proceedings of the conference appear less important than its symbolic value and its coincidental timing with events in Korea. Various themes essential to liberal anticommunism did find reaffirmation in a number of the speeches. Arthur Koestler, Franz Borkenau, and Sidney Hook all gave variations of the end-of-ideology theme. Robert Montgomery echoed the liberals' notion that the times required an activist attitude. And Borkenau sounded an old theme when he called World War II "a second edition of the Popular Front."[147] The real significance of the congress, however, was the statement made by its very existence. "The first great achievement is to have held the Congress in Berlin," Sidney Hook reported in *Partisan Review*, "and to have strengthened the feeling of solidarity with those struggling for freedom." The second great achievement "is to have created a nucleus for a Western community of intellectuals who will have no truck with 'neutrality' in the struggle for freedom either at home or abroad."[148] Hook's enthusiasm seems to have colored his reporting, for on the basis of reports from H. R. Trevor-Roper, Christopher Lasch concluded in his short history of the congress that the meetings "broke up in a spirit of rancor," resulting from the withdrawal of a "resolution excluding totalitarian sympathizers 'from the Republic of the Spirit.' . . . 'Professor Hook and Mr. Burnham,' according to Trevor-Roper, 'protesting to the end.' "[149]

Hook may have lost sight of the rancor amid the spirit of adventure which he felt pervaded the congress. The invasion of Korea occurred during the meeting, prompting Hook to announce to the delegates, "I suppose [the Communists] will explain the advance into South Korea as an attempt to bring about peace."[150] By the time Hook reported on the congress in the July *PR*, his sarcasm had changed to memories of the excitement which accompanied danger:

The news of the invasion of Korea broke just before the first session when it seemed uncertain whether the Russians would march in Germany too; in which event every delegate would have been a prisoner of the M.V.A in a few hours. West Berlin, defenseless in an iron ring of Soviet armor, remained outwardly calm. Nor was there any overt sign of nervousness or anxiety among the Congress members. On the contrary . . . the Korean events, if anything, had given a fillip to the spirit of the delegates.[151]

The delegates, of course, did not end up as prisoners in Germany. The meeting ended without incident, with a resolve to maintain the organization, and with a plan to establish an international headquarters and national affiliates.

Paris became the home of the congress, which eventually sponsored a series of international meetings and publications. In November 1950 a meeting in Brussels sought to create a fund to assist refugee intellectuals. Graham Greene, John Dos Passos, Aldous Huxley, and Arthur Koestler joined this effort by promising to contribute a percentage of the royalties from specific works to the venture.[152] In early 1951 a large international conference, of the type held the past year in Berlin, was planned for New Delhi. The choice of India proved as symbolic as that of divided Germany. Seeking to dissuade emerging nations from adopting the neutral stand favored by the Indian government, anti-Communist intellectuals traveled to the subcontinent in March. The Americans Norman Thomas, James Burnham, and Louis Fischer joined W. H. Auden, Stephen Spender, Ignazio Silone, Denis de Rougemont, and others as delegates to the conference. At one session, de Rougemont suggested to nonaligned Indians that their position was comparable to that "of the lamb that is neutral between the wolf and the shepherd." One Indian responded that the shepherd, after saving the lamb, "shears the lamb and possibly eats it."[153]

Among the various national affiliates established under the leadership of the congress was the American Committee for Cultural Freedom, founded in 1951. Attempting to create a broad-based anti-Communist movement among American intellectuals, the ACCF initially attracted individuals of various political strains. Anticommunism became the only major prerequisite. Former radicals heading toward the extreme right—such as James Burnham, Max Eastman, James T. Farrell, Whittaker Chambers, John Chamberlain, and John Dos Passos—joined with liberals like Arthur Schlesinger, Jr., David Riesman, Richard Rovere, and Elmer Rice. New York Intellectuals, however, provided the solid center of the organization and filled many of the official positions. Sidney Hook became the ACCF's first chairman and Irving Kristol its first executive director. Diana Trilling and Daniel Bell served as officers, along with Norman Thomas and Merlyn Pitzele.[154] In subsequent years editors of the three main liberal anti-Communist journals—William Phillips of *Partisan Review*, Elliot Cohen of *Commentary*, and Sol Levitas of the *New Leader*—joined the board.

The relation between the Congress for Cultural Freedom and the American Committee for Cultural Freedom never grew as close as its organizational ties suggest. The differences stemmed in part from intellectual disputes and in larger part from the Americans' uneasiness with the rumors circulating about the congress's source of funding. While most of the members of the ACCF have claimed that they had no knowledge of the CIA support for the CCF, recent revelations have suggested less sharp distinctions between the government-supported CCF and the independent ACCF. The total dismay with which some intellectuals responded to the revelations of the 1960s was belied by Diana Trilling's memories of her early suspicions. "Even before I came onto the Executive Board of the American committee," she wrote, "I was aware, and it was my clear impression that everyone else of the board was also in some measure aware, that the international body with which we were associated was probably funded by the government." Trilling recalled, "We strongly suspected that the Fairfield Foundation, which we were told supported the Congress, was a filter for State Department or CIA money."[155]

Trilling speculated that the CIA and not the State Department probably supplied the congress's funding, as the intelligence agency had to spend its money outside the United States and the American committee received no financial assistance. That speculation turned to certainty at an ACCF board meeting. Discussing the committee's financial difficulties, the chairman at the time, Norman Thomas, announced that they lacked the money even to pay the upcoming rent. "Mr. Thomas," Trilling wrote in 1977,

> could see but a single solution: he would phone "Allen"; he returned from the telephone to tell us that a check for a thousand dollars would be in the mail the next morning. None of us could fail to know that the "Allen" who tided us over was Allen Dulles, head of the CIA, and that in the strictest sense it was even a breach of legality for him to give us help. But none of us, myself included, protested.[156]

Eventually, the ACCF separated from the parent body, becoming after 1955 an "independent affiliate."

Thus, despite calls for intellectual openness and cultural independence, the Congress for Cultural Freedom began under shadowy circumstances, and part of its administrative structure remained in the shadows for years. Both the CCF and the ACCF geared their public activities to the open light, however. Both organizations undertook a variety of tasks aimed at publicizing their anti-Communist intellectual position. For the New York Intellectuals, connections with the congress and the committee facilitated the public proclamation of their ideas. Through a series of activities and publications, the CCF and ACCF argued a hard-line brand of anticommunism, while steadfastly sounding the call for intellectual freedom. The most prominent activities of both organizations were a series of public forums and the sponsorship of intellectual journals and publications. The initial Berlin congress, with its topical sessions and presentations by CCF members, set the form for future gatherings. In its first year of existence, the ACCF held a lecture series in New York organized by Kristol and chaired by Hook, with Diana Trilling, Arthur Schlesinger, and

Arthur Koestler among the featured speakers.[157] Subsequent annual forums were on topics like "The Ex-Communist: His Role in a Democracy" and "Anti-Americanism in Europe." In 1952 the anti-Communists returned to the Waldorf for a conference entitled "In Defense of Free Culture," which included as speakers Max Eastman, Mary McCarthy, Sidney Hook, and Lionel Trilling.[158] The publication program of the organization developed in two areas. The ACCF put out a variety of pamphlets and books on topics of particular importance for their political undertaking. Hook's *Heresy, Yes—Conspiracy, No*, originally an article in the *New York Times Magazine* and later expanded into a book, came out as a pamphlet under ACCF sponsorship. In 1954 James Rorty and Moshe Decter published *McCarthy and the Communists*, a liberal anti-Communist critique of McCarthy's activities, written under the sponsorship of the American committee.

In the area of intellectual magazines, the congress and the committee followed two lines of activity. Late in the decade *Partisan Review* lost its independent tax exemption and nominally became a publication of the American Committee, "purely for the purpose of being able to gain tax-exempt gifts from individuals and foundations," Daniel Bell recalled.[159] While the American committee came to an already existing publication, the Congress for Cultural Freedom helped found a number of international journals, including the French *Preuves* and the Italian *Tempo Presente*, edited by Ignazio Silone and Nicola Chiaromonte. Most prominent for Americans in general and New York Intellectuals in particular was the London-based *Encounter*.[160] This journal emerged out of the desire of the British CCF affiliate to publish its own magazine and that of the Paris headquarters for an English-language publication. The British choice for editor had been the poet Stephen Spender. The Paris office wanted Irving Kristol. Kristol had left *Commentary*, he recalled, "because I found it increasingly difficult to work for Elliot Cohen, who was in the process of having a breakdown, although at the time I was too inexperienced to know what was happening."[161] The Paris office asked Hook to recommend someone, and he suggested Kristol, who had been running the series of meetings for the ACCF. Moving to London, Kristol joined Spender as coeditor, and they brought out the first issue of *Encounter* in October 1953.

Encounter's initial number represented three interwoven groups. Based in England and edited by one of Britain's preeminent poets, the first issue included articles by a number of well-known literary persons—Christopher Isherwood, C. Day Lewis, Albert Camus, Spender himself, and Virginia Woolf (an excerpt from her diary). From the Congress for Cultural Freedom, the composer Nicholas Nabokov, CCF secretary-general, and Denis de Rouge-mont, president of the executive committee, contributed. Kristol's connection with the New York Intellectuals was no less evident. He wrote the unsigned opening editorial as well as a signed piece. There were also articles by Leslie Fiedler and Nathan Glazer.[162] Fiedler contributed his piece on the Rosenbergs, quoted above. Kristol's editorial promised, "*Encounter* seeks to promote no 'line,' though its editors have opinions they will not hesitate to express." He noted, too, the diversity of the Congress for Cultural Freedom's sponsors, including John Dewey, Karl Jaspers, Jacques Maritain, and Bertrand Russell. He asked, "What caused them to come together? Two things: a love of liberty and a respect for that part of human endeavor that goes by the name of culture." Thus, Kristol concluded, the magazine would "represent both this community and this diversity" and aim "not at slurring over differences of opinion, but rather at the uninhibited exploration of them"[163]

Spender recalled that while *Encounter* remained editorially independent of the Paris office of the CCF, the relationship between the journal and the headquarters did not always correspond to the unqualified freedom some of the other editors and contributors later described. "It would be untrue to write that the Congress never tried to influence editorial policy," Spender stated, "although the influence it attempted to exercise was by no means always political: simply, the people in Paris had bright ideas about the kind of articles we should put in." Both Spender and Kristol resisted one bit of intrusion, a suggested monthly column of congress activities. *Encounter* thus became "an independent magazine, partly of literature and the arts, partly of politics," Spender declared.[164] Yet, even by his reckoning, the independence was not absolute.

One further insight into *Encounter* editorial policy which Spender provided concerned the division of editorial work between the editors. "The political articles were the domain of the American editors," he wrote. (Melvin Lasky later replaced Irving Kristol as Spender's coeditor.)[165] This is telling both for the kinds of political articles which appeared, such as Fiedler's piece on the Rosenbergs, and for a personnel conflict which erupted in the mid-1950s. As Kristol remembered, "I think Stephen, understandably, rather resented being coeditor with me. He was a very distinguished poet and writer, and I was not particularly distinguished, certainly not in England. We got along reasonably well—no single editorial issue caused a fight." But sentiment grew for Dwight Macdonald to replace Kristol. Kristol surmises that Spender very likely thought "Dwight was older and better known. So there was a moment when it looked as though Dwight was going to take my place."[166] When the proposed change came before the Congress for Cultural Freedom, Kristol's backers, particularly Sidney Hook, fought against Macdonald. Although he was not present, Kristol later maintained, "People who knew Dwight well fought hard against [the change]. I ended up being asked to stay on, and Dwight came to us for a year." Hook concured in Kristol's assessment, recalling his intervention to keep Kristol on. Macdonald had a "plague-on-both-of-your-houses attitude toward the Kremlin and the West," Hook declared, adding, "I admired his editorial independence, but I regarded Macdonald as irresponsible." Threatening to resign from the CCF board if Kristol was dumped, Hook prevailed.[167]

In 1958, Kristol did leave *Encounter* to return to New York. Melvin Lasky, Kristol's old City College comrade and one of the founders of the CCF, took his place alongside Spender. When CIA activity was exposed in the mid-1960s, attention focused on *Encounter*. The ex-CIA official Thomas Braden's admissions included the direct role the CIA took in both the congress and its magazine. "We had placed one agent in a Europe-based organization of intellectuals called the Congress for Cultural Freedom," Braden reported in the *Saturday Evening Post*. "Another agent became an editor of *Encounter*."[168] The guessing game as to which editor had been the agent settled on Lasky, given his background with the congress, his postwar activities in Germany, and his admission that he knew about CIA funding. Peter Steinfels recently questioned whether the CIA could wait five years—from *Encounter*'s founding to Lasky's editorship—and felt a bit uncomfortable with Kristol's professed innocence. For his part, Kristol wrote in 1968 that he would have not taken the job had he known about the CIA, but not because he "disapproved of the CIA or even secret subsidies." Rather, Kristol maintained, he would have declined because he valued his "reputation as an independent writer and thinker" and because after his experience in the Army he had taken "a solemn oath . . . never again [to] work as a functionary in a large organization, and especially not for the United States government."[169]

The larger question of whether the London editors, as well as the ACCF officers in New York, knew of the link to the CIA continued to cause disagreements among the participants. Stephen Spender, for example, waxed indignant about the duplicitous treatment he received. He recounted responding to rumors of secret funding by asking the head of one foundation about *Encounter*'s backers. He received an irate letter from the foundation's director, restating the announced sources of *Encounter*'s money. When revelations in 1966 exposed the channeling of CIA funds, Spender, then corresponding editor, and Frank Kermode, his English replacement as coeditor, resigned in protest. Spender's former coeditor, Irving Kristol, believed his former colleague. "He had a right to be annoyed," Kristol said in 1976.[170] Others connected with the CCF found Spender's protestations less convincing. Arnold Beichman, said in 1976 that Spender was "full of shit!" Diana Trilling was more measured in her assessment:

> While it seems hard to believe, I think it is possible for Stephen [Spender] to have done as much work as he did for the Congress for Cultural Freedom without realizing that it was being funded by some department or agency of the United States government and reporting back to it. It's not only that he's a poet and poets can be pretty vague characters, but I have reason to know that he's a very trusting person—my husband and I lived in his house in London for a summer; he didn't know me at all well, but he had me open and read all his mail and decide what to forward him in France. Still, when he and Nicky Nabokov were sent by the congress to India to see Nehru, I should think that even a poet would begin to ask questions about the purpose of the visit.[171]

Thus, the seemingly innocent and intellectually reputable project of publishing a serious magazine became enmeshed in American intelligence operations—clouded by rumored connections to the American government. Against the declared purposes of intellectual independence and cultural freedom, the congress, the American committee, and *Encounter* all lived in a gray world of public pronouncements and private motives. The discrepancy between the declared openness and the covert operations extended beyond financial backing. The American Committee for Cultural Freedom, for example, while proclaiming its belief in intellectual independence and cultural diversity, sought to support a particular kind of intellectual activity and to undermine the activities of those it regarded as opponents. The organization's function, Hook told an early meeting of the ACCF executive committee, was "to expose Stalinism and Stalinist liberals wherever you may find them."[172]

The ACCF set itself the goal of clearly identifying those groups and individuals practicing what it considered Stalinist-oriented politics or un-revised, Popular Front liberalism. In this context, it went beyond political discussion or policy papers. In keeping with the activist element in postwar liberalism, the ACCF initiated a series of aggressive attacks on groups and individuals. The most striking of these campaigns centered on the Emergency Civil Liberties Committee. The ECLC had been formed in 1951 to fill the vacuum its organizers felt had been left by the American Civil Liberties Union's unwillingness to become actively involved in the most controversial civil liberties cases of the McCarthy era. Although declaring itself non-Communist, rather than anti-Communist, the ECLC included among its founding members several old Popular Fronters and opponents of the liberal anti-Communists.[173] In early 1953, when the ECLC decided to hold a public forum on the Bill of Rights, the ACCF responded with a campaign to discourage the announced participants. At a meeting of the executive board, the ACCF approved sending a telegram to all concerned. Drafted by Kristol, then the ACCF's executive secretary, and going out under George Counts's signature, the January 16 telegram read,

> Distressed to learn you are participating in forum of Emergency Civil Liberties Committee. Are you aware that this organization is a Communist front with no sincere interest in liberty in the United States or elsewhere? Urge you reconsider.[174]

The ECLC responded by defending its record, citing that the organization had been formed by 150 educators, clergymen, and professionals and that it had not been placed on the attorney general's list of subversive organizations. The ECLC further announced that its program would go on as planned, with Frank Lloyd Wright, Walter White of the NAACP, Professor Thomas Emerson of Yale Law School, the *Nation*'s Carey McWilliams, and the Princeton political scientist H. H. Wilson among the participants. Battles for support and countersupport raged, as both the ACCF and the ECLC sought to line up intellectual backers. The ACCF announced that Paul Tillich, theologian at Union Theological Seminary, had resigned from the ECLC because of the

ACCF revelations. The ECLC chairman, Paul Lehmann of Princeton Theological Seminary, offered the public response to the ACCF, with the support of Robert Lynd of Columbia and Broadus Mitchell of Rutgers. In the war of words, the ECLC demanded that the ACCF prove its charges of Communist connections. Kristol replied that since the ECLC had made the telegrams public, the burden of proof rested with them. He did admit that though non-Communists were taking part, there was no one who could "be legitimately described as anti-communist." The ECLC conference went on as planned, but the event did not end the friction between the two organizations.[175]

In June of 1953 Albert Einstein stirred ACCF ire by arguing that intellectuals called to testify before congressional committees should refuse to cooperate. Hook and Counts drafted the response, calling the physicist's views "ill-considered and irresponsible" and asserting that such a position only aided "the camouflage of the Communists." Einstein's advice, the ACCF statement argued, "would accomplish what both reactionaries and Communists want—to split the intellectual community from the rest of society." Instead, the ACCF called for "clean hands" and "speaking out."[176]

When the ECLC planned a conference on academic freedom in honor of Einstein's seventy-fifth birthday, the ACCF sought to discredit the conference and to dissuade Einstein from lending his name. J. Robert Oppenheimer served as intermediary between the ACCF and Einstein. Oppenheimer reported to the ACCF that though Einstein might be willing to say that the conference "wasn't his idea of a birthday celebration," he nonetheless could not retract a letter he had sent the ECLC on matters of academic freedom. "I do not know what we can do," Oppenheimer concluded, "unless we get someone to choke them [the ECLC] off and stop it."[177]

Sol Stein, Kristol's successor as the ACCF's executive director, urged Oppenheimer to continue to press Einstein. Stein himself wrote to the famed scientist, as did Norman Thomas. As the conference approached, the ACCF prepared a press release to support the charge that the ECLC was a Communist front. The evidence included the ECLC protest of teachers fired for having failed to declare their political affiliations, opposition to the conviction of those indicted under the Smith Act, and the background of various ECLC leaders. The ACCF admitted that though individually these did not provide "evidence of Communist views," together these facts were "revealing." The ECLC aimed to "monopolize the American anti-McCarthy fight," the ACCF claimed, and "to eliminate decent anti-totalitarian and anti-Communist organizations."[178]

A variety of American intellectuals found their way to the Congress for Cultural Freedom and to the American Committee for Cultural Freedom. The primary rallying force, hard anticommunism, allowed individuals of varying political stances to join together. Increasingly, these differences caused irritation and friction between members, the more conservative and the more liberal alike. Ex-radicals moving to the extreme right became an increasing embarrassment. Max Eastman's seeming defense of McCarthyism cast "an unclear shadow" on the ACCF, Hook told an executive committee meeting in 1952. When, in April 1952, Bell and Kristol submitted a resolution condemning both communism and "certain types of anti-communism," James Burnham objected and the resolution was tabled. Events came to a head the following year, when Burnham wrote the preface to a book accusing American scientists of relaying atomic secrets to the Soviets. Scientists rose in protest, including Oppenheimer, Hermann Muller, and Harold Urey, demanding Burnham's ouster from the ACCF. Nathan Glazer and Daniel Bell, while not defending Burnham, cautioned against his expulsion. Amid this tumult, Burnham resigned from the *Partisan Review* advisory board over his position on Senator McCarthy. In July 1954 he left the ACCF, believing that those "anti-communists who consider themselves to be anti-McCarthyites have fallen into a trap."[179]

The withdrawal of Burnham and Eastman on the right matched the resignation of some liberals a year or two later. Arthur Schlesinger, Jr., grew uncomfortable with the ACCF attitude toward McCarthy, from the perspective of a New Deal–ADA liberal. Objecting to the conclusions of James Rorthy and Moshe Decter in the ACCF-sponsored *McCarthy and the Communists*, Schlesinger disagreed with their interpretation of Yalta and State Department infiltration. In 1955 he also wrote to James T. Farrell, the ACCF's chairman, that the organization had lost sight of cultural freedom in its obsession with anticommunism. David Riesman concurred in Schlesinger's view, further objecting to the ACCF position against Owen Lattimore. Riesman, Schlesinger, Richard Rovere, and Herbert Muller publicly disavowed an ACCF statement which described Lattimore as "a willing instrument of the Soviet conspiracy."[180]

The middle ground, occupied in large part by the New York Intellectuals, remained the cohesive force at the ACCF. This proved true in regard both to personnel and to political philosophy. The organization initially hoped to join together diverse anti-Communist intellectuals. In reality, the consistent membership, as well as the consistent line, represented this central group. With several notable exceptions—Irving Howe, Meyer Schapiro, and Philip Rahv, among them—most of the New York Intellectuals belonged to the ACCF. Many held official positions—Hook, Kristol, Bell, Glazer, Diana Trilling, Phillips, Elliot Cohen. Most important, the political arguments the New Yorkers had been espousing in the postwar years became the official positions of the ACCF. The ideas of their revised liberalism and, especially, their liberal anticommunism gained wide circulation and a kind of "official sanction" from the ACCF.

The reprinting of Hook's article "Heresy, Yes—Conspiracy, No!" in the form of an ACCF pamphlet set the philosophical basis for the committee's attitude and marked the acceptance of Hook's distinctions between tolerable and intolerable political activity. As Michael Harrington noted in the mid-

1950s, adopting Hook's argument "in effect endorsed his systematic, explicit efforts to minimize the threat to civil liberties . . . the American Committee cast its weight not so much in defense of these civil liberties which were steadily being nibbled away, but rather against those few remaining fellow-travelers who tried to exploit the civil liberties issue."[181] To complement Hook's views, the ACCF also reprinted and circulated Kristol's famous *Commentary* article "Civil Liberties 1952—A Study in Confusion."

Since the foundation of liberal anticommunism followed the New York Intellectual design, the public positions which the ACCF took echoed the arguments individual New Yorkers had been making. In December 1952 the ACCF gave its approval to the banning of entry visas to Stalinists, while supporting the right of left anti-Stalinists to gain entrance. In a similar vein, the committee publicly argued in favor of J. Robert Oppenheimer during his security hearings. Admitting the scientist's previous political associations, the ACCF maintained that his record of the past few years, with its strong anti-Communist tendency, demonstrated his changed, secure position. He "resisted Communist efforts to exploit him," the committee announced, and "twice aided in anti-Communist activities," although it did not indicate whether these activities included contacts with Einstein concerning the ECLC.[182]

The ACCF position on the Rosenbergs reflected many of the liberal anti-Communist views in the debate, including the insistence that their guilt be admitted by anyone arguing for clemency. "Those who allow the Communists to make use of their name in such a way as to permit any doubt to arise about the Rosenbergs' guilt are doing a grave disservice to the cause of justice—and of mercy, too." The ACCF statement also repeated the cynicism expressed by Daniel Bell and others over the source of Communist concern for the accused spies. "Dead, the Rosenbergs are Communist martyrs. Alive, they are potential informers. There is no doubt as to where the Communist preference lies."[183]

The question of academic freedom fell to an ACCF committee, composed of Paul R. Hays, Arthur O. Lovejoy, George Counts, and Sidney Hook. Their statement reasserted the position Hook and others had been arguing. The trouble, this committee believed, stemmed not from overzealous patriots or witch-hunters but from "the implacable threat of Communist aggression. The existence of the Communist conspiracy in our own midst has stirred deep and natural anxieties." Admitting that these anxieties had been "exploited by unscrupulous politicians," the group nonetheless held that "hard and urgent questions" had been raised, "not easily answered by the familiar formulas of civil freedom." The ACCF's response to these "hard questions" reinforced the liberal anti-Communist position. "Where does the Communist teacher fit into the scheme of academic freedom? The only reasonable answer is: He does not." The justification for this view followed the familiar reasoning of the New Yorkers: "A member of the Communist party has trangressed the canons of academic responsibility, has engaged his intellect to servility, and is therefore professionally disqualified from performing his functions as a scholar and teacher." But fearing the intrusion of reactionaries and publicity seekers—especially of those unqualified to distinguish heretics from conspirators—the ACCF committee stated that "a teacher's opinions are no concern of the state so long as he reaches them in the course of honest inquiry." The committee concluded, "We see no reason why this matter cannot be left in the hands of the colleges and their faculties, themselves."[184]

The American Committee for Cultural Freedom publicly embraced the various anti-Communist positions, while it reinforced the arguments of individual New York Intellectuals. The impact of these views, taken as a whole, supported another aim of the New Yorkers—in fact, a basic drive of their anticommunism. This effort became clear in one of the ACCF's most important projects, the study by James Rorty and Moshe Decter published in 1954 under the title *McCarthy and the Communists*. Despite some opposition among ACCF liberals like Schlesinger and among conservatives like Burnham, the conclusion of the study dovetailed with the initial motivation for creating a liberal alternative to right-wing anticommunism. In assessing McCarthy's various activities, Rorty and Decter concluded that the true evil was not anticommunism per se but the type practiced by McCarthy. Real, serious anticommunism suffered from its association with this specious version. Their opening chapter, "The Divided Front Against Communism," argued that while "no real disagreement or confusion [existed] among our people about the necessity of resisting Communist military and diplomatic aggrandizement abroad, or of exposing and suppressing Communist espionage and subversion in the United States," McCarthy's actions nonetheless undermined the national unity needed to combat communism. "National unity is precisely what the Communist Party dreads more than anything else. . . . The strategy of the Party line is . . . to confuse, to divide, and ultimately to weaken and sap the strength of this nation." By overplaying his hand and by using unscrupulous methods, McCarthy helped achieve the party's aim. McCarthy's hyperbole—"instead of presenting Owen Lattimore as the skillful, effective and influential Party-lining propagandist he was, [McCarthy] characterized him as the 'top Soviet espionage agent' in America"—only undermined the national effort.[185]

The book's last chapter, "The Real Issue: How to Combat Communism Responsibly," reiterated the liberal anti-Communist position. Rorty and Decter there suggested the similarity between the methods of McCarthy and the Communists, both of which "foster disorder, internal divisions, and the confusion of issues." The "chief damage" of McCarthy's actions "is that genuine anti-Communists have allowed themselves to be set at odds . . . diverted from the serious business of fighting Communist subversion at home and Communist aggrandizement abroad."[186] Liberals must reassert their central position in the anti-Communist struggle, win back the preeminent role from McCarthy and the right. They should do this, the authors stated, to fight communism responsibly and effectively, in order to protect themselves against the wide-ranging assaults of the reactionaries.

As early as 1946 William Phillips had written that "the Left must not permit the struggle against Stalinism to be appropriated by the Right," and many of his New York Intellectual comrades had concurred. Liberal anticommunism emerged to counter the McCarthyite right. Nineteen fifty-four marked the beginning of the end for McCarthy, not because of the indictment by the ACCF or by Rorty and Decter, but because of his reckless assault on the Army, an institution hardly perceived as "soft" on communism and dear to the nation's president-general.

It would be several more years before the right was pushed fully to the periphery, but by the mid-1950s the liberal alternative was firmly in place. The organizational centers of the Congress and the American Committee for Cultural Freedom, with their hard core of New York Intellectuals, provided the institutional (and even quasi-governmental) legitimation of the liberal position. The potential threat that a right-wing hysteria would sweep moderates, liberals, and socialists away with the Communists had been eliminated. Self-protection, as well as a continuation of anti-Stalinism, had been a prime motive for the liberal development, and it succeeded. In addition, the nationwide preoccupation with the "Communist menace" focused new attention on the New York Intellectuals. They found a wider audience for, and more government interest in, their anticommunism than any earlier intellectual or political position had enjoyed. The issue of anticommunism opened previously closed magazines, helped create a new intellectual journal, and brought them into association with public and governmental figures once far removed. Even covert CIA funding provided a measure of satisfaction. "The fact that the CIA knew about *them*," Norman Podhoretz observed, "was itself a measure of how far, for better or worse, they had already traveled from their monastic confines of the thirties."[187]

Their drive for the center meant not only taking a moderate political position but also being accepted into what later became known as the establishment. They gained political influence, modest at first, to complement their intellectual reputation. They had long argued that society should turn to them for guidance, and with the successful establishment of liberal anticommunism it seemed that it had finally begun to happen. All their intellectual and political efforts had been serious and hard-fought—from their youthful socialism and belief in proletarian literature to their revised liberalism. This time, the historical moment matched the intellectual effort, and they won the day. The achievements of liberal anticommunism extended far beyond the questions asked, and the successes long outlived the resolution of the issues at hand.

Chapter 12

Sensations of Wisdom, Stamina, and Poise

In 1947, at the age of forty-two, Lionel Trilling published his only novel, *The Middle of the Journey*. Various political and intellectual themes swirled through the book, including the thinly disguised portrait of Whittaker Chambers. One significant underlying theme, embodied in Trilling's hero John Laskell, spoke to a changed perspective settling in among a number of Trilling's fellow intellectuals. Beyond any specific political issue, Laskell experienced the sense . . . that there really was no future.

> He did not mean that *he* had no future. He meant that the future and the present were one—that the present could no longer contrive and manufacture the future by throwing forward, on the form of expectation and hope, the desires of the present moment. It was not that he "lost hope," but only that he did not make a distinction between what he now had and was and what he expected to have and be.
>
> What happened to Laskell, all at once, was that he realized that you couldn't live the life of promises without yourself remaining a child. The promise of the future might have its uses as a way of seducing the child to maturity, but maturity itself meant that the future and the present were brought together, that you yourself lived *now* instead of preparing and committing yourself to some better day to come.[1]

Forty-two might seem an advanced age at which to begin to think about the transition from childhood to maturity. There is no question that in many respects, Lionel Trilling and the other New York Intellectuals had felt themselves mature individuals for many years. In fact, many of them had been required to take on adult responsibilities earlier than usual. Diana Trilling told of the enormous family burden which weighed on her husband at a very young age. Philip Rahv found himself a fourteen-year-old immigrant boy in

Providence schools and as a young man had bummed about the West, sleeping on park benches. Daniel Bell had delivered street-corner speeches for Socialist candidates while still a teenager. Yet these are all personal experiences reflecting individual concerns and family matters.

What Trilling was saying about John Laskell pertains to a larger sense of development and maturity. From the first, the New York Intellectuals' own sense of time and normal progression had been distorted. Throughout their younger days, the traditional signposts by which to judge one's own growth and that of one's peers—even of one's generation—had been discarded. As children they had felt the undue pressures for success at a very early age and been made aware of the degree to which their own achievement was bound up with that of their parents. Those of the first generation were poised to embark on careers in the late 1920s when the Depression disrupted their lives. Success was postponed, replaced by visions of a better day to come. Their radicalism during the 1930s provided some comfort amid the hard times, but it looked to a brighter future rather than to a secure present. The younger intellectuals, entering college during the Depression years, faced a different, but equally unusual, situation. They experienced a sense of "airlessness" brought on by the belief that few prospects awaited their generation. Finally, the war changed them all again. The younger group moved abruptly from a sense of having no prospects to the prospect of battle and death. Even the older intellectuals found themselves affected by the war. The sense of stasis on the home front during wartime added a new kind of limbo to that of the 1930s. In a short story published two years before his novel, Trilling had one character express the growing understanding of both the sense of distortion and the change under way beneath the surface. Like Trilling, the character Elwin had been too young for the First World War, "for the other too old, though by no means, of course, old." The war and the awareness of age which it brought prompted "the desire to have 'wisdom.' More and more in the last few months, Elwin had been able to experience the sensation of being wise, for it was indeed a sensation, a feeling of stamina, poise, and illumination."[2]

The members of the elder generation felt old, but they were by no means old. They had, as Bell and Trilling pointed out, been extremely young in the 1930s, in their late twenties or early thirties during the first days of the "new" *PR*.[3] Trilling and his characters Laskell and Elwin did not really feel "old." Instead, in the postwar years, with the Depression and the war behind them, the New York Intellectuals began to have a new sense of themselves and of the world around them—a realization that, as Laskell observes, "the future and the present were one." This realization, so long in coming and so vital in overcoming past notions about the world, might bring on feelings of aging. Having spent so much of their lives looking ahead and seeking change, they might, like John Laskell, remember "with a kind regret that [they] once dreamed of fame, even of immortality, where [they] were now concerned with only a sound professional reputation."[4] They had dreamed for years as immigrant youths and as young radicals of brighter tomorrows. After World War II they began to look around at their contemporary situation and tended to find it not displeasing at all.

For the younger intellectuals, the times had played different tricks. Feeling many of the same pressures in their youth as the elders, those of the second generation had been subject through much of their young lives to the added impact of the Depression. Crucial years had been jammed with events— adolescence and college mixed with Depression, radicalism, and war. So much had happened, and yet Irving Howe could recall, "The crucial fact for me was that [in 1949] I still was only twenty-nine years old."[5] The drives of past days remained—Howe identified them as "personal intensity, ambition, energy." For both generations normal development had been thrown off, intensified and distorted by Depression and war. The elders, in their middle and late forties in 1950, and the second generation, in their late twenties and early thirties, had finally arrived in the postwar years. To a degree, they became more equal partners. The older generation had not been cast aside by the younger; rather it led its own "counter-revolt," as Bell noted. Together they set about creating the main elements of their postwar philosophy—revised liberalism, the social utility of intellectuals, liberal anticommunism. As before, they did not always agree. But they all came into their own, the older and the younger. *Partisan Review* remained in the hands of two "elders," Phillips and Rahv, while *Dissent* was founded by one of the second generation, Howe. *Commentary* continued under Cohen, an older intellectual, and would ultimately pass, though not smoothly, to Norman Podhoretz, a member of the small third generation. Reputations of second-generation members—Kazin, Bell, Howe, Fiedler— grew to a level close to that of the most influential elders.

The first generation had carried on the two essential tasks of creating the community and of bringing it to prominence. In this second endeavor it had been joined by the members of the second generation, the young intellecuals and writers who had looked to *PR* and its writers as the source of their intellectual inspiration in the late 1930s. Coming of age, these younger individuals began to attach themselves to both the journals and the world of the elders. They helped each other make the transition to the postwar years. In some cases, the ideas of the second generation helped carry the first along. Podhoretz remembered that these younger intellectuals, "Schwartz, Bellow, Rosenfeld, Kazin, Fiedler, and Howe—products every one of Yiddish-speaking households—all proclaimed their Jewishness, took relish to it."[6] They preceded the first generation in this search, which they pursued with an intensity the once-cosmopolitan older ex-radicals could never really feel. Then too, the interest in Freud grew more strongly among the second generation—which helped raise the status of Lionel Trilling to the level of the most significant of the first generation.

The members of the second generation showed as much variety and aggressiveness as their older counterparts. And they did not join the community as passive acolytes, devoted to the words of their elders. Passivity in intellectual matters was never the style of any of these individuals, in either generation. They did reject particular elements of the earlier intellectual positions once argued by the *Partisan* writers, but so did the *Partisan* writers. They all joined in the revisions and understandings of the postwar years. Still, some conflict arose—personal and intellectual, as well as generational. Lionel Trilling for a time felt estranged from the *Commentary* editor Robert Warshow, for example. While some tension obviously stemmed from Trilling's commitment to highbrow cultural standards and Warshow's interest in popular culture, especially movies, there were other causes as well. "The reason for the hostility was one of those undefined but powerful antagonisms between members of different literary and cultural generations," Trilling admitted. "Our first alienation from each other was in part a matter of generations of, as it were, the cultural family."[7]

As the cultural family developed, a small third generation emerged. Its connections and relationships proved significantly different, however, from the ties between the first two. Whereas the second generation had been drawn to the radical intellectuals at *Partisan Review*, the third generation came under the influence of the academic eminence of some older members, particularly Lionel Trilling. "There is a kind of laying on of hands," Leslie Fiedler said, regarding this connection. "Norman Podhoretz and Steven Marcus are products of Lionel Trilling." The interrelation extended beyond the classroom. "Diana [Trilling], who played a very active role in this, always took a motherly role to both of them," Daniel Bell recalled. "Lionel was very pleased to have students, people who really acknowledged him as a strong intellectual influence."[8] Others would at times be identified as third-generation members—Midge Decter, Norman Mailer, Susan Sontag, Michael Harrington, Theodore Solotaroff, Jason Epstein, Philip Roth—but the changing times and world made it impossible for the third generation to take hold as the first two had done. Fame came to a number of these—Mailer, Sontag, Roth—and carried them in various directions before connections ever became really firm. There were also political differences, exacerbated by the upheavals of the 1960s. Most important, the first two generations had avoided too many serious splits because the maturing second generation joined the first at a point of transition and because they carved out new positions together. The third generation arrived when the orientation had shifted from future to present, when ideas were more firmly rooted, and the desire of the young to create their own identity led them to reject the old individuals and not just the old ideas. And finally, the community itself did not maintain the kind of cohesion it had once possessed. The youngest intellectuals found themselves drawn to individuals—Podhoretz and Marcus to Trilling, Harrington to Howe—rather than to the group.

These newest members did find a social network firmly established of which they could now become a part. The Upper West Side, Wellfleet, and Martha's Vineyard now replaced City College and the Village as centers of their social whirl. They all still attended each other's parties, still gossiped to one another. Dwight Madonald wrote to F.W. Dupee, filling him in on the latest events:

It now seems that Diana was wrong about Mary [McCarthy] and Jim [West] splitting.... Hannah Arendt tells me she had heard nothing of it from Mary. Speaking of Mary, had a run-in with Kazin other night at party.... He got huffy instantly.... He reminded me of Bellow in [the] way he responded to criticism. Not that any of us are stars in that dept.... However, to adapt Trotsky's famous mot re[garding] me: We're all human but Kazin abuses the privilege."

In another note Macdonald asked Dupee, "Why don't you and Andy [Dupee's wife] join us, if you are on the town New Year's Eve, in going to Dan Bell's party and then Hannah Arendt's."[9] Alfred Kazin described summers at Wellfleet, where Irving Howe, Richard Hofstadter, Edmund Wilson, Jason Epstein, and Philip Roth were also to be found. Despite Wellfleet summers together, Kazin and Howe never "hit it off," according to Kazin. "Irving is a man I don't regard myself at all like." Similarly, Kazin said in 1976 that he was never especially close to Daniel Bell—"even though he is my brother-in-law."[10] Success may have led the New Yorkers to move to better neighborhoods or classier summer retreats, but the mixture of their friendship and abrasiveness followed them.

One significant change can be seen in the manner in which the new young members attached themselves to the group. Norman Podhoretz recounted the exhilaration of being drawn into the circle—the thrill not merely of being asked to publish in the major journals but of knowing the prominent intellectuals personally and being made privy to their personal world. Regarding his start as a critic, Podhoretz wrote,

> Any praise I got and any attention I could attract would be all to the good, but it was the attention of the family I most dreamed of arousing. . . .there was nothing I loved better than to sit around with Warshow or Greenberg and listen (my wide-eyed worshipful fascination egging them on) to tales of the patriarchal past: how "Mary" had left "Philip" to marry Edmund Wilson . . . how "Dwight" had once organized nude swimming parties on the Cape, how "William" really felt about "Delmore," how "Isaac" really felt about "Saul." Oh to be granted the right to say "William" and "Philip" and "Dwight," as I could already say "Bob" and "Clem" and "Nat" [Glazer].[11]

In the early chapters of his memoir *Making It*, Podhoretz told the tale of his coming to feel he was truly a "New York literary intellectual." The significant change is not that Podhoretz or any bright young critic could or would want to move into this circle but that his attachment was to a group already established in the intellectual world and full of a past for which its members feel nostalgia and which its young devotees regret having missed. The memoirs of the elders spoke of the coming together of the group. The second generation remembered how it joined a coterie distinctly on the margin of intellectual life. But a young intellectual like Podhoretz felt he was joining a group at the very center. And that is where they were. The older intellectuals—first and second generation— came into their own in the years after the war and eventually shared with

Trilling's character "the sensation of being wise, . . . a feeling of stamina, poise, and illumination." Having looked to a brighter future for years, they found a satisfactory present. They possessed the "wisdom of age," without being old and while maintaining much of their youthful energy. They arrived in the 1950s with an ideal combination of drive and perspective and with the security of an established intellectual community. They intended not to rest on their laurels but to increase them.

DISSENTERS AND DISSENT

The New York Intellectuals did not settle into a postwar complacency. Nor did they appreciably soften their intellectual aggressiveness or approach to one another. They remained abrasive and tough, in print as well as in person. The style that had brought them into prominence remained. What changed in their internal discussions and interpersonal frictions was not readily apparent at the time. Only in later years did the intellectuals begin to understand that when they had been on the periphery, when the only people listening to them were other intellectuals, the combativeness had helped keep the community alive. The testing of ideas against each other in the 1930s, the gossiping and sniping in a social world of which only they were fully aware provided much of the community's forward momentum. The acceptance in the larger society of their ideas and of themselves changed the results of aggressive interactions. The intellectual criticisms and petty personal gibes ceased to be a cohesive force and began to weaken the fabric of the community. They no longer looked at the future as a path out of the unhappy present. Instead, they saw a satisfactory today evolving into a more satisfactory tomorrow. The liberal notion of progress replaced the radical beliefs of the past years. Their criticisms of each other became critiques of what they had become—the people they had chosen to be.

All this, however, could be understood only in hindsight. They had always battled, carried grudges and dislikes, even fought with their fists. And they continued to do so. Various New Yorkers found it difficult to accept certain portions of the postwar package of revised liberalism, intellectual relevancy, and liberal anticommunism. Some of these individuals began to be perceived as a kind of permanent minority camp within the community, and they organized a journal, *Dissent*, to present their contrary views. They remained vitally aware of one another even as they expressed their criticisms in extremely harsh terms. Like prizefighters in a traveling carnival, they might be combatants but they remained part of the same show.

The postwar precepts of the New York Intellectuals did not sit comfortably with every member of the community. Alfred Kazin, whose reactions against the failure of thirties radicalism were more a pulling back from politics than a finding of a new political position,[12] expressed his concern with the revised or "new" liberalism advanced by Schlesinger, Trilling, and the others. He found the same motives at work in the 1950s as in the 1930s, but with a new vocabulary and place on the political spectrum. Kazin felt unhappy with the "infatuation with abstractions," the "wish to believe names equal to things." This derived from revised liberalism's "extreme self-consciousness as an educational elite, from the academic tendency to see the artists as a corpus of knowledge . . . and from the old alienation that still sits deeper than its grateful affection for the American advantage in the struggle against totalitarianism."[13] Irving Howe pushed the critique even further, arguing against the connections being made, especially by Trilling, between liberalism and literature. Rather than a natural outpouring of positive Americanism, Howe felt the acceptance to be "largely a product of the will, a forced march of the intellect." A true period of affirmation, Howe believed, brings "energy, enthusiasm, hope." As for the liberal writers "who find comfort in the virtues of moderation and mildness, why is their work so often drenched in gloom?" Succinctly, Howe criticized the notion of the liberal imagination by asking how the intellectuals of liberalism can "believe the ADA program offers a proper amelioration for our social problems while they find Kafka the image of the quality of our life."[14]

The newly found place for intellectuals, down from the ivory tower and in the thick of contemporary questions, also troubled some dissenters. While not arguing for scholarly isolation or pure abstraction, some of the intellectuals found that the ease with which some of their peers accepted American society, and with which it accepted them, compromised their proper intellectual roles. A preoccupation with "the ideal of practicality, of a politics and social philosophy stripped of 'myth' and 'ineffectiveness,' of a subordination to 'reality' "—all these trends troubled Harold Rosenberg. "This is the drug that has transformed the fighting Dr. Jekyll into the bureaucratic and 'responsible' Mr. Hyde." The real trouble, Rosenberg argued, "is that the somnambulist Hyde dreams not only that he alone is awake but that he is vigorously bringing into being the very same world that his original could only feebly imagine."[15]

Irving Howe launched a more complete attack on the changes in intellectual activity, publishing an important article which was widely discussed among the New York Intellectuals. "This Age of Conformity," published in *Partisan Review* in 1954, took direct aim at the choices made by Howe's contemporaries. In its most recent stage, capitalism "had found an honored place for intellectuals," Howe claimed, and they "have been enjoying a return to the bosom of the nation." Howe's critique was directed not at those who he believed had "sold out" but rather at the "far more prevalent and far more insidious . . . slow attrition which destroys one's ability to stand firm and alone." Even those, like himself, who tried to retain a critical stance had become "responsible and moderate [and] tame." For others, the slippage into conformity occurred almost unnoticed, piecemeal rather than in some large confessional conversion. "Conformity," Howe wrote, paraphrasing Arthur Koestler, "is often a form of betrayal," and "betrayal may consist of a chain of small compromises." Two years earlier Lionel Trilling had argued that intellect had "associated itself with power as perhaps never before in history." Howe found this general trend disturbing: "Whenever [intellectuals] become absorbed into the accredited institutions of society they not only lose their traditional rebelliousness but to one extent or another *they cease to function as intellectuals.*"[16]

What is telling about Howe's analysis is its appreciation both of the slow evolution of this attitude and the degree to which it is more difficult to resist the trend than accept it. He was aware, he said, that "what one conforms to most of all—despite and against one's intention—is the *Zeitgeist.*" One drifts along, anxious and compliant, on the forward assumptions of the moment, and "not a soul in the intellectual world can escape this." Harking back to their radical days in the 1930s, Howe reminded his fellow intellectuals that once before they resisted the zeitgeist, when "those who hovered about the *New Masses* were mere camp-followers of success." The break with Stalinism, the *New Masses*, and the League of American Writers and the forming of *Partisan Review* to preserve their radicalism exhibited a determination to swim against the tide without casting off essential ideas. As difficult as that resistance had been, the contemporary zeitgeist proved even more seductive: "Today the *Zeitgeist* presses down upon us with a greater insistence than at any other moment of the century . . . established power and dominant intellectual tendencies have come together in a harmony such as this country has not seen since the Gilded Age; and this, of course, makes the temptations of conformism all the more acute. The carrots, for once are real." A "weariness" had settled in among intellectuals, Howe believed, stemming from "an age of defeat and their yearning to remove themselves from the bloodied arena of historical action and choice."[17] While understanding this tendency, Howe warned against it, fearing that complacency, lethargy, and even sleep would result from weariness.

Howe's piece caused something of a stir when it was published and was later frequently cited, especially by cold-war critics, as an example of intellectual independence during these years.[18] Among his contemporaries it provoked a hostile reaction. Robert Warshow answered in a long letter to *PR*, taking issue with Howe's points and his actions. Warshow opened his rejoinder with a story about Howe:

> The story is told during the years when Professor (then Mr.) Irving Howe worked as a writer for *Time*—on a part-time basis—he met one day in the corridors of the Time-Life Building an acquaintance whom he had known only in the less commercialized world. "My God," said Mr. Howe, immediately taking the offensive, "what are *you* doing here?" "Why, I'm working here," said his acquaintance. "*Full-Time?*" said Mr. Howe.

With this one story Warshow was not through; rather, he went on to chastise Howe for his criticisms of the "methods" by which literary criticism was taught in America. "What are we to say, then, to the advertisements for the summer session of the School of Letters of Indiana University," Warshow inquired, "offering 'courses on the graduate level in the theory and practice of literary criticism,' and listing Professor Howe as one of the Fellows of the School (not yet a Senior Fellow, to be sure)?"

From these personal attacks, Warshow then turned to a personal defense of those under criticism. "Let us ask, then, what Professor Howe is saying. Who are these 'conformists' who have put the deadly stamp of uniformity on our 'age'?" Warshow listed a number of individuals and groups, beginning with "Lionel Trilling, Sidney Hook, Russell Kirk, Arthur Schlesinger, Jr., Peter Viereck, Mary McCarthy," and going on to include "the editors of *Commentary*" and "the membership of the Committee for Cultural Freedom." Warshow aimed to show great diversity among the "conformists." "Certainly they are not conforming to each other," he declared. But the defense of individuals, especially those associated with the New York Intellectuals, forms the core of his argument. His mock list of what "non-conforming" intellectuals must do includes the following:

- You must not be pleased at anything in the present cultural situation. (That's where Lionel Trilling made his mistake.)
- You must not discover any justification for the Smith Act. (That takes care of Sidney Hook.)
- Don't suggest that class barriers are becoming less rigid in America. (There goes Mary McCarthy.)[19]

There is no question that Howe, in making his criticism, and those responding to it, clearly saw this question in personal as well as intellectual terms. What some individuals had become was under attack, and they rose to defend one another. Despite their vaunted independence and nonconformism, the intellectuals provided surprisingly little written support for Howe's position. Rosenberg did continue his critical assessment of the path intellectuals had taken. And a new voice on the periphery of the community, Norman Mailer's, also chided intellectuals for their current style.[20]

One intellectual's attitude is particularly telling, especially in its relation to Howe's article. Philip Rahv, one of the central forces, if not *the* central force, behind the formation of the community, had begun to drift away from the intellectual road taken by his peers. Personally aggressive, Rahv did not, however, initially chastise his contemporaries—at least not in print. Instead, he encouraged Howe. Howe recalled the origin of "This Age of Conformity" simply: "Philip put me up to it."

He wasn't a very courageous person; he wouldn't stick his neck out. He wanted such a piece to be written, but he wouldn't write it himself. So he commissioned me to do it, and I didn't suffer for it . . . . Rahv was so cautious he out-smarted himself . . . . I got the attention and he didn't.[21]

Rahv's views did not remain entirely under wraps during the 1950s. Rather, he seemed unwilling to blaze the trail of resisting intellectual conformity. By 1956 his position had became sufficiently apparent for Diana Trilling to complain in *Commentary* that Rahv possessed a "careful tolerance for anti-Americanism," deriving, she believed, "from the fear of conformity, that bogeyman of contemporary intellectual life."[22] Beyond his fear of conformism, Rahv began to express another viewpoint which deviated from the basic postwar position. Gradually, his old friend William Barrett recalled, Rahv dropped his hard anti-communism. One of the most vehement anti-Stalinists and critics of fellow travelers, Rahv now began to criticize anti-communism. Barrett believes that Rahv's intense focus on the person of Stalin accounts for this change. After the death of the Russian leader—"the diabolic figure who had corrupted the revolution"—Rahv hoped for a revitalization of revolutionary purity and a liberalization of the Soviet regime.[23]

Rahv had been critical of portions of the liberal anticommunism from the outset, although he never took an anti-anti-Communist position. He believed that some ex-radicals and ex-Marxists had gone too far, had become "scarcely distinguishable from the common run of philistines." Their anti-Stalinism had grown to be a "professional stance . . . exclud[ing] all other concerns and ideas." He feared that anti-Stalinism had become "a total outlook on life, no less, or even a philosophy of history."[24] Rahv's political ideas would continue to diverge from his fellow New Yorkers during the 1950s, especially after he left New York for a teaching job at Brandeis. This straying from the central line toed by most New York Intellectuals marked an important turning point for the community. While William Phillips maintained a hard liberal anticommunism and served on the ACCF's executive board, Rahv demurred. The internal wars at *Partisan Review*, rekindled, ultimately separating the two editors. For the moment, however, the divergence of the two founders of *PR* was a symbol of the drifting apart of the community these two had helped create.

Rahv did not stand alone in his criticism of liberal anticommunism. None of the New York Intellectuals exhibited much "softness" on communism, none argued the anti-anti-Communist view, and, certainly, none could be accused of Stalinism or fellow traveling. But a few felt that the stridency of the liberal position and the qualified critique of McCarthy—opposing his methods rather than his ends—were inappropriate. Meyer Schapiro, for one, later recalled that while willing to join any movement which would resist political repression worldwide, he declined to join the Congress for Cultural Freedom because of its sole focus on the Soviet Union. Furthermore, he disagreed with Elliot Cohen and Sidney Hook, both of whom he considered too tolerant of McCarthyism. "Elliot Cohen was nearly hysterical on the subject," Schapiro said. "And it was astounding to me that Hook, as a Deweyan, could separate means from ends."[25]

Irving Howe, once again standing in public opposition to other New York Intellectuals, extended his criticisms to the methods of the liberal anti-

Communist position. He argued that *Commentary* had taken the wrong tack in the civil liberties debate, citing articles by Kristol, Cohen, and Nathan Glazer. Howe thought "the magazine was more deeply preoccupied . . . with the dangers to freedom stemming from people like [the *Nation* editor] Freda Kirchwey and Arthur Miller than the dangers from people like Senator McCarthy." Howe did not seek to defend the *Nation's* kind of liberalism. In fact, he bemoaned the fact that though the *Nation* provided more information about civil liberties violations that any other journal, it aimed for a "quasi-appeasement of Stalin." This demonstrated "the failure of the other, more powerful wing of liberalism to do its job . . . those sophisticated liberals who read *Commentary* and think of Sidney Hook as their intellectual spokesman." Howe also found the rigidity of the liberal anti-Communist line inappropriate. When Diana Trilling served as executive secretary of the ACCF, Howe felt she was behaving "like the 'general secretary' of a radical sect, whose main joy in life is hunting for deviations among the other sects and chastising those who stray from the proper 'line.' "[26]

More than individual issues emerged from this questioning of liberal anti-communism, more even than the relative merits of the entire anti-Communist position. It went to what Rahv called the "total outlook on life." Recalling the divergent positions between Howe and some of his fellow anti-Communist intellectuals, Daniel Bell thought a key difference "between Irving and some of us—myself, Kristol, Hook, Lasky—is that I don't think Irving had a deep involvement in European intellectual life." Their belonging to and working with the Congress for Cultural Freedom provided a "first-hand experience with the events of the 1950s—the postwar purge trials, the murder of Masaryk, and such," Bell explained.

> Living in London and Paris, we became aware of the power of Communist domination in the intellectual milieu. Anti-Communist intellectuals were isolated, with no possibility of finding outlets. We may have overreacted, but Irving could maintain a more distant stance. Irving never has had the feeling of being harassed—a tangible feeling of conflict. People on the sideline never get involved.[27]

Here Bell made a distinction drawn directly from the changed position of intellectuals in the postwar years. Howe was never an ivory-tower intellectual. His ties to radical groups, for example, lasted longer than those of most other New Yorkers. And his anti-Soviet attitude—including purge trials, Masaryk, "and such"—never flagged. Nonetheless, it is his failure to have a "deep involvement" which Bell saw as crucial. By "deep involvement" Bell meant joining with a group which would provide "first-hand experience," such as the CCF, especially of the true European scene. Howe stayed on the "sideline," refusing to join the intellectual army out to defend freedom. That Howe surely believed that he, too, was defending freedom was irrelevant, in Bell's analysis. Intellectuals now had the opportunity to function at the center. They had to seize it. "There were only a few of us . . . who didn't go along with that,"

Howe recalled. "We were decidedly in the minority."[28] The minority was to become, in many ways, a permanent one.

A measure of the degree to which this group began to think of itself as a permanent minority came with the founding of a new intellectual journal, intended to represent its position most directly. Clearly, *Commentary* and the *New Leader* proved inhospitable, since they offered the hardest line in the liberal anti-Communist camp. Even *Partisan Review*, which had published Howe's intellectual attack on conformity, while being, "of course, opposed to McCarthy's campaign . . . failed to take the lead on the issue of freedom," Howe recalled. "The magazine," despite its share of critical articles, "failed to speak out with enough force and persistence, or to break past the hedgings of those intellectuals who led the American Committee for Cultural Freedom."[29] Thus, *Dissent* was born, attempting to draw together intellectuals critical of the postwar liberal line. The major force behind the magazine, from its initial appearance to the present day, Irving Howe later saw the reasons for the journal's founding as twofold: "First, the reaction to what was going on in the intellectual milieu. But perhaps more importantly, a reaction to the gradual but steady disintegration of the socialist movement." Looking at the current intellectual and political drift, the founders of *Dissent* felt "the life of the political sect had become intolerable and it was necessary to break out and try something fresher, newer, or better." Maintaining a commitment to socialism, Howe perceived their task as keeping an idea alive for the future. Meyer Schapiro, another founder, remembered the impetus more simply. Because of McCarthyism, the journal aimed to "defend 'dissent' and socialist ideas," wanting the journal to appeal to ex-Communists and ex-Trotskyists, critical of both the right and the Soviet Union.[30]

Dissent began on a small scale. "We thought if we could raise $10,000, we could publish," Schapiro recalled. "There was another group—Arthur Schlesinger, Mary McCarthy, Dwight Macdonald—who wanted to start a journal. They thought they needed $100,000. They raised $60,000 and didn't do it. *Dissent* raised $6,000 and started." In the winter of 1954 the first issue appeared, with a six-person editorial board, including Howe and Schapiro.[31] Among the contributing editors were Erich Fromm, Norman Mailer, and A. J. Muste. *Dissent* attempted to gather a wide variety of socialist intellectuals, relying less heavily on New York Intellectuals than either *Commentary* or *Partisan Review*. These journals had their large share of "outsiders" among the writers—*PR* always had various literary contributors, *Commentary* its Jewish ones. But *Dissent*, while always in the hands of Irving Howe, aimed to create a new grouping within the larger intellectual world of New York. In the recently collected *25 Years of Dissent*, only Howe and Harold Rosenberg, of the twenty-seven contributors, could be counted as central New York Intellectuals.[32]

The opening editorial of *Dissent* promised the kind of alternative Howe and the others had been seeking: "to dissent from the bleak atmosphere of conformism . . . from the support of the *status quo* . . . from the idle assumption that a new war is necessary or inevitable." Proudly proclaiming that the "accent of *Dissent* will be radical," the editors promised to keep it in the "tradition of democratic socialism": "We shall try to reassert the libertarian values of the socialist ideal, and at the same time, to discuss freely and honestly what in the socialist tradition remains alive and what needs to be discarded or modified." Despite these bold claims—made bolder by the times—*Dissent* showed itself to be a part of the postwar ethos by the description of its future contributors. "Our magazine will be open to a wide arc of opinion," the editors promised, "excluding only Stalinists and totalitarian fellow-travelers on the one hand, and those former radicals who have signed their peace with society as it is, on the other."[33] *Commentary* and *PR* also excluded ex-radicals who went all the way to the McCarthyite right, such as Burnham or Eastman. *Dissent* enlarged the group it felt had capitulated to contemporary society. But in setting itself between the two hostile camps, Stalinists and extreme American patriots—the division all liberals made in the postwar world—the editors at *Dissent* put their dissent on the preestablished basis of postwar liberalism, rather than going off into a new territory. They were as locked in by their diminishing radicalism, anti-Stalinism, fear of the McCarthyite hysteria, and commitment to cultural standards as were the liberals they assailed. The magazine played the role of permanent devil's advocate in the increasingly complacent world of postwar liberalism. But it was a fixed part of the postwar constellation, spinning around the liberal anti-Communist center but never shooting off into uncharted and unexplored realms.

A good part of the momentum for *Dissent* stemmed from the personality of its chief editor, Irving Howe. Howe had for years been associated with the New York Intellectuals, beginning with his days in the City College lunchroom. He was, as Bell remembers, the "commissar" of the Trotskyists. Yet Howe always had a kind of adversary relation with his fellow intellectuals, critical of some of their ideas but always connected to them. In 1942, for example, he published a critique of *Partisan Review* in the Trotskyist journal *New International*. Yet Howe later admitted that the first thing people said, when introducing him to an audience in the late 1940s and early 1950s, was "Mr. Howe writes for *Partisan Review*!" "That didn't totally define me," Howe remarked, "but it was almost sufficient."[34] Howe earned the grudging respect, if not the warm friendship or admiration, of some of his peers. This was due in part to his politics, in part to his personality, and in part to the career adjustment he made in the early 1950s. Having committed himself to politics in his early years, Howe went on to do a year and a half of graduate work in English. But his main attention remained on political questions. "He sort of entered literature via the backdoor," Leslie Fiedler observed. Fiedler, to whom Howe made a number of unkind references, assessed Howe's coming to literary criticism by quoting Randall Jarrell: "The only trouble with Mr. Howe is that he hates literature. He's just without an occupation since his politics collapsed." Yet, Howe's persistence and prolific publishing earned him acceptance by others. "Howe is ability incarnate," Clement Greenberg observed. "He has tremendous confidence. Irving now is a famous critic, but I can't read him myself."[35]

Howe himself always proved no less aggressive in his characterizations of other intellectuals. Taking careful aim at the larger philosophical position cast by the postwar liberals, Howe criticized it in both intellectual and personal terms. The "dominant school of liberalism—the school for which Sidney Hook is philosopher, David Riesman sociologist, and Lionel Trilling literary moralist—exempts itself from its own analysis and recommendations," Howe asserted. "Few things are more dogmatic today than the anti-dogmatism of the liberal intellectual, few things more closed than the famous open mind." In another article, Howe took exception to the positions Hook had been arguing. While he did not name the NYU philosopher, the connections were unmistakable. "How easy it is to attack and destroy 'the ritual liberals,' those that is, who favor unconditional civil liberties with respect to the Stalinist problem. How easy it is to offer the 'sophisticated' notion that Stalinists have no claim upon civil liberties because they are intent upon destroying them."[36]

Howe did not confine his criticisms to personal attacks or liberal naysaying. He did stake out some positions in marked contrast to the hard liberal anti-Communist ones. Rather than minimizing the McCarthyite threat, as Kristol and Cohen had done, or opting for a the-best-defense-is-a-good-offense strategy, he declared his concern over the fate of intellectual freedom and civil liberties. Again casting himself between the stringent anti-Communists and the "ritual liberals," Howe thought real problems did exist: "Between the willfulness of those who see only terror [the anti-anti-Communists and the fellow travelers] and those who see only health [the hard anti-Communists] there is need for simple truth: that intellectual freedom in the United States is under severe attack and that the intellectuals have, by and large, shown a painful lack of militancy in defending the rights which are a precondition of their existence." Yet even when arguing the case for concern over questions of civil liberties, he could lapse into the biting style of his intellectual coterie. He related the story of an Indiana State textbook commissioner who wanted to investigate Robin Hood, believing that the outlaw's robbing from the rich to give to the poor demonstrated a Communist attitude. "Can one, should one, laugh today? Is it really funny?" Howe asked. "To be sure, there are some quarters that don't feel worried at all, that seem to imply, in fact, that there is no need for concern until Sidney Hook is accused of robbing the rich to help the poor."[37]

Howe's largest concern, the one which was the real impetus for *Dissent*, did distinguish him from other New York Intellectuals. Whereas many of his contemporaries began to accept a revised liberal view, complete with a pragmatic approach to social ills and with the New Deal–style of problem solving, Howe maintained a radical stance. Although his was a relatively mild radicalism, he nonetheless did not abandon it for liberalism. In the "Our Country and Its Culture" symposium of 1952, Howe reaffirmed the older beliefs: "Marxism seems to me the best available method for understanding and making history. Even at its most dogmatic, it proposes a more realistic theory of society than the currently popular liberalism." This liberalism, "in an age of catastrophe, forsees an America blandly coasting through a series of New Deals." And while persisting in his anti-Stalinism, he saw it in the more traditional, late-1930s mold of a radical alternative. The threat of Stalinism, he believed, might require "temporary expedients in the area of *power*," but this did not demand "conformity in the area of *ideas*." Intellectuals should not "become partisans of bourgeois society," he declared.[38]

Dissent's initial attack on the liberal support for the status quo and its call for the maintenance of a socialist tradition brought an equally strident response from those it criticized. Perhaps fearing that *Dissent* would, in fact, draw intellectuals away from postwar liberalism and back toward the radicalism of the past, *Commentary* ran a long critique of the new magazine, written by Nathan Glazer. In "Philistine Leftism," Glazer characterized the brand of radicalism preached by *Dissent* as "left-wing socialism." He contended that many people, himself included, considered themselves socialists and yet dissociated themselves from *Dissent*. Charging that the *Dissent* crowd showed the same innocent myopia as the civil libertarians or unwitting fellow travelers, Glazer suggested that if the " 'independent radicals' editing *Dissent* had had their way in the last ten years, the NKVD would be comfortably established today in Rome, Paris, and London, at least." In an example remarkable for its prophetic qualities, Glazer scored one particular article in *Dissent*, an attack by Lewis Coser on American policy in Indochina. Coser in 1954 described the American policy as "imperialism." Glazer remarked, "It would seem that one of the 'immediate demands' of *Dissent* is that we hasten to permit the NKVD to set up its quarters in Saigon and Hanoi." A shortsighted approach to foreign policy was not the only fault Glazer found with the magazine. Quoting from the opening editorial, which promised a "wide arc of opinion," Glazer countered with the most severe analogy available. "Perhaps no more remarkable spectrum has been conceived of since *Mein Kampf*. One wonders what the editors plan to do about Royalists, aristocrats, anti-Semites, and the other non-signers of peace with society."[39] Glazer had used the most potent weapon in his intellectual arsenal, an implicit claim that *Dissent* was soft on communism and as wrongheaded as Nazism.

Within a few years, however, the attitude toward *Dissent* had become more benign, being closer to a dismissal for irrelevance than to a fear of its critique. In 1959 Daniel Bell noted that most of *Dissent*'s polemics remained "in that large, exotic cauldron that is the New York intellectual world." "*Dissent* attacked *Partisan Review* and *Commentary* for not being radical," Bell wrote. "But, other than attacking these magazines, there was little in *Dissent* itself that was new; it never exemplified what it meant by radicalism; and it has not been able, especially in politics, to propose anything new."[40] To younger intellectuals, making their way into the New York Intellectual world, *Dissent* did not generate much electricity. Norman Podhoretz, who despite his connections with Trilling and with *Commentary* found himself unfulfilled by postwar liberalism by the late 1950s, still did not consider *Dissent* an appealing alternative. In 1958 Podhoretz wrote that *Dissent* spoke "largely in the tired accents of an old-fashioned central European socialism." Of its growing influence, he could conclude only that it represented "a nostalgia for the grand passions and selfless dedication that democratic socialism once had no trouble breeding in its adherents."[41]

Dissent settled, quite comfortably, into its role as the minority voice among the 1950s intellectuals and has continued to maintain it, despite the rise (and fall) of various left journals. In part, despite Glazer's initial characterization, its continuance stems from the mildness of its radicalism. "I've never understood what Howe and [Michael] Harrington mean by socialism exactly," Dwight Macdonald said, "if all they mean is what you have in the German socialist democracy today or the British Labour party. I don't see that that is anything radical." "*Dissent*," Leslie Fiedler summarized, "turns out not to be dissenting at all."[42]

Fiedler is both right and wrong. For Howe, as for the others, the experiences of the 1930s marked the beliefs of the 1950s. Howe came to *Dissent* with neither the "tired accent of European socialism" which Podhoretz heard nor the radical distinctiveness which the journal itself proclaimed. He came, instead, with the same battle scars and intellectual evolution as the other New York Intellectuals, perhaps offering different answers but seeing world problems from the same perspective. "It would be a great error if we did not insist upon reminding people that we were right—whatever our shade of socialist or radical opinion," Howe wrote in *Dissent* in 1956, "we who for thirty bitter years kept up the fight against Stalinism. Modesty or immodesty is irrelevant here: there is a deep moral-political necessity for keeping the record clear."[43] On crucial questions, especially anti-communism, and, most important, in the way they saw the world, the dissenters were not very dissenting. Their opposition emerged on smaller questions, on particulars of the postwar view. Daniel Bell felt that Howe had stayed on the sidelines—and out of the Congress for Cultural Freedom—and therefore could never understand the necessities of a cold-war position. Midge Decter, a younger intellectual and once Elliot Cohen's secretary, was critical of *Dissent* for its intellectual isolation. "It hasn't been affected by events. It could always stay on its own ground. This is why it never had any impact. You are always pure and morally superior, but there are no implications and no consequences."[44]

Radical utopianism had once been the style of them all. In the postwar world, though, "implications and consequences" became important—keys to the new liberal mentality. Here Howe and *Dissent* dissented. They carried older ideas into the postwar world, where they came into conflict with some of the newer concerns being argued by their peers. Theirs was more a critique of specific elements in the postwar liberal mind than a full assault on the larger liberal mentality and philosophy. It might seem, in hindsight, a relatively small distinctiveness. Among those who keenly listened and wrote to each other, however, these small rumblings might come to resemble the earth's tremblings—a kind of satisfying undercurrent which gave the impression that a relatively static view was fluid and dynamic.

SAUL BELLOW AND THE "AXIAL LINES" OF LIFE

When Saul Bellow received the Nobel Prize for literature, in 1976, John Leonard wrote the front-page appraisal which accompanied the news of the award in the *New York Times*. Attempting to place Bellow in the cultural context most often associated with the Chicago novelist, Leonard opened his assessment as follows: "If Saul Bellow didn't exist, someone exactly like him would have had to have been invented, just after the Second World War by New York intellectuals, in a backroom at *Partisan Review*." Amid the congratulations and celebrations accompanying the honor, several of Bellow's friends rose to take issue with Leonard. Writing in the *New Republic*, Alfred Kazin reasserted Bellow's uniqueness: "I have known Bellow since 1942, and I can testify that the only person capable of inventing Saul Bellow is Saul Bellow."[45]

The discussion of Saul Bellow's relationship to *Partisan Review* and to the New York Intellectuals did not begin with John Leonard, but flourished for years. The basic question emerges whether Saul Bellow was "made" by *Partisan Review*. Reviewing his years as an editor of *PR* in the 1940s, William Barrett addressed the matter directly: "Nobody discovered Saul Bellow but Saul Bellow. He appeared with a manuscript, and that was the beginning of a career."[46] Even if the answer was as simple as this—if Bellow had knocked on the doors at *PR* one day, carrying his first published story, "Two Morning Monologues," under his arm—the matter would not be settled so easily. *Partisan Review* did publish Bellow's first work.[47] Connections go even further in the late 1930s, when a number of young intellectuals began to gather in Chicago, forming a group similar to that of the young radicals in the City College lunchroom. Among this midwestern contingent, which the *PR* editors called the Chicago school, were Isaac Rosenfeld, H. J. Kaplan, Oscar Tarkov, and Saul Bellow. When Leslie Fiedler did graduate work at the University of Wisconsin, he felt himself close to this Chicago group. "Midwestern" provides only a geographical location for this group, however, for they possessed the same urban toughness, intellectual aggressiveness, and verbal brilliance as their New York counterparts.

In 1941 Philip Rahv had gone to Chicago with his wife, Nathalie, who had work there as an architect. In April he wrote back to Fred Dupee, talking about the life in Chicago. "So far we've managed to meet quite a few people, and the best of them by far are the apprentice writers like Bellow and Harold Kaplan," Rahv wrote to his fellow *PR* editor. "I am quite enthusiastic about these two youngsters—they are the Delmore Schwartz type: brilliant and yet at the same time methodical and responsible."[48] In the May—June 1941 issue of *PR*, "Two Morning Monologues" appeared. Over the next ten years Bellow published six stories, in addition to his first two novels. Five of the stories appeared in *PR* and one in *Harper's Bazaar*. From the first, Bellow established a recognizable and, ultimately, uneasy relationship with the New York Intellectuals as friends and patrons. Yet he has resisted any notion that they made him famous. "Bellow himself always resented that connection," Fiedler would recall, but "on the other hand, he really owed a big debt to them, because they did help introduce him to the world. Rahv thought of him as one of their boys."[49]

The relationship between Saul Bellow and the New York Intellectuals went beyond sponsorship or editorial assistance. The ties between them were intricate and complicated. Rahv's considering Bellow "one of his boys" implies a kind of patronage relationship which does not fully describe the situation. There is no question of Bellow's innate abilities and his creative autonomy. "You can't push Bellow," Dwight Macdonald argued. "Bellow is an extremely brilliant writer. From the beginning his stuff was very good." But there is also no question of the push which *PR* and the New Yorkers, in general, gave to Saul Bellow. "On the basis of these two novels," Elizabeth Hardwick wrote in *PR* of *Dangling Man* and *The Victim* in 1948, "it would be hard to think of any young writer who has had a better chance than Bellow to become the redeeming novelist of his period." With Bellow's next novel, *The Adventures of Augie March*, the praise in *PR* went further. "Saul Bellow's new novel is a new kind of book," Delmore Schwartz declared. "The only other American novels to which his can be compared with any profit are *Huckleberry Finn* and *U.S.A.*" Schwartz went on to claim the superiority of *Augie March* to both these novels "by virtue of the complexity of its subject matter and . . . of a realized unity of composition." He also compared Bellow favorably to Henry James and Walt Whitman.[50]

The importance of Saul Bellow to these individuals goes to an even deeper level, however. As Norman Podhoretz later put it, Bellow "was the family's White Hope, as it were, in fiction."[51] Among intellectuals ever conscious of questions of creativity, criticism, and culture, Bellow set out to be a creative person, a novelist of the first order. Rahv immediately liked Bellow's combination of abilities: "Brilliant and yet at the same time methodical and responsible." Schwartz, to whom Rahv first compared Bellow, never regained the brilliance of his debut and became increasingly irresponsible—personally as well as professionally—as the years passed. Isaac Rosenfeld, for whom many had such high hopes, died young, his one novel, *Passage from Home*, revered by the New York Intellectuals but largely unknown. Lionel Trilling's literary ambitions seemed to be stifled by the mixed reaction to his novel, *The Middle of the Journey.* His long-promised second novel never reached publication. Some of the other first- and second-generation intellectuals, such as Leslie Fiedler and William Phillips, wrote fiction, long and short. Like Trilling's, however, their careers centered on criticism and kept fiction as a sideline.

Saul Bellow set out to be a novelist and planned to be a great one. Alfred Kazin remembered that even before the publication of Bellow's first novel, he "carried around with him a sense of destiny as a novelist that excited everyone around him. Bellow was the first writer of my generation . . . who talked of Lawrence and Joyce, Hemingway and Fitzgerald, not as books in the library but as fellow operators in the same business." Kazin understood the differences between Bellow and intellectuals like himself. Among aggressive young intellectuals, ghetto-bred and seeking big reputations, Bellow seemed something more.

> He was measuring the world's power to resist *him*, he was putting himself up as a contender. Although he was friendly, unpretentious, and funny, he was ambitious and dedicated in a style I had never seen in an urban Jewish intellectual; he expected the world to come to him. He had pledged himself to a great destiny. He was going to take on more than the rest of us were.[52]

With a precision and a regularity which distinguish him from many writers—New York Intellectuals as well as others—Bellow has produced a series of important works for over thirty years. The largest gap between any two novels is six years. His output has alternated between the tight "depressive" novels, as the critic Mark Shechner calls them, begun with *Dangling Man* and *The Victim*, and the "expansive" style adopted first in *Augie March*. But Bellow has produced steadily as well as intelligently. His "brilliance" has been matched by his "methodical" and "responsible" attributes. The destiny Kazin foresaw in 1942 came true.[53] In the process, he pushed beyond the New York Intellectuals, not stepping over or on them, but putting them into the larger chorus which began to sing his praises. He remained their friend but he went beyond being their novelist.

By the middle 1950s Bellow had achieved the position *PR* had envisioned for him. Elizabeth Hardwick's hopes of 1948 materialized. "With the publication of *Seize the Day*," Leslie Fiedler wrote in 1957, "Saul Bellow has become not merely a witer with whom it is possible to come to terms, but one with whom it is *necessary* to come to terms." Fiedler felt that of all the contemporary novelists Bellow was "the one we need most to understand, if we are to understand what the novel is doing at the present moment." As the years passed, Bellow's importance grew. "Probably the most significant American novelist to come to maturity since World War II has been Saul Bellow," began one critical assessment of his work in the 1960s; "Saul Bellow is America's most important living novelist," began another.[54] The Nobel Prize capped his achievement.

Although he moved beyond the smaller intellectual world of the New Yorkers and although he spent most of his life outside of New York, Bellow's success was more than just personal. Whether or not he was "made" by the *Partisan* writers is less significant than the degree to which his success and the history and achievement of the New York Intellectuals in general intertwined. Whatever the resentments or differences which grew, he had been, was still, one of them—Isaac Rosenfeld's old pal from Chicago, their friend. This was "Saul Bellow? Saul? Saul??!!" who had won the Nobel Prize, as Alfred Kazin put it.[55] Bellow's career complemented that of other intellectuals gaining recognition. Lionel Trilling, for example, made it clear that a Jew could be a great literary critic; Meyer Schapiro, a great art historian, and Saul Bellow, a great American novelist. No longer did Jewish novelists suffer from the parochialism Trilling found objectionable in writers like Ludwig Lewisohn, nor did they burn out or fail to live up to their initial promise. Bellow was ready to go the distance, and "putting himself up as a contender," he emerged as the champion.

More than his success or his longevity bound Bellow to the New Yorkers. His writing complemented emerging intellectual positions, just as his career complemented other intellectual successes. He offered the kind of novel which Jews in America had not yet published, or which, as Trilling suggested, Americans had not yet published. In a recent survey of Jewish writing in America, Mark Shechner suggested that Bellow's novels answered Trilling's criticism, made in *The Liberal Imagination*, that a true fiction of manners was impossible in America because of the thinness of American social institutions. An American novelist could not capture "a culture's hum and the buzz of implication." Bellow, for the first time since Henry James, captured "the textures and habits of urban life."[56] The particular urban life—the "hum" and "buzz" which Bellow transcribed—spoke to these intellectuals on a personal as well as a critical level. Bellow was, in fact, still *their* novelist because he wrote about them, sometimes literally but more often socially and culturally. "Bellow was not one of the family's own only because he was a Jewish intellectual," Podhoretz observed; "he also spoke for and embodied the impulse to lay a serious claim to their identity as Americans and to their right to play a more than marginal role in the literary culture of the country." Among the New York Intellectuals, Podhoretz wrote, "there was a sense in which the validity of a whole phase of American experience was felt to hang on the question of whether or not he would turn out to be a great novelist."[57]

Saul Bellow's fiction is more than a literary rehashing of the themes and issues floating through the New York Intellectual world. If it had been only that, the larger audience and critical response which lifted him to the pinnacle of contemporary American letters would not have come. But Bellow's work took many of the central questions which plagued the New York Intellectuals and formed them into the stuff of literature. Concerns and ideas they all shared in life became the themes of this work. From the earliest days of the "new" *Partisan Review*, they had all believed that cultural notions, philosophical issues, and literary creation helped move society along. Now Bellow chose as the material for his novels the very experiences of all of their own lives, offering these as crucial elements in the cultural flow. "Bellow was in effect acting out or testing out the possibilities of this complex fate of American-Jewishness within his work as a novelist," Norman Podhoretz remarked in 1976, "both validating or legitimizing it and testing its possibilities and limits."[58]

Bellow's novels chart many of the crucial questions the New Yorkers tackled in other contexts. In *Dangling Man*, his first, the ex-radical diarist awaits an army induction notice, seeking escape from the aimlessness and meaninglessness of his present condition. Many of the second generation had gone through college without any notion of careers and had seen the touchstone of their radicalism diminish. "In all the unease of his youth," Alfred Kazin wrote of Bellow's character Joseph, he is "consciously [trying] not merely to save his life but to find some foundation for life itself." Anti-Semitism served as the central theme for *The Victim*, Bellow's next novel, published in 1947, amid all the evaluation of Jewishness and Jewish identity. *Augie March* and *Seize the Day*, both published in the mid-1950s, mark the breakthroughs for Bellow. The novelist himself said he felt constrained in his earlier books, despite the sense of destiny Kazin perceived: "I still felt the incredible effrontery of announcing myself to the world (in part I mean the WASP world) as a writer and an artist." Bellow also claimed to have suffered the same exclusions as the others. "I had good reason to fear that I would be put down as a foreigner, an interloper." It was made clear to him when he studied literature in the university, as it was to Trilling, Elliot Cohen, and so many others, "that as a Jew and the son of Russian Jews [he] would probably never have the right *feeling* for Anglo-Saxon traditions, for English words."[59] Bellow believed that he broke out of these constraints with *Augie March*. Alfred Kazin, whose own attempt to bridge the gap between Jewish marginality and American literature had occurred with *On Native Grounds*, found *Augie March* "constructed entirely as a passageway to 'America,' . . . an attempt to break down all possible fences between the Jew and this larger country, so abundant and free in possibility that Augie is a conscious mythological creation."[60] They really could become "*our* forests," belonging to Alfred and Saul and all the other Jews from the concrete world of the immigrant ghettos.

Seize the Day is of all of Bellow's works the one most frequently praised by other New York Intellectuals. Despite its brevity, the novella grasps two themes which the intellectuals quickly identified—one from their past and one from the present. "He had cast off his father's name, and with it his father's opinion of himself," Bellow wrote of his character Tommy Wilhelm. "It was, he knew it was, his bid for liberty." Yet, the character realizes, the "changed name was a mistake." Bellow returned to the crucial theme of fathers and sons, to "the emotional transactions of males inside the family," as Leslie Fiedler called it, which was for the intellectuals a theme as old as themselves. What makes *Seize the Day* so compelling is that Bellow coupled the father-son theme with the larger question, which Alfred Kazin identified as "the painfully exact tragedy of our affluent day": "Tommy Wilhelm is a weakling, a passive sufferer, a *nebbish* in the crowded storm of New York life. Only his illusions about 'making it' have made him an interesting fabulist." For Fielder, "it is the price of failure in a world dedicated to success that Bellow is dealing with now . . . the bitterness of success and failure become pawns in the deadly game between father and son"; it "is the emotional range of our relationships that is the emotional stuff of his best work."[61]

"What makes Bellow's work so unusual," Alfred Kazin concluded in 1959, "is the fact that his characters are all burdened by a speculative quest, a need to understand their particular destiny." The New York Intellectuals shared this fate. They had searched for answers and a brighter future in the 1930s. That failing, they became twice-born and began the search anew. They had always felt that some kind of destiny beckoned; it just took them time to discover its true nature. "The problem of destiny," Kazin wrote,

> is the need to accept one's whole fate as a human being, to recognize the "axial lines" of life, as Augie March puts it. But to know whether the axial lines that we see, or think that we see, are what fate *had* to draw, is not merely the theme of Bellow's fiction, it is the overriding passion of his characters. And it is the extraordinary prominence of his speculation in Bellow's novel that gives him his unusual, his involuntarily provocative, place in American fiction.[62]

Saul Bellow was "their" writer not because he was their friend or because *Partisan Review* first championed his cause and published his work or even because he was a Jewish intellectual. He was "their" writer because he seized the themes which mattered most to them—the questions of their lives and their fate—and turned them into literature, offering insights into their dilemmas as he validated their lives.

Complementing Bellow's individual success was his preeminence in what has been called the emergence of Jewish-American literature in the postwar years. Bellow's sustained career, his brilliance as well as his methodical and responsible outpouring, made him the star of his constellation—the Nobel laureate of the group—but he was in well-known company. What is striking about the writers included in this literary category is the degree to which they all had close connections with the New York Intellectuals. Personal fame carried some of them, like Bellow, beyond the smaller intellectual world of the New Yorkers, but their roots often reached back to that community. Mark Shechner's evaluation of postwar Jewish writing puts the emergence of Jewish writers in the 1940s, when the older, more parochial styles of Abraham Cahan, Daniel Fuchs, Michael Gold, Howard Fast, and Albert Harper "gave way to the subtler and more evocative writing of Delmore Schwartz, Saul Bellow, Isaac Rosenfeld, and Norman Mailer." This development corresponds to the emergence of a group of "bookish and impecunious boys" who once might have been talmudic scholars but who now pursued the literary culture of Western civilization; Shechner cites Kazin, Trilling, Rahv, Schwartz, Howe, and Fiedler as examples. These are New York Intellectuals all, the writers and the critics. If one adds the two other writers who became most clearly associated with Jewish-American literature, Philip Roth and Bernard Malamud, the list is complete and the essential role of the New York Intellectuals very apparent.[63]

Bellow's arrival ushered in the new generation of young Jewish writers. He was not the only candidate for the role of leadership. Other contenders fell away as Bellow succeeded. Delmore Schwartz and Isaac Rosenfeld attracted at least as much early attention as Bellow, if not more. Both left careers of unfullfilled early promise; both died in lowly circumstances. Schwartz's demise would not come until the 1960s, but Rosenfeld receded just as his old friend Bellow advanced. Rosenfeld once seemed destined for literary stardom. He won the first *Partisan Review* fiction prize in 1946. Yet he proved irresponsible and unreliable. "Unlike Bellow, who could use every morsel of his experience," Kazin observed, "Isaac lived his fantasies, and in company." According to Mark Shechner, he became a "center of activity among second-generation Jewish intellectuals who congregated in New York during the 1940s."[64] As he became more flamboyant and less productive, the support of his mentors diminished. When he was young and promising, William Barrett later recalled, Philip Rahv included Rosenfled as an occasional dinner guest, "until Rahv decided [Isaac] was on the skids and was no longer a 'winner.'" The literary attitude of the *PR* editor also changed. "What an editor can do for a writer, once he has broken through, is give him encouragement and even flattery in moods of depression," Barrett believed. "Philip withheld these from Isaac when in fact Isaac needed them most." Rahv "was one of the few people of whom Isaac spoke with a real grudge."[65]

As Bellow grew ever more important, Rosenfeld grew increasingly estranged from his New York friends. He taught at the University of Minnesota and, finally, at the downtown extension of the Universtiy of Chicago. He died in a furnished room in Chicago, in 1956, the same year in which Bellow published *his* highly praised novel about fathers and sons, *Seize the Day*.

Of the Jewish writers who gained prominence during the postwar years, Bellow, Mailer, Roth, and Malamud emerged as the central figures. The themes of their works varied widely, and few tapped the issues so close to home as did Saul Bellow. Their ages and relationship to the New York Intellectuals also differed. Bernard Malamud, though a classmate of Alfred Kazin's at City College, taught at Oregon State University and did not gain public recognition until the 1950s. His first novel, *The Natural*, appeared in 1952. Many of Malamud's earliest stories, like Saul Bellow's, first appeared in *Partisan Review* and *Commentary*.[66] Norman Mailer, whose first novel *The Naked and the Dead* burst on the literary scene in 1946, had been closer to the Trotskyists in the late 1940s than to postwar liberalism and wrote frequently for *Dissent* in the mid-1950s. Philip Roth came last, publishing *Goodbye Columbus* in 1959. He was the novelist of the third generation, *Letting Go* being the story of Jews in postwar graduate schools, for example. But each had clear connections to the New York Intellectual world, although by the time the later ones emerged, the bonds were loosening among all of them.[67]

A body of literature began to appear, clearly diverse in style and theme, but identifiable as it captured the experiences of Jews in modern America. The larger questions of Jewish existence as well as the narrower ones of Jewish intellectuals—the themes best mined by Saul Bellow—became the material for a growing literary *oeuvre*. Here was another demonstration of the importance, relevance, and central role for these individuals in modern society—another sign of arrival.

BOHEMIANISM WITHOUT BOHEMIANS

The success of Saul Bellow and the emergence of Jewish-American literature made the arrival of the New York Intellectuals the subjects, as well as the creators, of the central literary current of postwar American society. Both the creative and the critical achievements rested on a larger victory, the completion of a cultural crusade begun in the 1930s. "The most pervasive event in American letters over the last ten years," Clement Greenberg wrote in *Partisan Review* in 1948, "is the stabilization of the avant-garde, accompanied by its growing acceptance by official and commercial culture."[68] The "new" *Partisan Review* was ten years old in 1948. Its initial commitment to modernism and avant-garde culture had succeeded. After 1945 critic and commentator alike came to recognize the degree to which the modernist cause and the notions of the avant-garde had won general acceptance.

The victory of modernist culture and the success of the avant-garde contained significant ironic elements as well as perplexing questions. "We grew up, the readers and writers of my generation, at the end of a desperate attempt to redeem the novel from success and the bourgeoisie," Leslie Fielder remembered, "to define a standard, a tradition of the avant-garde for what had already become the stuffiest of forms." They had carried through their efforts, for "the avant-garde novel has become a tradition; which is to say, it no longer exists."[69] The very success of the avant-garde approach meant that it could no longer possess its original attributes. It had modified the culture from which it dissented "and had in return been granted a recognition and place that do not dissatisfy it," Greenberg noted. "The avant-garde has been professionalized, so to speak, organized into a field for careers; it is no longer the adventure beyond ratified norms, the refusal in the name of truth and excellence to abide by the categories of worldly success and failure." The *Partisan* critics had set themselves off from the other radical critics of their day with the staunch defense of high culture, modernism, and the social function of the avant-garde. The New York Intellectuals had carried their special political and cultural view to positions of increasing intellectual importance in the postwar world. They had built careers on exclusions—as Jews, as anti-Stalinists, as modernists—turning them into the means to prominence. But the situation had changed. "The avant-garde writer *gets ahead* now," Greenberg observed, "and inside established channels: he obtains university or publishing or magazine jobs."[70] Promoting a cultural view which consciously dissented from the society's cultural norms, they had achieved positions as important "inside" critics, cultural arbiters of the very culture they had once reacted against.

This ironic twist led some of the critics to reevaluate their precise role, especially given their long-held belief that their views retained a vestige of their thirties radicalism in more appropriate postwar terms. Once they became central arbiters, that belief grew increasingly untenable. "The issue ought to be faced by writers on art," Harold Rosenberg put it directly, "that it is not possible to be both a revolutionist and a critic applying esthetic laws without becoming a bit ridiculous. The radical thinker cannot be for Art."[71] Rosenberg, always conscious of maintaining distinctiveness from his fellow intellectuals and among the most steadfast champions of "the tradition of the new," as he called it, took a very definite stand on this issue. Many of the others found that the questions raised were difficult to answer absolutely. It is also apparent that their own views began to change as they tried to resolve the implicit contradiction inherent in the success of an advocacy of the avant-garde.

A self-definition based on exclusions or oppositions provided an essential element of their 1930s identity. They heralded the radical implications of a cultural position predicated on contradiction. They defined who they were by the intellectual positions they held—radical and modernist, not bourgeois and philistine. Now, William Philips observed, "the avant-garde questions of the 30s have become the mass questions of today." These attitudes permeated the society, rather than just propelling particular intellectuals. The notions filtered down, through mass higher education, to shape popular culture as well as elite standards.[72] Thus, instead of standing in opposition to the prevailing cultural flow—mass, popular, middlebrow—highbrow thought and an avant-garde orientation now molded society. In the process it began to lose some of its punch, if not to run out of steam altogether.

Phillips noted the changes taking place. "The avant-garde is everywhere on the run," the *PR* editor observed, "serious and sustained avant-garde, not the chic variety that moves to TV and Hollywood before anyone has time to be shocked." But Phillips understood the new cultural trend, in which clear oppositions no longer stood out. Just as society had accepted some of the attitudes of thirties avant-garde culture, so did it seek to change the relation between mainstream culture and avant-garde critiques. "Even a genuine avant-garde would be in danger of becoming immediately fashionable," Phillips understood, "because what we have today is not so much an outright opposition to anything serious or extreme as a zeal to make it palatable."[73]

This new relation between the avant-garde and society—both the general acceptance of an avant-garde attitude and the desire to incorporate avant-garde notions immediately—led to basic questions about individual roles, especially among intellectuals whose avant-garde stance had been a chief element of their intellectual identity. "In place of avant-garde ideas we now had the *style of fashion*," Irving Howe suggested in 1968. Intellectuals bounced from one intellectual or cultural position to another. "Leslie Fielder," Howe remarked acerbically, "no doubt by design, seemed to go though more of such episodes than anyone else, even his admirerers could not always be certain whether he was *davenning* or doing a rain dance." The trouble, Howe concluded, was not any one style currently in fashion but the tyrannical dynamic of fashion, "the ruthlessness with which, to remain in fashion, fashion had to keep devouring itself."[74]

At the center of the cultural dilemma facing the aging revolutionary modernists were the growing contradictions between their cultural and political attitudes—or, more precisely, the orientation provided by the coupling of their political and cultural positions. At one time their political and cultural attitudes had been joined to create a fusion of radical ideology with a radical sensibility. Now they had moved into American society, especially political society. They had "chosen" the West, supported the Democratic candidates, joined organizations whose aim was to promote the American political system. American democracy is mass democracy, and as the *PR* editors wrote in 1952, this reality entailed specific cultural elements. "Political democracy seems to coexist with the domination of the 'masses.' Whatever the cultural consequences may be, democratic values which America either embodies or promises are desirable in purely human terms." In the world of hard political realities, the questions of cultural standards might have to be modified or given a lesser priority. But a parallel reduction in cultural standards had led the radical critics to react strongly in the 1930s. Stalinism and proletarian art made literature philistine and inferior to politics. A radical movement aimed at the masses produced a lowbrow mass art. In the postwar years the New Yorkers had abandoned radical values and embraced American liberal democracy. These political values were producing a questionable mass culture, yet to the *PR* editors they remained the "necessary conditions for civilization and represent[ed] the only immediate alternatives as long as Russian totalitarianism threaten[ed] world domination."[75]

This explanation might soothe political hearts, but it still left the question of defining a new cultural position which might bring together the political notions of a mass democracy with the highbrow standards to which the critics felt allegiance. They grappled with the problem but could never achieve a definitive position or consenus, as they had in the late 1930s. Robert Warshow tried to carve out a new middle ground, between highbrow and lowbrow sensibilities. He felt that the main cultural dynamic in postwar America was "the mass culture of the educated classes—the culture of the middle-brow." This described the new synthesis of a popular culture which responded to and incorporated avant-garde notions. "For the first time," Warshow believed, "popular culture was able to draw its ideological support from the most advanced sector of society." Yet, Clement Greenberg thought that this middle-brow culture, not lowbrow culture, posed the real threat to standards. It "cut the ground from under high culture." The merging of popular taste and highbrow attitudes depressed Alfred Kazin: "Have the yahoos taken over here, as everywhere; the beatniks with their infernal smirks, the chorus girls who just adore Lolita—it's so cute."[76]

Another critical line of argument sought to analyze the emerging mass culture. The old favorite term "kitsch" reappeared in a new assault on mass culture and in explanations for contemporary society. But again, no convergence of opinion occurred. Dwight Macdonald railed against "Midcult"; Harold Rosenberg attacked Macdonald. "While Macdonald's taste for kitsch is largely negative, it is genuine," Rosenberg asserted, "at least genuine enough to yield him the time to become familiar with it." The result, Rosenberg discovered, was that "the counterconcept to kitsch is more kitsch. When Macdonald speaks about kitsch he seems to be speaking from the point of view of art; when he speaks against art it is plain his ideas are kitsch."[77]

The crucial question was really which part of the avant-garde had actually succeeded. Particular ideas on culture had been discussed, but so had a belief in the inherent social function of any avant-garde approach. Modernism as a literary movement had gained legitimacy, and the heroes of the 1930s had been enshrined in the pantheon of modern literary giants. But the social function of the avant-garde had not really taken hold, nor was it clear that these intellectuals really wished it to continue. The revolutionary modernists had abandoned their cultural style while carrying their cultural ideas to promi-nence. No longer seeking to undermine the established, bourgeois order, they could no longer support a cultural approach subversive of that order. No consensus on a new function for the avant-garde or a new role for modernist criticism could emerge. It became more difficult to fashion a theory of modernism based on a defense of cultural standards than one based on a critique of them. As Irving Howe later wrote, modernism "is a dynamism of asking and learning not to reply. The past was devoted to answers, the modern period confines itself to questions." Modernism redefined "the very idea of a question . . . no longer an interrogation but now a mode of axiomatic description." But now these intellectuals *were* providing answers. "The intellectuals who had failed at revolution were to succeed as intellectual arbiters, " Alfred Kazin wrote. "The more history comes to be seen as static (in the Marxist idiom: a locomotive stalled in the inescapable present)," Howe observed, "the more art must take on a relentless dynamism."[78] But art had stalled along with history, the bourgeois order having been accepted politically and culturally. Modern culture no longer had a clear function. What did become clear, however, was that any new attempts to revive the social function of the avant-garde—to rekindle the culturally subversive mode—would only threaten the achievements which had been won. On this, at least, a relative consensus emerged. With a good deal more precision and agreement than on questions of what had become of their avant-gardism, ex-revolutionary modernists turned to face the newly proclaimed avant-gardism of others.

The success of the avant-garde and the respectability the old revolutionary modernists earned combined to cast a nostalgic glow over the efforts which had brought about these achievements. Memories of the pre-World War I Greenwich Village days, the expatriatism of the 1920s, the radical styles of the 1930s, took on an aura of folk mythology. To the younger intellectuals now joining the community, those past days looked like the best of times, when "people lived lives of great moment," Midge Decter recalled. The precision of the cultural and political issues matched the poignancy and intensity of those past lives. "The Bohemianism of the 1920s represented a repudiation of the provinciality, philistinism, and moral hypocrisy of American life, " Norman Podhoretz observed in 1958. "The radicalism of the 1930s was marked by a deep intellectual seriousness and aimed at a state of society in which the fruits of civilization would be more widely available—and ultimately available to all." By contrast, "the Bohemianism of the 1950s is another kettle of fish altogether."[79]

There continues to this day a debate about the literary worth and radical commitment of the 1950s bohemianism to which Podhoretz referred—the Beats. Among the New York Intellectuals a negative consensus clearly emerged with the first appearances of these would-be heirs to the avant-garde tradition. Some dismissed the Beats casually, as when Alfred Kazin spoke of "the beatniks at one [cultural] extreme personifying the ridiculous ideal of sensation for its own sake."[80] Longer analyses also came, notably from Diana Trilling and Norman Podhoretz. These contained telling themes, especially considering the ages of the two critics and their own relationships to these bohemians.

Diana Trilling's article took, in Leslie Fiedler's assessment, "a funny maternal tone; these are our children, what the hell are they doing?"[81] There is an explanation for this attitude. Trilling's article is based on a poetry reading at Columbia by Allen Ginsberg, Gregory Corso, and Peter Orlovsky. On one level, Trillng found "Ginsberg and his friends" outdated. How much better "if they had come of age ten or fifteen years sooner." They exhibited a kind of "embittered fond funniness" which was representative of the thirties but which had now "all but disappeared among intellectuals." Trilling commented, that "I hadn't quite realized how much I missed [this style] until Thursday night. . . ." But the pang of recognition came from nostalgic memory rather than from contemporary relevance. The poems "were still funny in that old radical-depressed way but not nearly as funny and authentic as they would have been had they been written before the Jews and the Italians and the Negroes, but especially the Jews, had been awarded a place as Americans-like-everyone-else instead of remaining outsiders."[82] The Beats seemed to offer imitations of a radical style no longer relevant, now that the exclusions of the thirties—those suffered by the New York Intellectuals, among others—had given way to the acceptance of the postwar world.

The characterization as pale imitations extended beyond literary themes to the Beats and their followers themselves. Trilling regarded the audience's "shoddiness" as a pose. She noted the "shock of so many young girls, so few of them pretty, and so many blackest black stockings; so many young men, so few of them—despite the many black beards—with any promise of masculinity." First viewing the crowd, Trilling was sure it "would smell bad." "But I was mistaken," she said. "These people may think they're dirty inside and dress up to it. But the audience was clean and Ginsberg was clean and Corso was clean and Orlovsky was clean." Beneath this pose, Trilling found, these were really just kids, engaging in a little late- or post-adolescent rebellion. "Certainly there's nothing dirty about a checked shirt or a lumberjacket and blue jeans; they're standard uniform in the best nursery schools." Under the uniforms they are clean. Real rebellion is not in their hearts, Trilling seemed to be saying, and the real avant-garde not in their souls.[83]

Trilling's attitude in these descriptions demonstrates the "maternal" tone Fiedler alluded to. There were personal as well as social reasons for this posture. She was the wife of a distinguished Columbia literary critic, and the new generation of students and literary figures came under his influence, direct and indirect. Norman Podhoretz and Steven Marcus, two important young critics, were Lionel Trilling's students. So was Allen Ginsberg. Ginsberg did not sail through his Columbia career with the praise and seeming promise of Podhoretz and Marcus. His time at Columbia had been troubled. Diana Trilling reports an episode which led to Ginsburg's suspension.

> It seems that Ginsberg had traced an obscenity in the dust of a dormitory window; the words were too shocking for the Dean of Students to speak, so he had written them on a piece of paper which he pushed across the desk to my husband: "Fuck the Jews." Even the part of Lionel that wanted to laugh couldn't; it was too hard for the Dean to have to transmit this message to a Jewish professor—this was still in the forties when being a Jew in the university was not yet what it is today. "But he's a Jew himself," said the Dean. "Can you understand his writing a thing like that?" Yes, Lionel could understand; but he couldn't explain it to the Dean. . . . It was ordinary good sense for the college to take protective measures with Ginsberg and for him.[84]

The Trillings had been keenly aware of Allen Ginsberg for some time. But Ginsberg did not act like the other, dutiful students who gathered around Lionel Trilling. He would come "with his lurid boasts which were also his confession." And certainly his career took a course different from that of other Trilling students. Yet Diana Trilling believed that beneath the Beat facade—just as under the dirty clothes of the Beat audience—beat the heart of a good child. "I suppose I have no right to say now, and on such early and little evidence, that Ginsberg had always desperately wanted to be respectable, or respected, like his instructors at Columbia, it is so likely that this is a hindsight which suits my needs." But Trilling continued, "It struck me, though, that this was the most unmistakable and touching message from platform to audience the other night, and as I received it, I felt I had known something like it all along."[85]

It was to Lionel Trilling and Mark Van Doren that Ginsberg came when he studied at Columbia, aiming with his flamboyance to impress or shock these two distinguished critics. Diana Trilling remembered saying to her husband, "He wants you to forbid him to behave like that. He wants you to take him out of it, or why does he choose people like you and Mark Van Doren to tell these stories to.' To which I received always the same answer: 'I'm not his father,' a response that of course allowed of no argument."[86] If Diana Trilling really believed, however, that Ginsberg's rebellious stance masked a personal drive for respectability and that it took someone like Lionel Trilling to pull him out of his current life-style, then the distinctiveness of the Beat rebellion can also be seen as a mask covering hidden motives. Ginsberg was somebody's good boy, if not the Trillings'. At the Columbia reading, he told the audience that his father was sitting among them. When Ginsberg read a poem about his mother and said he cried because of his father's presence, Trilling assumed his father must have been proud: proud of the poem, proud of his son reading his poetry in a university auditorium, proud that the last poet to read in the hall had been T.S. Eliot. And Trilling herself admitted to having been "moved" by a poem, "Lion in the Room," which Ginsberg dedicated to Lionel Trilling—a "passionate love poem," she thought. After the reading Diana Trilling returned home and found that a meeting was in progress in her living room. When W.H. Auden chided her for enjoying the reading, she responded, "It's different when it's human beings and not just a sociological phenomenon." And she told her husband, "Allen Ginsberg read a love-poem to you, Lionel. I liked it very much."[87] Trilling may not have been Ginsberg's father or have had enough fatherly influence to steer Ginsberg toward respectability, but the message of Diana Trilling's assessment is that the two worlds were closer than the Beats acknowledged. Allen Ginsberg was a dutiful son honoring his mother, pleasing his father, and reaching out to his teacher. This was not a real rebellion, a new avant-garde, or a major revision in literary tastes. It was the age-old story of the sons, even defiant ones, defining themselves in relation to their fathers. Diana Trilling believed that Ginsberg, although a prodigal, was never as far from home as he or his listeners assumed.

If Lionel Trilling declared that he was not Allen Ginsberg's father, Norman Podhoretz bellowed that he was not his brother. "Norman had always been told that he was going to be the spokesman for his generation," Daniel Bell recalled. "In the late fifties, he turned around and found a whole phenomenon called the Beats, who were far out, doing things that Norman never dreamed of—being on the road, taking hashish, screwing madly. Norman's reaction was to write 'The Know-Nothing Bohemians.'"[88] Podhoretz's attack on the Beats appeared in *Partisan Review* in 1958, the same year as Diana Trilling's assessment in *Commentary*. If her tone was condescending and maternal, his was aggressively hostile. "The plain truth is that the primitivism of the Beat Generation serves first of all as a cover for an anti-intellectualism so bitter that it makes the ordinary American's hatred of eggheads seem positively benign," Podhoretz claimed. From the Beat viewpoint, he continued, "to be articulate is to admit that you have no feelings . . . that you can't respond to anything . . . and that you are probably impotent." This worship of primitivism, however, arose "from a pathetic poverty of feeling" on the part of the Beats.[89] Their claims to be rebels also rang hollow. They might be

> rebels, all right, but not against anything so sociological and historical as the middle
> class or capitalism or even respectability. This is the revolt of the spiritually
> underprivileged and the crippled of soul—young men who can't think straight and
> so hate anyone who can; young men who can't get outside the morass of self and so
> construct definitions of feeling that exclude all human beings who manage to live,
> even miserably, in a world of objects; young men burdened unto death with the
> specially poignant sexual anxiety that America . . . seems bent on breeding, who
> therefore dream of the unattainable perfect orgasm, which excuses all sexual failures
> in the real world.[90]

These cripples could hardly be individuals tapping that cultural current which molds and drives society by fashioning an avant-garde critique. These were poor, "spiritually underprivileged," self-indulgent, sexually anxious, bitter young men. This movement did not capture the spirit of the avant-garde and did not extend logically from the bohemianism of the past, Podhoretz declared.

Whatever the value of the Beat literary contribution, Podhoretz's reaction in 1958 far exceeded their impact or place. Diana Trilling did not seem to take the Beats seriously enough, thinking them clean kids led by outcasts who actually sought respectability. Podhoretz took them too seriously, as a threat not for society but for young intellectuals—those, like himself, who signed on right out of college and faithfully followed the path to intellectual importance and respectability which was being forged by older intellectuals. This course the Beats rejected. Podhoretz noted "a suppressed cry" in the works of Jack Kerouac: "Kill the intellectuals who can talk coherently, kill the people who can sit still for five minutes at a time, kill those incomprehensible characters who are capable of getting seriously involved with a woman, a job, a cause." Ultimately, being for or against the Beats came down to "being for or against intelligence itself."[91] It also came down, for Podhoretz, to being for or against the kind of life Podhoretz had made for himself in the 1950s.

In the 1960s some of these attitudes would change or adjust. Podhoretz would loosen the bonds which held him to Trilling and the other elders and even embrace the new radicalism for a short time. While Podhoretz went one way, Trilling went the other. The Columbia critic began to have reservations about what he called the "adversary culture" of the modernist writers.[92] But in the late 1950s the victory of modernism remained fresh, and the intellectuals rode that victory to prominence. *Their* avant-garde had succeeded; *these* modernist critics now got ahead. They were not sure what form their avant-garde ideas should take, now that they had moved from the outside to the center, or how they were to keep alive a notion of a cultural critique predicated on the subverting of bourgeois sensibilities. But they did know that they were not yet ready to relinquish the banner of modernism or the avant-garde to new or younger claimants. They were far more specific in criticizing those who offered a new version of cultural rebellion than in fashioning an appropriate style of their own. If they could hold off these newer elements long enough to develop a clear theory of modernism which fit their new roles, they could continue in the forefront of both the intellectual and the avant-garde worlds— stand for Art and help generate art, in Harold Rosenberg's distinction. All they needed was time.

STATUS AND CONSENSUS

The literary critics were not alone in seeking new approaches to their discipline in the face of changing personal and political realities. Attitudes and interpretations change frequently, schools of thought rise and fall, revisions and counterrevisions abound in the scholarly and the literary worlds. The paradox confronting the literary critics stemmed from their new-found position in the mainstream of American society and from the success of their critical approach. Difficulties emerged over the adjustment or revision of a doctrine predicated on exclusions and marginality. In other disciplines—notably history and sociology—new themes corresponding to the postwar mentality appeared. Spared the internal dilemma of their literary counterparts, these sociologists and historians articulated new notions and approaches which more neatly fit their own new positions, reinforcing personal as well as professional needs.

One major turn among sociologists was discussed above. Daniel Bell's pronouncement of an "end to ideology" joined a larger chorus sounding this theme. Bell's book, published in 1960, collected articles written in the 1950s. In the same year, another City College graduate, Seymour Martin Lipset, published *Political Man*, which also brought together articles written over the past decade. Lipset's final chapter, "A Personal Postscript," is entitled "An End to Ideology?" It seconds Bell and goes on to cite the work of other analysts who concur.[93] Older notions, especially those derived from Marx, had become "exhausted," to use Bell's term. In the first chapter of *Political Man*, Lipset focused on a central issue which marked the changing attitudes, "Class and Conflict: Marx and Tocqueville." Lipset did not break new ground here; rather he addressed issues which had occupied numerous scholars and analysts for years. The revisions and ultimate abandonment of Marx had been a topic among New York Intellectuals for two decades. Historians were paying more and more attention to Tocqueville's observations on American democracy.

In 1948, a year before *The Liberal Imagination*, Richard Hofstadter wrote in the introduction to *The American Political Tradition* of "the rudderless and demoralized state of American liberalism." Whereas Trilling had suggested, as befit a literary critic, the need for "imagination," Hofstadter, the historian, called "for a reinterpretation of our political traditions which emphasizes the common climate of American opinion. The existence of such a climate of opinion has been much obscured by the tendency to place political conflict in the foreground of history." Hofstadter did not deny the presence of conflict in American history or American society, but he felt that beneath the arguments existed a common set of assumptions and a "kind of mute organic consistency."[94] The notion of "consensus" came to name the entire school of American historical writing which grew to prominence after World War II. Large, synthetic works, notably by Louis Hartz and Daniel Boorstin, attempted to translate the idea of a consensus into sweeping historical explanations.[95] Hofstadter later claimed that he had always held an ambivalent view of the consensus approach and that by the mid-1960s it was no longer as satisfying to him as it had been ten or twenty years earlier.[96] But at its outset, and in the minds of most students of American historiography, Richard Hofstadter stood at the center of consensus history.

Unlike other consensus historians like Hartz and Boorstin, Hofstadter also had a direct link to the New York Intellectuals. Because he did not frequently write for their main journals or share all of their other concerns, he was not truly a central member. Yet he was not a distant colleague or a scholar convenient for citation. "My closest friend," said Alfred Kazin in 1976, "was Richard Hofstadter." Kazin and Hofstadter worked together during the late 1930s in the main reading room of the New York Public Library, Kazin writing *On Native Grounds*, Hofstadter *Social Darwinism in American Thought*. Kazin wrote movingly and lovingly of Hofstadter, especially of the young Kazin's friendship with Hofstadter and his first wife, Felice Swados.[97] Hofstadter did his graduate work at Columbia and joined the faculty in 1946, a colleague of Trilling, Schapiro, and Dupee and later of Bell, Lipset, and Marcus. Bell recalled meeting both Hofstadter and Kazin at Sunday brunches which various intellectuals attended in the early 1940s.[98] Hofstadter not only had personal ties with the New York Intellectuals but also grew up in the same environment as many of them. "Richard Hofstadter was one of the first major American historians to come out of the cultural life of New York City," Arthur Schlesinger, Jr., remarked. And Hofstadter himself noted, "What started me off as an historian . . . was . . . engagement with contemporary problems. As one who matured in the 1930s, my interest has centered mainly in politics."[99]

Hofstadter's personal ties supplemented his professional contributions. In addition to bringing the notion of consensus to the writing of American history, he helped pioneer new areas of historical analysis, which both reinforced the consensus approach and brought history closer to the social sciences. In the mid-1950s Daniel Bell complained that most historians failed "to make adequate use of the sophistications (status, generational differences, character type) which sociologists have influenced." Among the "few talented individuals" who had incorporated these insights, Bell named Hofstadter, particularly his essay on pseudo-conservatism and his book *The Age of Reform*.[100] Bell's citing of these two works is extremely significant. *The Age of Reform* spanned a wide stretch of American history, as is suggested by its subtitle, "From Bryan to F.D.R." Of its central contentions, however, two reflected the recent contributions from social scientists and the New York Intellectual world. Revising the standard thinking about the Populist movement of American farmers in the late nineteenth century, Hofstadter suggested that a prime motivation for the movement could be traced to "rank in society. That was close to the heart of the matter, for the farmer was beginning to realize acutely not merely that the best of the world's goods were to be had in the cities and that the urban middle and upper classes had much more of them than he did but also that he was losing in status and respect compared with them." Hofstadter also discussed the deep strain of anti-Semitism in populism, even referring to a nearly forgotten article by Bell, "The Grass Roots of American Jew Hatred," published in 1944. Bell, Hofstadter wrote, "is one of the few writers who has perceived that there is any relation between latter-day anti-Semites and the earlier Populist tradition."[101]

The connection between the Populist tradition and anti-Semitism was taken a step further with the publication of *The New American Right*, which Bell edited. This work grew out of a Columbia faculty seminar in political behavior, attended by Bell, Hofstadter, and Lipset, among others. Attempting to analyze the phenomenon of McCarthyism, Bell wrote that the "most fruitful approaches seemed to be those worked out by Richard Hofstadter and Seymour Martin Lipset." Bell remarked that Hofstadter, "from a historian's vantage point, argued that a preoccupation with status has been a persistent element in American politics and that McCarthyism as a social phenomenon could best be explained as a form of status anxiety." Lipset, Bell noted, as "a sociologist, distinguished between 'class politics' . . . . and 'status politics.'. . . McCarthyism, he argued, was a species of status politics."[102] The importance of the analysis of the new American right derives not only from the insights of the contributors but also from the merging of the historical and the sociological investigations. "The main thrust of the essays in the volume identify and deal with the emergence of the 'status groups,'" Bell wrote in his contribution, and both Hofstadter and Lipset fully supported Bell's assertion in their arguments.[103]

What emerges beyond the explanations offered by the historians and sociologists is the relevance of contemporary events and personal experience to their positions. Conflict had been replaced by consensus—underlying sets of shared assumptions—and yet antagonisms remained. But as Bell also pointed out in his essay, "this is turbulence born not of depression, but of prosperity . . . we see that prosperity brings in its wake new social groups, new social strains, and new social anxieties."[104] If we look at the analysts and at their central themes, we can gain insights into their own place and their "social anxieties." Essential to the maturation and success of the New York Intellectuals was their desire to achieve something in the society which had excluded their parents. In the 1930s the path seemed to lead through radical change in American society itself. But their successes were ultimately won within the system. "Normally there is a world of difference between one's sense of national identity or cultural belonging and one's social status," Hofstadter wrote. "However, in American historical development, these two things, so easily distinguishable in analysis, have been jumbled together in reality, and it is precisely this that has given such a special poignancy and urgency to our status-strivings." Hofstadter here used "our" for all Americans, but the narrower usage—"our" young Jewish intellectuals from New York— fits precisely. "In this country a person's status—that is, his relative place in the prestige hierarchy of his community—and his rudimentary sense of belonging to the community—that is, what we call his 'Americanism'—have been intimately joined."[105]

The personal victories of the New York Intellectuals did not contain all the satisfactions they expected. Having risen on the social ladder to positions of intellectual and social prominence, they began to see American society in new terms. As Lipset noted, "Status politics, status insecurities and status aspirations are most likely to appear as sources of frustration, independent of economic problems, in periods of prolonged prosperity." Those with "status aspirations" became the subjects of various investigations—historical and contemporary— from the Populists to the McCarthyites. Those with "status insecurities" could usually be found in historical literature, as Lipset discussed in *Political Man*, citing David Donald's work on upper-class abolitionists and Hofstadter's on the Progressives. But the New York Intellectuals and many of their ghetto-bred generation experienced both. Having felt the "aspirations" in their youth, they now felt the "insecurities" that accompany success. Prosperous times, Lipset argued, "make it possible for individuals and groups who have moved up to constitute a visible threat to the established status groups; while at the same time the successfully mobile begin to search for means of improving their status."[106] In academic and intellectual circles, the New York Intellectuals belonged to the most "successfully mobile" group.

The literary critics who had risen to prominence on the tide of modernism faced difficult intellectual challenges in the postwar years. They sought to fashion a new avant-garde and modernist approach, more in keeping with their newfound status. In addition, they tried to fend off the new avant-garde claimants, the Beats, contesting their right to wear the avant-garde mantle. Still, no new modernist theory emerged which transposed earlier notions to the postwar setting. The historians and sociologists had better luck. Consensus replaced conflict and status replaced class as dominant norms in the two disciplines. And the work in each area complemented the other, strengthening the intellectual position of both. Numerous historians and sociologists participated in these revisions, which cannot be viewed merely as the workings or rationalizations of a few New York Intellectuals. But New York Intellectuals did figure prominently among the chief proponents of the revisions. These ideas neatly fit broad views of American society and history, and the narrower area of their own personal development. To insiders, the idea of a general consensus appealed much more than that of conflict. Having gained a central place in American society, the New York Intellectuals found that notions of status aspirations and anxiety rang true. Once again, their own place influenced their intellectual perspective and reinforced their personal position. These academics were more fortunate than the literary critics in forging a new framework. Like the critics, however, they would find themselves under attack within a few years, from forces not seeking status and willing to accept conflict. For the time, however, a consensus did seem to take shape. It emerged, as the authors in *The New American Right* noted, out of the prosperity of the postwar years—a prosperity which catapulted a number of New York Intellectuals to prominence.

THE "SHMALTZ-GRUB"

The small world of the New York Intellectuals grew larger in the years after the war. Their numbers did increase as a few younger intellectuals began to attach themselves. But the sense of greater size derived more directly from the enlarged importance of the group. The already established reputations of some continued to grow, and additional members of the second generation began to make names for themselves. Life became easier, "the world seemed to be opening up, with all its charms, seductions, and falsities," Irving Howe recalled. At the most basic level, "there was work to be had." This might not always be the kind of work that best exploited intellectuals' gifts, Howe admitted, but it did mean "a serious writer could find a nook in publishing, he could pick up some money by free-lancing, sometimes for the well-paying mass-circulation magazines . . . he could do book reviewing." Yet, beyond the new availability of jobs or assignments, recognition increased because "culture was coming into fashion as a sign of a more comfortable and refined mode of living. . . . And intellectuals who had done their best work in a state of neglect found themselves becoming minor celebrities."[107]

The move to the center was by no means simply a matter of society's drawing unwilling intellectuals in from the periphery. They began to seek out places at the center as well. Their attitudes changed along with their prospects. "In a way they are like people to whom the doctor says, 'You're gonna die in five years,'" Leslie Fiedler suggests. "If you live past the five years, what do you do with your life?" In Fiedler's assessment, "the vision these people had growing up in the thirties was that the whole system was going to collapse. And, the one thing that was absolutely true, 'I'm never going to make it.'" Instead, the society sustained itself and even prospered—and so did the intellectuals. "These people were unprepared for the continuation of the American social, economic, political system or for their own personal successes. It simply unnerved them," Fiedler explained. "What a lot of us said in the depths of our hearts was, 'If the system has been this good to us, it can't be as bad as we thought it was.' If it has been this good to *us!*"[108]

Thus, for a number of reasons, personal and social, New York Intellectuals began, in a phrase which became infamous in time, to "make it" in the postwar world. Postwar prosperity, the fewer exclusions of Jews, a greater interest in intellectual undertakings and highbrow culture, and the growth of the university—all these external changes combined to create a cultural situation which offered much. At the same time, the New Yorkers did not hesitate to accept the fruits of this changed scene, or even to pursue them.

In the 1930s, as part of their cultural highbrowism and in defensive response to the exclusions they felt, the *Partisan* writers had disdained those magazines considered middlebrow. In particular, the *New Yorker* seemed the epitome of this kind of suspect intellectual undertaking. Daniel Bell later explained the circuitous logic by which the highbrow writers prided themselves on their exclusion. "You had been writing for a sophisticated audience, and you could be bright, sparkling, and witty with all your allusions. Would you be writing the same for these [middlebrow] magazines? If you're writing the same and they appreciate it, what's so special about you? If you write down, isn't this dreadful, because you're denaturing your thought." Among the *Partisan* editors, "Dwight Macdonald would almost lead the pack in dismissing the *New Yorkers,*" Bell remembered. By the 1950s things were changing. Most symbolically, Edmund Wilson began to write for the *New Yorker* and then Macdonald did. "Some writers began to discover," Howe observed, "that publishing a story in *The New Yorker* or *Esquire* was not a sure ticket to Satan." In fact, the relationship to the *New Yorker* shifted so much that Norman Podhoretz recalled that when as a young critic he was invited to write for the magazine, Lionel Trilling "regarded this invitation as an extraordinary event—a kind of confirmation . . . of his ideas as to the nature of the changes which were obviously beginning to take place in the American cultural situation."[109] Even the *Saturday Evening Post*, once the most of disdained of magazines, began to publish articles by intellectuals. In the 1930s Philip Rahv had difficulty considering Faulkner a great writer, becaue he had published in the *Saturday Evening Post*, Clement Greenberg remembered. In the 1950s Greenberg became one of the contributors to its "Adventures of the Mind" series.[110]

Once excluded, the New York Intellectuals acquired increasing prominence in the world now open to them. "The writers for *Partisan Review* now came to dominate the *New Yorker*," Bell asserted. To Midge Decter, "*Partisan Review* was getting to be like a farm team for the *New Yorker*."[111] It is impossible to know whether, had the *New Yorker* or the *Saturday Evening Post* offered work to the *Partisan* writers in the 1930s, they would have accepted. Needing money, they might have. Deeply committed to intellectual standards and highbrow culture, they might have declined. What is sure is that when in the fifties the offers did come, their old idealism gave way to a new cultural practicalism and a new view of the larger American cultural scene.

A second area of exclusion which broke down after World War II was academe. Both as Jews and as intellectuals, the New Yorkers reaped the benefits of the changing attitudes of American universities. Many in the older generation had experienced anti-Semitic reactions to their attempts to move ahead as scholars, such as Schapiro's rejection from Princeton, Trilling's experiences at Columbia, or the advice given to Elliot Cohen not to pursue graduate study. By the 1930s hard times had compounded the anti-Semitism, and only a few of the second generation pursued academic careers immediately. This kind of prejudice lessened after 1945, and the path of Jews into colleges at all levels became markedly smoother. A second and, for these individuals, more significant change also occurred after the war, corresponding to the overall changed status of intellectuals in American society. Previously, universities had been the province of scholars; cafés, the little magazines, and publishing, the realm of intellectuals. Meyer Schapiro and Sidney Hook took academic jobs in their areas of scholarly expertise. Edmund Wilson functioned as an intellectual, apart from university life. The two streams merged in the postwar years.

Most of the New York Intellectuals, even those without advanced degrees, eventually found their way to the university. In part, the crush of war veterans and the enormous growth of the university accounted for the need for more professors. But a good portion of the demand came from the new appreciation of intellectuals. The arguments that intellectuals had a vital function in society began to take hold. Those without a Ph.D. (Howe, Kazin, Phillips), or even without a B.A. (Rahv) became professors. At Columbia, Daniel Bell and Nathan Glazer were awarded Ph.D.'s by the university after they had been hired to teach, on the basis of research already published.[112]

Before the war the exception among the New York Intellectuals had been those with academic jobs. The balance now shifted in the other direction. "The very idea of the intellectual not tied to an institution but following the imperatives of his own thought [became] harder to keep alive," Howe wrote "Edmund Wilson was still there, a great model of toughness and devotion: but who had his energy or his opportunities? Paul Goodman and Harold Rosenberg held out, getting by with marginal jobs, but they would soon be the exceptions."[113] In time, even Goodman and Rosenberg would join university faculties. The shift in perspective can be seen in the evolving attitude of Phillip Rahv. In 1950 Rahv taught one course at NYU, explaining to a friend, "Everybody on *PR* is now teaching—which shows how far things have gone." In 1957 Rahv could tell Allen Tate, "I have accepted an appointment [at Brandeis] for two years. If I stay longer it will be because the situation proves altogether congenial—which I doubt." Rahv remained at Brandeis until his death in 1974. Despite his hesitations, Rahv may have sensed the change more accurately than he could admit. "A little too late for me to start an academic career," he wrote Tate, "but there I go anyway. The *Zeitgeist* has got me down. There's no escaping it."[114]

The zeitgeist, which Howe had warned against in "This Age of Conformity," drew Rahv to Brandeis in 1957. It had drawn Howe there in 1954. The magnetism came from both sides, combining to create the cultural attraction. The university, Alfred Kazin saw clearly in 1955, began "to play the active role of patron: to support the creation of literature, to take writers into the academic community, and thus to show that it regards them as assimilated, harmonious—and necessary." Understating the case, Kazin observed, "This represents a very great change." He also detected the other dynamic, the awareness on the writer's part that "he is in the university because he wants to be there." In the postwar world, attachment to the university allowed the writer and intellectual to fulfill the role once sought outside academe:

> It enables him to play a role—as moralist, as philosopher, as literary guide and teacher to his tribe—which American writers have always loved to play, which the country has wanted them to play, and which in a culture so devoted to self-improvement as ours, the university best enables them to play.[115]

The stock of intellectuals, in general, rose dramatically in the postwar years. The New York Intellectuals became some of the great beneficiaries of this development. They began to taste prominence soon after the war, and their reknown kept rising. In 1947 Rahv expressed to Arthur Schlesinger his delight that an article by Schlesinger in *PR* had been passed around in the State Department. "I am very pleased to hear the response to your piece in Washington," Rahv wrote. "One thing that one can say about *Partisan Review* is that the pieces in it do get read by the right people."[116] By 1960 some of these individuals were being invited to Washington.

The importance of *Partisan Review* in particular and of the New York Intellectuals in general took on new aspects as the years progressed. Norman Podhoretz remembered that "no young novelist, whether successful elsewhere or not, could feel secure about his status as a serious writer until he had been favorably reviewed, or better still published, in *Partisan Review*." And a young critic like himself, "whether in the academy or not," could not "be altogether happy about his career until Phillips and Rahv had conferred upon him the honor of an invitation to do something for them." This kind of prominence and importance continued to grow. "These people are the Diors and Schiaparellis of intellectual fashion," the novelist George P. Eliot observed in the 1960s. "What they think today, you're apt to find yourself, in a Sears Roebuck-ish sort of way, thinking tomorrow."[117]

This kind of reputation, combining public importance with high intellectual standards, had been an underlying goal of the New York Intellectuals for years. The moment of achievement had arrived, and they took advantage of the opportunities. Yet, the successes did not come without correspondent sacrifices. A few were immediately apparent; others grew clear only as the prosperous years progressed. Most obviously, the move to the university brought a geographical dispersion. A number took academic jobs in New York, but others went to Boston, to Chicago, to California. Philip Rahv wrote ruefully to Allen Tate in 1953, "There is little doing in New York this winter. What with the lure of Europe on the one hand and the necessity of teaching on the other, there are few writers left in the city." Rahv wistfully admitted, "The old literary life—with its proud autonomy, absorbing gossip, and keen expression of personality—now belongs to the historical past." Rahv found himself equally displeased with the new individuals he began to meet in New York. As successes piled up for the older generations, the new aspiring intellectuals arrived with an outlook different from that of their counterparts in the prewar years. "The young writers are much too respectable and prudent," he complained; "they get married early, settle down and dream of the book-of-the-month club selection and other prizes of commercial success."[118]

Rahv did not indulge in fictitious nostalgia or in romanticizing his past at the expense of the present. Attitudes had undergone significant change. Compared with the boisterous, charged interactions of the *Partisan* writers—from their hand-to-mouth existence to their intense personal affairs—the attitude of Norman Podhoretz, for example, seemed amazingly strange and tame. "I *had* chosen a life of middle-class respectability in many essential respects. I was married and I believed in marriage; I had children and I believed in having them; I had a steady job and I believed in working hard," Podhoretz wrote, in regard to the 1950s. "As a child I couldn't wait to grow up; as a young man I was eager to get married, and so far from unwilling was I to become a father that when I did get married it was to a woman who already had two little children for me to raise while waiting for my own to be born." Times had changed. To Rahv, intellectuals had gone from lumpen-proletariats to lumpen-bourgeoisie.[119]

For the generation of Podhoretz, the acceptance of this new mentality came more easily than for the older intellectuals. Because they had defined themselves by their exclusions and their marginal existence, the elders' new status brought about some personal disorientation. As Howe succinctly put it, "Poverty is attractive only to the prosperous," but he also admitted that as "intellectuals started enjoying some of the good things of life," there emerged "some uneasiness." Personal uneasiness was accompanied by gossip and asides. "People made jokes or nasty remarks about getting rich or bourgeois. But really that was childishness, of course. By American standards, very few did more than achieve a modest sort of middle-class existence," Howe noted. "I mean, all right, so people had wine on the table when they served someone dinner; it is nothing to shoot anyone for."[120]

They did do some shooting, however, at least with barbed phrases and innuendos. Midge Decter recalled great discussions over Daniel Bell's acceptance of an editorship at *Fortune:* "a whole debate about should Dan Bell have done this or should he not have done this and become so rich. And he actually bought nice furniture. I think he was making around $15,000 a year."[121] As Decter concluded, a variety of factors converged to allow for this intellectual advancement, but the success was always tinged with envious attacks or personal digs. "They left bohemia because they had grown to appreciate American society and American life, and they appreciated it as being the last democracy." Furthermore, "there were jobs, but no sooner did somebody get a job than there was an essay published saying 'You people sold out!' " Looking back on the salaries of the *Commentary* editors or of an assistant professor, Decter called this whole debate "an absurdity."[122] Yet she is the woman—with the two small children—Norman Podhoretz married.

For the preceding generations of intellectuals, these matters seemed less absurd, because they went to the heart of questions about identity, more than to the individual debates over salary or furniture. "Children of the Depression, the intellectuals were astonished to gain modest comforts," Howe recounted. Howe's essay "This Age of Conformity" is an example Decter used to illustrate her point about the internal bickering over petty issues. But, as Howe realized, "it was ideology rather than money which was the main prompter."[123]

In 1959, at the beginning of his essay "Mass Society and Post-Modern Fiction," Howe offered a parody of Dostoevsky's *Crime and Punishment.* Raskolnikov's misery is ended when he receives a Guggenheim Foundation Fellowship and thus no longer needs to murder the hunchbacked pawnbroker. While personal issues remain for Dostoevsky's character, the social setting for the novel is now removed.

> Gliding from fellowship to fellowship, Raskolnikov may now end his life as a sober Professor of Literature. Like the rest of us, he will occasionally notice in himself those dim urges and quavers that speak for hidden powers beyond the assuagement of reason. He may remember that once, unlikely as it has now come to seem, he was even tempted to murder an old woman. But again like the rest of us, he will dismiss these feelings as unworthy of a civilized man.[124]

Whether Howe ever contemplated killing anyone we do not know. We do know that he was fired from his first job within six weeks for attempting to organize factory workers and that he has become a distinguished professor of literature at the City University of New York. Howe is hardly alone in having made this transition. It is the exceptional intellectual who held out against the zeitgeist and the opportunities. "If you play the game, go the the right parties, talk to the right people and review books in the right way," Paul Goodman held, "then you get the patronage—the literary plums." For example, "you get $2000 for collecting the short novels of Henry James and pasting together an introduction from stuff somebody else had written. I don't want to collect the short novels of Henry James." Goodman still adhered to an older intellectual model, one Howe had defended in his 1954 attack on conformity. But as Howe came to realize, things were different. "That power corrupts everyone knows by now, but we ought also to recognize that powerlessness, if not corrupting, can be damaging—as in the case of Paul Goodman, a very courageous writer who stuck to his anarchist beliefs . . . [but who] could also come to seem, in his very rectitude, an example of asphyxiating righteousness."[125]

Intellectuals moved into the newer postwar style—some readily, some reluctantly. Diana Trilling remembered that "once upon a time—that was in the thirties—one had had to defend even having a comfortable chair to sit in, or a rug on the floor. But by the forties things had changed; one's most intransigent literary friends had capitulated, everybody had a well-upholstered sofa." But some of the vitality had been drained away, traded in for the rug on the floor, perhaps. They still wrote as much—often more, because the opportunities became greater—and their words frequently had the same sharp edge. Yet the personal intensity declined. Reading intellectual journals in Boston and Palo Alto, where he had academic appointments, Howe sensed that things were, from his "own sort of socialist view, getting better." When he returned to New York, he realized that "it didn't make much difference what was being said in the intellectual journals and in the quarterlies and the weeklies, because the style of life, the kind of comfort that people lived, wasn't changed by their opinion."[126]

Being an intellectual became a profession rather than a way of life. Still serious, articulate, and prolific, they became less *engagé*. Arnold Beichman, close to many of these individuals through the American Committee for Cultural Freedom, recalls that in the late 1950s and early 1960s he had tried to rally intellectuals to his work organizing hospital workers, among the lowest-paid workers in New York. "In the old days you could always get the intellectuals to picket, so for the hell of it I sent a telegram to about fifty leading intellectuals asking their support during the New York hospital workers' strike. The only one who showed any interest at all was Steven Marcus, then a young Columbia College English professor. Nobody else." Despite the intellectuals' working-class backgrounds and previous commitments to political change from the bottom up, Beichman now found that "trade unions had become—to intellectuals anyway—a great irrelevance to cultural, political, and intellectual activity. The proletariat was no longer to be trusted as Marx's gravedigger of capitalism."[127]

Intellectual life had been stood on its head. Howe came to realize that, rather than exclusions and alienation, a new chief problem was plaguing intellectuals: "He's too much in society, he's too assimilated. . . . He's overwhelmed with the possibilities of making a dollar, for doing jobs. . . . It's not a matter of selling out. . . . It's just that you end up not doing the work for which you have presumably devoted your life."[128] There grew, as Saul Bellow labeled it, a "swamp of prosperity."

> Love, duty, principle, thought, significance, everything is being sucked into a fatty and nerveless state of "well-being." My mother used to say of people who had had a lucky break, in the Old Yiddish metaphor, "they've fallen into the *shmaltz-grub*"—a pit of fat. The pit has expanded now into a swamp, and the lucky ones may be those who haven't yet tasted the fruits of prosperity.[129]

Their falling into the *shmaltz-grub* brought another significant change for these intellectuals, which like many other changes became apparent only with the passage of time. They had always been a combative group, knocking each other as they battled their most hated enemies. The cohesive force, which had overcome the interpersonal tensions, had been the sense that they shared a common outlook and that while few others might be aware of their existence, they keenly knew and cared about each other. The postwar prosperity and the achievement of intellectual eminence changed all this. They dispersed physically, scattering across the country. Furthermore, success did not come at a single moment, but sooner to some, later to others, causing jealousies to erupt on both sides. Finally, and most significantly, they no longer lived on the margin with their exclusions, but at the center, accepted in ways they had never experienced. Their literary style, their political outlook, and their intellectual reputation enjoyed great prominence. Once, "they were themselves, if not the only, the main, people who knew what they were talking about," Norman Podhoretz observed.[130] That was no longer true. They were known and understood, respected and rewarded.

The centripetal force which had kept their circle together began to lessen. They still saw one another, interacted socially, and cared intensely about what the others wrote. But the forces pushing the community apart now grew stronger than those holding it together. In the 1960s their world would come undone, not by a sudden shattering into disparate pieces but by the gradual pulling away of groups and single members. Although the label New York

Intellectual would still identify an individual, the community itself would no longer have the same cohesiveness. In fact, during the next decade they would grow so far apart that new clusters of individuals would be discernible—new intellectual constellations would emerge. Their personal identification remained, but their intellectual world began to recede into the historical past.

Chapter 13

Things Fall Apart: Dispersions

The New York Intellectuals had come together on the periphery, united by their exclusions and talking to one another. They argued about radicalism and literature, intellectual roles, and the subversiveness of modernism. Jews in Gentile America, radicals in a world of liberal corporate capitalism, intellectuals in an anti-intellectual society—they formed an intellectual community on the margin and moved together toward the center. The history of the New York Intellectual community is the history of that progress, of the ways ideas changed or were tailored to facilitate the journey, of the intellectual and political costs it involved. With each success, with each arrival, the bonds which held the community together weakened. By the 1960s, their personal victories complete, they saw the cohesion of their world come undone. Once cohesiveness was no longer a practical necessity, internal tensions became the community's major dynamic force.

Personal tragedy struck the New York Intellectual community in the mid-1950s, and, in a sense, it never fully recovered. The shocks were centered at *Commentary* but reverberated throughout the intellectual world of New York. In 1955, at the age of thirty-seven, Robert Warshow dropped dead of a heart attack. In 1956 Isaac Rosenfeld died in Chicago. And in these years *Commentary's* editor, Elliot Cohen, became increasingly depressed. "Utterly paralyzed," Norman Podhoretz recalled, "he sat day after day in his office, unable to do anything but stare listlessly at the desk. . . . "[1] All the pressures of Cohen's lifetime finally took their toll: the pain of the years when he was in intellectual exile, writing press releases; the ambiguous relations with authorities, from Yale to the American Jewish Committee; his own, personal inadequacies as a writer. New anxieties piled up on top of the older problems.

He struggled within the Committee to maintain a hard line on communism. "Violent controversies" erupted, according to Morris Fine. "Elliot's temper" added intensity to the debate, and he "precipitated serious run-ins with Committee counsel Ed Lukas." Yet, Lionel Trilling later recalled that "what tormented [Cohen] was an irrational remorse over the antagonisms he had in the past directed to Communists and to sympathizers with Communism."[2] In 1956 Cohen entered a psychiatric hospital. His absence from *Commentary* caused additional problems. A struggle grew among the editors who remained to oversee the magazine. The name-calling and finger-pointing provoked by this rivalry has continued to the present. The rivals—Clement and Martin Greenberg, on the one had, and Norman Podhoretz, on the other—provided their versions of and observations on the conflict. None painted pictures of harmony. Podhoretz's disdain for the Greenberg brothers led him to refuse to call them by name in *Making It*, his memoir of these years. Referring to them only as "The Boss," Podhoretz portrayed the Greenbergs' actions toward him as petty, vindictive, and ruthless. When Podhoretz objected that his title and salary were less than Cohen had promised, The Boss "answered testily that Cohen was out of the picture and might never return to the magazine. . . . He was now The Boss." Clement Greenberg later questioned Podhoretz's assertions. "Norman never did complain to either of us about his title or salary, let alone get the answer he reports. He knew full well that those questions lay not at all with us, but with the American Jewish Committee in Cohen's absence." Podhoretz felt, in addition, that The Boss would do anything to maintain power. "If Cohen ever came back The Boss was planning to make life so miserable for him that the return would last only long enough to induce a relapse and set the stage for a coup." This assertion was "sheer invention," Clement Greenberg believed. "How did Norman know what was in our minds?" In fact, Greenberg said, neither he nor his brother ever wanted to run *Commentary*. "My brother and I both had reservations about the value of the magazine; Martin wanted his job there, nothing more." Greenberg later admitted that he and his brother were "disgusted" by Podhoretz, seeing him as someone with a "lack of convictions." Nonetheless, he noted, "Norman happens to be a superb editor; he's done with *Commentary* what neither of us could have done—or would have: in some part because we don't have his sheer ability, in other part because we didn't see magazine-editing as a career."[3]

The turbulence was not confined to the editorial offices of *Commentary*, but became a topic of discussion in the New York Intellectual world. Dwight Macdonald recalled hearing stories about Clement Greenberg's needling of Elliot Cohen. According to Greenberg this derived from a single outburst of "accumulated anger" which he aimed at Cohen a week before Cohen's hospitalization. He also recalled Cohen's wife thanking him for standing by Cohen when the editor was falling into his depression.[4]

Podhoretz's built-up rage finally burst, he wrote, and he quit *Commentary* "in a voluptuous emission of obscene expletives shouted at The Boss in the highest register [his] cigarette-roughened vocal cords could attain." However, the Committee refused to accept his resignation, investigated the charges made against the Greenbergs, and, in the end, reorganized the interim editorship. Martin Greenberg remained, along with Podhoretz and George Lichtheim, all as associate editors. Clement Greenberg left the magazine, told later that Cohen could not return as long as he, Greenberg, remained.[5]

Throughout these years, Elliot Cohen suffered continual personal doubts. Arnold Beichman visited Cohen in the hospital and found him burdened with self-recrimination. "How do I know I was right?" Cohen asked Beichman. At other times, during his hospitalization, Cohen seemed "very lucid," Morris Fine recalled, "full of ideas for the magazine of remarkable creativity." Cohen wanted to return to *Commentary*, and Podhoretz desired Cohen's return as well. The new, triple editorship worked more smoothly, "but it could not generate excitement or urgency."[6] The resumption of Cohen's editorship promised much.

In 1958 Elliot Cohen came back to his magazine but was no longer the dynamic force he had been during its formative years. A "shrunken, shaken man," Podhoretz recalled, Cohen lapsed into the same state which had preceded his hospitalization. "He just sat there, paralyzed," Morris Fine remembers. "His speech was impaired." It compounded the problems, at least from Podhoretz's perspective, that Cohen began siding with Martin Greenberg. To Clement Greenberg, Cohen's siding with Martin Greenberg seemed significant. "After his dose of therapy, such as it was, Elliot recognized that Martin didn't want control, didn't want to replace him; all he wanted was more comfort in his job."[7] Rather than cause the kind of explosive confrontation which had accompanied his first resignation, Podhoretz this time withdrew more quietly, going to work for his friend Jason Epstein, then at Doubleday. A resolution, if not an altogether easy one, now appeared to have come to the troubled personnel questions at *Commentary*. But in 1959 Elliot Cohen, unable to overcome the depression and doubts which haunted him, killed himself. The New York Intellectual world changed its course once again.

DIVING INTO THE PLAZA FOUNTAIN

In the history of the three chief journals of the New York Intellectuals— *Partisan Review*, *Commentary*, and *Dissent*—there has been only one total editorial change. In 1959 the American Jewish Committee set out to replace Elliot Cohen. Irving Kristol was first offered the job, but he refused it. Approached informally, Daniel Bell and Alfred Kazin also declined.[8] Two front-running candidates emerged, the former protagonists Martin Greenberg and Norman Podhoretz. According to Podhoretz, the acting editor Greenberg expected the appointment—an assertion Clement Greenberg disputed—but "never had a chance." Brimming with ideas, but publicly disdaining any interest in the job, Podhoretz met with the Committee to discuss the problems with the magazine and his ideas about the direction *Commentary* should take. As both the insider and the outsider, Podhoretz later acknowledged, he appeared experienced and fresh. He remained outwardly uninterested, although he continued through a series of interviews leading up to a direct offer, which he said he always planned to decline. Anger over The Boss rather than an actual desire for the editorship prompted his actions. But in the end, against the advice of Jason Epstein, Irving Kristol, Diana Trilling, William Phillips, and his own first instincts, he took it. At another level, however, as Podhoretz himself advised, "the best way to get a job you really want is to believe that you really don't want it."[9]

Podhoretz's failure to listen to the advice of his older friends—all but Jason Epstein represent first- and second-generation New York Intellectuals—is telling for the course he took in the next few years. In his heart, if not yet in his head, Podhoretz planned to strike out on his own, to light a new star in the intellectual constellation he inhabited. To begin with, however, one of his immediate resolves for revitalizing the magazine was "to take *Commentary* out of the hands of the largely academic types on whom it had come to rely so heavily and to bring it back into the family."[10] The first issue of the "new *Commentary*" fully reflected this change. In addition to Podhoretz's opening editorial, articles by Lionel Trilling, Alfred Kazin, and F. W. Dupee appeared, along with reviews by Steven Marcus and Irving Kristol. The family "cousins" Paul Goodman, Murray Kempton, George Lichtheim, Richard Chase, and Arthur Koestler also contributed. The second issue added Daniel Bell, Sidney Hook, Leslie Fiedler, William Barrett, Nathan Glazer, and Midge Decter.

The Podhoretz and Trilling contributions to the first new number dealt with the man Podhoretz replaced. Trilling's "On the Death of a Friend" talked about Cohen's life; Podhoretz's "The Issue" tried to establish the place of Cohen and *Commentary* in the context of the 1950s. After years of despair and dissension, Podhoretz observed, intellectuals in the 1950s "undertook to demonstrate that the Protestant-liberal-bourgeois synthesis had *not* broken down," and "*Commentary* was an important participant" in this endeavor.[11]

Podhoretz quoted Yeats's famous words "things fall apart" to describe the mentality of the prewar years, the mentality Cohen and *Commentary* had helped change. The irony is that, having claimed the role of *Commentary* in helping "our civilization" adapt without "losing form or identity," Podhoretz took *Commentary* in a direction in the early 1960s which helped undermine the form and identity of the smaller intellectual world he inhabited. While drawing members of his intellectual community to *Commentary*, he began to pull away from that very community.

One of his strongest attributes in his securing of the *Commentary* editorship, Podhoretz later believed, was his youth. America had embarked on its fascination with youthfulness in these years and was about to elect a young president. Having once committed himself wholeheartedly to the intellectual style and community of his elders, Podhoretz had already evidenced increasing doubts about this choice. "What makes it especially difficult to characterize the younger generation of intellectuals in this country is that they have not yet been articulate about themselves," he wrote in 1957. "They have found no spokesman to voice their protests or to proclaim their aspirations." Even while disparaging the Beats as "know-nothing Bohemians," Podhoretz criticized the intellectual complacency typical of his generation. Convinced that this mentality originated in "an intensive campaign against the pieties of American liberalism," he carried his criticism to ideas and individuals. Among those central to this attack on naïve liberalism, "there were, finally, and perhaps most important, the literary critics who implicitly (the New Critics) and explicitly (Lionel Trilling) brought the liberal picture of human nature into utter disrepute." This constituted, if not a conservative reaction, at least an attempt to "redress an imbalance of opinion . . . to show that liberalism was guilty of a failure to take a sufficiently complicated view of reality. Complexity became a key work [exercising] a thaumaturgic hold on the imagination of the young."[12]

The elders understood the path by which they had come to this revised and complex liberalism. The younger intellectuals merely knew they must "get down to the business of adult living as quickly as possible. And get down to business the young generation did. A great many of them married early. . . . As befitted responsible adults there was nothing playful or frisky about these young people . . . they struck a perfect attitude of the civilized adult: poised, sober, judicious, prudent." They achieved too easily and at the cost of real engagement. "The world is seen at a distant remove, commented on quietly and wisely, never struggled with or confronted full in the face." Podhoretz was ultimately harsh on his generation, on himself. We are really a "non-generation," he observed, "a collection of people who, for all their apparent command of themselves, for all the dispatch with which they have taken their places in society, for all their sophistication, for all their 'maturity,' know nothing, stand for nothing, believe in nothing."[13]

With *Commentary* under his control, Norman Podhoretz set out to establish what his generation stood for and how it differed from that of his intellectual mentors. He coupled his first major foray in his new effort with his first editorial coup. Having read a segment of a much longer work by Paul Goodman in *Dissent*, Podhoretz contacted Goodman about the entire manuscript. Admitting that it had been turned down by nineteen publishers, Goodman showed Podhoretz *Growing Up Absurd*. "It was everything I wanted for the new *Commentary*, and more: it was the very incarnation of the new spirit I had been hoping would be at work in the world, as it had been at work in me." Podhoretz excitedly persuaded Jason Epstein, now at Random House, to publish the book and edited three long serializations for his first three issues of *Commentary*. These created "so great a sensation that they put the 'new *Commentary*' on the map from the very first minute."[14]

Goodman's articles should also have put the older New York Intellectuals on the defensive from the very first minute, for though they continued to appear in the *Commentary* table of contents, Podhoretz began to steer the magazine away from the intellectual and political harbors of his elders. He broke with the hard anticommunism of the late 1950s—of which Elliot Cohen and his "Grand Design" had been an integral part—and began a short-lived flirtation with the left. This new effort caused personal frictions as well as intellectual disputes. "There are a lot of people you have to kill when you are young and you've made your mark early," Arnold Beichman observed. Podhoretz "had to kill Trilling, Hook, Bell, and Elliot Cohen." Bitter antagonisms erupted between Podhoretz and Lionel Trilling, Podhoretz's intellectual mentor and the preeminent pillar of the 1950s mentality Podhoretz had begun to cast off. Daniel Bell recalled four or five episodes between Podhoretz and Trilling, including a dinner for Manès Sperber. Podhoretz became almost abusive of Sidney Hook, saying, "You call yourself a Socialist?" Since the dinner was a public event and since Trilling did not want to subject himself to the outburst, he walked out. Podhoretz has subsequently denied this incident, although others recall it. Diana Trilling told of another encounter, about the same time, at a party at Arnold Beichman's. Amid other New York Intellectuals, Podhoretz verbally attacked Trilling. Diana Trilling remembered, "My hands began to tremble with rage, and I could see that it was taking a great effort for Lionel to keep himself under control, but he spoke very quietly to Norman and said he was sure they could find some basic premise in common and start off from there. To this Norman replied very violently that they had nothing in common!"[15] For his part, Podhoretz and others recall the abuse directed toward him. William Phillips tells of a dinner at which Lionel and Diana Trilling attacked Podhoretz and *Commentary*, while "Midge and Norman were trying to stay cool." Podhoretz himself remembers the abuse he took. "Daniel Bell exploded at me in rage over my sponsorship of Norman O. Brown, whom he considered dangerous and irresponsible." He also tells of other heated arguments, including a lunch where the philosopher Sidney Morgenbesser "became so nasty and insulting that, right in the middle of the meal, I stormed out of the restaurant."[16]

In 1957 Podhoretz foreshadowed his own, personal course in describing his entire generation. "[It] would be a mistake to accept the sobriety and composure of the young generation at face value," he asserted. "The truth is that this is a restless generation, and as it grows older it gets more and more restless; it is beginning to feel cheated of its youth (that, I suspect, is the meaning of the recent revival of interest in the 20's)." Alluding to his own life, Podhoretz noted that since "this generation . . . willed itself from childhood directly into adulthood, it still has its adolescence to go through—for a man can never skip adolescence, he can only postpone it." He concluded his essay optimistically: "And something very wonderful may come about when a whole generation in its late thirties breaks loose and decides to take a swim in the Plaza fountain in the middle of the night."[17]

In the early 1960s Podhoretz went, in Stanley Edgar Hyman's description, from being "the youngest of the old to . . . the oldest of the young."[18] In assuming the most important position of his life, he also embarked on his delayed adolescence. Fueled by driving ambition, he revived a sagging magazine. With the rebelliousness and often the tactlessness of adolescence, he marked himself off from his intellectual fathers. And if he did not dive into the Plaza fountain at midnight, he at least began to swim against the current of his intellectual world in New York, permanently diverting its flow.

SOMEBODIES AND NOT NOBODIES

> *All of us in the family knew and were even friendly with members of the White House staff; they read our magazines and the pieces and books we ourselves wrote, and they cared—it is even said that the President [Kennedy] himself cared—about w*ʰ*at we thought. Would Roosevelt have cared? Would Truman? Would Eisenhower?*
>
> *—Norman Podhoretz*[19]

If Norman Podhoretz helped change the world of the New York Intellectuals, outside forces also influenced the direction of their lives. After the New Yorkers had for years proclaimed the social function and utility of American intellectuals, there came a time in the 1960s when the message seemed to have reached the highest echelons in the nation. "The main thing that Kennedy did," Podhoretz told A. Alvarez, "was to give intellectuals a sense of connection to power. This was quite unprecedented in the experiences of most of us."[20] Intellectuals began to feel and seek these ties, adding to their own power and prestige. Hannah Arendt, something of an elder sage, believed that a significant change in the 1960s was "beyond doubt the new status of the intellectuals. Professors, for instance, today are somebodies and not nobodies; and this is entirely new and it dates back really only a few years."[21]

Intellectuals established intimate connections with government as never before. Some took jobs in Washington, including Nathan Glazer, the vital-center advocate Arthur Schlesinger, and a new "cousin," at least of *Commentary*, Daniel Patrick Moynihan. While most did not take employment, they nonetheless felt the connections. Kennedy was "the first major public figure who was genuinely of our time. One felt him to be a contemporary," Podhoretz remembered. "He was a man who was post-Freud, post-Marx, post-Einstein; he was a man who lived in the twentieth-century." Furthermore, "he began to flatter the intellectuals," Midge Decter recalled, "which is to say he invited them to his house for supper." After the Eisenhower era, which was "very dreary and very boring, very dull and very bad," the intellectuals "were enormously cheered up for three years."[22]

Not everyone felt immediate elation, but all felt the change. More than a good job or influence was at stake, Norman Mailer believed. "We became just a touch like minor royalty. Dispossessed of our natural lands . . . there was always Versailles. . . . And Kennedy did very much act like a king *vis-à-vis* the intellectuals." The question of how a politician could seduce this group of perceptive and hardheaded thinkers produced much analysis in later years.

Midge Decter found that Kennedy's "youth, his beauty, his—odious word—style, his being unlike our—even more odious word—image of a politician," all contributed to his personal appeal.[23] Elizabeth Hardwick sought out the intellectual underpinnings and touched on a theme central to the role of the New Yorkers in defining their place in the 1950s. The avant-garde and revolutionary modernism to which they had once been committed had lost its drive and meaning in the 1950s. Kennedy seemed "rather sweeter than he would have otherwise to people," Hardwick concluded, because "there's no real avant-garde. To find a president who at least keeps up with what is chic, alas, connects him with the intelligentsia in some funny way." If there were a "real avant-garde," Hardwick held, intellectuals "would feel that they had something that could be kept apart from chicness."[24]

While avant-garde implied a conscious opposition to the prevailing norms of the culture, "chicness" connoted style and fashion. Once intellectuals had come in from the cold and established connections with power, it became clear that their intellectual endeavors no longer represented opposition to the prevailing ethos. They were "chic" because they were "in"—they had achieved what they had long ago set out to achieve.

The New York Intellectuals had finally become fashionable. They no longer spoke only to each other: their audiences had grown, and their words fell on important and influential ears. "Intellectuals could and did dream of influencing the taste for change being expressed by their government and the society around them," Midge Decter reflected in 1968. Their thinking became "chic," as Elizabeth Hardwick suggested, not avant-garde, no longer subversive of the social order. Instead, it sought to reaffirm, while reforming, that order. The coming to power seemed a happy occasion. "This moment had arrived," Decter continued, "without apocalypse, without even the help of most intellectuals in bringing it, and without appearing to threaten those comforts the society had already provided."[25] Decter spoke of the general comforts Americans had acquired during the years of postwar prosperity, but her analysis points more directly to her intellectual colleagues. They had earned place and recognition, found more-comfortable positions and life-styles, and gained the social role they had long sought.

Lionel Trilling participated in this achievement but, according to his own sense of complexities and nuances, began to detect the problems with this victory just as he experienced its pleasures. "In a curious way Kennedy thickened things up and gave people—gave me at any rate, and I think a good many of my friends—a certain sense of our actuality in the social structure. The intellectual seemed to be more important." Trilling grew troubled, however, by the lack of a "strongly critical function"; he warned that intellectuals ought to be "leery" of their "easier acceptance."[26] Other intellectuals shared Trilling's doubts as the years progressed, especially after many intellectuals became personally entwined in the policies of the Vietnam War. In the first

years of the 1960s, the headiness of their new fashionableness carried
intellectuals along. "Those who received [White House] invitations were of
course flattered and delighted," Podhoretz recalled; "those who did not were
dejected and upset."[27]

As radicals and liberals, modernists and avant-gardists, the New York
Intellectuals always maintained that they held a critical view of American
society, an adversary relationship. Over the course of the 1950s, they had
modified their political outlook to create and conform with postwar liberal
attitudes and liberal anticommunism. They searched for a new meaning for
their vaunted avant-gardism and could only reject the claims of others trying to
define its new characteristics. In academic disciplines they helped develop
explanations of the historical process and social dynamics which praised
consensus over conflict, status anxieties over class antagonisms. Their ideas took
hold, established themselves, became fashionable. They were "in," "chic." The
public came courting. Having spent so many nights home alone, the New
Yorkers could not resist the advances. As Norman Podhoretz later concluded,
"While intelligence, learning, wide knowledge, and even wisdom were in
abundant supply with the intellectual community of New York, worldliness was
not one of its salient qualities." "For all their gloss of sophistication, they had
not really moved very far into the world," Irving Howe concluded. "The
immigrant milk was still on their lips."[28]

Having attained prominence, the New Yorkers sought to expand their
influence, to capitalize on their newfound prestige. Their path had always been
through important journals, and in the early 1960s it seemed that this would be
their route once again. For several years there had been talk of a creating a
New York equivalent to the *Times Literary Supplement* of London. Among those
thinking about such a publication were the two wunderkinder of the New York
Intellectual world, Norman Podhoretz and Jason Epstein. The moment for
launching such an endeavor came with the New York newspaper strike of 1963.
Epstein, a vice-president at Random House, knew that publishers had books
ready to bring out and advertisements to run. Moreover, reviewers had
available time. Seizing the opportunity, Epstein helped organize a number of
his fellow New Yorkers in creating the *New York Review of Books*. Robert Silvers
formerly at Harper's, and Epstein's wife, Barbara, became editors. The
contributors to the new magazine read like a who's who of contemporary
letters. New York Intellectuals formed the solid core of the *Review's* first
writers: Hannah Arendt, Saul Bellow, F. W. Dupee, Nathan Glazer, Clement
Greenberg, Irving Howe, Alfred Kazin, Irving Kristol, Dwight Macdonald,
William Phillips, and Philip Rahv, among others.[29] Other luminaries included
W. H. Auden, Ralph Ellison, Lillian Hellman, Robert Lowell, Stephen
Spender, and Edmund Wilson.[30] In the second year of the *Review*, Harold
Rosenberg, Diana Trilling, and Midge Decter contributed; Daniel Bell and
Norman Podhoretz did so in the third. The degree to which the *New York*

Review swept the field of contemporary writers and critics led Richard Hofstadter to refer to it jokingly as "The New York Review of Each Other's Books." Philip Nobile, who chronicled the *Review*'s early history, characterized the first issues as prey to "nepotism, fratricide, and incest, and even a dose of narcissism."[31]

The "fratricide" was extremely rare at the start. The *Review's* relationship with various segments of the New York Intellectual world would not always remain so warm. In time there were hostilities between factions of the community which would rival the old *Partisan Review–New Masses* debates in intensity. For the moment, however, rivalries remained relatively quiet. A few antagonisms rippled the calm. Mary McCarthy took objection both to a hostile review of *The Group* by Norman Mailer and to a pseudonymous parody called "The Gang," actually written by McCarthy's old friend Elizabeth Hardwick. Mailer himself took exception to Philip Rahv's being given *An American Dream* to review, an objection he later published in *Cannibals and Christians*.[32] Apart from these personal frustrations, things seemed relatively harmonious and promising.

In the course of the *New York Review*'s rise, two of its prime movers joined the upper ranks of the New York Intellectual world. Robert Silvers, whose tenure at *Harper's* had been marked by an interest in literary rather than in political issues, climbed slowly up the intellectual social ladder. Jason Epstein sprang to the top. He had already secured an upper rung before the *Review*'s appearance. Norman Podhoretz remembers his astonishment in the 1950s when Epstein, a classmate but not a friend at Columbia, made his first, striking marks in the publishing world. Considered "unserious" during his student days, Epstein had helped create the paperback revolution at Doubleday, lived "romantically with his new wife in the village," and threw "parties to which, it was said, famous writers always came, including (incredibly) W. H. Auden himself."[33] Podhoretz and Epstein did become friends in the 1950s, Epstein offering Podhoretz publishing jobs during several periods of tension at *Commentary* and joining him in bringing out *Growing Up Absurd* and Norman O. Brown's *Life Against Death*, two publishing coups. But Epstein differed from the New York Intellectuals, at least outwardly. If they all possessed aggressiveness and a bit of the hustler beneath their intellectual exterior, Epstein wore his ambition more openly. "Jason has the mind of a scholar and the instincts of a pushcart peddler," remembered a colleague at Doubleday. Dwight Macdonald observed, "Jason is a caricature of a New York Intellectual . . . a nineteenth century entrepreneur, a robber baron, only his market is not copper, but intellectuals."[34] It is not clear if Epstein would ever have been fully accepted as a member of "the family." Perhaps his entrepreneurial brusqueness would have kept him from the inner circles in any era. By the 1960s, however, despite the attraction of so many of the community to the *New York Review*, the group itself had begun to lose its function and cohesion. No solid community existed for Epstein to join. Instead the intellectual realm of the New Yorkers expanded into new areas and incorporated new personalities. In this much looser collectivity, more an intellectual environment than an intellectual community, Jason Epstein moved to a place of great prominence. And the *New York Review of Books,* more than any intellectual journal, served this new, enlarged constituency.

In a small corner of this enlarged world, a second journal appeared in the mid-1960s. Launched with less fanfare and a far more limited scope, the *Public Interest* never aimed to embrace the large world sought by the *New York Review*. Instead, moving somewhat against the emerging ethos of the 1960s, the *Public Interest* aimed to institutionalize the hardheaded, problem-solving approach which characterized the postwar mentality. Writing in 1961 in *Dissent*, Daniel Bell had clarified his notion of an end to ideology. As was noted above, Bell suggested that the ladder to the City of Heaven must be an "empirical one;" "a utopia has to specify *where* one wants to go, *how* to get there, the costs of the enterprise, and some realization of, and justification for, *who* is to pay."[35] Bell's description could unwittingly serve as a stylesheet for the *Public Interest*. The specific impulse for the journal's birth came, as Irving Kristol remembered, from decisions by Bell and himself. One of the motivations, Kristol said, came from "Dan's experience on the Commission for the Study of Automation, when he discovered that most of what was being written was absolute nonsense. I discovered . . . that we had very little solid, good information available to us about social and economic problems." The information existed in the academy, Kristol and Bell believed; "it just wasn't filtering through to the public or even us." They decided to start a magazine to bring this information to light but failed to raise the money for about a year and a half. "One evening we were having dinner at Sidney Hook's with Warren Manshel, and Warren, who is rather affluent, listened to us describe the magazine and said, 'I'll put up $10,000.' So we said, 'okay.' "[36]

The *Public Interest* remained in its small corner during its first years of publication, as Bell and Kristol held on to their 1950s approach, despite the changes taking place in the 1960s. Norman Podhoretz recalled that when first taking over *Commentary*, Bell and Kristol had proposed that he shape the magazine in accordance with "the ladder of practicality." Podhoretz, then in the flush of his newfound radicalism and adolescent liberation, would have none of it, at least for the time being. Instead, the idea had to wait five years, when "thanks to Kristol's great editorial talents and Bell's insatiable curiosity," the *Public Interest* sprang to life—a very quiet and unassuming life, considering the world in which it was born. Operating, in Podhoretz's words, within "the limits of the immediately possible and the terms of the given situation," the *Public Interest* carved out its small niche, attracted its particular contributors, and developed its own style.[37] Its self-imposed limits seemed totally inappropriate for the period. While the *New York Review* headed in the direction of the New Left and *Partisan Review* became caught up in the spirit of the counterculture, the *Public Interest* kept the flame of the 1950s mentality flickering. Out of time with the tempo of the late 1960s, it awaited a period when the world would come back to its senses, or at least to its sensibleness.

STIRRING UP THE MELTING POT

Two publishing events of 1963 marked, in extraordinarily different ways, the revival of a crucial theme for the New Yorkers. Rarely considered in the same light—and in most analyses properly viewed separately—the appearance of *Beyond the Melting Pot*, by Nathan Glazer and Daniel Patrick Moynihan, and *Eichmann in Jerusalem*, by Hannah Arendt, signaled a return to questions about Jewishness and ethnic identity, with added concerns over race elicited by events of the 1950s and early 1960s. The responses to these books proved quite disparate, and the issues varied widely. But looking at the earlier and later thinking of New York Intellectuals, we can see in these books and the issues they raised the resurfacing of old themes and the forming of new ones.

Hannah Arendt's work occasioned fireworks rarely seen in New York Intellectual circles. Appearing first in the *New Yorker* and then in book form, it reported on the trial of the accused Nazi but ranged beyond the events in the courtroom to comment on the questions of Nazi guilt and Jewish complicity. Subtitled "A Report on the Banality of Evil," Arendt's book applied her idea of totalitarianism to the Eichmann case. She argued against the notion of Eichmann as a larger-than-life villain and instead perceived him as a person caught in a system which inverted traditional morality. "Evil in the Third Reich had lost the quality by which most people recognize it—the quality of temptation. Many Germans and many Nazis, probably an overwhelming majority of them, must have been tempted *not* to murder, *not* to rob, *not* to let their neighbors go off to their doom . . . but, God knows, they had learned how to resist temptations." Even more disturbing for Jews, Arendt argued that the excessive passivity of European Jews had played into Nazi hands. She describes the Jewish councils which the Nazis established. "Without Jewish help in administrative and police work . . . there would have been either complete chaos or an impossibly severe drain on German manpower," Arendt wrote. "The members of the Jewish councils were as a rule the locally recognized Jewish leaders, to whom the Nazis gave enormous power . . . until they, too, were deported."[38]

Arendt's book provoked a hailstorm of criticism and enormous debate, well beyond mere political discussion. Irving Howe has suggested that repressed feelings—the tongue-tiedness of the late 1940s which had left questions of six million Jewish deaths unanswered—gave way as "the long-suppressed grief evoked by the Holocaust burst out. It was as if her views, which roused many of us to fury, enabled us to finally speak about the unspeakable."[39] A second reason, perhaps less bonedeep than the issue of the destruction of the Jews, also touched the personal beliefs of the New Yorkers. Arendt's thesis on totalitarianism served as a key foundation for the emerging liberal anti-Communist ideology of the postwar years. The Nazis and the Soviets both appeared as manifestations of this new totalitarian condition. But if the logical extension of this notion led to characterizations of Nazis as "banal" villains or to charges of Jewish complicity in the Holocaust, many intellectuals felt it necessary to reevaluate her thesis. Although he had considered her earlier book "a great work," Norman Podhoretz noted, "The time has come to re-examine the whole concept."[40] Podhoretz had plenty of company. Lionel Abel wrote a long critique in *Partisan Review,* ending with this statement: "In all this, I hear beneath the hate-paean to totalitarianism Miss Arendt's praise for her own theory about it, a theory which I believe is now invalidated." In addition to finding the thesis objectionable, Irving Howe argued that the publication of the work in the *New Yorker* would produce further difficulties. "Hundreds of thousands of good middle-class Americans will have learned from those articles that the Jewish leadership in Europe was cowardly, inept, and even collaborationist," Howe feared, "and that if the Jews had not 'cooperated' with the Nazis, fewer than five to six million Jews would have been killed. No small matter: and you will forgive some of us if we react strongly to this charge."[41]

React strongly they did. Howe not only published objections but also helped organize a public forum sponsored by *Dissent,* "a debate sometimes ugly and outrageous," he later admitted, "yet also urgent and afire." Norman Podhoretz described this forum as "a kind of protest meeting against the book." Alfred Kazin, one of Hannah Arendt's close friends, attended the meeting. "My defense of her was personal," he recalled; "I was outraged by the mob spirit." Rising to respond to the criticisms of the book, "I was tight and Howe was in his element." Kazin admitted "I did it as a defense of Hannah. Frankly, it wasn't too much later when I read the book more objectively, that I realized that she had taken very great liberties. The 'banality of evil' was a dangerous and glib concept. What she meant by this illusory phrase was that the Nazis did not *think* of what they were doing. She was mistaken," Kazin later asserted. "They knew exactly. Hannah was the prisoner of German philosophy, which traditionally trivialized evil people as lacking the mentality of German philosophers. The same arrogance is found in Marx, who of course made worse use of it than Hannah Arendt." Mary McCarthy noted the division along Jewish–non-Jewish lines. Believing the book "splendid," McCarthy commented, "Apparently this is so because I am a Gentile. . . . I don't 'understand.'. . . It is as if *Eichmann in Jerusalem* had required a special pair of Jewish spectacles to make its 'true purport' visible."[42]

William Phillips, who often provided the grease to keep the parts at *Partisan Review* moving, tried to calm the turbulent waters of this debate. Calling the participants by their first names—"Mary," "Hannah," "Lionel," "Dwight,"—"William" admitted being "saddened and bewildered by the confusion." "A historical disaster," he wrote, "had been transformed, I am sorry to say, into a journalistic occasion. . . . And some people seemed to think that what was being said [by everyone in the debate] was more awful than the events themselves."[43] While Phillips admittedly exaggerated in trying to quell the hostility which raged, his exaggerations contained more truth than he knew. Clearly, no one thought the book or the debate an evil equivalent to the Nazi terror. Yet the emotions which the debate tapped, whether because of an outpouring of suppressed grief as Howe suggests or because of other considerations about Jewish identity, demonstrated the degree to which Jewishness remained a sensitive issue. Having worked out their own, personal sense of Jewishness in the first postwar years, after the decade of cosmopolitan universalism, the New York Intellectuals had not fully resolved the more general questions of Jews in society. Did Jews constitute a particular social grouping with unique collective attributes? Or did individual Jews share connections only with a historical past? Did only commonalities but no ties with their Jewish contemporaries exist? Or were they an identifiable contemporary ethnic unit? The New Yorkers had gained a better sense of who they were as Jews in the 1940s and 1950s, but they still were unclear as to where, as Jews, they belonged.

Beyond the Melting Pot dropped itself more quietly into the discussion of race and ethnicity than Arendt's work did. While the thesis argued by Glazer and Moynihan produced significant debate, it in no way matched the storm over the Eichmann book. Written as "a piece of neutral (or 'value-free' . . .) social science,"[44] as Podhoretz later characterized it, the book is often cited as an early example of the current reassertions of ethnicity. Discussing several ethnic groups in New York—Jews, Irish, Italians, Blacks and Puerto Ricans—the book attempted to determine whether identifiable ethnic characteristics advanced or hindered economic and social growth by these groups. Praised and attacked since, the book figures prominently in any current discussion of racial and ethnic factors in American society. But for the New Yorkers and many other American Jews this work held a special significance. Its thesis and similar statements helped resolve some of the doubts about ethnic identity and offered an explantation for what a number of Jews felt were the troubling aspects of the movement for racial equality sweeping America.

In the postwar years Jews had been replaced by other minority groups as the newest candidates seeking entry into American society. The young 1930s radicals and intellectuals had, like many Jews, moved from the periphery toward the center, rapidly following the traditional lines of ethnic assimilation. Some of these children of immigrants had become full professors and intellectual arbiters. As both society's analysts and recent ethnic arrivals, they felt they had a dual expertise to offer new candidates. While rendered in the "value-free" language of social science, these observations were full of autobiographical elements. Writing in the "old" *Commentary* in 1958, Glazer discussed the status of New York's Puerto Ricans. Arguing that they "have been

subjected to less discrimination than any previous large immigrant group,"
Glazer did admit that they had inferior jobs and poorer quarters, but "this is
mostly because they are newcomers." What troubled Glazer was the failure of
the Puerto Ricans to follow the path of other immigrant groups, particularly
Jews. They showed little interest in education or in owning the garment houses
in which they worked. Rather, they appeared all too ready to rely on
goverment services.[45]

As the civil rights movement heated up and turned its attention northward,
issues concerning urban blacks demanded further attention. In *Beyond the
Melting Pot* Glazer and Moynihan suggested that the lack of community
institutions, save for churches, presented one serious problem for blacks.
Daniel Bell, noting this finding, offered the example of an alternative system.
"A cursory acquaintance with Jewish community life in New York City, for
example, reveals the dense network of community organizations and services
set up by the Jewish community itself . . . and the reason [the black community
lacks this structure] is that these tasks have been shirked or ignored by the
Negro middle-class." Irving Kristol seconded these notions, arguing that blacks
merely represented the latest in a line of urban immigrants. "Pushing a cart in
the garment centers is the traditional point of departure for pushing one's way
into the garment industry." And Kristol, too, found the potential for resolving
the problem in the black middle class.[46]

The solutions for racial problems taking hold in the 1960s did not point in
the direction suggested by Bell, Moynihan, Glazer, Kristol, and a host of other
social scientists. Rather than the traditional paths toward ethnic assimilation—
the one trod so successfully by the Jews—blacks suggested other routes. In
addition, many blacks began to focus on Jews not as pathfinders but as
antagonists. The slow emergence of these two themes marked the turning of a
significant segment of New York Intellectuals away from a main current of civil
rights activities. In 1964, a decade before the Supreme Court began to face the
question, Daniel Bell sounded a warning about preferential quotas. "Making a
special place for less qualified Negro students [at the city colleges] may
eliminate an equally poor Italian or Jewish boy. What then?" The problem with
quotas—what Nathan Glazer later called "affirmative discrimination"—was
not only their unfairness but also their threat to Jews. Many New Yorkers had
worked with driving ambition to succeed in the public school system and at
City College. Minority status had been a hindrance to their advancement, one
to be overcome. For the new minorities it might be an advantage.

The questions about the relative treatment of Jews and blacks coincided with
the beginning of the discussion of problems between the races. One racial trend
in the early 1960s was toward black separateness, as was shown by the growth
of groups like the Black Muslims and by the increasing admission by various
analysts that difficulties in race relations extended well beyond institutionalized
southern segregation. James Baldwin, once a favored black writer among the
New York Intellectuals, brought the intensity, rage, and bitterness of blacks

home to white audiences with the publication of *The Fire Next Time,* first in the *New Yorker* and then in book form. Podhoretz originally commissioned the piece for *Commentary.* In an angry confrontation over selling the piece to another magazine, Baldwin suggested that Podhoretz do an article on his own feelings about race. This appeared as "My Negro Problem—and Ours," which was published in 1963 and which Podhoretz later called the most radical act of this radical phase of the "new" *Commentary.*[47] Essentially a memoir of his youth in a racially mixed ghetto in Brooklyn, Podhoretz's piece deals with the central antagonisms between Jews and blacks, specifically between himself and the young blacks in his neighborhood. "In my world it was the whites, the Italians and Jews, who feared the Negroes, not the other way around." Believing his radical sister's stories about the plight of blacks in general, he nonetheless "still hated them with all [his] heart." Podhoretz then recounted a number of vivid examples of brutal treatment, battles for turf, and general antagonisms. One incident clearly depicts how the internalized drives of the young Jews fed this antagonism. In class a black student had been unable to answer the teacher's question. "As usual I had waved my arm eagerly ('Be a good boy, get good marks, be smart, go to college, become a doctor') and, the right answer bursting from my lips, I was held up lovingly by the teacher as an example to the class." That afternoon the black youth confronted Podhoretz, finally striking him with a baseball bat. There are other stories of Podhoretz succeeding, in school or at athletic events, and then being threatened by angry blacks. This perhaps explains why they hated him, but the reason he hated them goes even deeper. Again the issues of personal drive enter. He admitted that "bad boys" existed among whites—the sound of "Sing Sing" for Alfred Kazin—but "the Negroes were *really* bad," Podhoretz remembered,

> bad in a way that beckoned to one, and made one feel inadequate. *We* all went home every day for a lunch of spinach-and-potatoes; *they* roamed around during lunch hour, munching on candy bars. In winter *we* had to wear itchy woolen hats and mittens and cumbersome galoshes; *they* were bareheaded and loose as they pleased. *We* rarely played hookey, or got into serious trouble at school, for all our street-corner bravado: *they* were defiant, forever staying out (to do what delicious things), forever making disturbances in class or in the halls, forever being sent to the principal and returning uncowed. But, most important of all, they were *tough*; beautifully, enviably tough, not giving a damn for anyone or anything. To hell with the teacher, the truant officer, the cop; to hell with the whole of the adult world that held *us* in its grip, and that we never had the courage to rebel against except sporadically and in petty ways.[48]

Podhoretz understood that he was projecting some of the pressures he had felt as a young boy—the incorporated parental desires of the young immigrant children—onto the seemingly liberated blacks. He said he would try to overcome his childhood prejudices with adult understandings but admitted that despite his consciously willing himself to new attitudes, some of his older hatred persisted. It explained "the insane rage that can stir in me at the thought of Negro anti-Semitism."[49] He was beginning to understand his "Negro problem."

Although Podhoretz believed that his reactions to particular events were personal, he also felt that these attitudes toward blacks were widely shared among his contemporaries. In *The Commentary Reader*, published at the magazine's twentieth anniversary in 1966, Podhoretz reprinted "My Negro Problem—And Ours" followed by Nathan Glazer's "Negroes and Jews: The New Challenge to Pluralism," originally published in 1964. Glazer picked up Podhoretz's themes of black-Jewish relations from a more analytical, less personal perspective. He described how early civil rights activities often received financial and personal support from Jews. Based on a common effort to end discrimination in general, that support, he said, has weakened as Jews "have been confronted for the first time with demands from Negro organizations that, they find, cannot serve as a basis for common effort." This split fed the growing antagonisms between the groups, especially as Jews resisted "such demands as preferential union membership and preferential hiring . . . . The 'white liberal,' who is attacked as a false friend . . . and as probably prejudiced to boot, is generally (even if this is not spelled out) the white *Jewish* liberal." Part of the problem, Glazer found, is that "the accidents of history have put the Jew just ahead of the Negro, and just above him." This has resulted from the Jews' earlier arrival and their success in the areas which help fill the ranks of the professional middle class, such as acquisition of academic degrees and performance on civil service examinations. "But when Negroes challenge—as they do in New York—the systems of testing by which school principals and higher officials in the educational bureaucracy are selected and promoted, they are also challenging the very system under which Jews have done so well." Here the theme of *Beyond the Melting Pot* enters. It is finally dawning on Jews, Glazer contended that "many Negro leaders are now beginning to expect that the pattern of their advancement in American society will take quite a different form from that of the immigrant ethnic groups." In response, the "white community into which the Negro now demands full entrance is not actually a single community—it is a series of communities. And all of them feel threatened by the implications of the new Negro demand for full equality." The underlying thrust of this pressure by blacks is to declare that "the sub-community, because it either protects privileges or creates inequality, *has no right to exist*. That is why these demands pose quite a new challenge to the Jewish community, or to any sub-community."[50]

As the progress toward civil rights stalled, with the rise of black-consciousness and black-power movements and with the mounting unrest in the nation's black ghettòs, the problems and anxieties expressed by Glazer and the others increased. In 1964, in his essay proposing that blacks look to the Jewish communities for examples of community organization, Daniel Bell also argued that "the Negro community has to choose its political spokesmen in a responsible way." Three years later Glazer found that the opposite had occurred. Responsible leaders were listened to less and less, "while leaders who may be for the first time themselves actually unemployed ghetto youth, perhaps with criminal records, now claim to speak for the ghetto communities." The degree to which these new leaders found an audience among mayors and city councils derived not from their intelligence or creative solutions, Glazer argued, but "through the threat that they can burn the city down."[51] Race relations moved in precisely the direction which would raise the anxiety of whites, especially white Jews, and opposite to the direction proposed by the social scientists among the New Yorkers. Rather than following the traditional path of gradual assimilation into American society, on the strength of particular ethnic characteristics, this latest group of "newcomers" wanted to rewrite the rules in such a way as to threaten the place and security of other groups who had recently assimilated—especially Jews. This troubled the New Yorkers throughout the 1960s and united individuals who otherwise saw themselves as widely scattered on the political spectrum: Norman Podhoretz, thinking himself a champion of the new radicalism; Nathan Glazer, calling himself a democratic socialist; Daniel Bell, the more traditional liberal; and Irving Kristol, already moving rightward in advance of many of his contemporaries. The uneasiness and anxiety grew until 1968, when one issue crystallized the positions and clearly drew the lines in this debate. The New York City teachers strike brought together solidly those Jews who feared the growing power and threats of blacks. And the debates which erupted between intellectuals, in general, and *Commentary* and the *New York Review of Books*, specifically, further dispersed the already drifting community of the New York Intellectuals.

The issues which led to the walkout by New York City's schoolteachers in the fall of 1968 are intricate and extend well beyond any discussion of New York Intellectuals. The issues raised during the strike, however, reflect the continuing concerns of a number of these individuals over questions of race and the widening cracks between former friends. The strike was complex for these intellectuals because it required the choice between two causes both previously assumed to be attractive to liberals. On one side stood the city's blacks and educational reformers, hoping to decentralize the massive school system and institute community control. On the other stood the city's teachers and their union, many of them the Jews Nathan Glazer described, who had poured out of City College and into the educational system, "the system where Jews had done so well." *The New York Review* and *Commentary* lined up on opposite sides. The relatively peaceful days of the *Review's* first years had given way to bitter infighting, as it had taken up the cause of the New Left, while *Commentary* and Podhoretz had consciously begun to move rightward. The debate on the New York teachers strike clearly delineated the alternative positions and created two hostile camps in the New York Intellectual world.

Jason Epstein, in one of his infrequent appearances in the *New York Review*, wrote the first analysis of the strike in October. While generally supporting the decentralization program and the reassignment of nineteen teachers in

Brooklyn by the local governing board, he noted the necessity of understanding the position of teachers who "have invested ten or twenty years in their jobs and who are now totally dependent on them" while he empathized with the plight of parents whose children's education was defective.[52] The conflict grew increasingly angry, and some of the anger was directed at Epstein, as he reported in his second piece on the school situation. In his first article Epstein had not mentioned the ethnic aspects of the conflict. By November that issue had erupted on all fronts. The initial "conflict between a complacent educational bureaucracy and its disaffected clientele has emerged as a struggle between Jews and Negroes." Making his sentiments more explicit, Epstein now lambasted the teachers' union, the United Federation of Teachers, and its president, Albert Shanker. He accused the UFT of circulating counterfeit leaflets supposedly published by the black-dominated community councils— anti-Semitic statements guaranteed to enrage the city's whites in general and Jews in particular. Epstein himself came under fire from one correspondent who, unintentionally, captured the simmering issues for Jews. "Dear Fellow-Jew," the note to Epstein began. "When they come to kill the Jews they will kill you too. You won't escape by buddying up with Oliver and McCoy [two black leaders in the Brooklyn district]. Remember Germany? Hannah Arend [sic] was right."[53]

When the sociologist Dennis Wrong tallied the sins of the *New York Review* in *Commentary* two years later, its position during the school strike figured prominently. Wrong admitted the complexity of the issues but accused the *Review* of minimizing the importance of the anti-Semitism of some of the black leaders and of displaying "insensitivity to specifically Jewish interests." Wrong concluded that the *Review's* position "was supportive in general of New Left sentiments on trade unions, black power, public bureaucracies, official liberalism, and—implicity—the concerns of Jews."[54] Epstein and the *Review* might be guilty of minimizing the concerns of Jews, but *Commentary* certainly never was. Podhoretz ran, in early 1969, not only an analysis of the New York strike by Maurice Goldbloom but also a series of articles on blacks and Jews. Goldbloom's assessment came down squarely on the side of the teachers and the union. Concluding the series on blacks and Jews, Nathan Glazer warned his fellow Jewish intellectuals that "the expansion and inflammation of anti-Semitism among blacks" was "abetted and assisted and advised by a white, predominantly Jewish, intelligentsia." As an example, Glazer cited an advertisement in the *Black Panther*, supporting Eldridge Cleaver and signed by Allen Ginsberg, Norman Mailer, Edgar Friedenberg, Susan Sontag, Jules Feiffer, Noam Chomsky, and Robert Silvers, among others. The same issue of the Panthers publication had run an article on Al Fatah, entitled "Palestine Guerrillas versus Israeli Pigs." The crucial concern which turned many Jews against the New Left—Israel—how entered the already knotted world of black-Jewish relations.[55]

Even without the explosive question of Israel, the once harmonious relationship between Jews and the movement for black advancement underwent severe strain in the 1960s, as various individuals reassessed the impact of further steps in American race relations. As the New York teachers strike so clearly demonstrated, Jews, intellectual journals, and even old friends could split sharply over these issues. Now, however, the rifts became more permanent.

The 1960s presented the New Yorkers with a new world for which their postwar positions left them largely unprepared. Serious questions confronted all Americans during these years, problems which plagued consciences as they confronted national policy. The New Yorkers faced personal attack as well as intellectual or political challenges, and they were forced to defend who they were as much as what they stood for. Having argued for an intellectual role at the center of American society, they began to see the center evaporating. Increasing pressures over the war in Vietnam, the growing activism of American college students, and the general rise of the New Left all contributed to the polarization and emotionalism which marked much of American life during these years. Intensely political people and frequently involved in university life, the New Yorkers found themselves directly drawn to these questions. In the past, they had been *engagé* by their own choosing. Now they found themselves engaged by the actions of others—pulled into conflicts because of their social positions rather than because of their ideas.

The central issue for all the actions of these years, the Vietnam War, did not always stir the feelings of these intellectuals. In fact, considering the frequency and vehemence with which they wrote on most subjects, their contribution to debates over the war was surprisingly small. In the early 1960s Norman Podhoretz did print several articles which advanced a moderate revisionist position with regard to the cold war in general and others which discussed problems in Vietnam. This, Podhoretz believed, was in keeping with his attempts to foster a new radicalism in the early 1960s. He did not call upon other New York Intellectuals to aid in this task, however, but published pieces by Staughton Lynd, on the cold war, and by Hans Morgenthau, on Vietnam. Podhoretz later recalled that he liked Lynd's initial position because it took an "evenhanded, almost neutralist stand as between the United States and the Soviet Union." Podhoretz found Lynd's increasing, hard-line revisionism objectionable as the war persisted and antiwar sentiments grew increasingly militant. The Vietnam articles by Hans Morgenthau likewise offered a moderate approach, given the tone eventually taken in critical assessments.[56] Despite the moderateness of Podhoretz's revisionism—and Podhoretz believed he was a full participant[57]—he found many of his intellectual contemporaries unmoved. Midge Decter recalled a party in the early 1960s: "I remember Norman being nagged at by Dwight Macdonald and Cal [Robert] Lowell, one night, saying to him, 'Why is your magazine so boring? Why do you keep publishing those boring pieces on Southeast Asia? Who gives a damn? Who is Hans Morgenthau?' "[58]

Between 1964 and 1966, attitudes among the New York Intellectuals underwent major adjustments, as they, like increasing numbers of Americans, began to turn their attention to the situation in Vietnam. Whereas before 1964 the New Yorkers had tended to find discussions of Vietnam boring, Decter recalled, by 1966 there were, "screaming fights at Jason Epstein's house about whether Lyndon Johnson was the same as Hitler. We who had been the earliest opponents of the war were fighting with those people about whether to spell America with a k."[59]

Not all the intellectuals went over to the most strident antiwar position. In truth, they fanned out across the spectrum. Only a few like Irving Kristol outwardly supported American policy. Some like Saul Bellow remained quiet. In the margin of a letter from Bellow to F. W. Dupee, the Columbia critic later penciled, "Start of big Vietnam protest activities. Bellow did nothing."[60] Most took a moderate antiwar position, akin to the one being publicly argued by Senator William Fulbright, for example. Irving Howe wrote a statement, printed in the *New York Review* and cosigned by Michael Harrington, Bayard Rustin, Lewis Coser, and Penn Kimble, which outlined this position. It was critical of the war but aired misgivings about the course of the growing protests. While feeling the war "morally and politically disastrous," Howe and the others nonetheless believed that a protest movement "cannot be organized around a full-scale analysis of the Vietnam situation; its task is not to assign historical responsibility for the present disaster to one or another side."[61] Staughton Lynd, once Norman Podhoretz's favorite revisionist, took exception to Howe's call "not to give explicit or overt political support to the Vietcong." "May I inquire why it is immoral to desire a Vietcong victory?" the then-Yale historian asked. Howe's reply resonated with the differences between the Old Left and the New. Drawing on the vocabulary of liberal anticommunism, Howe responded, "A victory for a communist or communist-dominated movement means another totalitarian dictatorship suppressing human freedoms."[62] Despite the growing opposition to the war, this more moderate antiwar approach tried to limit the critique to the fighting itself. Like Hans Morgenthau's in *Commentary* several years before, the position which Howe and others began to take sought a middle ground in an increasingly polarized debate. And they attempted to limit the criticisms to the war itself. "I cannot accept the idea," Nathan Glazer wrote in 1967, "that the fundamental character of American society, its political or economic life, is the prime cause of the horror of Vietnam. In the end, I cannot help believing that Vietnam must be understood as the result of a series of monumental errors."[63]

As the critique of the war expanded from analyses of Vietnam itself to larger questions about American actions and perceptions since 1945, some of the New Yorkers found themselves assigned to the side of the guilty, despite their opposition to the war. Noam Chomsky's wide-ranging attack "The Responsibility of the Intellectuals" assailed Daniel Bell, Irving Kristol, and Arthur

Schlesinger, as well as more-public targets like McGeorge Bundy and Walt Rostow. "I have *never* defended American policy in Vietnam," Bell asserted, "but Chomsky, to be fair, does not name me as a supporter of the war. I am attacked for propounding a 'pragmatic,' 'instrumental,' and 'technocratic' view of the society which abets those who use such analysis in support of the war."[64] Many of the New Yorkers, according to Chomsky, had helped create the intellectual climate of postwar American society or had at least publicly supported it. Criticisms of the policy regarding Vietnam in terms of larger social questions emerging from the mentality and activities of the society added this general societal support to the discussions of guilt over the extension of American foreign intervention. Better, the New Yorkers believed, to find fault with military blunders and tactical miscalculations.

As questions about the relation between liberal anticommunism and the war began to surface widely, *Commentary* held one of its famous symposia in September 1967. In "Liberal Anti-Communism Revisited," Podhoretz asked a number of individuals, "As someone whose name has been associated with the anti-Communist Left, do you feel in any way responsible for American policies in Vietnam?" The responses generally followed the line of the two camps emerging among the New Yorkers, those whose view of Vietnam remained narrowly defined and those who saw the problems growing beyond that country and that war. Those who felt some responsibility did so ambivalently. While Dwight Macdonald rejected direct responsibility, because of his visible antiwar activities, he noted that " 'the anti-communism of the left' did help create a favorable climate of opinion for Johnson's war." Harold Rosenberg found that containment was the real issue and that, given its requirements, anti-communism of all varieties led potentially to Vietnam. "My will to 'contain' Communism," he said, "cannot carry the precondition that there be socialists in the White House or philosophers in the Pentagon." William Phillips and Phillip Rahv, each for different reasons, also expressed qualified agreement with the question.[65]

The denials were more explicit and absolute. The charge "makes no sense to me," wrote Daniel Bell; it "is a myth," claimed Sidney Hook. "Do I feel any responsibility for American policy in Vietnam?" Irving Howe asked himself. "None whatever." "I cannot give even the beginning of credence to the idea that my views as a liberal anti-Communist helped bring about the war," Lionel Trilling stated. The positions in this debate did not neatly divide between those of hawks and of doves. Rather, they tapped deeper beliefs about American society and the course of postwar politics—the war as a symptom of America's system or as an aberration. Most New Yorkers opposed the war, but for a variety of reasons and in very different ways. Dwight Macdonald, prominent in many antiwar demonstrations, found few of his friends on the line: "I do not recall seeing Irving Howe marching."[66]

The camps divided publications as well as individuals. Once again, the *New York Review of Books* and *Commentary* came to represent the two positions, though in less direct opposition to one another than they were over the teachers' strike. After his early articles on the situation in Vietnam, Podhoretz cooled down his criticism as it heated up elsewhere. In 1966 he organized a symposium, balancing two critics of government policy, George McGovern and Bernard Fall, with two of its defenders, Richard Goodwin and John Roche. The New York Intellectuals, for the most part, stayed out of these early discussions on the war. The *New York Review's* first contributions on Vietnam came from I. F. Stone, Marcus Raskin, Joseph Kraft, Jean Lacouture, and Bernard Fall.

As the sides became clearer, the New Yorkers entered the fray more directly. Chomsky's attack on cold-war intellectuals, first printed in the *Review*, prompted various responses, including an assessment by Lionel Abel in *Commentary*.[67] Mary McCarthy, traveling to Vietnam for the *Review*, sent back a number of long articles critical of the war and of the proposed moderate solutions being offered in America. Diana Trilling responded to McCarthy with the phrases of liberal anti-communism. Declaring her opposition to the war and her belief in American withdrawal, Trilling nonetheless believed that "in withdrawing from Vietnam we consign untold numbers of Southeast Asian opponents of Communism to their death and countless more to the abrogation of the right of protest which we American intellectuals hold so dear."[68] Only in May 1971 did *Commentary* come out foursquare for withdrawal, despite those articles from the early 1960s by Lynd and Morgenthau. Nathan Glazer did the honors, admitting that "one is embarrassed to add new words on Vietnam. Already there have been millions." Norman Podhoretz, in his "Issues" column of that month agreed with Glazer without mentioning the embarrassment or his having come full circle, back to his earlier position. Despite all the words which had been printed and the broad movement of Americans toward antiwar views during the decade, Podhoretz's position moved away from the new radicalism he believed he had helped create. Rather than criticize America's cold-war role, the *Commentary* editor stated his long-held belief "that [nothing] good would ever come for us or for the world from an unambiguous American defeat." "Unhappily" he was forced to the position of American withdrawal because of his dislike of the Nixon policy of Vietnamization, supported by the "indefinite and unlimited bombardment by American pilots in American planes." Only through total withdrawl he held, could Vietnamization come "truly and seriously into play."[69]

By 1971, however, the divisions within American society and among intellectuals had grown so deep that *Commentary's* declaration favoring American withdrawal could hardly bind the wounds. The intellectuals' debate on the war concerned not specific pro- and antiwar views but degrees of opposition and discussions over America's role and liberals' culpability. The differences on the responsibility for and the implications of the war came to be almost as heated as the debate on the war itself. The perception of America's involvement in Vietnam as an isolated mistake or a problem created by overzealous military figures provided a quite different perspective from the belief that the trouble stemmed from America's imperial role and the course of postwar American development. Other conflicts in American society contributed to this latter appraisal, Vietnam being only the most flagrant action of a severely flawed system. Crucial to the formation of this larger critical perspective were the developments on America's campuses and the emergence of the loosely defined political movement which sought to articulate this opposition, the New Left. The philosophy of the New Left took dead aim at the centers of American power. The process caused many New York Intellectuals a crisis of conscience and forced self-definitions in ways they would probably rather have avoided.

The New Yorkers had been intimately connected with the campus radicalism of the 1930s. Some still considered themselves leftists, especially those clustering around *Dissent*, as well as individuals like Philip Rahv and Sidney Hook. On the other hand, many had helped create the postwar liberal consensus, articulated the belief that ideology had ended, and felt themselves growing close to the centers of power in American society, as intellectual arbiters or, more directly, through visits and jobs in Washington. Finally, most had followed the path to academe after the Second World War, rising to prominent places in their university communities. When society in general and the university in particular came in for severe criticism and denunciation, their position became increasing problematic. They discovered themselves caught between their prewar inclinations and their postwar beliefs and places. In an era when the middle ground began to disappear, when lines became clearly drawn between "us" and "them," between the establishment and the antiestablishment, the New Yorkers found they had to choose one side or be assigned places on the basis of their actions and reactions. Many hoped to weather these storms by maintaining an attitude of moderation and by making subtle distinctions. As the decade wore on and social antagonisms intensified, that possibility receded.

The difficulty often began at home—at the university. Even before campus affairs became directly linked with the situation in Vietnam, problems emerged and camps began to form. In the fall of 1964 the troubles at Berkeley confronted a number of these intellectuals, just as it captured national attention. The situation for Seymour Martin Lipset is telling. Once a Trotskyist at City College, national chairman of the Young People's Socialist League, and delegate to the American Student Union in the 1930s, Lipset was teaching at Berkeley in the first years of the new student radicalism. As faculty adviser to the same YPSL, Lipset found himself more closely connected than other faculty to the emerging free-speech movement, the cause on which the first campus unrest centered. Favoring the "moderate" proposals of the movement, Lipset later said he opposed the confrontation tactics being advocated by the radicals. After a sit-in at the administration building, Lipset and the political scientist Paul Seabury wrote an analysis of the demonstration, severely critical of civil disobedience. "This new style of campus political action may affect other campuses, and eventually our national political life.... Extremism in the pursuit of liberty was quite recently a slogan of the radical right. Berkeley has shown that anyone can play this game." Lipset and Seabury issued a warning that "students at other universities will have learned how easily a great university can be brought to its knees." They added, "universities are probably more vulnerable to civil disobedience tactics than any other institutions in this country precisely because those in authority, whether administration or faculty, are liberal."[70]

Lipset and Seabury published their analysis in the *Reporter*, but another assessment of the situation at Berkeley directly entered the journalistic fray of the New York Intellectual world. Robert Silvers initially asked Nathan Glazer, then also teaching at Berkeley, to report on the student revolt for the *New York Review*. When the *Review* rejected the piece, Norman Podhoretz published it in *Commentary*. Glazer, like Lipset, took a moderate approach, suggesting difficulties and problems with each position and noting that Berkeley was "more than a local story." The *New York Review* published instead a prostudent assessment by the Berkeley political scientists Sheldon Wolin and John Schaar. Podhoretz later commented on the significance of this publishing development. "Rejecting Glazer's article and publishing the one by Wolin and Schaar, the *New York Review* for all practical purposes announced that it was signing on with the new radicalism." By publishing Glazer, *"Commentary* was in effect saying that it now had serious reservations about the new radicalism."[71]

After Berkeley, the discussion of a single campus gave way to a general appraisal of the larger student movement, as the next five years found one campus after another experiencing student unrest. Out of the general reaction to these events, a position began to emerge among those New Yorkers who found themselves moving against this tide. The lead in developing this position was taken by the writers associated with the *Public Interest*, although it was argued in various places and journals. The intention of their journal, to develop sound pieces of social analysis within the framework of the postwar liberal order, ran counter to the thrust of student sentiment. Admitting that liberals had failed to mount effective social programs, Daniel Bell and Irving Kristol argued in the introduction to a collection of essays on the student revolt that rather than seeing "the complexity of our social problems" students merely believed that the "government had 'copped out' of their responsibilities," relying on a "conspiracy theory of history," based on "such amorphous terms as 'the system' and 'the establishment.'" Instead of seeking clear solutions to specific problems, "goals which can be fought for, negotiated, or compromised," the "politics of confrontation" did not really seek to satisfy grievances at all. Its true goal was "the destruction of authority itself."[72]

These intellectuals had achieved positions of authority in society and in the university. If Bell and Kristol were right, they would have good reason to fear the students. In all fairness, however, it must be said that more than self-protection prompted their opposition. The university embodied certain values which the students seemed to be threatening. Despite "the disasters of American foreign and military policy or domestic policy," Nathan Glazer argued, there existed distinctive characteristics of the universities—"the commitment to free inquiry, free discussion, free teaching"—which needed protection. Glazer noted that this was the line he drew on the student revolt and that it made him "an enemy": "academic freedom did not need to be sacrificed to either a 'relevant' or 'politically repressive' or 'involved' university." This general threat emanated from all the groups in the student movement—radical whites, militant blacks, and faculty defenders. Together they "have effectively intimidated professors so they cannot give courses they were prepared to give."[73] There is considerable debate as to whether the student movement limited or expanded openness on America's campuses. It is striking in this discussion that a decade earlier these same intellectuals had willingly sacrificed or limited academic freedom as it applied to Communists and fellow travelers. "What is of first importance," Sidney Hook declared in 1968, "is to preserve, of course, the *absolute* intellectual integrity of our classrooms." With an apparently short memory, Hook stated, "I do not recall any other period in the last 50 years when intellectuals themselves have been so intolerant of each other, when differences over complex issues have been the occasion for denunciation rather than debate and analysis." Hook needed only to look to his willingness to drive individuals out of academe in the 1950s or to his descriptions of anti-anti-Communists like Henry Steele Commager to find examples only fifteen years back. Perhaps he felt that the prestige of his personal position made him immune to charges of intolerance in the 1950s. For in the 1960s the harsh words came from those with inferior academic status. Hook found it "preposterous for callow and immature adolescents . . . to set themselves up as authorities on what research by the teachers is educationally permissible." If this situation, already exaggerated by Hook, was allowed to persist, these students would ultimately "be presuming to dictate the conclusions their teachers should reach." Lapsing into cold-war rhetoric, Hook concluded, "This is standard procedure in totalitarian countries."[74]

Irving Kristol took an equally dim view of the students, especially considering all that American society had done for them. Amid general prosperity and a liberal administration, why do these students feel alienated, Kristol wondered. They "'go left' for the same reason so many high school students 'go delinquent.' *They are bored.*" This is Kristol's 1965 perception. By 1968 he had refined his position, a bit, but still employed the same metaphor. The students "are indeed for the most part rebels without a cause—and without a hope of accomplishing anything except mischief and ruin." Once a 1930s radical in Alcove No. 1 at City College, Kristol considered the student radicals of the 1960s "a mob who have no real interest in higher education or in the life of the mind, and whose passions are influenced by a debased popular culture that prevails unchallenged on the campus."[75]

The crisis on America's campuses touched even closer to home, for the New Yorkers, when in 1968 attention turned to Columbia. By the late 1960s positions had hardened and lines had been more clearly drawn between intellectuals, as the war debate intensified and the presidential campaign heated up. Questions of race compounded the Columbia situation because the proposed construction of a university gymnasium on college-owned property in Harlem sparked the initial conflict. Furthermore, Columbia was home to a number of prominent New York Intellectuals, including Lionel Trilling, Daniel Bell, F. W. Dupee, and Richard Hofstadter, all of whom became directly involved in the activities surrounding the strike and its attempted mediation. Trilling had held an informal meeting in his home, near Columbia, the night before the strike began, attended by Bell and several other Columbia faculty. When the strike began, Bell and Trilling took differing roles. The sociologist figured prominently in the ad hoc faculty group, which tried to mediate between students and administration and to keep the police off campus. The group's resolutions included placing themselves physically between the police and the demonstrators as well as between demonstrators and conservative student counterdemonstrators. Dupee served as one of these marshals. Trilling served on a committee appointed to work out the delicate problems of establishing a disciplinary group to handle the university's response to the students. This role warranted, at least once, a police escort from the campus to his home, two blocks away.[76]

Despite the efforts of Bell, Trilling, and countless other Columbia faculty as well as of outside mediators, negotiations broke down, and hundreds of New York tactical-squad policemen ultimately cleared the buildings of the demonstrators, putting a number of Columbia students and faculty in jail or in hospitals. In the outrage which followed the police action, during which nearly one hundred people were injured and seven hundred arrested, the faculty met to vote on the announced student strike. Trilling did not take a direct role, but the reporter for the *Columbia Daily Spectator* noted the impact of Trilling's position in the hall. While the historian Fritz Stern argued against an unconditional joining of the strike, "seated next to him was Lionel Trilling, nodding approvingly at each point his colleague made."[77] When, after a series of other demonstrations and strikes, Columbia held its commencement that June, Richard Hofstadter was asked to give the commencement address, breaking the tradition of having Columbia's president speak. That change was necessary because Grayson Kirk, head of the university, was by this time anathema to large segments of the campus, students and faculty alike. Hofstadter's first words became the signal for three hundred students and a few faculty to walk out in protest, not of Hofstadter, but of the university's actions over the last several months.

After the dust had settled and the students gone home for the summer, Dupee and Diana Trilling set down their analyses of the spring's events for the *New York Review* and *Commentary*, respectively. The differences between the two articles marked the two camps which had emerged among New York Intellectuals. Expressing the view of the majority of New Yorkers, Diana Trilling had harsh words for the students. Although never directly involved in the strike or the negotiations, she wrote from a personal closeness to Columbia. "When one marries a university teacher one marries into his university as much as one might have married into one's husband's family: there develops a not insignificant attachment and a perhaps distorting intimacy." She did feel a personal, if peripheral involvement in the strike. "A faculty wife became the short-order chef at any hour of the day or night for her husband and his exhausted colleagues." Because of her intimate connection to the Columbia family, Trilling had difficulty understanding the complaints being voiced against Columbia. She expressed an inability "to locate sufficient reason for revolution at Columbia . . . for protest, yes . . . but surely no reasonable reason to tear the place to pieces."[78] Instead, she seized on the position of a small minority of radical students and made it the central theme of the unrest. "The Columbia uprising had the declared intention of large social destructiveness, the largest." She found special significance in an open letter to Grayson Kirk from the Students for a Democratic Society leader Mark Rudd, issued the day before the students took over the four buildings. "We will destroy your world, your corporation, your University." Trilling made much of the order Rudd chose. The university might have been the first to come under attack, but the intentions of the radical students extended far beyond the boundaries of the Morningside Heights campus.

While Trilling admitted that the "brutality of the police on the morning of April 30 outraged virtually everyone," she nonetheless reminded everyone including the faculty who placed themselves between police and students and were also beaten, "that were it not for student lawlessness the law would never have been brought to the campus." Ultimately, Trilling could not rest with general descriptions, however. She was "married" to the university family—if her husband was paterfamilias in this new view of in loco parentis, she had to be the mother. As she had in her attitude toward Allen Ginsberg in the 1950s, she assumed this maternal role again. A student, "fresh out of jail a few short hours after the police bust," she reported, "grabbed an immediate phone to demand why one's writer-husband had not been present to protect the writer-student against the police." Trilling was caught between her two conflicting instincts of the moment, political and maternal. On the one hand, she heard in the student's complaint "revolutionary scorekeeping. . . . Its tone couldn't have been nastier and it spoke of guillotines or their later historical manifestation, the concentration camp, the knock on the door in the night." Trilling heard echoes of the political battles and fears of past decades in the student's verbal attack and saw how she had changed from one of the young radicals of the 1930s to one "well up on the list of those who, come the tribunals of the young, would never be missed." But she also heard something else, "the wail of a child coming out of a tantrum, when, before he takes quieter, crueler stock of his new-found power he touches home base, makes a sentimental ploy of the family sentiment."[79] Trilling remained the "university mother," despite her frustrations with the direction of these youths and the wrongheadedness of their politics.

For F. W. Dupee the uprising at Columbia meant something quite different. He understood that those with authority got "hung-up" on it, including some of his colleagues. "One of them said to me of the defiant students, 'As with children, there comes a time when you have to say no to them.' But the defiant students weren't children," Dupee countered, "and saying no meant exposing them to more than a 'good spanking.' The War was doing far more 'violence' to the University than they were." Dupee drew comparisons with the thirties, as did Trilling, but reached different conclusions. "Compared to the radicals of the Thirties, so stodgy and uninventive, these youths seemed to unite the politics of a guerrilla chieftain with the aesthetic flair of a costumer and an interior decorator." Dupee also discussed the role and ultimately the impotence of the Columbia faculty, whose function was clearly defined in academic matters but less so administrative affairs. He came to see that despite the efforts of many faculty members, the university's plan for resolving the situation "had been more or less predetermined, both as to the date and to the means (i.e., police action)." When he next met his Shakespeare class after "the bust," "several wore bandages, one was on crutches, one had his arm in a sling, and the teacher had a black eye." Rather than seeing the students as destroyers of the educational framework, Dupee ended his piece by noting their suggestions on how to continue the semester. "After six days in the liberated building," one wrote, "which seems like two years ago, I would like to re-connect with Western Civilization's past, after a rather exhausting vision of the future."[80] This was not the "large social destructiveness" which Diana Trilling found; rather, it was Dupee's belief in these students as serious, radical adults and not children.

"You must come right up, Dwight," Dupee had told Dwight Macdonald on the telephone. "It's a revolution! You may never get another chance to see one." After being initially opposed to the student strike, Macdonald heeded Dupee's words. "I came up and he was right." Macdonald found "an atmosphere of exhilaration, excitment." What really changed his perception, he reported, were visits to Mathematics Hall—"the Smolny Institute of the revolution, the ultra-Left SDS stronghold"—and to Fayerweather Hall—"the Menshevik center." Macdonald described these two as "communes" and found that the spirit within was strong, the decision making rational, and the process totally democratic. Macdonald was most impressed by the way the "communards" established a working society in the building and confronted problems they had never before considered.[81] Dupee's and Macdonald's descriptions of the Columbia strikers reveal an excitement about the spiritual elements which the students possessed, the vigor and enthusiasm they brought to the political conflict. For these Old Leftists, wearied from decades of political fights, this exuberance seemed refreshing, perhaps reminiscent of the spirit which had infused young radicals in the 1930s.

The New Left, in general, appeared to have recaptured the radical fire which had either gone out of so many of the old thirties radicals or had, at best, died down to a dim glow. A few—Macdonald, Dupee, Philip Rahv, William Phillips, and some others—found encouragement in this emerging spirit. For most, from the ever-more conservatives like Irving Kristol to the declared Old Left survivors like Irving Howe, these new trends did not inspire optimism. Many Americans feared the New Left and the attacks its members made on American society and American policies. But among the majority of New York Intellectuals hostility toward the young radicals arose for particular and often different reasons. By the 1960s these intellectuals might have shared few other political viewpoints, but most came to agree on their opposition to the New Left.

Those New Yorkers who found hope, optimism, or merely excitement in the revived political activity of the 1960s did, however, earn the enmity of their former intellectual comrades. Amid the crumbling cohesion of the community and the forming of new political and cultural constellations among the New Yorkers, some of these disputes, unlike many past antagonisms were permanent. And even if the wounds healed, the scars would continue to show ever after. Positions on the young shifted, and the support, even from the minority of New Yorkers who gave it, often varied. Some found the cultural aspects of the New Left encouraging; others took heart in the political developments. A few like Podhoretz began as supporters and ended as critics. Others like William Phillips came as skeptics and were converted. In both cases, however, their roles were never central. This was a revolt of the young, and even those who found favor with it, like Dwight Madonald on the Columbia campus, came as enthusiastic onlookers, supportive of rather than integral to the events and the ideas. Only those who stood against the New Left held a key role—not being part of the solution, they became, in the phrase of the time, part of the problem.

It is ironical that the two elder critics William Phillips and Philip Rahv came in some ways to symbolize the reawakened interest in radicalism and the attraction of the New Left among some New York Intellectuals. They had, in a sense, begun it all in the 1930s, sparking the birth and rebirth of *Partisan Review*, the central locus for the emerging community. Now, in the 1960s, growing personally estranged and each enjoying academic appointments and literary eminence, they found a new cause for optimism in the revolt of the young. They focused, however, on different aspects of the movement. For Rahv politics always played the dominant role, and he stood ready to enter the political wars once again. He did not like the students—"middle-class dilettantes" he called them—and did not like the counterculture. But the radical fire which had burned in the 1930s rekindled in the 1960s. "Rahv developed a peculiar kind of reversion to his early Marxist period, he didn't go back to Stalin's period, but he certainly developed an extreme, though a kind of ultra-left attitude politically," Macdonald recalled. His own, particular kind of radicalism reemerged, steeped in his past, reawakened by but critical of the present. To Norman Podhoretz he was a "born again" radical.[82]

For William Phillips the attraction had other sources. Focusing on the "new sensibility" which emerged from the cultural side of the New Left, Phillips became increasingly positive about these new developments. This was due in part to the new critics gathering at *PR*, particularly Richard Poirier, and to Phillips's own tendency to swing more sharply than some of his contemporaries. To his critics he appeared too easily swayed, too willing to tack with the prevailing winds. Phillips in 1979 saw himself as "more objective." He added, "People sometimes lose objectivity completely. I don't like to dismiss all radical groups or conservative ones. One has to make distinctions. Despite its political mindlessness and anti-intellectualism, some new idealism emerged that you had to become aware of. The old smug and conservative spirit that was around was deadening."[83] In particular, Phillips's approach allowed *PR* to become a vehicle for many of the new critical pieces which appeared, ranging from intellectual assessments of the Beatles to numerous contributions by Susan Sontag.

Rahv and Phillips again broke off from the prevailing consensus—liberal in the fifties as opposed to Communist in the thirties—and set out to revive the radical spirit. But significant differences set the sixties apart from the thirties for them. They no longer blazed the trails; rather, they now followed in the wake of a new radicalism and a new sensibility. Furthermore, they went off not together but at different paces and inspired by different aspects of the movement. And finally, they took very few of their old intellectual comrades with them. Dwight Macdonald, F. W. Dupee, and Mary McCarthy came along. Ironically, these three had been, with Rahv, Phillips, and George Morris, the founding editors of the "new" *Partisan Review* in 1937. A few younger intellectuals joined the New Left—Sontag, Mailer, and Leslie Fiedler. By and large, though, the New York Intellectuals held their ground, that liberal plot they had staked out in the postwar years. And those who remained felt nothing but enmity for those who strayed.

Nowhere did this hostility come out so clearly as in the exchange between Rahv and Irving Howe which ran in the *New York Review of Books* in the fall of 1967. The provocation was a review by Rahv of an edited work by Howe and Michael Harrington, *The Radical Imagination*, which drew together pieces previously published in *Dissent*. In addition to the Howe and Harrington book, Rahv also reviewed a work by the SDS founder Carl Oglesby. Although critical of Oglesby's attempt to "manufacture out of whole cloth" a political theory for the contemporary scene, Rahv held no "hope for political success in the used-up formulas of the Old Left as exemplified by Howe and Harrington." Rahv accused Howe of merely seeking to extend welfare capitalism, while calling it democratic socialism.[84] Howe rose to defend himself and to respond to Rahv—

the intellectual and the *ad hominem* once again emerging in the New York Intellectual style. Current political activities represented no true radicalism. Instead, this "crude, fashion-driven, smugly moralistic" variety was a " 'radicalism' of posture, gesture, and *frisson.*" And taking aim at the older converts to the new styles, Howe found it "a 'radicalism' of a vicarious and thereby corrupt apocalyptic fantasy . . . a 'radicalism' of the attic and the playground: old souvenirs dusted off, creaky limbs pressed to swing baby swing." But Howe was not through with a general dismissal of the New Left and its older converts. He struck out at his fellow New York Intellectuals who had signed on. "Lemming-like, the 'herd of independent minds' rushes after the latest thing. . . . Guerrilla squadrons will be formed as soon as midterms are graded: will they assemble at the *Paris Review* ball?" And finally, "now after nearly twenty years of planful circumspection, appears Philip Rahv offering Michael Harrington and myself Little Lessons in Leninism. . . . Rip Van Winkle wakes up and fancies himself at the Smolny Institute."[85]

Howe continued his riposte with a detailed restatement and defense of his radicalism, coupled with a critique of Rahv. He quoted from Rahv's 1948 views on the conditions of Stalin's Russia and then asked, "At which point, dear Philip, did the Soviet Union cease being a society of 'state serfdom?' When were the serfs freed—I mean the second time?" In conclusion, Howe reaffirmed his democratic and socialist principles—"unbreakably linked," he claimed—"the lesson to which I dedicate my voice."[86]

Rahv's reply was no less stinging and personal. There was truth to Howe's thrust that Rahv's radicalism had reawakened and that the dreams of his past were being dreamed anew. But the sting of truth also came from Rahv's assessment of Howe. "Irving Howe seems to be very angry," Rahv began; "obviously he cannot face any challenge to his comprehensive claims . . . of being a leader of the left and ready expert in matters of strategy and theory. How else explain his obsessive raging against the young people of the New Left?" Rahv took aim: "Can it be that he is infuriated with them because they refuse to accept him as the *éminence grise* of American radicalism? In their view there is very little radicalism left in him." Despite his declaration not to continue with the "punch and swagger" style of Howe's personal attacks, Rahv got in a few licks of his own. He accused Howe of employing a phenomenon of cold-war America, "Red-baiting with a liberal slant," citing Howe's attempt to apply to Rahv the label Leninism. And in response to Howe's quoting a 1948 article by Rahv, the latter said, "I might quote certain pieces of Howe's, written in the late Forties, including the one chiding the editors of *Partisan Review* for 'supporting the State Department' against Stalinist Russia . . . . But I will refrain."[87]

Rahv's final criticism went right to the question of Howe's ultimate impact in the political arena. After suggesting that the kind of "democratic-socialism" Howe proffered might be suitable for a European cabinet member like Germany's Willy Brandt, Rahv suggested that Brandt's party did represent considerable power at the polls. "But for an inconsequential group of political-minded intellectuals"—the *Dissent* crowd—"who are by no means activists, to set itself up as the mentor and guide of the entire Left is an exercise in sheer illusionism."[88] To Rahv, as to the New Left, the *Dissent* alternative did not look like much of an alternative at all.

The exchange between Rahv and Howe went well beyond the issues under discussion and the normal bruised feelings among the New Yorkers. In the past they had all lambasted one another, in print and in person. Philip Rahv had put Irving Howe up to his wide-ranging attack on his fellow intellectuals in "This Age of Conformity," fifteen years before, without having created the permanent breaches which developed in the 1960s. Now working relationships and friendships ended. Howe included the *New York Review* by name in his attack on the "lemming-like" intellectuals following the New Left. For the next ten years, Howe's name did not appear as a contributor to that magazine. Between Howe and Rahv the anger which set in after the *New York Review* exchange lasted until Rahv's death. Howe believed that "Rahv felt like an old general who sees troops marching off in the wrong direction and runs to jump in front of them and lead them the right way." Howe preferred to remain in place, perhaps waiting for the army to be defeated or to turn back to him. Nonetheless, each thought the other was upset by not being allowed to march to the head of the line. "We were both literary people, but in some sense politics counted for more," Howe concluded. "You could differ on literary issues and maintain a friendship. Not on politics."[89] Howe and Rahv never spoke to one another again.

Heated words about the New Left did not come only from the editors of *Dissent* and of *Partisan Review*. They abounded in the 1960s and continued in subsequent assessments of the movements. Midge Decter recalled her anger at William Phillips, which erupted during an evening at Phillips's home in the mid-1960s. "We sat in William's living room, and we began to argue about the young." To her later surprise, "I heard myself screaming—and you don't scream at William Phillips, because he's a very frail fellow and gets very fussed." Decter recalled her incredulity at the change in Phillips's position." 'I don't believe you,' " she remembered saying. " 'Is this you sitting here saying these things? You know better!' William was beginning to turn from somebody who was just very upset by everything to somebody who was really signing on with the left again."

In Decter's view Phillips was not alone in this return to the past. "In the sixties the elders thought they were given the chance of a second youth. . . . You could literally see it in them." If some of the elders seemed to be heading back to their youth, several significant younger members began to swing the other way. While Phillips, Rahv, Macdonald, and Dupee grew increasingly enthusiastic about the New Left, others became increasingly skeptical. This included Norman Podhoretz, who had once believed he stood in the vanguard of the new radicalism. *Commentary's* swing to the left "lasted about three or four years," Decter noted, "and then Norman began [to realize] it was not what he meant at all." Podhoretz has recently claimed that his radicalism lasted longer, that though he began to question some of the precepts of the movement, he was still in the radical camp through the late 1960s. By the mid-1960s his doubts had certainly begun to show. Although he later claimed his radicalism helped account for the harsh reception his memoir *Making It* received, nonetheless in *Making It* he admitted "I began to be disturbed by a certain tone or emphasis in these more and more coalescent moments which seemed to me to be turning them away from the necessary impulse to reexamine the cliches of the fifties and toward a disastrous surrender to the equally vicious clichés of the thirties."[90] If some of the elders seemed bent on returning to the mistaken paths of their youths, Podhoretz would carry on the lessons he learned from them about those years.

In this effort he began to gather as company a number of individuals from whom he had grown estranged during his fling with the new radicalism. "Podhoretz's older brothers like Dan [Bell] and Irving Kristol and, to a lesser extent, Nat Glazer were very, very unhappy" with the left turn *Commentary* had taken, Midge Decter remembered. "They felt they were being squeezed out and so they were."[91] Slowly they all began to come back. Whereas a small group of New York Intellectuals rallied to the support of the New Left, a large coalition of New Yorkers spoke out against it. From the democratic socialists at *Dissent* through the *Commentary* writers and on to the increasingly conservative voices at the *Public Interest*—from Howe to Podhoretz and Glazer to Lipset, Bell, and Kristol—the accusations and criticisms rang.

The assumption that ideology had come to an end in the 1950s was challenged by its reawakening in the 1960s. While still discussing the details and implications of his basic theory, Daniel Bell took note of the early rumblings of a new radical movement. For him and his contemporaries, "the end of ideology closes the book, intellectually speaking, on an era." But even as he bid farewell to the desires of his youth, Bell cautioned those no longer moved by ideological thinking to pay attention to newer individuals who were. Closing a book "is not to turn one's back upon it," he argued in 1961. "This is all the more important now, for a 'new Left,' with few memories of the past, is emerging. It has passion and energy, but little definition of the future."[92] This was a prescient appraisal both of relations between the Old Left and the New Left and of the general attitude of many New Yorkers toward this revived radical spirit. In time the hostility and the critical assessments would grow increasingly intense, but as early as 1961 we can see the dim outlines of the New York Intellectuals' emerging positions and their prime concerns about the New Left.

Much of the rhetoric of the New Leftists stressed their desire not to recapitulate the mistakes of the past and to have, in fact, little to do with anyone not of their generation. This conscious focus on the role of the young and the special insight youth afforded confronted both the careers and the cultural place of the New Yorkers. The older intellectuals had worked long to establish themselves as cultural and political arbiters. They could bring something else to any newly emerging radicalism—their firsthand experience with the previous left political upsurge in America. A number had made their own intellectual marks by describing that experience and radicalism in general. Thus, beyond being generally prominent intellectuals, they saw themselves as experts on radicalism, to whom mainstream America turned. The young did not agree and, from the first, rejected them.[93]

Rahv and Howe accused one another of testiness deriving from the failure to be recognized as a leader by the New Left. Both were correct. Underlying all the criticisms of the New Left by the New York Intellectuals is this dual theme of the failure to understand and learn from the experiences of the thirties and of an awareness of the generational conflict. In an essay in *The End of Ideology* initially written in 1957, Daniel Bell noted that a number of his intellectual contemporaries were still identified as "young": Richard Hofstadter, Alfred Kazin, Saul Bellow, and Leslie Fiedler among them. By the 1960s no one perceived these men and their generation as young any more.[94]

Assessments drawn from contrasts between the New Left and the Old—the sixties and the thirties—tried to play it two ways. Having abandoned their own radicalism for some variant of the postwar liberal ethic, the New Yorkers called attention to the New Left's repetition of the old radical mistakes of the Depression years. Yet, though they had abandoned their own radicalism they had never fully repudiated it. Instead, they saw it as a necessary step in their intellectual progress. While they thus felt it necessary to warn against the repetition of past lapses, they also took care to demonstrate the qualitative difference between the "important" radical argument of the 1930s and the more frivolous nature of the 1960s variety. Lionel Trilling admitted that while "a certain element of gratuitousness" existed in thirties radicalism, "now, it seems to me, the gratuitous element is considerably greater than it was in the thirties. For young people now, being political serves much the same purpose as being literary has long done—it expresses and validates the personality."[95]

Even Norman Podhoretz, the self-proclaimed champion of the new radicalism, found the unwitting recapitulation of the thirties cause for alarm. It was not Podhoretz's personal past which was being repeated but that of his intellectual mentors. Despite efforts to blaze his own trail, he had incorporated much more of his teachers' mentality than he would admit. Podhoretz's swing left had been part of his attempt to break away from those fathers and from what he called the conformity of the fifties. As long as the new radicalism stuck to that, he stuck to it. His concerns rose, however, as he began to see a turning away from this reexamination of the postwar consensus and a return to attitudes reminiscent of those of the 1930s.[96]

The problem centered on an unresolvable conflict. The older ex-radicals wanted the younger radicals to avoid the mistakes of their radical past which meant to come to see the world as the ex-radicals did, which meant to be no longer radical. "No sensible radical over the age of thirty," Irving Howe said of himself and his generation, "wants young people to merely rehearse his ideas, or mimic his vocabulary, or look back upon his dusty articles." Perhaps not. But what Howe did want was for the young to avoid "the tags of the very past they believe themselves to be transcending." To do that, however, required that on a few crucial issues, "above all those regarding totalitarian movements and societies, there should be no ambiguity, no evasiveness."[97] No quibbling, that is with basic assumptions from the 1950s.

If the New Left refused to see its link and similarity to the Old Left, the old ex-leftists happily pointed these out. For some, the missed connections caused concern. Irving Howe and Lewis Coser looked on alarmed as the New Left, they believed, dismissed " 'old political quarrels' as largely meaningless." The young, Howe and Coser feared, "dismiss as equally *passé* those who had the acumen to oppose the Moscow Trials and those deluded or cynical enough to support them." This view of the 1930s struggles is, in and of itself, enormously telling. But beyond the definitive way in which they described the right and wrong positions of the thirties, there emerges their incredulity that the younger radicals did not care—or at least did not care as much as the veterans of the prewar battles. Along the same lines, Howe and Coser found it striking that the young do not have much attachment to Russia or to China, "but dislike intensely the idea of an anti-Communist crusade. They are not very interested in distinguishing between kinds of anti-Communism, whether of the right or left."[98] This would emerge as a significant issue when the New Left moved from politics to scholarship, but even in its political phase the definitions and debates of the 1930s or 1950s just did not persuade the radicals of the 1960s.

If the young could not see the importance of the older issues in the current context, the former radicals could perceive parallels between the radicalism of the two periods—turns in the sixties which corresponded to the problems of the thirties. To Daniel Bell the New Left's modeling itself on the black militants mimicked "the young middle-class rebels of the 1930s ap[ing] the Revolutionary Proletariat." In Midge Decter's analysis, developments within the New Left revived the notions of the Popular Front. And the New Left's critical attitude toward America reminded Sidney Hook of "the early Forties," when the extreme left "maintained that there was no difference between the United States and totalitarian countries."[99] Whatever the accuracy of the perceptions, their drawing on these earlier events as evidence of movements gone wrong served to reaffirm for the New Yorkers the errors of the New Left and the validity of their critique of this new radicalism.

Past events mattered to the New York Intellectuals. Early battles, political victories, and the evolution of cultural positions marked their own history and the growth of their ideas. Whether because they were more radical or more innocent, the young disregarded this history. To them it either appeared irrelevant or exemplified radicalism gone wrong. Furthermore, the reason a "new" left had to emerge was that the old had withered away. To the young as well as the old, the generational differences soon became readily apparent. For Irving Howe, one of the few New Yorkers still claiming to be radical, this spilt proved particularly problematic. "The generational conflict breaks out with strong feelings on both sides," Howe noted in 1965, "the older people feeling threatened in whatever they have been able to salvage from past experiences, the younger people feeling the need to shake off the dogma and create their own term of action." While not going as far as some in reducing the entire New Left to a generational conflict, Howe nonetheless noted that "the present rupture between the young and their elders seems especially deep." He did not blame only the young for this situation. This signified that society failed "to transmit with sufficient force its values to the young, or, perhaps more accurately, that the best of the young take the proclaimed values of their elders with a seriousness which leads them to be appalled by their violation in practice."[100] Here was Howe again cutting it two ways—critical of American society and critical of the positions of the young—still the correct radical.

Yet, Howe and the others opened themselves up to the very kind of criticism they rejected, when they began to define more precisely the problems with the New Left. Howe was troubled by the employment of "establishment" as an epithet of New Left rhetoric. The term derived from England, Howe said, where the characteristics of its members could be clearly identified: "an Oxbridge education, closely related values to the ruling class, and setting the cultural standards which largely dominate both the London literary world and the two leading universities." Asking rhetorically whether such an establishment existed in America, Howe responded, "Perhaps. There may now be in the process of formation, for the first time, such an intellectual class."[101] If such a class was forming or had formed since World War II, Howe and the other New York Intellectuals were clearly among its key members. Their university dispersion was greater, but then no two universities dominate America as do Oxford and Cambridge in England. Surely, the New Yorkers joined the central group which set "cultural standards" and dominated "the literary world and the . . . universities." The New Left aimed its venom at the establishment and, in so doing, at the New York Intellectuals.

The New Left's critique directly confronted the notions which the New Yorkers had helped articulate in the postwar years—and which had helped turn them into an "establishment." Nathan Glazer, for example, argued that the kinds of "freedoms" suggested by the New Left would only lead to an undoing of the positive benefits of contemporary society. "The mild discipline of free countries, which makes it possible for large numbers to withdraw to nonproductive styles of life, chafes [the young]," Glazer noted. But any attempts to "dismantle the structure of modern society will mean a radical reduction in the standard of living for most people." For Glazer the choice was clear: either "destroy the large organization [and] introduce a larger degree of freedom from control, from work, from family discipline," or "maintain a high standard of living."[102] Both were not possible. In the years after 1945 the older ex-radicals had chosen the latter.

Furthermore, the basis on which an evaluation like Glazer's was made also came under attack during the 1960s—or so the social scientists believed. "At the moment it is fashionable among radicals," Glazer wrote, "to ignore these details [of solutions to social problems] and to justify their indifference by an assault on the idea that work is necessary to society." Seymour Martin Lipset, Glazer's colleague in the social sciences, saw this as a "kind of left-wing 'intellectual *Poujadisme*,' . . . a back-lash to systematic and quantitative social science, to large-scale social research, to the very conception of the utility of efforts at value-free objective scholars upon policy-relevant fields."[103] The acceptance both of the potential benefits of liberal American society and of the internal, problem-solving approach in place of systematic, ideological thinking marked a significant turn in the creation of the postwar mentality. Now it seemed the New Left wanted to turn back.

It is hardly surprising that the harshest critical position of the 1950s soon entered the analysis of the 1960s, as several New Yorkers brought a number of the points of their anti-Communist position into the discussion of the New Left. Irving Howe commented on the SDS phrase "liberal fascism," used to describe American society. He dismissed it as both unserious and indicative of an argument already laid to rest decades before. "Having lived through the ghastliness of the Stalinist theory of 'social fascism' (the grand-daddy of 'liberal fascism') I cannot suppose any literate person really accepts this kind of nonsense."[104] Glazer tried to sew up the case by suggesting that the New Left echoed the Nazis as well as the Stalinists. The young radicals argue that "any so-called 'objective' or 'scientific' education is really a fraud," he asserted. "The argument is not new. It is in effect the argument that was fought out in Russia over the question of whether all education and all science must reflect 'dialectical materialism.' . . . Or the battle that was fought out in Nazi Germany over 'Aryan' science and 'non-Aryan' (and therefore 'Jewish science)." Glazer then expressed his own incredulity at confronting these arguments once again. To him, "these positions became so outrageous and untenable in the eyes of Western intellectuals"; the answers "have long lain quiescent and unused. But called into play they must be."[105]

The identification of the New Left as another example of myopic radicalism or ideological thinking served as the obvious beginning point for the critique of New Left politics. The subsequent equations of the New Left with the Soviets and the Nazis closed the book, politically. Intrinsic criticisms matched extrinsic problems, old patterns reemerged in new settings, and old arguments were hauled out to do battle. It became necessary, in Glazer's phrase, to "remember the answers." This implied that the New Yorkers had heard it all before. There was really nothing new, they concluded, in the New Left.

What may have been new, the New Yorkers discovered, was a group of intellectuals who emerged out of the New Left, a kind of intellectual cadre not exactly like any of those which had sprung up in the 1930s. Many of the older intellectuals found themselves immediately struck by the difference in roles between the radical intellectuals of the two eras. The Depression left gathered around journals, held odd jobs which supported their writing and political activity, and shared their exclusions. By the 1960s young intellectuals, as well as the old, had secured university positions.[106] Although the intellectuals who moved to the campuses and into prominence in the 1950s thus became, as Irving Kristol suggested, "a kind of power-elite . . . a permanent brain trust," there was another result of academic expansion. "What has also happened at the same time," Kristol discovered, "is that a whole new intellectual class has emerged as a result of the explosive growth." And rather than forming "any kind of elite, [they] are a mass—and have engendered a mass movement." Moreover, their credentials as well as their politics are suspect. "Some of them, of course, are intellectuals . . . the majority unquestionably is not."[107]

Kristol compared the radicalism of the thirties and sixties and found the new version wanting. "Our radicalism was highly intellectual and much less a matter of psychological expression," he noted. "Whereas in the 1960s, the psychological and personal became more important, none of us were looking for self-fulfillment of any kind or searching for an identity." Instead, "we dealt in ideas and as a result were rather precociously intellectual. The radicalism of the students in the 1960s had a very powerful anti-intellectual bent." But Kristol was not asking for a better radicalism, as Howe or Rahv might have claimed to be. He was unhappy with any turn to radicalism, especially by that class of "mass" intellectuals. "What is certain," he wrote in 1967,

> is that the national prestige and the international position of the U.S. are being adversely affected by this *sécession des clercs*. Imperial powers need social equilibrium at home if they are to act effectively in the world. It was possible to think, in the years immediately after World War II, that the U.S. had indeed achieved this kind of equilibrium—that consensus and equipose at home would permit our statesmen to formulate and pursue a coherent foreign policy. But the academic revolution of the 1950s and 1960s raises this issue again, in a most problematic and urgent way.[108]

While the issues might be reheated versions of old battles and while one needed only to "remember" the answers in order to dispense with this upstart radicalism, the "upstart" radicals themselves did not seem to come from the old molds. Mass or not, they represented a new class of radicals, especially since many of them came from an economic class different from that of the young immigrant children of the 1930s. The New Left grew up in an entirely different era, and its paths to college and careers had been significantly easier than those of the Depression youths. Political ideas might reflect past years, but these ideas were rooted in a changed culture. From that new context, new cultural ideas developed to complement the political. A "new sensibility" matched the new ideology—and this too grated on the New Yorkers.

Just as Irving Kristol found the political atmosphere of the 1950s conducive to harmonious political development, so Daniel Bell saw in these years a proper atmosphere for cultural flowering. "The sensibility of the 50's was largely a literary one," Bell wrote in *Commentary*. "In the writings of such representative critics of the period as Lionel Trilling, Yvor Winters, and John Crowe Ransom, the emphasis was on complexity, irony, ambiguity, and paradox. These are properties of the mind." The worst that could come from this outlook, Bell found, was "a form of quietism," but at best there emerged "a mode of self-consciousness," as well as a guarding "against any overwhelming involvement, absorption, immolation in a creed or an experience." By contrast, "the sensibility of the 60's rejected that mood in savage, even mindless fashion. In its fury with the times, the new sensibility was loud, imprecatory, prone to obscenity, and given to posing every issue, political or otherwise, in disjunctive correlatives." Bell minces few words, continuing his assault by suggesting that the sixties sensibility also added "a concern with violence and cruelty; a preoccupation with the sexually perverse; a desire to make noise; [and] an anti-cognitive and anti-intellectual mood."[109]

Bell's criticisms threw down the gauntlet to a number of his old friends as well as his new, young adversaries. While *Partisan Review* published articles on the cultural implications of the Beatles, Bell found that "beginning with the 'new sound' of the Beatles in 1964, rock reached such soaring crescendos that it was impossible to hear oneself think: and that may indeed have been its intention." The critical positions represented by Susan Sontag, one of the most influential young critics at *PR*, could be best characterized, Bell wrote, as the "anti-cognitive, anti-intellectual mood . . . an attack on 'content' and interpretation . . . a sensibility, in Susan Sontag's words, 'based on indiscriminateness, without ideas [and] beyond negation.' " Here Philip Rahv shared Bell's perception, rallying against Sontag and Fiedler for failing to expose the counterculture as a "degeneracy . . . masquerading as the boldest and bravest spirit of experiment and liberation."[110]

Most New York Intellectuals cared as little for this "new sensibility" as for the entire New Left. Irving Howe also echoed Daniel Bell's sentiments, finding fault with *Partisan Review* for its failure of nerve. Howe imagined the possibility of "a journal like *Partisan Review* stripping the pretensions of the current scene with the vigor it showed in opposing the Popular Front." But that was the *PR* of Howe's youth, the old vehicle of the alienated radical intellectuals collecting on the periphery. In fact, he complained in 1968, *PR* betrayed "a hopeless clash between its editors' capacity to apply serious standards and their yearnings to embrace the moment."[111] It was more than the failure of one journal to live up to its old level of achievement which frustrated Howe. He feared that much of the structure of the cultural position the New York Intellectuals had helped create would be dismantled. The "new phase in our culture" sought "to shake off the bleeding heritage of modernism and reinstate one of those periods of collective naïf which seem endemic to American experience." Howe believed that this newly developing cultural position wanted to undo what he and his intellectual group had spent their careers establishing.

> The new sensibility is impatient with ideas. It is impatient with literary structures of complexity and coherence, only yesterday the catchwords of our criticism. It wants instead works of literature—though literature may be the wrong word—that will be absolute as the sun, as unarguable as orgasm, and as delicious as a lollipop. It schemes to throw off the weight of nuance and ambiguity, legacies of high consciousness and tired blood. It is weary of the habit of reflection, the making of distinctions, the squareness of dialectic, the tarnished gold of inherited wisdom. It cares nothing for the haunted memories of old Jews. It has no taste for the ethical nail-biting of those writers of the Left who suffered defeat and could never again accept the narcotic of certainty. It is sick of those magnifications of irony that Mann gave us, sick of those visions of entrapment to which Kafka led us, sick of those shufflings of daily horror and grace that Joyce left us. It breathes contempt for rationality, impatience with mind, and a hostility to the artifices and decorums of high culture. It despises liberal values, liberal cautions, liberal virtues. It is bored with the past: for the past is a fink.[112]

Howe's characterization is stunningly harsh, as are the other critiques of the New Left by Bell, Glazer, and Kristol. The New Yorkers always saved their most strident words for those with whom they competed for territory— Communists and proletarian writers in the 1930s or fellow-traveling academics and anti-anti-Communists in the 1950s. Logical adversaries—Hitler, McCarthy, Nixon, Goldwater—while drawing criticism, never provoked the same storm of words and intensity of argument. The far right always existed to contend with liberals and leftists. But the left with whom the New Yorkers fought, in the thirties or fifties or sixties, represented a different kind of adversary. They stood in the path of personal achievement, the acceptance of the New Yorkers as the intellectual and political representatives who could best counter the right. During the Depression and in the postwar years, this often came down to a matter of arguing about which group best carried the left or liberal position. But in the 1960s the New Left identified many New York Intellectuals not as misguided leftists but as part of the very establishment the new radicalism sought to overturn. For the New Yorkers this was a new development; now it was a question not of whether their liberalism served best but whether they were liberal at all. Furthermore, the young radicals minced no words about how old these intellectuals had grown, identifying the "young" intellectuals of the 1950s as part of the older generation under attack. Finally, those New Yorkers who stood against the New Left found that their hard-won recognition as cultural arbiters mattered little to these new radicals. The young had little use for authority in general and therefore for individual authorities. On a number of fronts—personal, political, cultural—the New Left posed a threat many New Yorkers found very troubling. In the end, all Nathan Glazer could suggest in 1970 was a full frontal assault.

I for one, indeed, have come to feel that this radicalism is so beset with error and confusion that our main task, if we are ever to mount a successful assault on our problems, must be to argue with it and to strip it ultimately of the pretension that it understands the causes of our ills and how to set them right.[113]

The turning of their ire so harshly on the New Left pushed those like Glazer further to the right. His call to action came in an article entitled "On Being Deradicalized." Having thought himself a socialist in the 1960s, Glazer would be identified as a neoconservative in the 1970s. The New Left pulled the New York Intellectuals further apart and pushed a number of them in the same direction as Glazer. Those horrified by the course of the New Left grew contemptuous of those who championed it. Even more important, though, the rise of the New Left set in dramatic relief what had become of the New York Intellectuals since their radical days of the 1930s. They had grown older, more conservative, more powerful. They had tried to carry with them into the present as much of their intellectual past as possible, often fooling themselves and their devotees about just how radical and avant-garde they remained. Events and their reactions to them cast new light on their social positions, a light perhaps more harsh and less flattering but one which provided a more realistic picture.

MAKING IT AND UNMAKING IT

For several years I toyed with the idea of doing a book about Mailer that would focus on the problem of success, but in the end I decided that if I ever did work up the nerve to write about this problem, I would have to do it without hiding behind him or anyone else. Such a book, I thought, ought properly to be written in the first person, and it ought in itself to constitute a frank, Mailer-like bid for literary distinction, fame, and money all in one package: otherwise it would be unable to extricate itself from the toils of the dirty little secret. Writing a book like that would be a very dangerous thing to do, but some day, I told myself, I would like to try doing it.
I just have.[114]

With this bold statement, Norman Podhoretz closed the first volume of his memoirs, *Making It*, and opened a can of worms from which, Lionel Trilling told him, it would take ten years to recover. *Making It* grew to become one of the great literary events of the 1960s. There seemed something in the book to offend everyone—at least everyone in "the family" which Podhoretz described. "I was raised intellectually to believe there was something admirable in taking risks," Podhoretz later observed, "but the people who raised me, in effect, punished me whenever I did what I was raised to do. I've never quite understood why."[115]

If the *Commentary* editor did not see the reasons for the hostility he provoked, many of his contemporaries supplied them in their responses to

Making It. The problem concerned what Podhoretz called the "dirty little secret," "the lust for success which I said (borrowing a phrase from D. H. Lawrence) had replaced sexual lust . . . especially for the writers, artists, and intellectuals among whom I lived and worked," Podhoretz later wrote. Podhoretz had spent most of the 1960s marking himself off from the intellectuals who inhabited his "family." *Making It* was the final act of family betrayal. It may also have truly signified the end of "the family." "Many members of this group resented being associated with any group," Podhoretz believed. "Others [exhibited] a certain degree of self-hatred, perhaps. I think people were afraid of being seen as taking themselves too seriously or to be self-important." This problem never seems to have bothered Podhoretz, according to Daniel Bell. "Norman is an overly serious person"; he lacks some "degree of distancing. He's so involved."[116] Involved Podhoretz became, not only in the book, but in the chapter of literary history about its publication and the reaction it stirred up.

Podhoretz was not always the target of interfamily antagonisms. Before *Making It* his colleagues would come to his defense. When the first collection of Podhoretz's articles and reviews appeared, Benjamin DeMott took the opportunity in the pages of the *New York Review of Books* to attack Podhoretz's sense of his intellectual group. Reading Podhoretz, DeMott observed, offered the example of a "new possibility in American letters—a critical intelligence that will have taught itself how to speak as the responsible voice of a community." In this era before the antagonisms had set in between intellectuals and publications, both Jason Epstein and William Phillips took exception to DeMott's characterization. Phillips chose sarcasm. "Since the next meeting of the New York Establishment to set the line on Mr. DeMott's review won't be held for another week, I'm writing this letter on my own," the *Partisan Review* editor answered. Turning serious, Phillips accused DeMott of maintaining a "provincial fantasy about New York 'literary life.' " Epstein responded to DeMott head-on. "Mr. Podhoretz's stength as a critic of literature and society lies partly . . . in his refusal to indulge in the trivial illusion that the New York literary community, which DeMott obsessively describes, really exists or, if it may be said to exist, that it matters."[117]

Three years later Podhoretz demonstrated how nonillusory this community was for him and how much it mattered in his life. Before this became evident to the world, the smaller literary community itself stirred with its reactions to Podhoretz's unpublished manuscript. From the moment he began showing it around—to his publisher, his agent, his friends—there were efforts to try to have it withdrawn. Initially, Podhoretz recalled, he had received a relatively large advance, "on the basis of a letter I wrote describing the book. When they read it, both my agent, Lynn Nesbit, and Roger Straus, who was going to publish it, were obviously horrified by the book. She didn't want to represent it, and he didn't want to publish it." Podhoretz had a contract, though, and Straus had received the completed manuscript. "What he had to do was maneuver me into withdrawing it, which he succeeded in doing by making it clear he would publish it with no enthusiasm, in effect hide it from the salesmen." Podhoretz thought his publishers and his agent were in collusion to stop publication. "I took the book away from her, much to her relief, and I took the book away from him, much to his relief, and I got a different agent, and we sold it to a different publisher." The book was ultimately brought out by Random House, but not by the division Jason Epstein controlled.[118]

Straus and Nesbit had good company in their opposition to Podhoretz. The *Commentary* editor had sent the manuscript to a number of friends for comment. Their reactions frequently matched that of Straus and Nesbit. F. W. Dupee responded pointedly, as Podhoretz noted in his reply. "I especially appreciate your directness in telling me what you think is wrong with the book. Let me be equally direct in response," Podhoretz wrote Dupee. "I fail to see in what sense I made a travesty of the 'family,' or of myself." Daniel Bell read the galleys and, though believing that people did not like the book for varying reasons, found his own response relatively simple. "What it lacks is a form of irony and self-distancing," he noted. Bell suggested to Podhoretz that if he would "add three or four pages at the end, it would blunt a lot of criticism." Podhoretz later observed that both Trilling and Epstein also suggested adding to the book. "I could, each said independently, add a new chapter at the end taking back everything I had written before."[119] Podhoretz rejected all these suggestions.

Epstein and Trilling did, in fact, have a good deal more to say to Podhoretz than just that he should add an extra chapter. "If I were God, I'd drown it in the river," Epstein reportedly said about the book. Being still friendly with Podhoretz, however, he also tried other avenues.[120] Epstein, who was never close to Trilling, telephoned the Columbia critic to ask, "Can you do anything to keep Norman from publishing the book?" Trilling agreed with Epstein that the book was "lamentable and shouldn't be published in its present form," Diana Trilling recounted. Early in 1967 Podhoretz, Midge Decter, and Lionel and Diana Trilling traveled to Germany as part of a group funded by the Ford Foundation. One evening in Berlin the Trillings undertook to have dinner alone with Podhoretz and Decter, so that "Lionel could make one more try at dissuading Norman from publishing it." When she saw that her husband could not shake Podhoretz's resolution, Diana Trilling turned to Midge Decter and said, "Midge, what do you think?" Decter responded, "Oh, I never interfere with these things." "Whatever the expression on my face, I hope it communicated the wryness I felt," Trilling added.

> I then turned to Norman and asked him what in the world other than something wrong with the book itself would make three such totally different people as Roger Straus, Jason Epstein, and Lionel Trilling all agree that the book shouldn't be published. To this Podhoretz answered without hesitation, "Oh, I've thought about that—Class!" It was surely the only time Lionel was ever put in the same economic class with Roger Straus![121]

Undaunted, then, Podhoretz proceeded with his plans to publish, and the New York literary world buzzed in anticipation. "I remember listening to Schlesinger, Diana Trilling, and James Wechsler at a party," recalled Arnold Beichman, who liked the book, "talking about Podhoretz as if he were mad, had gone off his rocker." Podhoretz so steeled himself for the onslaught of abuse that when the book finally appeared he found the critical reaction not nearly as bad as he had anticipated. "But by any measure other than the dire expectations Jason and Lionel had aroused in me, the response was very nasty indeed."[122]

Podhoretz's assessment of the book's reviews is essentially correct, although he did receive some kind words. Unfortunately, as Norman Mailer pointed out, they were not in the places Podhoretz really cared about. Kind words in the *Wall Street Journal*, the *Cleveland Plain Dealer*, or the *St. Louis Post-Dispatch* could not balance harsh appraisals in the *Atlantic,* the *New Republic*, or the *New York Review*. Wilfred Sheed's *Atlantic* review found the book a "tease." Recalling Edith Wharton's questioning of F. Scott Fitzgerald—"But what did you *do* in the bordello, Mr. Fitzgerald?"—Sheed asked the same question of Podhoretz.

What does Mr. Podhoretz do in the bordello? Simply sits up there and purrs, as far as we can make out. His ruthless confession must rank with the great literary teases of all time; or with the fake pornography they used to fob off on teen-agers in the bad old days.

The point of the book, Sheed concluded, is not really to expose, "but to rationalize and justify his own living standard. It is as if he wanted the reader to say, it's OK, you can keep the money."[123]

Despite the growing tensions between *Commentary* and the *New York Review*, Edgar Friedenberg's comments in the *Review* were far milder than might have been expected. He did find Podhoretz's tone so impersonal that he suggested an alternative title might be "Manhole in the Promised Land." Still, he felt that beneath the swagger and brashness, some potential good might still emerge. "We may surely hope that successive volumes will permit us to follow the career of this remarkable, still young man," Friedenberg concluded his review. "And they may be more mellow; sometimes, as we age, memory softens our perceptions of reality. In *Podhoretz Returns* and *Son of Podhoretz*, the monster may turn out to have a heart of gold."[124]

The further adventures of Norman Podhoretz took turns even his harshest 1968 critics probably did not expect. His politics veered sharply to the right, and this came to color even his assessment of the hostile reaction to *Making It.* "Podhoretz Returns," turned out to be *Breaking Ranks*, the second installment of his memoirs, published in 1979. In this work, he recounted the reaction to the first volume in political terms. He believed that the criticism he received was politically motivated, not because of disagreements over political philosophy or proposed actions, but because of the "informing idea of the whole book—an idea implicit in the title and summed up toward the end in the statement that the pursuit of success was not necessarily 'a corrupting force in American culture.' " By any traditional standard, this would not sound very political, he believed, but in the context of 1967 any position which did not harshly criticize American culture remained open to attack from the New Left. Beyond individual issues like the war or race relations, Podhoretz contended, the "idea that the worship of success lay at the root of the sickness of a 'sick society,' became the central, the organizing theme of the strictly cultural arm of the Movement. . . . And it was above all else because it challenged this idea about success in America that *Making It* provoked such a storm."[125]

Diana Trilling objected to Podhoretz's characterizations, especially as they concerned her husband:

> Does Norman Podhoretz really think that Lionel wanted Norman to remove his attacks on important persons of the left and that that's why he tried to persuade him against publishing *Making It?* If Norman can believe that, I guess he can believe anything that suits his purposes. Lionel was trying to protect *Norman* from exactly what happened to him when the book was published. Norman had been his old student; Norman had been his friend.[126]

Others have also quarreled with Podhoretz's analysis. In his recent review of Jewish writers, Mark Shechner talked of *Making It* as a novel, not because of its fabrication of events but because it "was and remains the only Jewish novel after the war . . . whose hero is allowed to achieve social success without paying a moral price." Shechner considered *Making It* a novel, as well as a memoir, because "the imagination of a life" is seen "in terms of a significant moral pattern. . . . Its myths cannot be separated from its recollected facts." In the end "the retribution and guilt that eventually catch up to the overreachers in proper moral fiction never arrive." Podhoretz sided with his readers as opposed to his intellectual peers, Shechner concluded; the middle-class Jews in the postwar world understood and approved of Podhoretz's course and his beliefs.[127]

Podhoretz is correct that the outside world found *Making It* less horrible than the New Yorkers themselves did. Their moral view, as Shechner suggested, was not being held up as a pose, covering a desire for fame and fortune. What made Podhoretz's view so irritating for New York Intellectuals was both its kernel of truth and its exaggerated application of that truth. From his opening words, Podhoretz took a very unsubtle and unambiguous position. "I am a man who at the precocious age of thirty-five experienced an astonishing revelation: it is better to be a success than a failure." He then described the corollaries of this intitial perception: "it was better to be rich than to be poor . . . to give orders than to take them . . . to be reconized than to be anonymous."[128] Podhoretz had come to the New York Intellectual community after all the battles of the 1930s had been fought, with Stalinists discredited, modernism firmly established, and intellectual eminence on the rise. Because of his age, he joined during the period of ascent. He saw his mentors in victory, moving toward the center, rather than on the periphery suffering defeats or being ignored. He was the young man who had missed adolescence, became old before his time. He tried to reverse this course, to dive into the Plaza fountain, but despite his short-lived flirtation with the left, too much of the stamp of his education in the 1950s remained. Like his mentors before him Norman Podhoretz had to break off from his intellectual parents, just as they had abandoned theirs in the 1930s. Like a rambunctious and arrogant adolescent, he abused his elders, particularly Lionel Trilling. But the lessons of the parents were too deeply imprinted ever to be fully thrown off. Podhoretz's problem had to do with the period of his coming of age. There is no question that the older New York Intellectuals possessed remarkable ambition and personal drive equal to those of the *Commentary* editor. But their years of exclusions and the path they followed to their postwar prominence provided a perspective which Podhoretz lacked. "In some sense," Daniel Bell observed, "Norman doesn't have a sense of irony— that sense which made Lionel so unique. What characterized Lionel was always a form of irony about himself. Great seriousness about himself, but also great wit."[129]

Making It demonstrated, unequivocally, the degree to which that once prominent aspect of the New York Intellectuals—the irony, the wit, the distancing—had receded in the wake of the successes they achieved in the postwar years. In the early days success had exhilarated them. Now it was something Podhoretz admitted he crassly sought: "Fame, I now saw (how courageous of me not to flinch), was unqualifiedly delicious. . . . "[130] In what Podhoretz had become—or, at least, in how he chose to picture himself—the New Yorkers could glimpse an exaggerated portrait of themselves and the course they had followed. In their achievements they had demonstrated the benefits of intellectual success, and now younger individuals sought to follow in their footsteps, without the humanizing touches which had made them unique. Podhoretz was not alone here, for in recent years other younger critics have popped up, eager to become New York Intellectuals. Unfortunately for them, it can no longer be done.

Throughout the 1960s the New Yorkers drifted apart, across the political map as well as the geographical one. The forces which held them together weakened, and currents which carried them away from one another grew. It is difficult to pinpoint a beginning of the end of the New York Intellectual community; it is easier to find an end to the end—*Making It*. This involved more than a desire to be dissociated from the family's "dirty little secret," to deny an interest in fame or fortune. It seems that personal drives alone could not keep intact a community which had already achieved success. The New Yorkers had stuck together for a good many reasons, among which their ambitions figured prominently. But the community existed for reasons other than that of individual development. The cohesion of the group, including a roughly shared agenda of political and cultural issues, had facilitated the personal advancement of its members. But they could not function as a static coterie in which membership provided only a ticket to prominence. Among a number of other things, Norman Podhoretz's memoir demonstrated that this was what the vestiges of the New York Intellectual community had become. Because no membership cards had ever been issued, no meetings held, no headquarters opened, there did not have to be any official closings, no motions to disband, no formal resignations. Instead, perhaps with some personal resignation, the intellectuals moved on as individuals, aware that what had made them could no longer be. Their old community could now only help create intellectuals like the one Norman Podhoretz described in *Making It*. It is little wonder that his picture of their world horrified them.

Chapter 14

What We Are Today

Should we not rather lament the passing of something extraordinary, which perhaps will never be seen again.

—Lionel Abel

It's the same as when two persons have been married. They may separate and never see each other for twenty years, but there is always that shared memory. They were members of the family.

—Daniel Bell[1]

As he looked at the changes which had occurred in the New York Intellectual world in the late 1960s, the "family cousin" David T. Bazelon felt that an "intellectual revolution" was going on. "Guys like [Jason] Epstein and [Norman] Podhoretz," he added, "are riding herd on a hurricane."[2] By 1970 the revolution was over and civil war had broken out. The piling up of issues between the two developing camps of the 1960s—some political, like the New Left and the New York teachers strike, some personal, like the hostilities over *Making It*—resulted in open warfare in the pages of their two major periodicals, *Commentary* and the *New York Review of Books*.

For any who might have missed the growing turmoil, *Commentary* laid the issues out in the clearest possible terms, with Dennis Wrong's "The Case of the *New York Review*," in November 1970. Writing at Podhoretz's request, Wrong chronicled the crimes of the *New York Review*, with 1967 as the point of no return. In that year the *Review* ran Jason Epstein's "The CIA and the Intellectuals," Noam Chomsky's "The Responsibility of the Intellectuals," Mary McCarthy's "Report from Vietnam," Andrew Kopkind's critique of Robert Kennedy, I. F. Stone's analysis of Zionism, and, in August, the single

366

issue which drove the final wedge between the factions. Andrew Kopkind, in "Soul Power," penned the infamous line "Morality, like politics, starts at the barrel of a gun." This was "perhaps the most offensive and offending sentence ever to have appeared in the *NYR*," Wrong declared. The same issue included "The Occupation of Newark," by Tom Hayden, which suggested that out of the urban disorders might come meaningful change. And finally, the cover illustration—a carefully executed line drawing showing the ingredients of a Molotov cocktail—would mark this forever as the "Molotov cocktail" issue. Not only the rightward emigrants at *Commentary* found this issue disturbing but also the self-proclaimed radicals at *Dissent*. Michael Harrington considered the drawing irresponsible and a "loud editorial."[3]

Wrong's most personal critiques were aimed at the two writers he thought most representative of the *Review*'s outlook—Noam Chomsky and Edgar Z. Friedenberg. His assessment of Chomsky was briefer, as he had already tabulated the sins of the MIT linguist in an article in *Dissent*, earlier that year.[4] Wrong did note a few of Chomsky's wrong turns, including his book *American Power and the New Mandarins*, which included "The Responsibility of the Intellectuals," with its attack on Bell, Schlesinger, and other cold-war intellectuals. Wrong spent more time on Friedenberg, the sociologist and educator who wrote *The Vanishing Adolescent* and *Coming of Age in America*. Wrong suggested that Friedenberg shared the "fashionable technophobia and juvenophilia of other *NYR* writers"; that he was "like Chomsky, given to such extreme and absolute statements imputing evil designs to large numbers of Americans that one is inclined to simply dismiss him as overwrought"; and that his "rejection of American society seem[ed] so extreme as to be beyond conceivable political rectification."[5]

Commentary's political position in 1970 remained in flux, and Dennis Wrong still comfortably wrote for it and for *Dissent*. He concluded his attack with a view satisfactory to the editors at both journals, resonant of issues fully alive only to the veterans of past intellectual wars. Calling up the debates of the 1950s and even the 1930s, Wrong declared that the major flaw epitomized by the *New York Review* was a failure to remember the lessons of the past. "The real lesson learned by the anti-Stalinist intellectuals of the 40's," Wrong wrote at the end of his piece, "was the menace of politicized will, feeding on its own self-righteousness, thrusting blindly forward in a frenzied activism until it finds or creates the resistance it seeks, a consumption which, now as then, can have disastrous consequences for us all."[6] In an unusual editorial addition, Podhoretz put below the article an offer of reprints at fifty cents each, with a 20 percent discount on orders larger than twenty-five. No other editorial comment was necessary to demonstrate how important Podhoretz considered the Wrong article and how widely he wished it circulated.

Podhoretz fired another salvo two months later, in assigning the Yale law professor Alexander Bickel to review several new books on the Chicago conspiracy trial which resulted from disruptions at the 1968 Democratic convention. Although several authors published works on the subject, including the defendant Tom Hayden and the *New York Times* reporter J. Anthony Lukas, the majority of Bickel's review was devoted to Jason Epstein's *The Great Conspiracy Trial*. When a frequent *Commentary* reviewer asked to do the Epstein book, the executive editor Neal Kozodoy responded, "Oh, no. We have something special in mind for that book."[7] Bickel not only took exception to Epstein's legal interpretations—"Epstein takes great pains to misread"—but also questioned Epstein's detachment in reporting. Bickel "recapitulates" and "translate[s]" Epstein's view of the Weathermen. "American society is so immeasurably culpable that random murders of any of its white members can be perceived as just" was how Bickel summarized Epstein's view. Furthermore, Bickel believed that Epstein had to employ "conspiratorial assumptions and fake historical analogies" because the real ills of American society call only for reform. "And the argument is for revolution not reform."[8]

By the early 1970s the division between *Commentary* and the *New York Review*, between Podhoretz and Epstein, between the old left-moving right and the New Left had become the stuff of literary gossip and a new guide for charting the New York Intellectual world. In March 1972 the *New York Times Magazine* chronicled all for the general public with Merle Miller's "Why Norman and Jason Aren't Talking." As such articles have a way of doing, Miller's piece became a spur to further hostility and argument, developing into an element in the battle rather than a report on the fray. Jason Epstein responded with a long letter, correcting minor factual errors and, more important, restating his editorial independence from the *New York Review*. Miller rebutted with a long defense of his own, ending with a sarcastic reference to what was purportedly Epstein's favorite adjective—"One other thing about Mr. Epstein's lengthy letter, it is boring." Lionel Trilling, Nathan Glazer, Tom Wolfe, the film critic Richard Schickel, and the former Doubleday editor Francis Price all added their corrections to and comments on Miller's assessment. And the battle went on.[9]

The political evolution of the 1970s and the decline of the New Left adjusted the position and tone of the two publications. *Commentary* continued rightward, ultimately arriving at its current neo-conservative position. The *New York Review of Books*, reflecting the decreasing intensity of the left in recent years, fell back on its literary-intellectual side. The political articles had a much milder tone. But if the guns between the two magazines cooled and a kind of undeclared cease-fire developed, at least in terms of direct attacks, no reconciliation took place. The split between *Commentary* and the *New York Review* represented symbolically the permanent division of the New York Intellectual world. Its third generation chose sides against one another, with the older members lining up as well. This ensured that whatever intellectual constellation might emerge, it would no longer represent a continuation of the old New York Intellectual community, but only one of its several spin-offs.

The largest single block of New York Intellectuals in a new political and journalistic grouping are those identified in recent years with neoconservatism. While this band of intellectuals includes a great number never previously connected to the New Yorkers, many of neoconservatism's intellectual mainstays and its two most prominent journals come right out of this world. The *Public Interest* and *Commentary* serve as the two intellectual bulwarks for this political position, supported by a host of other periodicals—from the editorial pages of the *Wall Street Journal* to *Daedalus* and the *American Scholar*. While the two most prominent figures in public life identified as neoconservatives were Daniel Patrick Moynihan and Jeane Kirkpatrick, the neoconservative brain trust includes Irving Kristol, Norman Podhoretz, Daniel Bell, Nathan Glazer, and Seymour Martin Lipset. These are the New York Intellectuals who led the rightward transition during the 1960s, Bell and Kristol at the *Public Interest* (later joined by Glazer) and Podhoretz, after a short veer left, at *Commentary*. Around these individuals have clustered a number of other analysts: Samuel P. Huntington, James Q. Wilson, Robert Tucker, Michael Novak, Edward Banfield, Robert Nisbet, and a host of others. For this latter group the motivations and intellectual paths to neoconservatism may vary. But for the New Yorkers who have ended up at this position the particular issues are telling.

It is usual to chart the development of neoconservatism as a reaction to the tumultuous days of the 1960s, whether among steadfast opponents of the New Left like Kristol or among reborn ex-radicals like Podhoretz. In fact, though, the roots go back to the positions of the 1950s and the era when these people called themselves liberals. It is probably more accurate to identify the New Left as a reaction to *them* than vice versa. In the introduction to his collected essays on student unrest, *Remembering the Answers*, Nathan Glazer asked rhetorically, "How does a radical, a mild radical . . . in the late 1950s end up a conservative, a mild conservative . . . in the early 1970s?" (This was written before the term "neoconservative" became fashionable.) His answer was to describe "mild radicals and radicalism" in the late 1950s. The issues he said were pressing then included demonstrations against civil defense, support for Fidel Castro, Jane Jacobs's stand against urban renewal, and support of public housing and tenant organizing. "Radicalism," Glazer wrote, "having rejected Marx, was in a state of peculiar openness."[10] More accurately, Glazer's radicalism was in a state of welfare liberalism.

Yet, Glazer was the self-proclaimed radical of the 1950s. Most of the other neoconservatives considered themselves liberals. What is striking is that despite changing labels, their ideas bear a close resemblance to those of the 1950s. For example, neoconservatives disapprove of preferential quotas and affirmative action programs—*Affirmative Discrimination* is the title of a book by Glazer.

Instead, they believe in hierarchies; they seek equal access, not equality. "Human talents and abilities . . . distribute themselves along a bell-shaped curve," Irving Kristol concluded, as do incomes and power. "In the United States, nature is triumphant: we are perfectly bell-shaped." Elsewhere Kristol remarked, "Nobody cares about equality as long as everything is getting better." Inappropriate commitment to equality led only to a populist leveling or, as Bell argued, a resentment against, "the authority represented in the superior competence of individuals."[11] But the neoconservative critique of populist sentiment did not begin with the "power to the people" slogans of the 1960s or with the calls for participatory democracy; it was appropriated from their own arguments of the 1950s. Populism was viewed as a conservative force—neoconservatives were liberals then—and the populist conservatives were responsible for Joseph McCarthy and, later, Barry Goldwater. Given its historical legitimacy in Hofstadter's *Age of Reform*, this view received its contemporary application in *The New American Right*, edited by Bell. Mass movements contesting the "authority" of "superior competence" disturbed Bell two decades before his neoconservative remarks in *The Coming of Post-Industrial Society*.

The role of intellectuals, often cited as a neoconservative linchpin, is also nothing new. The "knowledge industry," Kristol called them, "a kind of permanent brain trust to the political, the military, the economic authorities. These are the men who commute regularly to Washington, who help draw up programs for reorganizing the bureaucracy . . . who analyze the course of economic growth."[12] Yet, that intellectuals should have social importance and utility is a claim the New Yorkers long made—first as radical intellectuals and then as postwar liberals. All through the 1950s they pressed for intellectuals' involvement in government. In the 1960s a number received the opportunity. During the 1970s this trend continued, only now they advised admittedly conservative presidents.

Foreign-policy considerations best demonstrate the continuity between the "liberal" attitudes of the 1950s and the "neoconservative" positions of the 1970s and 1980s. The neoconservative view of the world is an attempt to pump new life into what once seemed a dead horse. Daniel Patrick Moynihan's belligerent defense of American power during his United Nations ambassadorship is only the most public example of this effort. Robert Tucker suggested in one *Commentary* article that the United States reconsider a kind of gunboat diplomacy to deal with the Arab oil crisis. More recently, Jeane Kirkpatrick's argument about a "double standard" in American foreign policy prompted praise from the then-candidate Ronald Reagan and her eventual appointment to the UN post. Kirkpatrick's assessment also initially appeared in *Commentary*.[13]

Nothing goes straight from pen to press at *Commentary*; everything passes across the desk of its editor, Norman Podhoretz. That Podhoretz assented to, in fact may have encouraged, these articles, is reinforced by his own recent foreign-policy pronouncemnts as well as by his editorial style. The impact of Vietnam, he contended, has been not to discredit cold warriorism but to spawn a new isolationism. Recent events, including those in Iran and Afghanistan, "have served so well and for so long to disguise and deny the ominous consequences of a tilt in the balance of power from the United States to the Soviet Union." The consequence of this change would be "the final collapse of an American resolve to resist the forward surge of Soviet imperialism." The subtitle of his book *The Present Danger* asks boldly, "Do we have the will to reverse the decline of American power?"[14] His cold-war rhetoric rings with assumptions of the 1950s, of the *Commentary* of Elliot Cohen, of the world with which Podhoretz himself brazenly broke in 1960. He begins by trying to rekindle the spirit of the Truman Doctrine and to revive the explicit policy of containment. Various factors work against this, he argues, including the growth of what he characterizes as "a culture of appeasement." Against this damaging tendency, he hopes, the revival of a "new nationalism"—epitomized by Moynihan's UN posture—will save us from wars or the "Finlandization of America."[15] Podhoretz's words have the ring of postwar liberalism. Arthur Schlesinger, Jr., argued that myopic, "Doughface progressives" remained naïve in the face of the Soviet challenge and that only pragmatic, action-oriented liberals possessed the correct ideas and style. Podhoretz finds contemporary intellectuals, including Schlesinger, equally naïve in that they hold a "mistaken point of view about Soviet intentions and the international situation in general."[16]

Podhoretz is, in fact, unhappy with the term "neoconservative." "I call myself a centrist liberal," he said in one conversation. In another, when asked whether he was not "similar to an 'old-fashioned liberal,'" he said, "Yes, That's the name we should use, but it's very difficult to dislodge the neoconservative label."[17] It seems just as hard to dislodge liberal ideas.

Irving Kristol has linked together the two elements of intellectual responsibility and American foreign policy. "It is much to be doubted that the U.S. can continue to play an imperial role without the endorsement of its intellectual class," he argued in the 1960s. Furthermore, Kristol wrote, "there is no way the United States . . . can avoid such an imperial role." The opposition of intellectuals would "enfeeble the resolution of our statesmen and diminish the credibility of their policies abroad."[18] In 1954 Sol Stein, the second executive director of the American Committee for Cultural Freedom, wrote to Elliot Cohen. The ACCF, Stein said, "is an active association of leaders of the American cultural community . . . devoted . . . to rallying intellectuals here and abroad in a serious and responsible opposition to Communism and all forms of totalitarianism."[19] Irving Kristol was the ACCF's first executive director, in 1951.

Beyond ideas, there are even organizations which seem to duplicate the past. In February 1981 the *New York Times* ran the announcement of a new "international committee" to lead a "struggle for freedom." Called the

Committee for the Free World, it had offices in New York and London, Midge Decter as executive director, and a roster of intellectual supporters including Podhoretz, Kristol, Glazer, Lipset, James Q. Wilson, and Sidney Hook. With covert CIA support, the Congress for Cultural Freedom had been created for postwar liberals. With direct conservative funding, this new organization now sought to band conservative intellectuals together in a similar grouping. The call to intellectuals—to stem the "increased danger to democratic societies" posed by the Soviet Union and "to defend the non-Communist world 'against the rising meanace of totalitarianism' "—seemed an idea whose time had come, again.[20]

All has not been smooth sailing even among those identified as neoconservatives. Daniel Bell has entirely rejected his inclusion. "Whenever I read about neoconservatism, I think, 'That isn't neoconservatism; it's just Irving.' "[21] Trying to maintain his tripartite self-description—"a socialist in economics, a liberal in politics, a conservative in culture"—Bell marked himself off from some of his peers. He believed that his ties to neoconservatives derived from a shared critique of domestic policy. In foreign policy, where Podhoretz came on, he got off. Even on domestic issues, Bell was recently chastised in *Commentary* by Michael Novak. For Novak, Bell's "socialist" side remains too strong, despite all his writing about the end of ideology. He does not sufficiently praise what Novak calls "the underlying spiritual power of capitalism." Capitalism, for Novak, is "intrinsically related to some core values—to liberty in the sense of self-discipline; to invention, creativity, and cooperation, the root of the corporation; to work, savings, investment in the future; to self-reliance, etc." Bell does not understand this, Novak argues, and this even undermines his analysis of Jewishness. Bell fails to "connect the deep impulses in the Jewish spirit with certain prerequisites for the emergence of capitalism." "Capitalism is *not* neutral with respect to values," Novak holds, and neoconservatives should not be neutral with respect to the value of capitalism. Daniel Bell's ambivalences have made his presence on the neoconservative roster problematic.[22]

Daniel Patrick Moyihan has found his difficulties with neoconservatives to be of a different sort. When he first won election to the Senate from New York, in 1976, it was hailed as a portent of a neoconservative trend in national politics. But, as the intellectuals and academics increasingly aligned themselves with the Republican party and then with the Reagan administration, Moynihan was caught trying to balance his views and his Democratic party credentials. In 1976 Podhoretz argued he was "much closer intellectually" to Moynihan than to Kristol. "I disagree with Irving Kristol about a lot of things; I don't disagree with Pat Moynihan about many things." Both Podhoretz and Moynihan have moved. Irving Kristol recalled having dinner with Podhoretz and Midge Decter in 1978, "and they were reproaching me for using the term capitalism. They felt very uncomfortable with the formulation that what we were doing was defending capitalism. Norman now accepts capitalism. That doesn't mean being anti-trade union, but distancing yourself."[23] Moynihan has had to be much more careful about maintaining his political base and thus about adopting positions outside the bounds of Democratic party orthodoxy. He has upheld many traditional Democratic positions and won reelection handily in 1982. While many of his old intellectual friends supported Ronald Reagan in 1984, Moynihan joined with most other Democratic party officials to back Walter Mondale, even in the primaries. Both Bell and Glazer also supported Mondale. Furthermore, Moynihan jousted with the Reagan administration over its failure to inform the Senate Intelligence Committee of the covert mining of Nicaraguan harbors in early 1984.

One particularly frustrating problem for neoconservative New York Intellectuals developed with the publication in 1981 of Jacobo Timerman's *Prisoner without a Name, Cell without a Number.* An Argentine journalist of leftist orientation, Timerman had been arrested by the military government and tortured. He claimed that severe anti-Semitism had played a significant part in his persecution and that the Argentine authorities represented a kind of neo-Nazism. Timerman's position was at odds with the Reagan administration's human-rights policy, which was based on arguments developed in *Commentary* by Jeane Kirkpatrick. Timerman challenged her authoritarian-totalitarian distinction, which suggested we apply different standards to right-wing and left-wing governments which abuse human rights. Sidney Hook, often perceived to be an intellectual father of neoconservatism and another cold-war liberal, defended Kirkpatrick against Timerman and his *New York Times* book reviewer, Anthony Lewis. "After all, despite Argentine anti-Semitism and anti-Zionism, the regime was compelled to let Mr. Timerman go," Hook noted. "Contrast this with the attitude of the Soviet regime toward Jewish leaders of the anti-Fascist resistance Victor Alter and Henryk Erlich . . . executed and degraded as Nazi spies by Stalin and his henchmen."[24] Hook's analogy was between Argentina in 1979 and Stalin's Russia. The Soviets of more recent times were compelled to let Solzhenitsyn go, for example. But Hook was viewing the world through cold-war lenses. Using phrases suggestive of his 1950s position, Hook found Kirkpatrick's concept "principled and commonsensical. Whenever we are confronted by an unhappy situation in which the only effective choice is between alternatives of different degrees of evil, we should always choose the lesser evil." Sidney Hook had once come around to choosing America and the West as a lesser evil than Communist Russia. By 1981 he was led to choose the military junta in Argentina.

Irving Kristol pressed the argument against Timerman even further. In fact, he took cognizance of the Solzhenitsyn analogy, believing that Timerman had "cast himself in the role of Solzhenitsyn-of-the-left." For Kristol an authoritarian regime is "generally hostile in practice" to our conception of human rights, "but not necessarily in principle, and therefore not irredeemably so," as are totalitarian ones. Kristol attacks Timerman for failing to mention his ties with a left-wing financier, David Graiver, who both practiced illegal financial dealings and supposedly financed left-wing urban guerrillas. Leaving out Graiver "is an extraordinary omission," to Kristol, for Graiver "was the immediate cause of Mr. Timerman's arrest and imprisonment." Furthermore, although "anti-Semitism may be rife in certain segments of Argentinian society, the government has been doing—and is doing—its best to render it ineffectual."[25] Irving Kristol was a leader of the renewed interest in Jewishness among the New York Intellectuals in the late 1940s, the one who stood at the synagogue door, "heart in—head out." Now his neoconservatism clashed with issues of serious concern to other Jews. Rabbi Morton Rosenthal, head of Latin American affairs for the B'nai B'rith Anti-Defamation League, called Kristol's article "a piece of character assassination." Other Jews were not so harsh. Nathan Perlmutter, executive director of the Anti-Defamation League, thought that Timerman exaggerated the danger to Argentine Jews. Nonetheless, as neoconservatives moved closer to the corridors of power—conservative power—they encountered incidents and arguments which did not as easily as Michael Novak sees, meld their political beliefs and their ethnic and religious attitudes. The strain of anti-Semitism in right-wing politics began to confront these conservative Jews, just as the existence of anti-Semitism in English literature confronted the literary modernists of the postwar years.

The neoconservative positions of Kristol, Podhoretz, and the others are not new. Much of the neoconservative—or, as Norman Podhoretz would have it, "old-fashioned liberal"—thinking is rooted in the 1950s and seems new only because it followed the hiatus of the 1960s and serves the 1970s and 1980s so well. Changes have certainly occurred. American foreign policy is not what it was in the Vietnam era; economic conditions are significantly different. Some of the neoconservatives, such as Podhoretz, have taken a circuitous path, flamboyantly breaking with the positions of their intellectual fathers and, like prodigal sons, working their way back. Once returned, they have joined with those intellectuals who have moved slowly, steadily rightward, led by Irving Kristol.

Neoconservatism is not what has happened to the New York Intellectual world; it is what has become of some of its members. For William Phillips, some have turned right and some to "a mindless left." It seems, to him, that his old associates have "gone crazy."[26] But to a degree which those not lured by neoconservatism might not like to concede, many essential neoconservative positions have evolved directly from "liberal" arguments previously offered by the New Yorkers. There is a continuity with past positions, not some wholesale conservative apostasy. Specifics have changed, and the willingness to support the avowed right is new. In 1964 Bell and others assessed the causality and dangers of the "radical right." In the 1980s many neoconservatives, including Kristol, Glazer, and Podhoretz, actively supported Ronald Reagan, heir to the Goldwater tradition. The neoconservatives may be a part of the new right constellation, but their path to it is very different from that of the other members. They come out of a liberal intellectual, academic milieu—the world of the New York Intellectuals.

Partisan Review always held a symbolic place in the New York Intellectual world, even after its intellectual centrality disappeared. Around its revived form in 1937 the community first gathered. Its pages resounded with the crucial arguments which set these individuals off from their radical and cultural competitors in the late 1930s. It also grew to represent the New Yorkers, as Leslie Fiedler succinctly put it in 1956: "I stand somehow for *PR* and *PR* for me."[27]

By 1956, however, it was already evident to those close to the magazine that the strong role of *PR* had weakened and that even the fragile cohesiveness of the journal was coming undone. The tensions associated with running an intellectual magazine and seeing it through so many changes, coupled with the unique personal interactions of the two editors, finally took their toll on Rahv and Phillips. There had been a series of flare-ups over the years, one serious confrontation coming in 1946 when Phillips, Delmore Schwartz, Clement Greenberg, and William Barrett joined to confront Rahv over his playing off of one editor against another and his behind-the-back verbal attacks.[28] After this a kind of uneasy truce developed, especially between the senior editors. By the 1950s the relations between them had, in Norman Podhoretz's view, "come to resemble nothing so much as a bad marriage being held together for the sake of the child." In part, the *PR* world diffused amid the postwar successes. The advent of new magazines like *Commentary* and *Dissent* and the opportunity for the New Yorkers to publish in previously closed ones lessened *PR's* influence. Geographical moves, especially into academe, scattered many in the *PR* crowd. And in 1957 one of the journals two pillars, Philip Rahv, left New York for Boston and a teaching job at Brandeis.

The relations between Rahv and Phillips continued to deteriorate during the 1960s. Rahv fumed in Boston, feeling that editorial control remained with Phillips in New York. "Since Rahv was a man with a great appetite for power," Podhoretz observed, Phillips's control "would have in itself been bad enough." But his absence from the inner workings of the magazine "deprived him the pleasure of conspiring with junior members of the staff against Phillips and even against his own writers." Although Rahv did less and less work on the magazine, according to Phillips, "he would make show of holding up his end. He wrote pompous letters, giving his long-winded opinions about manuscripts he insisted be sent to him, saying either irrelevant or obvious things." When he showed up in New York, he spent "most of his time gossiping" and then would "disappear again."[29]

Phillips now moved to the center of the magazine. The new forces lined up behind him. When the critic Richard Poirier joined the magazine, Dwight

Macdonald felt, he "gave Phillips countersupport," and "Poirier had a very different view of contemporary literature than Rahv did."[30] Macdonald's feelings matched Rahv's worries. Writing to Fred Dupee in 1966, about a negative review of a book by Dupee soon to appear in *PR*, Rahv said that he went to see Phillips and demanded that the review be shelved. "He was evasive on the subject . . . my impression was that he was being pushed by Poirier to print it after all . . . . So far as Steve [Marcus, an associate editor] is concerned, I am sure that you can expect nothing from him. He is . . . quite incapable of asserting himself in the face of the combined operation of W. and Richard P."[31]

The arrival of Richard Poirier on the *Partisan Review* editorial board was part of a larger change at the magazine. In 1963 *Partisan Review* moved to Rutgers University, to which Poirier had also just come. The offices and files moved to New Brunswick. Like its contributors and editors, the magazine itself could not resist the call of academe. *PR* did maintain general financial independence and editorial autonomy. Poirier, after some debate, became an editor, not a member of the editorial board, as Phillips initially proposed, and Phillips became a member of the Rutgers English department, with release time for editing the magazine.[32]

With Phillips and the magazine located in New York and New Brunswick and with Rahv in Boston, *PR* took a new turn and so did Philip Rahv. He bristled at the Rutgers connection, demanding a desk in the new offices but then never using it. He met Phillips and Poirier in New York every month or two. An old friend, Dorothea Straus, commented on the increasingly negative tone Rahv took in *PR* matters: "[He] mainly used his power of veto now. It seemed to overcome his genius for the discovery of talent. His conversation grew more negative too. 'It's no good—no good,' he would reiterate on almost every subject." In 1965, in an attempt to have titles reflect the work being done, the editorial board voted to name Phillips editor in chief. Rahv objected vehemently and brought a lawsuit against Phillips. After much haggling, Phillips agreed to be listed as chairman of the editorial board. Rahv "was to have visitation rights to the office," Phillips wrote. "It was stipulated that if either of us started another publication, that would constitute a conflict of interest and would amount to withdrawal."[33] The bad marriage had ended, and the lawsuit was a settling of custody rights.

Some of Rahv's frustration and jealousies came out in a series of critical attacks on old friends published in the 1960s. While finding new hope in the political radicalism of the decade, Rahv had nothing but contempt for the cultural side of the movement, the counterculture. He saw it as a "degeneracy . . . masquerading as the boldest and bravest spirit of experiment and liberation." *Partisan Review* and Richard Poirier, in particular, had been much more accommodating to the spirit of the counterculture.[34] Rahv's writings, during these years, took on their most intense and bombastic tone since his proletarian-literature days in the early 1930s. But pessimism rather than optimism now permeated his criticism.

Leslie Fiedler and Norman Mailer drew Rahv's special ire. Remembering Fiedler's initial *PR* publication, "Come Back to the Raft Ag'in, Huck Honey," as a talented young man's *jeu d'espirit* but "not all that weighty"; Rahv found Fiedler's subsequent career lacking. *Waiting for the End* seemed "long on generalizations, most of them dubious, and short on evidence." Rahv felt Fiedler played the enfant terrible. "If he fails to curb his appetite for histrionic blatancy of statement," Fiedler "will soon be officially certified by the publicity-media as the perennial bad boy of literary criticism." Norman Mailer came off no more lightly. In a review of *An American Dream*, Rahv claimed that if Mailer "aspires to be something more than an intellectual version of Mickey Spillane," he must consider the "multiple consequences" of "so portentous a theme as murder." And as Rahv chastised Fiedler for his bad-boy image, so he criticized Mailer for his self-stylings. "If Mailer ever extricates himself from his entanglement with the hocus-pocus of power and the glamour dream of romantic denunciation, both physical and psychic, of existence, he might yet emerge as one of our greater talents."[35]

Rahv's life, during the late 1960s and early 1970s, remained marred by negativism and personal tragedy. He had divorced his wife Nathalie in 1941. He was married again, to Theodora Jay Stillman, and settled on Beacon Street, spending summers on Martha's Vineyard. Dorothea Staus recalled that the Beacon Street town house never seemed right for Rahv; "neither Philip nor Theo were at ease there . . . it remained strictly Boston Brahmin. . . . It was as though Philip and some glowering witch-hunting minister out of the American past were locked in combat."[36] The house brought tragedy for Rahv as well. One evening, while Rahv was away, his wife fell asleep holding a lighted cigarette. Rahv returned to find the house gutted and Theo suffocated.

Outward appearances suggested that Rahv was making a new start in the late 1960s. Frustrated with *Partisan Review*, he finally resigned in 1969 from the editorship of the magazine he had helped create thirty-five years before. In 1970 he brought out *Modern Occasions*, a Boston-centered and Rahv-dominated alternative to *PR*. At first the new journal promised to revive the old spirit of the "new" *PR*, of the 1930s. Mark Krupnick, an associate editor, recalled the early organizational meetings as the magazine's best times. One occasion, a summer 1970 meeting in New Hampshire with Rahv, Krupnick, Philip Roth, and the writer and associate editor Alan Lelchuk, must have seemed to Rahv like the old *PR* meetings of the thirties. "There we were," Krupnick wrote, "four Jewish literary types and our four Gentile women." Roth, flushed with his *Portnoy* success, even offered to help in editing the magazine. But Rahv "treated the idea as a joke." He accepted happily, however, Roth's "Salad Days" for the first issue and later published an excerpt from *Our Gang*.[37]

In the fall of 1970 the new journal appeared. Rahv, with a new wife and a new magazine, seemed headed for better times. But once publication began, "it was downhill all the way." In the 1930s Rahv had possessed a talent for discovering brilliant young writers. Now his negative assessments of American culture came to dominant the magazine's tone. The first number of *Modern*

Occasions exemplified Rahv's combination of political radicalism, cultural conservatism, and overt negativism, especially to old friends. While Noam Chomsky contributed a piece in praise of the New Left, "Revolt in the Academy," Robert Brustein, then head of the Yale drama department, attacked the students in his "Decline of Professionalism." A piece in the "Art Chronicle" section took issue with Clement Greenberg, warning that "whatever the attractions of his bedside manner, contemporary artists are well advised to view Mr. Greenberg's claims with caution and yield reluctantly to his anesthetic, if not his knife."[38]

A less-than-glowing analysis of Lionel Trilling by Mark Krupnick, in the second number, prompted the resignation of Hilton Kramer, who had written a "New York Letter" in the first issue. Rahv greeted this, Krupnick recalled with "a delightful snort and some choice remarks about petty-bourgeois fetishists of culture."[39] Trilling was not the only old comrade to suffer harsh words in the magazine's second number. Much more scathing than Krupnick's piece was Saul Bellow's assault on old friends in "Culture Notes: Some Animadversions, Some Laughs." His bitterest words were saved for Leslie Fiedler and, especially, for William Phillips. Reading Phillips in *PR* on Susan Sontag, Bellow offered, is "much like trying to go scuba diving at Coney Island in urinous brine and scraps of old paper, orange rinds and soaked hot dog buns." This must have given Rahv special pleasure, not least because Bellow continued with an attack on what Richard Poirier had done to *PR*. "Mr. Poirier has made *PR* look like a butcher's showcase, shining with pink, hairless pigginess and adorned with figures of hand-carved suet which represent the very latest in art, literature and politics." Rahv commented on Bellow's piece in the fourth issue of *Modern Occasions*, saying that it was "brilliantly phrased and exceptionally witty" and that Bellow had laid out "certain degenerate manifestations of the cultural life in America at the present time."[40]

Rahv himself could not resist joining the scathing intellectual attack. He called "Dr. Leslie Fiedler, a swaggering titillator of the most recent cultural naughtiness." He also found fault with Daniel Bell and Norman Podhoretz, on the right, and with the countercultural views of Charles Reich and his "greening of America," which Rahv dismissed as "kid stuff."[41] But this negative tone soon took its toll at *Modern Occasions*. "Rahv increasingly wanted not literary criticism but literary assassinations," Krupnick later wrote. He "tended to rely on old friends," according to the managing editor, Carol Schloss, "and to want the young people around him to think up topics and writers."[42] The topics and the writers, however, seemed to have to fit Rahv's style of attack. "He contracted with America's No. 1 cultural hit-man, the movie critic John Simon, to do a job on Nabokov: he was being taken too seriously." Simon never came through, but others did, attacking Levi-Strauss and R. D. Laing, as well as Greenberg, Fiedler, Phillips, Poirier, and Reich. Rahv pushed Mark Krupnick to "perform demolition jobs," especially on Norman Mailer. Finally, Krupnick split with Rahv over the elder critic's persistence. Writing to Rahv, Krupnick tried to bring all the negativism into proper perspective:

> I don't wish to be the instrument of your hatred. . . . You've been trying for a long time to get someone to put the knife into Mailer, and people have put you off not only out of timidity (as you think) but because it's demeaning to wield the knife as the tool of someone else's will. The Ahab side of you has never been the side I admired, and I'm getting too old to play Ishmael or Starbuck in this scenario.[43]

A note in the sixth issue said that "the Summer issue of *Modern Occasions* will not be published. Instead a special double issue of the magazine will appear in the Fall, *The Editors*." The "special double issue" never appeared.[44]

Rahv's health deteriorated, his new marriage crumbled, and the magazine stopped publication. He engaged in a bitter dispute with his last wife. He revised his will, leaving his money to Israel. This stunned his friends. Some found hidden truths about his abandoned Jewishness, while others saw it as a means of keeping the money from his ex-wife. In December 1973 Rahv died in his Cambridge apartment, at age sixty-five. He looked much older, friends recalled. By contrast he had looked and been so young when he first brought out *Partisan Review* in the 1930s. Those were not only his younger days but also his great days. The corpus of Rahv's published works is small. His academic career came late, and he never fully adjusted to the role. His greatest skills were talking and editing. He once ran a magazine which published new writers destined for greatness—Mary McCarthy, Saul Bellow, Bernard Malamud, John Berryman, Delmore Schwartz, William Styron, and more. And he lived at the center of an intellectual world, in which he could pontificate in his broken English, his jutting finger punctuating the points. That intellectual world vanished. Even in the 1950s, when its political and cultural outlines were still easily perceptible, the personal intensity was declining. Old friends, beginning with William Phillips, became adversaries. In 1973, without *Partisan Review* or even *Modern Occasions*, without many of his friends, and without the intellectual world he had helped create, Philip Rahv died. "It was a sad way to go," Mark Krupnick remembered Rahv saying at Edmund Wilson's death in 1972. The same words would be spoken of Rahv himself a year later.[45]

PASSINGS

Death had struck the New York Intellectual community before—untimely deaths shocking friends and colleagues. Isaac Rosenfeld and Robert Warshow, for whom so much seemed promised, died young, only their closest friends and associates ever appreciating their true worth. Elliot Cohen unraveled in the late 1950s, finally committing suicide. Delmore Schwartz never regained the heady confidence which accompanied his first published story and poetry or achieved the perhaps unreachable heights others thought awaited him. In the end—

living alone in a West Side residential hotel, frequenting the reading room of the New York Public Library, continuing to write pages of unpublished fiction, Schwartz degenerated before the eyes of his old friends. Saul Bellow saw Schwartz on the street but could not face going up to him. Instead, he described the incident in *Humboldt's Gift*. "I knew that Humboldt [Schwartz] would die soon because I had seen him on the street two months before and he had death all over him. He didn't see me. He was gray stout sick dusty, he had brought a pretzel stick and was eating it. His lunch." Schwartz died in his room—alone amid books of poetry and the *Kama Sutra, Pilgrim's Progress* and crumpled girlie magazines—of a heart attack on July 11, 1966.[46]

These had been the untimely deaths, the shocks of careers too short or of promises unfulfilled. But the death of Philip Rahv meant something else. Rahv's great days may have been in the 1930s and his final years might not have been as happy as those of his youth, but when he died it seemed that his time *had* come. And if Rahv's time was at hand, so was that of some of the other "elders" of the community. In the few years following Rahv's death, other New York Intellectuals passed away, their lives not abruptly ended but fully run.

After the death of W.H. Auden, Hannah Arendt wrote a touching "Reflection" in the *New Yorker*, which ended with an obsevation of the "price" a great poet had to pay for his gifts: "We, in any event—his audience, readers and listeners—can only be grateful that he paid his price up to the last penny for the everlasting glory of the English language."[47] A year later William Phillips would offer a similar evaluation of Arendt herself, after her death in December 1975: "Hannah had in its highest form what I've always taken to be the supreme quality of intelligence, the instantaneous ability to cut through the nonsense surrounding most ideas and situations and to see them in a fresh way." Perhaps remembering the tumult surrounding *Eichmann in Jerusalem*, Phillips added, "Occasionally, this led to quirkiness or one-sidedness. . . . But this is the price one often has to pay for originality."[48]

Arendt's work on totalitarianism in the early 1950s had helped crystallize the developing postwar conceptions taking form as the revised liberal position which replaced the radical orientation of the 1930s. Her book on Eichmann helped undo the weakening community in the early 1960s. She never fully joined the New York Intellectual community. Her background, training, and late arrival in America and in intellectual circles made her something of an "elder sage" rather than an insider. Yet, she had her partisans among the New Yorkers: Alfred Kazin, Mary McCarthy, Robert Lowell, and others. And even those who ultimately came to publicly reject her ideas respected her intelligence and learning. She seemed a living tie with the European tradition to which these American intellectuals attached themselves philosophically but never personally. Many of the obituraries and tributes recalled her apartment on the Upper West Side, looking "quaintly European" William Phillips observed. "Hannah's high apartment house on the lower Hudson always gave me a feeling of apprehension," Robert Lowell recalled of his frequent afternoon visits, "the thrill, hesitation, and helplessness of entering a foreign country, a north German harbor, the tenements of Kafka." Her passing occasioned sadness, not shock. "One can only hope that as a generation goes," Phillips wrote, "its values will not also go."[49]

An unnatural death may shock friends, but often the life which preceded it shades the memories. Elliot Cohen's suicide seemed shocking, F.W. Dupee's oddly touching. In poor health, and retired from Columbia, Dupee had in 1971 moved west, where he hoped his health might improve in his ocean-front home in Carmel. His strength returned, at times, and then flagged. Always known for his subtle rather than bombastic personal style, Dupee went quietly. He wrote very little in his retirement, fading as a New York presence even while he still lived in California. In the end and even though by his own hand, F.W. Dupee slipped quietly away—another passing which fit its life.[50]

In keeping with his personal style, F.W. Dupee had faded away from the New York scene. Harold Rosenberg, who to the critic Seymour Krim "looked and shone like the Lion of Judah," remained a vibrant presence until his death in the summer of 1978. For Hilton Kramer, Rosenberg represented the "quintessential New York intellectual."[51] Rosenberg had begun his early career on a wide front of intellectual activities—poetry, literary criticism, political analysis, and art criticism. Although he was most often associated with art, he remained interested in and engaged with numerous topics. The last decade of his life he spent as an art critic for the *New Yorker*, but he taught part-time at the University of Chicago and wrote for other publications as well. While the art world might best remember him for coining the phrase "action painting" to describe the style of the New York school of abstract expressionists, his other notable phrase, "the herd of independent minds," is equally remembered by the New York Intellectuals. Always fiercely self-proclaimed in his intellectual independence, Rosenberg lived what he described. While his own man, he remained one of them nonetheless. Kramer talks about "the fate of these intellectuals" in his memoir of Rosenberg; Seymour Krim wrote, "Rosenberg's going sweeps a period with it. Most of the surviors of the *Partisan Review* heyday are now tired or quiet." What Krim also noted, and he was hardly the only one to do so, was the degree to which the younger intellectuals—he was fifty-six when he wrote—felt the loss of these elders. "It is a loss that is impossible to communicate: those we would never imagine dying are passing into mist, and we who are left feel naked and unworthy, no matter what good things might come our way." "It is no exaggeration to say," Hilton Kramer, another "younger" critic, observed, "that we are witnessing the closing of a period."[52]

Dwight Madonald had, since the first, boisterous meetings of the "new" *PR* at William Phillips's house, been a friendly adversary and adversary friend. He left *PR* at the beginning of World War II, breaking with the other editors over support for the war. He remained an anti-Communist in the postwar years, but never a member of the Congress for Cultural Freedom. In the 1960s he seemed to sign on more heartily than the rest with the New Left and the students. After Macdonald died in December of 1982, it was striking that the published remembrances and eulogies came not from contemporaries but from three younger men, all of whom felt Macdonald's influence. James Atlas, the biographer of Delmore Schwartz, used a longer piece in the *Atlantic* to pay his respects to Macdonald and publicly acknowledge Macondald's painstaking assistance on the Schwartz book. Walter Goodman, writing in the *New York Times*, observed, "In a very funny way, Dwight Macdonald was a very serious man. And in every way, he was his own man." And *Partisan Review*, of which Macdonald had once been editor and in whose pages some of his best-known early pieces had appeared, chose to print the eulogy the critic John Simon had delivered at Maconald's funeral, rather than any comment from the editors. Simon suggested that Macdonald's "living presence was so dazzling that it tended to eclipse his words" but that now they would surely be collected and properly appreciated. Goodman was right in saying that Macdonald was his "own man" and Simon right in commenting on Macdonald's "living presence." Both of these traits often rubbed against some other New York Intellectuals. In death, even as in life, Macdonald's distinctiveness and the ambivalence in his personal relations with old comrades showed. They left it for others to speak the unambiguous praise which decorum demands in eulogies.[53]

No death better marked the passing of the New York Intellectual community or more strikingly stirred the varied and ambivalent feelings of the generations of intellectuals who had come afterward than that of Lionel Trilling in 1975. Perhaps like no other intellectual of his generation—certainly not of his community—Lionel Trilling had risen to supreme intellectual eminence. Had he been English like his friend Isaiah Berlin, Norman Podhoretz suggested, he would have become "Professor Sir Lionel Trilling."[54] In fact, Diana Trilling recalled that they discussed retiring to Oxford—she for it, he opposed. What Trilling could not abide, his widow remembered, was becoming institutionalized in his own educational institution. "The young men, the new men don't drop into my office and sit on my desk and fight me. They treat me like an institution." Even when he became a University Professor at Columbia, Trilling refused to leave his old office in the English department for the one he was entitled to occupy in another building.[55]

For all his attempts to overcome his dignified place, Trilling *had* become something of an institution by the time of his death. The *New York Times* carried his obituary on the front page; *Time* noted his death not in its

"Milestones" section but with a two-page article under "Education." In his recollection in the *New Republic*, Irving Howe paid Trilling the compliment the Columbia professor would probably have enjoyed more than any other. "With the exception of Edmund Wilson, Lionel Trilling was the most influential literary critic in America these past few decades."[56] The young Trilling had revered Wilson, gazing across the street from his Village apartment to the window where Wilson worked, and feeling that this verified his arrival in the intellectual world. By his life's end Trilling had achieved a literary stature equivalent to Wilson's, with the added solemnity and prestige of a high university position.

Intellectual position and literary eminence stirred not only awe but also envy. Thus though Diana Trilling felt that her husband tried to avoid the trappings of an institutionalized man of letters, Alfred Kazin wrote in 1978 that Trilling possessed a "look of consciously occupying an important place."[57] The relations between Trilling and Kazin had never been smooth, but Kazin did not offer the only dissenting opinion about Trilling in the last decade of his life. One of Trilling's own best students, Norman Podhoretz, for whom Trilling served as an intellectual father, never seemed happy with the role or style of Trilling in his last years.

It is, in fact, the observations of three of Trilling's students which demonstrate how much the New York Intellectuals and their world had drifted. Podhoretz's battles with Trilling extended back to his own break with the liberalism of the 1950s and to the turn he took on assuming the editorship of *Commentary*. But from the middle 1960s to the early 1970s Podhoretz underwent a second political transformation, passing Trilling again as Podhoretz moved from the left to the right. Further complicating their personal relations was the Columbia critic's view of *Making It*. By the time Podhoretz came to reassess everyone's motives, including his own, in the second installment of his memoirs, he concluded that by the end of his life Trilling had lost his nerve. Podhoretz felt that Trilling having engaged in the radical wars of the 1930s, lacked "the stomach to enter the lists again." Although he opposed the new radicalism, Podhoretz thought that Trilling feared suffering the fate of Sidney Hook. "For Trilling, Hook was the cautionary figure of his own generation— the one who had gone too far in the rebellion against radicalism." As a result, the *Commentary* editor believed, Trilling exhausted himself in his last years, unable to secure the place of an Isaiah Berlin, afraid of being perceived as a Sidney Hook.[58]

When Trilling's fatal illness was diagnosed, Podhoretz called on Trilling. "Not long before Lionel died, Norman came to see him and was absolutely wonderful," Diana Trilling recalled. "Lionel didn't talk about his illness and so neither did Norman; he acted as if it were just a normal visit; he was very gentle, but he didn't treat Lionel like a dying man. They discussed all sorts of things—it was Norman at his very best." Although the personal ties remained, intellectual issues still divided the critic and his former student. Diana Trilling remembered hearing of Podhoretz's dissatisfaction at Trilling's funeral, where no formal eulogy was read. "Now I read *Breaking Ranks*," she stated, "and think of the way he writes about Lionel there, and I want to ask him, 'Is that the eulogy you would have wanted your old friend and teacher to have from you?' "[59] If Mrs. Trilling is correct, it is a very ambivalent eulogy at best.

Another of Trilling's students and Podhoretz's contemporaries, Steven Marcus, set out a more traditional and unambivalent eulogy in the *New York Times Book Review*. Describing Trilling as "our historian of the moral life of modernity, our philosopher of culture," Marcus also called him "our teacher." With his death, his writings "are now a permanent part of our cultural heritage."[60] In keeping with this belief, Diana Trilling has since Trilling's death been editing the "uniform edition" of her husband's works, reissuing older books and collecting previously uncollected pieces. This strikes some as an effort to turn Trilling into a cultural institution, others only as a way to ensure the "permanency" Marcus thought appropriate. Whatever the motive, those like Steven Marcus felt that Trilling's presence should not fade with his death and that his ideas or importance were not "exhausted" in the last years of his life.

Yet a third retrospective view of the Columbia critic came from a younger student, Morris Dickstein. Trilling had called attention to the notion of an "adversary culture," as he called it, a phrase which embodied the earlier discussions of the antagonistic function of modernism and the avant-garde. As Dickstein observed, however, this had come to be "identified exclusively with high culture."[61] With the rise of the new radicalism, with its cultural as well as political components, Trilling sensed the implications of his teachings and moved to a new context. In *Beyond Culture*, published in 1965, he distinguished between "two cultural environments": the first "philistine and dull, satisfied with its unexamined, unpromising beliefs." The second and true environment possessed a "commitment to the sources of life . . . to the imagination of fullness, freedom, and potency of life." For Norman Podhoretz, Trilling did not go far enough in this line of argument. While opposed to the new radicalism, he proved hesitant and reticent. Dickstein agreed that Trilling reacted ambivalently, but he still saw his own path to the new cultural radicalism leading from this teacher: "When [the] new consciousness began to emerge . . . Trilling's work had helped prepare me to receive it."[62]

For Dickstein the problem with Trilling was that he "came increasingly to admire and defend bourgeois values themselves."[63] For Norman Podhoretz it was that he did not defend them strongly enough. In between sit the perceptions of Steven Marcus. These are not the only ways of interpreting Trilling's work, nor are these the only voices worthy to speak. Trilling's ideas and influence have received and will receive wide discussion. What these views demonstrate is both the divergence among his own students and the degree to which a central concern of the New York Intellectual community, especially in the 1950s, had become the source of widely differing intellectual paths by the

1970s. The eulogy Podhoretz may have wanted is not his assessment of Trilling in *Breaking Ranks* or that of Marcus or Dickstein or any other single appraisal. The extent to which so many disparate intellectuals have tied their own thinking to that of the Columbia critic bespeaks Trilling's pervasive influence and lasting impact. What it does not represent is the continuance of a unified intellectual or cultural conception—a philosophical position for an intellectual community. By the 1970s Trilling stood as an intellectual pillar in the thinking of a number of intellectuals, but not as the spokesman for a single intellectual group. He had become a New York intellectual of widespread influence, not the representative of an influential community of New York Intellectuals.

THE PAST RECAPTURED

The New York Intellectuals have gone their various ways. Those still alive range from neoconservatives to "old-fashioned" liberals and democratic socialists. Some are in political and personal retirement. The community they once helped create no longer exists. Its members still hold great importance, but as individuals or as parts of new groupings. Personal antagonisms, political disputes, and cultural disagreements have severed many ties. They live and operate in separate worlds—so different, in fact, that those unfamiliar with their shared history might be surprised to learn of any past connections. Yet, despite the political and personal dispersion, a few common threads remain— ties to the past from which they all came. Forever identified as New York Intellectuals, they will forever share some common bonds.

Most of the New Yorkers were the children of immigrant Jews, growing up in the ghettos on the edge of American cities. They moved away—to college, radical politics, academic appointments, and intellectual prominence. In the years when they turned to take a renewed interest in their Jewish roots, that world began to slip away. "The story of the immigrant Jews is all but done," Irving Howe wrote at the end of his massive history of these people, *World of Our Fathers*. He added, "Let us now praise obscure men."[64] And praise they did, not only the East European Jews but Irving Howe as well. For the literary critic Pearl Kazin Bell, *"World of Our Fathers* is history and celebration, memory and judgement. And memory is the thread on which Yiddish life hangs. For the child of East European Jews, whose first language was Yiddish, that I was and will be to the end of my time, this book, more than a book, is an act of redemption."[65] For Nathan Glazer, Howe's book affirmed the history not only of the East European Jews in America but also of the intellectual world from which both Howe and Glazer came. Beyond Howe's "triumph" in character- izing Yiddish culture and his ability to "enrich" and "deepen" familiar stories of Jewish immigrants, "Howe has done more . . . he justifies in this book the marriage of historical and sociological materials with that high seriousness, that grasping for brilliance, that is the special mark of the New York Jewish intellectual tradition."[66] Howe himself gave an explanation for the book's success. Jews "hurried out to buy it," he believed, not in a search for "roots" but from a "readiness to say farewell in a last fond gesture . . . an affectionate backward glance at the world of their fathers before turning their backs forever and moving on, as they had to." He noted "My book was not a beginning, it was still another step to the end."[67]

If the intention of Howe in *World of Our Fathers* was to praise obscure men, other recent efforts have been made to evaluate prominent ones—the New Yorkers themselves. Individuals from the group have taken to setting down their memories, either in book-length memoirs or in autobiographical essays. Howe, William Phillips, William Barrett, Sidney Hook, Lionel Abel, Diana Trilling, and others have joined Norman Podhoretz in offering their own visions of the past. And in typical New York Intellectual fashion, they have continued to be as hard on one another as ever.

The past is not theirs alone, however. They have had to share the memories with others who came through these years and to share the assessments with younger analysts now coming to view the lives and times of the New Yorkers historically. Some of the conclusions being drawn by these analysts contradict the views of the New Yorkers and, more important, often cite their guilt and responsibility. As revisionist historians have come to reassess the cold war and the McCarthy years, many have argued against the position set out by the New York Intellectuals, as well as against that of the State Department and more-conservative anti-Communists. "Many young people who were scarcely born at the time and have now become historians," Nathan Glazer wrote in 1976, are "calling us to account." Glazer summarized the position of these "young scholars." They believe

> that the congressional committees investigating Communism represented a totally unjustified attack on the freedom of thought, speech, and action of progressive-minded Americans, undertaken only for mean political motives, and that those investigations posed a greater danger to this country's liberties than Communism ever did. Those of us who did not stand single-mindedly against this threat were culpable, guilty of a new "treason of the intellectuals."[68]

Many of the victims of McCarthyism have contributed to this turn in historical thinking, both in the form of traditional memoirs and analyses and in a series of plays, movies, and literary works. Hilton Kramer, defending liberal anticommunism, labeled this trend "a form of cultural chic," dismissing the academic as well as the cultural revisionism. Kramer said the position was reducible to a belief on the part of revisionists "that the Cold War was somehow a malevolent conspiracy of the Western democracies to undermine the benign intentions of the Soviet Union." He was further troubled by films like *The Front* and the documentary *Hollywood on Trial*, both of which portray the blacklisted as victims spawning a "false imagery of innocence."[69] While a number of revisionist historians answered back, Kramer received support for his views from expected quarters. Arthur Schlesinger, Jr., applauded Kramer: "I wish Hilton Kramer's article could be made required reading for everyone born after 1940."[70]

One specific target of Kramer's ire was shared by most New York Intellectuals. In Lillian Hellman's *Scoundrel Time* their worst fears about the impact of cold-war revisionist history came together. The third piece in her series of memoirs, *Scoundrel Time* leapt to the *New York Times* best-seller list in 1976 (and stayed there for twenty-one weeks, Kramer noted). Both Hellman and her longtime lover Dashiell Hammett suffered from anticommunism— Hammett going to jail, Hellman facing the blacklist. But her story is not just another anti-McCarthy tale, pointing the finger at the Wisconsin senator or other opportunistic politicians. Hellman assessed blame with a wide brush and put among the "scoundrels" a number of the cold-war intellectuals. Furthemore, Garry Wills introduced the book with what William Phillips called "an unfortunate example of pop revisionist history."[71] *Scoundrel Time* seemed to represent all the worst in revisionism. Down the line—or across the political spectrum—the New York Intellectuals answered back.

Garry Wills provoked the harshest treatment, perhaps because he was not their old friend as was Hellman and more likely because he tried to sketch out a general historical context into which Hellman's story could be set. Whatever he disliked about Hellman, Irving Howe found "nothing, to be sure in her book . . . as false and certainly nothing as vulgar as the Introduction Garry Wills has written for it." Sidney Hook remarked "Wills has unconsciously reconstructed the Kremlin propaganda line."[72]

It was Hellman, however, who sat at the center of the controversy. It was her story which was being told, and she accused directly—sometimes by name. "I suddenly wanted to go home and did, to spend the rest of the day asking myself how Diana and Lionel Trilling, old, respected friends, could have come out of the same age and time with such different political and social views from my own." When it was not by name, it was by publication. "Certainly the good magazines, the ones that published the most serious writers, should have come to the aid of those who were persecuted. *Partisan Review* . . . made no protest when people in this country were jailed or ruined. In fact, it never took an editorial position against McCarthy himself. . . . *Commentary* didn't do any-thing."[73]

In response, a number of the contributors to both magazines argued that they *had* done something, but even among them there were disagreements about what and how much. Nathan Glazer believed that "opposition to McCarthyism was so taken for granted by magazines like *Commentary* and *Partisan Review* that the main intellectual contribution they could make was to examine and clarify the many questions surrounding the phenomenon." Glazer included among these "examinations" one of his own contributions to *Commentary*, "The Method of Senator McCarthy." Irving Howe, the one liberal anti-communist credited by Hellman as writing a "distinguished" piece on the topic, disagreed with Glazer. "As for *Commentary* . . . its record on McCarthyism was, let us say, shabby." He even disputed Glazer by name. "His attempt retrospectively to exonerate the magazine from Miss Hellman's charges seemed to me, on this point, feeble."[74] But, Howe did credit both *Partisan Review* and his own *Dissent* with having fought a better fight. William Phillips also rose to *PR*'s defense.

Apart from standing behind their own journals, however, the intellectuals took deadly aim at Lillian Hellman. More was in question, they felt, than Hellman's incorrect analysis. She had come through many of the same political wars—but on the other side. Hellman helped sponsor the Waldorf conference in 1949, supported Henry Wallace, and remained a radical during the years when postwar liberalism developed. If her book gained acceptance, she would have, in Sidney Hook's view, "duped a generation of critics devoid of historical memory and critical common sense."[75] And so they all took shots at her, from Irving Kristol—"Lillian Hellman's memoir is so misleading"—to Dwight Macdonald—"I think it is extraordinary that she should get away with this pose of being a morally wronged woman. She was actually a Stalinist, even then."[76] Historical events were repeated, once-exhausted issues revived, and old lines of argument brought out again. Irving Howe chastised Hellman and Wills for failing to mention the event which "sent shivers through the hearts of intellectuals," the 1948 Communist coup in Czechoslovakia. Nathan Glazer brought back the Waldorf conference, asking, "Where did the threat to freedom lie—with those who picketed and exposed it; or with those who . . . were willing to join in a scheme designed by Communists to advance the greatest tyranny in the world?" And Sidney Hook opened his lengthy attack on Hellman with the most basic liberal anti-Communist attack, the Nazi-Soviet equation. He considered the fictitious memoir of a supporter of the Nazi German-American Bond in the late 1930s: "What would one think of the woman in this parable who, in 1976, strikes a pose of a heroine?"[77]

Naming names was what this was once all about, and it again added to the intensity of the discussion. Diana Trilling, having been named in *Scoundrel Time*, set out to defend herself, Lionel Trilling having died before Hellman's book appeared. Trilling chose a slightly awkward manner of response. About to publish a collection of her own essays, she annotated and footnoted her 1967 contribution to the *Commentary* symposium "Liberal Anti-Communism Revisited." Her article was a mix of specific points rebutting Hellman's charges and a more general discussion of the impact and course of anticommunism in the 1960s and 1970s. But the antagonisms did not end there. Trilling had orginally contracted for the collection with Little, Brown, Hellman's publisher. They requested that four passages critical of Hellman be deleted. According to Little, Brown's president, the passages were "of a more personal nature" than the criticism of the Trillings in *Scoundrel Time*. Diana Trilling's defenders suggested that Hellman's place on the best-seller lists prompted the publisher's concerns. Nonetheless, these old antagonisms once again stirred the New York literary world. Refusing to edit, Trilling took her book from Little, Brown to Harcourt Brace Jovanovich.[78]

The old disputes, as Irving Howe noted, proved the "formative passions of our lives," and they will not go away. As the world moves on, as new political and cultural issues emerge, the New Yorkers come back to these questions. One does not expect positions to change or one side to admit error and agree with a position it dismissed twenty or thirty years ago. What is striking, however, is that these old matters still call them to battle. In January 1980, during an appearance on "The Dick Cavett Show," Mary McCarthy was asked about "overpraised writers." "Lillian Hellman," she replied, "who I think is terribly overrated, a bad writer and dishonest writer . . . every word she writes is a lie including 'and' and 'the.' " In response Hellman sued. The *Times* aptly entitled its story about the tiff "Hellman-McCarthy Libel Suit Stirs Old Antagonisms." Its reporter assessed intellectual opinion on the matter and found the old lines still holding. Macdonald, Podhoretz, Howe, Diana Trilling, and Meyer Schapiro stepped to McCarthy's defense; Malcom Cowley and Richard Poirer were among those siding with Hellman. Poirier captured the underlying tension in the dispute. Mary McCarthy, he said, "brought some old toys from the New York intellectual attic and some of the old gang will want to play just like the 40's and 50's. Too bad."[79]

"It's not just two old ladies engaged in a catfight," Irving Howe argued. The issues had deep personal and historical meaning for them, for him, and for the others—for those who had come through the intellectual wars, thirty years earlier. Those years are now history, and historians have begun to assess the times and judge the participants. A number of them have offered negative appraisals of the role taken by the New York Intellectuals. The disputes of the 1930s and the 1950s "for many of us . . . for good or bad . . . made people what they are today," Howe commented.[80] But they are not what "made" the people now assessing this past. The world of the New York Intellectuals, that electrified environment of thirties radicalism and the transitional tensions of postwar liberalism, has dissipated like the world of their fathers. Many of the intellectuals are still around, however, and for them the issues remain alive in ways others cannot wholly understand.

The New York Intellectuals have gone—passed on to new attachments or passed away all together. The dead are praised as legends, pathfinders, great teachers. The living remain as individuals, more widely quoted than ever, attaining heights their first sponsors in the ethnic ghettos could not have envisioned. They advise presidents, hold endowed chairs at America's distinguished universities, write for the most prestigious journals, win the best prizes, and fill the card catalogues with works by and about themselves. For us, they no longer present a single entity or a unified intellectual position. They seem instead like some battle-hardened veterans of a team now disbanded, playing in a variety of different locales. They themselves, however, for all their different paths and new attachments, will always carry with them memories and connections to those past years—the seasons when they were young and fresh and had the world to win.

Notes

Introduction   "The Herd of Independent Minds"

1. Irving Howe, "The New York Intellectuals: A Chronicle and a Critique," *Commentary*, Oct. 1968, p. 42; Norman Podhoretz, interview, June 3, 1978; Midge Decter, interview, June 1, 1978.
2. Recent memoirs from members of the community include Alfred Kazin, *New York Jew* (New York, 1978); Norman Podhoretz, *Breaking Ranks* (New York, 1979); William Barrett, *The Truants: Adventures among the Intellectuals* (New York, 1982); William Phillips, *A Partisan View: Five Decades of the Literary Life* (New York, 1983); Lionel Abel, *The Intellectual Follies* (New York, 1984).
3. See assessment of Lionel Trilling, on p. 5, below, which was made by David Daiches in 1957.
4. Norman Podhoretz, *Making It* (New York, 1967), 116–17.
5. Daniel Bell, "The Intelligentsia," in *Tomorrow's American*, ed. Samuel Sandmel (New York, 1977), 38.
6. Howe and Phillips, quoted in Victor S. Navasky, "Notes on Cult: or, How to Join the Intellectual Establishment," *New York Times Magazine*, March 27, 1967, pp. 151, 125, 128.
7. David Daiches, "The Mind of Lionel Trilling," *Commentary*, July 1957, p. 66; Hilton Kramer, "An Era Comes to an End," *New York Times*, July 23, 1978, sec. 2, p. 23; Barrett, *Truants*, 69.
8. Leslie Fiedler, "*Partisan Review*: Phoenix or Dodo?" in *The Collected Essays of Leslie Fiedler*, vol. 2 (New York, 1971), 42.

Chapter 1   Young Men from the Provinces

1. Robert Warshow, "Poet of the Jewish Middle Class," *Commentary*, May 1946, pp. 17, 18.

2. Alfred Kazin, "Alfred Kazin: The Critic as Creator," *Horizon*, July 1962, p. 99.

3. Irving Howe, "A Memoir of the Thirties," in *Steady Work: Essays in the Politics of Democratic Radicalism, 1953–1966* (New York, 1966), 352.

4. Sidney Hook, interview, Jan. 4, 1978.

5. Howe, "Memoir," 356–57.

6. Alfred Kazin, interview, Oct. 23, 1976; Howe, "Memoir," 353–54.

7. Irving Howe, *World of Our Fathers* (New York, 1976), 256.

8. Daniel Bell, interview, July 13, 1979.

9. Kazin, "Alfred Kazin," 99.

10. Sidney Hook, "Experimental Naturalism," in *American Philosophy Today and Tomorrow*, ed. Horace Kallen and Sidney Hook (New York, 1935), 207.

11. Howe, "Memoir," 352–53.

12. Delmore Schwartz, "The Ballad of the Children of the Czar," *Partisan Review*, Jan. 1938, p. 29; Irving Howe, Twentieth Century Authors, First Supplement (New York, 1971), 464.

13. Howe, *World of Our Fathers*, 252.

14. Irving Howe, "Of Fathers and Sons," *Commentary*, Aug. 1946, 191.

15. Alfred Kazin, *A Walker in the City* (New York, 1951), 56.

16. Ibid., 21–22.

17. Ibid., 21.

18. Howe, "Fathers and Sons," 191.

19. Howe, *World of Our Fathers*, 252.

20. Delmore Schwartz, "America! America!" *Partisan Review*, Mar.–Apr. 1940, p. 123.

21. Robert Warshow, "Poet of the Jewish Middle Class," 21.

22. Irving Howe, "The Lost Young Intellectual," *Commentary*, Oct. 1946, p. 356; Kazin, interview, Oct. 23, 1976.

23. Isaac Rosenfeld, *Passage from Home* (Cleveland, 1946), 7; Warshow, "Poet of the Jewish Middle Class," 20.

24. Daniel Bell, "Reflections on Jewish Identity," in *The Ghetto and Beyond: Essays on Jewish Life in America*, ed. Peter I. Rose (New York, 1969), 472; "Talk with Lionel Trilling," *New York Times Book Review*, Feb. 13, 1955, p. 21. Bell was clearly generalizing for his contemporaries, because his own father died when he was an infant and his mother did not remarry until he was twelve.

25. Howe, "Fathers and Sons," 190–91.

26. Bell, interview, July 13, 1979; Howe, "Lost Young Intellectual," 364.

27. Delmore Schwartz, in "Under Forty: A Symposium on American Literature and the Younger Generation of American Jews," *Contemporary Jewish Record*, Feb. 1944, p. 12; Norman Podhoretz, *Making It* (New York, 1967), 14; Bell, interview, July 13, 1979.

28. Howe, "Lost Young Intellectual," 364.

29. Rosenfeld, *Passage from Home*, 80.

30. Bell, interview, July 13, 1979.

31. Mary McCarthy, "Philip Rahv, 1908–1973," *New York Times Book Review*, Feb. 17, 1974, p. 2; Bell, "Reflections," 472.

32. Kazin, in "Under Forty: A Symposium," 10.

33. Trilling and Kazin, in "Under Forty: A Symposium," 15–16, 11.

34. Lionel Trilling, "A Light to the Nations," *Menorah Journal*, 14 (Apr. 1928), 402.

35. Rosenfeld, in "Under Forty: A Symposium," 35.

36. Diana Trilling, "Lionel Trilling: A Jew at Columbia," *Commentary*, Mar. 1979, pp. 44, 46.

37. Trilling, "Funeral at the Club, with Lunch," *Menorah Journal*, 13 (Aug. 1927), 386.

38. Kazin, *Walker in the City*, 22.

39. Schwartz, in "Under Forty: A Symposium," 13.

40. Trilling, in "Under Forty: A Symposium," 32.

41. Bell, interview, July 13, 1979.

42. Greenberg, in "Under Forty: A Symposium," 32.

43. Kazin, *Walker in the City*, 172.

44. Lionel Trilling, "Notes on a Departure," *Menorah Journal*, 16 (May 1929), 424; Alfred Kazin, *Starting Out in the Thirties* (Boston, 1965), 45.

45. Lionel Trilling, *The Liberal Imagination: Essays on Literature and Society* (New York, 1950), 62.

46. Podhoretz, *Making It*, 3–4.

47. Irving Howe, "The New York Intellectuals: A Chronicle and a Critique," *Commentary*, Oct. 1968, p. 31.

48. Irving Howe, interview, June 16, 1976. Lionel Trilling suffered the reverse fate; people assumed that his name was changed, when it was not. "One of the very great acts of malice in the intellectual community," Diana Trilling remarked, "has been the attempt to discredit him by saying that his name had really been Cohen and that he changed it to Trilling." Cohen was Trilling's mother's maiden name. (Diana Trilling, interview, Oct. 3, 1979.)

49. Podhoretz, *Making It*, 4.

50. Trilling and Greenberg, in "Under Forty: A Symposium," 17, 33.

51. Podhoretz, *Making It*, 4–5.

52. Trilling, *Liberal Imagination*, 63.

Chapter 2   A New York Education

1. Irving Howe, "A Memoir of the Thirties," *Steady Work: Essays in the Politics of Democratic Radicalism, 1953–1966* (New York, 1966), 350–51.

2. Alfred Kazin, *A Walker in the City* (New York, 1951), 98–99.

3. Abraham Cahan, *The Rise of David Levinsky* (New York, 1960 [1917]), 169.

4. Stephen Steinberg, *The Academic Melting Pot: Catholics and Jews in American Higher Education* (New York, 1974), 9; Heywood Broun and George Britt, *Christians Only: A Study in Prejudice* (New York, 1931), 72. The figures in Broun and Britt are 22.5 percent for Columbia and 36.53 percent for NYU. Steinberg's study, which is more recent, gives the figures of 40 percent for Columbia and the imprecise "probably higher" for NYU. It lists the Harvard figure in this period as 20 percent.

5. In addition, Harold Rosenberg began his college career at City College but ultimately took his bachelor's degree from St. Lawrence. Clement Greenberg received his degree from Syracuse.

6. One business school in New York wrote a prospective applicant in 1928, "My

Dear Miss Cohen—We are sorry to inform you that it is our policy not to accept students of Jewish nationality. We are, therefore, not forwarding our catalogue unless we hear from you further." Quoted in Broun and Britt, *Christians Only*, 87. General discussions of the institution of quotas can be found ibid., 72–124; Steinberg, *Academic Melting Pot*, 18–31; John Higham, *Send Them to Me: Jews and Other Immigrants in Urban America* (New York, 1975), 159–61.

7. Among the second generation, Alfred Kazin did take his master's degree from Columbia. With the small third generation in the postwar years, we find a number returning to Columbia, including Norman Podhoretz, Steven Marcus, and Jason Epstein. This was due in part to the relaxing of anti-Jewish attitudes following World War II and in part to the presence of the first-generation fixture Lionel Trilling in the Columbia English department, along with Richard Hofstadter in history and Meyer Schapiro in art. Undoubtedly, the changed economic picture since the 1930s accounted for a portion of the swing away from tuition-free, public universities and toward private ones.

8. Lionel Trilling, "Young in the Thirties," *Commentary*, May 1966, pp. 46–47; Alfred Kazin, *New York Jew* (New York, 1978), 42–43. For a general discussion of anti-Semitism in college fraternities and social activities, see Broun and Britt, *Christians Only*.

9. Meyer Schapiro, interview, Oct. 30, 1978. See Broun and Britt, *Christians Only*, 183, for a discussion of the anti-Semitism of English departments. There were several New York Intellectuals in the second generation who earned doctorates, but in some cases not for quite a number of years. Leslie Fiedler, Richard Hofstadter, Seymour Martin Lipset, and Irving Kristol's wife, Gertrude Himmelfarb, all earned Ph.D's within a few years of their bachelor's degrees. Nathan Glazer completed his master's in 1944 but did not get his doctorate until 1962. Daniel Bell began graduate school right after college but soon quit. He finally took his doctorate in 1958. Steven Marcus, of the third generation, does have a Ph.D., but he received it only in 1961, having taken an M.A. in 1949.

10. Bell's cousin Teddy Cohen was "probably the brightest student in his class, '38, in American history at City College. But as City College had a rule that no more than 50 percent of its faculty could be from City College and that number had already been reached, his chances of getting another academic job were slim. Instead, he went to Columbia and studied Japanese. When the war broke out, he became one of the top advisors to MacArthur and wrote the Japanese labor code. He met a Japanese woman and married her. He stayed on in Japan, became head of one of the largest import-export companies and a millionaire. He retired to a ranch in Guadalajara, Mexico. And like the old story, 'If he knew how to write his name, he'd have become the shamus of the synagogue.' " (Daniel Bell, interview, July 13, 1979.) Cohen finally achieved his ambition to be a historian when he wrote a history of the American occupation of Japan. The book was published in Japan in 1984, but Cohen died before it was published in America. (Bell, interview, May 5, 1985.)

11. Quoted in Broun and Britt, *Christians Only*, 182. The differences between these figures and the ones for NYU given in n. 4, above, exist because when the less Jewish Bronx campus is counted, the percentage of Jews at NYU declines markedly.

12. Irving Howe, *Twentieth Century Authors, First Supplement* (New York, 1971), 464.

13. All but a few of the New York Intellectuals grew up in relatively impoverished circumstances. Except for Schwartz, Trilling, Warshow, and Macdonald, the others came from immigrant working-class families. Schwartz vacillated between luxury and poverty, while Trilling's father was a custom tailor but hardly a wealthy man. The quote is from Kazin, *New York Jew*, 43.

14. Malcolm Cowley, *Exile's Return: A Literary Odyssey of the 1920s* (New York, 1976 [1934]), 269–309; Alfred Kazin, *On Native Ground: An Interpretation of Modern American Prose Literature* (New York, 1942), 364.

15. Kazin, *On Native Grounds*, 364.

16. Dwight Macdonald, interview, Dec. 3, 1976.

17. Alfred Kazin, interview, Oct. 23, 1976.

18. Irving Kristol, interview, June 17, 1976; Irving Howe, interview, June 16, 1976.

19. Clement Greenberg, "The Late Thirties in New York," in *Art and Culture* (Boston, 1961), 231.

20. Wallace Phelps [William Phillips], "Three Generations," *Partisan Review*, Sept.–Oct. 1934, p. 52.

21. Lionel Trilling, "Edmund Wilson: A Backward Glance," in *A Gathering of Fugitives* (Boston, 1956), 55.

22. Kazin, interview, Oct. 23, 1976. Bernard Malamud presents something of an enigma in any chronology of the New York Intellectuals. In age he belongs with the second generation. Yet his emergence as an important figure coincides with the coming of the third generation, during the postwar years. As such, he is a part of both groups, belonging comfortably in neither. Albert Wohlstetter is professor emeritus in political science at the University of Chicago and a founder of the RAND Corporation.

23. Howe, interview, June 16, 1976; Kristol, interview, June 17, 1976.

24. Kazin took his B.A. in history from City College and only then discovered that his real interest was literature. When he went on to graduate school, it was in English, at Columbia. Saul Bellow graduated from Northwestern in anthropology and even did graduate work in that field at Wisconsin. Bellow has obviously carved out his career not in anthropology but in literature. His novels are, however, filled with a wide variety of topics and investigations, drawing on philosophy, history, and other disciplines quite frequently. As such, his fiction captures something of the intellectual sampling many of these intellectuals did in college.

25. Sidney Hook, "Professor Morris R. Cohen, Teacher," in *A Tribute to Professor Morris Raphael Cohen* (New York, 1928), 90. For a general discussion of Morris R. Cohen, see David A. Hollinger, *Morris R. Cohen and the Scientific Ideal* (Cambridge, Mass., 1975); Irving Howe, *World of Our Fathers* (New York, 1976). Cohen's other prominent students include Lewis Feuer, Ernest Nagel, Paul Weiss, Morton White, Herbert Schneider, and Joseph Ratner, all professional philosophers.

26. Hollinger, *Morris R. Cohen*, xii; Sidney Hook, "Morris Cohen: Fifty Years Later," *American Scholar*, Summer 1976, pp. 430–31.

27. Meyer Liben, "CCNY—A Memoir," *Commentary*, Sept. 1965, p. 68; Hook, "Morris Cohen: Fifty Years Later," 429; Hook, "Professor Morris R. Cohen," 92; Hook, "Morris Cohen: Fifty Years Later," 429.

28. Benjamin Nelson, quoted in Hollinger, *Morris R. Cohen*, 75; Hook, "Morris Cohen: Fifty Years Later," 428; Howe, *World of Our Fathers*, 284–85.

29. Hook, "Morris Cohen: Fifty Years Later," 430.

30. Howe, interview, June 16, 1976.

31. Hook, "Morris Cohen: Fifty Years Later," 432. Hook here claims that Cohen's "brilliant and pioneering text," *An Introduction to Logic and Scientific Method*, was in fact the work of Ernest Nagel.

32. An example both of Cohen's differences with his students and of the subsequent resurfacing of Cohen's ideas can be found in the *Modern Monthly* symposium of 1934 on communism. Cohen, along with Dewey and Russell, wrote under the heading "Why I Am Not a Communist," and Hook responded with "Why I Am a Communist," *Modern Monthly*, 8, no. 3 (Apr. 1934). Several of Cohen's contentions reemerged after World War II in the era of redefined liberalism, as argued by Trilling and Arthur Schlesinger, Jr., among others.

33. Liben, "CCNY—A Memoir," 64; Irving Kristol, "Memoirs of a Trotskyist," *New York Times Magazine*, Jan. 23, 1977, p. 51.

34. Liben, "CCNY—A Memoir," 64, 65.

35. In addition to the future New York Intellectuals who inhabited the anti-Stalinist alcove, Kristol recalled several others who went on to academic careers, including Philip Selznick, Morroe Berger, Bernard Bellush, Seymour Melman, and I. Milton Sacks. (Kristol, "Memoirs," 55.)

36. Kristol, "Memoirs," 56.

37. "Among the more cosmopolitan universities," Heywood Broun and George Britt reported in 1931, "Chicago probably has exhibited less prejudice against Jews in recent years than any." (Broun and Britt, *Christians Only*, 100.)

38. Daniel Bell, "The Mood of Three Generations," in *The End of Ideology: On the Exhaustion of Political Ideas in the Fifties* (New York, 1965 [1960]), 302.

39. Isaac Rosenfeld, "Life in Chicago," in *An Age of Enormity: Life and Writing in the Forties and Fifties*, ed. Theodore Solotaroff (New York, 1962), 332–33 (originally published in *Commentary*, June 1957).

Chapter 3 The Radical Vanguard

1. Thomas's presidential vote in 1932 was 881, 951; Deb's 1912 count was 900,672. These figures are deceptive in two ways. First, in 1912 only men voted, and though the percentage of women voting Socialist in 1932 is not known, the potential voters in 1912 accounted for only one-half the adult population. Second, the total vote for all candidates increased nearly threefold between 1912 and 1932. Approximately 15 million votes were cast in 1912 and 40 million in 1932. In the 1932 election Foster received 102,991 votes. The Socialist Labor candidate polled 33,175. Other splinter parties included the Prohibitionists (81,869), Liberty (53,425), and Farm Labor (7,309). In terms of student radicalism, the largest national radical student organization, the American Student Union, had a membership of 20,000, at its high point, out of a total college population of a

"million or so." (Daniel Bell, *Marxian Socialism in the United States* [Princeton, 1952], 148.)

2. The literature on American radicalism in the twentieth century is vast and growing. For good introductions to the course of radicalism in general, see James Weinstein, *Ambiguous Legacy* (New York, 1975); Milton Kantor, *The Divided Left* (New York, 1978). On specific radical parties see, from among many other sources, David A. Shannon, *The Socialist Party of America: A History* (Chicago, 1955); Theodore Draper, *The Roots of American Communism* (New York, 1957); idem, *American Communism and Soviet Russia* (New York, 1960); Irving Howe and Lewis Coser, *The American Communist Party* (Boston, 1957); James P. Cannon, *The History of American Trotskyism* (New York, 1944). Recent scholarship includes Frank Warren, *Liberals and Communists: The Red Decade Revisited* (Bloomington, Ind., 1966); idem, *An Alternative Vision: The Socialist Party in the 1930s* (Bloomington, Ind., 1974); Richard Pells, *Radical Visions and American Dreams* (New York, 1973). The Hook-Dewey debate ran in the *Modern Monthly*, Apr. 1934. A discussion of Dewey's position can be found in R. Alan Lawson, *The Failure of Independent Liberalism* (New York, 1971). Bell, *Marxian Socialism in the United States*, offers a general introduction, as well as a discussion of the formation of the American Workers party. The best introduction to the labor disputes of the 1930s is Irving Bernstein, *Turbulent Years: A History of the American Worker, 1933–1941* (Boston, 1969).

3. Irving Kristol, "Memoirs of a Trotskyist," *New York Times Magazine*, Jan. 23, 1977, p. 50; Irving Howe, "The New York Intellectuals," *Commentary*, Oct. 1968, p. 33.

4. *Culture and the Crisis* (League of Professional Groups for Foster and Ford, 1932); Alfred Kazin, *Starting Out in the Thirties* (Boston, 1965), 85.

5. Howe, "New York Intellectuals," 31; William Phillips, "The Wholeness of Literature," *American Mercury*, Nov. 1952, pp. 104–5.

6. Dwight MacDonald, introd. to *Memoirs of a Revolutionist: Essays in Political Criticism* (New York, 1957), 3; Lionel Trilling, "Young in the Thirties," *Commentary*, May 1966, pp. 47–48.

7. Howe, "New York Intellectuals," 32.

8. Meyer Schapiro, interview, Oct. 30, 1978; Clement Greenberg, interview, June 22, 1979; Diana Trilling to author, Nov. 27, 1979.

9. William Phillips, "How *Partisan Review* Began," *Commentary*, Dec. 1976, p. 42.

10. Harcourt, Brace and Company had given the authors a contract to publish, but nothing ever came of the project. In addition to Hook, Schapiro, Cohen, and Trilling, the other listed contributors were Lewis Corey, Clifton Fadiman, Newton Arvin, Bernard Smith, Granville Hicks, Hyman Rosen, Howard Doughty, Jr., Frederick Schuman, H. A. Potamkin, John Dos Passos, James Rorty, and Herbert Solow. (Cited in Daniel Aaron, *Writers on the Left: Episodes in American Literary Communism* [New York, 1961], 245.)

11. Irving Howe, interview, June 16, 1976. See, below, Chapter 6, for a complete discussion of the *Partisan* circle and Trotsky.

12. Daniel Bell, "A Symposium on Morality," *American Scholar*, Summer 1965, p. 351; idem, interview, July 13, 1979.

13. Quoted in Ron Chernow, "The Cultural Contradictions of Daniel Bell," *Change*, Mar. 1979, p. 12.

14. Kazin, *Starting Out*, 48–50.
15. Irving Howe, "A Memoir of the Thirties," in *Steady Work: Essays in the Politics of Democratic Radicalism, 1953–1966* (New York, 1966), 349–50; Alfred Kazin, *A Walker in the City* (New York, 1951), 144–45.
16. Kazin, *Starting Out*, 3–4; Irving Howe, "The Stranger and the Victim," *Commentary*, Aug. 1949, p. 153; Howe, interview, June 16, 1976.
17. Kazin, *Walker in the City*, 61.
18. Kazin, *Starting Out*, 46–48.
19. Malcolm Cowley, *Exile's Return: A Literary Odyssey of the 1920s* (New York, 1976 [1934]), 18.
20. Shannon, *Socialist Party*, 185.
21. London (1871–1927), a garment union laywer, had run for Congress twice before, in 1910 and 1912. The only Socialist in Congress, he suffered from the party's antiwar stand. He lost narrowly in 1918 but was reelected in 1920. By 1922 his Lower East Side district had been gerrymandered, and he lost for the last time. (See Irving Howe, *World of Our Fathers* [New York, 1976], 316–19.)
22. Kazin, *Starting Out*, 48; Howe, *World of Our Fathers*, 602.
23. Howe, "Memoir," 362; idem, *World of Our Fathers*, 321–22.
24. Howe, "Memoir," 351–52.
25. William Phillips, "New York City's Intellectual Life in the 30s," *New York Times*, Jan. 14, 1978.
26. Arnold Beichman, interview, May 25, 1976; Fiedler, interview, May 14, 1976.
27. Howe, "Memoir," 358.
28. Dwight Macdonald, "Politics Past—II," *Encounter*, Apr. 1957, p. 65–66.
29. Kristol, "Memoirs," 50.
30. *Culture and the Crisis*, 29.
31. Alfred Kazin, *On Native Grounds: An Interpretation of Modern American Prose Literature* (New York, 1942), 410; Daniel Bell, "The Failure of American Socialism," in *The End of Ideology: On the Exhaustion of Political Ideas in the Fifties* (New York, 1965 [1960]), 297.
32. Nathan Glazer, *The Social Basis of American Communism* (New York, 1961), 130, 147.
33. Isaac Rosenfeld, *Passage from Home* (Cleveland, 1946), 69.
34. Leslie Fiedler, "The Fear of Innocence," *Partisan Review*, Aug. 1949, p. 779.
35. Howe, "New York Intellectuals," 32. See ibid, 33–34, for a further discussion of this observation.
36. Lionel Trilling, "The Promise of Realism," *Menorah Journal*, May 1930, p. 481; idem, "Is Literature Possible?" *Nation*, Oct. 15, 1930, p. 406.
37. Michael Gold, "Towards Proletarian Art," *Liberator*, Feb. 1921, p. 23. For general discussions and examples of proletarian literature, see Granville Hicks et al., eds., *Proletarian Literature in the United States* (New York, 1935); Walter B. Rideout, *The Radical Novel in the United States, 1900–1954* (Cambridge, Mass., 1956); Aaron, *Writers on the Left*; Harry Swados, ed., *The American Writer and the Great Depression* (Indianapolis, 1960); Pells, *Radical Visions and American Dreams*.
38. "Draft Manifesto—John Reed Club," *New Masses*, June 1932, pp. 3–4.
39. William Phillips, *A Sense of the Present* (New York, 1967), 14. For Richard Wright, see Richard Crossman, ed., *The God That Failed* (New York, 1950), 103–46.

40. Malcolm Cowley, *The Dream of the Golden Mountains* (New York, 1980), 134–35.

41. William Phillips, "How *Partisan Review* Began," *Commentary*, Dec. 1976, pp. 42–43; Aaron, *Writers on the Left*, 298.

42. The other founding editors of the *Partisan Review* were Nathan Adler, Edward Dahlberg, Sender Garlin, Alfred Hayes, Milton Howard, Joshua Kunitz, Louis Lozowick, Leonard Mins, and Edwin Rolfe.

43. "Editorial Statement," *Partisan Review*, Feb.–Mar. 1934, p. 3. The other contributors to the first issue included Ben Field, Edwin Rolfe, Arthur Pense, Obed Brooks, and Waldo Tell. The journal also printed the "John Reed Club Notes." Contributors to subsequent numbers in 1934 included Isidor Schneider, Georg Lukacs, Genevieve Taggard, Edwin Newhouse, Jack Conroy, Jerre Mangione, Nelson Algren, Kenneth Fearing, William Rollins, Jr., Alan Calmer, and Meridel Le Sueur. During 1935, notable writers, among them André Malraux, Newton Arvin, Horace Gregory, Kenneth Patchen, Richard Wright, John Strachey, and Louis Aragon, published in *PR*.

44. Phillips, "How *Partisan Review* Began," 43.

45. Ibid.

46. Whatever the quality of the literature being produced, it was difficult to argue with Rahv as to its abundance. His particular remarks came out of a review of two proletarian novels—*Parched Earth*, by Arnold Armstrong, and *The Shadow Before*, by William Rollins, Jr. Other proletarian novels of the era include Jack Conroy, *The Disinherited*; Robert Cantwell, *The Land of Plenty*; Michael Gold, *Jews without Money*; James T. Farrell's *Studs Lonigan* trilogy, *Young Lonigan, The Young Manhood of Studs Lonigan,* and *Judgment Day*; Edward Dahlberg, *Bottom Dogs*; Edwin Seaver, *The Company*; Mary Horton Vorse, *Strike!*; Maxwell Bodenheim, *Run, Sheep, Run*; Grace Lumpkin, *To Make My Bread*; Josephine Herbst, *Pity Is Not Enough*; Waldo Frank, *The Death and Birth of David Markind*; Albert Harper, *The Foundry*; Edward Newhouse, *You Can't Sleep Here*; Nelson Algren, *Somebody in Boots*; Tom Kromer, *Waiting for Nothing*; Clara Weatherwax, *Marching! Marching!*

  Similarly, magazines sprang up across the country. The John Reed Clubs alone accounted for not only *Partisan Review* but also *The Anvil* (which for a brief period in 1936 merged with *PR*), edited by Jack Conroy in Moberly, Missouri; *Leftward*, in Boston; *Partisan*, Hollywood; *Cauldron*, Grand Rapids; *Left Front*, Chicago; *Left Review*, Philadelphia; *New Force*, Detroit; the *Hammer*, Hartford. By January 1934 the number of John Reed Club chapters had jumped to thirty. (The list of journals and clubs is from Aaron, *Writers on the Left*, 431.)

47. Philip Rahv, "The Novelist as a Partisan," *Partisan Review*, Apr.–May 1934, p. 50.

48. Wallace Phelps [William Phillips], "Three Generations," *Partisan Review*, Sept.–Oct. 1934, p. 52.

49. Wallace Phelps [William Phillips] and Philip Rahv, "Problems and Perspectives in Revolutionary Literature," *Partisan Review*, June–July 1934, p. 3.

50. Wallace Phelps [William Phillips] and Philip Rahv, "Criticism," *Partisan Review*, Apr.–May 1935, pp. 17–22.

51. William Phillips and Philip Rahv, "Recent Problems of Revolutionary Literature," in Hicks et al., eds., *Proletarian Literature in the United States*, 369.

52. Ibid.

53. Cowley quoted in "Symposium: Thirty Years Later—Memories of the First American Writers' Congress," *American Scholar*, Summer 1966, pp. 496–97; Newton Arvin, "The Democratic Tradition in American Letters," in *The Writer in a Changing World*, ed. Henry Hart (New York, 1937), 35. (This collection is the printed proceedings at the Second American Writer's Congress.)

54. "The Coming Writers' Congress," *Partisan Review*, Jan.–Feb. 1935, p. 94.

55. "Editorial," *Partisan Review*, Apr.–May 1935, 3; "Symposium: Thirty Years Later," 499.

56. Among the other speakers at the congress were Louis Aragon, Edward Dahlberg, Joseph Freeman, Waldo Frank, Jack Conroy, Kenneth Burke, Granville Hicks, Isidor Schneider, John Howard Lawson, Michael Blankfort, Meridel Le Sueur, Friedrich Wolf, Harry Ward, Moissaye Olgin, Edwin Seaver, Joseph North, Nathaniel Buchward, Eugene Gordon, Eugene Clay, Moishe Nadir, Clarence Hathaway, Henry Hart, and Alexander Trachtenberg. Waldo Frank was chosen president, and the executive council included Kenneth Burke, Harold Clurman, Cowley, Frank, Freeman, Michael Gold, Hart, Herbst, Hicks, Josephson, Alfred Kreymborg, Lawson, Albert Maltz, Schneider, Seaver, Genevieve Taggard, and Trachtenberg. The national council consisted of Nelson Algren, Blankfort, Maxwell Bodenheim, Brooks, Alan Calmer, Robert Cantwell, Conroy, Dahlberg, Farrell, Kenneth Fearing, Horace Gregory, Sidney Howard, Joshua Kunitz, Meridel Le Sueur, Grace Lumpkin, Mumford, Nadir, Odets, Joseph Opatoshu, Paul Peters, William Rollins, Jr., George Sklar, and Wright. (See "Discussion and Proceedings," in *American Writers' Congress*, ed. Henry Hart [New York, 1935], 165–92.)

57. Harold Rosenberg, "The American Writers' Congress," *Poetry*, July 1935, 226–27.

58. "Discussion and Proceedings," in *American Writers' Congress*, 68, 190.

59. Granville Hicks, "The Dialectics of the Development of Marxist Criticism," in *American Writers' Congress*, 94–96.

60. Ibid., 97–98.

61. William Phillips and Philip Rahv, "Private Experience and Public Philosophy," *Poetry*, May 1936, pp. 100–104.

62. Cowley, *Dream of the Golden Mountains*, 281; "Symposium: Thirty Years Later," 509.

Chapter 4 The *Partisan* Family

1. William Phillips, "How *Partisan Review* Began," *Commentary*, Dec. 1976, p. 45; F. W. Dupee to Newton Arvin, June 14, 1937, F. W. Dupee Papers; note attached to Arvin letter by Dupee, 1972. The best general introduction to *Partisan Review* remains James Gilbert, *Writers and Partisans: A History of Literary Radicalism in America* (New York, 1968).

2. Dwight Macdonald, interview, Dec. 3, 1976.

3. Ibid.

4. Phillips, "How *PR* Began," 45.

5. William Phillips, *A Partisan View: Five Decades of the Literary Life* (New York, 1983), 51.

6. William Phillips, interview, Aug. 30, 1979.

7. Both McCarthy and the "disgruntled listener" are quoted in Doris Grumbach, *The Company She Kept* (New York, 1967), 61, 76.

8. Macdonald, interview, Dec. 3, 1976.

9. William Barrett, *The Truants: Adventures among the Intellectuals* (New York, 1982), 36, 38–39; idem, "The Truants: *Partisan Review* in the Forties," *Commentary*, June 1974, p. 49.

10. Mary McCarthy, "Philip Rahv, 1908–1973," *New York Times Book Review*, Feb. 7, 1974, pp. 1–2; Barrett, *Truants*, 29; Alfred Kazin, *Starting Out in the Thirties* (Boston, 1965), 159–60.

11. Macdonald, interview, Dec. 3, 1976; Clement Greenberg, interview, June 22, 1979; Barrett, "Truants," 49.

12. Phillips, interview, Aug. 30, 1979. On Phillips's radical beginnings see above, p. 47. Émile Coué practiced a 1920s variety of self-help philosophy, making famous the phrase "Day by day in every way I am getting better and better." Fletcherizers chewed their food many times before swallowing. See also Phillips, *Partisan View*, 15–45.

13. Barrett, *Truants*, 37.

14. "Editorial Statement," *Partisan Review*, Dec. 1937, p. 3.

15. From Schwartz's work "Genesis," quoted in James Atlas, *Delmore Schwartz: The Life of an American Poet* (New York, 1977), 31.

16. Dwight Macdonald, "Delmore Schwartz," *New York Review of Books*, Sept. 8, 1966, p. 16; Schwartz, quoted in Atlas, *Delmore Schwartz*, 98; ibid., 97–100.

17. Lionel Trilling, "The America of John Dos Passos," *Partisan Review*, Apr. 1938, pp. 26–32.

18. See above, p. 23.

19. Diana Trilling to author, Nov. 27, 1979.

20. Wallace Markfield, *To an Early Grave* (New York, 1964), 188.

21. Sidney Hook, "Some Social Uses and Abuses of Semantics," *Partisan Review*, Apr. 1938, pp. 14–25.

22. *PR* was able to follow up on the publication of well-known figures in subsequent issues. Over the next few years, the famous contributors included Ignazio Silone, E. E. Cummings, Leon Trotsky, James Agee, André Breton, Diego Rivera, André Gide, Allen Tate, W. H. Auden, Henry Miller, Sherwood Anderson, and John Dos Passos.

23. Irving Howe," Edmund Wilson: A Reexamination, *Nation*, Oct. 16, 1948, p. 430.

24. Lionel Trilling, "Edmund Wilson: A Backward Glance," in *A Gathering of Fugitives* (Boston, 1956), 53, 55.

25. Meyer Schapiro, interview, Oct. 30, 1978; Irving Howe, interview, June 16, 1976; Barrett, *Truants*, 53.

26. Irving Kristol, interview, June 17, 1976; Irving Kristol, "Memoirs of a Trotskyist," *New York Times Magazine*, Jan. 23, 1977, p. 57; Daniel Bell, interview, July 13, 1979.

27. Other important or emerging American literary figures publishing in *PR* during the late 1930s included the critics Harry Levin, William Troy, and Arthur Mizener and the poets Randall Jarrell, Julian Symons, Theodore Roethke, Richard Eberhart, and Karl Shapiro.

28. Quoted in Andrew James Dvosin, "Literature in a Political World: The Career and Writings of Philip Rahv" (Ph.D. thesis, New York Univ., 1977), 60–61.

29. W. H. Auden to F. W. Dupee, Mar. 18, 1939, F. W. Dupee Papers.
30. Phillips, interview, Aug. 30, 1979.
31. The difference between a "Trotskyite" and a "Trotskyist" was in the mind of the labeler. Those who followed Trotsky called themselves Trotskyists, while their Communist opponents labeled them Trotskyites. Trotskyists argue that using the suffix "ite" would make Socialists "Socialites." In this work the groups are called by whichever name they themselves preferred. The use of the term "Trotskyite" signifies that a Stalinist made the appraisal. For such a Stalinist appraisal of *Partisan Review*, see the *New Masses*, Oct. 4, 1937, p. 21.
32. For a fuller discussion of the relationship between *PR* and Trotsky, which neither *PR* nor its opponents fully explained or, probably, understood, see below, pp. 107–13.
33. The other contributors to this number were James Agee, George L. K. Morris, and Elizabeth Bishop.
34. Malcolm Cowley, *"Partisan Review,"* in *Years of Protest*, ed. Jack Salzman (Indianapolis, 1967), 297–300.
35. "Ripostes," *Partisan Review*, Jan. 1938, p. 61.

Chapter 5 · The *Partisan* Mind: Cultural Turns

1. William Phillips and Philip Rahv, "In Retrospect: Ten Years of *Partisan Review*," in *Partisan Reader* (New York, 1946), 683.
2. "Ripostes," *Partisan Review*, Feb. 1938 p. 62.
3. "Editorial Statement," *Partisan Review*, Dec. 1937 p. 3.
4. Malcolm Bradbury and James McFarlane, "The Name and Nature of Modernism," in *Modernism: 1890–1930*, ed. Malcolm Bradbury and James McFarlane (New York, 1976), 26. The literature on modernism is enormous, encompassing as it does most forms of artistic expression, as well as the social and cultural history of Europe and America from the late nineteeth century forward. The anthology by Bradbury and McFarlane is a useful introduction, with an extensive bibliography.

    A number of New York Intellectuals wrote directly about modernism. Beyond the articles cited in this chapter, these publications include Irving Howe, *The Decline of the New* (New York, 1970); Lionel Trilling, *The Liberal Imagination* (New York, 1951); idem, *The Opposing Self* (New York, 1955); idem, *A Gathering of Fugitives (Boston, 1956)*. Edmund Wilson, *Axel's Castle: A Study in the Imaginative Literature of 1870–1930* (New York, 1931), served as an important statement about modernism for many of the young New Yorkers.
5. Lionel Trilling, "The Situation of American Writing," *Partisan Review*, Fall 1939 p. 111.
6. Philip Rahv, "The Slump in American Writing," *American Mercury*, Feb. 1940 pp. 188, 187.
7. Philip Rahv "Two Years of Progress—From Waldo Frank to Donald Ogden Stewart," *Partisan Review*, Feb. 1938 p. 28.
8. William Phillips, "Koestler and the Political Novel," *Nation*, Aug. 26, 1944, p. 241; Rahv, "Slump in American Writing, 185.
9. Philip Rahv, "Proletarian Literature: A Political Autopsy," *Southern Review*, 4 (1939), 619, 620.

10. William Phillips, "The Esthetic of the Founding Fathers," *Partisan Review*, Mar. 1938, pp. 13–14.

11. Philip Rahv, "Twilight of the Thirties," *Partisan Review*, Summer 1939, p. 6; William Phillips, "The Intellectual's Tradition" (1941), in *Partisan Reader*, 485–91.

12. Among the other signers of the LCFS statement were Lionel Abel, James Burnham, V. F. Calverton, Eleanor Clark, James T. Farrell, Clement Greenberg, Kenneth Patchen, Harold Rosenberg, Meyer Schapiro, Delmore Schwartz, James Wheelwright, and Bertram Wolfe. ("Statement, League for Cultural Freedom and Socialism," *Partisan Review*, Summer 1939, pp. 125–27).

13. Philip Rahv, "The Artist as Desperado," *New Republic*, Apr. 21, 1941, pp. 558–59.

14. Philip Rahv, "Dostoevsky and Politics: Notes on *The Possessed,*" *Partisan Review*, July 1938, pp. 25–36.

15. Dwight Macdonald, "Soviet Soceity and Its Cinema," *Partisan Review*, Winter 1939, pp. 89, 90.

16. *Twentieth Century Authors, First Supplement* (New York, 1971), 386–87; *Who's Who in World Jewry* (New York, 1971), 351.

17. Dwight Macdonald, interview, Dec. 3, 1976.

18. Clement Greenberg, "Avant-Garde and Kitsch" (1939), in *Partisan Reader*, 380, 390–91; idem, "Mr. Eliot and Notions of Culture: A Discussion," *Partisan Review*, Summer 1944, pp. 306–7.

19. Lionel Trilling, introd., *Partisan Reader*, xv.

20. Rahv, "Twilight of the Thirties," 14; idem, "Proletarian Literature," 623. Albert Maltz, Clifford Odets, and John Howard Lawson were all associated with proletarian literature, and all ended up in Hollywood. In the postwar years Odets became a "friendly" witness before the House Un-American Activities Committee, while Maltz and Lawson were two of the jailed "Hollywood Ten."

21. For Rahv's earlier characterization of proletarian literature, see esp. above, pp. 61–62.

22. William Phillips, "Thomas Mann: Humanism in Exile, "*Partisan Review*, May 1938, p. 3.

23. Rahv, "Slump in American Writing," 191.

24. Philip Rahv, "Trials of the Mind," *Partisan Review*, Apr. 1938, pp. 3–4, 9.

25. Rahv, "Slump in American Writing," 191; Lionel Trilling, "Dreiser and the Liberal Mind," *Nation*, Apr. 20, 1946, p. 466.

26. Rahv, "Twilight of the Thirties," 8.

27. Ibid., 15.

28. Phillips, "Thomas Mann," 5.

29. Phillips, "Intellectual's Tradition," 486.

30. Ibid.

31. William Phillips, "Mr. Eliot and Notions of Culture: A Discussion," *Partisan Review*, Summer 1944, p. 309; Isaac Rosenfeld, in "Under Forty: A Symposium on American Literature and the Younger Generation of American Jews," *Contemporary Jewish Record*, Feb. 1944, p. 36.

32. Phillips, "Koestler," 241.

Chapter 6 The *Partisan* Mind: Political Turns

1. Irving Kristol, interview, June 17, 1976; Irving Howe, "The New York Intellectuals," *Commentary*, Oct. 1968, p. 44.
2. Eastman, quoted in John P. Diggins, *Up from Communism: Conservative Odysseys in American Intellectual History* (New York, 1975), 46. For the entire discussion of Eastman's Marxism, see 39–59, 173–79.
3. Sidney Hook, "Marxism, Metaphysics, and Modern Science," *Modern Quarterly*, May 1928, p. 393. The attacks were often personal and direct. Eastman suggested in one piece that Hook's antagonism stemmed from Eastman's having beaten Hook to publication, after Hook had told Eastman of his own study of Marxism. "The publication of my book," Eastman wrote, "must have been a keep disappointment to him." Hook defended his own position and morality. "They need no defense against a man who has been found guilty time and again of systematically abusing texts and contexts to save his own face and discredit others." Max Eastman, "As to Sidney Hook's Morals," *Modern Quarterly*, Nov.– Feb. 1928–29, 87; Sidney Hook, "As to Max Eastman's Mentality," ibid., 91.
4. Sidney Hook, "John Dewey and His Critics," *New Republic*, June 3, 1931, p. 74; idem, "On Workers Democracy," *Modern Monthly*, Oct. 1934, p. 529; idem, *Towards the Understanding of Karl Marx* (New York, 1933), ix. On John Dewey's thinking and political activity in the 1930s, see R. Alan Lawson, *The Failure of Independent Liberalism* (New York, 1971), 99–130.
5. Sidney Hook, telephone interview, May 29, 1976.
6. Sidney Hook, "The Philosophy of Dialectic Materialism," *Journal of Philosophy*, Mar. 1, 1928, p. 123; idem, "Marxism: Dogma or Method?" *Nation*, Mar. 15, 1933, p. 285; idem, "The Meaning of Marxism," *Modern Quarterly*, Winter 1930– 31, p. 431.
7. Hook, "Philosophy of Dialectic Materialism," 114; idem, "Marxism Dogma or Method?" 284; idem, "Meaning of Marxism," 435; idem, "The Marxian Dialectic," *New Republic*, Mar. 22, 1933, p. 154.
8. Calverton, quoted in Diggins, *Up from Communism*, 54.
9. Hook, "Marxian Dialectic," 154.
10. Hook, *Towards the Understanding of Karl Marx*, 76, 79, 84.
11. Sidney Hook, "An Epic of Revolution," *Saturday Review of Literature*, Feb. 27, 1932, p. 551; idem, "Pictures of the Past," ibid., Apr. 30, 1932, p. 700; idem, "Philosophy of Dialectic Materialism," 114.
12. Hook, *Towards the Understanding of Karl Marx*, 114, 164–65.
13. William Barrett, "The Truants: *Partisan Review* in the 40s," *Commentary*, June 1974, p. 52.
14. Irving Howe, "The Thirties: Fact and Fantasy," *Dissent*, Autumn 1955, p. 333; Daniel Bill, interview, July 13, 1979; Sidney Hook, interview, Jan. 4, 1978.
15. Alfred Kazin, interview, Oct. 23, 1976; Alfred Kazin, *Starting Out in the Thirties* (Boston, 1965), 72–73.
16. Hook was properly respectful of his mentors as well as clear about his own version of communism. "If by communism one means an acceptance of the present principles and tactics of the Third International or any of its affiliated organizations, I am not a communist. . . . I believe that communist principles are more important than communist organizations." Hook thought that Cohen

defined "the essence of liberalism to be freedom of thought and inquiry, freedom of discussion and criticism." "Now communism," Hook wrote, "as I understand it, would not dream of denying the value of liberalism in this sense. . . . Genuine liberalism in the sense which Professor Cohen defines it, is possible in *all fields* only when vested interests have been abolished." (Sidney Hook, "Why I Am a Communist—Communism without Dogmas," *Modern Monthly*, Apr. 1934, pp. 143, 148. The entire article is on 143–65. The Dewey, Cohen, and Russell articles appear in the same issue, 133–42.)

17. Sidney Hook, "Metaphysics, War, and the Intellectuals," *Menorah Journal*, Oct.–Dec. 1940, p. 335.
18. Sidney Hook, "Experimental Naturalism," in *American Philosophy Today and Tomorrow*, ed. Horace M. Kallen and Sidney Hook (New York, 1935), 223–24.
19. Sidney Hook, "Dialectic and Nature," *Marxist Quarterly*, Aprl.–June 1937, pp. 255, 281–83. Herbert Marcuse's *Reason and Revolution*, which argued for a revolutionary interpretation of Hegel, was greeted by Hook with a negative review in the *New Republic*, July 21, 1941, pp. 90–91.
20. Meyer Schapiro, interview Oct. 30, 1978. It should not be assumed that Hook capitulated to Eastman's position by dropping the dialectic. They still had significant differences, such as their attitudes toward Freud. Rather, Hook's abandonment in the 1930s of what Eastman had dropped in the 1920s demonstrates the growing frequency with which American intellectuals adjusted or revised their Marxism along similar but not identical lines.
21. Sidney Hook, "Violence For and Against: A Symposium," *Common Sense*, Jan. 1938, p. 23.
22. William Phillips, "The Devil Theory of the Dialectic," *Partisan Review*, Jan. 1938, p. 23.
23. Lionel Abel, "New York City: A Remembrance," *Dissent*, Summer 1961, p. 257.
24. Edmund Wilson, "The Myth of the Marxist Dialectic," *Partisan Review*, Fall 1938, p. 77; Wilson and Phillips, cited in Diggins, *Up from Communism*, 62–63.
25. Michael Gold, *Daily Worker*, Oct. 1937.
26. Dwight Macdonald, interview, Dec. 3, 1976.
27. Isaac Deutscher, *The Prophet Outcast: Trotsky, 1929–1940* (New York, 1963), 430–31.
28. William Phillips and Philip Rahv, "In Retrospect: Ten Years of *Partisan Review*," in *Partisan Reader* (New York, 1946), 683.
29. McCarthy, quoted in Doris Grumbach, *The Company She Kept* (New York, 1967), 75; Mary McCarthy, *Twentieth Century Authors, First Supplement* (New York, 1971), 609.
30. Cited in M. S. Venkataramani, "Leon Trotsky's Adventure in American Radical Politics: 1935–37," *International Review of Social History*, 4 (1964), 10ff.
31. Kristol, interview, June 17, 1976.
32. Philip Rahv, "Trials of the Mind," *Partisan Review*, Apr. 1938, p. 3.
33. Kristol, interview, June 17, 1976.
34. Barrett, "Truants," 52.
35. Leon Trotsky, *The Revolution Betrayed* (London, 1937), 173.
36. Leon Trotsky, "Art and Politics," *Partisan Review*, Aug.–Sept. 1938, p. 10.
37. Dwight Macdonald, "Soviet Society and Its Cinema," *Partisan Review*, Winter 1939, p. 82.

38. Dwight Macdonald, "Soviet Cinema: 1930–1938," *Partisan Review*, July 1938, p. 38.

39. Philip Rahv, "Dostoevsky and Politics: Notes on *The Possessed*," *Partisan Review*, July 1938, p. 32.

40. James T. Farrell, "The Cultural Front: Leon Trotsky," *Partisan Review*, Sept.–Oct., 1940, p. 388; Sidney Hook, "Russia in Solution," *Saturday Review*, Apr. 8, 1932, p. 521. Other *PR* contributors shared Farrell's view. "For brilliance, solidity, and sheer volume," Dwight Macdonald wrote, Trotsky's body of work "had no parallel in the literature of Marxism." Alfred Kazin later recalled that Trotsky "personified the highest intransigence and brilliance." Not all the more recent appraisals have been favorable, however. To Leslie Fiedler, "Trotsky was an intellectual and a dandy." What the anti-Stalinist radicals wanted "was a beautiful loser, and Trotsky is your original beautiful loser. To begin with he was articulate, and then he became the victim of an assassin. There is great romance about him." (Dwight Macdonald, "Trotsky Is Dead: An Attempt at an Appreciation," *Partisan Review*, Sept.–Oct. 1940, p. 347; Alfred Kazin, "The Ghost of Trotsky," in *Contemporaries* [Boston, 1962], 412; Leslie Fiedler, interview, May 14, 1976.)

41. Irving Howe, "Leon Trotsky," in *Steady Work: Essays in the Politics of Democratic Radicalism, 1953–1966* (New York, 1966), 118.

42. Macdonald, "Trotsky Is Dead," 344–45; Dwight Macdonald, "Introduction: Politics Past," in *Memoirs of a Revolutionist* (New York, 1957), 15.

43. William Phillips to F. W. Dupee, Aug. 22, 1938, F. W. Dupee Papers. For the heated debates concerning this issue of the magazine, see above, pp. 82–83.

44. Trotsky, "Art and Politics," 10.

45. Sidney Hook, "The Fallacy of the Theory of Social Fascism," *Modern Monthly*, July 1934, p. 394; Elliot E. Cohen and Louis Berg, "May Day—1934: Record and Prospect," ibid., June 1934, p. 88.

46. Philp Rahv, "Versions of Bolshevism," *Partisan Review*, Summer 1946, p. 370.

47. Sidney Hook, "The Faiths of Whittaker Chambers," *New York Times Book Review*, May 25, 1952, p. 34; Diana Trilling, "The Oppenheimer Case," in *Claremont Essays* (New York, 1964), 125; idem, "A Memorandum on the Hiss Case," *Partisan Review*, May–June 1950, p. 490.

48. Philip Rahv, "Two Years of Progress: From Waldo Frank to Donald Ogden Stewart," *Partisan Review*, Feb. 1938, p. 25.

49. Sidney Hook, "The Anatomy of the Popular Front," *Partisan Review*, Spring 1939, p. 40; Philip Rahv, "The Sense and Nonsense of Whittaker Chambers," *Partisan Review*, July–Aug. 1952, pp. 478–79.

50. Kenneth Burke, "Revolutionary Symbolism in America," in *American Writers' Congress*, ed. Harry Hart (New York, 1935), 87–93; Newton Arvin, "The Democratic Tradition in American Letters," in *The Writer in a Changing World*, ed. Harry Hart (New York, 1937), 35–37, 43.

51. F. W. Dupee, "The Americanism of Van Wyck Brooks," *Partisan Review*, Summer 1939, pp. 81–85.

52. Archibald MacLeish, "The Irresponsibles," *Nation*, May 18, 1940, p. 623.

53. Van Wyck Brooks, "What Is Primary Literature?" *Yale Review* Sept. 1941, p. 29.

54. Dwight Macdonald, "Kulturbolshewismus Is Here," *Partisan Review*, Nov.–Dec. 1941, pp. 443–51.

55. "Statement, League for Cultural Freedom and Socialism," *Partisan Review*, Summer 1939, p. 125. See above, pp. 88–89, 110, for the LCFS statement on intellectual activity and radical politics

Chapter 7 *Partisan* Warfare

1. "The War of the Neutrals," *Partisan Review*, Fall 1939, p. 11.

2. Lionel Abel, "New York City: A Remembrance," *Dissent*, Summer 1961, p. 258.

3. Edmund Wilson to F. W. Dupee, May 16, 1940, F. W. Dupee Papers.

4. Mary McCarthy to F. W. Dupee, n.d., F. W. Dupee Papers.

5. William Phillips, interview, Aug. 30, 1979; Phillip Rahv to F. W. Dupee, Apr. 5, 1941, F. W. Dupee Papers; Barrett, quoted in Andrew James Dvosin, "Literature in a Political World: The Career and Writings of Philip Rahv (Ph.D. thesis, New York Univ., 1977), 103.

6. Sidney Hook, "Radicals and War: A Debate," *Modern Monthly*, Apr. 1936, p. 14; "This Quarter—Munich and the Intellectuals," *Partisan Review*, Fall 1938, pp. 7–8; Philip Rahv, "Trials of the Mind," ibid., Apr. 1938, p. 10.

7. Dwight Macdonald, "This Quarter," *Partisan Review*, Spring 1939, p. 10.

8. The only original signer who did not sign this second statement was Parker Tyler. Among the new endorsers of the LCFS position were Kay Boyle, Ralph Manheim, Kenneth Rexroth, and William Carlos Williams.

9. "Statement: League for Cultural Freedom and Socialism," *Partisan Review*, Fall 1939, pp. 125–26.

10. "This Quarter," *Partisan Review*, Fall 1939, p. 4.

11. Dwight Macdonald, "Notes on a Strange War," *Partian Review*, May–June 1940, pp. 174–75.

12. Clement Greenberg and Dwight Macdonald, "Ten Propositions on the War," *Partisan Review*, July–Aug. 1941, pp. 271–73. Sidney Hook did not join the LCFS and became, ahead of the other New York Intellectuals, committed to the war effort. As with his Marxist revisions, others ultimately adopted Hook's position.

13. Philip Rahv, "Ten Propositions and Eight Errors," *Partisan Review*, Nov.–Dec. 1941, pp. 499–502.

14. Dwight Macdonald, interview, Dec. 3, 1976.

15. Macdonald, cited in James B. Gilbert, *Writers and Partisans: A History of Literary Radicalism in America* (New York, 1968), 248; Phillips, interview, Aug. 30, 1979.

16. "Statement by the Editors," *Partisan Review*, Jan.–Feb. 1942, p. 2.

17. Irving Howe, "The Dilemma of *Partisan Review*," *New International*, Feb. 1942, p. 22; Macdonald, interview, Dec. 3, 1976.

18. Dwight Macdonald, "Resignation Letter," *Partisan Review*, July–Aug. 1943, p. 382; "Letters," ibid.

19. Sidney Hook, *The Hero in History: A Study in Limitation and Possibility* (Boston, 1943), 7, 102.

20. For a fuller discussion of this question, see above, pp. 99–105.
21. Hook, *Hero in History*, 114, 116, 184.
22. Ibid., 232–33.
23. Sidney Hook, "The New Failure of Nerve," *Partisan Review*, Jan.–Feb. 1943, pp. 2–3.
24. Ibid., 3, 8, 23.
25. Sidney Hook, "The Failure of the Left," *Partisan Review*, Apr. 1943, pp. 168, 175–76.
26. George Orwell, "Pacifism and War," *Partisan Review*, Sept.–Oct. 1942, p. 419.
27. Harold Rosenberg, "On the Fall of Paris," in *Tradition of the New* (New York, 1960), 209, 210, 217 (originally published in *Partisan Review* in 1940).
28. William Peterson, "What Has Become of Them?" *Partisan Review*, Jan.–Feb. 1941, pp. 59–62.
29. Philip Rahv, foreword, *Image and Idea* (New York 1949).
30. Rosenberg's remark, quoted in William Barrett, *The Truants: Adventures among the Intellectuals* (New York, 1982), 59.
31. Midge Decter, interview, June 1, 1976.
32. Howe, "Dilemma of *Partisan Review*," 21.
33. Alfred Kazin, *Starting Out in the Thirties* (Boston, 1965), 6–10, 122; idem, *New York Jew* (New York, 1978), 3–18; Irving Kristol, interview, June 17, 1976; Irving Howe, interview, June 16, 1976; Daniel Bell, interview, May 5, 1985. Daniel Bell did get some free-lance work at the *New Leader*, Nathan Glazer continued as a student at City College until 1944, and Seymour Martin Lipset took his B.A. in 1943 and went directly on to graduate school.
34. Irving Kristol, interview, June 17, 1976.
35. Bell, interview, July 13, 1976.
36. *Enquiry*, Nov. 1943, p. 2.
37. See William Ferry [Irving Kristol], "Auden: The Quality of Doubt," *Enquiry*, Nov. 1942, unpaginated; idem, "A Christian Experience," ibid., Jan. 1943, pp. 19–20; idem, "Other People's Nerve," ibid., May 1943, pp. 3–6; idem, "James Burnham's *The Machiavellians*," ibid., July 1943, pp. 20–24; idem, "The Moral Critic," ibid., Apr. 1944, pp. 20–23.
38. Saul Bellow, "Notes on a Dangling Man," *Partisan Review*, Sept.–Oct. 1943, p. 403.
39. Clement Greenberg to F. W. Dupee, Apr. 4, 1943, F. W. Dupee Papers; Kazin, *New York Jew*, 99, 4.
40. Alfred Kazin, "The Critic as Creator," *Horizon*, July 1962, p. 99.
41. Alfred Kazin, *On Native Grounds: An Interpretation of Modern American Prose Literature* (New York, 1942), 489.
42. Norman Podhoretz, *Making It* (New York, 1967), 123.
43. Bell, interview, July 13, 1976.
44. David T. Bazelon, *Nothing but a Fine Tooth Comb* (New York, 1969), 19.
45. Alfred Kazin, interview, Oct. 23, 1976; Irving Howe, "The New York Intellectuals: A Chronicle and Critique," *Commentary*, Oct. 1968, p. 43.
46. Sidney Hook, "The Tragedy of German Jewry," *New Leader*, Nov. 26, 1938, p. 8.
47. Hook stated in 1937, "Jews are in more deadly danger from this anti-fascist movement *in its present form* than from almost any other possible false utopia."

(Hook, "Promise without Dogma," *Menorah Journal*, Oct.–Dec. 1937, p. 281.)

48. Kazin, interview, Oct. 23, 1976; Bell, interview, July 13, 1979.

49. Alfred Kazin, "In Every Voice, In Every Ban," *New Republic*, Jan. 10, 1944, pp. 45–46.

50. Kazin, interview, Oct. 23, 1976.

51. Elliot E. Cohen, "An Act of Affirmation," *Commentary*, Nov. 1945, p. 2.

52. Sidney Hook, "Reflections on the Jewish Question," *Partisan Review*, May 1949, p. 466.

53. Isaac Rosenfeld, "The Meaning of Terror," in *An Age of Enormity: Life and Writing in the Forties and Fifties*, ed. Theodore Solotaroff (Cleveland, 1962), 197 (orginally published in *Partisan Review*, in 1949); Howe "New York Intellectuals," 43.

Chapter 8   Heart In—Head Out

1. Lionel Trilling, "Notes on a Departure," *Menorah Journal*, May 1929, p. 424.

2. Norman Podhoretz, "Jewishness and Young Intellectuals," *Commentary*, Apr. 1961, pp. 307–8.

3. Harold Rosenberg, "Does the Jew Exist?" *Commentary*, Jan. 1949, p. 18.

4. Harold Rosenberg, "Jewish Identity in a Free Society," in *Discovering the Present: Three Decades in Art, Culture, and Politics* (Chicago, 1973), 259–61 (originally published in *Commentary* in 1950).

5. Irving Kristol, interview, June 17, 1976; Norman Podhoretz, interview, June 3, 1976; Leslie Fiedler, "Plight of the Jewish Intellectual," in *Mid-Century: An Anthology of Life and Culture in Our Times*, ed. Harold N. Ribalow (New York, 1955), 164–65.

6. Clement Greenberg, in "Under Forty: A Symposium of American Literature and the Younger Generation of American Jews," *Contemporary Jewish Record*, Feb. 1944, p. 32; Irving Howe, *World of Our Fathers* (New York, 1976), 600.

7. Lionel Trilling in "Under Forty," 17.

8. Alfred Kazin, *A Walker in the City* (New York, 1951); idem, interview, Oct. 23, 1976.

9. Clement Greenberg, "Self-Hatred and Jewish Chauvinism," *Commentary*, Nov. 1950, p. 426.

10. Ibid.

11. Ibid., 426, 432.

12. Ibid., 433.

13. Harold Rosenberg, "Jewish Identity in a Free Society," *Commentary*, June 1950, p. 501; idem, *Discovering the Present*, 269.

14. Irving Kristol, "How Basic Is 'Basic Judaism'?" *Commentary*, Jan. 1948, p. 27.

15. Daniel Bell, interview, July 13, 1979. Bell had been in an earlier study group in Chicago, which included Daniel Boorstin, Benjamin Nelson, William Irwin, and Ralph Marcus.

16. Rosenberg, *Discovering the Present*, 269.

17. Harold Rosenberg, "Sartre's Jewish Morality Play," in *Discovering the Present*, 278–79 (originally published in *Commentary* in 1949); Daniel Bell, "Reflections on Jewish Identity," in *The Ghetto and Beyond: Essays on Jewish Life in America* (New York, 1969), 469–70 (originally published in *Commentary* in 1961).

18. The selection committee for the Bollingen Prize included W. H. Auden, Allen Tate, and Robert Lowell. Allen Tate objected to Barrett's "insinuation" of anti-Semitism and concluded, "I hope that persons who wish to accuse me of cowardice and dishonor will do so henceforth personally, in my presence, so that I may dispose of the charge at some other level than that of public discussion. Courage and honor are not subjects of literary controversy, but occasions of action." (William Barrett, "A Prize for Ezra Pound," *Partisan Review*, Apr. 1949, pp. 344–47; Allen Tate, comment, ibid., May 1949, p. 520.)

19. The problem of anti-Semitism in English and American literature was not confined to dead British authors or American modernist expatriates like Eliot and Pound. Henry James, Henry Adams, and other late-nineteenth-century American writers expressed their anti-Semitic sentiments in their works. In addition, major twentieth-century figures like William Carlos Williams, E. E. Cummings, and Ernest Hemingway made anti-Jewish remarks.

20. Leslie A. Fiedler, "What Can We Do about Fagin?" *Commentary*, May 1949, p. 412.

21. "The Jewish Writer and the English Literary Tradition: A Symposium," *Commentary*, Sept. 1949, p. 209.

22. William Phillips in "The Jewish Writer and the English Literary Tradition," 210; Isaac Rosenfeld, ibid., 213–24.

23. Diana Trilling, in "The Jewish Writer and the English Literary Tradition," 215; Phillips, ibid., 210.

24. D. Trilling, in "The Jewish Writer and the English Literary Tradition," 215.

25. Alfred Kazin, in "The Jewish Writer and the English Literary Tradition—II," *Commentary*, Oct. 1949, p. 367.

26. Phillips, in "The Jewish Writer and the English Literary Tradition," 210; Kazin, interview, Oct. 23, 1976.

27. Fiedler's piece "What Can We Do about Fagin?" raised the issue of the relation between Jews and the anti-Semitic strain in English literature and led to the *Commentary* symposium.

28. Leslie A. Fiedler, "The State of American Writing, 1948: Seven Questions," *Partisan Review*, Aug. 1948, p. 873.

29. Ibid., 873–74.

30. Fiedler, "What Can We Do about Fagin?" 418.

31. Leslie A. Fiedler, "What Makes Herman Run?" *New Leader*, Oct. 3, 1955, p. 23. Herman Wouk was not alone among Jewish writers turning out popular novels which pandered to the glories of postwar American prosperity and material culture. Harold Robbins, Jacqueline Susann, and Sidney Sheldon were other Jews who wrote best-selling, lowbrow novels. Wouk's work, which clearly stands above that of these writers, earned special criticism because of its higher quality. It is easy to summarily dismiss *The Carpetbaggers* or *Valley of the Dolls* as worthless trash. When subtler writing introduced subtler themes, as did *Marjorie Morningstar*, it became the duty of the Jewish critic to make sure the incorrectness of these themes did not go unnoticed.

32. Nathan Glazer, "The 'Alienation' of Modern Man," *Commentary*, Apr. 1947, p. 378.

33. Ibid.; Daniel Bell, "A Parable of Alienation," in *Mid-Century: An Anthology of Jewish Life and Culture in Our Time*, ed. Harold N. Ribalow (New York, 1955), 134 (orginally published in *Jewish Frontier* in 1946).

34. Isaac Rosenfeld, in "Under Forty," 35–36.
35. Fiedler, "State of American Writing, 1948," 872; Bell, "Parable of Alienation," 134.
36. Clement Greenberg, "The Jewishness of Franz Kafka," *Commentary*, Apr. 1955, 321–22.
37. Ibid.
38. Fiedler, "State of American Writing, 1948," 872.
39. Trilling's hesitations about Jewish connections were overcome, in part, by his sense that the differences between Jews and non-Jews were growing less distinct. This became especially apparent in academe, where he had felt himself so different during the 1920s. By 1950 he found the "the individual Jewish student is likely to be closer in type to the general image of the American student than his father was; his manners and habits distinguish him less from the generality." (Lionel Trilling, "Seven Professors Look at the Jewish Student: A Symposium," *Commentary*, Dec. 1951, p. 527.)
40. Elliot E. Cohen, "The Intellectuals and the Jewish Community," *Commentary*, July 1949, pp. 20, 22.
41. Ibid., 20, 23.
42. Ibid., 25.
43. Ibid., 30.

Chapter 9 Into the Promised Land

1. Elliot E. Cohen, "An Act of Affirmation," *Commentary*, Nov. 1945, p. 2; Cohen, quoted in Norman Podhoretz, *Making It* (New York, 1967), 99–100.
2. In the mid-1940s the *Contemporary Jewish Record* became a minor "family publication." In October 1943 Philip Rahv took over as managing editor, a position he held for five issues, until April 1944. Before that time Lionel Trilling had been the only New York Intellectual to publish in the journal. In Rahv's five issues appeared the "Under Forty" symposium as well as pieces by Harold Rosenberg, Saul Bellow, Sidney Hook, and Isaac Rosenfeld. Rosenfeld was an assistant editor from June 1944 to August 1944.

The last issues of the journal, before it was superseded by *Commentary*, were put together by Clement Greenberg, who followed Rahv's pattern of publishing New York Intellectuals. Greenberg ran articles and reviews by Delmore Schwartz, David T. Bazelon, Nathan Glazer, Rosenfeld, Rosenberg, Hannah Arendt, and Hook as well as by himself. Glazer was an editorial assistant from February until June of 1945.
3. Meyer Schapiro, interview, Oct. 30, 1978.
4. The first issue of *Commentary* listed Cohen as editor, Greenberg as managing editor, Glazer and Evelyn Shefner as editorial assistants, and Frances Green as business manager. The contributing editors were Hook, Salo Baron, J. L. Lurie, Jacob R. Marcus, and Shalom Spiegel. By the second issue, Greenberg's title had changed to associate editor. A new managing editor joined with the fifth issue, Hanna F. Desser. With the sixth, Glazer was promoted to assistant editor. The second issue of volume 2 (July 1946) listed Robert Warshow as a second assistant editor. Irving Kristol joined the magazine in September 1947, as assistant editor.
5. Among the other contributors to the first issues were a number of New York

Intellectual fellow-travelers, including James Rorty, Randall Jarrell, Reinhold Niebuhr, Lewis Coser, Martin Greenberg (brother of Clement), Pearl Kazin (Alfred's sister and later the wife of Daniel Bell), and Arthur Schlesinger, Jr.

6. Elliot Cohen, interview in *Time*, Jan. 29, 1951, p. 72
7. Podhoretz, *Making It*, 133–34.
8. Lionel Trilling, introd., Robert Warshow, *The Immediate Experience* (New York, 1962), 13–14.
9. Arnold Beichman, interview, May 25, 1976; Midge Decter, interview, June 1, 1976; Cohen, interview in *Time*, 72–73.

   Morris Fine, who worked for many years for Committee, recounted a story which illustrates Cohen's editorial persistence and influence. Having read the work of a young historian who had published in *Commentary*, Cohen hired him to work at the Committee. When he read this person's memos, he was extremely unhappy with their quality and asked Cohen about it. Cohen told Fine how heavily he had edited this fellow's work. (Morris Fine, interview, Aug. 24, 1979.)

10. Decter, interview, June 1, 1976; Elliot Cohen, "The Promise of the American Synagogue," *Menorah Journal*, Aug. 1918, p. 278. For Trilling's description of Cohen's rejection of a graduate career, see above p. 30.
11. Podhoretz, *Making It*, 129; Dwight Macdonald, interview, Dec. 3, 1976.
12. Podhoretz, *Making It*, 129.
13. Irving Kristol, interview, June 17, 1976; Podhoretz, *Making It*, 128, 130.
14. Macdonald, interview, Dec. 3, 1976; Decter, interview, June 1, 1976.
15. Isaac Rosenfeld, "Adam and Eve on Delancey Street," *Commentary*, Oct. 1949, p. 387.
16. *Commentary*, Nov. 1949, p. 501.
17. Macdonald, interview, Dec. 3, 1976.
18. Decter, interview, June 1, 1976.
19. Podhoretz, *Making It*, 134–35.
20. Norman Podhoretz, "The Issue," *Commentary*, Feb. 1960, pp. 182–83.
21. Lionel Trilling, quoted in Podhoretz, *Making It*, 127; Lionel Trilling, "On the Death of a Friend," *Commentary*, Feb. 1960, p. 93; Irving Howe, "This Age of Conformity," *Partisan Review*, Jan.–Feb. 1954, pp. 7–33.
22. Elliot E. Cohen, "The Intellectuals and the Jewish Community," *Commentary*, July 1949, p. 22.
23. Daniel Bell, "A Parable of Alienation," in *Mid-Century: An Anthology of Jewish Life and Culture in Our Time*, ed. Harold N. Ribalow (New York, 1955), 139 (orginally published in *Jewish Frontier* in 1946).
24. Irving Howe, "The Lost Young Intellectual," *Commentary*, Oct. 1946, p. 361.
25. Ibid., 366–67 (italics Howe's).
26. Bell, "Parable of Alienation," 139.
27. Howe, "Lost Young Intellectual," 361; Cohen, "Intellectuals and the Jewish Community," 24
28. Howe, "Lost Young Intellectual," 362; idem, "This Age of Conformity," 14–15.
29. Daniel Bell, "The Mood of Three Generations," in *The End of Ideology: On the Exhaustion of Political Ideas in the Fifties* (New York, 1965 [1960]), 302 (orginally published in *Saturday Review* in 1955); idem, "Parable of Alienation," 144; Howe, "Lost Young Intellectual," 362.

30. Daniel Bell, "Reflections on Jewish Identity," in *The Ghetto and Beyond: Essays on Jewish Life in America*, ed. Peter I. Rose (New York, 1969), 471 (originally published in *Commentary* in 1961).
31. Ibid.
32. Alfred Kazin, *New York Jew* (New York, 1978), 209; idem, interview, Oct. 23, 1976. Howe's works on Yiddish literature include Irving Howe and Eliezer Greenberg, eds., *A Treasury of Yiddish Stories* (New York, 1954); idem, eds., *A Treasury of Yiddish Poetry* (New York, 1969); idem, eds., *Voices from the Yiddish: Memoirs and Diaries* (New York, 1972).
33. Bell, "Reflections on Jewish Identity," 473.
34. For the reaction of the New York Intellectuals to Rosenfeld's novel, see above, p. 19.
35. Isaac Rosenfeld, *Passage from Home* (Cleveland, 1946), 241–42; Alfred Kazin, interview, Oct. 23, 1976.
36. Sidney Hook in "Our Country and Our Culture: A Symposium," *Partisan Review*, May–June 1952, p. 570.
37. Howe, "Lost Young Intellectual," 367.
38. Bell, "Reflections on Jewish Identity," 475.

Chapter 10   The Postwar Mentality: Imagination and Affirmation

1. "Our Country and Our Culture: A Symposium," *Partisan Review*, May–June 1952, pp. 282–84.
2. Lionel Trilling, *The Liberalism Imagination: Essays on Literature and Society* (New York, 1950), ix. For Hook and Cohen, see above, pp. 39, 104, 404–5.
3. Diana Trilling, "'Liberalism' vs. Liberalism," *Commentary*, Apr. 1947, p. 387; Leslie Fiedler, "Hiss, Chambers, and the Age of Innocence," in *An End to Innocence* (Boston, 1952), 8.
4. Daniel Bell, "Has America a Ruling Class?" *Commentary*, Dec. 1949, p. 603
5. Arthur Schlesinger, Jr., "Liberty and the Liberal," *Commentary*, July 1952, p. 84. F. O. Matthiessen's radicalism extended over a number of years; Daniel Boorstin's was extremely short-lived.
6. Arthur Schlesinger, Jr., *The Vital Center: The Politics of Freedom* (Boston, 1962 [1949]), 163; Sidney Hook, "The Future of Socialism," *Partisan Review*, Jan.–Feb. 1947, p. 33.
7. Schlesinger, *Vital Center*, 41, 159.
8. Diana Trilling, "'Liberalism' vs. Liberalism," 387; Sidney Hook, *New York Times*, Aug. 13, 1949, p. 19.
9. Fiedler, "Hiss, Chambers, and the Age of Innocence," 24.
10. Arthur Schlesinger, Jr., "The Perspective Now" (The Future of Socialism: Part III in a Symposium), *Partisan Review*, May–June 1947, p. 236; Leslie Fiedler, "Hiss, Chambers, and the Age of Innocence," 24.
11. William Phillips, "America the Beautiful and Damned," *Commentary*, Nov. 1951, p. 508.
12. Dwight Macdonald, "Liberal Soap Opera," *Partisan Review*, n. 4, 1954, p. 341.
13. William Phillips, "The Politics of Desperation," *Partisan Review*, Apr. 1948, p. 45.
14. Dwight Macdonald, "Politics Past—I" *Encounter*, Mar. 1957, pp. 39–40.
15. Daniel Bell, "The Refractions of the American Past" (1958), in *The End of*

Ideology: On the Exhaustion of Political Ideas in the Fifties (New York, 1965 [1960]), 98.

16. Schlesinger, "Perspective Now," 232–33.

17. Schlesinger, *Vital Center*, xxi–xxii.

18. Daniel Bell, "America's un-Marxist Revolution," *Commentary*, Mar. 1949, p. 203; Norman Podhoretz, "Truman and the Idea of the Common Man," ibid., May 1956, p. 472.

19. Schlesinger, "Perspective Now," 231; Hook, "Future of Socialism," 25. For Hook, the "growth of a socialist economy never was, and certainly is not now, a matter of economic law but of political decision based upon the verifiable relations between social organization, human values, and the needs and interests at their root." This led to a "theory of piecemeal socialism through the democratic process." (Ibid., 29.)

20. Hook, "Future of Socialism," 30–33.

21. Much subsequent scholarship has suggested different assessments of the New Deal as a radical force. See, e.g., Barton J. Bernstein, "The New Deal: The Conservative Achievements of Liberal Reform, in *Towards a New Past*, ed. Barton J. Bernstein (New York, 1968), 263–88; Howard Zinn, introd., *New Deal Thought* (Indianapolis, 1966); Paul Conkin, *The New Deal* (New York, 1975).

22. Elliot E. Cohen, "The Free American Citizen, 1952" *Commentary*, Sept. 1952, p. 229.

23. Irving Kristol, "Urban Civilization and Its Discontents," in *On the Democratic Idea in America* (New York, 1972), 16 (orginally published in *Commentary*, July 1970).

24. Sidney Hook, "Unpragmatic Liberalism," *New Republic*, May 24, 1954, p. 18.

25. Alfred Kazin, interview, Oct. 23, 1976; Leslie A. Fiedler, interview, May 14, 1976; Nathan Glazer, "The Study of Man," *Commentary*, Nov. 1945, p. 84.

26. Nathan Glazer, "Government by Manipulation," *Commentary*, July 1946, p. 81.

27. Daniel Bell, "Ideology and the Beau Geste," *Dissent*, Winter 1961, p. 75. Bell incorporated this essay into his revision of *The End of Ideology*, in 1965.

28. "Talk with Lionel Trilling," *New York Times Book Review*, Feb. 13, 1955, p. 21.

29. Ibid.; Sidney Hook, quoted in "Parnassus: Coast to Coast," *Time*, June 11, 1956, p. 66.

30. Bell, *End of Ideology*, 393. Bell has continued to attempt to explain what he meant. In 1979 he told a writer for *Change* magazine, "Alienation—if you think of it as a form of distancing yourself—can be a very positive thing, because you don't go overboard in terms of total commitment. The virtue of total commitment can be overexaggerated if it leads to the view, 'I know the truth, you are in error, therefore I've got a right to exterminate you.'" (Quoted in Ron Chernow, "The Cultural Contradictions of Daniel Bell," *Change*, Mar. 1979, p. 13.)

31. Bell, *End of Ideology*, 402–3.

32. Daniel Bell, "Sociodicy: A Guide to Modern Usage," *American Scholar*, Autumn 1966, p. 712.

33. Bell, "Ideology and the Beau Geste," 75.

34. Harold Rosenberg, "Twilight of the Intellectuals," in *Discovering the Present: Three Decades in Art, Culture, and Politics* (Chicago, 1973), 167.

35. Lionel Trilling, The *Middle of the Journey* (New York, 1947), 32–33; Norman Podhoretz, *Making It* (New York, 1967), 316.

36. Schlesinger, *Vital Center*, xxii–xxiii; Irving Kristol, "Flying off the Broomstick," *Commentary*, Apr. 1951, p. 400.

37. Schlesinger, *Vital Center*, 1, xxiii.

38. Daniel Bell, interview, July 13, 1979.

39. Reinhold Niebuhr, *The Children of Light and the Children of Darkness* (New York, 1944), x.

40. Ibid., 29, 41.

41. Reinhold Nebuhr, "Two Forms of Utopianism," *Christianity and Society*, Autumn 1947, p. 6.

42. Schlesinger, "Perspective Now," 235.

43. Reinhold Niebuhr, *The Irony of American History* (London, 1952), 16.

44. Daniel Bell, interview, July 13, 1979.

45. Podhoretz, *Making It*, 126

46. Trilling, *Liberal Imagination*, ix, x.

47. Ibid., xii–xiii, xiv.

48. Ibid., 56–57, 263.

49. Lionel Trilling, "The Progressive Psyche," *Nation*, Sept. 12, 1942, p. 216; idem, *Freud and the Crisis of Culture* (Boston, 1955), 22; idem, *Liberal Imagination*, 34.

50. Trilling, *Liberal Imagination*, 53.

51. Ibid., 42.

52. Ibid., xiv–xv.

53. Ibid., 3–8.

54. Ibid., 10.

55. Ibid., 10–13, 20–21.

56. Vernon L. Parrington, *The Beginning of Critical Realism in America, 1860–1920* (New York, 1930), 241.

57. Trilling, *Liberal Imagination*, 11.

58. Ibid., 292–93.

59. Ibid., 9, 266.

60. Ibid., 267–68, 275.

61. Ibid., 302. Trilling's "active" writers included Yeats, Eliot, Pound, Joyce, Lawrence, and Gide. The American writers whose styles troubled him were John Dos Passos, Eugene O'Neill, and Thomas Wolfe.

62. Trilling, *Liberal Imagination*, 303.

63. Trilling, *Freud and the Crisis of Culture*, 33. See above, pp. 89–90, Rahv's views on Dostoevsky's subversive qualities as exemplified in *The Possessed*.

64. "Our Country and Our Culture: A Symposium," 282–84.

65. William Barrett, "The Truants: *Partisan Review* in the 40's," *Commentary*, June 1974, pp. 53–54.

66. Sidney Hook, in "Our Country and Our Culture," 569–70; Diana Trilling, "America through Dark Spectacles," *Twentieth Century*, July 1953, pp. 39–40.

67. Bell, "The Mood of Three Generations," in *End of Ideology*, 311 (parts of the essay appeared in 1955, 1957, and 1959).

68. The movement of these intellectuals to the university is more fully discussed below, pp. 311–12.

69. Nathan Glazer, "Revolutionism and the Jews: The Role of the Intellectuals," *Commentary*, Feb. 1971, p. 55; Bell, *End of Ideology*, 314.

70. Bell, *End of Ideology*, 313–14 (originally published in *Encounter* in 1959); Lionel Trilling, in "Our Country and Our Culture," 320.

71. Harold Rosenberg, "The Intellectuals and the American Idea," *Commentary*, May 1951, p. 508.

72. Philip Rahv, in "Our Country and Our Culture," 306.

73. Ibid., 304–5.

74. William Phillips, "The Intellectual's Tradition" (1941), in *Partisan Reader*, ed. Phillips and Philip Rahv (New York, 1946), 486. See above, Chapter 5, for Phillips's view in the 1930s.

75. Irving Kristol, "The Troublesome Intellectuals," *Public Interest*, Winter 1966, p. 6; Daniel Bell, "The Writer as Independent Spirit: As Public Figure," *Saturday Review of Literature*, June 4, 1966, p. 18; Lionel Trilling, quoted in Marcus Cunliffe, "The Intellectuals—2: The United States," *Encounter*, May 1955, p. 24.

76. Philip Rahv, "Twilight of the Thirties," *Partisan Review*, Summer 1939, p. 8.

77. Lionel Trilling in "Our Country and Our Culture," 321; Trilling, quoted in David Daiches, "The Mind of Lionel Trilling," *Commentary*, July 1957, p. 66.

78. William Phillips, "The Wholeness of Literature," *American Mercury*, Nov. 1952, pp. 103–4.

79. Schlesinger, "Perspective Now," 236–37; Diana Trilling, "A Memorandum on the Hiss Case," *Partisan Review*, May–June 1950, p. 489.

80. Diana Trilling, "A Communist and His Ideals," *Partisan Review*, July 1951, pp. 437–38.

81. Ibid., 439.

82. Bell, *End of Ideology* (1961 ed.), 396. This section was deleted in the 1965 revision.

83. Diana Trilling, "A Communist and His Ideals," 440.

84. Sidney Hook, in "Our Country and Our Culture," 573.

85. Diana Trilling, "The Other Night at Columbia: A Report from the Academy" (1958), in *Claremont Essays* (New York, 1964), 172, 163–64.

86. Diana Trilling, "The Oppenheimer Case: A Reading of the Testimony" (1954), in *Claremont Essays*, 123.

87. Lionel Trilling, in "Our Country and Our Culture," 320.

88. Trilling and Barzun were closely associated at Columbia, teaching a famous course together. The other intellectuals pictured in the *Time* article were George Kennan, the French Dominican Raymond-Leopold Brickberger, the physicist George Gamow, Paul Tillich, Thornton Wilder, the jurist Arthur T. Vanderbilt, Walter Lippmann, the economist Sumner Slichter, Frank Lloyd Wright, and Russell Kirk. Among those quoted in the article were Daniel Boorstin, David Riesman, J. A. Brogan, Edmund Wilson, Newton Arvin, Crane Brinton, and Mortimer Adler.

89. "Parnassus: Coast to Coast," 65.

Chapter 11 Liberal Anticommunism

1. See David Caute, *The Great Fear: The Anti-Communist Purge under Truman and Eisenhower* (New York, 1978), 43.

2. Diana Trilling, "The Oppenheimer Case: A Reading of the Testimony" (1954), in *Claremont Essays* (New York, 1964), 124–25.

3. William Phillips, "The Politics of Desperation," *Partisan Review*, Apr., 1948, pp. 450, 452.

4. Douglas, quoted in R. H. S. Crossman, "The Plight of U.S. Liberalism," *New Statesman and Nation*, Oct. 16, 1954, p. 461.

5. Phillips to Koestler, quoted in James B. Gilbert, *Writers and Partisans: A History of Literary Radicalism in America* (New York, 1968), 261; "The Liberal Fifth Column: An Editorial," *Partisan Review*, Summer 1946, p. 292.

6. Irving Kristol, "Civil Liberties: 1952—A Study in Confusion," *Commentary*, Mar. 1952, p. 234.

7. Irving Kristol, "Liberty and the Communists," *Partisan Review*, July–Aug. 1952, p. 495; Elliot E. Cohen, "The Free American Citizen, 1952," *Commentary*, Sept. 1952, p. 229; Nathan Glazer, "The Method of Senator McCarthy," ibid., Mar. 1953, p. 266.

8. Diana Trilling, "From an Autumn Journal," *Partisan Review*, Jan.–Feb. 1953, p. 26.

9. Ibid.; Sidney Hook, *New York Times*, May 8, 1953; idem, "Rigors of Heresy," *Saturday Review*, Apr. 24, 1954, p. 17.

10. Robert Warshow, "Father and Son—And the FBI," in *The Immediate Experience* (New York, 1974), 167, 171 (originally published in *American Mercury* in 1952).

11. Irving Kristol, "On 'Negative Liberalism,'" *Encounter*, Jan. 1954, p. 2.

12. Diana Trilling, "A Memorandum on the Hiss Case," *Partisan Review*, May–June 1950, p. 500.

13. Sidney Hook, *New York Times*, May 8, 1953, 24; idem, in "Our Country and Our Culture: III," *Partisan Review*, Sept.–Oct. 1952, p. 574.

14. William Phillips, "Changing Fathers in Midstream," *American Mercury*, Jan. 1953, p. 104.

15. Melvin J. Lasky, "Why the Kremlin Extorts Confessions," *Commentary*, Jan. 1952, p. 5.

16. Sidney Hook, *Heresy, Yes—Conspiracy, No* (New York, 1953), 26; "The Liberal Fifth Column," 285; Diana Trilling, "America through Dark Spectacles," *Twentieth Century*, July 1953, p. 38.

17. Kristol, "Civil Liberties: 1952," 230.

18. Sidney Hook, "Does the Smith Act Threaten Our Liberties?" *Commentary*, Jan. 1953, p. 68.

19. Sidney Hook, "On the Battlefront of Philosophy," *Partisan Review*, Mar. 1949, p. 252.

20. "The Liberal Fifth Column," 286–88.

21. Arthur Schlesinger, Jr., *The Vital Center: The Politics of Freedom* (Boston, 1962 [1949]), 144.

22. Trilling, "Memorandum on the Hiss Case," 497.

23. In France, Hannah Arendt worked for Youth Aliyah, a relief agency that placed Jewish orphans in Palestine. In the United States she was employed by the American Conference on Jewish Relations from 1944 to 1946, served as chief editor of Schocken Books from 1946 to 1948, and was executive secretary of Jewish Cultural Reconstruction, Inc., from 1949 to 1952.

24. Alfred Kazin, interview, Oct. 23, 1976. Kazin is the only New York Intellectual thanked by name in *The Origins of Totalitarianism*.

25. The publication of Arendt's *Eichmann in Jerusalem* elicited enormous controversy and a reevaluation of the basis of her thesis. This is discussed below, Chapter 13.

26. Hannah Arendt, *The Origins of Totalitarianism* (New York, 1951), 301–2, 355, 394, 429, 367.

27. Melvin J. Lasky, "The Red and the Brown," *Twentieth Century*, Mar. 1951, pp. 199, 200.

28. The general theme of the equation of fascism and communism has been dealt with by a number of scholars. The most succinct review of this is Les K. Adler and Thomas G. Patterson, "Red Fascism: The Merger of Nazi Germany and Soviet Russia in the American Image of Totalitarianism, 1930s–1950s," *American Historical Review*, 75 (Apr. 1970), 1046–64.

29. Irving Howe, "The Choice of 'Comrades,'" *Dissent*, Summer 1957, pp. 333–35.

30. Sidney Hook, "Introduction: Communism's Postwar Decade," *New Leader*, Dec. 19, 1955, pp. 52–54.

31. Nathan Glazer, *The Social Basis of American Communism* (New York, 1961), 4.

32. Kristol, "Civil Liberties: 1952," 235.

33. Ibid., 235–36.

34. Daniel Bell, *Marxian Socialism in the United States* (Princeton, 1967 [1952]), 186.

35. Sidney Hook, "Communism and the Intellectuals," *American Mercury*, Feb. 1949, p. 136.

36. Robert Warshow, "The 'Idealism' of Julius and Ethel Rosenberg," *Commentary*, Nov. 1953, p. 47.

37. Harold Rosenberg, "The Communist," *Commentary*, July 1949, pp. 3–4.

38. Irving Howe, "Freedom and the Ashcan of History," *Partisan Review*, Spring 1959, p. 266.

39. Schlesinger, *Vital Center*, 104.

40. Hook, *Heresy, Yes*, 21–22.

41. Kristol, "Liberty and the Communists," 494.

42. Sidney Hook, "One Hit, One Miss," *Twentieth Century*, July 1952, p. 46.

43. Kristol, "Liberty and the Communists," 496; Warshow, "Father and Son," 170; Bell, *Marxian Socialism*, 186.

44. Hook, *Heresy, Yes*, 27.

45. Hook, "Does the Smith Act Threaten Our Liberties?" 68.

46. Hook, *Heresy Yes*, 19–21.

47. Hook, "Does the Smith Act Threaten Our Liberties?" 68.

48. Vinson, quoted in Caute, *Great Fear*, 194. For a general discussion of *Dennis* v. *U.S.*, see 187–97.

49. Schlesinger, *Vital Center*, 201.

50. Kristol, "Liberty and the Communists," 496.

51. Sidney Hook, "Uncommon Sense about Security and Freedom," *New Leader*, June 21, 1954, p. 9.

52. William Barrett, "Cultural Conference at the Waldorf," *Commentary*, May 1949, p. 487.

53. William Phillips, in "Our Country and Our Culture," 589.

54. D. Trilling, "Memorandum on the Hiss Case," 486–87.

55. Daniel Bell, "'Hard' and 'Soft' Anti-Communism," *New Leader*, May 17, 1954, p. 24.

56. Hook, "Communism and the Intellectuals," 136.

57. D. Trilling, "Memorandum on the Hiss Case," 486; Alfred Kazin "Old Revolutionists," *Partisan Review*, Winter 1958, p. 138

58. D. Trilling, "Memorandum on the Hiss Case," 486.
59. Sidney Hook, "From Alienation to Critical Integrity: The Vocation of the American Intellectuals," in *The Intellectuals*, ed. George B. de Huszar (Glencoe, Ill., 1960), 532 (orignally published in *Partisan Review*, in 1952).
60. Sidney Hook, "Academic Integrity and Academic Freedom," *Commentary*, Oct. 1949, p. 330.
61. Ibid., 329, 330.
62. Irving Kristol, "Ordeal by Mendacity," *Twentieth Century*, Oct. 1952, p. 321.
63. Sidney Hook, "The Fellow-Traveler: A Study in Psychology," *New York Times Magazine*, Apr. 17, 1949, p. 9.
64. Ibid., 20.
65. Hook, "Academic Integrity and Academic Freedom," 331.
66. Schlesinger, *Vital Center*, 36–40.
67. Irving Howe, "The Sentimental Fellow-Traveling of F. O. Matthiessen," *Partisan Review*, Oct. 1948, 1126–27; D. Trilling, "Oppenheimer Case," 126–27.
68. Hook, "Fellow-Traveler," 9.
69. "*The Nation* Censors," *New Leader*, Mar. 12, 1952, pp. 16–18.
70. Richard Rovere, "How Free Is *The Nation?*" *New Leader*, July 14, 1952, pp. 12–14.
71. *Nation*, Sept. 24, 1955.
72. "Liberalism, Libel, and André Gide," *Partisan Review*, May–June 1951, p. 368. Schlesinger wrote, "As an occasional contributor to the *Nation*, I would like to associate myself with the sentiments expressed by Clement Greenberg." Niebuhr's resignation letter stated he was "sick of del Vayo's animadversions on foreign affairs." (Schlesinger and Niebuhr, quoted in Mary Sperling McAuliffe, *Crisis on the Left: Cold War Politics and American Liberals, 1947–1954* [Amherst, Mass., 1978], 114.)
73. Among the books by anti-anti-Communists were Henry Steele Commager, *Freedom, Loyalty, Dissent* (New York, 1954); Alan Barth, *Government by Investigation* (New York, 1955); idem, *Loyalty of Free Men*, with an introd. by Zechariah Chafee, Jr. (New York, 1951); William O. Douglas, *An Almanac of Liberty* (Garden City, N.Y., 1954).
74. Kristol, "Civil Liberties: 1952," 228.
75. Warshow, "Father and Son," 163.
76. Kristol, "Civil Liberties: 1952," 228. Kristol's article became notorious immediately on publication and has remained provocative ever since. The letters to *Commentary* came both from supporters and from critics. Among the published letters supporting Kristol were those from Ludwig Lewisohn, the author and then chairman of the Brandeis English department, Jay Lovestone, Arnold Beichman, Richard Chase, and Ernest Angell, chairman of the board of directors of the American Civil Liberties Union. Angell wrote as an individual, not for the ACLU. Norman Thomas and the lawyer Arthur Garfield Hays wrote letters expressing agreement as well as disagreement. Letters of opposition came from Joseph L. Rauh, Jr., the lawyer, and Robert M. MacIver, the sociologist. (*Commentary*, May 1952, pp. 491–500.) Arthur Schlesinger, Jr., wrote a few months later, calling the Kristol article "feeble." (Ibid., July 1952, p. 83.)

Kristol recalled, "I really was rather bored with politics" at the time. He first wrote a review of a book by Carey McWilliams, "and then when the Commager article appeared I just got irritated and wrote the article." (Kristol, interview, June 17, 1976.)

Daniel Bell tried to soften the article initially. "I said to Irving, 'Be a little more ironic, you know, balance it.' Well, he's paid for it, time and time again." (Bell, interview, July 13, 1979.)

77. Hook, *Heresy, Yes*, 11–12.
78. Kristol, "Civil Liberties: 1952," 233.
79. Commager was professor of history at Columbia from 1938 to 1956.
80. Kristol, "Civil Liberties: 1952," 230.
81. Sidney Hook, "Unpragmatic Liberalism," *New Republic*, May 14, 1954, p. 20.
82. Lionel Trilling, introd., *Middle of the Journey* (New York, 1975), xx.
83. Kristol, "Civil Liberties: 1952," 229.
84. Ibid., 236.
85. Hook, "Communism and the Intellectuals," 19.
86. Kristol, "Civil Liberties: 1952," 235–36.
87. Sidney Hook, "What Is Guilt by Association?" *American Mercury*, Nov. 1952, pp. 37–38.
88. Kristol, "Liberty and Communists," 493.
89. Sidney Hook, *Common Sense and the Fifth Amendment* (New York, 1957), 12, 143.
90. Kristol, "Civil Liberties: 1952," 234–35.
91. Kristol, "Liberty and the Communists," 495.
92. Irving Kristol, "Mr. Kristol Comments," *Commentary*, May 1952, p. 500. In 1958, in *Kent* v. *Dulles*, the Supreme Court ruled that the right to travel could not be abridged without due process and that the secretary of state did not have the authority to withhold passports.
93. Hook, "Does the Smith Act Threaten Our Liberties?" 73.
94. Sidney Hook, "The Ethics of Controversy," *New Leader*, Feb. 1, 1954, p. 14.
95. Hook, "Ethics of Controversy," 14; Hook, *Heresy, Yes*, 19–21.
96. Nathan Glazer, letter to the *New York Times*, Jan. 17, 1953, p. 14; Kristol, "Mr. Kristol Comments," 500.
97. Norman Podhoretz, *Making It* (New York, 1967), 294.
98. Kristol, "Liberty and the Communists," 493.
99. Quoted in Caute, *Great Fear*, 424. For a broad discussion of campus anti-Communist activities, see ibid., 403–30. On the dispute between McGeorge Bundy and Sigmund Diamond, see *New York Review of Books*, Apr. 28, May 26, June 9, and July 16, 1977.
100. Sidney Hook, "Should Communists Be Permitted to Teach?" *New York Times Magazine*, Feb. 27, 1949, p. 26.
101. Hook, "Academic Integrity and Academic Freedom," 334. Irving Howe distinguished his position from Hook's, claiming that "the discipline imposed by the CP might seem uniform on paper but was not so in fact" and "that judgments about professors should be made individually, case by case." (*A Margin of Hope* [San Diego, 1982], 212.)
102. Hook, "Academic Integrity and Academic Freedom," 330.
103. Philip Rahv, in "Our Country and Our Culture," 308ff.
104. Hook, "Academic Integrity and Academic Freedom," 334.
105. Kristol, "Mr. Kristol Comments," 499.

106. Joseph McCarthy, quoted in Caute, *Great Fear*, 413. The case involved the Harvard physicist Wendell Furry, who first took the Fifth before McCarthy's committee. At his second appearance, Furry abandoned this defense to "avoid undue harm to me and the great institution with which I am connected."

107. Kristol, "Mr. Kristol Comments," 499; Hook, "Academic Integrity and Academic Freedom," 334.

108. Hook, "Academic Integrity and Academic Freedom," 330, 334–37, 339.

109. *New York Times*, Nov. 18, 1953, p. 28.

110. Lionel Trilling, letter to the *New York Times*, Nov. 26, 1983, p. 30.

111. A number of other American colleges and universities dismissed faculty members who claimed Fifth Amendment protections, including Rutgers, New York University, Ohio State, the University of Kansas City, Temple, Michigan, and Fisk. For a full discussion, see Caute, *Great Fear*, 414–18.

112. Lionel Trilling, letter to the *New York Times*, Nov. 26, 1953, p. 30.

113. In 1976 Philip Nobile polled a variety of intellectuals about Hiss's guilt. Those who still believed Hiss guilty included William F. Buckley, Jr., Sidney Hook, Clare Boothe Luce, Dwight Macdonald, and Norman Podhoretz. Among those who felt Hiss was innocent were Alexander Cockburn, Abe Fortas, Gus Hall, Lillian Hellman, Carey McWilliams, Arthur Miller, and Robert Sherrill. Those "undecided" in Nobile's survey included James MacGregor Burns, Norman Cousins, Anthony Lewis, Norman Mailer, David Riesman, and C. Vann Woodward. (Philip Nobile, "The State of the Art of Alger Hiss," *Harper's*, Apr. 1976, pp. 67–76.)

For the Alger Hiss case, see Whittaker Chambers, *Witness* (New York, 1952); Fred J. Cook, *The Unfinished Story of Alger Hiss* (New York, 1958); Alistair Cooke, *A Generation on Trial: USA v. Alger Hiss* (New York, 1950); Alger Hiss, *In the Court of Public Opinioin* (New York, 1957); Edith Tiger, *In Re Alger Hiss: Petition for a Writ of Error Coram Nobis* (New York, 1979–80); Allen Weinstein, *Perjury: The Hiss-Chambers Case* (New York, 1978).

On the Rosenbergs, see Alvin Goldstein, *The Unquiet Death of Julius and Ethel Rosenberg* (New York, 1975); Robert Meeropol and Michael Meeropol, *We Are Your Sons* (Boston, 1975); Walter Schneir and Meriam Schneir, *Invitation to an Inquest* (Garden City, N.Y., 1965); Ronald Radosh and Joyce Milton, *The Rosenberg File: A Search for the Truth* (New York, 1983).

114. Morton Sobell was sentenced to thirty years in prison, David Greenglass to fifteen, and Harry Gold to thirty.

115. Nathan Glazer, letter to the New York Times, Jan. 17, 1953, 14; Daniel Bell, "The Rosenberg Case," *New Statesman and Nation*, Jan. 31, 1953, pp. 120–21.

116. D. Trilling, "Memorandum on the Hiss Case," 484; Sidney Hook, "The Faiths of Whittaker Chambers," *New York Times Book Review*, May 25, 1952, p. 1; Kristol, "Ordeal by Mendacity," 321; William Phillips, "In and Out of the Underground," *American Mercury*, June 1952, p. 92.

117. Warshow, "The 'Idealism' of Julius and Ethel Rosenberg," 415.

118. Leslie A. Fiedler, "Hiss, Chambers, and the Age of Innocence," in *An End to Innocence* (Boston, 1952), 6 (originally published in *Commentary* in 1950); Philip Rahv, "The Sense and Nonsense of Whittaker Chambers," *Partisan Review*, July–Aug. 1952, p. 478.

119. Harry Dexter White had been assistant secretary of the Treasury under Henry

Morgenthau, Jr., during the Roosevelt administration, with responsibilities for foreign relations and connections with the armed forces. In 1946, Truman nominated him to head the International Monetary Fund. Accused by Chambers and Elizabeth Bentley, White appeared voluntarily before the House Un-American Activities Committee, where he denied having Communist ties. He died of a heart attack three days after his appearance.

120. Rahv, "Sense and Nonsense of Whittaker Chambers," 477; Phillips, "In and Out of the Underground," 92–93.

121. Sidney Hook, "The Faiths of Whittaker Chambers," 1.

122. Bell, "Rosenberg Case," 121.

123. Leslie Fiedler, "The Rosenbergs: A Dialogue" (1952), in *Collected Essays of Leslie Fiedler*, vol. 2 (New York, 1971), 201–2. Irving Kristol took an odd position on the "decline" of the spy profession. "Instead of the glamorous and gay Mata Hari we have the grim *tricoteuse* Ethel Rosenberg. The profession has become overcrowded, and standards have deteriorated. Above all, the business has become too serious." (Kristol, "Web of Realism," *Commentary*, June 1954, p. 609.)

124. *New York Times*, June 10, 1949, p. 8.

125. Sidney Hook, "The Strange Case of Whittaker Chambers," *Encounter*, Jan. 1976, pp. 80–81; Lionel Trilling, introd., *Middle of the Journey*, vii.

126. D. Trilling, "Memorandum on the Hiss Case," 496.

127. Ibid., 493.

128. Fiedler, "Hiss, Chambers, and the Age of Innocence," 13.

129. Phillips, "In and Out of the Underground," 96.

130. Fiedler, "Hiss, Chambers, and the Age of Innocence," 14.

131. D. Trilling, "Memorandum on the Hiss Case," 493; Phillips, "In and Out of the Underground," 96.

132. Robert Warshow, "The Liberal Conscience in 'The Crucible,'" *Commentary*, Mar. 1953, p. 271.

133. Fiedler, "Hiss, Chambers, and the Age of Innocence." 14.

134. Fiedler, "Rosenbergs: A Dialogue," 202, 204.

135. D. Trilling, "Memorandum on the Hiss Case," 499; Fiedler, "Hiss, Chambers, and the Age of Innocence," 4.

136. D. Trilling, "Oppenheimer Case," 141–42. Some critics did not agree with Trilling's assessment. Answering her in *PR*, the philosopher Hans Meyerhoff reiterated the anti-anti-Communist position, finding that Trilling placed guilt on the wrong party. The transfer, Meyerhoff claimed, of "the political and moral responsibility for this case from the present enemies of freedom to the collective unconscious of the liberal movement" was another example of an inappropriate invocation of psychological theorizing. "Surely there is something wrong with this species of liberal conscience and imagination." (Hans Meyerhoff, "Through the Liberal Looking Glass—Darkly," *Partisan Review*, Spring 1955, p. 247.)

137. Harold Rosenberg, "Couch Liberalism and the Guilty Past," *Dissent*, Spring 1955, p. 319.

138. William Phillips, "Sleep No More," *Partisan Review*, Mar. 1949, p. 250.

139. Macdonald, interview, Dec. 3, 1976; Hook, interview, Jan. 4, 1978. For the LCFS, see above, pp. 88–89, 110, and 126.

140. *New York Times*, Mar. 25, 1949; Tom O'Connor, "News Tailored to Fit," *Nation*, Apr. 16, 1949, p. 439; Arnold Beichman, interview, May 25, 1976. See also Dwight Macdonald, "The Waldorf Conference," *Politics*, Winter 1949, 32B.

141. *New York Times*, Mar. 25, 1949. Among the other sponsors were Newton Arvin, Daniel Aaron, Robert Bendiner, Lewis Corey, Bernard De Voto, Paul Douglas, Max Eastman, James T. Farrell, Horace Kallen, Hans Kohn, Merle Miller, Perry Miller, Reinhold Niebuhr, Lewis Mumford, A. Phillip Randolph, Ralph DeToledano, Edmund Wilson, and Bertram Wolfe.

142. Macdonald, "Waldorf Conference," 32A–32D; Beichman, interview, May 25, 1976.

143. *Time*, Oct. 20, 1947, p. 31; ibid., Sept. 20, 1954, pp. 48–52. Lasky's attitude toward the roots of the European problem can be seen in his "Berlin Letter" in *PR* in 1948: "The die, I am afraid, was cast when Eisenhower made his rather ignorant decision that the taking of Berlin would be 'a mere show' and allowed the Soviets to enter the capital and to reach the Elbe. Moscow's machine for the occupation dug in." (*Partisan Review*, Apr. 1948, p. 488.)

144. Among the announced titles of sessions were "Challenge of Cultural Freedom," "Science and Totalitarianism," "Art, Artists, and Freedom," "Citizen in a Free Society," "Defense of Peace and Freedom," and "Free Culture in a Free State."

145. *Time*, May 1, 1950.

146. *New York Times*, June 17, 1950. Irving Brown was the AFL's chief international officer in Europe. For a further discussion of American labor's postwar international policy, see Peter Weiler, "The United States, International Labor, and the Cold War: The Breakup of the World Federation of Trade Unions," *Diplomatic History*, 5 (Winter 1981), 1–22.

147. See Christopher Lasch, "The Cultural Cold War: A Short History of the Congress for Cultural Freedom," in *Towards a New Past*, ed. Barton Bernstein (New York, 1968), 324–25. Koestler argued, "The words 'socialist' and 'capitalist,' 'Left' and 'Right' have today become virtually empty of meaning." Hook looked forward "to an era when references to 'right,' 'left,' and 'center' will vanish from common usage as meaningless." Robert Montgomery stated, "No artist who has the right to bear that title can be neutral in the battles of our time. . . . Today we must stand up and be counted."

148. Sidney Hook, "The Berlin Congress for Cultural Freedom," *Partisan Review*, Sept.–Oct. 1950, p. 722.

149. Lasch, "Cultural Cold War," 328.

150. *New York Times*, Nov. 28, 1950.

151. Hook, "Berlin Congress for Cultural Freedom," 715.

152. *New York Times*, Nov. 28, 1950.

153. Lasch, "Cultural Cold War," 332–33.

154. Merlyn Pitzele, an economist, was labor editor of *Business Week* from 1940 to 1955, as well as the labor adviser to Thomas Dewey in 1944 and 1948, and to Eisenhower in 1952.

155. Diana Trilling, "Liberal Anti-Communism Revisited," *We Must March My Darlings* (New York, 1977), 60.

156. D. Trilling, "Liberal Anti-Communism Revisited," 61. See Arnold Beichman.

"Disputed History," *Society*, Sept.–Oct., 1984, p. 5, for his explanation of the CCF-ACCF division.

157. *New York Times*, May 18, 1951. Diana Trilling's talk entitled "A Communist and His Ideas," was later published in *Partisan Review*.

158. Other speakers included George Counts, Elmer Rice, Richard Rovere, Conway Zirkle, F. S. C. Northrup, Arthur Koestler, and Bertram Wolfe.

159. Bell, interview, July 13, 1979.

160. Other CCF journals included *Forum* (Austria), *Cuadernos and Examen* (Latin America), *China Quarterly*, and *Survey: A Journal of Sopviet and East European Affairs*.

161. Kristol, interview, June 17, 1976.

162. Other contributors to the first issue included Tom Scott, Dazai Osamu, Alberto de Lacerda, Edith Sitwell, Mark Alexander, Hugh Seton-Watson, and John Kenneth Galbraith.

163. "After the Apocalypse" (editorial), *Encounter*, Oct. 1953. p. 1. Stephen Spender discussed Kristol's authorship of the editorial in *The Thirties and After* (New York, 1978), 127.

164. Spender, *Thirties and After*, 127–28.

165. Ibid.

166. Kristol, interview, June 17, 1976.

167. Sidney Hook, interview, Jan. 4, 1978.

168. Thomas Braden, "Speaking Out," *Saturday Evening Post*, May 20, 1967, p. 10.

169. Peter Steinfels, *The Neoconservatives* (New York, 1979), 84–87; Irving Kristol, "Memoirs of a 'Cold Warrior.'" *New York Times Magazine*, Feb. 11, 1968, p. 25.

170. Spender, *Thirties and After*, 128; Kristol, interview, June 17, 1976.

171. Beichman, interview, May 25, 1976; D. Trilling, interview, Oct. 3, 1979.

172. Hook, quoted in McAuliffe, *Crisis on the Left*, 116.

173. Ibid., 89–107. Among the ECLC founders were the *Nation* editor Carey McWilliams; the left journalist I. F. Stone; Paul Lehmann, chairman and professor at Princeton Theological Seminary; Henry Pratt Fairchild, professor emeritus of sociology at NYU; E. Franklin Frazier, chairman of the sociology department at Howard University; Thomas Emerson, professor at Yale Law School; and Harold Wilson, professor of politics at Princeton. (Ibid., 173 n. 66.)

174. *New York Times*, Jan. 20, 1953.

175. *New York Times*, Jan. 20, 21, 1953; McAuliffe, *Crisis on the Left*, 118.

176. *New York Times*, June 12, 13, 1953.

177. Oppenheimer, quoted in McAuliffe, *Crisis on the Left*, 119.

178. ACCF statement, quoted ibid., 120.

179. See John P. Diggins, *Up from Communism: Conservative Odysseys in American Intellectual History* (New York, 1975), 215–22, 317–28, 329. The book for which Burnham wrote the preface was Medford Evans's *The Secret Fight for the A-Bomb*.

180. McAuliffe, *Crisis on the Left*, 125, 126–27; Schlesinger to Farrell, quoted in Diggins, *Up from Communism*, 330.

181. Michael Harrington, "The Committee for Cultural Freedom," *Dissent*, Spring 1955, p. 115.

182. Ibid., 117; *New York Times*, Apr. 18, 1954.

183. *New York Times*, Jan. 5, 1953.
184. Ibid., July 19, 1953.
185. James Rorty and Moshe Decter, *McCarthy and the Communists* (Westport, Conn., 1972 [1954]), 1, 13.
186. Ibid., 125.
187. Podhoretz, *Making It*, 136.

Chapter 12   Sensations of Wisdom, Stamina, and Poise

1. Lionel Trilling, *The Middle of the Journey* (New York, 1947), 139.
2. Lionel Trilling, "The Other Margaret," *Partisan Review*, Fall 1945, p. 488.
3. Daniel Bell, "The Mood of Three Generations" (1957), in *The End of Ideology: On the Exhaustion of Political Ideas in the Fifties* (New York, 1965 [1960]), 299–300; Lionel Trilling, "Young in the Thirties," *Commentary*, May 1966, pp. 43–51.
4. Trilling, *Middle of the Journey*, 33.
5. Irving Howe, "Mid-Century Turning Point: An Intellectual Memoir," *Midstream*, June–July 1975, p. 28.
6. Norman Podhoretz, *Making It* (New York, 1967), 122.
7. Lionel Trilling, introd. to Robert Warshow, *The Immediate Experience* (New York, 1962), 13, 15.
8. Leslie Fiedler, interview, May 14, 1976; Daniel Bell, interview, July 13, 1979.
9. Dwight Macdonald to F. W. Dupee, Nov. 11, no year, Dec. 21, no year, F. W. Dupee Papers.
10. Alfred Kazin, *New York Jew* (New York, 1978), 236; Alfred Kazin, interview, Oct. 23, 1976. In a letter to F. W. Dupee, Philip Rahv noted the cluster of intellectuals at Martha's Vineyard. "Saul B., Styron, L. Hellman, [Robert] Brustein, host of others. . . . As an intellectual colony, it will soon rival Wellfleet," Rahv wrote. Rahv to F. W. Dupee, July 1964, F. W. Dupee Papers.
11. Podhoretz, *Making It*, 146–47.
12. "I was so sick and tired of the radical, political intellectual who always had a position," Kazin commented. "Nowadays I meet Lionel Abel on Fifth Avenue, and he opens up by explaining how proletarianized America is becoming. I have to laugh. Who the hell cares about the positions. Needless to say Abel has gone from left to right and seems much exercised about intellectuals who unlike himself have not gone from Sartre to Reagan." (Kazin, interview, Oct. 23, 1976, revised 1985.)
13. Alfred Kazin, "On Melville as Scripture," *Partisan Review*, Jan.–Feb. 1950, p. 69.
14. Irving Howe, in "Our Country and Our Culture: A Symposium: III," *Partisan Review*, Sept.–Oct. 1952, pp. 579–80.
15. Harold Rosenberg, "Twilight of the Intellectuals," *Dissent*, Summer 1958, p. 228.
16. Irving Howe, "This Age of Conformity," *Partisan Review*, Jan.–Feb. 1954, pp. 8, 10, 11, 13; Lionel Trilling, in "Our Country and Our Culture," 320.
17. Howe, "This Age of Conformity," 20, 25.
18. Howe's piece is the only one praised by Lillian Hellman in *Scoundrel Time* (New York, 1976), 86. See below, Chapter 14.
19. Robert Warshow, "Letter to *PR*," *Partisan Review*, Mar.–Apr. 1954, pp. 235–37.

20. See Harold Rosenberg, "A Discussion," *Commentary*, Jan. 1957, p. 84; Norman Mailer, in "Our Country and Our Culture," 299–300.

21. Howe, quoted in Andrew James Dvosin, "Literature in a Political World: The Career and Writings of Philip Rahv" (Ph.D. thesis, New York Univ., 1977), 126.

22. Diana Trilling, "America and 'The Quiet American,' " *Commentary*, July 1956, p. 67.

23. William Barrett, "Portrait of the Radical as an Aging Man," *Commentary*, May 1979, 42–43.

24. Philip Rahv, in "Our Country and Our Culture," 307.

25. Meyer Schapiro, interview, Oct. 30, 1978.

26. Howe, "This Age of Conformity," 19; Irving Howe, "Does It Hurt When You Laugh?" *Dissent*, Winter 1954, p. 5; idem, "Some Critics of *Dissent*," Ibid., Fall 1956, p. 437.

27. Bell, interview, July 13, 1979.

28. Howe, interview, June 16, 1976.

29. Irving Howe, "The New York Intellectuals: A Chronicle and a Critique," *Commentary*, Oct. 1968, p. 38.

30. Howe, interview, June 16, 1978; Schapiro, interview, Oct. 30, 1978.

31. Ibid. In *Margin of Hope* (San Diego, 1982), 235, Irving Howe tells of raising "a bit more than a thousand dollars" to start *Dissent* and then "another thousand" from Joseph and Muriel Buttinger. The other members of the editorial board were Travers Clement, Lewis Coser, Harold Orlans, and Stanley Plastrik.

32. Schapiro, long associated with *Dissent*, was not represented. Among those who were included were Michael Harrington, Robert Heilbroner, Paul Goodman, Theodore Draper, Roy Medvedev, Octavio Paz, Ignazio Silone, and Michael Walzer.

33. "A Word to Our Readers," *Dissent*, Winter 1954, pp. 3–4.

34. Howe, quoted in Dvosin, "Literature in a Political World," 114.

35. Fiedler, interview, May 14, 1976; Clement Greenberg, interview, June 22, 1979.

36. Irving Howe, "America the Country and the Myth," *Dissent*, Spring 1955, p. 241; idem, "Does It Hurt When You Laugh?" 6.

37. Howe, "This Age of Conformity," 18; idem, "Does It Hurt When You Laugh?" 5.

38. Howe, in "Our Country and Our Culture," 577; idem, "This Age of Conformity," 15.

39. Nathan Glazer, "Philistine Leftism," *Commentary*, Feb. 1954, pp. 202–5.

40. Bell, *End of Ideology*, 311.

41. Norman Podhoretz, "The New Nihilism and the Novel," *Partisan Review*, Fall 1958, p. 579.

42. Dwight Macdonald, interview, Dec. 3, 1976; Fiedler, interview May 14, 1976.

43. Irving Howe, "Notes on the Russian Turn," *Dissent*, Summer 1956, p. 309.

44. Midge Decter, interview, June 1, 1976.

45. *New York Times*, Oct. 22, 1976; Alfred Kazin, "Mr. Bellow's Planet," *New Republic*, Nov. 6, 1976, p. 7.

46. William Barrett, "The Truants: *Partisan Review* in the 40's," *Commentary*, June 1974, p. 51.

47. Bellow's first four stories appeared in *Partisan Review*: "Two Morning Monologues," May–June 1941, pp. 230–36; "The Mexican General," May–June 1942, pp. 178–94; "Spanish Letter," Feb. 1948, pp. 217–30; "Sermon by Doctor Pep," May 1949, pp. 455–62.

48. Philip Rahv to F. W. Dupee, Apr. 5, 1941, F. W. Dupee Papers.

49. Fiedler, interview, May 14, 1976.

50. Macdonald, interview, Dec. 3, 1976; Elizabeth Hardwick, "Fiction Chronicle," *Partisan Review*, Jan. 1948, p. 114; Delmore Schwartz, "Adventure in America," ibid., Jan.–Feb. 1954, pp. 112–15.

51. Podhoretz, *Making It*, 156.

52. Kazin, *New York Jew*, 40, 41.

53. Mark Shechner, "Jewish Writers," in *Harvard Guide to Contemporary American Writing*, ed. Daniel Hoffman (Cambridge, Mass., 1979), 221. Shechner sorts Bellow's books into the "depressive"—*Dangling Man*, 1944; *The Victim*, 1947; *Seize the Day*, 1956; and *Mr. Sammler's Planet*, 1970—and the "expansive"—*The Adventures of Augie March*, 1953; the play *The Last Analysis*, 1964; *Herzog*, 1964; and *Humboldt's Gift*, 1975. *Henderson the Rain King* (1959) is not included in this classification.

54. Leslie Fiedler, in *Saul Bellow and the Critics*, ed. Irving Malin (Carbondale, Ill., 1969), 1; Earl Rovit, *Saul Bellow* (Minneapolis, 1967), 5; John Jacob Clayton, *Saul Bellow: In Defense of Man* (Bloomington, Ind., 1968), 3.

55. Kazin, "Mr. Bellow's Planet," 7.

56. Shechner, "Jewish Writers," 219–20.

57. Podhoretz, *Making It*, 161, 165.

58. Norman Podhoretz, interview, June 3, 1976. Leslie Fiedler echoed Podhoretz's view. "*Partisan Review* becomes, for Europe and *Life* magazine, the mouthpiece of intellectual America, not despite but because of its tiny readership and its specially determined contributors; and in Saul Bellow a writer emerges capable of transforming its obsessions into myths." ("Saul Bellow," in *Collected Essays* [New York, 1971], 58.)

59. Bellow, quoted in *Writers at Work: The "Paris Review" Interviews*, 3d ser. (New York, 1966), 182–83.

60. Alfred Kazin, introd. (1968) to Saul Bellow, *Seize the Day* (New York, 1956), ix.

61. Ibid., ix; Fiedler, in *Saul Bellow and the Critics*, 7; idem, "Saul Bellow," 62.

62. Alfred Kazin, "The World of Saul Bellow," in *Contemporaries* (Boston, 1962), 218–19.

63. Shechner, "Jewish Writers," 193.

64. Kazin, interview, Oct. 23, 1976; Mark Shechner, "Isaac Rosenfeld's World," *Partisan Review*, Winter 1976, p. 524.

65. William Barrett, *The Truants* (New York, 1982), 112; idem, "Truants," 51.

66. Of the eleven stories Malamud published independently, before collecting them in *The Magic Barrel*, his first volume of stories, published in 1958, eight appeared in either *Partisan Review* or *Commentary*: "The First Seven Years," *Partisan Review*, Sept.–Oct. 1950, pp. 661–71; "The Prison," *Commentary*, Sept. 1950, pp. 252–55; "The Bill," ibid., Apr. 1951, pp. 355–58; "The Loan," ibid., July 1952, pp. 56–59; "The Magic Barrel," *Partisan Review*, Nov. 1954, pp. 587–603; "The Angel Levine," *Commentary*, Dec. 1955, pp. 534–40; "The Last Mohican,"

Partisan Review, Spring 1958, pp. 175–96; and "Behold the Key," *Commentary*, May 1958, pp. 416–27. The others were "Girl of My Dreams," *American Mercury*, Jan. 1953, pp. 62–71; "The Mourners," *Discovery*, Jan. 1955, pp. 37–95; and "A Summer's Reading," *New Yorker*, Sept. 22, 1956, pp. 149–50.

67. Philip Roth published a bit more widely in his early days, but, then, *Partisan Review* and *Commentary* were much more institutionalized by the late 1950s and the publishing possibilities for Jewish writers much wider. Still, two early Roth stories appeared in *Commentary* ("You Can't Tell a Man by the Song He Sings," Nov. 1957, pp. 445–50, and "Eli, the Fanatic," Apr. 1959, pp. 292–309). Roth's stories also appeared in *Paris Review* and in the *New Yorker*.

68. Clement Greenberg, "The State of American Writing—1948: Seven Questions," *Partisan Review*, Aug. 1948, p. 876.

69. Leslie Fiedler, "The Novel in the Post-Political World," *Partisan Review*, Summer 1956, pp. 358–59.

70. Greenberg, "State of American Writing," 876. Greenberg did feel that the avant-garde survived in painting "because painting has not yet reached the point of modernization where its discarding of inherited convention must stop lest it cease to be viable as art." ("American-Type Painting," *Partisan Review*, Spring 1955, p. 179.)

71. Harold Rosenberg, "The Sum of Many Colors," *Saturday Review*, June 6, 1953, p. 44.

72. William Phillips, *A Sense of the Present* (New York, 1967), 25.

73. William Phillips, "The American Establishment," *Partisan Review*, Winter 1959, pp. 107–8.

74. Howe, "New York Intellectuals," 39–40.

75. "Our Country and Our Culture," 285.

76. Robert Warshow, "Legacy of the 30's," *Commentary*, Dec. 1947, p. 539; Clement Greenberg, "Works and Leisure under Industrialism," ibid., July 1953, p. 55; Alfred Kazin, "Lady Chatterley in America," in *Contemporaries*, 106–7.

77. Harold Rosenberg, "Popular Culture and Kitsch Criticism," *Dissent*, Winter 1958, p. 16.

78. Irving Howe, "The Culture of Modernism," in *The Decline of the New* (New York, 1970), 8–9; Alfred Kazin, *Starting Out in the Thirties* (Boston, 1965), 157; Howe, "Culture of Modernism," 8.

79. Decter, interview, June 1, 1976; Norman Podhoretz, "The Know-Nothing Bohemians," *Partisan Review*, Spring 1958, p. 307.

80. Kazin, "Lady Chatterley," 167.

81. Fiedler, interview, May 14, 1976.

82. Diana Trilling, "The Other Night at Columbia: A Report from the Academy" (1958), in *Claremont Essays* (New York, 1964), 159–60.

83. Ibid., 165–66.

84. Ibid., 155.

85. Ibid., 158.

86. Ibid.

87. Ibid., 173.

88. Bell, interview, July 13, 1979.

89. Podhoretz, "Know-Nothing Bohemians," 313–15.

90. Ibid., 315–16.

91. Ibid., 318.

92. Lionel Trilling, *Beyond Culture* (New York, 1965), ix–xviii.

93. Seymour Martin Lipset, *Political Man: The Social Bases of Politics* (Garden City, N.Y., 1960), 43.

94. Richard Hofstadter, *The American Political Tradition and the Men Who Made It* (New York, 1948), vii–viii.

95. Among the numerous works cited as examples of consensus history, in addition to Hofstadter's, the following are frequently mentioned: Louis Hartz, *The Liberal Tradition in America: An Interpretation of American Political Thought* (New York, 1955); Daniel Boorstin, *The Americans: The Colonial Experience* (New York, 1958); idem, *The Genius of American Politics* (New York, 1953).

96. Richard Hofstadter, *The Progressive Historians* (New York, 1968), 444n.

97. Kazin, interview, Oct. 23, 1976; Kazin, *Starting Out in the Thirties*, 100. In this book Kazin gave Hofstadter and his wife pseudonyms—John and Harriet. He called them by their true names in *New York Jew*, 14–17.

98. Bell, interview, July 13, 1979.

99. Arthur M. Schlesinger, Jr., "Richard Hofstadter," in *Pastmasters*, ed. Marcus Cunliffe and Robin Winks (New York, 1969), 278, 279.

100. Daniel Bell, "The Antique Dream," *New Leader*, Dec. 5, 1955, p. 16.

101. Richard Hofstadter, *The Age of Reform: From Bryan to F.D.R.* (New York, 1955), 33, 81n.

102. Daniel Bell, preface to *The Radical Right*, ed. Daniel Bell (Garden City, N.Y., 1963), ix. The original book, published in 1955, was entitled *The New American Right*. The 1963 edition added new essays on Goldwater conservatism and the John Birch Society. Nathan Glazer coauthored, with David Riesman, a 1955 chapter, "The Intellectuals and the Discontented Classes."

103. Daniel Bell, "Interpretations of American Politics," in *Radical Right*, 61.

104. Ibid., 47.

105. Richard Hofstadter, "The Pseudo-Conservative Revolt," in *Radical Right*, 83. Later in the same essay, on p. 88, Hofstadter reinforced this point with regard to American immigrants. "In their search for new lives and new nationality these immigrants have suffered much, and they have been rebuffed and made to feel inferior by the 'native stock,' commonly being excluded from the better occupations and even what has bitterly been called 'first-class citizenship.' Insecurity over social status has thus been mixed with insecurity over one's very identity and sense of belonging. Achieving a better type of job or better social status and becoming 'more American' have become synonymous, and the passions that ordinarily attach to social positions have been vastly heightened by being associated with the need to belong."

106. Seymour Martin Lipset, "The Sources of the 'Radical Right,'" in *Radical Right*, 339–40. See Lipset, *Political Man*, 319.

107. Howe, "New York Intellectuals," 40; idem., "Mid-Century Turning Point," 25.

108. Fiedler, interview, May 14, 1976.

109. Bell, interview, July 13, 1976; Howe, "New York Intellectuals," 40; Podhoretz, *Making It*, 174.

110. Greenberg, interview, June 22, 1979.

111. Bell, interview, July 13, 1979; Decter, interview, June 1, 1976.

112. "When I came to Columbia," Daniel Bell recounted, "Jacques Barzun was the provost. After everything had gone through and I was already appointed with tenure, Jacques said, 'Does Dan have a Ph.D.?' Bob Merton said, 'Do you have a Ph.D.?' I said, 'No.' They said, 'Why?' I said, 'I never submitted a thesis.' Jacques said, 'If he's going to be giving graduate courses and examining other people, he ought to have a Ph.D.' There had been an interesting precedent. When Robert Lynd came to Columbia in '29–'30, he was brought in to do empirical work, and he didn't have a Ph.D. He'd already written *Middletown*. So, since a Ph.D. was supposed to be a designation of an achieved piece of work, the administration said they would give Lynd a Ph.D. for *Middletown*. *The End of Ideology* became my Ph.D. thesis. Glazer got his Ph.D. the same way, although there was a traditional examination." (Bell, interview, July 13, 1979.)

113. Howe, "Mid-Century Turning Point," 26–27.

114. Philip Rahv to Morton Zabel, Mar. 7, 1950; Philip Rahv to Allen Tate, Mar. 7, 1957, quoted in Dvosin, "Literature in a Political World," 133–34.

115. Alfred Kazin, "The Writer in the University," *Atlantic*, Oct. 1955, pp. 79, 81.

116. Philip Rahv to Arthur Schlesinger, Jr., Sept. 4, 1947, quoted in James B. Gilbert, *Writers and Partisans: A History of Literary Radicalism in America* (New York, 1968), 189.

117. Podhoretz, *Making It*, 238–39; Eliot, quoted in Victor S. Navasky, "Notes on Cult: or, How to Join the Intellectual Establishment," *New York Times Magazine*, Mar. 27, 1966, p. 128.

118. Philip Rahv to Allen Tate, Feb. 19, 1953, quoted in Dvosin, "Literature in a Political World," 131–32.

119. Norman Podhoretz, *Breaking Ranks* (New York, 1979), 28; Philip Rahv, "Testament of a Homeless Radical," *Partisan Review*, Summer 1945, p. 400.

120. Howe, "Mid-Century Turning Point," 27; idem, interview, June 16, 1976.

121. Decter, interview, June 1, 1976. Bell's explanation of his taking the position at *Fortune* is that, among a number of reasons, he needed the money for alimony and child support. (Bell, interview, July 13, 1979.)

122. Decter, interview, June 1, 1976.

123. Howe, "Mid-Century Turning Point," 27.

124. Irving Howe, "Mass Society and Post Modern Fiction," *Partisan Review*, Summer 1959, pp. 420–421.

125. Goodman, quoted in Navasky, "Notes on Cult," 126; Howe, "New York Intellectuals," 40–41.

126. Diana Trilling, "The Other Night at Columbia," 154; Howe, quoted in A. Alvarez, *Under Pressure: The Writer in Society: Eastern Europe and the U.S.A.* (Harmondsworth, Eng., 1965), 114.

127. Arnold Beichman, interview, May 25, 1976.

128. Howe, quoted in Alvarez, *Under Pressure*, 114.

129. Saul Bellow, "The Swamp of Prosperity," *Commentary*, July 1959, p. 79.

130. Podhoretz, interview, June 3, 1976.

Chapter 13   Things Fall Apart: Dispersions

1. Norman Podhoretz, *Making It* (New York, 1967), 197.

2. Morris Fine, interview, Aug. 24, 1979; Lionel Trilling, letter to the *New York Times*, Apr. 16, 1972.

3. Podhoretz, *Making It*, 200–201, 229; Clement Greenberg to author, Apr. 7, 1985.

4. Dwight Macdonald, interview, Dec. 3, 1976; Clement Greenberg to author, Apr. 7, 1985.

5. Podhoretz, *Making It*, 226; Greenberg, interview, June 22, 1979.

6. Arnold Beichman, interview, May 25, 1976; Fine, interview, Aug. 24, 1979; Podhoretz, *Making It*, 232.

7. Podhoretz, *Making It*, 232; Fine, interview, Aug. 24, 1979; Clement Greenberg to author, Apr. 7, 1985.

8. Daniel Bell, interview, May 5, 1985; Alfred Kazin, interview, Oct. 23, 1976.

9. Podhoretz, *Making It*, 274.

10. Ibid., 287.

11. Norman Podhoretz, "The Issue," *Commentary*, Feb. 1960, p. 183; Lionel Trilling, "On the Death of a Friend," ibid., 93–94.

12. Norman Podhoretz, "The Young Generation" (1957), in *Doings and Undoings* (New York, 1964), 105–7.

13. Ibid., 111.

14. Podhoretz, *Making It*, 296–97.

15. Beichman, interview, May 25, 1976; Bell, interview, July 13, 1979; Diana Trilling, interview, Oct. 3, 1979.

16. Norman Podhoretz, *Breaking Ranks* (New York, 1979), 54–55; William Phillips, *A Partisan View: Five Decades of the Literary Life* (New York, 1983), 73–74.

17. Podhoretz, "Young Generation," 111.

18. Hyman, quoted in Podhoretz, *Making It*, 298.

19. Ibid., 313.

20. Podhoretz, quoted in A. Alvarez, *Under Pressure: The Writer in Society: Eastern Europe and the U.S.A.* (Harmondsworth, Eng., 1965), 105–6.

21. Arendt, quoted ibid., 109.

22. Podhoretz, quoted ibid., 102; Midge Decter, interview, June 1, 1976.

23. Mailer, quoted in Alvarez, *Under Pressure*, 108; Midge Decter, "Anti-Americanism in America," *Harper's*, Apr. 1968, p. 41.

24. Hardwick, quoted in Alvarez, *Under Pressure*, 107.

25. Decter, "Anti-Americanism in America," 43.

26. Lionel Trilling, quoted in Alvarez, *Under Pressure*, 111.

27. Podhoretz, *Breaking Ranks*, 105.

28. Ibid., 105; Irving Howe, *World of Our Fathers* (New York, 1976), 606.

29. Other early contributors to the *New York Review* included Lionel Abel, David Bazelon, Paul Goodman, Gertrude Himmelfarb, Richard Hofstadter, Norman Mailer, Steven Marcus, Mary McCarthy, and Susan Sontag.

30. Also contributing were Elizabeth Hardwick, Frank Kermode, William Styron, Allen Tate, David Riesman, and Arthur Schlesinger.

31. Philip Nobile, *Intellectual Skywriting: Literary Politics and the "New York Review of Books"* (New York, 1974), 28, 29.

32. Mailer reprinted a letter he wrote to Robert Silvers which complained of the *Review*'s duplicitous treatment of him. Saying that Silvers could find no one not "afraid" to review *The Group*, Mailer wrote, "would I do it, you begged, as a special favor to you. Perhaps, you suggested, I was the only man in New York who had the guts to do it. A shrewd appeal. I did it. Two months later my book

(Presidential Papers) came out. You had given the copy to Midge Decter for review. Her submitted piece was, in your opinion—I quote your label—'overinflated.' That is to say, it was favorable. Changes were requested. The reviewer refused to make them. The review was not printed. . . . Now, we have my new book, *An American Dream.* I hear you have picked Philip Rahv to review it, Philip Rahv whose detestation of my work has been thundering these last two years into the gravy stains of every literary table on the Eastern Seaboard." (Norman Mailer, *Cannibals and Christians* [New York, 1966], 228.)

33. Podhoretz, *Making It*, 173.
34. Joe Marks and Macdonald, quoted in Nobile, *Intellectual Skywriting*, 85–86, 84.
35. Daniel Bell, "Ideology and the Beau Geste," *Dissent*, Winter 1961, pp. 75–77.
36. Irving Kristol, interview, June 17, 1976.
37. Podhoretz, *Making It*, 315–16.
38. Hannah Arendt, *Eichmann in Jerusalem* (New York, 1963), 134, 104.
39. Irving Howe, "Mid-Century Turning Point: An Intellectual Memoir," *Midstream*, June–July 1975, p. 25
40. Podhoretz, *Breaking Ranks*, 162; Norman Podhoretz, "Hannah Arendt on Eichmann," *Commentary*, Sept. 1963, p. 206.
41. Lionel Abel, "The Aesthetics of Evil," *Partisan Review*, Summer 1963, p. 230; Irving Howe *"The New Yorker* and Hannah Arendt," *Commentary*, 1963, p. 319.
42. Irving Howe, "The New York Intellectuals: A Chronicle and a Critique," *Commentary*, Jan. 1969 p. 43; Podhoretz, *Breaking Ranks*, 162; Kazin, interview, Oct. 23, 1976; Mary McCarthy, "The Hue and Cry," *Partisan Review*, Winter 1964, p. 82.
43. William Phillips, "Arguments: More on Eichmann," *Partisan Review*, Spring 1964, p. 281. See also idem, *Partisan View*, 109–10.
44. Podhoretz, *Breaking Ranks*, 136.
45. Nathan Glazer, "New York's Puerto Ricans," *Commentary*, Dec. 1958, p. 471, 474–76.
46. Daniel Bell, "Plea for a 'New Phase' in Negro Leadership," *New York Times Magazine*, May 31, 1964, p. 31; Irving Kristol, "The Negro Today Is Like the Immigrant Yesterday," ibid., Sept. 11, 1966, p. 138; idem, "A Few Kind Words for Uncle Tom," *Harper's*, Feb. 1965, p. 98.
47. Podhoretz, *Breaking Ranks*, 124. As the civil rights movement turned to more-specific questions of black identity and Afro-American heritage, the position of both James Baldwin and Ralph Ellison in the otherwise white literary world of the New York Intellectuals grew problematic. Leslie Fiedler recalled that the New Yorkers played a kind of "Jewish Mother" role for Ellison and Baldwin and that they were often criticized for it. By 1967 Ellison had sufficiently broken with *Commentary* to accuse its writers of being "new apologists for segregation." When Podhoretz demanded an apology, Ellison responded by citing "My Negro Problem—And Ours" and pieces by Glazer and Moynihan as examples of his accusation. (Leslie Fiedler, interview, May 14, 1976; "'A Very Stern Discipline': An Interview with Ralph Ellison," *Harper's*, Mar. 1967, p. 85; Norman Podhoretz, letter, ibid., May 1967, p. 11; Ralph Ellison and Norman Podhoretz, letters, ibid., July 1967, pp. 4–20.)
48. Norman Podhoretz, "My Negro Problem—And Ours" (1963), in *Doings and Undoings*, 363–64.

49. Ibid., 367.

50. Nathan Glazer, "Negroes and Jews: The New Challenge to Pluralism" (1964), in *The Commentary Reader* (New York, 1966), 388–98.

51. Bell, "Plea for a 'New Phase' in Negro Leadership," 11; Nathan Glazer, "The Ghetto Crisis," *Encounter*, Nov. 1967, pp. 15–16.

52. Jason Epstein, "The Brooklyn Dodgers," *New York Review of Books*, Oct. 10, 1968, p. 38.

53. Jason Epstein, "The Issue at Ocean Hill," *New York Review of Books*, Nov. 21, 1968, p. 3. Dwight Macdonald wrote to the *New York Review*, accusing the United Federation of Teachers of doing "their best to increase fear and hatred driving Negro and Jew in this city." ("An Open Letter to Michael Harrington," ibid., Dec. 5, 1968, p. 48.)

54. Dennis H. Wrong, "The Case of the *New York Review*," *Commentary*, Nov. 1970, p. 55.

55. Maurice Goldbloom, "The New York School Crisis," *Commentary*, Jan. 1969, pp. 43–58; Nathan Glazer, "Blacks, Jews and the Intellectuals," ibid., Apr. 1969, p. 35. Other articles in the *Commentary* series were Earl Rabb, "The Black Revolution and the Jewish Question," ibid., Jan. 1969; pp. 23–33; Milton Himmelfarb, "Is American Jewry in Crisis?" ibid., Mar. 1969, pp. 33–42.

56. Podhoretz, *Breaking Ranks*, 183–89.

57. Podhoretz wrote, "The new radicalism which Lynd and I had been working together to create would be new in nothing so much as its freedom from the illusions about Communism that had corrupted the last great wave of radicalism in America." (Podhoretz, *Breaking Ranks*, 189.)

58. Decter, interview, June 1, 1976.

59. Ibid.

60. See Irving Kristol, "Civil Disobedience Is Not Justified by Vietnam," *New York Times Magazine*, Nov. 26, 1976, pp. 128–30. Dupee's comments are noted in the margin of Saul Bellow's letter to F. W. Dupee, June 21, 1965, F. W. Dupee Papers.

61. Irving Howe, "The Vietnam Protest Movement," *Steady Work: Essays in the Politics of Democratic Radicalism, 1953–1966* (New York, 1966), 95.

62. Lynd and Howe, quoted in Nobile, *Intellectual Skywriting*, 35.

63. Nathan Glazer, "The New Left and Its Limits," *Remembering the Answers: Essays of the American Student Revolt* (New York, 1970), 189. This essay derives from a debate with Saul Alinsky in the fall of 1967 and originally appeared in *Commentary*, July 1968, pp. 31–39.

64. Bell, quoted in Lionel Abel, "Vietnam, the Cold War and Other Matters," *Commentary*, Oct. 1969, p. 26. For Chomsky's full remarks on Bell and others, see "The Responsibility of Intellectuals," in *American Power and the New Mandarins* (New York, 1969), 323–66.

65. "Liberal Anti-Communism Revisted: A Symposium," *Commentary*, Sept. 1967, pp. 31, 55, 66. For the response of Phillips and Rahv, see 56–58 and 63–64.

66. Ibid., 36, 44, 51, 76; Macdonald, interview, Dec. 3, 1976.

67. Lionel Abel, "The Position of Noam Chomsky," *Commentary*, May 1964, pp. 35–44.

68. Diana Trilling, "On Withdrawing from Vietnam: An Exchange," *New York Review of Books*, Jan 18, 1968, p. 5. Mary McCarthy's articles on Vietnam are

"Report from Vietnam I: The Home Program," ibid., Apr. 20, 1967, pp. 5–11; "Report from Vietnam—II: The Problem of Success," ibid., May 4, 1967, pp. 4–9; "Report from Vietnam—III: Intellectuals," ibid., May 9, 1967, pp. 4–11.

69. Nathan Glazer, "Vietnam: The Case for Immediate Withdrawal," *Commentary*, May 1971, pp. 33–37; Norman Podhoretz, "Issues," ibid., 6–9.

70. Seymour Martin Lipset, introd., *Rebellion in the University* (Chicago, 1971), xvi–xx.

71. Nathan Glazer, "What Happened at Berkeley," *Remembering the Answers*, 99; Podhoretz, *Breaking Ranks*, 207.

72. Daniel Bell and Irving Kristol, introd., *Confrontation: The Student Rebellion and the Universities* (New York, 1967), x, xi.

73. Glazer, introd., *Remembering the Answers*, 16–19; Nathan Glazer, "Student Politics and the University," *Atlantic*, July 1969, p. 44.

74. Sidney Hook, "The Prospects of Academe," *Encounter*, Aug. 1963, pp. 63–65.

75. Irving Kristol, "What's Bugging the Students," *Atlantic*, Nov. 1965, pp. 109–10; idem, "Toward a Restructuring of the University" (1968), in *On the Democratic Idea in America* (New York, 1972), 115.

76. Jerry L. Avorn and Robert Friedman, *Up against the Ivy Wall* (New York, 1970), 67–70, 131.

77. Ibid., 210.

78. Diana Trilling, "On the Steps of Low Library: Liberalism and the Revolution of the Young," *Commentary*, Nov. 1968, pp. 36–39.

79. Ibid., 39, 46.

80. F. W. Dupee, "The Uprising at Columbia," *New York Review of Books*, Sept. 26, 1968, pp. 20, 26, 38.

81. Dwight Macdonald, "An Exchange on Columbia," *New York Review of Books*, July 11, 1968, p. 42.

82. Macdonald, interview, Dec. 3, 1976; Podhoretz, *Breaking Ranks*, 274.

83. William Phillips, interview, Aug. 30, 1979.

84. Philip Rahv, "Left Face," *New York Review of Books*, Oct. 12, 1967, pp. 10, 13.

85. Irving Howe and Philip Rahv, "An Exchange on the Left," *New York Review of Books*, Nov. 23, 1967, p. 36.

86. Ibid., 38, 39.

87. Ibid., 39, 40.

88. Ibid., 41.

89. Howe, quoted in Andrew James Dvosin, "Literature in a Political World: The Career and Writings of Philip Rahv" (Ph.D. thesis, New York Univ., 1977), 207, 179.

90. Decter, interview, June 1, 1976; Podhoretz, *Making It*, 317.

91. Decter, interview, June 1, 1976.

92. Bell, "Ideology and the Beau-Geste," 75–76.

93. See, e.g., Daniel Bell, *Marxian Socialism in the United States* (Princeton, 1967); Nathan Glazer, *The Social Roots of American Communism* (New York, 1961); numerous works by Sidney Hook; Irving Howe and Lewis Coser, *The American Communist Party* (Boston, 1957); Lionel Trilling, *The Middle of the Journey* (New York, 1947).

94. Daniel Bell, "The Mood of Three Generations," in *The End of Ideology: On the*

Exhaustion of Political Ideas in the Fifties (New York, 1965 [1960]), 200 (parts of the essay originally appeared in 1955, 1957, and 1959).

95. Lionel Trilling, quoted in "Columbia: Seven Interviews," *Partisan Review*, Summer 1968, p. 387.

96. See Podhoretz, *Making It*, 317.

97. Irving Howe, "New Styles in 'Leftism,'" (1965), in *Beyond the New Left* (New York, 1970), 24.

98. Irving Howe and Lewis Coser, "New Styles in Fellow-Traveling," *Dissent*, Autumn 1961, p. 497.

99. Daniel Bell, "Columbia and the New Left" (1967), in *Confrontation*, 105; Decter and Hook, quoted in Nobile, *Intellectual Skywriting*, 143, 140.

100. Howe, "New Styles in 'Leftism,'" 24, 23.

101. Ibid., 26.

102. Glazer, introd., *Remembering the Answers*, 28.

103. Glazer, "New Left and Its Limits," 175–76; Seymour Martin Lipset, "The Activist: A Profile" (1968), in *Confrontation*, 48.

104. Howe, "The New York Intellectuals," 45.

105. Nathan Glazer, "Remembering the Answers," in *Remembering the Answers*, 292–93.

106. Ibid., 277.

107. Kristol, "American Intellectuals and Foreign Policy," in *On the Democratic Idea in America*, 84–85. Seymour Martin Lipset believed, "Many professors find solace in student militancy directed against forces they hold responsible for their felt sense of status inferiority or insecurity." This same description was applied to the supporters of Senator McCarthy in the 1950s. (Lipset, "Activist," 49.)

108. Kristol, interview, June 17, 1976; idem, "American Intellectuals and Foreign Policy," 87.

109. Daniel Bell, "Sensibility in the 60s" *Commentary*, June 1971, p. 63.

110. Ibid., 64; Rahv, quoted in Podhoretz, *Breaking Ranks*, 274.

111. Howe, "New York Intellectuals," 50.

112. Ibid., 47.

113. Nathan Glazer, "On Being Deradicalized," *Commentary*, Oct. 1970, p. 70.

114. Podhoretz, *Making It*, 356.

115. Norman Podhoretz, interview, June 3, 1976.

116. Podhoretz, *Breaking Ranks*, 223; Podhoretz, interview, June 3, 1976; Bell, interview, July 13, 1979.

117. Benjamin DeMott, "City Light," *New York Review of Books*, Apr. 30, 1964, p. 9; William Phillips and Jason Epstein, letters, ibid., June 11, 1964, p. 22.

118. Podhoretz, interview, June 3, 1976.

119. Norman Podhoretz to F. W. Dupee, Dec. 19, 1967, F. W. Dupee Papers; Bell, interview, July 13, 1979; Podhoretz, *Breaking Ranks*, 220.

120. Epstein, quoted in Nobile, *Intellectual Skywriting*, 12.

121. Diana Trilling, interview, Oct. 3, 1979.

122. Beichman, interview, May 25, 1976; Podhoretz, *Breaking Ranks*, 221.

123. Wilfrid Sheed, "*Making It* in the Big City," *Atlantic*, Apr. 1968, pp. 97, 98. See Norman Mailer, "Up the Family Tree," *Partisan Review*, Winter 1968, pp. 238–52.

124. Edgar Z. Friedenberg, "Du côté de chez Podhoretz," *New York Review of Books*, Feb. 1, 1968, pp. 12, 13. Other reviews of the book included Granville Hicks,

"How to Succeed at an Early Age," *Saturday Review*, Jan. 13, 1968, pp. 77–81; Mordecai Richler, "Climbing Norman's Ladder," *Nation*, Feb. 5, 1968, pp. 180–81; Stanley Kauffmann, "The Challenge of Success," *New Republic*, Jan. 27, 1968, pp. 27, 37–38.

125. Podhoretz, *Breaking Ranks*, 224–26.
126. D. Trilling, interview, Oct. 3, 1979.
127. Mark Shechner, "Jewish Writers," in *Harvard Guide to Contemporary American Writing*, ed. Daniel Hoffman (Cambridge, Mass, 1979), 204.
128. Podhoretz, *Making It*, xi.
129. Bell, interview, July 13, 1979.
130. Podhoretz, *Making It*, xi.

Chapter 14 What We Are Today

1. Lionel Abel, "New York City: A Remembrance," *Dissent*, Summer 1961, p. 259; Daniel Bell, interview, July 13, 1979.
2. David T. Bazelon, quoted in Victor S. Navasky, "Notes on Cult: or, How to Join the Intellectual Establishment," *New York Times Magazine*, Mar. 27, 1966, p. 128.
3. Dennis H. Wrong, "The Case of the *New York Review*," *Commentary*, Nov. 1970, p. 54; Philip Nobile, *Intellectual Skywriting: Literary Politics and the "New York Review of Books"* (New York, 1974), 50.
4. See Dennis Wrong, "Chomsky: Of Thinking and Moralizing," *Dissent*, Jan.–Feb. 1970, pp. 75–81.
5. Wrong "Case of the *New York Review*," 58–59.
6. Ibid., 63.
7. Kozodoy, quoted in Merle Miller, "Why Norman and Jason Aren't Talking," *New York Times Magazine*, Mar. 26, 1972, p. 109.
8. Alexander Bickel, "Judging the Chicago Trial," *Commentary*, Jan. 1971, pp. 38, 33, 34–35.
9. Miller, "Why Norman and Jason Aren't Talking," 34–35, 104–11; letters, *New York Times Magazine*, Apr. 16, 1972, pp. 39–42; Apr. 23, 1972, p. 48; Apr. 30, 1972, p. 48.
10. Nathan Glazer, *Remembering the Answers: Essays on the American Student Revolt* (New York, 1970), 3–4.
11. Irving Kristol, quoted in Peter Steinfels, *The Neoconservatives: The Men Who Are Changing America's Politics* (New York, 1979), 240; Irving Kristol, quoted in Geoffrey Norman, "The Godfather of Neoconservatism (And His Family)," *Esquire*, Feb. 13, 1979, p. 41; Bell, quoted in Steinfels, *Neoconservatives*, 215.
12. Irving Kristol, "American Intellectuals and Foreign Policy" (1967), in *On the Democratic Idea in America* (New York, 1972), 85.
13. See Robert Tucker, "Oil: The Issue of American Intervention," *Commentary*, Mar. 1975, pp. 31–44; Jeane Kirkpatrick, "Dictatorships and Double Standards," *Commentary*, Nov. 1979, pp. 34–45.
14. Norman Podhoretz, *The Present Danger: Do We Have the Will to Reverse the Decline of American Power?* (New York, 1980), 12.
15. Ibid., 58–60.
16. Ibid., 74.
17. Norman Podhoretz, interview, June 3, 1976.

18. Kristol, "American Intellectuals and Foreign Policy," 83.
19. Stein, quoted in Mary Sperling McAuliffe, *Crisis on the Left: Cold War Politics and American Liberals, 1947–1954* (Amherst, Mass., 1978), 116.
20. *New York Times*, Feb. 19, 1981.
21. Bell, interview, July 13, 1979.
22. Bell, interview, May 5, 1985; Michael Novak, "Class, Culture and Society," *Commentary*, July 1981, p. 72.
23. Podhoretz, interview, June 3, 1976; Kristol, quoted in Sidney Blumenthal, "The Intelligentsia of the Right," *Boston Globe Magazine*, Mar. 14, 1981, pp. 36–38.
24. Sidney Hook, letter, *New York Times Book Review*, Aug. 2, 1981, p. 24.
25. Irving Kristol, "The Timerman Affair," *Wall Street Journal*, May 29, 1981.
26. William Phillips, interview, June 17, 1976.
27. Leslie Fiedler, *"Partisan Review*: Phoenix or Dodo?" (1956), in *The Collected Essays of Leslie Fiedler*, vol. 2 (New York, 1971), 42.
28. For differing accounts of this "confrontation," see William Phillips, *A Partisan View: Five Decades of Literary Life* (New York, 1983), 273–74; William Barrett, *The Truants: Adventures among the Intellectuals* (Garden City, N.Y., 1982), 39–43.
29. Norman Podhoretz, *Breaking Ranks* (New York, 1979), 270–71; Phillips, *Partisan View*, 274.
30. Dwight Macdonald, interview, Dec. 3, 1976.
31. Philip Rahv to F. W. Dupee, June 20, 1966, F. W. Dupee Papers. Despite Rahv's disdain, Steven Marcus was by 1966 well on the way to the distinguished position he came to hold in American academic circles.
32. Phillips, *Partisan View*, 263–65.
33. Ibid., 275, 276; Dorothea Straus, *Palaces and Prisons* (New York, 1976), 86.
34. Philip Rahv, quoted in Podhoretz, *Breaking Ranks*, 274. It is easy to see where a sensibility like Rahv's might clash with that of Richard Poirier, especially on the subject of contemporary music, and specifically on the Beatles. In Poirier's 1966 estimate, *Sgt. Pepper's Lonely Hearts Club Band* deserved evaluation in a style equivalent to that used in the evaluating of literature. He found a "stately Wagnerian episode" in "A Day in the Life" and thought the Beatles' use of Indian sitar operated "in the manner of classical allusion in Pope." "But," he added, "as in Pope, the instrument of ridicule here, the sitar, is allowed in the very process to remain unsullied and eloquent." This was grist for the mill of a highbrow scoffer like Rahv. (Richard Poirier, "Learning from the Beatles," *Partisan Review*, Fall 1966, pp. 526–46.)
35. Philip Rahv, "Lettuce and Tomatoes," *New York Review of Books*, July 9, 1964, p. 6; idem, "Crime without Punishment," ibid., Mar. 25, 1965, p. 4.
36. Straus, *Palaces and Prisoners*, 85–87.
37. Mark Krupnick, "He Never Learned to Swim," *New Review*, Jan. 1976, pp. 33–34.
38. Flora Natapoff, "The Abuse of Clemency: Clement Greenberg's Reductive Aesthetic," *Modern Occasions*, Fall 1970, p. 117. In addition to the Chomsky piece and the Brustein article, the other contributions to the first number of *Modern Occasions* included stories by Philip Roth ("Salad Days") and Alan Lelchuk ("Cambridge Talk"), an interview with Mary McCarthy, and poetry by Robert Lowell and Richard Moore.
39. Krupnick, "He Never Learned to Swim," 36.
40. Saul Bellow, "Culture Now: Some Animadversions, Some Laughs," *Modern*

Occasions, Winter 1971, pp. 164–65; Philip Rahv, "Cultural Malaise and Ultimate Culpability," ibid., Fall 1971, p. 461.

41. Rahv, "Cultural Malaise and Ultimate Culpability," 461–68; Philip Rahv, "Kid Stuff: The Myth of Consciousness—III," *Modern Occasions*, Spring 1971, pp. 307–13.

42. Krupnick, "He Never Learned to Swin," 38; Schloss, quoted in Andrew James Dvosin, "Literature in a Political World: The Career and Writings of Philip Rahv" (Ph.D. thesis, New York Univ., 1977), 217.

43. Krupnick, quoted in Dvosin, "Literature in a Political World," 220.

44. *Modern Occasions*, Spring 1972, n.p.

45. Krupnick, "He Never Learned to Swim," 39.

46. Saul Bellow, *Humboldt's Gift* (New York, 1973), 7. For the details of Schwartz's death, see James Atlas, *Delmore Schwartz: The Life of an American Poet* (New York, 1977), 376.

47. Hannah Arendt, "Reflections: Remembering Wystan H. Auden . . . ," *New Yorker*, Jan. 20, 1975, p. 46.

48. William Phillips, "Hannah Arendt and Lionel Trilling," *Partisan Review*, 43, no. 1 (1976), 10–11.

49. Ibid., 11; Robert Lowell, "On Hannah Arendt," *New York Review of Books*, May 13, 1976, p. 6.

50. For a touching remembrance of F. W. Dupee, see Morris Dickstein, "Remembering F. W. Dupee," *Partisan Review*, 46, no. 3 (1979), 433–37.

51. Seymour Krim, "Remembering Harold Rosenberg," *Commentary*, Nov. 1978, p. 67; Hilton Kramer, "An Era Comes to an End," *New York Times*, July 23, 1978, p. 23.

52. Kramer, "Era Comes to an End," 23, 1; Krim, "Remembering Harold Rosenberg," 67.

53. James Atlas, "Unsentimental Education," *Atlantic*, June 1983, pp. 79–92; Walter Goodman, "A Traditionalist Who Wore Radical Stripes," *New York Times*, Dec. 26, 1982; John Simon, "Dwight Macdonald: 1906–1982," *Partisan Review*, 50, no. 2 (1983), 279–81. Simon was prophetic, because Da Capo Press plans to reissue Macdonald's works.

54. Podhoretz, *Breaking Ranks*, 300.

55. Diana Trilling, interview, Oct. 3, 1979.

56. Irving Howe, "On Lionel Trilling," *New Republic*, Mar. 13, 1976, p. 29.

57. Alfred Kazin, *New York Jew* (New York, 1978), 43.

58. Podhoretz, *Breaking Ranks*, 296, 300.

59. Diana Trilling, interview, Oct. 3, 1979.

60. Steven Marcus, "Lionel Trilling, 1905–1975," *New York Times Book Review*, Feb. 8, 1976, pp. 32–34.

61. Morris Dickstein, *Gates of Eden: American Culture in the Sixties* (New York, 1977), 254.

62. Lionel Trilling, *Beyond Culture: Essays on Literature and Learning* (New York, 1965), 196–97; Podhoretz, *Breaking Ranks*, 297–98; Dickstein, *Gates of Eden*, 264.

63. Ibid., 266.

64. Irving Howe, *World of Our Fathers* (New York, 1976), 646.

65. Pearl K. Bell, "The Past Recaptured," *New Leader*, Mar. 1, 1976, p. 18.

66. Nathan Glazer, "World of Our Fathers," *New Republic*, Apr. 24, 1976, p. 20.

67. Irving Howe, *A Margin of Hope* (San Diego, 1982), 18.

68. Nathan Glazer, "An Answer to Lillian Hellman," *Commentary*, June 1976, p. 36.

69. Hilton Kramer, "The Blacklist and the Cold War," *New York Times*, Oct. 3, 1976.

70. Among the letters critical of Kramer's piece were those by Eric Foner, Michael Meeropol, Ronald Radosh and Louis Menashe, and Bruce Cook. Alfred Kazin wrote in support of Kramer. (*New York Times*, Oct. 17, 1976.)

71. William Phillips, "What Happened in the Fifties," *Partisan Review*, Fall 1976, p. 340.

72. Irving Howe, "Lillian Hellman," in *Celebration and Attacks* (New York, 1978), 206; Sidney Hook, "Lillian Hellman's *Scoundrel Time*," *Encounter*, Feb. 1977, p. 90.

73. Lillian Hellman, *Scoundrel Time* (Boston, 1976), 84, 85–86.

74. Glazer, "Answer to Lillian Hellman," 37; Howe, "Lillian Hellman," 209, 209ff. For Glazer's "opposition to McCarthyism," see above, pp. 212–13.

75. Hook, "Lillian Hellman's *Scoundrel Time*," 83.

76. Irving Kristol, interview, June 17, 1976; Macdonald, interview, Dec. 3, 1976.

77. Howe, "Lillian Hellman," 208; Glazer, "Answer to Lillian Hellman," 37; and Hook, "Lillian Hellman's *Scoundrel Time*," 82–83.

78. Diana Trilling, *We Must March My Darlings* (New York, 1977), 41–66; *New York Times*, Sept. 29 and 30, 1976.

79. *New York Times*, Mar. 19, 1980. The suit had not yet gone to court when Hellman died in 1984.

80. Ibid.

Index

Abel, Lionel, 386
  in "new" *Partisan Review*, 76;
  on Rosenberg and Marxism, 106;
  Trotsky, 108;
  on Nazi-Soviet Pact, 123;
  on Eichmann and Jews, 330;
  on end of New York Intellectuals, 366;
  Kazin on politics of, 425n.12
Academe
  Glazer on Phillips and Rahv, 200;
  and anticommunism, 244-50, 246-47, 248-50;
  academic freedom in 50s: 247-48, 271,
    Rahv on, 247, Hook on, 247, Kristol
    on, 247, 248;
  academic freedom in 60s, 343, Glazer on,
    343, Hook on 343;
  postwar attraction, 311-13
Acheson, Dean, 210
Adamic, Lewis, 234
Adams, Henry, 147, 149
Agee, James, 76, 172
Alger, Horatio, 152, 256
Alter, Victor, 373
Altman, Jack, 44
American capitalism, Bell and Schlesinger
  on, 182
American Committee for Cultural Freedom
  (ACCF), 259-73;
  founding, 263;
  and CIA, 264;

lecture series by Kristol, 264-65;
  publications, 265, 270-71, 272;
  and Emergency Civil Liberties Commit-
    tee, 266-69;
  and Einstein, 269;
  on academic freedom, 271;
  on Oppenheimer, 271;
  on passports, 271;
  on Rosenbergs, 271
American Committee for the Defense of
  Leon Trotsky, 108
American Forum for Socialist Education,
  221
American Marxist Association, 106
American Student Union, 41
American Writers' Congress, 53, 86, 110,
  113, 400n.56
Americanism, Elliot Cohen and Kristol on,
  184
Americans for Intellectual Freedom, 260,
  423n.141
Anderson, Sherwood, 191
Anti-anticommunism, 235-38, 343
Anti-Semitism
  and academe, 23, 30-31, 311;
  German, 138;
  and English literature, 146-49, 410n.19;
  and Populists, 301, 307;
  and New York Teachers' strike, 336;
  and race, 336
Aragon, Louis, 92, 132

441

on communism and idealism, 222;
communism as a conspiracy, 225-26;
liberalism and anticommunism, 228-29;
on the Rosenbergs, 253;
on Waldorf Conference, 261;
on the American Committee for Cultural
  Freedom, 263;
and liberal anticommunism, 270;
on Lionel Trilling and 3rd generation, 277;
on Howe's anticommunism, 284;
gets Ph.D., 311, 394n.9, 430n.112;
on *Dissent*, 288;
on Podhoretz in 50s, 303;
on Podhoretz in 60s, and Lionel Trilling,
  323, and Hook, 323, abuse of
  Podhoretz, 323, criticism of *Making It*,
  361;
on Podhoretz in 70s, 360, 364;
on meeting Hofstadter, and Kazin, 306:
on Hofstadter, status anxiety, and
  consensus history, 307;
The New American Right, 307;
on New York Intellectuals and *The New
  Yorker*, 310, 311;
in "new" *Commentary*, 321, Decter on,
  351;
in *New York Review*, 326;
founds *Public Interest*, 328;
race and ethnicity, 332, 334;
Chomsky on, 339;
Vietnam and anticommunism, 339;
on 60s campus unrest, 342;
Columbia strike, 344;
on New Left vs. Old, 353;
on 50s vs. 60s sensibility, 357;
on Susan Sontag, 357;
on Lionel Trilling, 364;
end of New York Intellectuals, 366;
on preferential quotas, 370;
Michael Novak on, 372;
and neoconservatism, 369, 370, 372;
Rahv on, 378;
Bell, Pearl Kazin, 385
Bellow, Saul, 352, 379;
  in "Chicago" crowd, 41;
  on intellectuals, 96;
  and World War II, 135;
  Fiedler on, 155, 292, 294;
  in early *Commentary*, 160;
  and Nobel Prize, 290;
  relationship to *Partisan* and early
    publishing, 291;
  Macdonald on, 291;

Elizabeth Hardwick on, 291;
Schwartz on, 291;
Podhoretz on, 291, 293-94;
Kazin on, 292, 294, 295;
works: 292, 294, Marc Shechner on, 292,
  recent appraisals, 292, 293;
novelist of New York Intellectuals, 293;
on postwar prosperity, 315-16;
in *New York Review*, 326;
and Vietnam (Dupee on), 338;
critique of Fiedler, Phillips, and *Partisan
  Review*, 378;
Schwartz and *Humboldt's Gift*, 380;
college, 395n.24
Benda, Julian, 78
Bentley, Elizabeth, 229, 255
Berkeley, 40, 341-42
Berkman, Alexander, 49
Berlin, Isaiah, 382
Bernanos, 149
Bernstein, Leonard, 260
Berryman, John, 82, 379
Beyond the Melting Pot, 329-32
Bickel, Alexander, 367-68
Biddle, Francis, 237
Biemiller, Andrew, 44
Bishop, Elizabeth, 82
Blackmur, R.P., 5, 82
Bollingen Prize, 146-47, 410n.18
Boorstin, Daniel, 180, 307
Borkenau, Franz, 262
Borghese, Guiseppe, 262
Bradbury, Malcolm, 85
Braden, Thomas, 267
Brando, Marlon, 260
Brandt, Willy, 349
Brooks, Van Wyck, 32, 65, 116-19
Browder, Earl, 44, 54, 65, 66, 123
Brown, Irving, 262
Brown, Norman O., 323
Brownson, Orestes, 179
Brustein, Robert, 378
Buber, Martin 142
Buckley, William, 255
Bukharin, 94
Bundy, McGeorge, 245, 334
Burke, Kenneth, 82, 116
Burnet, Thomas, 192
Burnham, James, 78, 82, 106, 263, 270
Butler, Nicholas Murray, 23, 37, 255

Cahan, Abraham, 29